The Palgrave Handbook of Romani Language and Linguistics

Yaron Matras · Anton Tenser
Editors

The Palgrave Handbook of Romani Language and Linguistics

palgrave
macmillan

Editors
Yaron Matras
School of Arts, Languages, and Cultures
University of Manchester
Manchester, UK

Anton Tenser
University of Helsinki
Helsinki, Finland

ISBN 978-3-030-28107-6   ISBN 978-3-030-28105-2   (eBook)
https://doi.org/10.1007/978-3-030-28105-2

© The Editor(s) (if applicable) and The Author(s) 2020
This work is subject to copyright. All rights are solely and exclusively licensed by the Publisher, whether the whole or part of the material is concerned, specifically the rights of translation, reprinting, reuse of illustrations, recitation, broadcasting, reproduction on microfilms or in any other physical way, and transmission or information storage and retrieval, electronic adaptation, computer software, or by similar or dissimilar methodology now known or hereafter developed.
The use of general descriptive names, registered names, trademarks, service marks, etc. in this publication does not imply, even in the absence of a specific statement, that such names are exempt from the relevant protective laws and regulations and therefore free for general use.
The publisher, the authors and the editors are safe to assume that the advice and information in this book are believed to be true and accurate at the date of publication. Neither the publisher nor the authors or the editors give a warranty, expressed or implied, with respect to the material contained herein or for any errors or omissions that may have been made. The publisher remains neutral with regard to jurisdictional claims in published maps and institutional affiliations.

Cover credit: jordi clave garsot/Alamy Stock Photo

This Palgrave Macmillan imprint is published by the registered company Springer Nature Switzerland AG
The registered company address is: Gewerbestrasse 11, 6330 Cham, Switzerland

Contents

1   Introduction   1
Yaron Matras and Anton Tenser

Part I   History

2   The Historical Origins of Romani   13
Michael Beníšek

3   Historical Sources on the Romani Language   49
Ignasi-Xavier Adiego

Part II   Structure

4   Romani Lexicon   85
Andrea Scala

5   Romani Phonology   119
Márton A. Baló

6   Romani Morphology   155
Viktor Elšík

7   Romani Syntactic Typology   187
Evangelia Adamou and Yaron Matras

v

vi   Contents

Part III   Contact

8   The Impact of Turkish on Romani   231
Victor A. Friedman

9   The Impact of Slavic Languages on Romani   261
Anna-Maria Meyer

10   The Impact of Hungarian on Romani   303
Zuzana Bodnárová and Jakob Wiedner

11   Romani and Contact Linguistics   329
Yaron Matras and Evangelia Adamou

12   Para-Romani Varieties   353
Peter Bakker

Part IV   Variation

13   Romani Dialectology   389
Viktor Elšík and Michael Beníšek

14   Language Policy and Planning in Romani   429
Dieter W. Halwachs

**15   Romani Bible Translation and the Use of Romani
in Religious Contexts**   459
Wilco van den Heuvel

Part V   Language Use

16   Romani in Child-Directed Speech   489
Pavel Kubaník

17   Romani on the Internet   515
Daniele Viktor Leggio

Contents   vii

18   Romani Language Literature   539
Sofiya Zahova

Author Index   571

Dialect Index   581

Subject Index   585

Notes on Contributors

Evangelia Adamou is Senior Researcher at the National Centre for Scientific Research in France (CNRS). She specialises in the analysis of under-described languages with a focus on language contact and bilingualism, combining corpus and experimental methods. She has conducted extensive fieldwork on Romani in Greece and in Mexico. She is currently Co-PI on a research project to study Romani repertoires (Riksbankens Jubileumsfond, 2019–2026).

Ignasi-Xavier Adiego is Professor of Indo-European Linguistics at the University of Barcelona. One of his research interests is the study of the varieties of Romani language. In 2002, he discovered and published the manuscript of the *Gypsy Vocabulary of Francesc de Sentmenat* (eighteenth century), one of the most important historical documents of the Romani language. Other research interests include the ancient Anatolian languages and the languages of ancient Italy. He is, together with John D. Ray and D. Schürr, one of the decipherers of the Carian alphabet and language.

Peter Bakker is Associate Professor of Linguistics at Aarhus University, School of Communication and Culture. He has published numerous academic articles on a variety of topics and languages, including Basque, Romani and Amerindian languages. His research interests revolve around new languages, such as pidgins, creoles and mixed languages. In his research on the genesis of these languages, he combines linguistics, anthropology and history. His publications on Romani include edited volume on Romani in contact, a Romani linguistics bibliography and articles on Para-Romani

Notes on Contributors

varieties, notably in Turkey, Scandinavia, the Basque Country and the Iberian Peninsula.

Márton A. Baló is a Research Fellow at the Research Institute for Linguistics of the Hungarian Academy of Sciences. His primary fields of interest are phonology, morphology and the Romani language. He has published articles on certain morphological and dialectological aspects of Romani. Besides his research, he has taught courses in general linguistics and on the grammar of Romani at Eötvös Loránd University. He has also conducted extensive fieldwork among the Hungarian Roma.

Michael Beníšek is Assistant Professor in Romani Studies at Charles University, Prague. His research focuses on the historical grammar of Romani, dialectology and descriptive work on Romani dialects, and he has conducted extensive fieldwork research on Romani varieties in Slovakia and Ukraine.

Zuzana Bodnárová holds a Ph.D. in General Linguistics from the Charles University in Prague, where she was a member of a research team working on the Atlas of Central Romani project. She is currently involved in Romani-related projects of the Plurilingualism Research Unit at the University of Graz. Her research interests include the sociolinguistic situation of Romani, and the linguistic variation and change in Romani in contact with Hungarian.

Viktor Elšík, Ph.D. is employed in the Department of Linguistics at the Charles University in Prague. His expertise includes Romani linguistics and language contact. He is a co-author of a monograph on the *Cross-Dialectal Variability of Romani from the Perspective of Linguistic Typology* (Mouton de Gruyter, 2006) and the author of papers on the structure, history and dialectology of Romani. He has long-time experience with linguistic field research in Romani communities in East-Central Europe.

Victor A. Friedman is Andrew W. Mellon Distinguished Service Professor Emeritus in the Humanities and Professor Emeritus in the Department of Linguistics at the University of Chicago and Honorary Adjunct at La Trobe University. He is a foreign member of the Macedonian Academy of Arts and Sciences, the Academy of Sciences of Albania, the Academy of Arts and Sciences of Kosova, and Matica Srpska. He has been awarded the "1300 Years of Bulgaria" jubilee medal, the Blaže Koneski Medal and the Medal of Service to the Republic of North Macedonia, as well as the degree of doctor honoris causa from the University of Skopje. In 2009, he received the

American Association of Teachers of Slavic and East European Languages' Annual Award for Outstanding Contributions to Scholarship. In 2014, he received the Association for Slavic, East European, and Eurasian Studies' Annual Award for Distinguished Contributions to Scholarship. His research focuses on all aspects of the languages of the Balkans and the Caucasus.

Dieter W. Halwachs is sociolinguist at the University of Graz; head of the *Plurilingualism Research Unit* at the University's language centre *treffpunkt sprachen*—the research unit is designed as a sociolinguistically based political project which aims for social cohesion, human rights and a politics of plurality; member of the *Committee of Experts of the European Charter for Regional or Minority Languages* at the *Council of Europe*; coordinator of various projects on dominated languages, urban multilingualism and language documentation (among them, *UNESCO World Atlas of Languages*). His research interests include *language politics, endangered languages and language contact.*

Pavel Kubaník is a graduate in the Romani Studies Seminar at Charles University, Prague. He combines his interests in sociolinguistics and linguistic anthropology with extensive fieldwork, especially among Roma in the Czech Republic and Slovakia.

Daniele Viktor Leggio holds a Ph.D. in anthropology and linguistics combined to explore the relationship between languages, identity and language codification on an online radio catering for diasporic Roma from Mitrovica, Kosovo. As part of the MigRom project, he has contributed to research that ethnographically explored the experiences, expectations, plans, interactions with local authorities and reception of Romanian Roma migrants in Western Europe. His research interests combine sociolinguistics, ethnolinguistics, migration and diaspora studies, language policy and planning, computer-mediated communication and Romani studies.

Yaron Matras is Professor of Linguistics at the University of Manchester. He has published widely on Romani linguistics, including the titles *Romani: A Linguistic Introduction* (Cambridge, 2002), and *Romani in Britain: The Afterlife of a Language* (Edinburgh, 2010), and has led a series of large-scale research projects and international research consortia devoted to Romani linguistics and Romani studies in general. He served as Editor of the journal *Romani Studies* from 1999 to 2017 and was co-founder of the European Academic Network on Romani Studies. His interests include contact linguistics and multilingualism, and he is the author of *Language Contact* (Cambridge, 2009; second edition 2019) and the founder of the Multilingual Manchester research unit.

xii   **Notes on Contributors**

Anna-Maria Meyer is a Postdoctoral Researcher in the Department of Slavic Studies at the University of Cologne (Germany). Apart from the language contact of Slavic and Romani, she has been researching Slavic constructed languages, the Polish-English mixed variety "Ponglish", Slavic alphabets and orthographies (Glagolitic, Cyrillic, Latin) as well as different aspects of Slavic sociolinguistics and pragmatics.

Andrea Scala is Associate Professor of Historical Linguistics, General Linguistics and Contact Linguistics at the State University of Milan (Italy). His research mainly focuses on Romani lexicon and grammar, Armenian language in its historical relations with neighbouring languages and Italo-Romance dialects. He is author of about sixty articles and three monographs on these subjects.

Anton Tenser holds a Ph.D. in Linguistics from the University of Manchester and a docentship in Romani Studies at the University of Helsinki. He is the author of a monograph on the grammar of *Lithuanian Romani* as well as several academic articles on Romani linguistics and ethnography. Anton has contributed to a number of large-scale Romani linguistics projects, including RMS, RomLex, Helsinki Romani project and the Russian Romani Corpus. In the past, he has taught at the University of Chicago, University of Helsinki and Vanderbilt University. He currently works as an analytical linguist at Google, Pittsburgh.

Wilco van den Heuvel is a linguist who has been active in the field of Austronesian, Papuan and Romani linguistics. From 2007 to 2009, he lived with his family in Transylvania, Romania, where he conducted a survey on Romani varieties and on the use of Romani in religious contexts. He currently works as an independent linguist and as a teacher of Dutch to refugees and newcomers in the Netherlands. Website: https://vu-nl.academia.edu/WilcovandenHeuvel.

Jakob Wiedner holds a Ph.D. in linguistics and currently works as postgraduate assistant in the Plurilingualism Research Unit at the University of Graz. Since 2010, he has been involved in several Romani-related projects, among them ROMLEX and the Norwegian Romani project. He has since also worked on the development of linguistic and other language-related software, especially with Romani linguistic data.

Sofiya Zahova is a Researcher at the Vigdís Finnbogadóttir Institute of Foreign Language, University of Iceland. Her main interests are in the field of Romani studies, history and ethnography of the Balkans and Eastern Europe. She is author of the books *Montenegro After Yugoslavia: Dynamics of Identities* (2013, in Bulgarian), *History of Romani Literature with Multimedia on Romani Kids' Publications* (2014) and UNICEF-Commissioned Report *Research on the Social Norms Which Prevent Roma Girls from Access to Education* (2016, in Bulgarian and English).

Abbreviations

1	First person
2	Second person
3	Third person
A	Agent-like argument
ABL	Ablative
ACC	Accusative
ADD	Additive connector
ADJ	Adjective, adjectivizer
ADV	Adverb
AGR	Agreement
AOR	Aorist
ART	Article
BCE	Before Current Era
CAUS	Causative
CE	Current Era
COMP	Complementizer
COND	Conditional
COP	Copula
CORR	Correlative particle
DAT	Dative
DEF	Definite article
DEM	Demonstrative
DIM	Diminutive
DMS	Dental modal subordinator
DO	Direct object
F	Feminine
FREQ	Frequentative

xvi **Abbreviations**

FUT	Future
GEN	Genitive
GER	Gerund
IMP	Imperative
IMPF	Imperfect
IND	Indicative
INDF	Indefinite
INF	Infinitive
INS	Instrumental
IO	Indirect object
ITR	Intransitive
LOAN	Loanword adaptation
LOC	Locative
M	Masculine
MID	Middle
N	Noun
NEG	Negative
NEUT	Neuter
NOM	Nominative
NOUN	Nominalizer
NP	Noun phrase
NPFV	Non-perfective
NPOS	Non-positive
NREM	Non-remote
NUM	Numeral
O	Object
OBL	Oblique
P	Patient-like argument
PFUT	Present–future
PFV	Perfective
PL	Plural
PLPF	Pluperfect
POSS	Possessive
PRF	Perfect
PRIV	Privative
PROG	Progressive
PRS	Present
PST	Past
PTC	Perfective participle
PTCP	Participle
Q	Questions
QNT	Quantifier

R	Recipient-like argument
REFL	Reflexive
REL	Relative pronoun
REM	Remote
RMS	Romani Morpho-Syntax database
ROMLEX	Romani Lexical database
S	Single argument
SG	Singular
SOC	Sociative
SOV	Subject-object-verb
SUBJ	Subject
SUBJ	Subjunctive
SUP	Superlative
SV	Subject-verb
SVO	Subject-verb-object
T	Theme argument
TAM	Tense-aspect-mood
TR	Transitive
TRN	Translative case
Txt	Text
V	Verb
VERB	Verbalizer
VO	Verb-object
VOC	Vocative
VS	Verb-subject
WALS	WORLD Atlas of Language Structures

Database Abbreviations

AL	Albania
BG	Bulgaria
CZ	Czech Republic
FIN	Finland
GR	Greece
HU	Hungary
LT	Lithuania
LV	Latvia
MK	Republic of North Macedonia
MX	Mexico
PL	Poland
RO	Romania
RUS	Russia
SK	Slovakia
UKR	Ukraine
YU	Yugoslavia

Language Abbreviations

Arm.	Armenian
Bulg.	Bulgarian
CR	Common Romani
Cz.	Czech
FPS	Piedmontese Sinti of Southern France
Fr.	French
Germ.	German
Gr.	Greek
IPS	Italian Piedmontese Sinti
It.	Italian
Kurd.	Kurdish
Latv.	Latvian
M. Pers.	Middle Persian
MIA	Middle Indo-Aryan
NIA	New Indo-Aryan
OChSl.	Old Church Slavonic
OIA	Old Indo-Aryan
Oss.	Ossetic
Pasht.	Pashto
Pers.	Persian
Piedm.	Piedmontese
Prov.	Provençal
Rom.	Romanian
Russ.	Russian
SCr.	Serbo-Croatian
Slk.	Slovak
Sln.	Slovene

List of Figures

Fig. 7.1	Linear order in the NP	188
Fig. 9.1	Borrowing of Slavic temporal and phasal adverbs in Romani	268
Fig. 9.2	Borrowing of Slavic local adverbs in Romani	269
Fig. 9.3	Borrowing of Slavic focus particles and intensifiers in Romani	269
Fig. 9.4	Borrowing of Slavic prepositions into Romani	290
Fig. 9.5	Borrowing of Slavic conjunctions into Romani	291
Fig. 10.1	Romani dialect groups influenced by Hungarian	305
Fig. 15.1	The core of a translation process	470
Fig. 15.2	Example of a translation process	471
Fig. 17.1	Group description of Romane Nevipena	521
Fig. 17.2	Jusuf Suleiman's personal website	524
Fig. 17.3	Messages in Romani, guestbook on Jusuf Suleiman's site	524
Fig. 17.4	Exchanges on RRM	526
Fig. 17.5	Romani message, with English translation, from Vikipidiya discussion page	528

List of Tables

Table 4.1	Indo-Aryan inherited lexemes in Romani	92
Table 4.2	Kinship terms in Romani varieties of Italy	96
Table 4.3	Borrowability of kinship terms based on distance from EGO	97
Table 5.1	Vowels in Romani	120
Table 5.2	Consonants in Romani	123
Table 6.1	Proto-Romani inflectional paradigm of the verb *ker-*	162
Table 6.2	Proto-Romani inflectional paradigm of the noun *gadžo*	165
Table 6.3	Proto-Romani inflectional paradigm of the adjective *lačho*	166
Table 7.1	Adverbial subordinators in Romani	209
Table 8.1	Romani 12PL person markers (Balkan and Vlax dialects)	239
Table 8.2	Romani dialects with Turkish conjugation	241
Table 8.3	Turkish conjugations occurring in Romani dialects	245
Table 12.1	Frequency of categories by language etymology in Conde's 150 sentences	361
Table 12.2	Romani and English in early sources of Romani in England	377
Table 14.1	Language policy and planning goals (Hornberger 2006)	434
Table 15.1	Overview of Romani New Testaments published since 1984	468
Table 15.2	Overview of entire Bibles in Romani	469
Table 15.3	Translations of 'baptise' and 'holy spirit' in six publications	474
Table 16.1	Baby-talk lexicon in four varieties of Romani	494

1

Introduction

Yaron Matras and Anton Tenser

Popular images of the Romani language are often wrapped in the mystique that surrounds perceptions of the Romani people as supposedly hidden, withdrawn, and subversive. There is still widespread belief that Romani is an array of different languages, some of them haphazardly put together as an internal means of communication aimed primarily at concealing interaction from others, lacking in systematicity and drawing on random elements from different sources. Even some contemporary scholars speak occasionally of the 'myth of the Romani language' (Canut 2011) or suggest that it might have emerged as a 'group ritual' (Willems 1997, p. 83) or an improvised mode of communication 'created along the trade routes' (Okely 1983, p. 9). Still widespread is the reference to Romani in the plural, as 'Romani languages', despite the fact that already Pott's (1844–1845) monumental work clearly demonstrated the diachronic unity of Romani and that political efforts since the early 1990s, in particular at the level of European institutions (see Matras 2013, 2015; Halwachs et al. 2013), have recognized the language as a marker of Romani identity and a potential access pathway to

---

Y. Matras (✉)
School of Arts, Languages, and Cultures,
University of Manchester, Manchester, UK
e-mail: yaron.matras@manchester.ac.uk

A. Tenser
University of Helsinki, Helsinki, Finland

College of Wooster, Wooster, OH, USA

© The Author(s) 2020
Y. Matras and A. Tenser (eds.), *The Palgrave Handbook of Romani Language and Linguistics*, https://doi.org/10.1007/978-3-030-28105-2_1

education and equal opportunities. Among the aims of this collection is to add yet another reference point to help dispel such myths and give a realistic perspective on Romani. Our principal agenda is to provide an up-to-date, state-of-the-art overview of research into the descriptive-historical linguistics and sociolinguistics of Romani.

Drawing on its early roots in the nineteenth century, the linguistic study of Romani in the first part of the twentieth century produced a number of reference grammars (Sampson 1926; Sergievski 1931; Barannikov 1934) and some substantial, groundbreaking research into historical relations with other Indo-Aryan languages (e.g. Grierson 1908; Woolner 1913–1914; Sampson 1923; Turner 1926; Bloch 1932). Post-war descriptive Romani linguistics saw the completion of a number of doctoral dissertations devoted to local and regional dialects (Kostov 1963; Kenrick 1969; Kochanowski 1963–1964) alongside more descriptive grammars (e.g. Gjerdman and Ljungberg 1963; Pobożniak 1964; Ventcel 1966), and the introduction of a Balkanist areal perspective on Romani (Friedman 1985; Boretzky 1986) as well as interest in contact phenomena and language attrition (Hancock 1970; Kenrick 1979; Boretzky 1985; Igla 1989).

The early 1990s saw growing interest in linguistic typology and the documentation of smaller and endangered languages. It was also the period of dramatic political developments surrounding the fall of communism and the opening of borders, allowing freedom of cultural and political association among the Romani communities of Central and Eastern Europe, and leading to a consequent increase in their public visibility. All this gave a new boost to interest in Romani. A new generation of doctoral dissertations examined typological features now in a theoretically informed perspective (Holzinger 1993; Matras 1994; Halwachs 1998), and new concepts were introduced into the study of contact and Romani-based mixed languages (Bakker and van der Voort 1991; Boretzky and Igla 1994). New forms of participatory research emerged, with linguists supporting language revitalization programmes, the development of literacy and educational resources, Bible translations, and various civil society and activist initiatives. The first International Conference on Romani Linguistics took place in Hamburg in 1993, bringing together specialist researchers from various countries. It has since been convening on a bi-annual basis, the thirteenth such event having taken place in Paris in late 2018. Enabled through grants from national and international research councils and partly in conjunction with a rising number of doctoral dissertations devoted to both individual Romani varieties and comparative studies, Romani has become the subject of considerable digital documentation work. Romlex, an online comparative dictionary of Romani dialects, was launched in 2001. The Romani Morpho-Syntax

(RMS) database, launched in 2006, remains one of the most comprehensive online dialectological resources for any language, offering structural sketches of well over a hundred varieties of Romani based on first-hand fieldwork, accompanied by audio files and search functions. The online Atlas of Central Romani combines detailed maps with extensive analytical commentaries on the structural distribution of forms. Online lexical database resources also exist for so-called Angloromani and Scandoromani (the use of Romani-derived lexicon in varieties of English and Scandinavian languages, respectively). Further online resources document Romani language publications and serve as repositories for literacy and education materials in Romani.

In the absence of historical records of the language that pre-date early modern times, the growing corpus of comparative dialect material has allowed researchers to substantially expand our understanding of the historical development of Romani. The study of Romani has also enriched general linguistic discussion. It has had a considerable impact on the study of language contact, in particular the postulation of borrowing hierarchies (see Matras 1998; Elšík and Matras 2006; Elšík 2009; see Matras and Adamou, this volume), and on our understanding of the formation and functions of so-called mixed languages (see Bakker 1998; Matras 2010; see Bakker, this volume). While formal linguistic theory has taken little interest in the language (but see McDaniel 1989), consideration has been given to Romani in various cross-linguistic typological compilations (e.g. van der Auwera 1998; Kortmann 2003; Hansen and de Haan 2009; Boye and Kehayov 2016). Romani linguistics has made prolific contributions to the field of language standardization and language policy, with specialists noting the 'paradigm shift' that is exemplified by plurilingual and trans-national standardization practices in Romani (see, e.g., Matras 2015). The geographical diffusion, the impact of contact, and the exceptional historical journey of Romani as an Indo-Aryan language spoken in Europe have prompted attention to Romani in discussions of phylogenetics and the interface of genetics and language (see Pereltsvaig and Lewis 2015).

While anchored primarily in linguistic methodology, contemporary research in Romani linguistics has also informed and engaged with the cross-discipline discussions in the field known more generally as Romani Studies. Work in linguistic ethnography (e.g. Leggio 2015; Abercrombie 2018) lies in the immediate interface of linguistics and anthropology. For many anthropologists, their own knowledge of Romani not only facilitated their immersion in Romani-speaking communities but also opened an avenue towards an interpretation of the symbolic value of particular Romani concepts (see Sutherland 1975; Stewart 1997; Tauber 2006; Engebrigtsen

2007). Other researchers in the social sciences have drawn on epistemological notions from Romani linguistics to address issues such as the performance of identity narratives (Lemon 2000; Silverman 2012) or group boundaries and community affiliation (Marushiakova and Popov 2004), or have illuminated historical aspects of language policy from a critical social science perspective (O'Keefe 2013; Marushiakova and Popov 2017). Language has also begun to figure in approaches to the educational integration of Roma (Payne 2017; New et al. 2017).

For more than a decade and a half, Matras's (2002) introductory overview of Romani linguistics has served as a principal reference work, outlining the language's historical origins, offering the first modern comparative discussion of its structural composition in phonology, morphology, and syntactic typology, and integrating a model of dialect differentiation and a discussion of contact behaviour and sociolinguistics including language policy. The present volume sets a new milestone in a similar trajectory. For the first time, we bring together a set of contributions in a joint effort to give an up-to-date state of the art that incorporates the most recent research findings in the field as well as the individual insights of authors with specializations in distinct sub-fields. The historical and structural aspects are covered by chapters on origins (Beníšek) and historical sources (Adiego), as well as lexicon (Scala), phonology (Baló), morphology (Elšík), and syntactic typology (Adamou and Matras). The extraordinary role of language contact is addressed in chapters on the impact of key contact languages, namely Turkish (Friedman), Slavonic (Meyer), and Hungarian (Bodnávorá and Wiedner), as well as an overview of contact developments (Matras and Adamou) and a discussion of Para-Romani or 'mixed' varieties (Bakker). These contributions all set the scene for an integrated discussion of dialect differentiation (Elšík and Beníšek) and of language policy endeavours (Halwachs). We then expand the coverage to a number of novel themes that have not been explored before in the context of integrated discussions of Romani language and linguistics and which reflect not just new areas of research but in some cases also new domains of language activity that are connected to globalization and the expansion of media technology and trans-national connections: particular features of child-directed speech in Romani (Kubaník), Romani Bible translations (van den Heuvel), Romani on the Internet (Leggio), and Romani literature (Zahova).

The descriptive chapters draw heavily on the Romani Morpho-Syntax (RMS) database, now a standard reference in Romani linguistics, and readers will have the opportunity to refer to the online resource to follow up on examples provided in the text, adding to the volume's coherence as a joint exploration and discussion platform. The RMS project began in 2000 with the compilation by Viktor Elšík and Yaron Matras, working together at the University of Manchester, of an overview of Romani dialect features based on published sources. From this, a questionnaire template emerged, in 2001, tailored to cover morpho-syntactic and some lexical and lexico-phonetic variation in a typologically informed perspective, which has since become a standard tool for the compilation of dialect descriptions in Romani (see Matras and Elšík 2006, Matras et al. 2009). A team of around fifty fieldwork and transcription assistants, technical assistants, and researchers contributed to the compilation of questionnaire-based elicitation as well as the collection of free speech samples from speakers in over 120 locations across Europe, giving in many cases first insights into dialect types and forms that had been largely unknown to the research community before. The resource has also transformed language documentation practices, introducing for the first time the model of the descriptive grammar in electronic form, accompanied by audio files and tag-searchable phrase transcriptions matched systematically to the cells of tables displaying inflectional paradigms and analytical features, with key structural categories marked for etymology and 'depth' of borrowing (from current or earlier contact languages).

While many of the authors are thus able to draw on a shared comparative resource, openly accessible to the readers and the public, this collection also highlights debates and current gaps in the study of Romani. For a start, the periodization of Romani into 'Proto-Romani' (the pre-European pre-cursor), 'Early Romani' (the form of the language spoken in contact with medieval Greek, possibly in Anatolia), and 'Contemporary Romani' (as known to us today in its dialectal variation) appears to remain consensual yet new terms are being introduced for some of the phases (see Beníšek, this volume). The unique position of Romani as a non-territorial Indo-Aryan language that developed into its present shape in contact with European languages prompts reflection on models of language divergence as well as convergence. The tension between so-called genetic or phylogenetic models of dialect differentiation and language divergence, and models of feature diffusion through contact and repertoire complexity still requires careful attention at least for certain dialect clusters and regions, as Elšík and Beníšek (this volume) flag for central Europe; it will, without a doubt, also require cross-discipline collaboration in order to better understand the historical circumstances that may have shaped contacts between Romani-speaking communities and their mobility and migrations in the past. And while we are now able to draw on a rich comparative descriptive corpus of structural material, extensive documentation of natural discourse and larger-scale surveys of variation are still lacking. The application to Romani of variationist sociolinguistics, discourse and conversation analysis, studies of language socialization, and critical sociolinguistic approaches to language repertoires, identity, and place is still at its very early beginnings. Some authors also point to the absence of a reliable modern etymological dictionary.

Discussions of language policy and the politics of language, language and faith, the use of language in the formation of online communities, and the links between literary production and activism, all serve to flag issues of agency in the shaping of language practices and their description and analysis. Interest in Romani linguistics emerged as the enlightenment brought about a quest for an understanding of origins, primordial connections, and divergence pathways. It was subsequently inspired, if not directly driven, by emerging methods and traditions of orientalism and colonial studies, both in respect of the Indo-Aryan connections of Romani and in regard to the marginalized social status of Romani-speaking communities in Europe and related communities in Western and Central Asia. In many countries, compilation of language samples for Romani was part of a law enforcement agenda from early modern times (see Adiego, this volume; Matras 1999), embedding the scientific study of the language into forensic services and a policy of control and containment. Our collection appears at a time when there is much discussion around the notion 'critical Romani studies' as a platform for a symbolic assertion of agency, with implications for a new epistemology (for a critical discussion, see Stewart 2017). Romani linguistics remains embedded into mainstream linguistics, and it draws on the mainstream discipline for its agenda and methods, seeking to uncover general and universal patterns, pertaining for instance to the mapping of cognition onto language, and to different forms of managing communication in different social contexts and units. While it has long broken away from both law enforcement and socio-political containment agendas, it has become attuned to issues of social justice and the responsibility to reach out to support and inform communities. We hope that this volume will be of interest both to linguists and to language enthusiasts including authors, translators, educators, and policy makers, as well as to specialists in neighbouring disciplines in the social sciences and humanities more generally. We wish to thank the contributors for publishing their work in this forum and Palgrave Macmillan for accommodating this collection in their programme of academic handbooks.

References

Abercrombie, Amelia. 2018. Language purism and social hierarchies: Making a Romani standard in Prizren. *Language in Society* 47 (5): 741–761.

Bakker, Peter. 1998. Para-Romani language versus secret languages: Differences in origin, structure, and use. In *The Romani element in non-standard speech*, ed. Yaron Matras, 69–96. Wiesbaden: Harrassowitz.

Bakker, Peter, and Hein van der Voort. 1991. Para-Romani languages: An overview and some speculations on their genesis. In *In the margin of Romani: Gypsy languages in contact*, ed. Peter Bakker and Marcel Cortiade, 16–44. Amsterdam: Institute for General Linguistics.

Barannikov, A.P. 1934. *The Ukrainian and South Russian Gypsy dialects*. Leningrad: Academy of Sciences of the USSR.

Bloch, Jules. 1932. Le présent du verbe "être" en tsigane. *Indian Linguistics* 2: 309–316.

Boretzky, Norbert. 1985. Sind Zigeunersprachen Kreols? In *Akten des 1. Essener Kolloquium über "Kreolesprachen und Sprachkontakte"*, ed. Norbert Boretzky, Werner Enninger, and Thomas Stolz, vom 26.1. an der Universität Essen.

Boretzky, Norbert. 1986. Zur Sprache der Gurbet von Priština (Jugoslawien). *Giessener Hefte für Tsiganologie* 3: 195–216.

Boretzky, Norbert, and Birgit Igla. 1994. Romani mixed dialects. In *Mixed languages: 15 case studies in language intertwining*, ed. Peter Bakker and Maarten Mous, 35–68. Amsterdam: IFOTT.

Boye, Kasper, and Petar Kehayov (eds.). 2016. *Semantic functions of complementizers in European languages*. Berlin: De Gruyter.

Canut, Cécile. 2011. La Langue Romani: Une Fiction Historique. *Langage et société* 136: 55–80.

Elšík, Viktor. 2009. Loanwords in Selice Romani, an Indo-Aryan language of Slovakia. In *Loanwords in the world's languages: A comparative handbook*, ed. Martin Haspelmath and Uri Tadmor, 260–303. Berlin: Mouton de Gruyter.

Elšík, Viktor, and Yaron Matras. 2006. *Markedness and language change: The Romani sample*. Berlin: Mouton de Gruyter.

Engebrigtsen, Ada. 2007. *Exploring gypsiness: Power, exchange and interdependence in a Transylvanian village*. New York: Berghahn Books.

Friedman, Victor A. 1985. Balkan Romani modality and other Balkan languages. *Folia Slavica* 7: 381–389.

Gjerdman, Olof, and Erik Ljungberg. 1963. *The language of the Swedish Coppersmith Gipsy Johan Dimitri Taikon: Grammar, texts, vocabulary and English word-index*. Uppsala: Lundequist.

Grierson, George A. 1908. India and the Gypsies. *JGLS*, n.s., 1: 400.

Halwachs, Dieter W. 1998. *Amaro vakeripe Roman hi – Unsere Sprache ist Roman: Texte, Glossar und Grammatik der burgenländischen Romani-Variante.* Klagenfurt: Drava.

Halwachs, Dieter W., Barbara Schrammel-Leber, and Simone A. Klinger. 2013. *Romani, education, segregation and the European Charter for Regional and Minority Languages.* Graz: Grazer Romani Publikationen.

Hancock, Ian F. 1970. Is Anglo-Romanes a creole? *JGLS*, 3rd ser., 49: 41–44.

Hansen, B., and F. de Haan (eds.). 2009. *Modality in European languages.* Berlin: Mouton.

Holzinger, Daniel. 1993. *Das Romanes: Grammatik und Diskursanalyse der Sprache der Sinte (= Innsbrucker Beiträge zur Kulturwissenschaft, 85).* Innsbruck: Verlag des Instituts für Sprachwissenschaft der Universität Innsbruck.

Igla, Birgit. 1989. Kontakt-induzierte Sprachwandelphänomene im Romani von Ajia Varvara (Athen). In *Vielfalt der Kontakte (Beiträge zum 5. Essener Kolloquium über "Grammatikalisierung: Natürlichkeit und Systemökonomie". 1. Band),* ed. Norbert Boretzky, Werner Enninger, and Thomas Stolz, 67–80. Bochum: Brockmeyer.

Kenrick, Donald S. 1969. *Morphology and lexicon of the Romany dialect of Kotel (Bulgaria).* Unpublished Doctoral dissertation. School of Oriental and African Studies, London.

Kenrick, Donald. 1979. Romani English. *International Journal of the Sociology of Language* 19: 79–88.

Kochanowski, Vania de Gila. 1963–1964. *Gypsy studies.* New Delhi: International Academy of Indian Culture.

Kortmann, Bernd (ed.). 2003. *Dialectology meets typology: Dialect Grammar from a cross-linguistic perspective.* Berlin: De Gruyter Mouton.

Kostov, Kiril. 1963. *Grammatik der Zigeunersprache Bulgariens: Phonetik unf Morpholigie.* Unpublished Doctoral dissertation. Humboldt University, Berlin.

Leggio, D. Viktor. 2015. Radio Romani Mahala: Romani identities and languages in a virtual space. In *Virtual citizenship? Roma communities, inclusion policies, participation and ICT tools,* ed. Alfredo Alietti, Martin Olivera, and Veronica Riniolo, 97–114. Milan: MacGraw-Hill.

Lemon, Alaina. 2000. *Between two fires: Gypsy performance and Romani memory from Pushkin to post-socialism.* Durham: Duke University Press.

Marushiakova, Elena, and Vesselin Popov. 2004. Segmentation vs. consolidation: The example of four Gypsy groups in CIS. *Romani Studies* 14 (2): 145–191.

Marushiakova, Elena, and Vesselin Popov. 2017. Politics of multilingualism in Roma education in early Soviet Union and its current projections. *Social Inclusion* 5: 48–59.

Matras, Yaron. 1994. *Untersuchungen zu Grammatik und Diskurs des Romanes. Dialekt der Kelderaša/Lovara.* Wiesbaden: Harrassowitz.

Matras, Yaron. 1998. Utterance modifiers and universals of grammatical borrowing. *Linguistics* 36: 281–331.

Matras, Yaron. 1999. Johann Rüdiger and the study of Romani in eighteenth century Germany. *Journal of the Gypsy Lore Society*, 5th ser., 9: 89–116.

Matras, Yaron. 2002. *Romani: A linguistic introduction*. Cambridge: Cambridge University Press.

Matras, Yaron. 2010. *Romani in Britain: The afterlife of a language*. Edinburgh: Edinburgh University Press.

Matras, Yaron. 2013. Scholarship and the politics of Romani identity: Strategic and conceptual issues. *European Yearbook of Minority Issues* 10 (2011): 209–245.

Matras, Yaron. 2015. Transnational policy and 'authenticity' discourses on Romani language and identity. *Language in Society* 44: 295–316.

Matras, Yaron, Christopher White, and Viktor Elšík. 2009. The RMS Database and web resource. In *Linguistic databases*, ed. Martin Everaert and Simon Musgrave, 329–362. Berlin: Mouton de Gruyter.

McDaniel, Dana. 1989. Partial and multiple wh-movement. *Natural Language & Linguistic Theory* 7: 565–604.

New, William S., Hristo Kyuchukov, and Jill de Villiers. 2017. 'We don't talk Gypsy here': Minority language policies in Europe. *Journal of Language and Cultural Education* 5 (2): 1–24.

O'Keeffe, Brigid. 2013. *New Soviet Gypsies: Nationality, performance, and selfhood in the early Soviet Union*. Toronto: University of Toronto Press.

Okely, Judith. 1983. *The traveller-Gypsies*. Cambridge: Cambridge University Press.

Payne, Mark. 2017. The inclusion of Slovak Roma pupils in secondary school: Contexts of language policy and planning. *Current Issues in Language Planning* 18 (2): 161–180.

Pereltsvaig, Asya, and Martin Lewis. 2015. *The Indo-European controversy: Facts and fallacies in historical linguistics*. Cambridge: Cambridge University Press.

Pobożniak, Tadeusz. 1964. *Grammar of the Lovari dialect*. Kraków: Państwowe wydawnictwo naukowe.

Pott, August. 1844–1845. *Die Zigeuner in Europa und Asien. Ethnographisch-linguistische Untersuchung vornehmlich ihrer Herkunft und Sprache*. Halle: Heynemann.

Sampson, John. 1923. On the origin and early migrations of the Gypsies. *JGLS*, 3rd ser., 2: 156–169.

Sampson, John. 1926. *The dialect of the Gypsies of Wales, being the older form of British Romani preserved in the speech of the clan of Abram Wood*. Oxford: Clarendon Press.

Sergievskij, Maksim V. 1931. *Cyganski Jazyk*. Moskva: Centraljnoe Izdateljstvo Narodov S.S.S.R.

Silvermann, Carol. 2012. *Romani routes: Cultural politics and Balkan music in diaspora*. Oxford: Oxford University Press.

Stewart, Michael. 1997. *The time of the Gypsies*. Boulder: Westview Press.

Stewart, Michael. 2017. Nothing about us without us, or the dangers of a closed-society research paradigm. *Romani Studies* 27: 125–146.

Sutherland, Anne. 1975. *Gypsies: The hidden Americans*. Prospect Heights: Waveland.

Tauber, Elisabeth. 2006. *Du wirst keinen Ehemann nehmen. Respekt, Bedueutung der Toten unf Flucht-Heirat bei den Sinti Estraixaria*. Berlin: LIT-Verlag.

Turner, Ralph L. 1926. The position of Romani in Indo-Aryan. *JGLS*, 3rd ser., 5: 145–189.

van der Auwera, Johan (ed.). 1998. *Adverbial constructions in the languages of Europe*. Berlin: De Gruyter Mouton.

Ventcel, Tatjana V. 1966. *Cyganskij jazyk (severnorusskij dialect)*. Moscow: Nauka.

Willems, Wim. 1997. *In search of the true Gypsy: From enlightenment to final solution*. London: Frank Cass.

Woolner, Alfred C. 1913–1914. The Indian origin of the Gypsies in Europe. *Journal of the Panjab Historical Society* 2: 136–141.

Part I

History

2

The Historical Origins of Romani

Michael Beníšek

2.1 Introduction

Romani is a group of Indo-Aryan varieties that are descended from a common ancestor (Late Proto-Romani also known as Early Romani) spoken in Greek-speaking areas of the Byzantine Empire at the beginning of the second millennium CE.

The Indo-Aryan group of languages constitutes one of the three divisions of the Indo-Iranian branch of the Indo-European language family, the other divisions being Iranian and Nuristani. It is primarily spoken in South Asia (Indian subcontinent, hence Subcontinental Indo-Aryan languages), in particular in its northern and central parts, where it forms a vast dialect continuum, and in the island countries of Sri Lanka and the Maldives. Indo-Aryan has a documented history spanning more than three thousand years, which provides an excellent opportunity to study its development. This history is linguistically divided into three stages: Old Indo-Aryan (OIA), which includes Vedic and Classical Sanskrit based on languages spoken between approximately 1500 and 600 BCE; Middle Indo-Aryan (MIA),

---

This chapter was supported by the Charles University project Progres Q10, Language in the shiftings of time, space and culture.

M. Beníšek (✉)
Charles University, Prague, Czech Republic
e-mail: michael.benisek@ff.cuni.cz

© The Author(s) 2020
Y. Matras and A. Tenser (eds.), *The Palgrave Handbook of Romani Language and Linguistics*, https://doi.org/10.1007/978-3-030-28105-2_2

which covers languages of a period roughly between 600 BCE and 1000 CE, such as Pāli, language varieties of Aśokan inscriptions, various Prākrits and Apabhraṃśa varieties of the final phase of MIA; and New Indo-Aryan (NIA), whose beginnings can be traced back to the first centuries of the second millennium; see Masica (1991) and Cardona and Jain (2003) for the general surveys of Indo-Aryan linguistics from recent times. The latest introduction to the general study of South Asian languages is provided by Hock and Bashir (2016).

Romani is one of the non-Subcontinental Indo-Aryan languages since it is neither part of the Indo-Aryan dialect continuum, nor spoken in any other part of South Asia, although some form of Early Proto-Romani was still spoken in the Indian subcontinent until the second half of the first millennium CE. Romani has often been associated with other Indo-Aryan 'Gypsy' languages spoken outside India. These include Domari, the Indo-Aryan language of the Dōm people of the Middle East (e.g. Macalister 1914; Herin 2012; Matras 2012), and Lomavren, which is a mixed language that consists of Armenian grammar with an Indo-Aryan lexicon (Finck 1907; Scala 2014). There were attempts to group Romani, Domari and Lomavren together in a genealogical sense by assuming a single ancestral 'proto-Gypsy' language (Sampson 1923; Kaufman's conference manuscript cited in Hancock 1995, pp. 28–29). However, despite shared ethnonyms (see Sect. 2.2) and a similar socio-economic profile of their speakers, it is now well established that Romani and Domari plus the Lomavren lexicon constitute three distinct groups of Indo-Aryan varieties that cannot be traced back to their exclusive common ancestor (Turner 1926; Hancock 1995; see also Boretzky and Igla 2004, pp. 12–15; Matras 2012, pp. 20–27 for a linguistic comparison of Romani and Domari from an historical viewpoint). The same holds true for Romani in relation to Ḍumāki (Ḍomaakí), a small Indo-Aryan language in northern Pakistan (Lorimer 1939; Weinreich 2008), which has also been compared to Romani (e.g. Lesný 1941).

This chapter introduces topics related to the origins of Romani and its Indo-Aryan inheritance. Section 2.2 discusses Romani ethnonyms of Indo-Aryan origin. Section 2.3 addresses the methodological issues of Proto-Romani reconstructions. Section 2.4 deals with the position of Romani in Indo-Aryan and presents a very brief overview of the Proto-Romani language contact. The largest part of the chapter (Sect. 2.5) provides a brief sketch of the major Indo-Aryan features in Romani phonology and grammar.

2.2 Ethnonymy

The original self-appellation of Romani speakers is based on Late Proto-Romani *rom* (feminine *romni*),[1] whose reflexes are widespread Romani auto-ethnonyms, spelled as *rom*, *rom*, *rrom* or *řom*, with various phonetic realisations of the initial rhotic. The name is cognate with the self-designations of the Domari- and Lomavren-speaking groups of West Asia, viz. *dōm* and *lom*, respectively, as well as with the names of certain non-agrarian castes inhabiting the northern parts of the Indian subcontinent, such as *ḍom* (e.g. in Hindi and Bengali) and *ḍum/ḍūm* (e.g. in Nepali). All these appellations are reflexes of the Sanskrit and Prakrit designation of a caste of musicians *ḍomba-* (with a rarer variant *ḍumba-*; CDIAL 5570), which is attested in literature dating back to the sixth century CE. The earliest mention of Ḍombas is found in the Sanskrit astrological text Bṛhatsaṃhitā of Varāhamihira (LSI.11, p. 143; Vekerdi 1981, p. 250; Beníšek 2007), while abundant references occur in the Sanskrit chronicle of Kashmir Rājataraṅgiṇī, written by Kalhaṇa in the twelfth century (see Beníšek 2009b).[2]

It has repeatedly been suggested that Ḍombas may have been named after their musical profession. Mayrhofer (2001, p. 232) suggests an onomatopoeic source for *ḍomba-*, with an original meaning 'maker of a *ḍom*-sound, drummer'. Other etymological proposals include Przyluski (1926, p. 35), who suggests a connection to Sanskrit *tumba-* 'gourd (Lagenaria vulgaris)', whose fruit is said to resemble a drum, and Kuiper (1948, p. 87), who directly associates *ḍomba-* with various Sanskrit and Prakrit words for drums, such as *dundubhi-*, *ḍamaru-*, *ḍiṇḍima-* and *āḍambara-*. Kuiper argues that all these words are Munda loanwords, but similar forms also occur in Dravidian languages (cf. DEDR 2949). The word's non-Indo-Aryan etymology supports the assumption that Ḍombas were recruited from non-Indo-Aryan tribal populations, either Dravidian or Munda, but the main arguments for such assumptions are a socio-economic profile of the caste, its low ('untouchable') status in the Brāhmaṇical ideology and even physical characteristics of Ḍoms in modern India (cf. Woolner 1913–1914; LSI.11; Briggs 1953; Vekerdi 1981). According to Sharma (1990, p. 290), the Ḍombas were probably one of the aboriginal tribes who were absorbed into caste-based society during the Gupta period, i.e. in the fourth to sixth centuries CE, which coincides with their first appearance in the literature. However, it should be pointed out that modern reflexes of the word *ḍomba-* in India are cover terms for various groups that share a similar socio-economic profile but not necessarily a common origin.

Along with its ethnic meaning, *rom* is commonly used in a matrimonial sense in Romani: *rom* means 'husband' and its feminine derivation *romni* is used to mean 'wife'. This usage, too, has clear Indian origins. In both major language families of India, Indo-Aryan and Dravidian, designations of castes (*jāti*), the principal endogamous units of the Indian social organisation, often occur in discourses in which their occurrence might seem irrelevant or redundant. Manifestations of such redundant employment occur when these designations are used instead of any general word for 'husband' and 'wife' or when they are employed as vocatives, not only by members of different castes but also reciprocally between husband and wife. This sociolinguistic feature of India was thoroughly discussed by Emeneau (1980, pp. 218–243). Emeneau cites examples in the Sanskrit epic and narrative literature that abound in references to interacting characters vie the designations of their caste membership. For example, *tasya brāhmaṇī* [his Brāhmaṇa.F] means 'his wife (he being a Brāhmaṇa)', *te kṣatriyā* [your Kṣatriya.F] is used to mean 'your wife (you being a Kṣatriya)' and *madīyā brāhmaṇī* [my Brāhmaṇa.F] occurs as a phrase meaning 'my wife (I being a Brāhmaṇa)'. Examples of vocative addresses in Sanskrit literature include *brāhmaṇa* 'O (my) husband (who is a Brahman)' and *brāhmaṇi* 'O wife (of mine, I being a Brahman)' (see Emeneau 1980, pp. 226–232 for references to literary passages where such expressions occur). The tradition continues into modern languages, for which there is evidence in both literary and oral tales. For example, a Panjabi narrative in Grierson (LSI.9, p. 700), quoted in Emeneau (1980, p. 241), contains examples such as *jāṭanī jāṭnai kahādī* [Jat.F Jat.DAT saying.F] 'the Jat's wife used to say to her husband (lit. to the Jat)'. Emeneau argues that such a strong emphasis on group nomenclature that displaces some general words for 'husband' and 'wife' is an expression of the far-reaching importance of caste-based social organisation of India. In Romani, this matrimonial reference of *rom* and *romni*, which was formerly a pragmatic option for referring to members of one's own community, was lexicalised, and such lexicalisation was only possible outside India in contact with languages that lack such a trait.

In some Romani varieties, particularly in those spoken in northern and western parts of Europe, the word *rom* has been maintained only in this lexicalised matrimonial reference, while other terms have replaced it as a group label. We encounter Romani autonyms such as *kalo* (< 'black') and its phonological variants in various parts of western and northern Europe, *manuš* (< 'human') in France and *sinto* (perhaps from a former cryptic formation and definitely unrelated to the name of the Pakistani province of Sindh; see Matras 1999, pp. 108–112), among groups from German-speaking areas. Significantly, members of these groups often still refer to their language using derivations of *rom* (adjective *romano*, adverb *romanes*). One particularly noteworthy ethnonym based on *rom* is represented by complex formations that are documented in uncontiguous communities in various parts of Europe, viz. *romanichal* or *romanichel* in Britain (and in immigrant communities in North America), *romnitschēl* in early nineteenth-century descriptions of German Romani (Graffunder 1835), *eromanitsel* or *errumantxel-* in the Basque country (Ackerley 1929; Bakker 1991), *roma(n)sēl* in Finland (Thesleff 1901; Granqvist 2013), *romacel* in Parakalamos of Greece (Matras 2004a) and *urumčel'* or *urmačel'* in Crimea (Marushiakova and Popov 2004), among others (see Bakker 1999, p. 200). The first part of these appellations contains *rom*, obviously as part of the historical adjective derivation in the feminine agreement form *romani*. The origin of the last part *-čel*, etc., is less clear. Turner (CDIAL 4911) suggests an origin in the reconstructed OIA noun **cella-* 'boy' of possible Dravidian origin, from which Hindi *celā* 'disciple, pupil' derives (cf. also Bakker 1999, p. 200 for other proposals). More likely, this segment is descended from the Late Proto-Romani feminine noun **čhel* 'clan, kin', for which there is evidence in the Latvian Romani noun *čhel'* 'family, kin, tribe, people' (Mānušs et al. 1997, p. 43). It follows that these complex autonyms are probably based on a morphologised and lexicalised Proto-Romani phrase **romani čhel* 'Romani clan', with a later semantic shift to 'a member of the Romani clan' (cf. also Elšík 2008, p. 212).

Romani dialects also possess common expressions that refer to outsiders. The widespread Romani designation for 'non-Roms' is *gadžo*, which is apparently related to words that mean 'man' in certain Indo-Aryan caste argots, such as *kajjā* in Sãsī, *kājā* in Naṭī, *kājaro* in Kanjarī and *kājwā* in Ḍom (LSI.11, pp. 11 and 96), as well as to the Domari and Lomavren words for outsiders *kadža* and *kača*, respectively. The origin of these expressions is unknown, and they might have an ultimate non-Indo-Aryan etymology. Finck's (1907, p. 63) proposal to derive *gadžo* from OIA *gārhya-* 'domestic' (via MIA **gajjha-*) is doubtful as *gārhya-* would have yielded **khadžo* in Romani.[3] Two other Indo-Aryan words for non-Roms, both of which are dialectally limited, are *goro* < MIA *gora-* < OIA *gaurá-* 'white, yellowish' (cf. Hindi *gorā* 'fair-skinned') and *das*, which usually means 'Slav', < MIA *dāsa-* < OIA *dāsá-* 'slave, non-Aryan'. Finally, there are differentiating words of Indo-Aryan origin for children: *čhavo* 'boy, son' (*čhaj* < **čhavi* 'girl, daughter'), from MIA *chāva-*, *chāpa-* 'young of an animal' (CDIAL 5026), refers to an in-group Romani child, while an alien child is called *raklo/rakli* (cf. Hindi *laṛkā* 'boy', *laṛkī* 'girl'; CDIAL 10924). Such differentiation in the words for children on the basis of their origin is also likely to have been inherited from India, where it is particularly common in some Dravidian languages (cf. Emeneau 1980, p. 221).

2.3 Proto-Romani

Romani is characterised by huge dialectal variation, which manifests itself in the existence of several dialect groups and numerous regional and group dialects (see Elšík and Beníšek, this volume). Via comparative reconstruction, we can arrive at a common forerunner of all Romani dialects, which is called 'Early Romani' by Matras (2002; also Elšík and Matras 2006). In line with practices common in historical linguistics, where an unattested and reconstructed predecessor of attested known varieties is generally called a 'proto-language', I will call this hypothetical language from which all Romani dialects have descended 'Proto-Romani' and more specifically 'Late Proto-Romani'. The attribute 'Late' indicates a final period in the development of the proto-language, which was followed by its split into individual dialects, and, at the same time, it distinguishes the period from earlier stages (see below). Many Late Proto-Romani forms, such as the genitive suffix *-ker-, are continued in at least some present-day dialects and are therefore well attested, whereas others, such as the form of the remoteness suffix *-asi, are merely hypothetical.[4]

There are both intralinguistic and extralinguistic pieces of evidence from which we are able to locate Late Proto-Romani in time and space. First, all Romani dialects share not only the inherited layer of Indo-Aryan forms and structures but also pre-European loan components and a strong Medieval Greek element, which indicate that Late Proto-Romani must have been spoken in a Greek-speaking environment of the Byzantine period. Second, historical evidence records the migration of Romani populations from the Balkans to other parts of Europe beginning in the fourteenth century (see Fraser 1995), and this places the last stage of a Romani unity in the first centuries of the second millennium. Late Proto-Romani was still a more or less homogeneous language but one that was undergoing radical, contact-induced changes and massive borrowing from Greek, which involved lexical and grammatical vocabulary, as well as inflectional and derivational morphology and patterns of syntactic typology.

Late Proto-Romani already displayed many Balkan characteristics, having departed much from a language typical of the Indian Sprachbund. A period prior to Late Proto-Romani that covered both the time when the language was still spoken on Indian soil and the time of the earliest migration can be designated 'Early Proto-Romani' (this is what Matras 2002 calls 'Proto-Romani'). Early Proto-Romani can be reconstructed by comparing Late Proto-Romani forms with those of other Indo-Aryan languages, among which those of the older (OIA and MIA) stages play the most significant

2 The Historical Origins of Romani 19

role. However, there is an important methodological difference between reconstructing Early Proto-Romani and reconstructing Late Proto-Romani. While Late Proto-Romani can be reconstructed as a more or less synchronic state that formed a starting point for the known dialectal variation, the Early Proto-Romani reconstruction aims at reconstructing a historical development in the earliest layers of Romani that led from its MIA predecessor to Late Proto-Romani. Let me illustrate different methods of both reconstructions on a single noun. The word for 'moon' in Romani dialects occurs as *čhon, čh'on, čon, č'on, šon, śon, chon*, plus forms with long vowels and certain rare forms in individual varieties (*čōn, cōn, sōn, čūn*, etc.).[5] From this variety of forms, the Late Proto-Romani masculine noun **čhon* can be safely reconstructed by the comparative method. This word has a known etymology in the MIA feminine noun *joṇhā-* 'moonlight' (< OIA *jyótsnā-*; CDIAL 5301), to which it exhibits regular sound correspondences. The Early Proto-Romani reconstruction should describe a sum of changes and their relative chronology (if relevant) that led from *joṇhā-* (i.e. *džoṇhā-* according to Romani orthography) to **čhon*. Thus, phonological changes involved the transfer of aspiration (**džhoṇā-*), the shift of the retroflex nasal to a dental or alveolar nasal (**džhonā-*), apocope of the final vowel (**džhon*) and, finally, the devoicing of the aspirate (**čhon*). Furthermore, there was a change in the grammatical gender of this noun (feminine > masculine) and a semantic shift in the meaning from 'moonlight' to 'moon'. The Early Proto-Romani reconstruction can also make an indirect inference to the original functions of a particular inherited form in Romani. For example, there are several Romani dialects that still possess the Indo-Aryan converb (absolutive or conjunctive participle) in *-i*. Evidence of the Subcontinental Indo-Aryan languages, taking into consideration various Indo-Aryan stages, can shed light on the range of functions the converb in **-i* had in Early Proto-Romani.

A comprehensive and systematic overview of the Early Proto-Romani development is still missing, but certain individual features of such a development have already been discussed in detail. Matras (2000) reconstructs the development of the system of demonstratives (also Matras 2002, pp. 106–112), while Bubeník (2000) deals with a reconstruction of an ergative morphosyntax in Early Proto-Romani. Much can be found in Matras (2002), but a discussion of the development of a perfective conjugation is particularly worthy of notice. Tálos (1999) presents a phonological reconstruction of what he calls Ancient Romani or Ḍommānī and describes as a Śaurasenī-like Prākrit, i.e. an unattested predecessor of Romani that still had characteristics of a MIA language. Beníšek (2010) discusses historical aspects of Indo-Aryan non-finite verb forms in Romani, and Oslon (2012) reconstructs the forms of some nouns in a Proto-Romani stage. A sketch of Late Proto-Romani (called 'Early Romani') is provided by Elšík and Matras (2006, pp. 68–84). Numerous historical discussions, along with outlines of what they often call 'original Romani forms', are found in Boretzky and Igla (2004).

2.4 The Classification of Romani Within Indo-Aryan

The dialectological position of Romani within Indo-Aryan can only be discussed in association with the internal genealogical classification of all Indo-Aryan languages. However, no such classification is universally recognised. The presence of a vast dialect continuum with no clear boundaries of languages and dialects, alongside the extensive contact of Indo-Aryan languages among themselves since earliest times, makes any classificatory attempt difficult and largely dependent on selected linguistic criteria.

Still, various schemes of Indo-Aryan historical taxonomy have been put forward since the nineteenth century (see Masica 1991, pp. 446–462 for a detailed survey). The most authoritative position, at least in terms of the importance it has had in subsequent discussions, was occupied by Grierson (LSI 1.1), who worked with a division of Indo-Aryan into three sub-branches—inner, outer and mediate—and their further differentiation into several groups, whose names are mostly geographically motivated (Central, Eastern, Southern, Northwestern and Pahari or Northern). Although Grierson's scheme is no longer accepted in its particulars (but cf. Southworth 2005 for its recent defence), his basic terminological framework has gained ground. Authors after Grierson generally worked with the linguistic groups introduced by Grierson, sometimes adding one or two, while they differed with respect to the categorisation of certain languages, although there are also languages whose classifications have never been disputed. Thus, for example, the group of Central (sometimes called Midland) languages is commonly understood to comprise Hindi and other languages of the Hindi Belt (the so-called Hindi dialects), but various other languages, such as Rajasthani languages, Panjabi, Gujarati and Nepali are put into the Central group by different scholars.

Leaving aside earlier unfounded speculations (see review in Hancock 1988), the first systematic scientific attempt to classify Romani within Indo-Aryan was that of Miklosich (1874–1878, IV, pp. 287–296). Miklosich suggested that Romani originated in Dardic, a group of languages spoken in the valleys of the northwestern mountainous area of the Indian subcontinent.[6] His arguments were centred on archaic features in Romani phonology that have parallels in some Dardic languages, such as the survival of two sibilants and the preservation of consonant clusters /Cr/, /st/ and /št/ (</ṣṭh/) (see below). Miklosich's view gained the general acceptance of the scholars of that time, e.g. Pischel (1883), Bloch (1919, pp. 21–22), and Grierson (LSI 8.2), who revised his earlier opinion about the Eastern (Māgadhī) origin of Romani (Grierson 1888), but it was put to doubt by Woolner (1913–1914, 1915) and Sampson (1923) and definitely disproven by Turner (1926) in his influential study on the position of Romani in Indo-Aryan. Turner's findings have not been seriously challenged since then and deserve more detailed attention.

2.4.1 Romani and Central Indo-Aryan

Turner (1926) analysed early phonological innovations that took place in Indo-Aryan—mostly during a transition from OIA to MIA and some during the MIA period itself—and showed that Romani reflects the sum of innovations typical of Central Indo-Aryan. In his view, the Central group comprises Rajasthani, Hindi, Central and Eastern Pahari (i.e. Nepali) and perhaps Bihari. The features discussed by Turner are as follows (see his paper for more details)[7]:

1. The OIA syllabic rhotic /ṛ/ was fully vocalised and developed into a close vowel /i/ or /u/, as in *ghṛtá-* 'clarified butter' > *khil* 'butter' (cf. Hindi *ghī*) and *pṛcchÁti* > *phučel* 'asks' (Hindi *pūche*).
2. The OIA consonant cluster /kṣ/ was assimilated and became the aspirated velar /kh/, as in OIA *ákṣi* > *jakh* 'eye' (Hindi *ãkh*).
3. The OIA consonant group of a sibilant plus /m/ developed into /m/ via MIA /mh/, as in the first- and second-person plural pronouns: OIA *asm-* (cf. ACC *asmÁn*) and **tuṣm-* (cf. ACC *yuṣmÁn*) > Romani *am-* (*ame* or *amen* 'we') and *tum-* (*tume* or *tumen* 'you.PL'); cf. also Hindi *ham* and *tum*.
4. The OIA consonant group of a dental plus /v/ or /m/ became a labial, as in the reflexive *(ā)tmán-* > *p-* (cf. Hindi *āp*).
5. The initial semivowel /y/ underwent affrication to the voiced post-alveolar /j/ (i.e. /dž/), as in *yā-* > *dža-* 'to go' (Hindi *jā-*).
6. The OIA intervocalic nasal /m/ was spirantised to /v/ (reflected in writing only in Late MIA), as in *grÁma-* > *gav* 'village' (Hindi *gãv*).

On the grounds of these shared innovations, Turner (1926, p. 159) arrived at the conclusion that Romani originated in the group of Central

22   M. Beníšek

Indo-Aryan languages. Then he dealt with Romani conservations that have been modified in other Central languages:

1. The OIA simple intervocalic dentals /t/, /d/ and perhaps /th/ have been preserved in Romani as /l/ but lost in other Central languages, as in *gatá-> gelo* 'gone' (versus Hindi *gayā*), *nadí-* (>*nel*) > *len* 'river' (versus Hindi *naī*), cf. also *ghṛtá-> khil* (versus Hindi *ghī*).
2. Romani preserves a two-way distinction in the sibilants /s/ and /š/ from the OIA inventory of three, /s/, /ś/ and /ṣ/, while all three sibilants have been reduced to /s/ in other Central languages. The alveolar sibilant /s/ continues that of OIA, as in *divasá-> dives* 'day', while the OIA palatal /ś/ and the retroflex /ṣ/ have merged into single /š/, as in *śatá-> šel* 'hundred' (versus Hindi *sau*) and *mắnuṣa-> manuš* 'human' (versus Hindi *mānus*).[8]
3. The OIA /r/ has been retained after dental and labial stops in consonant groups, as in *trḯṇi> trin* 'three' (versus Hindi *tīn*), *drắkṣā-> drakh* 'grape' (versus Hindi *dākh*) and *bhrắtā* (*bhrátṛ-*) > *phral* 'brother' (versus Hindi *bhāī*). After velars, /r/ has been lost even in Romani (cf. *grắma-> gav* 'village').
4. Finally, perhaps the most striking phonological retention in Romani, the OIA consonant groups /st(h)/ and /ṣṭ(h)/ in intervocalic position have been maintained as /st/ and /št/, as in *hásta-> vast* 'hand' (versus Hindi *hāth*) and *kāṣṭhá-> kašt* 'piece of wood' (versus Hindi *kāṭh*).

Apart from the preservation of the intervocalic dentals, which still occur in the midland Śaurasenī Prākrit of the Middle MIA period (e.g. in *gada-* 'gone'), these features were apparently innovated quite early in the Central languages. Since /st(h)/ and /ṣṭ(h)/ are no longer reflected in the Early MIA varieties of Aśokan inscriptions set up in Kalsi, Topra and Meerut (third century BCE), which were taken by Turner as representatives of Central dialects, Turner concluded that Romani had broken its relations with the Central group before the time of the Mauryan emperor Aśoka. However, this time determination of the separation of an Early Proto-Romani idiom from the rest of Central Indo-Aryan is the weakest point of Turner's study, as shown by Woolner (1928). The language of the Aśokan inscriptions in the locations mentioned is in fact based on an Eastern dialect of Aśoka's government headquarters in Pāṭaliputra (modern Patna) and does not represent a local Central Indo-Aryan vernacular of that period as it has the features typical of Eastern MIA languages, such as /r/ > /l/ and the NOM.SG.M ending *-e*. Central Indo-Aryan is not represented in the edicts of Aśoka (cf. also Woolner 1924, pp. xx–xxii), so the languages of these inscriptions cannot provide evidence of when Romani split from Central Indo-Aryan.

2 The Historical Origins of Romani   23

There is at least one more innovation that has affected the Central languages up to Western Pahari and is shared by Romani: the merger of initial /v/ with /b/, as in *vāś-> baš-* 'to make a noise' (often about an animal) and *vivāha-> biav* 'marriage' (cf. Hindi *byāh*). According to Turner (1926, pp. 171–172), this innovation took place in Romani independently of the Central group due to its late (NIA) occurrence, like in most Dardic languages, where it is also documented (in contrast to other Northwestern languages such as Sindhi, Panjabi and Kashmiri, in which initial /v/ is retained; see Masica 1991, pp. 202–203).

2.4.2 Romani and Northwestern Indo-Aryan

Romani, though shown by Turner (1926) to be a Central Indo-Aryan language, also exhibits certain innovations typical of languages spoken in the northwest of the Indo-Aryan continuum. Turner argued that these innovations were introduced into the language after its speakers had migrated from a midland area to the northwest.

The most convincing phonological innovation shared by Romani and Northwestern languages is the voicing of voiceless stops after nasals, as in OIA *dánta->* Romani *dand* 'tooth', *káṅkata-> kangli* 'comb' and *páñca> pandž* 'five'. Besides Romani, this innovation occurs in Sindhi, Panjabi and Kashmiri and in most Pahari and Dardic languages. It also partly affected the language of Kharoṣṭhī documents from Central Asia, which represents a Northwestern MIA language from the first centuries CE. Matras (2002, p. 149) adds the development of a perfective conjugation from older pronominal enclitics as an important grammatical innovation that links Romani with Sindhi, Western Panjabi ('Lahnda'), Kashmiri and other Dardic languages (see Sect. 2.5.4). Finally, some lexical items in Romani also point to their Northwestern origin, although in general, the Romani vocabulary is closer to that of Central languages (see Turner 1926, pp. 172–174). A striking example of such a loanword (unmentioned by Turner) is the Romani word for 'apple' *phabaj*, which has cognates only in some Dardic languages (e.g. Torwali *babaí*, Palula *babaái*, etc.; cf. CDIAL 9387).

Recently, Zoller (2010) tried to show that there had been a heavy lexical impact on Romani from Dardic, Western Pahari and even Nuristani. Some of his suggestions are worthy of consideration; for example, he points out that [HEAD-MODIFIER] compounds, such as *šer-nango* [head-bare] 'bareheaded', and verbal expressions with the conjunct verb 'to give', such as *brišind d-* [rain give] 'to rain', have parallels in some Dardic languages and

24 M. Beníšek

may represent loan translations (see Zoller 2010, pp. 292–294). However, most of his other suggestions are at least controversial or even outright wrong. For example, Zoller (2010, p. 255 and elsewhere) maintains that all Romani words in which /l/ stands for OIA /t/ are Dardic loans. The arising questions of what a regular reflex of the OIA intervocalic /t/ in inherited words would be—and where such words are—are left unanswered by him. Zoller fails to notice that /l/ < /t/ is also in the 3SG suffix *-el* (< OIA *-ati*); otherwise, he would have to assume that this verbal inflectional suffix was also borrowed. It is possible that lateralisation of the old dental stops was triggered by contact with a Northwestern language (the same development characterises Dardic Kalasha), but this is different from lexical borrowing.[9]

The question of when Early Proto-Romani found itself in contact with Northwestern languages, which is also connected to the issue of when it split from Central languages, remains unresolved. Turner's reference to the time before Aśoka, based on an erroneous assumption, is almost certainly too early. It would indicate a period of at least one thousand or even more years of presence in the environment of Northwestern languages before Early Proto-Romani speakers definitely left South Asia. It is reasonable to assume that such long-term contact with related languages would probably have led to the radical overshadowing of the Central basis of Romani, if not to a complete shift to a Northwestern language. Moreover, such an early date is in conflict with the fact that some Central innovations reflected in Romani are definitely post-Aśokan, e.g. /m/ > /v/ between vowels.

Turner seems to have been too dependent on the Stammbaum scheme by assuming a strict separation of Romani from the Central group in a given point of time and the loss of contact once and for all. Early Proto-Romani might have originated in a transitional area of a dialect continuum, on a more conservative periphery of the Indian midland area that had been affected by innovations spreading from Northwestern languages to some extent. Such a source in transitional dialects would explain the conservative features that are no longer reflected in the midland Śaurasenī Prākrit, as well as some Northwestern innovations that may have already occurred in situ without a migration somewhere to the Indus valley or to the Hindu Kush. After all, the voicing of voiceless stops after nasals occurs as far east as in Nepali, which is classified by Turner as a Central language. Still, some ultimate migration of Early Proto-Romani speakers to the northwest of the subcontinent, followed by contact with Dardic languages, must have occurred, but it may not have taken place earlier than the first millennium CE.

2.4.3 Departure

Another question is when Early Proto-Romani separated from other Subcontinental languages and became an outlier spoken in non-Indo-Aryan surroundings. The general phonological, grammatical and even lexical makeup of Romani indicates that its predecessor in India passed through the whole MIA stage (see also Sect. 2.5). Romani features that go back to OIA and have no known parallels in MIA are conservative phenomena inherited from MIA varieties that are not attested in literary languages. Still, it is not necessary to assign the separation from Subcontinental Indo-Aryan only to the literary period of NIA languages in the second millennium. Linguistic innovations that appear in writing often have a longer history in vernaculars, and their development always predates their first occurrence in a literary variety, especially in India.

Outside of India, Proto-Romani was in contact with non-Indo-Aryan languages. Berger (1959) suggested contact with Burushaski, a language isolate in the Karakoram Mountains, but his discussions of possible Burushaski etymologies for thirteen Romani words seem to be too hypothetical (cf. Matras 2002, p. 24). An historical analysis reveals that Proto-Romani must have been in contact with Iranian languages, in particular with Persian, perhaps also with Kurdish and Ossetian (Hancock 1995), and with Armenian (Boretzky 1995a; Scala 2013). Several lexical items also point to a Georgian source (Friedman 1988), although Georgian (as well as Ossetian) words may have been transmitted to Romani via other sources (Matras 2002, p. 25). The most profound influence on Proto-Romani was exercised by Byzantine Greek (e.g. Miklosich 1872–1880, III; Tzitzilis 2001; Grant 2003; Boretzky 2012a). The traditional view (dating back to Pott 1844–1845; Miklosich 1872–1880) is that loans from Iranian, Armenian and Greek were acquired successively and are indicative of a gradual migration from India westward. This view has recently been challenged (see Matras 2002, p. 25) as contact with all these languages could at least partly have taken place simultaneously in medieval Anatolia. This alternative scenario also means that migration from India to Byzantium could have been rapid rather than gradual (see also Elšík and Matras 2006, p. 69), which is compatible with the absence of genuine Eastern Iranian loanwords in Romani. Furthermore, there is evidence that Proto-Romani must have been in contact with some of these languages by the end of the first millennium. Toropov (as cited in Elšík 2009, p. 269) shows that contact with Armenian must have occurred by the ninth century, and Tzitzilis (2001) argues for contact with Greek dialects in Anatolia by the tenth century. Thus, it becomes clear from the linguistic evidence that the departure of Proto-Romani speakers from the Indian subcontinent must have taken place no earlier and no later than during the second half of the first millennium CE.

A view that puts the departure after 1000 is maintained mostly by a group of Romani and Indian scholars who claim that Roms have an origin in warrior clans (Rājpūts) that resisted the Islamic invasion of India in Medieval times (e.g. Kochanowski 1968; Rishi 1974; Hancock 2006, etc.; see Matras 2004b for a critical assessment of some of their arguments). Hancock (e.g. 2000) maintains that Romani emerged as a military koiné, which he calls 'Rajputic', that was based on diverse Indo-Aryan varieties. This koiné, he states, later became a native language when isolation from the original Indian homeland led to the social and cultural amalgamation of the composite population of Indian warriors and their camp followers. Hancock associates the departure from India with invasions led by Mahmud of Ghazni in the eleventh century. His recurrent linguistic argument for this period is that Romani has no neuter gender like other NIA languages and unlike MIA, which still had it (e.g. Hancock 2001; 2006, pp. 74–77). However, the neuter did not disappear abruptly in the history of Indo-Aryan languages around the year 1000. Its loss was a gradual process that had been ongoing during the whole MIA period and was finally accomplished in NIA languages, except for those spoken in the southwest (see Masica 1991, p. 220). As early as in Pāli and in Aśokan inscriptions, the earliest MIA varieties dating back to the pre-Christian era, there is evidence of confusion of the neuter gender with the masculine, while in Late MIA the old gender system was already disintegrated to an advanced degree (see Tagare 1948, pp. 105–106; Bubeník 1996, pp. 69–72). The eventual loss of the neuter in NIA is, therefore, a result of a long history covering the whole MIA stage. Moreover, as Oslon (2012) convincingly argues on morphological grounds, the loss of the neuter seems to have been accomplished relatively late in Proto-Romani (cf. also Sect. 2.5.2).[10]

2.5 An Outline of the Indo-Aryan Legacy

The following subsections provide a brief sketch of the major Indo-Aryan features in Romani phonology and grammar. (See also Sects. 2.4.1 and 2.4.2 for the phonological features of Romani that are diagnostic for its classification within Indo-Aryan.) Lexicon, including derivational morphology, is left out of the discussion here. There are altogether 700 or so Indo-Aryan lexical

2 The Historical Origins of Romani   27

roots in Romani; discussions of their etymologies go back to the works of Pott (1844–1845) and Miklosich (1872–1880), which are critically reviewed in exhaustive etymological notes in Sampson (1926, IV). Another important work on Indo-Aryan words is the comparative dictionary of all Indo-Aryan languages by Turner (1962–1966, i.e. CDIAL). There are also dictionaries of Romani dialects with etymological notes such as Wolf (1960), Valtonen (1972), Mānušs et al. (1997) and Boretzky and Igla (1994), while Soravia (1988), Boretzky (1992, 2012b), Tálos (1999), Scala (2005) and Elšík (2009) contribute with historical discussions of a selected lexical material (see also Scala, this volume).

2.5.1 Phonology

The MIA simple velar, dental and labial stops and post-alveolar affricates in initial position plus their geminates (often from OIA consonant clusters) in internal position are continued in Romani as simple consonants, as in MIA *tatta-* (OIA *taptá-*) > Romani *tato* 'warm'. Most OIA simple intervocalic stops were already reduced in MIA (cf. OIA *yūkā-* > MIA *jūā-* > Romani *džuv* 'louse'), but the intervocalic dental has become /l/ in Romani, cf. MIA *muda-* (OIA *mr̥tá-*) > *mulo* 'dead'. The MIA intervocalic /v/ (sometimes from OIA /p/) and /m/ have merged together as /v/, cf. MIA *tāv-* (OIA *tāp-(áyati)*) 'to heat' > *tav-* 'to cook', MIA *nāma-* (OIA *nā́man-*) > *nav* 'name'. Liquids and nasals generally remain, but non-initial /m/ in Romani is descended from consonant clusters such as /mm/ (*kham* 'sun' < *ghamma-* 'heat'), /mh/ (*am-* 'we' < *amhe*) and /mb/ (*rom* < *ḍomba-*). The MIA glottal fricative /h/ usually disappears between vowels, as in MIA *muha-* > Romani *muj* 'mouth', and often in initial position as well (MIA *hijjo* > *idž* 'yesterday'; but cf. *hasa-* alongside *asa-* 'to laugh' < MIA/OIA *has-*). For sibilants, see Sect. 2.4.1. Non-etymological initial, /j/ and /v/, as in *jakh* 'eye' (< MIA *akkhi*) and *vast* 'hand' (< *ast < OIA *hásta-*), result from morphological assimilation of older determiners (Turner 1932) or from a later prothesis (*ilo - jilo* 'heart' < MIA **hidaa-*, OIA *hr̥daya-*).

Distinctive aspiration, a feature typical of Indo-Aryan consonantism, has been preserved in Romani. However, there are only voiceless aspirates / kh, čh, th, ph/ retained in Romani, as in MIA *dukkha-* > *dukh* 'pain', while their voiced counterparts /gh, jh (= džh), dh, bh/ have been devoiced, as in MIA *ghara-* > *kher* 'house'. Although voiced aspirates are missing in a number of Northwestern NIA languages (cf. Masica 1991, p. 102), the devoicing was an independent and relatively late development in Proto-Romani, possibly triggered by contact with Armenian (Boretzky and Igla 2004, p. 15). It must have occurred after two other changes took place, viz. after the transfer of aspiration from the internal consonant to the initial one, as in MIA *gabbhiṇī->khabni* 'pregnant', and after fricativisation of the initial voiceless velar in words such as MIA *khā->xa-* 'to eat' as there are no cases /gh/ > /x/. The fricative /x/ is a foreign sound in Indo-Aryan, which was probably introduced into Proto-Romani through the contact with Iranian. Miklosich (1874–1878, II, pp. 771–792), Aichele (1957), Turner (1959) and Boretzky and Igla (1993, pp. 15–16) provide more detailed discussions on the development of Romani aspirates.

Indo-Aryan retroflexion is generally lost in Romani. Retroflex nasals and sibilants have merged with reflexes of /n/ and /ś/, respectively, while retroflex stops have changed into a rhotic (except for internal /ṣṭh/ > /št/). In some dialects, there is a distinctive rhotic consonant (usually a geminate or uvular trill) that occurs as a reflex of certain retroflex stops (see already Gilliat-Smith 1911). This indicates that Late Proto-Romani must have had two rhotic consonants: alongside a dental or alveolar trill from MIA and OIA /r/, there was another rhotic (perhaps still a retroflex flap) that developed from /ḍ/ in initial position (*ḍomba->*ṛom*) and in the consonant cluster /ṇḍ/ (OIA *āṇḍa->*anṛo* 'egg') and from retroflex geminates in internal position (OIA *aṭṭa->*aṛo* 'flour'). See Matras (2002, pp. 36–38), Boretzky and Igla (2004, pp. 45–47), and Elšík and Matras (2006, pp. 70–71) for more details.

Romani has inherited the five MIA short vowels /a, i, u, e, o/ with no essential changes. The most conspicuous shift affected /a/ in open syllables of MIA, which has become /e/ in Romani, as in *divasa->dives* 'day' (but not at the edge of words, cf. *avara->aver* 'other'). In original close syllables, the regular reflex of MIA /a/ is /a/ irrespective of the current syllable structure, as in *danta->dand* 'tooth' and *matta->mato* 'drunk'. It should be pointed out that /a/ was realised as [ə] in older stages of Indo-Aryan (Deshpande 1975), as it is still in many non-Eastern NIA languages, so the development of MIA /a/ in Romani can be described as fronting in open syllables and lowering in close syllables (cf. also Boretzky and Igla 1993, pp. 14–15; Tálos 1999, pp. 218–219 for various historical scenarios). MIA long vowels merged with short vowels in Proto-Romani perhaps due to contact with either Armenian or Greek (Boretzky and Igla 2004, pp. 33–34), and final MIA vowels have been apocopated, like in most other NIA languages.

2.5.2 Nominal Morphosyntax

Like Central and Northwestern NIA languages, Romani has a two-way gender distinction, masculine versus feminine (cf. below for possible traces of the old neuter). The overt gender markers of indigenous ('oikoclitic') nouns and adjectives in the nominative singular are -o in masculine nouns (*bar-o rakl-o* 'big boy') and -i in feminine nouns (*bar-i rakl-i* 'big girl'). Both suffixes have developed from the nominative singular suffixes extended by a velar (formerly diminutive) suffix in OIA, e.g. **manṛ-o* 'bread' < MIA *māḍ-ao* < OIA *maṇḍ-akaḥ* 'a sort of pastry or baked flour', *makh-i* 'fly' < MIA *makkh-iā* < OIA *mákṣ-ikā*. While the feminine suffix -i (-ī) is common in NIA, the Subcontinental NIA languages differ as to whether their overt masculine suffix is -o or -ā. The languages that have -o like Romani include Nepali, Central and some Western Pahari languages in the north, some languages of the Hindi area (Bundeli, partially Braj), Rajasthani languages, Gujarati and Sindhi in the southwest and some Dardic languages in the northwest (see Masica 1991, pp. 220–223). An exceptional Indo-Aryan masculine noun in -i in Romani is *pani* 'water', which has developed through apocope from the OIA gerundive formation *pānī́ya-* 'drinkable' via MIA *pāṇia-* (cf. also Hindi masculine *pānī* 'water').

Romani nouns that end in a consonant (hence 'consonantal nouns') are unmarked with respect to gender in the nominative singular. The class of consonantal masculine nouns continues the MIA and OIA class of thematic (*a*-stem) nouns unextended by the aforementioned velar suffix, e.g. *kher* 'house' < MIA *ghara-*, *vast* 'hand' < OIA *hásta-*. The class of consonantal feminine nouns consists of two subclasses that continue two distinct feminine classes of *ā*-stems and *ī*-stems. They differed in Proto-Romani by presence or absence of iotation from the former *ī*-stem suffix in all forms save the nominative singular (cf. Elšík 2000a). The iotated subclass (< *ī*-stems) had /j/, as in **phen*, PL **phen-j-a*, 'sister' < MIA *bhaïṇī-* (OIA *bhaginī-*), **suv*, PL **suv-j-a*, 'needle' < MIA *sūī-* (OIA *sūcī́-*), while the uniotated subclass (< *ā*-stems) did not, as in **čhib*, PL **čhib-a*, 'tongue' < MIA *jibbhā-* (OIA *jihvā́-*), **džuv*, PL **džuv-a*, 'louse' < MIA *jūā-* (OIA *yū́kā-*).

Romani has inherited two number categories, singular and plural, from MIA. The nominative plural marker of the masculine nouns marked for gender, as well as of all marked adjectives, is -e (*bar-e rakl-e* 'big boys') from OIA -*akāḥ* via MIA **-ayā/*-aya*. The same suffix also occurs in Hindi (including Braj), Panjabi, 'Lahnda', Marathi, Konkani, Shina and in most

Western Pahari languages (see Masica 1991, pp. 226–229), i.e. in those languages, with the exception of Shina, Western Pahari and partially Braj, that have the singular masculine suffix *-ā*. The connection of Romani with NIA languages in this particular feature is thus partially different from that in singular marking as languages with the masculine suffix *-o* often take another plural marker *-ā*. The plural suffix of the feminine nouns marked for gender is identical to that of consonantal feminines discussed in the next paragraph.

In Late Proto-Romani, the consonantal masculine nouns were split in their plural marking: some nouns had **-a*, as in **kher-a* 'houses', and some had no plural marker, as in **vast* 'hand(s)' (Elšík 2000a, p. 14). Oslon (2012) argues that differentiation between these two subclasses of consonantal masculines continues the old gender differentiation between neuter and masculine nouns. He proposes to derive *-a* from the OIA plural suffix of neuter nouns *-āni* (MIA *-āī*), while the zero marker reflects the regular development of the MIA plural suffix of masculine nouns *-ā* (< OIA *-āḥ*). Alternatively, the plural *-a* in consonantal masculines might go back to MIA *-āo*, in which the thematic plural suffix *-ā* (< *-āh*) is 'reinforced' by the athematic plural suffix *-o* (< *-ah*) (cf. Pischel 1900, p. 299). While rare in masculines, the plural suffix *-āo* is common in MIA *ā*-stem feminines and must be the source of the plural *-a* in Romani feminines, as in *čhib-a* 'tongues' < MIA *jibbh-āo* (also extended to iotated feminines, as in *suv-j-a* 'needles', and to marked feminines, as in *rakl-j-a* 'girls').

Like other NIA languages, Romani shows at least three historical and typological layers of case marking (see Matras 1997, following Masica 1991). The first layer comprises the nominative and general oblique markers inherited from MIA and OIA. The nominative suffixes are discussed in the previous paragraphs in connection with gender and number marking. The oblique suffixes are descended from MIA dative-genitive suffixes (< OIA genitive), and they are noteworthy for having relatively conservative shapes that can be traced back to the Middle (Prākrit) stage of MIA rather than to Late MIA (Apabhraṃśa): SG.M *-es/-as* < MIA *-assa* (< OIA *-asya*), SG.F *-a* < MIA *-āe* (< OIA *-āyai* or *-āyāḥ*), PL *-en* < MIA *-āṇā* (< OIA *-ānām*). The oblique markers of adjectivals are different from those of nominals in lacking the final consonant, i.e. SG.M and PL *-e*. In addition, some vestigial locative and ablative suffixes of MIA origin have been retained in adverbialised forms in Romani. They include the locative *-e* < MIA *-ahī* (< OIA *-asmin*), as in *kher-e* '(at) home' < Late MIA *ghar-ahī*, and the ablative *-al* < MIA *-ādo* (< OIA *-āt* plus *-tah*), as in *kher-al* 'from home' < MIA (Śaurasenī) *ghar-ādo* (Beníšek 2009a).

The general oblique in Romani functions as a base to which Layer II case markers are attached (see below). Besides, it has several 'independent'

2 The Historical Origins of Romani   31

functions, some of which date back to older stages of Indo-Aryan. Its most conspicuous conservative functions inherited from functions of the MIA dative-genitive are the marking of the possessor in predicative possession ('to have') and the marking of the recipient of the verb 'to give'. Of more recent origin is the function of the independent oblique in marking the animate direct object. The inanimate object in Romani is marked by the nominative, which is a legacy of the nominative/accusative merger in Late MIA. It follows that Romani has differential object marking, which is in general typical of NIA languages, although individual languages differ among themselves with respect to formal means and semantic-pragmatic patterns that are involved in object marking (cf. Masica 1991, pp. 364–369).

The second layer of case marking consists of agglutinative suffixes that have developed from older postpositions (see Friedman 1991), which are attached through the mediation of the oblique base. The dative (benefactive) suffix *-ke* (*-ge* after nasals) continues Late MIA *kehī* 'for the sake of' (Bubeník 2000, p. 225). The instrumental-comitative suffix *-sa* goes back to one of the MIA comitative adpositions, such as *sahū*, *samā* and *saddhī* (cf. OIA *sahá*, *sahitam*, *samám* and *sārdhám*) 'together/along with'. The locative suffix *-te* (*-de*) is from MIA *tahī* 'there, in that place' (< OIA *tásmin* 'in that'), while the ablative suffix *-tar* (*-dar*) is probably from its ablative counterpart **tādo* 'from there' (attested as *tāo* in Ardhamāgadhī), albeit with an irregular development of /d/ > /r/ (Beníšek 2009a). Finally, the genitive suffix *-ker-* (*-ger-*) has its origins in MIA *keraa-/keria-* 'belonging to' (from OIA *kāryà-* 'proper to be done' via **kāira-*; see Chatterji 1926, p. 753). Like its counterparts in Subcontinental languages, the Romani genitive agrees with its head through the Suffixaufnahme (Koptjevskaja-Tamm 2000) and is generally preposed.

The third layer of case marking is represented by adpositions, which, unlike in Subcontinental NIA languages, are mostly preposed in Romani. See Matras (1997) for more details.

2.5.3 Pronominal Forms

The most stable stock of Indo-Aryan forms in Romani comprises first- and second-person pronouns. The 1SG pronoun *me* 'I' is descended from the MIA 1SG instrumental pronoun *maī*, *mai*, *mae* (< OIA *máyā*), which indicates that it was formerly an agentive (ergative) form (Woolner 1915, p. 120; Bubeník 2000, p. 218). In contrast, the 2SG pronoun *tu* 'you' is supposed to go back to the Late MIA nominative form *tuhū* (Woolner 1915,

p. 125; Bubeník 2000, p. 218). The 1PL and 2PL pronouns are based on stems *am-* 'we' and *tum-* 'you.PL', which continue MIA *amh-* and *tumh-*, respectively (<OIA *asm-* and **tuṣm-*). Like the 1SG pronoun, the 1PL and 2PL pronouns are also based on historical non-nominative forms. Their present-day nominative forms in Romani dialects are in general either identical to oblique forms *amen* and *tumen* (<MIA dative-genitive *amhāṇā* and *tumhāṇā*) or end in *-e*, i.e. *ame* and *tume*, which, for phonological reasons, cannot be directly derived from the MIA nominatives *amhe* and *tumhe*. Elšík (2000b, pp. 71–72) is inclined to view *ame* and *tume* as secondary forms reduced from *amen* and *tumen* and assumes that Late Proto-Romani can be reconstructed as having homonymy of nominative and oblique plural pronouns (also Boretzky and Igla 2004, p. 89). However, if we concede that *ame* and *tume* were the original nominative forms, there is an appropriate etymology for them in MIA instrumental pronouns *amhehī* and *tumhehī* or in Late MIA (Apabhraṃśa) instrumental forms *amha(h)ī* and *tumhaī*. In other words, the 1PL and 2PL pronouns may also be descended from older instrumental forms like the 1SG pronoun. There is no space here to discuss possessive forms of personal pronouns, nor peculiar oblique forms of the 1SG and 2SG pronouns; readers are referred to consult Woolner (1915) and Elšík (2000b) for more detailed information. Just a passing mention can be made of the reflexive pronominal root *p-*, which originates in MIA *appā* < OIA *ātmán-* (also *tmán-*) 'breath, soul, self'.

Third-person pronouns in Romani are based on older demonstratives. The MIA and OIA demonstrative stem in *ta-* (in Śaurasenī also *-da-*) survives in the Romani root *l-*, which occurs in oblique forms of the third-person pronouns, such as M *les* < MIA *tassa* (*edassa*), F *la* < MIA *tāe* (*edāe*) and PL *len* < MIA *tāṇā* (*edāṇā*) (cf. Turner 1928), as well as in oblique and plural forms of the article and some demonstratives. Proto-Romani also had a set of distal demonstratives M **ova*, F **oja* and PL **ona* (alongside **ola*), which have given rise to nominative forms of the third-person pronouns (*ov, oj, on/ol*), as well as to nominative forms of the definite article (*o, e/i*, etc.), but their etymology is not so straightforward. Some authors (Woolner 1915, p. 127; Sampson 1926, IV, pp. 405–406; Bloch 1965, p. 195) compared them to NIA distal demonstratives *o, ū, vo*, etc. (<OIA *asáu* 'that' according to CDIAL 972; cf. also Masica 1991, p. 225), but cf. Matras (2002, pp. 106–112) for an explanation in an internal Proto-Romani development. One of the possible sources of the plural form **ona* might be the MIA demonstrative stem *ṇa-*.

Inherited interrogatives of Indo-Aryan origin comprise *kon* 'who' < Late MIA *kavaṇa-* (<OIA *kaḥ punar*; CDIAL 2575), including the oblique

form *kas* < MIA *kassa* (< OIA *kásya*), *kaj* 'where' < MIA *kahī* (< OIA *kásmin* 'in what') and *keti* 'how much/many' < MIA *kettia-*. Less clear is *so* 'what' with the initial sibilant (also reflected in *savo* 'which' and *sar* 'how'), which is likely to be descended from MIA *kīsa-, kīdisa-* 'of what kind' (< OIA *kīdŕśa-, kīdŕś-*), while *kana* 'when' has not been satisfactorily explained yet. In contrast to other Central NIA languages, Romani makes use of interrogatives in the function of relativisers at the expense of Indo-Aryan relative pronouns in *ja-* (< OIA *yá-*). Indefinites in Romani rely on either loan elements or on later (post-Indian) developments, but some dialects contain traces of Proto-Romani **k(h)aj* 'some' < OIA *káścid* 'some(one)'.

2.5.4 Verbal Morphosyntax

There are two aspectual verb stems in Romani, both of which can be traced back to older stages of Indo-Aryan. The non-perfective stem represents a direct continuation of the present indicative stem of MIA and OIA, while the perfective stem is based on the MIA and OIA past passive participle.

The non-perfective stem, also called the present stem, is the default base (root or stem) of the verb to which personal subject suffixes are added. The personal suffixes continue the so-called primary endings of MIA and OIA: 1SG *-v* < MIA/OIA *-mi*, 2SG *-s* < MIA/OIA *-si*, 3SG *-l* < MIA *-di*, OIA *-ti*, 1PL *-s* < OIA (Vedic) *-masi* (versus *-maḥ/-mo* in Classical Sanskrit and *-ma* and *-mo* in MIA), 3PL *-n* < MIA/OIA *-nti*. The 2PL suffix is identical to the 3PL suffix *-n*. It is generally assumed that the 3PL suffix has taken over the 2PL, but Turner (1927, p. 237) suggested that the 2PL *-n* might be from the OIA (Vedic) 2PL suffix *-thana*, which is a very rare variant of the more common 2PL suffix *-tha* (MIA *-dha, -ha*). A conspicuous feature is the retention of the sibilant in the 1PL suffix, which also has its parallel in the earliest form of OIA. Although the sibilant form must have survived on into MIA vernaculars,[11] it does not occur in literary varieties of MIA.

In most Romani verbs, the non-perfective personal suffix is preceded by a historical thematic vowel, which is *-a-* in the first person (< MIA/OIA *-ā-*) and *-e-* in the second and third persons (< MIA/OIA *-a-*). See the singular forms of the Romani verb *phuč-* 'to ask' and their MIA (Śaurasenī) and OIA precursors:

1SG *phuč-a-v* < MIA *pucch-ā-mi* < OIA *pṛcch-ā́-mi*,
2SG *phuč-e-s* < MIA *pucch-a-si* < OIA *pṛcch-á-si*,
3SG *phuč-e-l* < MIA *pucch-a-di* < OIA *pṛcch-á-ti*.

Since the thematic vowel always follows a consonant in the Romani verb, thematic verbs are usually called consonantal verbs in Romani linguistics. Due to apocope of MIA final vowels, the thematic vowel is not present in the 2SG imperative (*phuč* 'ask' < MIA *pucch-a*). Romani has also inherited vestiges of the historical athematic conjugation in which the personal suffix is attached directly to the root. Unlike in OIA, but much like in MIA (cf. Bubeník 1996, p. 110), athematic verbs represent a marginal and unproductive class that is virtually restricted to verbs whose roots end in the vowel /a/ (hence vocalic verbs), e.g. *dža-* 'to go', 3SG *dža-l* < MIA (Śaurasenī) *jā-di* (< OIA *yā̆-ti*).

The perfective inflection is based on the overt perfective stem, also called the past or preterite stem, to which special personal suffixes are attached. The perfective conjugation has developed from finitised past passive participles, which replaced the OIA finite past tenses during the MIA period. As discussed by Matras (2001; 2002, pp. 146–151), a new finite paradigm later emerged as a result of incorporation of agentive pronominal enclitics into participles, which challenges the older assumption that the personal suffixes are descended from copular forms. Matras also argues that the system of pronominal suffixes developed in Early Proto-Romani during its contact with Northwestern Indo-Aryan languages. Furthermore, the development of the perfective inflection from passive constructions and the origin of personal subject markers in non-nominative pronouns provide evidence that Early Proto-Romani participated in the NIA shift towards split ergative typology that was later disposed of (see Bubeník 2000; Matras 2002, pp. 144–151 for more details).

The perfective stem markers have their origin in MIA and OIA suffixes of past passive participles. The most common OIA participial marker *-tá-* and its MIA (Śaurasenī) reflex *-da-* (but *-a-* in some less conservative varieties) have three common reflexes in Romani: *-l-*, as in *xal-* (*xa-* 'to eat'), *-t-*, as in *bešt-* (*beš-* 'to sit, to dwell') and *-d-*, as in *kerd-* (*ker-* 'to do'). Romani has also retained several perfectives directly from MIA and OIA participles. Such conservative formations now occur as irregular forms that cannot be synchronically derived from their non-perfective bases; for example, *ov-* 'to become' (3SG *ovel* < OIA *bhávati*) has the perfective counterpart *ul-*, which is based on the MIA participle *bhūda-* (< OIA *bhūtá-* 'become, been'). Other examples are *mul-* (versus non-perfective *mer-*) 'to die' < MIA *muda-* (< OIA *mr̥tá-* 'dead') and *sut-* (versus non-perfective *sov-*) 'to sleep' < MIA *sutta-* (< OIA *suptá-* 'slept, asleep'). The verb 'to go' is suppletive (perfective *gel-* < MIA *gada-* < OIA *gatá-*, versus non-perfective *dža-* < MIA *jā-* < OIA *yā-*). In contrast, the verb *ker-* 'to do' has the regular perfective stem *kerd-* in Romani,

2 The Historical Origins of Romani   35

unlike in other NIA languages that show direct reflexes of the OIA participle *kr̥tá-* 'done' (e.g. Hindi *kiyā*).

Another perfective suffix in Romani is *-(i)n-*, which is mostly found in forms that continue participial formations of MIA with no attested counterparts in OIA (cf. Bubeník 1996, p. 123), e.g. *din-* (*d-* 'to give') < MIA *diṇṇa-* 'given' (versus OIA *dattá-*) and *run-* (*rov-* 'to weep') < MIA *ruṇṇa-* 'wept' (versus OIA *rudita-*). Another perfective suffix *-il-*, which is common in some middle verbs, originates in the MIA adjectival suffix *-illa-*, whose original function was to turn passive participles into active ones, and its cognates are found in Marathi and some other NIA languages (cf. Bloch 1965, pp. 267–268; Bubeník 2000, p. 214).

As mentioned above, the perfective subject suffixes are historically derived from cliticised pronouns. The pronouns were attached to the participles by means of iotation, which is argued by Matras (2002, p. 147) to have been an ezafe-like mediating particle. The conservative forms of the personal suffixes are: 1SG *-om* (e.g. *xal-j-om* 'I ate') < MIA/OIA *me*, 2SG *-al* (*xal-j-al* 'you ate') < MIA *te/de*, OIA *te*, 3SG (in transitive verbs) *-as* (*xal-j-as* 's/he ate') < MIA *se* (unattested in OIA but dating back to Proto-Indo-European; cf. Bubeník 1996, p. 94). The 1PL suffix *-am* (*xal-j-am* 'we ate') seems to be related to the 1PL pronoun *am-* (MIA instrumental *amhehĩ*?), while the 2PL suffix *-an* (*xal-j-an* 'you.PL ate') has an uncertain origin. According to Matras (2002, p. 149), who points to the 1PL suffix *-en* in Domari, *-an* might originate in the MIA 1PL oblique clitic pronoun *ṇe* (also *ṇo*, OIA *naḥ*), which could have infiltrated the 2PL during a Proto-Romani period. Matras suggests that this suffix later underwent a change to *-am* in the 1PL under the influence of the 1PL pronoun *amen*. Finally, the 3PL suffix *-e* is from the plural marker of adjectives, which reflects the participial nature of the 3PL perfectives, albeit in the active meaning (*xal-e* 'they ate'). Adjectival inflection also occurred with intransitive 3SG perfectives in Late Proto-Romani, as it still does in some modern dialects, e.g. *gel-o* 'he went', *gel-i* 'she went'.

The copula in Romani is suppletive, having two historical roots: the indicative *s-* (sometimes debuccalised to *h-* and with vocalic forms such as *is-*, *es-* and *eh-*) and the non-indicative *ov-*. The latter root is from MIA/OIA *bhava-* (*bhū-*) 'to become' and has been replaced by *av-* 'to come' in a number of dialects (see Boretzky 1997). The copula in *s-* exhibits significant dialectal variation of forms that has yet not been satisfactorily explained in all details. Traditionally, the indicative copula and its inflection were described as a direct continuation of the OIA copular verb *as-* in highly irregular and odd forms (e.g. Sampson 1926, III, p. 208; Boretzky 1995b). However, already Bloch (1932a) argued that this copula might at least partly be based

36   M. Beníšek

on an old participle. This is indicated by the fact that personal marking in the indicative copula often mirrors that of the perfective inflection, at least in the first and second persons; cf. the forms common in Central and Northeastern dialects and beyond, which are deemed 'original' by Boretzky and Igla (2004, p. 126): 1SG *s-om*, 2SG *s-al* or *s-an*, 1PL *s-am*, 2PL *s-an*. Thus, the indicative copula may have emerged as part of the same development as finitisation of the past participle, although its current personal forms have a present-tense reading (see also Matras 2002, pp. 150–151). The OIA participial base of the Romani indicative copula seems to be *āsitá-* 'seated, being at rest, one who has sat down, etc.', the past participle of the OIA verb *ās-* (3SG *áste*) 'to sit, to rest, to exist, etc.'. The conservative third-person copula in Romani is *si* (*isi*, *hi*, *ehi*, etc.), which has probably developed through erosion from the plain participle with no personal marking rather than from OIA *ásti* 'is', as is usually claimed. Finally, it cannot be ruled out that the third-person forms ending in a nasal, such as *hin* in Eastern North Central dialects, which occur even with an adjective-like inflection (SG.M *hin-o*, SG.F *hiň-i*, PL *hin-e*), continue the OIA present participle of the same verb *ásīna-* 'seating'.

Early Proto-Romani had two temporal-modal particles that became agglutinated to verbs by the Late Proto-Romani period and are now continued as endings attached to personal suffixes. The first one was **asi* < MIA general past copula *āsi*, *āsī* from the OIA 3SG imperfect copula *ásīt* 'was' (see Bloch 1932b). Like its modern reflexes in present-day dialects (*-as*, *-ys*, *-s*, *-ahi*, *-e*, etc.), Late Proto-Romani **-asi* had various past (imperfect, pluperfect) and conditional (potential, irrealis) functions, all of which are subsumed under a single temporal category of 'remoteness' by Matras (2001; see also 2002, pp. 152–155). The other particle was **a*, whose current reflexes (*-a*) have either indicative or future-tense functions in Romani dialects. On these grounds, there is no general consensus as to what was its original function in Late Proto-Romani. According to Matras (2001, 2002; also Elšík and Matras 2006, pp. 82–83), **-a* had a purely indicative function as the general present/future tense (as opposed to the zero-marked subjunctive). Matras (2001, p. 167) even draws a parallel between the subjunctive-indicative (zero versus *-a*) dichotomy in Romani and the injunctive-indicative (zero versus *-i*) dichotomy in early forms of OIA, but any historical link between the two is to be ruled out as there is no evidence for such a dichotomy in post-Vedic phases (apart from vestiges of some injunctive formations), and there is nothing reminiscent of such a dichotomy in MIA. Another view is that the original function of *-a* was that of a future-tense marker, which seems to be assumed by Boretzky and Igla (2004, pp. 137–138), who see the present-future polysemy a secondary and partly contact-induced development in the dialects where it occurs. Bubeník (1995, pp. 3–6) works on the assumption that *-a* has developed from a future auxiliary and draws a comparison with future markers grammaticalised from deverbal particles in some NIA languages. There are no traces of the OIA and MIA synthetic future formations in Romani.

Romani has retained a synthetic morphology for valency-increasing operations (see Hübschmannová and Bubeník 1997). The inherited causative marker is *-av-*, as in *naš-av-* 'to expel' (*naš-* 'to escape' < OIA *naś-* 'to get lost, to perish'). The suffix continues the MIA causative marker *-āve-* (older *-āpe-*), which developed through a reanalysis of morpheme boundaries in causatives of OIA roots in *-ā* (e.g. OIA *sthā-páya-* [stand-CAUS-] 'to make stand'). Another inherited transitivising suffix *(-j)-ar-* goes back to MIA *-āḍ-* or *-ār-* (Bubeník and Hübschmannová 1998, p. 31), and its cognate suffixes occur in various NIA languages (Masica 1991, p. 318). Valency-decreasing morphology in Romani is more recent. It has developed from analytic passive constructions that consisted of the passive participle and the copular auxiliary *ov-* 'to become' (see Bubeník and Hübschmannová 1998). Although Bubeník (2000, pp. 221–222) finds traces of such periphrases in some Late MIA varieties, the Romani formation of the passive by cliticisation of 'to become' is unique within NIA and may have been triggered by contact with Iranian languages (Matras 2002, p. 125). No relics of the MIA passive suffix *-(i)jja-* (< OIA *-yá-*) are present in Romani.

Several MIA and OIA non-finite formations are continued in various adjectival, nominal, adverbial and verbal forms of Romani. First, the Romani perfective participle continues the category of past passive participles of MIA and OIA. Second, the thematic OIA gerundive (also called the future passive participle or the participle of necessity) in *-(i)tavya-* (MIA *-davva-*, *-tabba-*, etc.) survives in the Romani nominaliser *-(i)ben*, whose form has been contaminated by another nominal suffix *-(i)pen* (< MIA *-ppaṇa-* < OIA *-tvana-*; cf. Schmid 1963). Cognates of *-(i)ben* in some western NIA languages are used as an infinitival marker, and the same may have been the case in Early Proto-Romani before verbal nouns were replaced by finite clauses in complementation (Beníšek 2010). Otherwise, there are no relics of the MIA and OIA infinitives. Third, there are two kinds of adverbial participles in Romani that function as converbs: those in *-(i)nd-* are based on the MIA present active participles in *-anta-* (< OIA *-ant-*), while the converbs in *-i* continue what is sometimes called the 'absolutive' in Indology (MIA *-ia*, OIA *-ya*). The latter formation is cognate with conjunctive participles in some NIA languages, but it constitutes a far less prominent category in Romani than in Subcontinental NIA due to the fact that clause linking largely relies on finite constructions, and it is in fact lacking in most present-day dialects. However, the absolutive/conjunctive participle must have played a role in forming some historical compound verbs in Romani, as it does in other NIA languages. Beníšek (2013) discusses the origin and development of compound verbs *lidža-* and *ledž-* 'to take away, to carry off' in Central Romani dialects, while other compound verbs in Romani still await a discussion from the Indo-Aryan point of view.

Romani has inherited two Indo-Aryan verb negators, including their complementary distribution: indicative *na* (< MIA *na*, OIA *ná*) and imperative (prohibitive) *ma* (< MIA *ma*, *mā*, OIA *mā́*). Changes in the system of verb negation are confined to individual Romani dialects.

2.6   Conclusion

More than two centuries have passed since Rüdiger's (1782) groundbreaking study on the Indian origin of Romani, which laid the foundation stone of modern Romani linguistics (see Matras 1999). Historical linguistics then dominated research on Romani for almost two centuries, when works of Pott (1844–1845), Miklosich (1872–1880, 1874–1878), Sampson (1926) and Turner (1926) were of milestone importance. Although perhaps overshadowed in recent years, historical work still occupies an important place in Romani linguistics, which is shown by a number of diachronic studies that have recently appeared, as well as by the position the historical discussions have in more general works (such as Matras 2002; Boretzky and Igla 2004; Elšík and Matras 2006).

Future historical and comparative research can benefit greatly from the recent boom in documentary and descriptive work on various Romani dialects. A significant amount of new data that has come to light offers fresh material for comparative work and historical reconstructions of Late Proto-Romani ('Early Romani'). Matras (2002), Boretzky and Igla (2004), and Elšík and Matras (2006) are important starting points for future work on a comprehensive grammatical description of Late Proto-Romani. Furthermore, there is no true etymological dictionary of Romani. Although there are dictionaries of individual dialects or groups of dialects that also contain etymological notes (see the introduction to Sect. 2.5), what is still missing is an exhaustive dictionary of the Late Proto-Romani vocabulary reconstructed from the lexical material of all Romani dialects and offering ultimate etymologies. A detailed, up-to-date overview of the Early Proto-Romani development in the historical context of Indo-Aryan languages is also missing. Here, comparative work can draw from recent descriptions of lesser-known Indo-Aryan varieties. There is also a good reason to assume that diachronic studies on individual phonological, grammatical and lexical features that take into account comparative Indo-Aryan evidence will continue to come up in future. Only some of the topics that offer promising directions for future research could be addressed in the space of this chapter.

Notes

1. The dot under the consonant letter, as in ṛ, denotes a retroflex sound. This has to be distinguished from r̥ with a circle, which points to the syllabic rhotic in OIA. I follow the Indological tradition of transliteration in forms of the Indian Subcontinental languages and the Romani academic tradition in writing the Romani forms. Note that there are certain contradictions between the two systems. The palatal approximant is written y in the languages of India and j in Romani, while j in Indian languages is a voiced affricate, i.e. dž in Romani. The letter c expresses the post-alveolar affricate in the Indian languages (= č in Romani) but the alveolar affricate in Romani.
2. The etymological connection between Romani *rom* and Sanskrit *ḍomba-* and Hindi *ḍom* was initially suggested by Hermann Brockhaus in a letter to Pott (Pott 1844–1845, I, p. 42) and independently by Leland (1882, pp. 333–335).
3. Matras (2002, p. 15), referring to Soravia (1988, p. 8), attributes this etymology to Pischel (1900). However, Pischel (1900) does not deal with the origin of Romani *gadžo*. He is referred to by Finck (1907, p. 63) only in association with the sound change /rhy/ > /jjh/ in OIA *gārhya-* > MIA **gajjha-*.
4. Unless a dialect is specified, Romani forms in this chapter are mostly cited in their conservative shapes that occur in at least some Romani dialects and represent a more or less intact legacy of Late Proto-Romani forms. The forms with an asterisk are explicit Proto-Romani reconstructions, regardless of whether such forms are attested in any Romani dialect. Thus, a single form may occur once with the asterisk and once without it according to the context, as in a statement that *-ker-* is a conservative genitive suffix in Romani dialects that continues the Proto-Romani genitive suffix **-ker-*.
5. There are also extended forms in Romani dialects, such as *čhonut* and *čhomut*, which probably developed from a historical compound of *čhon* 'moon' and *udud* 'light'.

6. Dardic languages, which were considered a third branch of Indo-Iranian by Grierson (LSI), are now understood in a purely geographical meaning as Indo-Aryan languages spoken in the mountainous valleys of an area from Eastern Afghanistan down to Kashmir. They do not constitute a genealogical subgroup of languages descended from a common proto-language (cf. Bashir 2003).
7. There are two additional features dealt with by Turner that are left out of the overview here. The first is the lack of retroflexion of the OIA dental after /r/ in Central languages (including Romani), which is, in fact, a shared retention. The second is the dropping of /y/ in OIA *-īya-* (common in passive verbs), evidence of which is too scarce in Romani to make any valid conclusion.
8. There are some exceptions from the regular development of sibilants in Romani that are discussed by Turner (1926, p. 162) and by Hamp (1987, 1993).
9. Some of Zoller's etymological proposals are also based on wrong interpretation of words. For example, *avdives* 'today' is from a demonstrative phrase *av(a) dives* 'this day' and has nothing to do with OIA *ā nūnam* 'up to now', as he claims. The adverb *eklik* 'a little' in Burgenland Romani is from *(j)ekh likh* 'one nit', and Vlax *avertehara* 'day after tomorrow' is *aver tehara* 'other tomorrow', to mention but a few words for which there is no need to invoke Dardic, Nuristani and other etymologies.
10. Also, Hancock's claim of the mixed nature of the Romani lexicon does not challenge in any way the long established fact that the Indo-Aryan layer of Romani consists of the inherited Central core supplemented by a loan Northwestern component. Moreover, some of Hancock's illustrations of Indo-Aryan synonyms in Romani do not reflect different Indo-Aryan languages but rather an inheritance of seeming synonyms from OIA. For example, two Romani words for 'to wash', *thov-* and *xalav-* (cf. Hancock 2006, p. 82), etymologically connected to OIA *dhāv-* and *kṣal-*, have probably been inherited from OIA with a semantic distinction, such as that between 'to wash' and 'to rinse', rather than originating in different speech varieties of Indian warriors.
11. See Turner (1927, p. 236) for reflexes of *-masi* (versus *-mo*) in NIA.

References

Ackerley, Frederick George. 1929. Basque Romani. *Journal of the Gypsy Lore Society*, 3rd ser., 8: 50–94.
Aichele, Walther. 1957. Die ursprünglich aspirierten Medien der Zigeunersprache. *Zeitschrift für Phonetik und Allgemeine Sprachwissenschaft* 10 (2): 101–107.

2 The Historical Origins of Romani   41

Bakker, Peter. 1991. Basque Romani—A preliminary grammatical sketch of a mixed language. In *In the margin of Romani: Gypsy languages in contact*, ed. Peter Bakker and Marcel Cortiade, 56–90. Amsterdam: Institute for General Linguistics.

Bakker, Peter. 1999. The Northern branch of Romani: Mixed and non-mixed varieties. In *Die Sprache der Roma: Perspektiven der Romani-Forschung in Österreich im interdisziplinären und internationalen Kontext*, ed. Dieter W. Halwachs and Florian Menz, 172–209. Klagenfurt: Drava.

Bashir, Elena. 2003. Dardic. In *The Indo-Aryan languages*, ed. George Cardona and Dhanesh Jain, 818–894. London: Routledge.

Beníšek, Michael. 2007. Varáhamihira a nejstarší zmínka o dómbech. Romano džaniben. Ñilaj, 12–26.

Beníšek, Michael. 2009a. Middle Indo-Aryan ablative and locative markers in Romani. *Indo-Iranian Journal* 52 (4): 335–362.

Beníšek, Michael. 2009b. References to the Ḍombas in Rājataraṅgiṇī. *Archiv Orientální* 77 (4): 349–366.

Beníšek, Michael. 2010. The quest for a Proto-Romani infinitive. *Romani Studies*, 5th ser., 20 (1): 47–86.

Beníšek, Michael. 2013. Central Romani lidža-/ ledž-: A vestige of an Indo-Aryan compound verb and its cross-dialectal variability. *Acta Orientalia Academiae Scientiarum Hungaricae* 66 (4): 471–486.

Berger, Hermann. 1959. Die Burushaski Lehnwörter in der Zigeunersprache. *Indo-Iranian Journal* 3: 17–43.

Bloch, Jules. 1919. *La formation de la langue marathe*. Paris: Édouard Champion.

Bloch, Jules. 1932a. Le présent du verbe "être" en tsigane. *Indian Linguistics* 2: 27–34.

Bloch, Jules. 1932b. Survivance de skr. āsīt en indien moderne. *Bulletin de la Société Linguistique* 33 (1): 55–65.

Bloch, Jules. 1965. *Indo-Aryan from the Vedas to modern times*. Paris: Librairie d'Amérique et d'Orient Adrien-Maisonneuve.

Boretzky, Norbert. 1992. Zum Erbwortschatz des Romani. *Zeitschrift für Phonetik, Sprachwissenschaft und Kommunikationsforschung* 45 (3): 227–251.

Boretzky, Norbert. 1995a. Armenisches im Zigeunerischen (Romani und Lomavren). *Indogermanische Forschungen* 100: 137–155.

Boretzky, Norbert. 1995b. Die Entwicklung der Kopula im Romani. *Grazer Linguistische Studien* 43: 1–50.

Boretzky, Norbert. 1997. Suppletive forms of the Romani copula: Ovel/avel. In *The typology and dialectology of Romani*, ed. Yaron Matras, Peter Bakker, and Hristo Kyuchukov, 107–132. Amsterdam: John Benjamins.

Boretzky, Norbert. 2012a. *Die lexikalischen Gräzismen des Romani. Ein Beitrag zur Wortgeschichte*. Grazer Linguistische Monographien 31. Graz: Karl-Franzens-Universität Graz.

Boretzky, Norbert. 2012b. *Studien zum Wortschatz des Romani*. Veliko Tarnovo: Faber.

Boretzky, Norbert, and Birgit Igla. 1993. *Lautwandel und Natürlichkeit. Kontaktbedingter und endogener Wandel im Romani*. Essen: Universität GH Essen.

Boretzky, Norbert, and Birgit Igla. 1994. *Wörterbuch Romani-Deutsch-English für den südosteuropäischen Raum. Mit einer Grammatik der Dialektvarianten*. Wiesbaden: Harrassowitz.

Boretzky, Norbert, and Birgit Igla. 2004. *Kommentierter Dialektatlas des Romani. Teil 1. Vergleich der Dialekte*. Wiesbaden: Harrassowitz.

Briggs, George Weston. 1953. *The Doms and their near relations*. Mysore: Wesley Press and Publishing House.

Bubeník, Vít. 1995. On typological changes and structural borrowing in the history of European Romani. In *Romani in contact: The history, structure and sociology of a language*, ed. Yaron Matras, 1–23. Amsterdam: John Benjamins.

Bubeník, Vít. 1996. *The structure and development of Middle Indo-Aryan dialects*. New Delhi: Motilal Banarsidass.

Bubeník, Vít. 2000. Was Proto-Romani an ergative language? In *Grammatical relations in Romani: The noun phrase*, ed. Viktor Elšík and Yaron Matras, 205–227. Amsterdam: John Benjamins.

Bubeník, Vít, and Milena Hübschmannová. 1998. Deriving inchoatives and mediopassives in Slovak and Hungarian Romani. *Grazer Linguistische Studien* 50: 29–44.

Burrow, Thomas, and Murray Barnson Emeneau. 1984. *A Dravidian etymological dictionary (DEDR)*. Oxford: Clarendon Press.

Cardona, George, and Dhanesh Jain. 2003. *The Indo-Aryan languages*. London: Routledge.

CDIAL = Turner 1962–1966.

Chatterji, Suniti Kumar. 1926. *The origin and development of the Bengali language*. Calcutta: Calcutta University Press.

DEDR = Burrow and Emeneau 1984.

Deshpande, Madhav. 1975. Phonetics of short A in Sanskrit. *Indo-Iranian Journal* 17 (3–4): 195–209.

Elšík, Viktor. 2000a. Romani nominal paradigms: Their structure, diversity, and development. In *Grammatical relations in Romani: The noun phrase*, ed. Viktor Elšík and Yaron Matras, 9–30. Amsterdam: John Benjamins.

Elšík, Viktor. 2000b. Dialect variation in Romani personal pronouns. In *Grammatical relations in Romani: The noun phrase*, ed. Viktor Elšík and Yaron Matras, 65–94. Amsterdam: John Benjamins.

Elšík, Viktor. 2008. Review of [Angǎcev, Ilija. Kratka morfologija na ciganskija dialekt na Ljaskovec (A brief morphology of the Gypsy dialect of Ljaskovec). Edited by Birgit Igla. Veliko Tărnovo: Faber 2008]. *Romani Studies*, 5th ser., 18 (2): 212–216.

Elšík, Viktor. 2009. Loanwords in Selice Romani, an Indo-Aryan language of Slovakia. In *Loanwords in the world's languages: A comparative handbook*, ed. Martin Haspelmath and Uri Tadmor, 260–303. Berlin: Mouton de Gruyter.

Elšík, Viktor, and Yaron Matras. 2006. *Markedness and language change: The Romani sample*. Berlin: Mouton De Gruyter.

Emeneau, Murray Barnson. 1980. The Indian linguistic area revisited. In *Language and linguistic area*, ed. Murray Barnson Emeneau, 197–249. Stanford: Stanford University Press. (Reprinted from Emeneau, Murray Barnson. 1974. The Indian linguistic area revisited. *International Journal of Dravidian Linguistics* 3 (1): 92–134.)

Finck, Franz Nikolaus. 1907. *Die Sprache der armenischen Zigeuner*. St Petersburg: Kaiserliche Akademie der Wissenschaften.

Fraser, Angus. 1995. *The Gypsies*. Oxford and Cambridge: Blackwell.

Friedman, Victor A. 1988. A Caucasian loanword in Romani. In *Papers from the eighth and ninth annual meetings, Gypsy Lore Society, North American chapter*, ed. Cara DeSilva, Joanne Grumet, and David J. Nemeth, 18–20. New York: Gypsy Lore Society.

Friedman, Victor A. 1991. Case in Romani: Old grammar in new affixes. *Journal of the Gypsy Lore Society*, 5th ser., 1 (1): 85–102.

Gilliat-Smith, Bernard J. 1911. The sound Ṛ. *Journal of the Gypsy Lore Society*, n.s., 4 (4): 292–296.

Graffunder, Alfred. 1835. *Ueber die Sprache der Zigeuner. Eine grammatische Skizze*. Erfurt: F. W. Otto.

Granqvist, Kimmo. 2013. Johdanto. In *Romanikieli ja sen tutkimusalat*, ed. Kimmo Granqvist and Mirkka Salo, 11–37. Helsinki: Suomalaisen Kirjallisuuden Seura.

Grant, Anthony P. 2003. Where East meets West: Observations on a list of Greek loans of European Romani. In *Papers in contact linguistics—Interface: Bradford studies in language, culture and society*, ed. Anthony P. Grant, vol. 6, 27–69. Bradford: Department of Languages and European Studies, University of Bradford.

Grierson, George Abraham. 1888. Ḍoms, Jâṭs, and the origin of the Gypsies. *Journal of the Gypsy Lore Society* 1 (2): 71–76.

Grierson, George Abraham. 1898–1928. *Linguistic survey of India (LSI)*, vols. I–XI. Calcutta: Superintendent Government Printing.

Hamp, Eric P. 1987. On the sibilants of Romani. *Indo-Iranian Journal* 30 (2): 103–106.

Hamp, Eric P. 1993. More on the sibilants of Romani. *Journal of the Gypsy Lore Society*, 5th ser., 3 (2): 67–68.

Hancock, Ian. 1988. The development of Romani linguistics. In *Languages and cultures: Studies in honor of Edgar C. Polomé*, ed. Mohammad AlivJazayery and Werner Winter, 183–223. Berlin: Mouton de Gruyter.

Hancock, Ian. 1995. On the migration and affiliation of the Ḍōmba: Iranian words in Rom, Dom and Lom Gypsy. In *Romani in contact: The history, structure and sociology of a language*, ed. Yaron Matras, 25–51. Amsterdam: John Benjamins.

Hancock, Ian. 2000. The emergence of Romani as a koïné outside of India. In *Scholarship and the Gypsy struggle: Commitment in Romani studies*, ed. Thomas Acton, 1–13. Hatfield: University of Hertfordshire.

Hancock, Ian. 2001. K upřesnění doby odchodu mluvčích protoromštiny z Indie. *Romano džaniben* 3–4: 6–12.

Hancock, Ian. 2006. On Romani origins and identity: Questions for discussion. In *Gypsies and the problem of identities: Contextual, constructed and contested*, ed. Adrian Marsh and Elin Strand, 69–92. Istanbul: Swedish Research Institute.

Herin, Bruno. 2012. The Domari language of Aleppo (Syria). *Linguistic Discovery* 10 (2): 1–52.

Hock, Hans Henrich, and Elena Bashir (eds.). 2016. *The languages and linguistics of South Asia: A comprehensive guide*. Berlin: Mouton de Gruyter.

Hübschmannová, Milena, and Vít Bubeník. 1997. Causatives in Slovak and Hungarian Romani. In *The typology and dialectology of Romani*, ed. Yaron Matras, Peter Bakker, and Hristo Kyuchukov, 133–145. Amsterdam: John Benjamins.

Kochanowski, Vania de Gila. 1968. Black Gypsies, white Gypsies: The Gypsies within the perspective of Indo-European migrations. *Diogenes* 16 (63): 27–47.

Koptjevskaja-Tamm, Maria. 2000. Romani genitives in cross-linguistic perspective. In *Grammatical relations in Romani: The noun phrase*, ed. Viktor Elšík and Yaron Matras, 123–149. Amsterdam: John Benjamins.

Kuiper, Franciscus Bernardus Jacobus. 1948. *Proto-Munda words in Sanskrit*. Amsterdam: N.V. Noord-hollandsche uitgevers maatschappij.

Leland, Charles Godfrey. 1882. *The Gypsies*. Boston: Houghton, Mifflin and Company.

Lesný, Vincent. 1941. Die Zigeuner sind ursprünglich die Indischen Ḍôms. Randglossen zu Lorimers Buch "The Ḍumāki Language". *Archiv Orientální* 12: 121–127.

Lorimer, David Lockhart Robertson. 1939. *The Ḍumāki language: Outlines of the speech of the Ḍoma, or Bēricho, of Hunza*. Nijmegen: Dekker & van de Vegt.

LSI = Grierson 1898–1928.

Macalister, Robert Alexander Stewart. 1914. *The language of the Nawar or Zutt, the nomad smiths of Palestine*. Gypsy Lore Society Monographs 3. London: Edinburgh University Press.

Mānušs, Leksa, et al. 1997. *Čigānu-latviešu-angļu etimoloģiskā vārdnīca un latviešu-čigānu vārdnīca*. Rīga: Zvaigzne ABC.

Marushiakova, Elena, and Vesselin Popov. 2004. Segmentation vs. consolidation: The example of four Gypsy groups in CIS. *Romani Studies*, 5th ser., 14 (2): 145–191.

Masica, Colin P. 1991. *The Indo-Aryan languages*. Cambridge: Cambridge University Press.

Matras, Yaron. 1997. The typology of case relations and case layer distribution in Romani. In *The typology and dialectology of Romani*, ed. Yaron Matras, Peter Bakker, and Hristo Kyuchukov, 61–93. Amsterdam: John Benjamins.

Matras, Yaron. 1999. Johann Rüdiger and the study of Romani in eighteenth-century Germany. *Journal of the Gypsy Lore Society*, 5th ser., 9 (2): 89–116.

Matras, Yaron. 2000. The structural and functional composition of Romani demonstratives. In *Grammatical relations in Romani: The noun phrase*, ed. Viktor Elšík and Yaron Matras, 95–122. Amsterdam: John Benjamins.

Matras, Yaron. 2001. Tense, aspect and modality categories in Romani. *Sprachtypologie und Universalienforschung* 54 (2): 162–180.

Matras, Yaron. 2002. *Romani: A linguistic introduction*. Cambridge: Cambridge University Press.

Matras, Yaron. 2004a. Romacilikanes—The Romani dialect of Parakalamos. *Romani Studies*, 5th ser., 14 (1): 59–109.

Matras, Yaron. 2004b. The role of language in mystifying and de-mystifying Gypsy identity. In *The role of the Romanies*, ed. Nicholas Saul and Susan Tebbut, 53–78. Liverpool: University of Liverpool Press.

Matras, Yaron. 2012. *A grammar of Domari*. Berlin: Mouton de Gruyter.

Mayrhofer, Manfred. 2001. *Etymologisches Wörterbuch des Altindoarischen*. III. Band. Heidelberg: Universitätsverlag C. Winter.

Miklosich, Franz. 1872–1880. *Über die Mundarten und Wanderungen der Zigeuner Europas*. I–XII. Vienna: Karl Gerold's Sohn.

Miklosich, Franz. 1874–1878. *Beiträge zur Kenntniss der Zigeunermundarten*. I–IV. Vienna: Karl Gerold's Sohn.

Oslon, Mixail V. 2012. Otrazhenie drevneindijskogo srednego roda v cyganskom. *Voprosy jazykovogo rodstva* 8: 93–101.

Pischel, Richard. 1883. Die Heimath der Zigeuner. *Deutsche Rundschau* 36: 353–375.

Pischel, Richard. 1900. *Grammatik der Prakrit-Sprachen*. Strasbourg: Karl J. Trübner.

Pott, August Friedrich. 1844–1845. *Die Zigeuner in Europa und Asien. Ethnographisch-linguistische Untersuchung, vornehmlich ihrer Herkunft und Sprache, nach gedruckten und ungedruckten Quellen*. Halle: Heynemann.

Przyluski, Jean. 1926. Un ancien peuple du Penjab: Les Udumbara. *Journal Asiatique* 28: 1–59.

Rishi, Weer Rajendra. 1974. *Multilingual Romani dictionary*. Chandigarh: Roma Publications.

Rüdiger, Johann Christian Christoph. 1782. Von der Sprache und Herkunft der Zigeuner aus Indien. In *Neuester Zuwachs der teutschen, fremden und allgemeinen Sprachkunde in eigenen Aufsätzen*, ed. Erstes Stück, 37–84. Leipzig: P. G. Kummer.

Sampson, John. 1923. On the origin and early migrations of the Gypsies. *Journal of the Gypsy Lore Society*, 3rd ser., 2: 156–169.

Sampson, John. 1926. *The dialect of the Gypsies of Wales, being the older form of British Romani preserved in the speech of the clan of Abram Wood*. Oxford: Clarendon Press.

Scala, Andrea. 2005. Contributi allo studio del lessico della romanī: note etimologiche e semantiche in margine ad alcuni lessemi di dialetti zingari italiani. *Quaderni di semantica* 26 (1): 131–139.

Scala, Andrea. 2013. A hitherto unnoticed Armenian loanword preserved in Southern-Italian and Dolenjska Romani. *Romani Studies*, 5th ser., 23 (1): 121–126.

Scala, Andrea. 2014. The mixed language of the Armenian Bosha (Lomavren) and its inflectional morphology: Some considerations in light of Armenian dialectal variation. *Annali del Dipartimento di Studi Letterari, Linguistici e Comparati, sezione linguistica* 3: 233–250.

Schmid, Wolfgang P. 1963. Das zigeunerische Abstraktsuffix -ben/-pen. *Indogermanische Forschungen* 68: 276–283.

Sharma, Ram Sharan. 1990. *Śūdras in Ancient India: A social history of the lower order down to circa A.D. 600*. New Delhi: Motilal Banarsidass.

Soravia, Giulio. 1988. Di alcune etimologie zingariche. *Archivio glottologico italiano* 73: 3–11.

Southworth, Franklin. 2005. *Linguistic archeology of South Asia*. London and New York: Routledge Curzon, Taylor & Francis Group.

Tagare, Ganesh Vasudev. 1948. *Historical grammar of Apabhraṁśa*. Poona: Deccan College Post-Graduate and Research Institute.

Tálos, Endre. 1999. Etymologica Zingarica. *Acta Linguistica Hungarica* 46 (3–4): 215–268.

Thesleff, Arthur. 1901. *Wörterbuch des Dialekts der finnländischen Zigeuner*. Helsingfors: Finnische Litteratur-Gesellschaft.

Turner, Ralph Lilley. 1926. The position of Romani in Indo-Aryan. *Journal of the Gypsy Lore Society*, 3rd ser., 5: 145–189.

Turner, Ralph Lilley. 1927. The phonetic weakness of terminational elements in Indo-Aryan. *The Journal of the Royal Asiatic Society of Great Britain and Ireland* 2: 227–239.

Turner, Ralph Lilley. 1928. Romani *les* and Sanskrit *tasya. Bulletin of the School of Oriental Studies* 5 (1): 43–51.

Turner, Ralph Lilley. 1932. So-called prothetic V- and Y- in European Romani. *Journal of the Gypsy Lore Society*, 3rd ser., 11: 115–120.

Turner, Ralph Lilley. 1959. Transference of aspiration in European Gypsy. *Bulletin of the School of Oriental and African Studies* 22: 491–498.

Turner, Ralph Lilley. 1962–1966. *A comparative dictionary of the Indo-Aryan languages (CDIAL)*. London: Oxford University Press.

Tzitzilis, Christos. 2001. Mittelgriechische Lehnwörter im Romanes. In *Was ich noch sagen wollte… A multilingual Festschrift for Norbert Boretzky on occasion of his 65th birthday*, ed. Birgit Igla and Thomas Stolz, 327–340. Berlin: Akademie Verlag.

Valtonen, Pertti. 1972. *Suomen mustalaiskielen etymologinen sanakirja*. Helsinki: Suomalaisen kirjallisuuden seura.

Vekerdi, József. 1981. On the social prehistory of the Gypsies. *Acta Orientalia Academiae Scientiarum Hungaricae* 35 (2–3): 243–254.

Weinreich, Matthias. 2008. Two varieties of Domaakí. *Zeitschrift der Deutschen Morgenländischen Gesellschaft* 158 (2): 299–316.

Wolf, Siegmund A. 1960. *Großes Wörterbuch der Zigeunersprache (romani tšiw). Wortschatz deutscher und anderer europäischer Zigeunerdialekte.* Mannheim: Bibliographisches Institut.

Woolner, Alfred C. 1913–1914. The Indian origin of the Gypsies in Europe. *Journal of the Panjab Historical Society* 2: 118–137.

Woolner, Alfred C. 1915. Studies in Romani philology I: Personal pronouns. *Journal of the Gypsy Lore Society*, n.s., 9: 119–128.

Woolner, Alfred C. 1924. *Asoka text and glossary.* Lahore: Oxford University Press.

Woolner, Alfred C. 1928. Asoka and the Gypsies. *Journal of the Gypsy Lore Society*, 3rd ser., 7: 108–111.

Zoller, Claus Peter. 2010. Aspects of the early history of Romani. *Acta Orientalia* 71: 243–312.

3

Historical Sources on the Romani Language

Ignasi-Xavier Adiego

3.1 Introduction

The arrival and dispersion of the Romani people in Europe from the fourteenth century onwards are well documented in historical sources, the impact of which has been studied in some depth. The same cannot be said of the Romani language: first, testimonies do not appear until the sixteenth century, and then snippets of information occasionally appear over the course of the next three centuries. Only at the end of the eighteenth century does the documentation begin to increase, in parallel with the development of the linguistic study of Romani. It is surprising to see how for years scholars have discussed and speculated on the origin of the Romani people and their language without resorting to direct information on the Romani language, particularly if one bears in mind that it was precisely the linguistic evidence which, from Rüdiger (1782) onwards, served to establish both the Indian origin of the people and the route they followed after leaving the Indian subcontinent. It is also worth emphasizing that most of the earliest documents remained practically unnoticed to their authors' contemporaries and have been recovered from little known editions or even from forgotten manuscripts in more recent times.

This chapter embraces all the known direct sources of the Romani language, from the very oldest ones until its identification as an Indo-Aryan

---

I.-X. Adiego (✉)
University of Barcelona, Barcelona, Spain

© The Author(s) 2020
Y. Matras and A. Tenser (eds.), *The Palgrave Handbook of Romani Language and Linguistics*, https://doi.org/10.1007/978-3-030-28105-2_3

49

50   I.-X. Adiego

language in the 1780s. This identification paved the way for a more comprehensive study of Romani, through the publication of descriptive grammars, comprehensive dictionaries and comparative works. Our attention is focused, therefore, on the period in which interest in Romani was spurious and very limited.

Despite the scarcity of the information provided by these first sources of Romani language, they often attract the attention of scholars since they offer some interesting linguistic details on the evolution and dialect diversification of Romani. The present chapter will try to take into account this kind of linguistic information, and where relevant, will try to align the historic Romani samples with documented dialects or dialect groups (for a discussion of Romani dialectology see Elšík and Beníšek, this volume).

3.2   The First Romani Language Samples

For many years, Vulcanius' list of Romani words (Vulcanius 1597) was taken as the earliest document on the Romani language and the only specimen dated from the sixteenth century. It appears as such in Pott's (1844) seminal work on Romani linguistics. It was Miklosich (1874) who first drew attention to a document that was earlier than Vulcanius, produced by Borde in 1542. In the twentieth century, the list of pre-Vulcanius sources increased with the inclusion of Ewsum's list, which was dated before 1570 (Kluyver 1911). Finally, in recent years two further specimens have been added to the dossier of sixteenth-century attestations: they included a Spanish theatre piece written before 1578 (Adiego 2013) and the vocabulary of Johannes ex Grafing, dated 1515, currently believed to be the oldest attestation of Romani (Knauer 2010).

Interestingly, from these five specimens, only two—Borde (1542) and Vulcanius (1597)—were published. However, Borde's book remained in obscurity until it was reprinted in 1870. The other three were transmitted in manuscripts discovered in the twentieth and twenty-first centuries. Thus, for many years, Vulcanius was the only source that had an impact on the study of Romani.

Before the vocabulary of Johannes ex Grafing (1515), there is no clear attestation of Romani in western sources. Crofton (1907, pp. 161–162) noted some 'uncouth' names given to Gypsies in Scottish documents from ca. 1500 onwards, which may contain Romani elements. An example is the name *Anthonius Gavino / Anthonius Gagino* given to a 'Lord / Count of Little Egypt' respectively in two copies of a letter dated 1505 (MacRitchie

3 Historical Sources on the Romani Language 51

1894, pp. 29–30); there may be a play on the Scottish name *Gawen* and Romani *gaveno* 'urban' < *gav* 'town' or *gadženo* < *gadžó* 'non-Gypsy', according to John Sampson (*apud* Crofton 1907, p. 161). In 1540, names such as *Barbara Dya Baptista* and *Sebastiane Lalow, Egiptiane*, are found (MacRitchie 1894, pp. 33, 37), in which Romani words like *daj* 'mother' or *lalo* 'red' can be recognized (Crofton 1907, p. 162). These etymological approaches are attractive but difficult to prove, as is usual when one is dealing with proper names for which no semantic explanation is possible.

In this section, all the oldest documents (i.e. those from the sixteenth century) are considered. The only exception is the Spanish play, which will be treated in Sect. 3.3, due to its dramatic character.

3.2.1 Johannes ex Grafing

The first specimen of Romani is a word list (accompanied by a few very short sentences) included in a manuscript by the Benedictine monk Johannes ex Grafing. This list was discovered by Georg Knauer, a classical philologist, when he was preparing an edition of the Latin version of pseudo-Homeric *Batrachomyomachia* by Johannes Reuchlin (1455–1522). One of the manuscripts he used in his edition was written by ex Grafing, then a student of Reuchlin's. The manuscript includes Romani words and sentences together with other examples from other languages. Knauer suggests that they were compiled by ex Grafing during his stay in Vienna between 1510 and 1515.

Ex Grafing's testimony is a bilingual Latin-Romani list that consists of some names of the zodiac signs, followed by some basic words (animals, body parts, personal denominations, food), three sentences and numerals. The fact that the list starts with the names of the zodiac signs seems to say more about the collector than about his informers; perhaps he began his inquiry by asking about the names of the zodiac signs, guided by the image of Gypsies as practitioners of fortune telling. The incompleteness of the list suggests that the informers were unable to offer systematic answers and tried to translate, word by word, some of the names suggested by the inquirer.

Despite the textual problems, the idiosyncrasies of the spelling (which is not always easy to explain) and the difficulty of interpreting several words, the language recorded in ex Grafing's list is genuinely Romani. The frequent odd spellings do not prevent us from recognizing typical Romani words such as *schügel* (*džukel*) 'dog', *müich* (*muj*) 'mouth', *oraclo* 'slave' (*o raklo* 'the (non-Gypsy) boy') *grast* 'horse', etc. The Maiden of the Zodiac (Virgo)

52   I.-X. Adiego

is ingeniously translated as *schukairānj* (*šukar rani*) 'beautiful lady'. The numerals, too, are those expected for Romani.

In spite of their brevity and scarcity, the sentences given by ex Grafing are also informative: *Quid dixisti* ('What did you say') is translated as *sopensal*, where we can guess an original *so phend(j)al* or similar, where the ending *-al* of the 2nd sg. preterite is clear. Note that *s* in *pensal* may represent a sort of palatalization of the preterite stem, as in many Romani dialects. Similarly, *non audivi* ('I did not hear') is translated as *naschimsū* (where *ū* is an abbreviation for *um*), behind which an original Romani *na šundjom* 'I did not hear' can be identified. Once again, *s* is possibly used to denote a palatalized sound or its outcome.

As for the possible dialectal affiliation of this document, Boretzky (apud Knauer 2010) tries to identify Sinte elements: (1) the preterite endings 1sg *-um*, 2sg *-al*, (2) the word for 'crab' *garaffeni*, (3) the form of the words *puiri* 'feet', *märo* 'bread', *scherheni* 'star' and (4) the use of *parni* for 'money'.

Even if this adscription to Sinte seems possible in principle, none of these traits is exclusive to this dialect. Moreover, the preterites *pensal* and *schimsū* point to a jotation (see Matras 2002, pp. 139–140) for perfective stems in *-d-*, a non-Sinte trait.

Perhaps the apparent Sinte traits should simply be interpreted as archaisms. The jotation may also be an archaism: as Matras points out, jotated forms of perfective stems must be postulated for Early Romani (except for the 3pl) and so the non-jotated forms of Sinte are a later analogous process.

Among the forms without a satisfactory explanation, *greischeich* 'dominus' ('lord') merits some attention. As Knauer rightly shows, the Common Romani [henceforth CR] form for 'lord' is *raj*, so the comparison is difficult to establish. Probably a better solution would be to interpret *greischeich* as *rašaj* 'priest' (note that here *ei* represents /aj/, as in modern German). The possible semantic problem can be easily resolved if we consider that among Benedictine monks (and Johannes ex Grafing was one) *Dominus* (shortened *Dom*) is an honorific title.

3.2.2 Borde

Borde's specimens of Romani are included in a book written in 1542, but not published until 1547 or later (Borde 1542). It was reprinted in 1870 by F. J. Firenwall, and it was this re-edition that came to the attention of Franz Miklosich, the most important scholar of Romani linguistics in the second half of the nineteenth century (Miklosich 1874).

3 Historical Sources on the Romani Language 53

This book was the first, and only, published volume of an ambitious work by Andrew Borde, an English physician and traveller who died in 1549. Each chapter of *The fyrste boke of knowledge* deals with the natural disposition of a certain people, their country and the money they use. Chapter 38 is titled 'treteth of Egypt, and of theyr mony and of theyr speche'. Borde equates Gypsies (though not mentioned by this name) with Egyptians. He affirms that 'ther be few or none of the Egipcians that doth dwel in Egipt, for Egipt is repleted now with infydele alyons'. Borde gives thirteen short phrases with their English translations for 'any man that wyl learne parte of theyr speche'. As Yaron Matras notes, the content of the phrases invites us to think that 'they were written down during a casual and spontaneous encounter in a bar' (Matras 2010, p. 58).

The examples are written in Romani, but they contain some errors and imprecisions. This does not come as a surprise: if we observe the examples of other languages given in the book, it is clear that Borde had a very superficial knowledge of many of them (for instance, the Spanish phrases provoke an unintended comical effect in a native speaker of that language). There are also some clear misspellings.

Despite the errors and false segmentations, most of the sentences are transparent: *Lach ittur ydyues* 'Good morow!' (i.e., *lačo tuti dives* 'Good day to you'[1]); *Lachira tut!* 'Good nyght' (i.e. *lači rat tut* 'Good night to you'); *A vaua tosa* 'I wyl go wyth you' (i.e. *avava tusa* 'I will go with you'), *pe, pe, deue lasse* 'Drynke, drynke! for God sake' (*pi, pi, develesa* 'Drink, drink, God willing!'). Other sentences are more difficult to interpret: *Hyste len pee* 'Sit you downe, and dryncke'. Here a typographical mistake (*h* for *b*) must be assumed: *Byste len pee: beš tale, pi* ('Sit down, drink!' cf. in Welsh Romani *beš talé* 'sit down' Sampson 1926, p. 35).

In the case of *Mole pis lauena* 'Wyl you drynke some wine', it is clear that the Romani sentence means rather 'you drink wine, beer' (*mol pis, lovina*). However, Borde erroneously takes *lauena* to mean 'wine' and extends the error to another sentence, incidentally full of misspellings: *achae, da mai manor la veue* 'Mayde, geue me bread and wyne'. The original form and meaning seem rather to correspond to something like *čhaj, de man manro, lovina* 'Maiden, give me bread, beer'; note *mai* for *man*, *manor* for *manro*, *la veue* for *lauena*. Initial *a* in *achae* is controversial: while Miklosich (1874, p. 764) takes it as an epenthetic vowel, Crofton (1907, p. 168) prefers to analyse *achae* as *ač čaj* 'stop, maid!' (CR *ačh-* 'stay'). Incidentally, note the use of the nominative *čaj* here instead of the vocative *čaja* (as in Welsh Romani, see Sampson 1926, p. 164.)

54   I.-X. Adiego

As in the case of ex Grafing, we are dealing with a kind of archaic Romani that is not easily identifiable as any specific dialect, but at the same time, nothing prevents us from considering it as the ancestor of British Romani dialects. Note, for instance, the presence of the word *lauena* for 'beer', a word of Slavonic origin, which spread to the Romani dialects of the north (North Russian, Latvian, Lithuanian, East Slovak, Finnish) and also appears in British Romani (both in mixed Angloromani and in Romani-inflected Welsh Romani).

3.2.3 Johan van Ewsum

In 1900, in a paper published in the *Yearbook of the Dutch Literature Society*, A. Kluyver edited a Romani vocabulary found in the archive of the van Ewsum family (Kluyver 1900). The papers belonging to this family from Groningen (the Netherlands) had been published in Dutch in 1889, but this important document remained unnoticed until Kluyver drew attention to it, first in Kluyver (1900) and later in an article in the *Journal of the Gypsy Lore Society* (Kluyver 1911).

The list was written by Johan van Ewsum and must therefore predate his death in 1570. Under the title *Clene gijpta sprake* (to be interpreted as 'little specimen of Gypsy language', according to Kluyver), the document contains fifty words and three sentences in Romani accompanied by a translation into a variety of Gronings, the Friso-Saxon language spoken in Groningen. The last word in the list (*atschaeij*) is not translated.

The reasons for van Ewsum's interest in Romani are unknown, as the list is not accompanied by any information other than the title. Kluyver recalls that van Ewsum was a magistrate and suggests that he may have obtained this vocabulary from Romani people whom he had arrested. If this is true, the document would be the first source of Romani in the context of law enforcement, which is seen in later examples such as the Winchester confessions and Waldheim's vocabulary (see below).

Most of the vocabulary is easy to identify as Romani. Only some words remain obscure. The most significant trait is the possibility of recognizing the change *s > h*, not only in the verb 'to be' *hi* (*< si*), but also—and more importantly—in the adverb *har* (*< sar*) 'how'. The change *si > hi* is beyond doubt attested in examples like *hirackilo* 'dat issen knegt' 'this is a boy', CR *si rakló* '(he) is a (non-Gypsy) boy'. More complicated is the case of *sar > har*, which hangs on the analysis of the phrase *de mar harde pyaer*, glossed by van Ewsum as 'geeft mij to drincken' ('give me to drink'). Kluyver proposed to interpret it as CR *de man sar te pijav* (literally 'give me how that I drink'). This implies a correction of *mar* in *man* (which is easy to accept, as other sentences present the same misspelling), recognition of an assimilation process *har + te > harde* and a correction of *pijaer* in *pijaeu = pijav*. These suggestions make sense, but the interpretation is weakened if it must rely on them. In any case, Kluyver's analysis of this phrase is quite reasonable, and if his interpretation is accepted, Ewsum's specimen of Romani must be assigned to Sinte because *sar < har* is a characteristic trait of that dialect.

3.2.4 Vulcanius

As mentioned above, unlike the two preceding examples, Vulcanius' vocabulary had an impact on subsequent scholarship. The work was quoted repeatedly by other scholars, it served as the basis for fakes like Gramaye's pseudo-Romani elaborations (Adiego 2016) and as mentioned above, it inaugurated the list of historical sources of Romani in Pott (1844).

In 1597, the Dutch humanist Bonaventura de Smet (Vulcanius is a Latinization of his last name, 'the blacksmith', as it alludes to the Roman blacksmith god Vulcan) (1538–1614) published *De literis et lingua Getarum sive Gothorum* ('On the letters and the language of the Getas or Goths'). This work offers a miscellany of linguistic materials, mostly from Germanic languages—for instance, it reproduces notes on Crimean Gothic taken from the work of the Flemish writer Ogier Ghiselin de Busbecq (1522–1592) and shows examples of the Gothic alphabet based on the *Codex argenteus*, the most important document in that language. The book turns out to be a sort of potpourri in which the author includes specimens of Basque and Romani—completely unrelated to the topic of the book. Vulcanius was aware of the irrelevance of these references in the study of German peoples and languages, but the desire to include notes on lesser known languages prevailed over other considerations.

As the source for his examples of Romani, Vulcanius used another important humanist: Joseph Justus Scaliger (1540–1609), a French scholar and a colleague of his at the University of Leiden. That is why some scholars (e.g. Barthélémy 1975) prefer to speak of 'Scaliger's list' although it is equally unclear whether Scaliger himself compiled the Romani specimens or whether they came into his possession from another source. In any case, 'Vulcanius' list' is the common way to refer to this document among scholars.

56   **I.-X. Adiego**

Compared with the previous materials, here we have fewer problems of reading and interpretation. It is true that the spelling is somewhat confusing, particularly the use of <ch> to represent CR *kh, x, š* and *č/čh*. For instance:

– *cheleue* 'tripudiare, h. fortis aspiratio' (Romani *khelava* 'I dance')
– *cheron* 'caput' (Romani *šeró* 'head')
– *chiral* 'caseus' (Romani *kiral* 'cheese'; <ch> here might represent a palatalized variant, the outcome of *k* before *i*, observed in some Romani dialects)
– *chor* 'barba, hic ch. pronuntiandum ut Hispanice' (Romani *čhor* 'beard')
– *chouri* 'culter, ch Hispanicum' (Romani *čurí* 'knife')
– *christari* 'scrinium' ('case, chest'; cf. Sinte *xistari* n. f. box, cabinet, chest, drawer, Spanish Caló *jastáris* 'arca', *jestári* 'arca' (Borrow), Finnish Romani *xistardi* 'trunk, coffin'.

The origin of this confusion seems to be clear: *ch* was used in some cases to represent the French value (CR *š*]), in others the Late Latin one (CR *x*), or a sound close to it (CR *kh*), and finally also its Spanish value (CR *č*, and by extension its aspirated counterpart *čh*).

Also puzzling is the use of the letter *x*. It is used for the word *xai* 'girl', *xauea* 'boy' and *taxtai* 'cup', and in the two latter cases, the list's author affirms that *x* must be pronounced as in Spanish. This is a very ambiguous statement, because at that time the pronunciation of Spanish *x* was changing from /ʃ/ to /x/ (the modern pronunciation). An example of this fluctuating situation is that, while there is evidence for an articulation /x/ of *x* at the end of the sixteenth century, the name of Cervantes' famous character *Don Quixote* (*Don Quijote* in modern Spanish spelling) was adapted to other European languages as if *x* still represented /ʃ/ (French *Quichotte*, Italian *Chisciotte*) when the first translations of the novel were published at the beginning of the seventeenth century. The ambiguity is compounded by the fact that, etymologically speaking, *taxtai* represents Romani *taxtaj* (with *x*) and *Xauea* is the vocative of Romani *čhavo* (*šavo* in some dialects). Also surprising is the fact that in other words in the list, Romani *čh, š* and *x* are represented by means of other letters (*ch* for *čh, sch* for *š, h* for *x*).

The list contains some obvious errors. For instance, *tirachan* is glossed as 'pallium' ('cloak'), when it is clearly the Romani *tirax* 'shoe', pl. *tirax-a* (well attested in many dialects). But perhaps the most curious and significant mistake is *kascht* 'bibis' ('you drink'): *kascht* is most probably the Romani word for 'wood' (*kašt*). As Miklosich already observed, the confusion comes from French, where the word *bois* can mean both 'wood' and 'you drink'

3 Historical Sources on the Romani Language 57

(Miklosich 1874, p. 769). The spelling <ou> for /u/ (*chouri, gourou*) or the use of <ch> for š in some forms also shows that these words at least were collected under French influence.

For some nouns, informant(s) gave the vocative form: *dade* 'father' (nominative *dad*), *daio* 'mother' (nominative *dai*)—for these vocatives, see Sampson (1926, p. 131)—and *xavea* 'son' (Romani *čhave(j)a*, of a nominative *čhavó*, cf. below).

For the first time, we have an approach based on a scholarly interest in Romani. Vulcanius—or Scaliger?—also tried to give some etymologies: a Greek origin for *foros* 'city' and *philatti* 'castle' and a 'Bohemian' origin for *krali* 'king' and for *maasz* 'flesh' are suggested. The first three etymologies are correct (but not *maasz*, Romani *mas*, of Indian origin). Like Borde, Vulcanius considers the Egyptian origin of Romani people to be uncontroversial.

Barthélemy (1975, p. 5) imaginatively recreated the possible context in which a list of Romani words of this kind was collected: 'One can imagine easily the framework: the humanist has invited a Gypsy family to drink a glass in the inn. In an evening, perhaps, he collects hastily, even a bit quickly, some dozens of words: Nothing is absent in this scene: the glasses, the bottle of wine, the candle, the man with his dagger, the woman with her typical hairstyle, the children. They eat too, by putting the knife on the bread and the cheese. They sing, they dance, and the *gadžo* pays a silver coin'. Therefore, the situation would not be very different to that proposed for the origin of Borde's list: a casual encounter in a bar.

However, the spelling inconsistencies pointed out above and some contradictory clues suggest that the list may have come from different sources, or that the Gypsy informants were of different origins. Some traits seem to point to an Iberian Romani dialect (cf. already Pott 1844; N.N. 1930, p. 20). For instance, the term *xauea* mentioned above shows the form of vocative attested in Spanish Romani, *chavea* (the word passed into Andalusian Spanish, Wagner 1937, p. 31). The use of *x* in this case for š (cf. above) could reinforce the idea that this word was collected not only from Iberian Gypsies, but also in a Spanish (or Catalan) context. The possible use of epenthetic *e* in *erani* 'lady' could also be interpreted as an Iberian trait, but the alternative explanation as article + noun cannot be ruled out (although there are no other examples of univerbation article + noun in Vulcanius). On the other hand, a form like *buchos* in *ser buchos?* 'what is your name?' points clearly to an Eastern origin: the verb *bučhol* 'be called' is attested in Vlax (under the variant form *bušol*) and Southern Central dialects, as well as Crimean. Finally, the (High) German loanword *Buchos* for 'book' indicates that informants were at some point in contact with that language.

According to Vulcanius, Romani was the language of 'Nubian vagabonds' (*Nubiani errones*), also known as Cingars, Bohemians or Egyptians, from the ancient region of Nubia. Significantly, Vulcanius offers not only a sample of the Romani language, but also a sample of the way of speaking of 'other certain vagabonds' (*alii quidam errones*), i.e. the Rotwelsch or German thieves' cant. He realizes that he is dealing with different linguistic materials, whose common feature is the nomadic character of speakers. For Vulcanius, Romani is a language in its own right, whereas Rotwelsch cannot be called a language (*neque enim linguam appellare libet*, Vulcanius 1597, p. 105), but an *idiotismus*, a idiosyncratic modality of speech. Therefore, Vulcanius inaugurates the clear-cut differentiation between Romani and marginal jargons, which will be repeated in later documentation.[2]

3.2.5 The Oldest Documents: An Assessment

These first word lists dating from the sixteenth century were all elaborated exclusively due to their authors' linguistic interest. Curiously, none of them served to ground a specific opinion regarding the origin of the Gypsies. In the case of Vulcanius or Borde, speculation about the Romani people is only an informative complement to the samples of the Romani language, and no attempt is made to link the assumed Egyptian or Nubian origin of the Gypsies to the words and phrases collected. In van Ewsum, the connection to Egyptian is only visible in the title of the word list. All the information is reliable, regardless of the spelling errors and inconsistencies or the inaccuracy of the translations. Finally, in ex Grafing, no information accompanies the specimens, not even the name of the language. Of the four lists, only Vulcanius offers etymological connections for some forms.

The dialectal adscription of the examples is not easy. Van Ewsum, Vulcanius and Borde show traits compatible with a 'Northern' adscription, but the nature of the Northern dialectal group as such is too generic and heterogeneous. A 'Western-peripheral' aspect seems more accurate. In van Ewsum, evidence for a change clearly identifiable as Sinte relies on the interpretation of a single sentence. Ex Grafing's vocabulary, coming from the Central zone, may also be related to Sinte according to Boretzky (pers. comm. in Knauer 2010, p. 4), but the evidence is controversial. Finally, in Vulcanius, the form *buchos* favours a contact with Central dialects, but other traits have been associated with Iberian Romani.

3.3 Romani on Stage: The Aucto del Finamiento de Jacob and the Signorina Zingaretta

The fascination with Roma people and the clichés fabricated around them favoured the appearance of Gypsies in fictional works. In general, these Gypsies followed the convention of speaking the same language in which the work was written. However, the desire for realism, or the search for comic effect, led some authors to present Gypsies with individual idiomatic traits. Whether or not these idiomatic traits are truly Romani is another matter and depends above all on the writer's knowledge of Romani. Given that in these fictional works Gypsy characters very rarely pronounce true Romani words or sentences, it is evident that only a few writers could access Romani for this purpose.

An example of 'false Romani' is found in an Italian comedy published in Mantua in 1546, called *La Cingana* ('the Gypsy woman'), written by Gigio Arthemio Giancarli Rhodigino. In this piece, Gypsy characters speak allegedly in Romani, but, as Ascoli already showed, they actually use a mixture of Colloquial Arabic and Italian thieves' slang (Ascoli 1865, pp. 122–127; Miklosich 1874, p. 5; Crofton 1907, pp. 162–163).

In Spanish classical literature (sixteenth–seventeenth centuries), the presence of Gypsies is well attested (see Leblon 1982). They speak Spanish but with a particularity: the letter *s* is systematically replaced by *z*. It is not totally certain, but very probable, that at that time the letter *z* already represented the sound /θ/ (not, as in Medieval times, the sound /dz/). This kind of pronunciation, called *ceceo* ('/θ/-speaking'), is also typical of some regions of Southern Spain, and it is not well regarded socially. The first example of the use of *ceceo* by Gypsy characters is a work by the Portuguese writer Gil Vicente (1465–1536?), entitled *Farça das Ciganas* ('Comedy of the Gypsy women', 1521): the eight Gypsies on stage speak Spanish with *ceceo* and also have a tendency to articulate *o* as *u* (for instance, *zeñuraz* for *señoras* 'ladies'). This latter trait is absent in later works.

3.3.1 Aucto del Finamiento de Jacob

The only known and sure example of the use of Romani in one of these Spanish classical plays is the *Aucto del finamiento de Jacob* (see Leblon 1982, pp. 102–103; Adiego 2013), dated before 1578—and therefore preceded only by ex Grafing, Borde and probably also van Ewsum among the earliest specimens of Romani. There is no doubt that the anonymous author of

60   I.-X. Adiego

this work had some idea of Romani (for instance, the word *monron* 'bread' is used, cf. CR *manró*), but the four verses pronounced by a Gypsy man are puzzling: although no clear Romani structure is visible, we can recognize some Romani words whose meanings make sense in the context of the plot. For instance, the sequence *tudoriquereza* is easy analysable as *tu dorikeresa* 'you (will) tell fortune', an order by the Gypsy man to the Gypsy woman that is accomplished in the following action. Similarly, *lesque reguno* admits an interpretation as Romani *leskero gono* 'his bag', precisely the bag that will be stolen by the man while the woman tells the victim's fortune. It gives the impression that the author may have obtained the translation into Romani of some words or short phrases and used them to create a free composition in these four verses. Also striking is the fact that the Romani material is fully integrated into the metrical structure and the rhyme pattern of the work.

3.3.2   Signorina Zingaretta

The other example of Romani in a play comes from Italy: a comedy published in 1646, entitled *Signorina Zingaretta* ('Little Miss Gypsy'), has some Gypsy characters who use sentences and words in Romani. The play is a free adaptation of the novel *La gitanilla* ('The little Gypsy girl', 1613) by Cervantes.

As usual in these earliest documents, the interpretation is not easy. In this case, it is compounded by the lack of a translation of the phrases. Modern scholarship (see particularly Ranking 1913; Piasere 1994) has offered tentative and in many cases satisfactory explanations for this Romani material. Some examples are easy to interpret. For instance, *gianes soca macherao* seems to be *džanes so kama-kerav* 'you know what I will do'; *camama mbro bacin = kamama mro bažin* 'I want my share'. Others are more difficult.

According to Piasere (1994), the traits of these examples point clearly to a Southern-Italian Romani, more precisely a Calabrese variety. Only the use of *-ao* (=*-aw*) for the 1st sg. present ending (in *kerav*, written *cherao*) recalls the Sinte spoken in Northern Italy.

3.4   The 'Winchester Confessions' (1616) and the Possible Emergence of Anglo-Romani

Among the earliest documents on Romani, the 'Winchester Confessions' occupy a particularly important place. The 'Winchester Confessions' are a document preserved in a family archive published by Alan McGowan

3 Historical Sources on the Romani Language   61

in 1996. The document consists of a series of depositions taken in 1615 and 1616 by a governor of the House of Correction for the County of Southampton. The final deposition was made by Walter Hindes, apprehended in the company of 'Counterfeit Egyptians'. This deposition is accompanied by a list of around a hundred Romani words and phrases translated into English, presented as 'Canting words as the Counterfett Egiptians use amongst themselves as ther Language' (McGowan 1996, p. 20).

This highly valuable attestation of Romani in seventeenth-century England caught the attention of Peter Bakker not only due to its intrinsic value, but especially because the phrases—mainly nominal phrases, but also a few short sentences—seem to show a mixed Para-Romani variety, similar to the Angloromani attested from the nineteenth century onwards (see Bakker, this volume):

> *to be corde* 'is to be whipped' (*kurde* pl. participle of the verb *kur-* 'to whip, to beat'
>
> *coore the gorife* 'goe beate the Cow'. *coore* imperative of *kur-* 'to beat' and *guruf* 'ox, bull' are Romani, but note the English article *the*).
>
> *swisht with a sayster in the end* 'a staff with a pike'. Besides *swisht* (of unknown origin) and *sayster* (cf. Welsh Romani *sastārn* 'iron; any implement made of iron', Sampson 1926, p. 327), note the English forms *with a* and *in the end*.

In his very brief review of the work (Bakker 1997, p. 50), Bakker noted that the word list showed the mixed character of Romani. In Bakker (2000), evidence from the 'Winchester Confessions' is used to assert that the change from an inflected British Romani to a mixed Angloromani 'happened rapidly and in the sixteenth century for the first time' (Bakker 2000, p. 29). However, Bakker (2002) qualified this statement considerably: he admitted that 'it is not certain, however, whether the group of Gypsies whose language was recorded, always expressed themselves in this way, or whether they had adjusted their language use to their companion' (Bakker 2002, p. 91). The point is that Walter Hindes, the deponent, was not a Gypsy but someone who had lived with Romani people during a period of time. This is an important detail, because, as Yaron Matras rightly points out, 'it is difficult to say whether these examples testify to the use of a mixed code in Romani households, or simply to the adoption of Romani-derived vocabulary as a special lexicon among other population sectors, a usage pattern which may well have arisen independently of the decline or the structural "erosion" of inflected Romani itself' (Matras 2010, p. 92). In sum, Walter Hindes probably offered the governor some examples of how he communicated with the members of the Gypsy group by means of a secret jargon that mixed the Romani lexicon with English grammar.

62   I.-X. Adiego

Therefore, Bakker's assumption that the 'Winchester Confessions' represent the emergence of Angloromani must be questioned. The most interesting point is the fact that this non-Gypsy informant 'mimicked' the procedures of a Para-Romani dialect. So the relevance of the example lies perhaps not in being the birth date of Angloromani, but in being a possible scenario in which a Para-Romani dialect could emerge from the contact between speakers of (fully inflected) Romani with adults who did not speak Romani.

As Bakker (2002) has convincingly demonstrated, the Romani elements of Winchester Romani must be clearly attributed to British Romani. All the words, except a pair of etymologically obscure forms, can also be found in other documents of this dialectal group. Two words are specifically attested only in British Romani: *jardoxa* 'apron' (unknown etymology) and *pokonyos* 'justice of the peace' (a Slavic loanword). Two words remain unexplained: *pusherrons* 'handkerchief' and *swisht* 'staff' (see above).

3.5   Other Seventeenth-Century Documents

Apart from the 'Winchester Confessions', seventeenth-century sources of Romani are desperately scarce. In fact, we know of only two documents that offer notes on Romani, of very different kinds: a travel book by a Turkish writer, Evliya Çelebi (1611–1684), and a historiographical work by a German scholar, Hiob Ludolf (1624–1704).

3.5.1   Evliya Çelebi's 'Book of Travels'

Thanks to the collaboration of a Turcologist, Robert Dankoff, and a specialist in Romani linguistics, Victor A. Friedman, we have access to an excellent edition and commentary of the Romani sentences included in book 8 of Evliya Çelebi's *Seyahat-name* 'Book of Travels', a large work written in Ottoman Turkish (Friedman and Dankoff 1991). More recently, in collaboration with Seyit Ali Kahraman and Yücel Dağlı, Dankoff has edited the whole of book 8 with a new transcription of Romani specimens (Kahraman et al. 2003, p. 39).

Evliya Çelebi wrote that he had collected these sentences in 1668 in Gümülcine, a city in the Greek region of Eastern Macedonia and Thrace (Greek Komotini), known as Rumelia during the time of the Ottoman Empire. The interest in this document lies above all in the fact that it is the first example of Romani as it was spoken in an Eastern area. The list is

3 Historical Sources on the Romani Language   63

accompanied by digressions about the origin and settlement of these Gypsies (see the translation of the passages in question in Friedman and Dankoff 1991, pp. 3–6). Unsurprisingly, an Egyptian origin is proposed by appealing to the Biblical and Koranic narration of the destruction of Pharaoh's army when pursuing Moses and the Israelites. According to Çelebi, 'Moses put a curse on the people of Pharaoh who were not present at that battle. As a result of the curse they could not remain in Egypt but were scattered abroad, condemned to wander from clime to clime and from town to town, hungry and homeless, dwelling in the mountains and the valleys, and raiding and thieving' (Friedman and Dankoff 1991, pp. 4–5).

Çelebi's collection of Romani examples includes typical Romani words, such as *yk* /yek/ 'one', *duwy* /duj/ 'two', *manruw* /manro/ 'bread', *duwduwm* /dudum/ 'gourd', *şa'x* /šax/ 'cabbage', etc. But perhaps the most curious and surprising feature of this source is a series of phrases characterized by their obscenity. For instance, *şuwş katah xal muruwm timinç* /soske te xal mo rom te mindž/ 'Why should my husband eat your cunt?', *tana' xala ma'xal mabuw ya'ta'r* /te na xala me xal me buljatar/ 'if he doesn't eat (my cunt), (let) him eat my ass'. Other sentences are inoffensive: *şuw karaz şuwpy kanka'n* /so keres, so bikengjan/ 'what are you doing, what did you sell?' After presenting these specimens of Romani, Çelebi asserts that Gypsies 'are always quarreling among themselves, day and night, and cursing each other out with obscenities' (Friedman and Dankoff 1991, p. 5). It is impossible to know whether this assertion serves to justify the 'naughty expressions' (Friedman and Dankoff 1991, p. 5) offered in the book or whether they are given to back up such a statement. In any case, both theory and examples contribute to producing a stereotyped image of Gypsies.

Friedman and Dankoff complete their edition and commentary of Çelebi's words and phrases with a convincing appraisal of this Romani material from a dialectal point of view (Friedman and Dankoff 1991, pp. 16–18). Çelebi's Rumelian Romani shows clear connections to one of the two Romani dialects that Paspati described in his study on the Gypsies under the Ottoman Empire: the non-Vlax, Sedentary dialect (as opposed to the Nomad dialect; Paspati 1870). However, some features of Çelebi's Romani are exclusive to Paspati's Vlax and Nomad dialects. As usual in dialectological studies, it is difficult to decide whether we are dealing here with parallel innovations, or contact and convergence, or even evidence of a common dialectal origin blurred by independent evolution and contact with other dialects. As features shared by Celebi's samples and Paspati's Vlax dialects, Friedman and Dankoff (1991, p. 17) mention Old Indian *ṇḍ* > *nr* (*manro* 'bread'), palatalization of *l, n* before *í, é* (*buye* < *bulé* 'ass'), palatalization of *t,*

64   I.-X. Adiego

d> *kʲ*, *gʲ* (*buti*> *buki* 'thing'), *ivé*> *í* (*dives*> *gis* 'day', note also palatalization of *d* in this example) and the presence of initial *a-* in the verb *akušela* 'swears'.[3] It is important to note that the first three traits are not exclusive to the Vlax group, as they are also shared with Iberian Romani (cf. Spanish Romani *manró* 'bread', *callí* (< *kalí*) 'Gypsy woman', *buchí* 'thing'): *ṇḍ*> *nr* and verbal *a-* forms may be archaisms, and palatalizations may be parallel innovations. Alternatively, and more probably, all these phenomena can be attributed to linguistic contact with other dialects, particularly Vlax ones.

In sum, though meagre, Çelebi's list is an interesting document as it is the first sample of a Romani dialect spoken in the Balkan Peninsula. The dialect it portrays is similar, but not identical, to the one recorded by Paspati among sedentary Romani people in the area two centuries later. The interest in showing Gypsies as a quarrelsome people who use curses and swearwords led to the first documentation of several Romani taboo words.

3.5.2 Ludolf's Commentary to His 'History of Ethiopia' (1691)

The second seventeenth-century document is the note on the Gypsies and their language, accompanied by a list of words, included in a work by the German orientalist Hiob Ludolf (*Iobus Ludolfus* in Latin, 1624–1704): the *Commentarius ad historiam suam Aethiopicam* ('Commentary to his own History of Ethiopia'), published in 1691. As the name indicates, this book is a kind of supplement to a prior work of Ludolf's, the *Historia Aethiopica* ('History of Ethiopia'), published in 1681. Chapter 15 of the first book of the *Historia* was dedicated to the languages spoken in Ethiopia. In the commentary, Ludolf discusses the number of the world's languages and criticizes previous work by Megiser, the author of a *Thesaurus polyglottus* (Megiser 1603). In his treatment of Romani, Megiser took the terminology and the examples from Vulcanius and classified it as a 'new Egyptian language of Nubian vagabonds'.

Ludolf questions the alleged Nubian origin of the Gypsies and, guided by a laudably scientific spirit, offers a list of Romani words he obtained. The list is not particularly long, but it serves to confirm that Vulcanius' list was authentic, not a fake (*contra* Megiser's insinuations) and that the Romani language had nothing to do with Coptic. In fact, Ludolf points out that the majority of these Romani words are of unknown origin. He offers some etymologies for a handful of them (in general erroneous), but he explains them as loanwords, logically acquired by Gypsies on their wandering.

The words are clearly Romani. Of special interest are the forms *si* for 'heart' and *wira* for 'grass'. The form *si* points to Sinte *dsi* 'heart' (< CR *ogi*). As for *wira*, it could be an error representing *wisa*, a German loanword (< *Wiese* 'field', cf. *wisa* in Wolf 1987, p. 252). Both forms point clearly to Sinte as the dialectal variety spoken by Ludolf's informants.

Ludolf indicates that he himself collected all these words 'from different bands of these (Gypsies), who came to me during their travels' (Ludolfus 1691, p. 214). From 1678 onwards, Ludolf lived in Frankfurt am Main, so in all probability, it was in that city that he collected the words. This is consistent with the adscription of these materials to Sinte.

In spite of the brevity of Ludolf's vocabulary, the inconsistency of etymologies and his inability to offer any hypothesis about the genetic classification of Romani, this author deserves credit as the first scholar to apply scientific criteria to the study of Romani. Questioning the principle of *auctoritas*, he wanted to check the validity of Vulcanius' list by collecting his own data from the Gypsies themselves; he proved that the list was authentic, but also demonstrated that the Romani vocabulary was unrelated to Coptic or the other languages spoken in Egypt. He also tried to give a reasonable explanation for some loanwords in Romani.

3.6 The First Half of the Eighteenth Century

If the documents attested during the seventeenth century are desperately meagre, the situation hardly changed until 1755. Apart from some documents of scarce interest, which we will consider briefly, the most important evidence of Romani is provided by the Waldheim report and La Croze's vocabulary.

3.6.1 'Bocskor Kódex'

The few forms in Romani found in the passages of the *Bocskor kódex* are difficult to analyse and so, despite József Vekerdi's commendable efforts to clarify them (Vekerdi 1962), the source is of little use.

This codex contains a great many texts copied (and perhaps also written) by János Bocskor, a Transylvanian landowner who lived around 1700. The date limit for the texts in the codex is 1739, but it is clear that it was produced during the preceding years. Vekerdi (1962, p. 123) contends that the

66   I.-X. Adiego

texts in which Romani words appear were copied at the beginning of the eighteenth century.

There are two texts: a composition entitled 'Gypsy Funeral' and an alleged Lord's prayer, copied twice in the codex. The Gypsy funeral is a text in Hungarian with non-Hungarian words, most of them more or less clearly identifiable as Romani words (for instance, *mandro* 'bread' or *avende* 'come!'). The 'Lord's prayer' is impossible to analyse, and in any case, it seems that it is not properly a version of the *Pater noster*. In fact, the text seems to have been composed in part by inserting words taken from the 'Gypsy funeral'.

3.6.2 The Waldheim Report

Much more informative are the Romani materials contained in the report for the year 1722 (published in 1726) of a correction-, orphan- and poor-house in Waldheim in Upper Saxony, Germany (N.N. 1726, pp. 145–158). As in the case of the 'Winchester Confessions', the information was obtained as the result of repressive measures. In this case, the notice makes clear that a suspicious boy was 'insistently pressed', even using punishment, to confess, and that the information given under this pressure contained a list of Romani and Rotwelsch words. This list, in which forms from each language are clearly separated into different columns and written in different scripts (Rotwelsch in Blackletter, Romani in Latin), comprises around 120 Romani items, including a number of phrases.

As Matras (1999, p. 107) observes, the list documents a Sinte variety. As notable traits, he points out the shift $v > b$ (*loby* 'money' < CR *love*), the raising $o > u$ (*bacru* 'goat' < CR *bakro*) and the change $s > h$ (*hau* /ho/ 'what' < *so, racker we ha* /rakerweha/ 'you say' < 2nd sg ending *-esa*), but with some exceptions (*so* 'what' besides the mentioned *hau*). One trait noted also by Matras (1999, p. 107) is the tendency to render *-i* as *-ing*: *ratting* 'night', *giling* 'song', which he attributes to a possible influence by the cryptolectal endings used productively in Rotwelsch (cf. *trittling* 'foot', *funkling* 'fire').

Not surprisingly, there are some borrowings from German (for instance, *schustaris* 'shoemaker', from German *Schuster*, *baua* 'building', from German *Bau*). Also typical Sinte is the word *isba* 'living room' (borrowed from Polish) or *kadwilgen* 'ducat (a kind of money)' (Sinte *xadvel*). Equally characteristic of a North-western dialect is the productivity of *-k(e)ro* for coining words: *Wastængri* 'glove' (*vastengri* from *vast* 'hand: cf. Finnish Romani *vastengiero* 'glove', Welsh Romani *vastengere* 'gloves', Sinte *vastengêro* 'glover', *vasteskêro* 'glove').

The phrases are short and very few. Note, for instance, *Hau pieke we ha?* 'what are you selling? (/ho pikəweha?/, *ho < so*, *pikəweha* 2sg present 'you sell', CR *bikin-* 'to sell', note the stem enlarged by the suffix *-əw-*, typical of Sinte, Finck (1903, p. 14).

3.6.3 Björckman's Dissertation on Gypsies (1730)

Despite the efforts of several authors to assign importance to the Romani materials in the doctoral dissertation of the Swedish scholar Samuel P. Björckman entitled *Dissertatio academica de Ciganis* (Björckman 1730; see also Ehrenborg 1909, pp. 111–113; Etzler 1944, pp. 178–179; Carling et al. 2014, p. 8), it is of little interest. Björckman states that he checked Vulcanius' list by reading the meaning of the words in Swedish to a Gypsy in an Uppsala prison, and the Gypsy confirmed the forms in front of witnesses. We need not doubt that the experiment took place, but Björckman limits himself to a partial reproduction of Vulcanius' Romani words and Latin meanings, in general with the same (often odd) spellings: for instance, *juket* 'canis' ('dog'), as opposed to Vulcanius *iuket* 'canis' (Björckman only spells *j* instead of *i*; the word is most probably a mistake in Vulcanius for *iukel*, cf. CR *džukel*.[4] On four occasions, Björckman deviates from Vulcanius: for *oculus*, besides Vulcanius' *achon* he gives *yaka*; for 'bread', he gives *manro* against Vulcanius' *manron*; for 'heaven', he gives Vulcanius' *cheron* but also *chiro* and instead of *tuochan* 'clothes', he gives *touchan*. Curiously, the first three alternative forms are also found in Ludolfus (1691)—*iaka, manro and scheiro*, an author quoted by Björckman. *Touchan* for *tuochan* is most probably a misspelling. If so, no new information is actually provided by Björckman.

3.6.4 Monsieur La Croze, Collectio Vocum e Lingua Cinganorum (1741)

Another list of Romani words appeared in the biography of Monsieur de La Croze, written by Charles Etienne Jordan and published in 1741 (Jordan 1741, pp. 310–312). Mathurin Veyssière de la Croze (1661–1739) was a French orientalist and librarian at the Berlin Royal Library. In the second part of the book, Jordan copied a selection (*un extrait*) of a manuscript volume by La Croze containing some of this scholar's reading notes. Among them, Jordan transcribes a list of Romani words, preceded by a Latin paragraph. In this paragraph, La Croze explains that it is a 'collection of words of the language of the Gypsies (*Cingani*), in part extracted from Ludolf's comments to Ethiopian History, in part from the mouth of a certain Gypsy prisoner in the citadel of Spandau,[5] a person not lacking intelligence, in the year 1727, 2nd June, in the second feast of Pentecost. Also other Gypsy prisoners were present, who, separately interrogated, gave the same words' (Jordan 1741, p. 310).

Between the words *stariben* 'prison' and *dadé* 'father', La Croze inserts the following comment: 'pronunciation of the Gypsies in France; for the dialects differ somewhat each from other' (*Pronunctiatio* [sic] *Cinganorum in Gallia: nam Dialectis* [sic: read *Dialecti*] *nonnihil inter se differunt*, Jordan 1741, p. 311). Possibly the note refers to the word for 'father', which appears with an accent mark (*dadé*) and differs from the form *dad* in *amaro dad* 'our father'.[6] This latter form was also collected by la Croze as an attempt by the informant to translate the Lord's prayer—*amarodad tu hal androboliben* 'our father, thou are in the heaven'. However, the informant was unable to continue (*caetera exprimere non potuit*). Most probably, *dadé* is simply the vocative case of *dad*, and La Croze erroneously interpreted both forms as dialectal variants.

In his analysis of La Croze's list, Windstedt (1908) pointed out the compilation's errors and deficiencies. In many cases, La Croze does not make it clear whether he independently obtained the same words collected by Ludolf. Only in the cases where the form was different does he note the particularity, but in the rest of cases, he gives the same form as Ludolf without explaining whether he is following Ludolf or also giving his own results. It must be said that the differences between Ludolf's and La Croze's forms are in general very slight.

Moreover, some words and phrases must be the result of a misunderstanding: for instance, *strebitza* is given for 'day', when it must mean 'ladder' (cf. Sinte *šterovica* 'ladder', apparently a Slavic loanword). Rather comical is the gloss *ne hom* 'I am sick' (Latin *aegroto*), when the actual meaning is 'I am not', and ludicrous the form *tu hal avatod* 'you love', undoubtedly an invention by La Croze, as Windstedt rightly observed, from a false analysis of *me kom avatod* 'I love' (actually *me kamava tut* 'I love you'): this *me kom* was erroneously equated to *me hom* 'I am', and a second person form was created from the combination of the segment *avatod* and *tu hal* 'you are'.

Despite these errors and distortions, La Croze's vocabulary offers a clear picture of a Sinte dialect, as one would expect given the place where the forms were collected. We can recognize the characteristic change of $s > h$ in different forms (*kercha = kereha < keresa* 'you do'; *hom < som*, *hal < sal*; the only exception is *so* 'what?' instead of *ho*. cf. the alternance *hau* /ho/ - *so* in the Waldheim report.

3.7 The Second Half of the Eighteenth Century: Vocabularies

3.7.1 Beytrag zur Rottwellischen (1755)

A book published in 1755 marks a turning point in the historical sources of Romani. Under the title 'Contribution to the grammar of Rotwelsch, or: Dictionary of the Gypsy Language' (*Beytrag zur Rotwellischen Grammatik, oder: Wörter-Buch von der Zigeuner-Sprache*), this work offers two crucial novelties: (1) for the first time, we do not have simply a brief list of Romani words, but a dictionary containing more than 800 entries, and (2) for the first time, a long text written in Romani is presented, together with a German translation: 'The letter of a Gypsy to his wife, where he gives notice on his miserable situation, in which he is'.[7]

Once again, we are dealing with specimens of Sinte Romani, as shown by the change *s > h*, the German loanwords and other traits.

The spelling oddities and the not entirely literal translation into German do not prevent us from recognizing true Romani sentences in the letter: for instance, *dowa Keer, kaime gaijam medre gazdias Tele*, translated in German as 'meine Herberge worinn ich eingekehret, brannte ab' ('my inn, where I stopped, burned down'). The sentence is roughly interpretable as *dova kher, kaj me gajam me dre, xačjas tele* 'that house, where we went in, burned down'.

3.7.2 Iberian Romani ca. 1750: Sentmenat's and López de Oliver's Vocabularies

Approximately two centuries after the first specimen of Romani in the Iberian Peninsula, we find two new documents, both in manuscripts and for a long time unnoticed, with contrasting characteristics. The first one is a short word list included in a miscellaneous handwritten book by an anonymous author (although it seems to be connected in some way to the Spanish family of López de Oliver). Preserved in the Spanish National Library, it was published for the first time in 1921 (Hill 1921) and a new edition, with commentaries, appeared in 1998 (Adiego 1998).

The second document, published in 2002, is a longer list of words and also some sentences copied by a Catalan nobleman interested in linguistic and antiquarian topics, the Marquis of Sentmenat (1697–1762) and preserved in the Library of Catalonia (Adiego 2002).

70   I.-X. Adiego

While the first word list shows Spanish Romani to be a mixed language (for instance, *avelar mal muy* 'to have bad face', where *avelar* is from CR *avel* but constructed as a Spanish infinitive), Sentmenat's Romani is still an inflected dialect, comparable to the specimens of Catalan Romani attested in the first half of the nineteenth century. For instance, *Latxi sib[é]r te deltút ro Dabél* 'Buenos días' ('Good day'), literally 'That my-God can give you (2nd sg) good days' (*lači siber te del tut ro-dəbél* < CR *lačhe dives te del tut m(i) ro-devel*). Note the influence of Catalan phonology in the word *devel*, spelled *dabel,* where *a* [ə] represents the treatment of *e* in unstressed position, typical of Central Catalan. Also characteristic of Catalan Romani is the univerbation of possessive and noun in the word 'God': compare present Catalan Calo *ruddəbel* 'God'.

3.7.3 Finnish Romani: Ganander (1780)

An important document which for a long time remained unpublished is the first collection of Finnish Romani words and a few short sentences, accompanied by a morphological description. This is the study by Christfrid Ganander (1741–1790), *Undersökning om de så kallade Tattare eller Zigeuner, Cingari, Bohemiens* ('Research on the so-called Tattare or Zigeuner, cingari, Bohemiens', Ganander 1780.[8]) As in the case of Sentmenat or Ludolf before him, linguistic interest is the fundamental reason for Ganander's collection. In fact, the book was sent to the Royal Swedish Academy of Sciences, where it was awarded a silver medal. As Valtonen (1969, p. 124) pointed out, Ganander was able to identify some loanwords but failed to establish more etymologies due to his lack of knowledge of Sanskrit. He established connections to Latin (for instance, *desso = decem* '10' or *devel =* 'Deus') which are etymologically related, since Latin and Sanskrit have a common ancestor.

3.8 The Second Half of the Eighteenth Century: The Comparative Study of Romani

In the middle of the second half of the eighteenth century, interest in Romani entered a new phase that paved the way for a truly scientific approach, based on a strictly linguistic study and applying a solid methodology. The key is the establishment of a connection between Romani and the

3 Historical Sources on the Romani Language 71

Indo-Aryan languages, which placed Romani within this group as a daughter of Proto-Indo-European, like Greek, Latin, Germanic, Balto-Slavic and other languages and linguistic groups of Eurasia.

3.8.1 The Beginning of the 'Indian Approach'

The connection of Romani with the Indo-Aryan (or, more generically, the Indo-Iranian) languages appeared in the literature in a sudden and insignificant way (Courthiade 2014). In 1771, the German scholar Christian Wilhelm Büttner (1716–1801) published the first part of a study of ancient and modern writing systems. In the preface of the book, which contains a long list of examples of the survival of ancient populations under the names of present peoples (for instance, the Iberians or Aquitanians under the Basques, the Gauls and Celts under the Irish and Scottish or the Medes and older Thracians under the Slavs), he concludes with the example of a Hindustani-Afghan branch that can be found today under the name of *Zigeuner* (Gypsies). Interestingly, for the other examples, there is a more or less precise geographical link between the ancient populations and the modern peoples, and the linguistic basis for the connection is in some cases very doubtful or simply non-existent (for instance, the alleged link between 'older Thracians' and Slavs). In the case of 'Hindustani-Afghan' and Gypsies, however, the absence of a geographical link leads us to assume that Büttner was thinking of linguistic evidence for the connection. As Courthiade rightly observes, Büttner does not seem to communicate anything new, so we must imagine that the idea was already present among scholars interested in language classification, although this idea had not yet been published.

The first direct and well-founded report of the connection of Romani with the languages of India was offered by Samuel Augustin ab Hortis (1729–1792). This Slovak scholar published a series of articles on the Romani people in the weekly gazette *Kaiserlich Königlich allergnädigst privilegirte Anzeigen* (published in Vienna) in 1775 and 1776. The issues of 13 and 20 March 1776 were devoted to the language of the Gypsies. In contrast to the earlier speculations on the possible parenthoods of Romani, ab Hortis adopts a very prudent position. For instance, he offers several specimens of Romani to stress that it is safer to present some words obtained from reliable sources than to construct stories and deductions on the origin of all the people from a simple similarity of names and words, which may often be purely accidental (ab Hortis 1776, p. 94). Together with a list of just over 70 words, including numerals, he gives two versions of the Lord's Prayer in

Romani. The list of words is attributed to an anonymous scholar and seems to have been obtained from Transylvanian Gypsies. As for the translations of the Lord's Prayer, the second one is also attributed to a reliable source: the version would be the one in use by Hungarian Gypsies at that time and had been collected directly from them by another scholar during a journey to Hungary. The first version is more enigmatic: ab Hortis only indicates that it is an 'old translation'. Both texts are written in Hungarian orthography.

But the most cited information in ab Hortis' work is the story of the Hungarian student in Leiden, Stephanus Váli (Istvan Vályi), later a Lutheran minister in the village of Almáss (today Almásfüzitő), in the province of Komárom (in North-western Hungary), who became friends with three classmates from Malabar. He learned more than a thousand words (*mille et plura uocabula eorum linguae*) of their tongue, and, on his return to Hungary, he confirmed that these words were understood by Gypsies from the neighbouring city of Györ. Therefore, Vali concluded that the Gypsies originated from the Indian region of Malabar. He even affirmed that in Malabar, there was a district called Czigania, which was the origin of the name Czigani or Czingani.

The veracity of this anecdote has long been debated. First and foremost, it must be noted that the narration was not directly obtained by ab Hortis; he reproduces a brief text written in Latin by the Hungarian soldier and writer Sámuel Székely Dobai (1704–1779), where he reports that in 1763 the printer Istvan Pap Szathmar Nemethi visited him and told him the story of Istvan Vályi. This is therefore FOAF ('friend of a friend') information, which means that, even if the general story may be true, some or many details may be wrong or distorted. It is interesting also that the anecdote ends with Székely's insistence on the credibility of Pap Szathmar Nemethi as a source of information: he is 'one of the scholars of our country' (*unum ex eruditis Patriae nostrae*), a person 'not so credulous to have tolerated that Váli, a minister from Almáss, would deceive him' (*nec ita credulum ut sibi passus fuisset imponi a Valio Pastore Almasiensi*).

The existence of Stephanus Váli-Istvan Vályi and his stay in Holland as a student is beyond doubt: a certain Stephanus Waali was enrolled at Utrecht University (not in Leiden!) in 1753, ten years before the date reported in the story (Willems 1997, p. 58). A certain Stephanus Váli also appears in Wallaszky (1785, p. 237), a list of Hungarian intellectual figures, in a section devoted to historians and antiquarians (*historici et antiquarii*). Furthermore, the presence of students from India attending classes in Dutch universities is well attested, and three Indian students from Ceylon (modern Sri Lanka), then a Dutch colony, are known to have studied in Leiden at the time of Stephanus Váli's stay in Holland (Willems 1997, p. 58). This is consistent with Sámuel Székély's narration, since at that time the term *Malabar* was used to refer not only to the modern region of Malabar in south-west of continental India where Malayalam is spoken, but also to the Tamil population of Ceylon. But both Malayalam and Tamil are Dravidian, non-Indo-European languages, a fact that makes Vályi's linguistic experiment very unlikely. The story gains credibility if we assume that these students spoke the other language of Ceylon, Sinhalese, an Indo-Aryan language like Romani. Certainly, there are notable differences between Sinhalese and Romani, and the idea of Hungarian Gypsies confirming one by one the thousand words collected by Váli appears extremely far-fetched. However, it is possible that the clear similarities between a few words in the two languages led the Hungarian minister to equate Gypsies with 'Malabars'. Words such as Romani *mas*: Sinhalese *mas* 'meat', Romani *lon* : Sinhalese *luṇu* 'salt', Romani *kan:* Sinhalese *kana* 'ear', Romani *devel*: Sinhalese *deviyā* 'god' and others are close enough to reach such a conclusion. This explanation seems preferable to the scenario drawn by Courthiade of a simple 'acoustic misunderstanding' between the Hungarian and the Indians speaking in broken Latin and speculating with the similarity between *zingari* and *Siṃhāla* 'Ceylon' (Courthiade 2014, p. 2).

3.8.2 Johann Christian Christoph Rüdiger

If Büttner and Váli (and secondarily ab Hortis) can be considered as the first scholars to mention the genetic relationship between Romani and Indo-Aryan languages, the first author to present evidence of this relationship, and consequently the true founder of the comparative study of Romani, was undoubtedly Johann Christian Christoph Rüdiger (1751–1822). Rüdiger's work has been unjustly eclipsed for many years by Heinrich Moritz Gottlieb Grellmann (1756–1804), whose work on Gypsies and Romani, although basically the fruit of plagiarism (of the work of Rüdiger and others), achieved great success and was translated or summarized in several languages. Only recently, thanks to Martin Rauch's dissertation (Ruch 1986) and articles such as Matras (1999) and Courthiade (2014), the figure of Rüdiger has obtained the credit he deserves. As Matras rightly points out, the importance of Rüdiger's work lies not only in its foundational character but also in the innovative methodology used.

Rüdiger's study of Romani appeared under the title 'Von der Sprache und Herkunft der Zigeuner aus Indien' ('On the language and the origin of

74   **I.-X. Adiego**

Gypsies from India') in a miscellaneous selection of author's articles (Rüdiger 1782, pp. 37–84).

Rüdiger confesses that the starting point of his research was the vocabulary contained in the *Beytrag* (N.N. 1755, cf. supra). Later, it was the St. Petersburg linguist Hartwig Ludwig Christian Bacmeister (1730–1806) who gave impetus to his work by sending him a sample text to enable him to collect linguistic data. Although Rüdiger did not give more information, this sample text was the one that Bacmeister published in 1773 in a multilingual version (Russian, French, Latin, German) entitled 'Project and request for a collection of samples of languages' (Bacmeister 1773, pp. 25–30) an ambitious plan of language comparison that the author later abandoned (see von Adelung 1815, pp. 24–25; Adelung was in possession of all the materials collected by Bacmeister).

With this sample text, Rüdiger was able to interview a Gypsy woman and obtain first-hand information on Romani. He checked this material with Benjamin Schultze's *Grammatica Hindostanica* (Schultze 1745) and, although the comparison could not be exhaustive as Schulze's book did not offer equivalences for all the vocabulary contained in Romani phrases, Rüdiger concluded that the genetic relationship of the two languages had been demonstrated. Moreover, the German scholar did not limit the comparison to vocabulary, but also offered parallels in the inflectional morphology.

The Romani recorded by Rüdiger belongs to the Sinte dialect. Matras (1999) has analysed the main linguistic traits that support this adscription. Note as an example the typical development of *s > h* affecting a great many morphological forms (copula *hom, hi, has,* etc., instrumental mark *-ha,* verbal endings *-eha, aha* and others).

Another scholar who supported the opinion that Romani was an Indo-Aryan language was Peter Simon Pallas (1741–1811), a German zoologist and biologist who was also interested in the world's languages (on Pallas as a linguist, see Archaimbault 2010). The book in which Pallas refers to the question is generally quoted as published in 1781, and therefore, prior to Rüdiger's decisive work, but in reality, the volume in which Pallas spoke about Romani appeared in 1782, as did Rüdiger's study.

Unfortunately, in Pallas (1782, p. 96), the reference to Romani is as superficial and frustrating as in Büttner (1771). In speaking about the language of the Indian merchants who lived in the southern Russian city of Astrakhan, he remarks that 'it has been pretended to note some resemblance of a few words with the language of Gypsies'. Immediately afterwards, he gives some words (numerals and five common nouns) of the language of those Indians.

The language is clearly identifiable as a Pakistan Punjabi dialect, which is hardly surprising since, as Pallas himself affirms some pages above, they came from the zone of Multan, in Pakistani Punjab. However, no forms in Romani are added for comparison. The numerals and the nouns mentioned by Pallas suggest clearly that he also used Bacmeister (1773) for his linguistic inquiry.

3.8.3 The British Branch of the Indian Approach: William Marsden and Jacob Bryant

In the journal *Archeologia* for the year 1784, two articles were published on the origin of Romani. The first was written by William Marsden, who, independently from Rüdiger, offered a list of 39 Romani words directly comparable to Hindustani (in a few cases to Bengali or to Marathi), which demonstrated the genetic relationship of these languages and the Indian origin of Romani (Marsden 1785). Despite the brevity of the list, in which Marsden combined British Romani with 'Turkish Gypsy' and Ludolf's words, and the absence of inflectional comparison, Marsden's list offered convincing evidence of the proposed connection.

The second article was a brief note by John Douglas accompanied by a vocabulary of Romani, including a linguistic comparison of a few Romani words to 'Persic or Hindustani', which Jacob Bryant would have produced some years before and which Douglas, having heard of Marsden's work, wanted to make known (Douglas 1785). This led John Sampson to claim that Bryant deserved priority over Rüdiger as the first to demonstrate the Indian origin of Romani (Sampson 1911). This priority is impossible to confirm. Sampson's suggestion 'that Bryant took down his words at Windsor on the 12th of August 1776' (Sampson 1911, p. 168) is the figment of an unbridled imagination, and even if this assertion were true, the discovery of the Indo-Aryan connection to Romani may have happened later and does not necessarily precede Rüdiger's. The discussion of Bryant's position in the history of the Indo-Aryan connection should not conceal the fact that, apart from the list of possible Indo-Aryan cognates for some Romani words, Bryant offers the first vocabulary of Angloromani of a certain length (250 words, in contrast to the two preceding repertoires (Andrew Borde and the Winchester Confessions). As Matras (2010, p. 58) points out, the vocabulary also contains some interesting examples of grammatical inflection (for instance, *crellis escochare* 'palace' = *krelis-es-ko kher*, literally 'house of the king').

3.9 After Rüdiger

From the end of the eighteenth century onwards, coinciding with the assertion of the Indo-Aryan affiliation of Romani and the general interest in linguistic taxonomy (the step immediately prior to the birth of comparative linguistics in 1814) materials on Romani began to proliferate. A good indicator of the dramatic increase in publications can be seen in the chapter on sources (*Quellen*) that opens August Pott's magnificent work *Die Zigeuner in Europa und Asien: ethnographisch-linguistische Untersuchung, vornehmlich ihrer Herkunft und Sprache, nach gedruckten und ungedruckten Quellen,* published in 1844 and which signified the inauguration of the comparative and exhaustive study of the Romani language. Prior to Rüdiger, Pott mentions only seven testimonies; after Rüdiger, forty-two. The literature that includes information on Romani in that period is varied: for instance, there is a series of travel books, a literary genre that became very popular during the nineteenth century, in which Gypsies are mentioned and specimens of their language are collected. But it is undeniable that the books by Rüdiger and particularly Grellmann heralded a new and different approach to Romani. Although sources comparable to those mentioned in this chapter continued to exist, the language began to be studied with the tools of linguistic sciences.

Notes

1. Thus Miklosich (1874), by assuming a misspelling *r* for *t*: this is not improbable, *pace* Crofton (1907, p. 164).
2. On Vulcanius' list, see Miklosich (1874), N.N. (1930), and Barthélémy (1975). On the personality and works of Bonaventura Vulcanius (though with scarce reference to Romani materials), see Cazes (2010).
3. They also consider the use of *š* for *s* in *maš* (CR *mas*) 'meat', as a possible Vlax trait, which is also present in Paspati's Nomad Romani (essentially Vlax).
4. The pretension that Björckman's *juket, cheron* and *manron* (sic! Björckman *manro*!) should be analysed as incorporating the Swedish postclitic article (*juke-t, chero-n, manro-n*) and would consequently be an example of the process towards a mixed language (Carling et al. 2014, p. 8) is simply ridiculous, as these forms were copied from Vulcanius (note above the remarks on the possible misspelling *iuket* for *iukel*).
5. Now a borough of Berlin.
6. Windstedt (1908, p. 116) thinks rather that the note refers to *stariben* 'prison', but in that case, it would be difficult to ascertain what La Croze was alluding to.

7. A transcription of the letter, accompanied by an interpretative re-transcription (in Romani standard spelling) and a translation into French can be found in Courthiade (2014, p. 9).
8. The Romani vocabulary and phrases included in Ganander's manuscript were extracted and edited in Etzler (1944, pp. 312–314).

References

ab Hortis, Samuel Augustin. 1776. "Von der Sprache der Zigeuner" and "Beschluß von der Sprache der Zigeuner". In Kaiserlich-Königlich allergnädigst privilegierte Anzeigen aus sämmtlich-kaiserlich-königlichen Erbländern, Jahrgang 6, 85–88 and 93–96.

Adiego, Ignasi-Xavier. 1998. The Spanish-Gypsy vocabulary of manuscript 3929, Biblioteca Nacional de Madrid (eighteenth century): A rereading. *Journal of the Gypsy Lore Society*, 5th ser., 8: 1–18.

Adiego, Ignasi-Xavier. 2002. *Un Vocabulario espanol-gitano del Marqués de Sentmenat (1697–1762)*. Edición y estudio lingüistico. Barcelona: Edicions de la Universitat de Barcelona.

Adiego, Ignasi-Xavier. 2013. The oldest attestation of the Romani language in Spain: The Aucto del finamiento de Jacob (sixteenth century). *Romani Studies* 23: 245–255.

Adiego, Ignasi-Xavier. 2016. Romani or Pseudo-Romani?: On the lord's prayer in 'Nubian' by Jean-Baptiste Gramaye (1622). *Romani Studies* 26: 175–182.

Archaimbault, Sylvie. 2010. Peter Simon Pallas (1741–1811), un naturaliste parmi les mots. *Histoire Épistémologie Langage* 32: 69–91.

Ascoli, Graziadio. 1865. *Zigeunerisches*. Halle: Heynemann.

Bacmeister, Hartwig. 1773. *Idea et desideria de colligendis linguarum speciminibus*. Petropoli: Typis Academiae Scientiarum.

Bakker, Peter. 1997. Review of McGowan (1996). *Journal of the Gypsy Lore Society*, 5th ser., 7 (1): 49–50.

Bakker, Peter. 2000. The genesis of Angloromani. In *Scholarship and the Gypsy struggle: Commitment in Romani studies: A collection of papers and poems to celebrate Donald Kenrick's seventieth year*, ed. Thomas Acton, 14–31. Hatfield: University of Hertfordshire Press.

Bakker, Peter. 2002. An early vocabulary of British Romani (1616): A linguistic analysis. *Romani Studies*, 5th ser., 12 (2): 75–101.

Barthélémy, André. 1975. Le glossaire tsigane-latin de Scaliger. *Etudes Tsiganes* 21 (4): 5–10.

Björckman, Samuel P. 1730. *Dissertatio academica de Ciganis*. Uppsaliae: Literis Wernerianis.

78   I.-X. Adiego

Borde [Boorde], Andrew. 1542(?). *The fyrst boke of the introduction of knowledge: The which doth teache a man to speake parte of all maner of languages and to knowe the vsage and fashion of al maner of coutreys. And for to knowe the moste parte of all maner of coynes of money, ye which is curraunt in euery region.* London: Wyllyam Copland.

Borde, Andrew. 1870. *The fyrst boke of the introduction of knowledge... edited by Frederik James Furnivall.* London: N. Trübner and Co.

Büttner, Christian Wilhelm. 1771. *Vergleichungs-Tafeln der Schriftarten verschiedener Völker in denen vergangenen und gegenwärtigen Zeiten.* Erstes Stück. Göttingen und Gotha: Johann Christian Dieterich.

Carling, Gerd, Lenny Lindell, and Gilbert Ambrazaitis. 2014. *Scandoromani: Remnants of a mixed language.* Leiden: Brill.

Cazes, Hélène (ed.). 2010. *Bonaventura Vulcanius, works and networks.* Leiden-Boston: Brill.

Courthiade, Marcel. 2014. Les premières approches linguistiques du rromani (1500–1800): entre présupposés, dégoût, ambitions et objectivité de méthode. Dossiers d'HEL, SHESL, 2014, Linguistiques d'intervention. Des usages socio-politiques des savoirs sur le langage et les langues, p. 10. Available at https://halshs.archives-ouvertes.fr/halshs-01115106/document. Accessed 11 November 2018.

Crofton, Henry. 1907. Borde's egipt speche. *Journal of the Gypsy Lore Society*, n.s., 1: 157–168.

Douglas, John. 1785. Collections on the Zingara, or Gypsey language; by Jacob Bryant. In *Archaeologia: Or miscellaneous tracts relating to antiquity* 7: 387–394 [= The annual register, or a view of the history politics and literature for the years 1784 and 1785 (Second edition: 1800), 83–89].

Ehrenborg, H. 1909. Swedish Tsiganologues. *Journal of the Gypsy Lore Society*, n.s., 3: 111–119.

Etzler, Allan. 1944. *Zigenarna och deras avkomlingar i Sverige.* Historia och språk, Uppsala: Almqvist & Wiksell.

Finck, Franz Nikolaus. 1903. *Lehrbuch des Dialekts der deutschen Zigeuner.* Marburg: N. G. Elwert.

Friedman, Victor A., and Robert Dankoff. 1991. The earliest text in Balkan (Rumelian) Romani: A passage from Evliya Çelebi's Seyähat-näme. *Journal of the Gypsy Lore Society*, 5th ser., 1: 1–20.

Ganander, Christfrid. 1780. *Undersökning om de så kallade Tattare eller Zigeuner, Cingari, Bohemiens.* Manuscript conserved in Stockholm: Kungl. Svenska Vitterhetsakademien.

Hill, John M. 1921. A Gypsy-Spanish word-list. *Revue Hispanique* 53: 614–615.

Jordan, Charles Etienne. 1741. *Historie de la vie et des ouvrages de M. La Croze.* Seconde partie, Amsterdam: Frabçois Changuion.

Kahraman, S. A., Yücel Dağlı, and Robert Dankoff. 2003. *Evliyâ Çelebi Seyahatnâmesi. VIII. Kitap.* İstanbul: Altan Matbaacılık Ltd.

3 Historical Sources on the Romani Language   79

Kluyver, A. 1900. Eene onuitgegeven lijst van woorden, afkomstig van Zigeuners uit het midden der zestiende eeuw. In *Mededeelingen van de Maatschappij der Nederlandsche Letterkunde in Leiden over het jaar 1899 en 1900*, 45–55. Leiden: E.J. Brill.

Kluyver, A. 1911. Un glossaire tsigane du seizième siècle. *Journal of the Gypsy Lore Society*, n.s., 4: 131–142.

Knauer, Georg Nicolaus. 2010. The earliest vocabulary of Romani words (c.1515) in the Collectanea of Johannes ex Grafing, a student of Johannes Reuchlin and Conrad Celtis. *Romani Studies*, 5th ser., 20 (1): 1–15.

Leblon, Bernard. 1982. *Les Gitans dans la littérature espagnol*. Toulouse: France-Ibérie Recherche.

Ludolfus, Iobus [= Hiob Ludolf]. 1691. *Ad suam historiam Aethiopicam antehac editam commentarius*. Francofurti Ad Moenum: Typis Martini Jacqueti.

MacRitchie, David. 1894. *Scottish Gypsies under the stewarts*. Edinburgh: David Douglas.

Marsden, William. 1785. Observations on the language of the people commonly called Gypsies. In *Archaeologia: Or miscellaneous tracts relating to antiquity* 7: 382–386 [= The annual register, or a view of the history politics and literature for the years 1784 and 1785 (second edition: 1800), 81–83 (without word list)].

Matras, Yaron. 1999. Johann Rüdiger and the study of Romani in eighteenth century Germany. *Journal of the Gypsy Lore Society*, 5th ser., 9: 89–116.

Matras, Yaron. 2002. *Romani: A linguistic introduction*. Cambridge: Cambridge University Press.

Matras, Yaron. 2010. *Romani in Britain: The afterlife of a language*. Edinburgh: Edinburgh University Press.

McGowan, Alan. 1996. *The Winchester confessions 1615–1616: Depositions of travellers, Gypsies, fraudsters, and makers of counterfeit documents, including a vocabulary of the Romany language*. South Chailley, East Sussex: Romany and Traveller family History Society.

Megiser, Hyeronimus. 1603. *Thesaurus polyglottus uel Dictionarium multilingue*. Francofurti ad Moenum [Frankfurt]: sumptibus authoris.

Miklosich, Franz. 1874. Die ältesten Denkmäler der Zigeunersprache. *Sitzungsberichte der Kaiserlichen Akademie der Wissenschaften* 77: 759–771.

N.N. 1726. Beschreibung des Chur-Sächsischen allgemeinen Zucht-, Waysen- und Armen-Hauses (....) Anno 1716. Bei dieser neuen Auflage mit einem Rotwelschen und Zigeunerischen Lexico (...) vermehrand et, Leipzig: Bei Christoph Hekels sel. Sohn.

N.N. 1755. Beytrag zur Rotwellischen Grammatik, oder: Wörter-Buch, von der Zigeuner-Sprache, nebst einem Schreiben eines Zigeuners an seine Frau ... Frankfurt und Leipzig: n.p.

N.N. 1930. Vulcanius' Romani vocabulary. *Journal of the Gypsy Lore Society*, 3rd ser., 9: 16–25.

Pallas, Peter Simon. 1782. *Neue nordische Beiträge zur physikalischen und geographischen Erd- und Völker-Beschreibung, Naturgeschichte und Ökonomie.* Bd. 3. St. Petersburg, Leipzig: Johann Zacharias Logan.

Paspati, Alexandre G. 1870. *Etudes sur les Tchinghianes ou Bohémiens de l'Empire Ottoman.* Constantinople: Antoine Koroméla.

Piasere, Leonardo. 1994. Il piu antico testo Italiano in Romanes (1646): una riscoperta e una lettura etnostorica. Universita' degli Studi di Verona, Facolta' di Lettere e Filosofia, Istituto di Psicologia, Report 56.

Pott, August, 1844. *Die Zigeuner in Europa und Asien: ethnographisch-linguistische Untersuchung, vornehmlich ihrer Herkunft und Sprache, nach gedruckten und ungedruckten Quellen.* Halle: Heyneman.

Ranking, D. F. de l'Hoste. 1913. An Italian Gypsy comedy. *Journal of the Gypsy Lore Society*, n.s., 7 (1): 59–68.

Ruch, Martin. 1986. Zur Wissenschaftsgeschichte der deutschsprachigen Zigeunerforschung von den Anfängen bis 1900. PhD thesis, University of Freiburg.

Rüdiger, Johann Christian Christoph. 1782. *Neuester Zuwachs der teutsche, fremden und allgemeinen Sprachkunde in eigenen Aufsätzen*, vol. 1. Stück Leipzig: P. G. Kummer.

Sampson, John. 1911. Jacob Bryant: Being an analysis of his Anglo-Romani vocabulary, with a discussion of the place and date of collection and an attempt to show that Bryant, not Rüdiger, was the earliest discoverer of the Indian origin of the Gypsies. *Journal of the Gypsy Lore Society*, n.s., 4: 162–194.

Sampson, John. 1926. *The dialect of the Gypsies of Wales.* Oxford: Clarendon Press.

Schulzius, Benjaminus [Benjamin Schultze].1745. *Grammatica hindostanica collectis in diuturna inter Hindostanos commoratione in justum ordinem redactis ac larga exemporum [sic] luce perfusis regulis constans et missionariorum usui consecrata.* Halae Saxonum: In typographia Instituti Judaici.

Valtonen, Pertti. 1969. Finnish Romani research. *Journal of the Gypsy Lore Society*, 3rd ser., 48: 124–127.

Vekerdi, József. 1962. Gypsy fragments from the early eighteenth century. *Acta Orientalia Academiae Scientiarum Hungaricae* 14 (1): 123–129.

Vekerdi, József. 1982. *A magyarországi cigány kutatások története.* Debrecen: Kossuth Lajos Tudományegyetem.

von Adelung, Friedrich. 1815. *Catherinens der grossen Verdienste um die vergleichende Sprachenkunde.* St. Petersburg: Friedrich Drechsler.

Vulcanius [= De Smet], Bonaventura. 1597. De literis et lengua Getarum siue Gothorum, Ludguni Batavorum [= Leiden]: ex officina Plantiniana, apud Franciscum Raphelengium.

Wagner, Max L. 1937. Stray notes on Spanish Romani. *Journal of the Gypsy Lore Society*, 3rd ser., 16: 27–32.

Wallaszky, Paullus [Pál]. 1785. *Conspectus reipublicae litterariae in Hungaria ab initiis regni ad nostra usque tempora delineatus.* Posonii et Lipsiae: Antonius Loewe.

Willems, Wim.1997. *In search of the true Gypsy. From enlightenment to final solution.* London-Portland: Frank Cass [= 2017, London and New York: Routledge].

Windstedt, E. O. 1908. Some old German-Gypsy word-lists. *Journal of the Gypsy Lore Society*, n.s., 2: 109–117.

Wolf, Sigmund A. 1987. *Großes Wörterbuch der Zigeunersprache (romani tšiw)*, 2nd ed. Hamburg: Helmut Buske.

Part II

Structure

4

Romani Lexicon

Andrea Scala

4.1 Introduction

This chapter aims to provide an overall introduction to the Romani lexicon, focusing mainly on its historical aspects, but without disregarding its structural dimensions. The Romani lexicon may be considered as a repository of important data on the history of the Romani people. The numerous loanwords that entered Romani allow us to reconstruct past phases of bilingualism and migrations of Romani speakers, often more than historical sources can. After a short presentation of some significant pre-scientific and scientific works dealing with the Romani lexicon and of the most important works in Romani lexicography, this chapter introduces the topic of the heuristic value that the study of the Romani lexicon can have for the history of Romani people. The different lexical layers attested in Romani are taken into separate consideration and discussed: notably, the native, i.e. directly inherited, Indo-Aryan layer; the Iranian and the Armenian layers; and the Greek layer, in part to be ascribed to a common lexical legacy present in all Romani varieties, and in part represented by dialect-specific loanwords. Further lexical layers, such as the Slavic and German ones, are examined through a case study on two Sinti varieties. After this mainly historical-linguistic part, the

A. Scala (✉)
Dipartimento di Studi Letterari, Filologici e Linguistici,
Università degli Studi di Milano, Milan, Italy
e-mail: andrea.scala@unimi.it

© The Author(s) 2020
Y. Matras and A. Tenser (eds.), *The Palgrave Handbook of Romani Language and Linguistics*, https://doi.org/10.1007/978-3-030-28105-2_4

86   A. Scala

chapter briefly examines the strategies other than loanwords used to enlarge the Romani lexicon, focusing on some of the most productive derivative morphemes and on metaphor- and metonymy-based lexical innovations. Some reflections are proposed on cultural and structural dimensions of the Romani lexicon, with special regard to the existence and persistence of some cultural taxonomies mapped by the lexicon. Lastly, the Romani lexicon is considered in its dialectal and geo-linguistic differentiation. Finally, some considerations are developed on possible key areas for future research on the Romani lexicon.

4.2   The Romani Lexicon and Understanding Its Coherence

The first collections of the Romani lexicon are random in nature and are essentially mono-dialectal. Sentences and word lists written up by individual scholars in the sixteenth century, such as Andrew Borde, Johan van Ewsum and Bonaventura Vulcanius, were probably elicited from a single informant (see Adiego in this volume). Moreover, even Bonaventura Vulcanius, the most learned and chronologically the last of the three, was probably unacquainted with the previous sources on Romani and had no possibility of establishing a comparison between his materials and those of Borde and van Ewsum (for more details cf. Adiego in this volume). The German orientalist Hiob Ludolf (or Leutholf) knew Bonavetura Vulcanius's word list and compared it with a set of 39 Romani words he had personally collected ("sciscitatus sum de vocabulis nonnullis rerum naturalium, quae facilius retinentur et minus corrumpuntur"; Ludolfus 1691, p. 214). Ludolf seems to consider the two sets of words as something coherent, but after demonstrating that the language of the so-called Gypsies or Egyptians was unrelated to the languages of Egypt ("vocabula…neque Aegyptiaca sive Coptica"), he developed no further research on the Romani lexicon. After all, until the end of the eighteenth century, the idea was very widespread that the language of the Rom was an invented code created by them precisely to conceal the meaning of their discourse and to deceive simple people, and that it coincided with the slang of tramps and criminals. As far as I know, this idea appeared for the first time in the Italian translation of Sebastian Münster's *Cosmographia Universalis* (Münster 1558, p. 304), in a paragraph absent from the many German editions, and survived at least until *Vocabulario Polyglotto* (1787) by Lorenzo Hervás y Panduro; in this work, a list of words clearly belonging to Italian criminal slang is presented as the language of the Gypsies (Hervás y

Panduro 1787, pp. 120–125). It bears noting that Bonaventura Vulcanius in 1597 had already rejected the identification of Romani with criminal slang like Rotwelsch; at any rate, until the nineteenth century, the labels used by different authors to indicate Romani are far from stable and consistent: an anonymous work published in 1755 titled *Beytrag zur Rottwellischen Grammatik, oder Wörter-buch von der Zigeuner-Sprache, nebst einem Schreiben eines Zigeuners an seine Frau*, surely also used by Johann Rüdiger, names 'Rotwelsch' what is clearly a Romani (Sinti) dialect.

The last two decades of the eighteenth century saw great advances in the comprehension of the unitary nature and historical meaning of the Romani lexicon, and there is no doubt that the study of the lexicon provided the starting point for intuiting the Indo-Aryan origin of Romani. Even the famous article by Johan Rüdiger (1782), which aimed to demonstrate the link between Romani and Urdu, found its strongest evidence in the lexical similarities. Rüdiger, significantly in a pre-Boppian period, attributed great relevance to grammatical similarities, especially morphological similarities, as proof of the genetic relationship between languages, but, as has been observed (Matras 1999, pp. 102–103), the grammatical similarities he cited between Romani and Urdu (e.g. the presence of adjectival and de-adjectival derivations, of a derivational prefix marking negation, of vowel suffixes to mark gender in nouns and adjectives, and of postposed declensional affixes; the lack of word composition patterns, etc.) refer almost entirely to morpho-syntactic structure and categories and are unsupported by any etymological link. All in all, in a demonstration intended to be based on similarities in the grammar, the most striking correspondences between Romani and Urdu come from the lexical and morpho-lexical ones. Between the late eighteenth and early nineteenth centuries, two encyclopaedic works, Pallas (1786) and Adelung (1806), devoted space to Romani. Collecting and comparing lexical data from different sources, Pallas and Adelung clearly show the unity and linguistic coherence of the Romani lexicon. In these works, concerning the lexicon of languages from all over the world, Romani is intentionally set among the languages of India, and this probably enhanced comparison with the lexicon of other Indo-Aryan languages.

4.2.1 Romani Lexicography: A Short Overview

Among the many works devoted to Romani in the nineteenth and twentieth centuries, several deserve to be remembered for their importance to the study of the Romani lexicon. August Friedrich Pott, in his monumental work

Zigeuner in Europa und Asien (1844–1845), was the first to offer a rich etymological examination of the Romani lexicon, which he gathered from published sources. But it was his pupil Franz Xaver von Miklosich who opened new perspectives on the understanding of the Romani lexicon, significantly expanding the lexical corpus available at that time, especially through personal collections in different parts of Europe (von Miklosich 1872–1880, 1874–1878). Both Pott's and Miklosich's research efforts have solid historical-comparative foundations, but while Pott's attention focuses mainly on the Indo-Aryan layer of Romani, Miklosich's work mainly investigates the numerous loanwords that are present in all varieties of Romani. Half a century after Miklosich, John Sampson published a comprehensive monograph on the dialect of the Welsh Gypsies (Sampson 1926). The third part of the work contains a detailed examination of the lexicon carried out through a synchronic-descriptive approach, paying particular attention to the contextual semantics of lexemes, exemplified by a rich set of sentences, and to word-formation. Moreover, each lexical entry is enriched by an etymological note. To this day, Sampson's work remains one of the most important points of reference both for the documentation of the Romani lexicon and for Romani etymology.

A very different kind of lexicographical work is represented by the dictionary by Siegmund Wolf (1960). It consists of a highly detailed compilation of all the sources on the Romani lexicon published earlier, starting from Andrew Borde, Johan van Ewsum and Bonaventura Vulcanius, and until 1957. Few lexical collections escaped Wolf's attention, among these, worthy of mention is Maksim Sergievskij and Aleksej Barannikov's dictionary (1938) devoted to Russian Romani. Each entry contains references to the source, definitions and a short etymological note. A second edition of this important work with some corrections was published in 1987. Wolf's dictionary represents a comprehensive compilation of the available corpus of lexical research on Romani, and this can be considered its main merit; unfortunately, the etymological explanations provided in the work are rather weak at times. After Wolf, Romani lexicography has produced mainly lexical collections from single dialects and areas, sometimes enriched by etymological explanations and sometimes only descriptive. Several works are devoted to large areas. The dictionary of Romani dialects spoken in the former Yugoslavia, collected by Boretzky and Igla (1994), bears mention as highly useful from both a descriptive and etymological perspective. The dictionary by Soravia and Fochi (1995), only descriptive, presents extensive lexical data from the Romani varieties of Italy, previously published from the 1970s to the 1990s in the review *Lacio drom*. For the Romani dialects spoken in Hungary, Vekerdi's (1983) dictionary is essential.

As for lexical descriptions of individual dialects, besides the aforementioned Sampson (1926), important works are those by Valtonen (1972) on Finnish Romani, and by Formoso and Calvet (1987) devoted to the Piedmontese Sinti spoken in southern France, both with etymological notes, and others, such as Cech and Heinschink (2002) on Dolenjski Romani, Halwachs and Ambrosch (2002) on Burgenland-Romani, Calvet (1982) on the dialect of the Erli of Sofia (Bulgaria), Calvet (2009) on the dialect of Kalderasha and Toporov (2003) on Crimean Romani. A very useful online instrument, developed in collaboration between the Romani projects and Graz and Manchester universities, is *ROMLEX*, a lexical database, which makes lexical collections from many different Romani dialects accessible. Lastly, the *Romani Morpho-Syntax Database* (RMS) also provides rich information on the lexicon and allows a comprehensive lexical comparison to be drawn among different Romani dialects throughout Europe.

4.2.2 The Romani Lexicon as an Archive

As stated earlier, Pott's work shows clear awareness that although a large part of the Romani lexicon is of Indo-Aryan origin, many words cannot be ascribed to this layer (Pott 1844–1845, vol. II). However, a systematic and detailed study of Romani's numerous loanwords was not developed by Pott, but by his talented pupil, Franz Xaver von Miklosich. In a famous series of studies published between 1872 and 1880, Miklosich proceeded to distinguish the different layers of loanwords present in the Romani lexicon. The first outcome of this operation was the possibility of reconstructing, at least in rough outline, the migrations of Romani-speaking people. Behind this idea, there was (and still is) a simple inference: loanwords require bilingualism and bilingualism among people without writing requires direct contact; such contact, in turn, implies physical presence in the territories and among the communities where the donor languages are spoken. In this perspective, the lexicon becomes a kind of unwitting archive, in which loanwords, not unlike index fossils, represent historical traces of use for reconstructing the migrations of the Romani people. Thanks to the study of the different layers of loanwords, the westward journey of the Rom became clearly visible to Miklosich: to understand where the ancestors of the Rom passed through to reach Europe, it sufficed to match the different donor languages the loanwords belonged to with the historical areas of settlement of their speakers. In this perspective, the linguistic history of the Romani people can be conceived as a long chain of bilingualisms. Definitive migrations forced Romani speakers to repeatedly change their linguistic repertoire, which however was generally organized in endo-communitarian code(s) (i.e. the language(s) spoken only inside the Romani community) and eso-communitarian code(s) (i.e. the language(s) used outside the community to communicate with the members of the majority community). During periods of movement between areas with different languages, some Romani communities may plausibly be thought to have continued to speak, besides Romani, the language of the previous area of settlement as well, while at the same time acquiring the language of their new place of settlement. Each new bilingualism replaced the previous one that left a historical trace in the continuation of some loanwords. Theoretically, this is not the only possible explicative model of the coexistence in Romani of different layers of loanwords, but it is the most likely one. Considering the Indo-Aryan layer as the native layer of Romani, it may be observed that the subsequent most ancient lexical layers (Iranian, Armenian, Greek) are consistent with a westward migration of Romanì speakers. Of course, it is hard to exclude a priori the possibility that some individual Iranian, Armenian or Greek loanwords could have been acquired almost contemporarily in Eastern Anatolia (Matras 2010, p. 35), where varieties of such languages have been spoken for centuries.

4.3   Lexical Layers Shared by All Romani Varieties

All Romani dialects share the same legacy of Indo-Aryan, Iranian, Armenian words and also a significant number of Greek loanwords. This fact is not easy to interpret; it might be assumed that the ancestors of the present-day Romani speakers migrated in a rather compact group at least as far as Hellenophone Anatolia, and their diaspora began within the Greek-speaking area, perhaps in the Hellenic peninsula. In this respect, it must also be stressed that no certain Arabic or Turkic loanwords can be found in the common Romani lexicon. This fact suggests that contact with these languages was absent or irrelevant, for geo- and sociolinguistic reasons or for chronological reasons. The absence of Turkic loanwords, combined with the chronology assumed by the Armenian loanwords (before eleventh century), suggests that the movements within Asia of the Romani people preceded the settlement of Turkic groups in Iran and Armenia. The first encounter of Romani people with the Turkic languages was to occur in the Balkans some centuries later. As for the lack of Arabic loanwords, both a geo- and sociolinguistic reason and a chronological reason must be taken into consideration.

Even in the period of the strong north- and northeastward expansion of the Caliphate of the 'Rightly Guided' caliphs (before 661), Arabic was never deeply rooted in northern Iran, Armenia and Eastern Anatolia. The lack of Arabic loanwords acquired via Iranian languages also seems to be significant. Although the role of geo- and sociolinguistic reasons and chronological ones is difficult to discern, the fact remains that Romani shows no traces of a period of their speakers' Arabic or Turkic bilingualism before the Modern Era.

4.3.1 The Indo-Aryan Layer

The native layer of Romani, which is to say the most ancient inherited layer to which both inflectional morphology and core vocabulary can be traced, is the Indo-Aryan one. A regular historical phonology and the broad comparability of inflectional morphology between Romani and Old, Middle and Modern Indo-Aryan languages demonstrate this genealogical affiliation (cf. Beníšek in this volume). With reference to the lexicon, the Indo-Aryan legacy in Romani embraces almost all semantic spheres. Of course, the number of Indo-Aryan inherited lexemes in the various semantic spheres differs, as some semantic domains and even some single items are more resistant, and others are more prone to lexical substitution through loanwords. Here is a concise sample of some Indo-Aryan lexemes continuing in Romani (regarding the semantic spheres listed in Table 4.1, cf. Elšík 2009, in Haspelmath and Tadmor 2009).

Of course, there are also many function words such as the verb 'to be', the personal and demonstrative pronouns, other indefinite pronouns such as *či* 'nothing', *vaver* 'other', etc., that are of Indo-Aryan origin. As for the semantic spheres proposed in the *World Loanword Database* by Martin Haspelmath and Uri Tadmor, Romani's lack of Indo-Aryan terms for warfare and hunting is worthy of attention. Obviously, the lexicon related to the semantic sphere labelled as 'modern world' also lacks Indo-Aryan roots.

As is often the case in languages with heavy borrowing, the Indo-Aryan layer is well preserved in Romani especially in its high-frequency lexicon; in its lexicon having a high cognitive salience in mapping the physical world, individuals' relationship with it, and everyday life objects and relationships; and, lastly, in its lexicon presenting a high salience in cultural and community identity (for a general discussion, cf. Tadmor 2009). These categories are rather different and not complementary; some lexemes can in fact be attributed to more than one category. In the high-frequency lexicon, we find

Table 4.1 Indo-Aryan inherited lexemes in Romani

Physical world	*pani* 'water', *bař* 'stone', *phuv* 'earth', *čik* 'mud', *brišind* 'rain', *iv* 'snow', *kham* 'sun', *čhon* 'moon', *jag* 'fire', etc.
Kinship	*dad* 'father', *dai* 'mother', *čhavo* 'son', *čhai* 'daughter', *phral* 'brother', *phen* 'sister', *kak* 'uncle', *řom* 'husband', *řomni* 'wife', *salo/-i* 'brother/sister-in-law', *sastro* 'father-in-law', *sasui* 'mother-in-law', *džamutro* 'brother/son-in-law', *bori* 'sister/daughter-in-law', etc.
Animals	*džukel* 'dog', *džukli* 'female dog', *bašno* 'cock', *xer* 'donkey', *xerni* 'she-ass', *guruv* 'ox', *guruvni* 'cow', *bakro* 'sheep', *balo* 'pig', *mačho* 'fish', *čiriklo* 'bird', *sap* 'snake', *džuv* 'louse', *pišom* 'flea', *ruv* 'wolf', *šošoi* 'hare', etc.
Body	*šero* 'head', *bal* 'hair', *jakh* 'eye', *nakh* 'nose', *mui* 'face, mouth', *(v)ušt* 'lip', *čhib* 'tongue', *dand* 'tooth', *čham* 'cheek', *kan* 'ear', *musi* 'arm', *vast* 'hand', *xer(oi)/čang* 'leg', *pinřo* 'foot', *peř* 'belly', *kar* 'penis', *pele* 'testicles', *xas* 'cough', *čhungar* 'saliva', *muter* 'urine', etc.
Food and drink	*manřo* 'bread', *ařo* 'flour', *mas* 'meat', *goi* 'sausage', *mol* 'wine', *thud* 'milk', *kiral* 'cheese', *khil* 'butter', *anřo* 'egg', *phabai* 'apple', *akhor* 'walnut', *lon* 'salt', etc.
Clothing and grooming	*gad* 'shirt', *kangli* 'comb', *suv* 'needle', *thav* 'thread' and some others
Agriculture and vegetation	*giv* 'wheat', *džov* 'barley', *rukh* 'tree', *patrin* 'leaf', *kanřo* 'thorn', *čar* 'grass', *khas* 'hay', *phus* 'straw', etc.
Basic actions and technology	*ker-* 'to do', *phag(ar)-* 'to break', *čhin-* 'to cut', *thov-* 'to wash', *čhuri* 'knife', *kat* 'scissors', *sumnakai* 'gold', *rup* 'silver', *sastri* 'iron', etc.
Motion	*dža-* 'to go', *(a)v-* 'to come', *per-* 'to fall', etc.
Possession	*l-* 'to take', *(a)star-* 'to hold', *d-* 'to give', *(a)rakhel-* 'to find', *naš(al/ar)-* 'to lose', *bikin-* 'to sell', *kin-* 'to buy', etc.
Spatial relations	*(a)vri* 'outside', *andr-el-al* 'inside', *paš-el-al* 'near', *angl-el-al* 'in front of', *pal-el-al* 'behind' *dur* 'far', *upr-el-al* 'up, above', *tel-el-al* 'down, below', *čhiv-* 'to put', *(a)čh-* 'to stay', *putar-* 'to open', *phand-* 'to close', etc.
Quantity	*jekh* '1', *dui* '2', *trin* '3', *štar* '4', *pandž* '5', *šov* '6', *deš* '10', *biš* '20', *šel* '100', *pherdo* 'full', *paš* 'half', *but* 'much, many', *gin-* 'to count', etc.
Time	*nevo* 'new', *terno* 'young', *phuro* 'old', *(a)kana* 'now', *dives* 'day', *rat* 'night', *berš* 'year', *nilai/nial* 'summer', *ivend* 'winter', etc.
Sense perception	*dikh-* 'to see', *šun-* 'to hear', *khand-* and *sung-* respectively 'to have a bad/a good smell', *parno* 'white', *kalo* 'black', *lolo* 'red', *tato* 'warm', *šilo* 'cold', *guglo/gudlo* 'sweet', *keřko* 'bitter', etc.
Emotions and values	*rov-* 'to cry', *(a)sa-* 'to smile, laugh', *kam-* 'to love, to want', *čum* 'kiss', *dukh* 'pain', *doš* 'blame', *ladž* 'shame', *šuker* 'beautiful', *čačo* 'true', *xoxano/xoxado* 'lying', *lačho* 'good', *mišto* 'well', *džungalo* 'bad', *dar/traš* 'fear', etc.
Cognition	*džan-/džin-* 'to know', *xaljar-/xaljov-* 'to understand', *sikav-* 'to teach' *na* 'no', *oja/ova* 'yes', *sar* 'how?', *so* 'what?', *kon* 'who?', *kai* 'where?', etc.
Speech and language	*gilav-* 'to sing', *vačar-/rakar-* 'to speak', *phen-* 'to say', *nav/lav* 'name', *phuč-* 'ask', *(a)khar-* 'to call', etc.
Social and political relations	*gav* 'village', *gadžo* 'individual of non-Romani origin', *raklo* 'young individual of non-Romani origin', *lubni* 'prostitute' and few others
Law	*sov-* 'to oath', *čor* 'thief', *čor-* 'to steal'
Religion and belief	*devel* 'God', *beng* 'devil', *rašai* 'priest', *(a)kuš-* 'to curse'

4 Romani Lexicon 93

words used quite often (e.g. the copula, verbs such as *dža-* 'to go', *av-* 'to come', *xa-* 'to eat', *dik-* 'to see'; adverbs of place and time, negative particles, and personal and demonstrative pronouns, etc.). In the high cognitive salience lexicon, we find words having particular relevance to speakers' general cognitive activity, although they are not necessarily used very frequently, often being closely linked to particular discourse contexts, e.g. body parts like *nakh* 'nose', *(v)ušt* 'lip', *dand* 'tooth', *peř* 'belly', *pele* 'testicles'; adjectives like *terno* 'young' and *nevo* 'new'; words referring to speech activities like *vačar-/rakar-* 'to speak', *xaljar-/xaljov-* 'to understand'; the lowest numerals; some psycho-physical states like *dar/traš* 'fear', *ladž* 'shame'; seasons like *nilai/nial* 'summer', *(i)vend* 'winter'; non-domestic prototypical animals cf. *čiriklo* 'bird', *mačho* 'fish', *sap* 'snake'; recurring atmospheric phenomena like *iv* 'snow', *balval* 'wind'; materials like *sastri/saster* 'iron', *rup* 'silver', *sumnakai* 'gold', etc. To the lexicon having a high cultural salience, words may be assigned that represent objects, processes and values with important functions in the culture of the community; some examples may be religious words like *rašai* 'priest', *drabar-* 'to tell fortunes', *(a)kuš-* 'to swear, to curse' and some others.

The Swadesh list (Swadesh 1952, pp. 456–457), which marks an attempt to establish a series of words that capture universal concepts, is based mainly on assumed high-frequency and high cognitive salience lexicon. These two parts of the lexicon are likely to be more stable (cf. Tadmor 2009, pp. 66–72), while those words that have a high salience in the cultural identity of a community should be less stable, because they are often replaced in cases of culture innovation (Tadmor 2009, pp. 64–65). Moreover, belonging to more than one of these categories appears to be the most favourable condition for preserving the inherited lexicon. This is the case for example with those words that have both high frequency and high cognitive salience, but other words are preserved over the centuries because they are frequent and culturally central; a good example of this is words expressing a human being who does not belong to the Rom community, like *gadžo/gadži* 'non-Romani men/women', *raklo/rakli* 'non-Romani boy/girl'. Although the doubts expressed by Matras (2002, p. 21) on the reliability of the Swadesh list are well justified, it may be useful to keep in mind that, according to Boretzky's (1992) survey of many Romani dialects, the loss of Indo-Aryan lexemes in the Swadesh 200 word list amounts to 33–37 items. Lastly, it is reasonable that some semantic spheres are in general more resistant to loanwords: this seems to be the case with Indo-Aryan terms related to kinship, quantity, spatial relations, emotions and cognition (Elšík 2009); but also within these spheres it is often important to evaluate each individual lexeme for frequency, cognitive salience and cultural centrality.

94   A. Scala

The lexical data of RMS, although rather limited in number and not collected specifically for lexical research, allow a wide range of comparison among many Romani varieties from all over Europe (the sample consists of more than 100 dialect surveys in 22 different countries) and can provide some interesting evidence about some conservative lexical types. For instance, with reference to animal names, the words for 'horse', 'dog', 'puppy', 'cat', 'hedgehog' and 'ant' are taken into consideration by RMS: in the whole sample, the type *džukel* 'dog' represents by far the most resistant Indo-Aryan term, only in some dialects do we find the lexical type *rikono*, whose etymology is uncertain (Boretzky and Igla [1994, p. 332] speak of an Armenian origin, but Orengo 2003 does not accept this hypothesis); *kir* 'ant' is also widely preserved, while other terms, although sometimes pre-European like the ubiquitous Armenian loanword *grast* 'horse', are not of Indo-Aryan origin. The lexical data of RMS can be usefully integrated with those of ROMLEX, which collects far more lexical types, but from a smaller sample of 27 Romani dialects. As for other animal names, ROMLEX shows that the Indo-Aryan lexemes *bakro* 'sheep', *guruvni* 'cow', *khaini/kaxni* 'hen, chicken', *mačho* 'fish' and *sap* 'snake' are also preserved in the whole sample and *džuv* 'louse' has been replaced only in Crimean Romani by *likh* 'nit', another word of Indo-Aryan origin. Moreover, *balo* 'pig', *čiriklo* 'bird' and *ruv* 'wolf' are highly resistant and have been lost respectively only in Sepečides Romani (*gruni* 'pig', cf. northern Greek *groýni*), Kosovo Arli Romani (*čavka* 'bird', cf. SCr. *čavka* 'jackdaw') and Sinti (*volfo* 'wolf', cf. Germ. *Wolf*). Lastly, a high degree of stability is also shown by *bašno* 'cock' and *pišom* 'flea', replaced in only two dialects. As is clear, the persistence of these words depends on different accounts, and some of these are not only animal names but also food names.

A lexical sphere generally considered highly resistant to lexical change is that of kinship terms. It bears noting that this semantic domain does not show a unitary inner behaviour; cf. the following data from five Romani varieties spoken in Italy (the kinship terms of Indo-Aryan continuity in italic type, loanwords in roman type; for lexical data cf. Soravia and Fochi 1995).

The Indo-Aryan heritage is less stable in terms indicating relatives by marriage, cf. *saštró/sasú* 'father-/mother-in-law', often replaced by loanwords (cf. e.g. *bopéro* < Fr. *beau-père*, *suóčero* < It. *suocero* or the semi-calque *svigerdát* < Germ. *Schwiegervater* for 'father in law' and *mánja* < Piedm. *mápa* 'aunt', *suóčera* < It. *suocera* or the semi-calque *svigerdái* < Germ. *Schwiegermutter* for 'mother in law'), such as *saló/salí* 'brother-/sister-in-law' as well (cf. *sugáro, sogáreso, svagári* for 'brother-in-law' and *sugára, sogáresi, svegártsa* 'sister-in-law' cf. SCr. *šogor*, Germ. *Schwager*). Inherited lexicon is better preserved within the terms for the nuclear family, where the basic terms *dad* 'father', *dai* 'mother', *čhavo* 'son', *čhai* 'daughter', *phral* 'brother', *phen* 'sister', *řom* 'husband' and *řomni* 'wife' have not been replaced by loanwords in any of the above-considered dialects. The preservation of inherited kinship terms is often sensitive to the distance from EGO (see Matras 2009, pp. 169–171). This is also the case with the Romani dialects taken into consideration in Table 4.2. In order to verify this relationship, we can assign in the single dialects 2 points to each Indo-Aryan kinship term neither replaced nor flanked by a loanword, 1 point to each Indo-Aryan term for which also a synonymic loanword is in use, and 0 points to each kinship term for which no Indo-Aryan word is still preserved. Inserting the average of these scores in a diagram representing the distance from EGO (following Matras 2009), we obtain the results shown in Table 4.3.

Some Indo-Aryan kinship terms, such as those for 'father', 'mother', 'son', 'daughter', 'brother', 'sister' and 'daughter-in-law', show a score of 2, i.e. they are preserved in all the considered dialects. Also rather high is the score for 'aunt' (1,6), which indicates that only a few dialects have replaced the Indo-Aryan word. On the contrary, there is no trace of Indo-Aryan kinship terms for 'nephew', 'niece', 'grandfather', 'grandchild', 'granddaughter' (score 0). Lexical items representing relatives closer to EGO are more likely to be Indo-Aryan and, interestingly, female kinship terms are more conservative than male ones. Such a situation suggests that in an internally structured semantic sphere such as kinship terminology, cognitive and cultural factors interact, determining in the competence of each speaker (EGO) a core and a periphery within the lexical sphere. Moreover, it bears noting that some kinship terms have been replaced by Indo-Aryan lexical items (cf. *sastrí*, etymologically 'mother-in-law' for 'daughter-in-law' and *pralë da vastë, penë da vastë* literally 'hand-brother' and 'hand-sister' for 'male cousin' and 'female cousin'). With reference to an analogous situation in Domari (and in English and Maltese), Matras (2009, pp. 169–171) has proposed the existence of a 'proximity' constraint. According to the 'proximity' constraint, in lexico-semantic domains, that which is closer, more intimate and possibly more connected with speech routines, tends to resist lexical substitution via loanwords.

As for the continuity of the Indo-Aryan lexicon in Romani, a major role is also played by word classes. Some lexical categories tend to be borrowed more easily than others: typically the most concise version of this hierarchy may be articulated as follows: nouns > verbs > adjectives (for a reflection on the topic, cf. Matras 2009, pp. 156–158), i.e. nouns are the lexical category more prone to borrowing than verbs and adjectives, and verbs are

Table 4.2 Kinship terms in Romani varieties of Italy

	Piedmontese Sinti	Lombard Sinti	Venetian Sinti	Abruzzian Romani	Calabrian Romani
father/mother	*dat/dai*	*dat/dai*	*dat/dai*	*datë/daj(ë)*	*datë/daj(ë)*
brother/sister	*pral/pen*	*pral/pen*	*phral/phen*	*pralë/penë*	*pralë/penë*
grandfather/grandmother	*papú/bibí, nóna*	*pápo, nóno/nóna*	*pápos/mamín*	*papú/nonnë*	*papú/nonnë*
son/daughter	*čavó/čai*	*čau/čai*	*čávo/čai*	*čavó/čai*	*čavó/čai*
uncle/aunt	*kakó, bárba/bibí, mánja*	*káku, bárba, ziu/bibí, zía*	*káko/bibin*	*kagë, tsitsí/bíbbë*	*tsitsi/bíbbë*
male cousin/female cousin	*kikidžaló/kikidžalí*	*kuzin/kuzína*	*kozino/kozína*	*prálë da vastë/penë da vastë*	*pralë, jemató/penë, jematí*
husband/wife	*rom/romní*	*rom/rómli*	*rom/rómni*	*rom/romní*	*rom/rombrí*
father-in-law/mother-in-law	*bopéro/bibí, mánja*	*suóčero/suóčera*	*svigerdát/svigardái, svogártsa*	*saštró/sasú*	*sastró, sóčërë/sasú*
son-in-law/daughter-in-law	*bofiso, saló/borí, salí*	*dženero/bóri*	*svigarčávo/bóri*	*džamutró/burí*	*jénërë/sastrí*
brother-in-law/sister-in-law	*sugáro/sugára*	*sálo, sogáreso/sáli, sogáresi*	*svagári/svegártsa*	*saló/salí*	*saló, džamutró/salí*
grandchild (and nephew)/grand-daughter (and niece)	*nebúdo/nebúda*	*nevúdo/nevúda*	*éngelo/éngela*	*nispjó/nispjí*	*nisprijó/nisprijí*

4 Romani Lexicon 97

Table 4.3 Borrowability of kinship terms based on distance from EGO

grandmother 0.2 /grandfather 0						
mother-in-law 0,8	aunt 1,6	mother 2	father 2	uncle 1		father-in-law 0,6
sister-in-law 1	female cousin 1	sister 2	**EGO**	brother 2	male cousin 1	brother-in-law 1
daughter-in-law 2	niece 0	daughter 2	son 2	nephew 0		son-in-law 0,4
grandchild 0/ granddaughter 0						

borrowed more easily than adjectives. Consequently, in Romani as well, the replacement of the native lexicon through luxury loanwords (i.e. loanwords introduced as alternative lexicalization for an existing concept. cf. also the label 'core loanwords' in Haspelmath 2009, p. 48) is expected to be more likely for nouns than for verbs. An example of research that pays attention to the lexical categories of loanwords is that by Elšík (2009), devoted to Selice Romani. In this variety of Romani spoken in Slovakia, in a corpus of 1430 lexemes, only 37.4% is of Indo-Aryan origin, the rest being loanwords; among these, the high number of Hungarian lexical borrowings (735, i.e. 52.7% of the corpus and 84.2% of the loanwords) attracts attention. Loanwords comprise 75.6% of all nouns (59.9% from Hungarian) and 54.9% of all verbs (41.2% from Hungarian). Conversely, among retained Indo-Aryan roots, 24.4% are nouns and 45.1% are verbs. Furthermore, function words seem to be highly resistant to lexical substitution: 69.1% of these words in Selice Romani are of Indo-Aryan origin (but see Matras and Adamou in this volume, for a more differentiated discussion of the borrowing of grammatical lexicon). Among the many loanwords present in Selice Romani, some are luxury (or core) loanwords, but a significant number are necessity loanwords connected to new objects and concepts encountered by Romani speakers when the Indo-Aryan layer had already lost part of its productivity.

On the whole, about 700 Romani roots may be traced back to Indo-Aryan; of course, different dialects show different degrees of retention of this common legacy. Despite its 62.6% of loanwords, Selice Romani appears to be a rather conservative dialect as concerns the native lexicon, preserving

98   A. Scala

at least 534 Indo-Aryan roots. Overall, the Indo-Aryan lexical layer tends to preserve a strong leading role in the lexical core of Romani, while it decreases to a considerable degree in the peripheral areas of the lexicon.

4.3.2 The Iranian Layer

The Iranian lexical layer of Romani is the less investigated one. Approximately 60 Romani words can be traced to an Iranian origin. The attempt made by Hancock (1995) to enlarge this corpus offers interesting material, which, however, needs to be verified with greater attention (Matras 2002, p. 23). As noted by Boretzky and Igla (1994, pp. 329–331), some Romani words allow a twofold etymological hypothesis; this is also the case with a handful of possible Iranian loanwords which show strong similarity, if not perfect identity, with Indo-Aryan or Armenian lexemes. These similarities are based on different premises. In the first case, they are due to the etymological closeness between the Indo-Aryan and Iranian languages, for which the reconstruction of a common prehistorical phase has long been proposed. Cases such as *angušt(o)* 'finger' and *kirmo* 'worm' can be formally traced either to Indo-Aryan (cf. OIA *aṅguṣṭha* and *kṛma*) or to Iranian (cf. e.g. Pers. *angušt* and *kirm*). Considerations of a lexico-semantic order might possibly lead to affirming that such words, belonging as they do to the lexical core of a language, should probably be considered Indo-Aryan, but it is clear that such criteria are less reliable than formal ones.

As for the lexical similarities between the Iranian languages and Armenian, it suffices to consider that a very large portion of the Armenian lexicon consists of Iranian loanwords, and it is no accident that until the studies by Heinrich Hübschmann (1875), Armenian had been considered an Iranian language. For example, for Romani words like *baxt* 'fortune', an Iranian origin (cf. M. Pers., Pers., Kurd. and Pasht. *baḫt*) is as possible as an Armenian one (cf. Arm. *baxt*, borrowed into Armenian from Middle Iranian before the 5th c.). The same uncertainty may be noticed for *zor* 'strength' and *xal* 'leprosy' (Scala 2004, p. 346). The items that are clear loans from Iranian include words belonging to different semantic domains, such as animal names (*kermuso/karmuso* 'mouse', *buz(n)o* 'billy goat', cf. Pers. *karmūš* 'mole' and *buz* 'billy goat'); edible fruits and vegetables (*ambrol* 'pear', *sir* 'garlic': cf. Pers. *amrūd*, Pers. and Kurd. *sīr*); and metals (*avsin* 'steel': cf. Oss. *äfsän* 'iron'). Among natural entities, the Iranian loanword *dorjav*, the oldest attested Romani word meaning 'sea' (cf. Pers. *daryā(b)* 'sea, big river'), is worthy of note. Some other Iranian loanwords concern small and large artefacts, like *zen* 'saddle', *poštin* 'fur coat', *sini* 'small table' (cf. Early Modern Pers. *zēn*, *pōstīn*, Pers. *sīnī* 'vessel'); a proto-industrial machine like *asjav* 'mill' (cf. M. Pers. *āsyāb*, Pers. *āsyā*); and a settlement name like *diz* 'city, fortress', cf. Pers. *diz/diž* 'fortress'). There are also some adjectives, like *kořo* 'blind', *xurdo* 'short, small', *tang* 'narrow' (cf. Early Modern Pers. *kōr*, Pers. *xurd* and *tang*), and verbs, e.g. *parvar-* 'nourish' and *res-* 'arrive' (cf. Pers. *parvardan* and *rasīdan*).

Another issue regarding the Iranian layer in Romani is the difficulty—sometimes the impossibility—of identifying the Iranian dialectal area from which the different loanwords were acquired. At times, the lexical type can be relevant in this sense; for example, *(a)mal* 'friend' seems to find correspondence only in Eastern Iranian cf. Pasht. *mal* and Oss. *ämbal*. With reference to Ossetic, it may be useful to keep in mind that, despite its actual position on the northern side of the Caucasus, this language belongs to the Eastern Iranian languages; the ancestors of the Ossetians, called Alani in the classical sources, moved westwards in the first half of the first millennium, leaving the eastern areas of the Iranian continuum. Among Western Iranian dialects, Kurdish may have played some role as a source for loanwords (Matras 2002, p. 23). But in fact there are no Iranian loanwords in Romani that can be traced back exclusively to Kurdish (for the debated case of *khulai/xulai* 'gentlman, landlord' cfr. Voskanian 2002, p. 177). However, in most cases, the dialectal origin of the Iranian loanwords remains ambiguous, cf. for instance *sir* 'garlic', which could derive from either Kurdish or Persian *sīr*. Iranian loanwords may be of some help to clarify the relative chronology of at least some sound changes that occurred in Romani. In Indo-Aryan words like *bal* 'hair' < OIA *vāla*, *bango* 'lame' < OIA *vaṅka*, *berš* 'year' < OIA *varṣa*, initial *v-* yielded *b-*. This phonetic innovation does not affect the Iranian loanwords, cf. *veš* 'wood, forest' < M. Pers. *wēša(g)*, Early Modern Pers. *weša* and *vurdon* 'caravan' < M. Pers. *wardyūn*. This fact suggests that the change *v- > b-* in Romani was already achieved before the ancestors of present-day Romani speakers entered the Iranian area. An important etymological corollary derives from this: Romani words beginning with *v-* cannot be traced back to an Indo-Aryan root having etymological *v-*. Such words as *vudár* 'door' and *vast* 'hand' have respectively undergone a metathesis (cf. OIA **duvāra < dvāra*) and a prothesis of *v-* (cf. OIA *hasta*). The *v*-prothesis is a relatively late phenomenon that also affected Slavic loanwords like *vódro* 'bed' (cf. OChSl. *odrŭ*). Lastly, other words showing *v-* can be loanwords from Armenian (cf. *val* 'early, soon' from Arm. *vał*) or from Greek (cf. *vront-* 'to thunder' from Gr. *brontáei*). As for the chronology of Iranian loanwords in Romani, it is difficult to find phonetic features that allow solid dating hypotheses. Nevertheless, the archaic form of some Iranian loanwords, such as the already quoted *veš* 'wood, forest', whose equivalent in Persian is *bīšé*, cannot be neglected. The chronology of the change *v*-(or better *ß*-) > *b*- in Iranian languages is problematic and of course varies according to different dialects; it may be noted that the Middle Iranian languages offer no traces of this innovation. Early Modern Pers. shows hesitation between the fricative and the occlusive, and in thirteenth-century Classical Persian, the change seems to be accomplished (Pisowicz 1985, pp. 148–149).

4.3.3 The Armenian Layer

The Armenian lexical layer in Romani, which has been the object of many studies over the past 25 years (Boretzky 1995; Orengo 2003, 2007; previously cf. Dowsett 1973–1974; Hancock 1987), consists of about 30 indisputable loanwords, with about 20 additional items of uncertain attribution, for which an Iranian or, in some cases, a Georgian origin may be possible. The fact that a very large part of the Armenian lexicon consists of Iranian loanwords and that many Armenian words entered Georgian makes it difficult to establish the language from which those words entered into Romani. It may be noted that in the past few years, it has been possible to ascribe to this layer some words whose origin was unknown. This is the case with *kurung* 'crow', *pendex* 'hazelnut' (Scala 2004) and *val* 'early, soon' (Scala 2013), respectively, from Arm. *kŕunk* 'crane', *pndeł* 'hazelnut', *vał* 'early'. Contact with the Armenian language has left significant traces in Romani, in different semantic domains: domestic equines such as *grast/grai* 'horse', *khuro* 'colt', probably *džoro* 'mule' (cf. Arm. *grast* 'beast of burden', *k'uŕak* 'colt', *ǰori* 'mule', but cf. also Georg. *ʒori* 'id.') and *gomež* 'horse' of interest for the semantic shift (cf. Arm. *gomeš* 'buffalo'); wild animals like the above-mentioned *kurung* 'crow'; edible fruits and vegetables like *mamux* 'wild plum', *dudum* 'pumpkin', *pendex* 'hazelnut' (cf. Arm. *mamux*, *dədum* and *pndeł* 'id.'); metals like *arčiči* 'lead, tin' (cf. Arm. *arčič* 'id.'); small and large artefacts like *bov* 'oven, stove', *kočak* 'button', *balani* 'tub' (cf. Arm. *bov* 'oven, furnace', *kočak* 'button', *bałanik'* 'bath'); and fabrics and cloths, like *vuš* 'linen', *thalik* 'cloak', *tirax* 'shoe' (Cf. Arm. *vuš* 'linen', *t'ałi* 'felt, cloak of felt', *trex* 'sandal'). Lastly, there are some very interesting loanwords referring to spiritual and religious dimension, such as *ogi* 'soul', *patragi* 'Easter', *xung/xonk* 'incense' (cf. Arm. *(h)ogi* 'soul', *patarag* 'mass', *xunk* 'incense').

Some phonetic evidence (notably the reflexes in Romani of the Arm. lateral / and of the occlusives and affricates) suggests that contact between

Romani and Armenian took place before the eleventh century and that Armenian loanwords were acquired from a variety of Armenian that is fully compatible with Old Armenian and with the modern eastern dialects of the Armenian continuum, but not with the western ones, spoken till the beginning of the twentieth century, in Eastern Anatolia (for a discussion cf. Orengo 2003, pp. 13 and 15; Scala 2004, pp. 346–347).

4.4 Between Common Legacy and Dialect-Specific Innovation: The Greek Layer

The post-Armenian lexical layers represent a large part of the lexicon in all Romani dialects. In particular, Greek lexical loanwords are quite abundant (at least 200 loanwords according to Boretzky and Igla [1994, pp. 333–338] just for the dialects of the former Yugoslavia) and can be divided into two different groups: the first group, when not replaced by more recent loanwords, is shared by all Romani dialects, while the second set is present and variously distributed only in some dialects. Two such nuclei refer to different ethno-historical and chronological phases, pointing to an early dialectal differentiation within Romani. The Greek loanwords in Romani include words related to all lexical categories and semantic spheres. Nouns such as *kakavi* 'kettle', *klidi(n)* 'key', *kokalo* 'bone', *kurko* 'Sunday, market, week', *papi(n)* 'goose', *papo* 'grandfather', *xoli(n)* 'anger', *zumi(n)* 'soup, broth' and many others, but also numerals like *efta* 'seven', *oxto* 'eight', *enjá* 'nine' and others; adverbs such as *pale* 'again' (homophone of *pale* 'behind', the latter of Indo-Aryan origin), *tasja/teisa* 'tomorrow, yesterday' are of certain Greek origin (cf. respectively Ģr. *kakkábē, kleidí, kókkalo, papí* 'duck', *pappoŷs, kholḗ, zoymí, ephtá, okhtō, enniá, pále, takhiá*) and, together with many others, are ubiquitous in the Romani dialects. In this nucleus, *drom* 'street' (Gr. *drómos*) has always been included as well; the fact that *drom* has been inserted in a consonant stem is unusual for Greek words ending in *-os*, and this makes the hypothesis of (Iranian or Armenian) intermediation possible. Interestingly, the plural of *drom* is regularly *droma* and the oblique *dromes-* (as *řom* 'man', pl. *řoma*, obl. *řomes-*), while the majority of Greek loanwords show plural markers borrowed from Greek (cf. Elšík in this volume). However, integration in Romani inflection is also well documented for sure Greek loanwords, such as *kurko* 'Sunday, market, week', pl. *kurke*, obl. *kurkes-* (cf. *gadžo*, pl. *gadže*, obl. *gadžes-*). The Greek loanwords listed above represent a lexical set common to all Romani varieties and can therefore be traced to the initial phases of contact between Romani and Greek.

102   A. Scala

Among these loanwords, those that are integrated into Indo-Aryan plural inflection appear to be older than those showing Greek inflection, cf. e.g. *foro* 'city, square, market', pl. *fori* (Gr. *fóros,* pl. *fóroi*). During the period of bilingualism with Greek, Indo-Aryan nominative plural endings ceased to be productive, and the earliest Greek lexical layer must reasonably be sought among the loanwords that preserve such endings (Matras 2002, pp. 80–81). The adoption of Greek endings produced a nominal loan morphology (Elšik 2000), a pattern of inflection that separates many Greek and all post-Greek loanwords from the pre-European Romani lexicon. The region that was unquestionably the first theatre for this meeting was Anatolia, where Greek remained in use even beyond the invasions of Turkic people. In the periodization of Romani, the common Greek loanwords act as a border between Early Romani and Romani; their historical value is therefore of particular relevance, dividing a still unitary phase of Romani from a phase of dispersion, which is still ongoing.

Besides this common set of Greek loanwords, many Romani varieties show other Greek words that are not shared among all dialects. For example, *foro* 'city, square, market' is extremely widespread, but southern Balkan dialects often use the Iranian word *diz*. Greek loanwords like *ciros/čiros/siro* 'time' (Gr. *kairós*), *filacin/filišin* 'castle, prison' (Gr. *phylakḗ*), *kambana/gambana* 'clock, watch' (Gr. *kampána* 'bell'), *vali* 'glass (material), bottle, window' (Gr. *gyalí* 'glass (material)'), *zervo/-a* 'left' (Gr. *zérbos/-a*) and some others are in use almost exclusively in Northwestern dialects of Romani. Some words like *drosin* 'dew' (cf. Gr. *drosiá*), *kukudi* 'hail' (Gr. *koykoýdi*), *silavi* 'tongs' (Gr. *oxylábē*) and others seem typical of Balkan Romani. Except for the persistence of *diz* in place of *foro*, in all other cases the dialects that do not have these Greek loanwords show more recent lexical borrowings. Moreover, it is clear that the duration of the contact with Greek can play a significant role in the amount of Greek loans acquired by different dialects. This is particularly evident in those southern Balkan dialects that have remained in contact with Greek for a longer time and therefore have some Greek loanwords whose equivalents in other dialects are pre-Greek, cf. *klono* 'grapes' (Gr. *klõnos*), *namburo, namboreme* 'ill' (Romani *na* 'not' + Gr. *mporeĩ* 'he can'), *fora* 'time, occasion' (Gr. *phorá* 'time'), *xasarel* 'to lose' (Gr. *khánō,* aor. *khas-*) in opposition to the pre-Greek forms existing elsewhere: *drak* 'grapes', *nasvalo* 'ill', *var* 'time(s)', *našal/-av-* 'to lose'. Some peripheral Romani dialects, whose speakers left the Balkans rather early, may preserve some rare Greek loanwords. This is the case with southern Italy Romani. Here, Calabrian Romani and Abruzzian Romani show words such as *firíta/firíddə* 'window', *íssjə* 'exact', *nispjó/nisprijó* 'grandchild, nephew', *xuxxúlə* 'cap', *vajínə* 'barrel' and others, that are undoubtedly of Greek origin, cf. Gr. *thyrídi, ísios, anipsiós, koykoýli, bagéni*, but that are very rare or not documented at all outside of these dialects (Scala 2006–2007). Lastly, some Greek loanwords appear to be very typical of Sinti dialects. This is the case, for example, with *korako* 'crow' (Gr. *koráki, kórakos*), whose equivalent in other dialects is the Armenian loanword *kurung*. The case of *korako*, like that of *foro*, can reflect a synonymy existing in Early Romani, which has been flattened in some dialects in favour of the Greek word and in others in favour of the pre-Greek one.

As for the semantic domain of Greek loanwords, words related to blacksmithing are particularly numerous, cf. *amoni* 'anvil' (Gr. *amóni*), *xarkuma* 'copper' (Gr. *khárkōma*), *karfin* 'nail, spike' (*karphí*), *kopidi* 'chisel' (Gr. *kopídi*), *ksilavi/silavi* 'tongs' (Gr. *oxylábē*), *mihani* 'bellows' (Gr. *mēkhanḗ*), *molivi* 'lead' (Gr. *molýbi*), *petalo* 'horseshoe' (Gr. *pétalo*), *piro(sar)el* 'to quench' (Gr. *pyrṓnō*), *rini* 'file' (Gr. *rínē*), *sfiri* 'hammer' (Gr. *sfyrí*), *vari* 'big hammer' (Gr. *bariá* 'big and heavy hammer'), *vraxtura* 'blacksmith's tool' (Gr. *brékhtoyra*). Such a rich set of smithery terms probably points to the fact that blacksmithing was an important domain of interaction between the Romani people and the Greeks. In fact, it may be thought that in the Byzantine Empire, Romani people had a recognized social role as metalworkers.

4.5 Additional Lexical Layers in Romani: A Case Study

After leaving peninsular Greece in several waves, Romani speakers proceeded in different directions and developed different and group-specific bilingualisms with Slavic, Romance, Germanic and Finno-Ugric varieties. In the late Middle Ages, some groups reached and long remained in the easternmost areas of the Balkans, moving mainly through the Danube valley and migrated westwards; in some cases, this movement is still underway. Other groups, whose dialects lack Balkan Romance loanwords, probably moved through the western part of the Balkans (Macedonia, Serbia, Croatia) and hence reached southern Italy (e.g. Abruzzian Rom, whose ancestors probably crossed the Adriatic Sea), the northwestern corner of the southern Slavic area (e.g. Doljenski Rom) or central and northern Europe (e.g. the Sinti of Germany, France and Italy; the Kale of Wales and Finland). For those groups that call themselves Sinti (regarding the denomination, cf. Matras 1999), their stay in German-speaking regions must have been rather long, as their lexicon consists of a very significant number of German loanwords. In this case, too, the lexicon is decisive for reconstructing the migration of the Rom in Europe. Of course, the new, group-specific loanwords acquired outside Greece have in many cases replaced the older lexical layers, causing further lexical differentiation between dialects.

A case study showing the complexity of post-Greek lexical layers in Romani is offered by the Piedmontese Sinti of southern France (Formoso and Calvet 1987; henceforth FPS) gathered in two different collections in 1956 and 1982–1983 among a number of Sinti families sedentarized near Saint-Priest (Rhône) and Grasse (Alpes-Maritimes). First of all, in FPS, a nucleus of Slavic loanwords may be identified, some very widespread in many Romani dialects and others typical only of Sinti dialects: cf. *dívjo* 'bad' (SCr. *divlji*, Sln. *divji*, Cz. and Slk. *divý*), *dóstar* 'enough' (SCr., Bulg. *dosta*), *krali* 'king' (SCr., Sln., Bulg. *kral*, Cz. *král*, Slk. *král'*), *kralísa* 'queen' (SCr., Sln. *kraljica*, Bulg., Mac. *kralica*), *pláxta* 'bed sheet' (cf. SCr. *plahta*), *trupo* 'back' (SCr., Cz., Bulg. *trup* 'body'), *vódro* 'bed' (cf. Bulg. *odŭr* 'bed'), *xoléb/xovél* 'trousers' (OChSl. *xóleva* 'boot', SCr. *chol'ovy*).

Abundant, but less so than in other Sinti dialects, is the German layer, cf. *béro* 'bear' (Germ. *Bär*), *blíndo* 'blind' (*blind*), *brantüína* 'liqueur' (*Branntwein*), *flínta* 'rifle' (*Flinte*), *líxta* 'light' (*Licht*), *pána* 'pan' (*Pfanne*), *štil* 'silent' (*still*), *švéstra* 'nun' (*Schwester*), *víza* 'grass' (*Wiese* 'meadow'). Some loanwords in this layer show a phonetic form compatible only with some German dialects, cf. *glei* 'quickly', *pléio* 'lead' both with -*ei*- instead of [ai] and the latter also with *p*- instead of *b*- (cf. standard German *gleich*, *Blei*), two characteristics that point to Upper German area and, in the case of -*ei*-, to the Alemannic area in particular (König 1998, p. 174). As for the diphthong -*ei*-, documented also in Rhenish dialects, this is a conservative trait that might, in some words, reflect an early loanword. Moreover, such loanwords as *féšta* 'feast' (*Fest*), *kíšta* 'case' (*Kiste*), *néšta* 'nest' (*Nest*) can in their -*št*- sequence be traced to an area that includes the southwestern German dialects and a part of the Palatinate (for the isogloss cf. König 1998, pp. 230–231). Comparison between the German loanwords of FPS and of Italian Piedmontese Sinti (IPS) reveals that FPS has many German loanwords that are lacking in IPS where we find pre-German words, cf. FPS *brúka* IPS *purt* 'bridge', FPS *šerf* IPS *sutló/sukló* 'sour', FPS *švéstra* IPS *rasaní* 'nun', FPS *štunda* IPS *kóra* 'hour' and others. On the whole, the lexicon of FPS appears more innovative than IPS. If after leaving Piedmont, as seems likely, FPS speakers had no more contact with German, it must be concluded that the two groups that call themselves Piedmontese Sinti are originally different groups that saw significant moments of formation in Piedmont or in the former Duchy of Savoy. This hypothesis, conceivably starting from the lexicon, agrees rather well with other phonological and morphological differences separating the two dialects (Scala, in press).

The Romance layer is also highly abundant in FPS and consists of Piedmontese, Italian, Provençal and French loanwords. This last layer is of course still evolving, French being the current contact language for FPS, while the others seem substantially closed, especially since the sedentarization of the group. In many cases, it is impossible to assign a loanword to Piedmontese, French or Provençal, because of the strong lexico-phonetic similarity among these Romance varieties; in other cases, a distinction is possible. As for the Piedmontese layer, it is represented by loanwords such as *gérčo* 'oblique' (Piedm. *gertʃ*), *gunfjav-* 'inflate' (*gumfjé*), *lüzérta* 'lizard' (*lyzérta*), *mak* 'only, just' (*mak*), *pjúmbo* 'lead' (*pjumb*). All these and many other forms point to a variety of Piedmontese identifiable with the regional koine dialect spoken in Piedmont and having as its model the dialect of Turin. Also noteworthy is the presence of Provençal loanwords, which bear witness to an earlier phase of bilingualism with this Gallo-Romance variety whose speakers have dramatically decreased in past generations, cf. *búsca* 'trunk' (Prov. *busca*), *kadenáto* 'sliding lock' (*cadenat*), *seríja* 'sawdust' (*serrilha*) and others. The presence of Italian loanwords is quite limited, and this can easily be explained by the relatively late spread of Italian in northwestern Italy. The Piedmontese Sinti of France probably used to frequent Piedmont before Italian became the reference language of this area in the twentieth century.

4.6 Internal Strategies of New Lexicon Production

As seen in the above paragraphs, direct loans have been a key strategy for the enrichment of the Romani lexicon; however, several internal strategies of new lexicon production also contributed towards creating new words. These internal modes of lexicon production, which create new words not transparent to the speakers of the majority language, can be divided into derivational strategies and metasemic strategies. Both these strategies have operated throughout the entire history of Romani and are still operative in the individual dialects, although with different degrees of productivity.

Some word-formation processes based on affixation are quite old and may be considered as inherited at least from Early Romani (Matras 2002, pp. 74–78). A highly productive affix is represented by the genitival suffix

-k(Vr)- (with the allomorph *-g(Vr)-* after the masculine plural stem ending in *-n*). This suffix, placed after oblique endings, results in adjectives having a very general meaning of relation/pertinence (cf. Koptjevskaja-Tamm 2000; Meli 2016). These adjectives are inflected and agree in gender and number with the nominal head represented by the referent they indicate. They are usually substantivized, cf. e.g. Piedmontese Sinti *bakréngero* ʻshepherdʼ (the one of the sheep), *brisandéskero* ʻumbrellaʼ (that of the rain), *droméskero* ʻroadmanʼ (the one of the road), *maréskero* ʻbakerʼ (the one of the bread), *narvaléskero* ʻmental institutionʼ (that of the crazy), *nasaléskro* ʻdoctorʼ (the one of the ill), *nasaléngeri* ʻmidwifeʼ (woman of the sick persons), *sodabéngero* ʻpistolʼ (that of the six shots). The semantic nature of the output is not predictable, but this strategy seems often used to create professional names and place names. This derivational strategy is well documented throughout Romani, but it is particularly productive in Northwestern dialects, such as Sinti dialects and Welsh Romani. As for the latter, the number of the nouns derived through *-k(Vr)-* quoted in Sampsonʼs lexicon (Sampson 1926) is enormous. It is not certain if this suffix is currently productive; for instance, in Lombard Sinti, the suffix in the synonymic forms *-eskro/-engro* attaches to German loanwords as well, cf. e.g. *feldéngro* ʻfarmerʼ, from *félda* ʻcountryside, fieldʼ (cf. Germ. *Feld* ʻfieldʼ), but there are no examples derived from a Romance lexical base. In such cases, it may be thought that the suffix is no longer productive, but it is also possible that the suffix attached only to words perceived as native by Romani speakers, i.e. all words not belonging to the current majority language. A number of other suffixes are highly productive; many of them contribute to predictable derivations (see Elšík in this volume).

As hinted above, metasemic processes such as metaphors and metonymies represent further strategies of Romani lexicon enlargement. A domain in which such processes act abundantly is that of police officers, cf. e.g. the very widespread metaphor-based lexemes *pořalo* ʻpotbelliedʼ and *šingalo* ʻhornedʼ both for ʻpolicemanʼ. In other cases, metonymy-based lexemes are created, cf. *sástri* ʻironʼ, which develops other meanings such as ʻtrainʼ and ʻnailʼ.

Examples of more or less creative lexical innovations are the ethnonyms and place names created by Rom and Sinti to name the people and places they encountered in Europe (Wolf 1958). Among the ethnonyms, it is possible to find original denominations such as *biboldo* ʻunbaptizedʼ, *čhindo* ʻcutʼ (i.e. ʻcircumcisedʼ) and *xalořo*, diminutive of ʻshabby, meagre manʼ, for ʻJewʼ, *loló* for ʻRussianʼ literally ʻredʼ, referring to the time of the Soviet Union, and loanwords like Sinti *velčo, valčo* ʻFrenchʼ (Germ. *Welsch*), Slovakian Romani *saso* ʻGermanʼ (Germ. *Sachse*), Romani of the former

Yugoslavia *njamco* 'German' (SCr. *nemac*) and many others. Highly productive in ethnonyms are also the roots *lal-* 'dumb/mute' and *čhib* 'tongue': some German Sinti use *laləro* for 'Lithuanian' and Rom of Norway *lall* for Finns and the Sami people. Albanians are called *čhibane* among the Rom of the Balkans and in the Romani of former Yugoslavia *čhibalo* refers to Germans. The interpretation of these derivatives of *čhib* is uncertain; both the meaning 'good-for-nothing (one who can only speak and cannot act)' and 'talkative' with reference to the reprimands made to Rom by non-Rom individuals in their own languages being possible. Also rather widespread is the term *xoraxai/xoraxano* 'Turkish' (also generalized as 'Muslim'), whose origin is uncertain and has been tentatively connected with a Turkic tribe called Karakhan, which ruled in Central Asia at the end of the first millennium (Matras 2010, p. 39; 2015, pp. 136–137). An interesting case is represented by the ethnonym *das* 'Slavs' attested in the Balkans; the word *das* is also used with the meaning of 'slave' in very few dialects, for instance in the dialect of Erli of Sofia. The origin of the ethnonym *das* must be related to a semantic calque on Gr. *Sklábos* 'Slav' and 'slave' (Matras 2002, p. 26).

Place names in Romani are often calques, imperfect calques or re-creative translations of local place names, sometime with some playful manipulations, cf. e.g. among German Sinti the calque *nevo foro* 'new city' for Neustadt, the imperfect calque *xačerdino them* 'burned country' for Brandenburg; in the case of *čovaxanjakro them* 'witches' country' for Hessen, cf. Germ. *Hexen* 'witches', the Romani version of an opaque German place name has been created by translating a transparent word having some phonetic similarity with it (Matras 2002, p. 27); similarly, southern Italy Romani *bul bangí* 'crooked ass' i.e. It. *culo torto* indicates *Colle Torto* 'crooked hill'. Finally, other place names are metonymic such as in southern Italy Romani *o baro rašái* 'the big priest', i.e. 'the pope' for 'Rome', *šukaribé* 'the beauty' for 'America' and *diliné* 'the fools' for Monacilioni according to the popular denomination of its inhabitants.

4.7 Cultural and Structural Dimensions of the Romani Lexicon

To what extent the inner structure of the Romani lexicon can reflect the culture of its users is a matter of debate. Of course, it is highly risky to reconstruct a material culture starting from lexicon. In this sense, a recent attempt to claim, on the basis of some lexical evidence, that Romani people were originally a group of warriors (Hancock 2002, pp. 10–14) clearly shows its

108   A. Scala

methodological limits (for a discussion cf. Matras 2004, pp. 201–205). The idea that the ancestors of present-day Romani people were sedentary warriors, who only later became blacksmiths, would be supported by the fact that many Romani words for metalwork are of Greek origin (but cf. *sumnakai* 'gold', *rup* 'silver' and *sastri* 'iron' surely belonging to the Indo-Aryan layer), while they would be of Indo-Aryan origin if blacksmithing were a skill brought from India (Hancock 2002, p. 10). This reconstruction is clearly untenable: the fact that blacksmithing terminology came from Greek merely means that metalwork was a domain in which Romani speakers and Greek speakers frequently interacted (Matras 2004, p. 204). Generally speaking, the absence of inherited words in a domain does not imply the absence of such words in a more ancient period as well. A look at present-day Lombard Sinti shows that no pre-Germanic words for 'ox' (*nósko*), 'cow' (*nóski*) and 'donkey' (*néslo*) are still in use. If Lombard Sinti were the only known Romani variety, we should infer that Lombard Sinti speakers had no words for such concepts before entering German-speaking areas and, of course, it would be a mistake. Moreover, the presence of Indo-Aryan words in some semantic domains testifies only that Romani speakers were, already in India, familiar with the concepts expressed by those words. In this methodologically more solid perspective, the fact that Romani shows some Indo-Aryan words (more or less closely) related to warfare (cf. e.g. *xanří* 'sword') and to domestic animals (cf. Table 4.1) or to parts of the house (cf. e.g. *vudár* 'door') cannot be considered as proof that Romani speakers were settled, as proposed by Hancock (2002, p. 14), and not nomadic people in India. If lexemes per se do not allow any reliable reconstruction of a people's past material and socio-economic life (Campanile 1993, pp. 19–22), some prudent inference on cultural taxonomies reflected by lexicon might still be possible (Lazzeroni 1998, pp. 3–11). In the case of Romani, an old taxonomy of individuals is represented by the lexical set indicating human beings according to whether or not they belong to the Romani community. Everyone who is not considered a member of the community is called ♂*gadžo*/♀*gadži,* a word that can be traced back to OIA *gārhya* 'domestic' and whose cognates in some itinerant groups of India are used to indicate 'farmer' (Matras 2002, p. 15). These words are used in opposition to ♂*řom*/♀*řomni,* which also means 'husband' and 'wife'. This fundamental distinction is also lexicalized with a specific term for young individuals, who are called ♂*čavo*/♀*čai* when belonging to the Romani community and ♂*raklo*/♀*rakli* when not belonging to it. Neutral terms like ♂*manuš*/♀*manušni* 'male/female person' and ♂*dženo*/♀*dženi* 'male/female individual of unspecified identity' also exist, but these lexemes, which behave as hyperonyms of both ♂*řom*/♀*řomni,*

4 Romani Lexicon 109

♂*čavo*/♀*čai* and ♂*gadžo*/♀*gadži*, ♂*raklo*/♀*rakli*, are retained only in some dialects, and this might suggest their lesser taxonomic centrality or utility in the Romani communities. Additional dialect-specific segmentations of this opposition exist, cf. e.g. Lombard Sinti *pírdo*, which designates 'an itinerant gadžo', who shares socio-economic status with the Sinti, but who does not belong to their community.

Religious terminology is characterized by some Indo-Aryan words such as *devel* 'God', *beng* 'devil', identifying a basic opposition between good and evil, and *rašai* 'priest' (interestingly connected with Vedic *ṛṣi* 'singer of sacred hymns'). The majority of the Rom identify Christianity as their religion of reference, but the term for the 'cross' *trušul* is of Indo-Aryan origin and can be connected to OIA *triśūla* 'trident'. For this word, a re-functionalization of the name of Śiva's trident has been proposed by Pott (1844–1845, II, p. 293), but the new meaning could be based only on the form of the cross having 3 extremities in the upper part. In the religious semantic sphere, some important words like *patragi* 'Easter', *ogi* 'soul' are of Armenian origin (cfr. Arm. *patarag* 'liturgy' and *(h)ogi* 'soul'). Some important words like *patragi* 'Easter', *ogi* 'soul' are of Armenian origin (cfr. Arm. *patarag* 'liturgy' and *(h)ogi* 'soul'). From a historical point of view, it is quite plausible that the Rom encountered Christianity for the first time when still in Armenia. Highly typical of Romani is the situation of numerals, which show a clear split between inherited and borrowed forms (Bakker 2001, p. 96). While Romani numerals 'one-six' and 'ten' are of Indo-Aryan origin, there are no pre-Greek words for 'seven', 'eight' and 'nine'. Many dialects have for these numerals the Greek loanwords *efta, oxto, enja*, but others show later loanwords. Of course, it cannot be thought that proto-Romani speakers lacked some of the first ten numerals, and more generally, the borrowing of numerals cannot be considered a gap-filling strategy (Matras 2009, p. 201). In fact, alongside Greek and post-Greek loanwords, additive, subtractive and multiplicative numerals are well documented for 'seven', 'eight' and 'nine', cf. e.g. Welsh Romani *trin t'ā štắr* '3 and 4', i.e. '7'; *dūvarī štắr* '2 times 4' or *dūī štắr* 'two 4' for '8'; *štắr t'ā panš* '4 and 5' or *deš bī yek* '10 without 1' for '9'. A possible hypothesis is that old complex numerals tended to be preferably replaced, in a more or less exclusive manner, by more compact and short forms borrowed from the majority language (Scala 2017); such a process could be interpreted as a case of pattern replication, a phenomenon not uncommon within numerals (Matras 2009, p. 248). Of course, the use of additive, subtractive and multiplicative numerals in some Romani dialects could also represent a strategy to avoid direct, and therefore transparent, borrowing from the majority language.

110   A. Scala

There are only three colour names of Indo-Aryan origin: *kalo* 'black', *parno* 'white' and *lolo* 'red'. This set of colour names perfectly fits the main prediction of Berlin and Kay's hierarchy of colour terms (Berlin and Kay 1969, pp. 16–35): according to Berlin and Kay, the basic colour names existing in a language could be predicted on the basis of the number of basic colour terms that a language has. If a language has three colour names, they must be 'white', 'black' and 'red'. In their research on colour terms, Berlin and Kay (1969) surveyed 110 languages and Romani was not in the sample; however, their prediction on colour names holds for Romani as well. Of course, it is impossible to say whether these colour names were the only ones present in proto-Romani, or if they are the most stable colour names—as some cross-linguistic surveys seem to suggest—and therefore the only three not replaced in Romani by loanwords (Matras 2009, pp. 187–188). For this latter possibility, cf. the case of Albanian spoken in Basilicata in southern Italy (Arbëresh), which has replaced with loanwords or, at times, with new formations all Albanian colour names except 'black', 'white' and 'red'. As for nature and the physical world, the names for the seasons interestingly number only two: *nilai/nial/linai/lilai* referring to the warmer season and *ivend* referring to the colder season. A two-term opposition in this domain is highly unusual in Eurasia; Indian tradition, too, distinguishes six seasons. It remains uncertain whether such a poor inventory of season names can be related to the fact that Romani people traditionally did not practise agriculture.

Equally of interest is the Romani lexicon for some parts of the body: for example, the semantic map of limbs shows some variation in the different dialects. Early Romani presented four words to map the space between hip and foot, namely *čang* and *heroi* for 'leg, thigh' (the original distribution is unclear), *koč* 'knee' and *pinřo* 'foot'. Today, very few dialects preserve the four terms, and many lexico-semantic combinations are attested (Boretzky and Igla 2004, p. 219). Where *heroi* 'leg' is present, *čang* means 'knee'; where *koč* is present for 'knee' and *heroi* has fallen into disuse, *čang* means 'leg'. Many Vlax dialects have only *čang* with both meanings. In some dialects, the same term can mean 'foot' and 'leg'; this is the case with *heroi* in Latvian Romani and with *piro* < *pinřo* in the Erli Romani spoken in Sofia. The neutralization of 'leg' and 'foot' may have arisen in the Balkans where this polysemy is quite common, cf. SCr. *noga*, Bulg. *krak*, Rom. *picior* all meaning both 'leg' and 'foot'. In some dialects, an identical neutralization can be observed for *vast* 'hand' and *musi* 'arm', cf. *vast* in Latvian Romani and *musi* in the Erli Romani of Sofia for both 'arm' and 'hand'. In this case, the role of Slavic and Baltic languages might have been relevant, cf. Bulg. *rŭka*, Russ. *ruka,* Latv. *roku* 'hand' and 'arm'.

4.8 The Romani Lexicon from the Dialect Perspective: Lexical Isoglosses

In Romani dialects, differences in the lexicon are obvious due to recent layers of loanwords: for example, Sinti dialects present German loanwords that are absent in Balkan Romani, whose speakers never reached Germany. Moreover, many new lexical isoglosses are continuously developing in all dialects, because the acquisition of new loanwords from different contact languages, which generates new synonyms, as well as inter-dialectal Romani contact, is incessantly reshaping the lexicon of contemporary Romani varieties. Perhaps less predictable and more interesting are the lexical isoglosses related to the most ancient layers of the lexicon, especially the Indo-Aryan native one. Boretzky and Igla (2004, pp. 217–225) provide a list of lexical isoglosses separating different dialects or dialect clusters (for the proposed dialectal segmentation, see Boretzky and Igla 2004, pp. 18–26). On the whole, old lexical isoglosses reflect phenomena of lexico-semantic innovations deriving from a synonymy resolved in a semantic differentiation or in a lexical neutralization, in this case with elimination of one of the two synonyms. At times, the synonymy stage may still be observed in some conservative dialects. The following are some examples of rather clearcut lexical isoglosses in Romani. In several cases, Vlax dialects behave differently from all the others: for example, the word *angušto* for 'finger' is in use in most of the dialects, but in Vlax dialects it has been replaced with *nai*, meaning originally 'nail'. Another word, not exclusive to but very characteristic of Vlax dialects, is *koř* 'neck'; for this meaning, other dialects use *men* instead. It is quite likely that the meaning of the two words was originally different, with *men* referring only to 'nape', that is the back of the neck. More complex is the case of the word for 'month'/'moon': the type *čhon* is used in Vlax dialects and in Northwestern, Northeastern, Northern-Central dialects, while *masek* is typical of southern Balkan dialects and the Southern-Central group. To the contrary, other lexical isoglosses join Vlax dialects, sometimes along with southern Balkan ones, as in the case of the Greek loanword *najis-* 'to thank', unknown to Northwestern, Northeastern and Central dialects that use only *pariker-*, and sometimes with all dialects except the Northwestern and Northeastern ones, as occurs with *thab-/phab-* 'to burn', whose equivalent in Northwestern and Northeastern dialects is *xač-*. Northwestern and Northeastern dialects show further lexical peculiarities in the words *gil/dʒi/zi* 'heart' (probably of Armenian origin, cf. Arm. *(h)ogi* 'soul') and *stariben* 'prison' that are not in use in the dialects of other areas, which prefer *ilo* and *phanglipen,* respectively (but Finnish Romani, although belonging to Northwestern dialects, still preserves both lexical types, cf. Valtonen 1972, pp. 92 and 112). A rather isolated example of a function word that shows dialectal distribution is represented by the interrogative adverb meaning 'how much…?': Northwestern, Northeastern and Central dialects have forms like *keci/kici/kisi*, whereas Balkan and Vlax dialects use *kazom, kabor* and *sode*. However, in the latter instances, the form *keti* is also attested, for example in the Romani dialect of Prilep (Boretzky and Igla 1994, *s.v.*). In some cases, there are also semantic isoglosses, in which the same Romani lexeme shows different meanings: for example, the verb *kuř-* means 'to hit' in Northwestern, Northeastern and North-Central dialects, while in South-Central and Balkan dialects the meaning is 'to have sexual intercourse'. This second meaning is clearly of metaphoric origin, and in some dialects, like Thracian Romani, as documented by Alexandre Paspati (1870), it appears beside the original meaning. An overview of these lexical isoglosses shows that a significant group of them opposes Northwestern and Northeastern dialects to Balkan dialects, while Central dialects sometimes match with the former and sometimes with the latter, and this group is often internally segmented. In other cases, Vlax dialects present significant lexical peculiarities. Of course, lexical isoglosses alone are not enough to differentiate Romani dialects, but they can be of some significance when considered in a more complete framework alongside other structural isoglosses (cf. Matras 2002, pp. 214–237; Matras 2005). In this sense, lexical differences not related to European loanwords form a bundle of isoglosses that seems especially to confirm the 'great divide' (Matras 2005, Map n. 2) that separates Northern dialects from Balkan and Vlax dialects. In some cases, there is also lexical evidence matching the so-called Southeastern divide (Matras 2005, Map n. 3) that distinguishes the Vlax dialects from the others. Lastly, the distribution of lexical differences in the inherited lexicon offers some further evidence of the behaviour of the central branch as a transitional zone.

4.9   Research on the Romani Lexicon: Some Desiderata and Future Perspectives

Research on the Romani lexicon still presents many desiderata. As for common lexical layers, Iranian and Greek loanwords lack comprehensive and detailed studies that also take into consideration, for instance, the dialectal articulation of the source languages. Such studies would perhaps better illuminate the timing and paths of the migrations of Romani speakers before their dispersion in Europe. A similar path of research could be carried out on some dialect-specific layers as well, for example on the German loan-words in Northwestern Romani dialects, and especially in those Sinti dialects that have been spoken for centuries inside Germanophone territories. As for individual dialects, there is no ignoring that many lack a comprehensive and etymological exploration of their lexicon, and some dialects lack a dictionary altogether: much work needs to be done in this area. For etymological issues, Sampson (1926) and Boretzky and Igla (1994) are probably the most useful and reliable works, but on the whole they explore few dialects, while many others have not yet undergone any etymological study; here, it bears mentioning that Soravia 1981 still remains the only detailed etymological analysis of a Sinti dialect. More generally, the study of the Romani lexicon still awaits a general etymological dictionary, a work that would greatly benefit from lexical research on individual dialects. Such a work might also define the true extent of the Indo-Aryan lexical legacy, which is still partially uncertain. Moreover, the research on inherited lexicon replacement represents a field of study of great interest for the general trends of language change, and for this purpose, Romani may be considered a very interesting case. However, the lack of both clear data on the original amount of the Indo-Aryan native layer and new detailed studies on individual dialects presents obstacles to empirical research on this subject. Further topics worthy of attention in reference to the Romani lexicon are lexical variation and semantic innovation. As for lexical variation, not a few loanwords in Romani are luxury (or core) loanwords, and such loanwords often require a very long time to prevail over the inherited term: the old and new words can coexist for decades (or even centuries). This fact emerges very rarely in lexical collections, in which the search for the oldest and most 'genuine' Romani lexemes obscures the true composition of the lexicon used by Romani speakers. Research on lexical variation is therefore another desideratum, which should be taken into serious account. As for semantic innovation, many dialect-specific cases still remain unexplored, especially in those semantic spheres that are internally highly structured (e.g. classification of individuals with regard to their belonging to one community or another, kinship terms, etc.). Moreover, the mechanisms of semantic enrichment of the inherited lexicon are still rather underexplored: in fact if loanwords have always been central in the research about Romani lexicon, phenomena such as semantic calques have received only scant attention thus far. The above-mentioned subjects represent only some possible future paths of research on the Romani lexicon. Some of these, and detailed lexical explorations of specific dialects in particular, can be carried forward by individual scholars. But for more ambitious projects, such as that of a comprehensive etymological dictionary of Romani, a large international network of researchers focusing on the Romani lexicon, from different countries and using different skills, would provide a highly useful perspective.

References

Adelung, Johann Ch. 1806. *Mithridates oder allgemeine Sprachenkunde*. Berlin: Vossischen Buchhandlung.

Bakker, Peter. 2001. Typology of Romani numerals. *Sprachtypologie und Universalienforschung* 54 (2): 91–107.

Berlin, Brent, and Paul Kay. 1969. *Basic color terms*. Berkeley: University of California Press.

Boretzky, Norbert. 1992. Zum Erbwortschatz des Romani. *Zeitschrift für Phonetik, Sprachwissenschaft und Kommunikationsforschung* 45: 227–251.

Boretzky, Norbert. 1995. Armenisches im Ziguenerischen (Romani und Lomavren). *Indogermanische Forschungen* 100: 137–155.

Boretzky, Norbert, and Birgit Igla. 1994. *Wörterbuch Romani-Deutsch-Englisch für den südosteuropäischen Raum*. Wiesbaden: Harrassowitz.

Boretzky, Norbert, and Birgit Igla. 2004. *Kommentierter Dialektatlas des Romani. Teil 1 Vergleich der Dialekte*. Wiesbaden: Harrassowitz.

Calvet, Georges. 1982. *Lexique tsigane. Dialecte des Erlides de Sofia*. Paris: Publications Orientalistes de France.

Calvet, Georges. 2009. *Dictionnaire Tsigane-Français: dialecte kalderash*. Paris: L'Ashiatèque.

Campanile, Enrico. 1993. Antichità indoeuropee. In *Le lingue indoeuropee*, ed. Anna Giacalone Ramat and Paolo Ramat, 19–43. Bologna: il Mulino (English translation: 2006. *Indo-European languages*. London and New York: Routledge).

Cech, Petra, and Mozes Heinschink. 2002. Vokabular der Dolenjski Roma aus Novo Mesto und Bela Krajna, Slowenien. *Grazer Linguistische Studien* 58: 1–42.

Dowsett, Charles J.F. 1973–1974. Some Gypsy-Armenian correspondences. *Revue des études arméniennes*, n.s., 10: 59–81.

Elšík, Viktor. 2000. Romani nominal paradigms: Their structure, diversity and development. In *Grammatical relations in Romani: The noun phrase*, ed. Viktor Elšík and Yaron Matras, 9–30. Amsterdam: Benjamins.

Elšík, Viktor. 2009. Loanwords in selice Romani, an Indo-Aryan language of Slovakia. In *Loanwords in the world's languages: A comparative handbook*, ed. Martin Haspelmath and Uri Tadmor, 260–303. Berlin: De Gruyter Mouton.

Formoso, Bernard, and Georges Calvet. 1987. *Lexique tsigane. Dialecte sinto piémontais*. Paris: Publications Orientalistes de France.

Halwachs, Dieter W., and Gerd Ambrosch. 2002. *Wörterbuch des Burgenland-Romani (Roman)*. Graz: Romani-Projekt.

Hancock, Ian. 1987. Il contributo armeno alla lingua Romani. *Lacio Drom* 23 (1): 4–10.

Hancock, Ian. 1995. On the migration and affiliation of the ḍōmba: Iranian words in Rom, Lom and Dom Gypsy. In *Romani in contact: The history and sociology of a language*, ed. Yaron Matras, 25–51. Amsterdam: Benjamins.

Hancock, Ian. 2002. *We are the Romani people: Ame sam e Rromane džene*. Hatfield: Centre de recherches tsiganes, University of Hertfordshire Press.

Haspelmath, Martin. 2009. Lexical borrowing: Concepts and issues. In *Loanwords in the world's languages: A comparative handbook*, ed. Martin Haspelmath and Uri Tadmor, 33–54. Berlin: De Gruyter Mouton.

Haspelmath, Martin, and Uri Tadmor (eds.). 2009. *World Loanword Database*. Leipzig: Max Planck Institute for Evolutionary Anthropology. Available at http://wold.clld.org.

Hervás y Panduro, Lorenzo. 1787. *Vocabulario poliglotto*. Cesena: G. Biasini.

Hübschmann, Heinrich. 1875. Ueber die Stellung des Armenischen im Kreise der indogermanischen Sprachen. *Zeitschrift für vergleichende Sprachforschung* 23 (1): 5–49.

König, Werner. 1998. *Dtv-Atlas: deutsche Sprache*. München: Deutscher Taschenbuch Verlag.

Koptjevskaja-Tamm, Maria. 2000. Romani genitives in cross-linguistic perspective. In *Grammatical relations in Romani: The noun phrase*, ed. Viktor Elšík and Yaron Matras, 123–149. Amsterdam: John Benjamins.

Lazzeroni, Romano. 1998. *La cultura indoeuropea*. Bari-Roma: Laterza.

Ludolfus, Iob. 1691. *Ad suam Historiam Aethiopicam anthac editam Commentarius*. Francofurti ad Moenum: Typis Martini Jacqueti.

Matras, Yaron. 1999. Johann Rüdiger and the study of Romani in eighteenth-century Germany. *Journal of the Gypsy Lore Society*, 5th ser., 9: 89–116.

Matras, Yaron. 2002. *Romani: A linguistic introduction*. Cambridge: Cambridge University Press.

Matras, Yaron. 2004. A conflict of paradigms. *Romani Studies* 5: 193–209.

Matras, Yaron. 2005. The classification of Romani dialects: A geographic-historical perspective. In *General and applied Romani linguistics*, ed. Barbara Schrammel, Dieter Halwachs, and Gerd Ambrosch, 7–26. Munich: Lincom.

Matras, Yaron. 2009. *Language contact*. Cambridge: Cambridge University Press.

Matras, Yaron. 2010. *Romani in Britain: The afterlife of a language*. Edinburgh: Edinburgh University Press.

Matras, Yaron. 2015. *The Romani Gypsies*. Cambridge, MA: The Belknap Press of Harvard University Press.

Meli, Giulia. 2016. From inflection to derivation: Outcomes of Early Romani genitive in Piedmontese Sinti. *SKASE Journal of Theoretical Linguistics* 13 (3): 29–45.

von Miklosich, Franz X. 1872–1880. *Über die Mundarten und Wanderungen der Zigeuner Europas I–IV*. Wien: Karl Gerold's Sohn.

von Miklosich, Franz X. 1874–1878. *Beiträge zur Kenntnis der Zigeunermundarten I–IV*. Wien: Karl Gerold's Sohn.

Münster, Sebastian. 1558. *Sei libri della cosmografia universale*. Basilea: A spese di Henrigo Pietro Basiliense.

Orengo, Alessandro. 2003. *I prestiti armeni nella romani*. Pisa: ETS.

Orengo, Alessandro. 2007. Ancora sui prestiti armeni nei dialetti romani. In *Studi linguistici e orientali in onore di Fabrizio A. Pennacchietti*, ed. Pier Giorgio Borbone, Alessandro Mengozzi, and Mauro Tosco, 565–571. Wiesbaden: Harrassowitz.

Pallas, Peter S. 1786. *Linguarum totius orbi vocabularia comparativa*. Petropoli: Typis Iohannis Caroli Schnoor.

Paspati, Alexandre G. 1870. *Etudes sur les Tchinghianés ou Bohémiens de l'Empire Ottoman*. Constantinople: Imprimérie Antoine Koroméla.

Pisowicz, Andrzej. 1985. *Origin of the New and Middle Persian Phonological Systems*. Kraków: Nakładem Uniwersytetu Jagiellońskiego.

Pott, August F. 1844–1845. *Die Zigeuner in Europa und Asien*. Halle: Heynemann.

Rüdiger, Johannes Ch. 1782. Von der Sprache und Herkunft der Zigeuner aus Indien. In *Neuester Zuwachs der teutschen, fremden und allgemeinen Sprachkunde in eigenen Aufsätzen, Bücheranzeigen und Nachrichten*, 37–84. Leipzig: P. G. Kummer (repr., 1990, Hamburg: Buske).

Sampson, John. 1926. *The dialect of the Gypsies of Wales*. Oxford: Clarendon Press.

Scala, Andrea. 2004. Armeno e dialetti zingari: note sparse e nuove proposte. In *Bnagirkʿ Yišatakacʿ. Documenta Memoriae. Dall'Italia e dall'Armenia. Studi in onore di Gabriella Uluhogian*, ed. Valentina Calzolari, Anna Sirinian, and Boghos Levon Zekiyan, 337–347. Bologna: Dip. di Paleografia e Medievistica.

Scala, Andrea. 2006–2007. Contributi alla conoscenza dei prestiti lessicali greci nei dialetti degli zingari dell'Italia meridionale di antico insediamento. *Atti del Sodalizio Glottologico Milanese*, n.s., 1–2: 46–52.

Scala, Andrea. 2013. A hitherto unnoticed Armenian loanword preserved in Southern-Italian and Dolenjska Romani. *Romani Studies* 23 (1): 121–126 (The printed version contains a crucial misprint, the only version corresponding to the will of the author is the electronic one).

Scala, Andrea. 2017. I numerali da 1 a 10 in sinto lombardo. In *Italiani di Milano. Studi in onore di Silvia Morgana*, ed. Massimo Prada and Giuseppe Sergio, 789–797. Milano: Ledizioni.

Scala, Andrea. In press. Codici storici della marginalità nel Nord-Ovest. In *Lingue e migranti nell'area alpina e subalpina occidentale*.

Sergievskij, Maksim V., and Aleksej P. Barannikov. 1938. *Cygansko-russkij slovar'*. Moskva: Gosudarstvennoe Izdatel'stvo Inostrannyx i Nacional'nyx Slovarej.

Soravia, Giulio. 1981. Vocabolario sinto delle Venezie. *Lacio Drom* 17: 2–55.

Soravia, Giulio, and Camillo Fochi. 1995. *Vocabolario sinottico delle lingue zingare parlate in Italia*. Roma: Centro Studi Zingari; Bologna: Istituto di Glottologia.

Swadesh, Morris. 1952. Lexicostatistic dating of prehistoric ethnic contacts. *Proceedings of the American Philosophical Society* 96: 452–463.

Tadmor, Uri. 2009. Loanwords in the world's languages: Findings and results. In *Loanwords in the world's languages: A comparative handbook*, ed. Martin Haspelmath and Uri Tadmor, 53–75. Berlin: De Gruyter Mouton.

Toporov, Vadim. 2003. Slovar' jazyka krymskix cygan. Moskva: Izdatel'stvo "Ivanovskij Gosudarstvennyj Universitet".

Valtonen, Pertti. 1972. *Suomen mustalaiskielen etymologinen sanakirja*. Helsinki: Soumalaisen kirjallisuuden seura.

Vekerdi, József. 1983. *A magyarországi cigány nyelvjárások szótára*. Pécs: Janus Pannonius Tudományegyetem Tanárképző Kara.

Voskanian, Vardan. 2002. The Iranian loan-words in lomavren, the secret language of the armenian gypsies. *Iran and the Caucasus* 6: 169–180.

Wolf, Siegmund. 1958. Völker- und geographische Namen im Romani (Zigeunersprache). *Beiträge zur Namenforschung* 9: 180–188.

Wolf, Siegmund. 1960. *Großes Wörterbuch der Zigeunersprache*. Mannheim: Bibliographisches Institut.

5

Romani Phonology

Márton A. Baló

5.1 Introduction

In its earliest stages, the main focus of research on Romani phonology was to sketch out the phonological systems of sundry dialects as part of the overall description of the given variety, a trend that has continued up to the present day. The historical development of various phonemes, both vowels and consonants, and phonological change under the influence of contact languages have also been widely researched, as well as the influence of Romani on other languages. Less work has been done on Romani phonology within various theoretical frameworks, although some recent contributions rely upon the utilisation of autosegmental phonology (e.g. Gardner and Gardner 2008) and Optimality Theory (for details, see Granqvist 2009). Romani intonation had been sadly neglected, but it has received more attention recently (e.g. Ariste 1978; Grigorova 2001; Arvaniti and Adamou 2011). Arvaniti (2016), while presenting an analysis of the intonational system of Greek Thrace Romani, highlights the problems posed by the use of data coming from spontaneous fieldwork in lieu of controlled speech recorded under laboratory conditions for traditional research on intonation.

This chapter will serve as a descriptive introduction to the complex sound system of Romani. It provides an outline of the core phoneme inventory

---

M. A. Baló (✉)
Research Institute for Linguistics,
Hungarian Academy of Sciences, Budapest, Hungary
e-mail: balo@nytud.hu

© The Author(s) 2020
Y. Matras and A. Tenser (eds.), *The Palgrave Handbook of Romani Language and Linguistics*, https://doi.org/10.1007/978-3-030-28105-2_5

120   M. A. Baló

common to all dialects, complemented by the various dialect-specific modification processes affecting both vowels and consonants and introducing a varied set of contact-induced additional phonemes. The chapter also describes the most outstanding phonological processes such as aspiration, lengthening, hiatus, gemination, diphthongisation and the reduction of vowels and consonant clusters, placing them in a cross-dialectal perspective and making reference to intra-dialectal variation where necessary. Phenomena such as palatalisation, including aspects of morphological jotation, the appearance and position of semi-vowels, the treatment of affricates and their relationship to fricatives and stops, the distribution of the schwa and the fate of the retroflex consonants are dealt with in detail. Other processes like truncation, elision, prothesis, metathesis and paragoge are also discussed. Stress and syllable structure, with reference to the sonority hierarchy, are given their separate sections, and processes across word boundaries are also touched upon. The various phenomena are primarily illustrated by data from the Romani Morpho-Syntax (RMS) Database, which contains a large number of dialect samples and is available at http://romani.humanities.manchester.ac.uk/rms/. Many of the examples in the paper come from sources in the database, which are accessible online, along with audio files and their transcripts.

5.2 The Sound System

5.2.1 Vowels

Table 5.1 summarises the core vowel inventory of Romani, originating from the Early Romani vowel system (cf. e.g. Matras 2002, p. 58; Boretzky 2003, p. 13; Boretzky and Igla 2004, p. 33). The precise phonetic quality of each vowel in present-day dialects may be influenced by the vowel distribution of the contact language, most commonly the main language of the country where the given Romani-speaking population lives.

The open central vowel is fairly stable in most dialects, but in some cases, it can be more front or more back, depending on certain factors, for

Table 5.1 Vowels in Romani

	Front	Central	Back
	Unrounded		Rounded
Close	i		u
Mid	e		o
Open		a	

example the specific, corresponding phones the contact language uses. The two back vowels are securely retained, although certain morphophonological processes may affect their relative distribution in some varieties. The front vowels are perhaps the most prone to modification processes, especially centralisation; the mid front vowel, for instance, may be realised as anything between mid and open, front and central, depending on the variety.

5.2.2 Additional Vowels

Additional vowels can be divided into two distinct groups: vowels emerging through various contact-induced modification processes and replacing or complementing core vowels in inherited words and vowels appearing in loanwords coming from contact languages only. The first group comprises the more open front vowels /ɛ/ and /æ/, the central vowels /ə/, /ɨ/ and /ɐ/, and the more open back vowels /ɒ/ and /ɔ/, while the second group may most commonly contain the front rounded vowels /y/, /ø/ and /œ/.

The back vowel /o/ is occasionally complemented or replaced by other back vowels through contact phenomena in some positions, like /ɒ/ from Hungarian in southern Slovakia (Elšík et al. 1999, p. 309). In Hungarian loanwords containing an unrounded /ɑ/ originally, like *pad* 'bench' or *csónak* 'boat', the /ɑ/ may be rounded and possibly heightened, for instance Romungro *pada* ~ [ˈpɒda] and *čonakos* ~ [ˈt͡ʃɒnɔkos], while the /o/ is lowered, cf. *homokos* 'sand' ~ [ˈhɒmɔkos] from Hungarian *homok* (RO-072, Glodeni, Romania).[1] A more open /ɔ/ instead of /o/ may also occur in Kalderaš (Boretzky 1994, p. 5).

In Vend Romani and other Central varieties, /e/ may be realised as more open, e.g. *edej* 'here' [ɛdej] ~ [ædej] (Bodnárová 2015, pp. 90–91; Elšík et al. 1999, p. 308), which can also take place in the Vlax dialect of Kalderaš (Boretzky 1994, p. 5). Gardner and Gardner (2008, p. 167) report that /e/ and /ɛ/ are distinct phonemes in Gabor Romani, another Vlax dialect, the latter one having been introduced under the influence of Hungarian and replacing grammatical endings like the feminine plural ending *-ja* and the /a/ of the intransitive marker *-av-*.

In certain Northeastern dialects, like Lithuanian Romani, Polska Roma or Čuxny, the velarisation of the aspirated articulation of aspirated stops, leading to the emergence of new clusters such as /px, tx, kx/, triggers centralisation and lowering of /e/, as in *lathel* 'find' ~ [lɐtxɐɫ] or *phen* 'sister' ~ [pxɐn] (LT-005, Šiauliai, Lithuania), merging it with the open central vowel in these positions (cf. *khangiri* 'church' [kxɐɲɪˈɽi]).

The central vowels /ə/ and /ɨ/ may replace /e/ and /i/, respectively, as a result of contact-induced phenomena under the influence of languages whose phoneme inventories contain the centralised vowels by default (see discussion in Sect. 5.3.1).

The second group of vowels, appearing in loanwords only, varies from dialect to dialect, with the most common vowels including /y/ and /ø/, as well as /œ/, cf. e.g. Bodnárová (2015, p. 92) for Vend. Naturally, other varieties, where the vowel system of the contact language includes these vowels, also borrow them, like *köprüs* 'bridge' ~ ['køprys] from Turkish *köprü* in Xoraxani (BG-015, Kaspičan, Bulgaria), *šöro* 'beer' ~ ['ʃøro] from Hungarian *sör* in Romungro (HU-009, Hugyag, Hungary) or *tjüteti* 'town' ~ [tʲy'teti] from Albanian *qytet* in Mečkari (AL-001, Fier, Albania). As we see in Vekerdi (1985), and as Elšík et al. (1999, p. 309) also remark, a strategy of unrounding to adapt these vowels is sometimes used; therefore, Hungarian *felhő* 'cloud' and *büntet* 'punish' may become [fel'he:vo] and [bintetisar-'], alongside [fel'hø:vo] and ['byntetin-].

5.2.3 Consonants

Table 5.2 summarises the core consonant inventory of present-day Romani. Most of the consonants included in Table 5.2 are originally inherited from Indo-Aryan, and only some of them are the results of later developments or borrowings. Palatal and palatalised consonants are to be discussed in a separate section and are therefore omitted from Table 5.2. Mostly contact-induced, dialect-specific, additional consonants are not part of Table 5.2, either.

The three basic voiceless stops, bilabial, alveolar and velar, and their voiced counterparts are essential to all Romani dialects. They can appear in virtually any position within a word: *ker-* 'do, make', *raklo* 'boy', *gili* 'song', *jag* 'fire', *rup* 'silver', *papin* 'goose', *mato* 'drunk', *trad-* 'drive', *perdo* 'full', *dad* 'father', *beš-* 'sit, live', *xabe* 'food', etc. Romani has a three-way distinction in stops: voiceless, aspirated and voiced, having devoiced Old Indo-Aryan breathy voiced consonants. There are a few dialect-specific instances where stops may also emerge as a result of a later development (see below, and cf. also Matras 2002, p. 50).

Sonorants in Romani include the nasals /m/ and /n/, the lateral /l/ and the dental and uvular trills /r/ and /ʀ/. The uvular trill, or, in some varieties, the uvular fricative /ʁ/, is most likely the continuation of historical /ř/ (Matras 2002, pp. 50–51) and is found in several, mainly Vlax dialects (cf. e.g. Gardner and Gardner 2008, p. 165). In these varieties, the dental

Table 5.2 Consonants in Romani

	bilabial	labiodental	alveolar	post-alveolar	palatal	velar	uvular	glottal
Stop	p pʰ b		t tʰ d			k kʰ g		
Fricative		f v	s z	ʃ ʒ		x		h
Nasal	m		n					
Trill			r				ʀ	
Lateral			l					
Approximant					j			
Affricate			t͡s	t͡ʃ t͡ʃʰ d͡ʒ				

and the uvular trill can actually represent separate phonemes, as seen in the minimal pair *bař* 'stone' and *bar* 'garden'. Another source of the uvular fricative /ʁ/ in the Sinti-Manuš group is a later development through contact with languages that already have it, like French and German. As for the dental trill, the extent of vibration varies from dialect to dialect, and it can also vary within a dialect. In certain Central varieties, the vibration can either be weak, as in *keres* 'you do', or heavy, as in *kerdjal* 'you did', and can reach a geminate-like level in an intervocalic position, as in *barreha* 'stone.SG.INS' in West Slovak (SK-016), *murri* 'my.F' alongside *muri* in Kalderaš (RO-065, Timišoara, Romania) and *arro* 'flour' in Romanian Romungro (RO-072).

The most widespread fricatives in Romani are the voiceless alveolar and post-alveolar sibilants /s, ʃ/, the voiced labiodental /v/, the velar /x/ and the glottal /h/, while the other fricatives fulfilled a marginal role in the Indo-Aryan component of the vocabulary or entered the language at a later stage. The voiceless labiodental /f/ and the voiced post-alveolar /ʒ/ only appear in *feder* 'better' and *užo* 'clean' (Matras 2002, p. 51). The voiced alveolar sibilant /z/ first occurred in lexical items of Persian origin, e.g. *zor* 'strength', while the glottal /h/ often alternates with the velar /x/.

Affricates most commonly include post-alveolar /t͡ʃ, d͡ʒ/, as well as alveolar /t͡s/ from the Byzantine and later periods, while the alveolar /d͡z/ is likely to be a later addition. Besides the continuation of inherited positions, affricates often emerge as a result of more recent sound changes in several dialects (see Sect. 5.4.7 in detail).

5.2.4 Additional Consonants

Similarly to vowels, additional consonants are comprised of two categories: consonants that are a result of phonological processes and consonants borrowed from contact languages. The first group primarily includes the palatal and palatalised consonants, now widespread in several dialects of Romani, discussed in detail in Sect. 5.4.10. The most prominent members of the second group are the dental fricatives /ð, θ/ and the voiced velar fricative /ɣ/, which appear under modern Greek influence in the Romani dialects spoken in Greece. Although these consonants have been known to occur only in recent loan elements from Greek (cf. Igla 1996, p. 12; Adamou and Arvaniti 2014, p. 228), they may in fact replace the alveolar stops and the glottal fricative, respectively, in the core component of the lexicon, as we see in the Greek Romani varieties of Sofades, Kapaki and Néa Smírni: *luludi* 'flower' ~ [lulu'ði] (GR-004, Sofades, Greece), *athe* 'here' ~ [a'θe] (GR-031), *čerhan* 'star' ~ [t͡ʃer'ɣā] (GR-032).

5.3 Processes Affecting Vowels

5.3.1 Centralisation

Centralisation is common in several dialects, not only after sibilants, velars and the trill, but in certain lexemes in other environments as well, especially where the contact language contains /ə/ either as a phoneme (e.g. Romanian, cf. also Boretzky 1991, pp. 5–6) or as a reduced vowel (e.g. Russian). Thus, in areas where Romanian is the majority language, we find *kher* 'house' ~ [kʰər], for example, and also frequently word-finally, e.g. *phralenge* 'brother.PL.DAT' ~ [pʰraˈleŋgə], *bare* 'big.PL' [baˈrə] in North Vlax dialects like Kalderaš (RO-008, Pitești, Romania). Further examples from the Vlax dialects include lexemes such as *veš* 'forest', realised as [vəʃ] in varieties of both certain North and South Vlax dialects, like Kalderaš, Gabor (Gardner and Gardner 2008, p. 169) and Gurbet (Boretzky 2003, pp. 143–145); *del* 'give' ~ [dəl] in Kalderaš and Gurbet, as well as *berš* 'year' ~ [bərʃ]. The latter item might be borrowed by Central dialects in contact with either Romanian or certain Vlax dialects, like Romungro (RO-001, Cluj, Romania). In Vlax varieties spoken in areas where the phoneme inventory of the majority language does not contain /ə/, like in Hungary, there is no such phenomenon.

Centralisation also takes place in Northeastern dialects in contact with Russian, like the Servi spoken in Kiev (UKR-003, UKR-004), North Russian Romani (RUS-006, Nižnij Novgorod, Russia; RUS-008, Ekaterinburg, Russia) and Lithuanian Romani (LT-007, Šiauliai, Lithuania; LT-008, Troškūnai, Lithuania): *kher* ~ [kˣər], *veš* ~ [vəʃ], *berš* ~ [bərʃ]. In addition, in North Russian Romani there are some cases where it seems that /e/ in a stressed position remains /e/, while the absence of stress triggers centralisation, for example *feder* 'better' ~ [fəˈdir], or *phen* 'sister' ~ [pˣen] but *phenja* 'sister.PL' ~ [pˣəˈɲa] (RUS-006). In certain Balkan dialects, this is not the case, however, and centralisation can be heavy in stressed Layer I oblique endings: *dades* 'father.SG.ACC' ~ [daˈdəs], *manušes* 'man.SG.ACC' ~ [manuˈšəs] (BG-001, Velingrad, Bulgaria), while centralising in other positions as well: *verda* 'car' ~ [vərˈda], *terno* 'young' [tərˈno] (BG-001; BG-014, Vălči Dol, Bulgaria).

In varieties where /e/ is centralised, centralisation may also affect the close front vowel, regardless of the dialect group they belong to. The realisation of /i/ as /ɨ/ is thus common in varieties spoken in Poland, Lithuania and Russia (e.g. LT-008; PL-018, Łódź, Poland; RUS-006), as well as in Moldova, although the distribution might differ slightly from that of the centralisation of /e/.

126   M. A. Baló

Common triggers are the trill and the sibilant, as in *brišind* 'rain' ~ [brɨˈʃɨnd/ brɨˈʃɨnt], *bakrori* 'sheep' ~ [bakˈrorɨ] (MD-006), *trin* 'three' ~ [trɨn] (LV-005, Riga, Latvia), *šilalo* 'cold' ~ [ʃɨɫaˈɫo] (RUS-006) or as in certain forms of the copula: *isi* 'is', *isis* 'was' ~ [iˈsɨ], [iˈsɨs] (LT-008), as well as the lateral approximant: *linaj* 'summer' ~ [lɨˈnaj] (RUS-006).

In the Northeastern and Balkan dialects, besides the position after the velars stops, centralisation also seems to affect the position following the alveolar stops, although the distribution of both is restricted. Centralisation after velar stops mostly occurs word-initially in certain lexemes, with variation among the different varieties. For instance, we find *kirmo* 'worm' ~ [kɨrˈmo] and *kirlo* 'throat' ~ [kɨrˈlo]/[gɨrˈlo] (RUS-008; BG-014; BG-016, Montana, Bulgaria), alongside [kerˈlo] (BG-012, Velingrad, Bulgaria) and [kərˈlo] (BG-014), but *kirjo(v)-* 'boil' remains unaffected: [kirˈjoɫ] (RUS-008). In certain varieties, there is intra-speaker variation, and both [kɨrˈlo] and [kirˈlo] exist, while the /i/ after the voiced velar stop is not usually centralised: *gili* 'song' ~ [giˈɫi] (LT-005).

The distribution of the centralised /ɨ/ after alveolars varies again, with some lexemes and varieties being more and others less prone to centralisation. Word-initially, centralisation appears to be triggered more frequently: *tikno* 'small.ᴍ' ~ [tɨkˈno], *tiro* 'your.ᴍ' ~ [tɨˈro], *dilino* 'stupid.ᴍ' ~ [dilɨˈno] (RUS-008), *dives* 'day' ~ [dɨˈves] (LT-005), as opposed to *pativ* 'honour' [paˈtiv] (RUS-006), and we also find intra-speaker variation: *dikhja* 'he/she saw' ~ [dɨkhˈja]/[dikhˈja] (RUS-008).

In addition to that, the centralised /ɨ/ may appear in other environments, after affricates, sibilants and palatals, for instance *dživel* 'he/she lives' ~ [d͡ʒɨˈveɫ] (RUS-008) and *cikno* 'small.ᴍ' ~ [t͡sɨkˈno] (UKR-010), [sɨkˈno] (BG-014), or *divo* 'day' (UKR-004, Kiev, Ukraine), accompanied by variation again: [ɟiˈvo]/[ɟɨˈvo].

5.3.2 Vowel Length

While no phonemic status is attributed to vowel length in Romani in general, and the emergence of long or lengthened vowels is not a historically inherited feature (see already Miklosich 1872–1880, pp. ix, 24; also cited in Matras 2002, p. 59), vowel lengthening does take place in several varieties of Romani.

One trigger of long vowels is compensatory lengthening. This often happens following the elision of /v/, and examples can be found in several dialects, especially in ones that are in contact with languages where long vowels exist. Thus, while *džuvli* 'woman' is realised as [d͡ʒuvˈli] in Polish Xaladytka (PL-014, Ełk, Poland), for instance, with no elision, it becomes [ˈd͡ʒuːli]/[ˈt͡ʃuːli]/[ˈjuːli] in Finnish Romani (FIN-005); similarly, *phuv* 'earth' becomes [pʰuː] (FIN-008), *avri* 'out' becomes [ˈaːri] (SK-052, Litava, Slovakia; HU-009), and *dive* 'day' becomes [diː] (SLO-001, Gornji Slaveči, Slovenia), although elision and lengthening do not always co-occur, cf. [d͡ʒuˈlʲi] in Gurvari (HU-007, Kiskundorozsma, Hungary) and [aˈri] in Romanian Romungro (RO-059, Bahnea, Romania; RO-072). In Čuxny, *džuvli* 'woman' is realised as [d͡ʒuːˈli] (LV-005), *javes* 'you come' as [jeːs] and *dikhava* 'I see' as [diˈkʰaː] (EST-005, Kohila, Estonia). However, the /v/ is not necessarily deleted; thus, it does not trigger lengthening, rendering variation, as seen in the accusative case, with [d͡ʒuvˈlʲa] and [d͡ʒuːˈlʲa] both existing (EST-005). In certain Romungro varieties, the deletion of the /v/ of the third person singular masculine personal pronoun also results in vowel lengthening: *ō* < *ov* (e.g. HU-009). The same can happen in Lithuanian Romani, where the first person singular present tense concord marker is *-ov*: *dikhov* 'I see' ~ [diˈkʰoː] (LT-008).

Compensatory lengthening can also accompany the word-final deletion of /j/ in Central dialects and in Northern Vlax. In Slovakian Rumungro, for example, the word *kaj* 'where' can be realised as both [kaj] and [kaː] (SK-052); in Hungarian Romungro, on the other hand, words like *kaj* 'where' and *duj* 'two' are always realised as [kaː] and [duː], respectively (HU-009). In Lovari, *vorbij* 'speak' can be realised as [vorˈbiː] (YU-015, Debeljača, Serbia), and in Kalderaš, *trajij* 'live' as [traˈjiː] (RO-065). After the reduction of *-ije-*, *pijel* 'he/she drinks' is realised as [piːl] in Vend (Bodnárová 2015, p. 86). In Molise Romani, the optional deletion of the word-final /r/ in *šukar* 'beautiful' results in lengthening: [ʃuˈgaː] (IT-007).

Another reason for the existence of long vowels is the influence of contact languages. Thus, for instance, Finnish Romani abounds in them, particularly in the first vocalic position of the word, often accompanied by a shift of stress to the first syllable, see *pani* 'water' ~ [ˈpaːni], *dives* 'day' [ˈdiːves], *hero* 'head' [ˈheːro], *dženo* 'person' [ˈd͡ʒeːno], *juvi* 'lice' ~ [ˈjuːvi] (FIN-012). Monosyllabic words may undergo lengthening as well: *cer* 'house' ~ [t͡seːr], *tat* 'father' ~ [taːt], although this seems to be optional, cf. *phen* 'sister' ~ [pʰeːn]/[pʰen], *(s)tar* 'four' ~ [star]/[taːr] (FIN-006). In words with three syllables, the vowel of the penultimate syllable may become longer: *brihino* 'rain' ~ [ˈbrihiːno] (FIN-012), which is in line with disyllabic words, where the first vocalic position also coincides with the penultimate syllable. Northeastern dialects, especially those under the influence of Latvian, exhibit vowel lengthening as well; see, for instance, *manuš* 'man' ~ [ˈmaːnuʃ], *nevo* 'new.ᴍ' ~ [ˈneːvo] and *phuro* 'old.ᴍ' ~ [ˈpʰuːro] in Čuxny (LV-005). Sinti may also be affected, as illustrated by examples such as *pani* 'water' ~ [ˈpaːni], *vudar* 'door' ~ [ˈvuːdər] and *mal* 'friend' ~ [maːl], accompanied by the deletion of the word-initial /a/, although in fast speech it may not take effect: [ˈpani], [ˈvudər] (RO-022, Timišoara, Romania).

The contact influence of languages with long vowels is present in varieties spoken in Slovakia, Slovenia and Hungary as well: *džene* 'people' ~ [ˈd͡ʒeːne], *balo* 'pig' ~ [ˈbaːlo] (HU-007), *čhavo* 'boy' [ˈt͡ʃʰaːvo] (HU-009); *žuvli* 'woman' [ˈʒuːvli], without the elision of the /v/, *šero* 'head' ~ [ˈʃeːro], *roma* 'men' ~ [ˈroːma], *džek* 'one' [d͡ʒeːk], *ič* 'yesterday' ~ [iːt͡ʃ] (SLO-001); *armin* 'cabbage' ~ [ˈaːrmin], *butji* 'work' ~ [ˈbuːtʲi], *foros* 'town' ~ [ˈfoːros], *gelas* 'he/she went' ~ [ˈgeːlas] (SK-016).

Consistent vowel lengthening in morphological endings may be regarded as a sign of grammatical functionalisation of vowel length (Matras 2002, p. 60), somewhat similar to multiple exponence (Harris 2017), where one feature or function is expressed through more than one realisation in the word. In Southern Central dialects, where the first vowel of adjectives is lengthened only in non-attributive position (Elšík et al. 1999, p. 311), the position and the vowel length can be considered as two realisations of the same syntactic function.

5.3.3 Vowel Reduction

Several dialects manifest optional or regular vowel reduction. These reduced vowels can be found in unstressed syllables, so, for example, *džučel* 'dog' can either be [d͡ʒuˈt͡ʃel] or [d͡ʒəˈt͡ʃel] in Arli (YU-011, Beočin, Serbia). In other varieties, reduction regularly takes place, at least in certain lexemes, cf. *purno* 'leg' ~ [pərˈno] in Servy (UKR-018, Dnipropetrovsk, Ukraine) and *purnenca* 'foot.ᴘʟ.ɪɴs' ~ [pərˈnenca] in Kubanska Vlaxurja (UKR-016, Krasnodar, Russia); *kirlo* 'throat' ~ [kərˈlo] in Arli (MK-005, Kumanovo, Macedonia) and *kirleha* 'throat. sɢ.ɪɴs' ~ [kərˈleha] in West Slovak (SK-016); *khelel* 'dance.3sɢ' ~ [kʰəˈlel], *geljom* 'I went' [gəˈlʲom] in Maj Vlaši (RO-058, Senereuş, Romania). In Sinti, where stress often shifts to the first syllable, reduction takes place in the second syllable: *džuvel* 'woman' ~ [ˈd͡ʒuvəl], *vudar* 'door' ~ [ˈvuːdər] (RO-022).

Reduction may eventually lead to the deletion of the vowel and, thus, the emergence of consonant clusters, frequently word-initially. This is most conspicuous in the genitive pronouns, see *mr-* 'my', *tr-* 'your', *leskr-* 'his', in

Central dialects such as Vend (Bodnárová 2015, pp. 69–75) and Romungro (RO-072; SK-052; SK-059, Diakovce, Slovakia), as well as Sinti (RO-022), and optionally in certain Romungro varieties, with the full vowel, the reduced vowel and the deleted vowel varying (RO-001), while in Polska Roma, only the third person singular genitive pronoun is affected: [ˈłeskro] (PL-019, Zielona Góra, Poland). The deletion may also affect other words in both Sinti and the Central dialects, like *vri < avri* 'out' (RO-022), *pro < punro* 'foot' (SK-016, SK-059).

This process may lead to the deletion of the /r/ on the one hand, as in the case of the genitive pronouns in attributive positions in varieties found in the Balkans: *m-, t-* (BG-001; YU-004, Aleksandrovo, Serbia; GR-002, Parakalamos, Greece) and also *lesk-* in the Rakarengo variety of Romania (RO-002), or the deletion of the /k/ in certain Polska Roma and Sinti varieties in the third person singular genitive pronoun: [łesro]/[lesru] (PL-018, RO-022). On the other hand, it can lead to the syllabification of the /r/ in Central, Southern Vlax and Southern Balkan dialects, particularly in the words *berš* 'year' and *brišind* 'rain', perhaps due to the Slavic contact languages: [brʃ] and [brˈʃind]/[brˈʃint]/[brˈʃin] (e.g. BG-014; HR-002, Zagreb, Croatia; RO-001; SK-016; SK-031, Šumiac, Slovakia; YU-017, Budva, Montenegro).

5.3.4 Hiatus

The most common occurrence of hiatus in Romani is at word boundaries, where the first word ends in and the second word begins with a vowel. In such cases, deletion of the final vowel of the first word is a widespread strategy to resolve hiatus in several Romani dialects.

Deletion of the last vowel of prepositions ending in a vowel, like *angle* 'in front of' *ande* 'in', *ke* 'by, at', *paša* 'to, next to', *pala* 'behind', *pe* 'on', *upre* 'above' (and their dialect-specific forms), often takes place before words beginning with a vowel, most notably the definite articles *o, i* and *e*, yielding *anglo, angli, ko, ki,* etc.

Other words with an initial vowel, when preceded by a preposition, may also trigger deletion, see, for example, *ek* 'one' in Vlax, as in *ande ek rjat* 'one evening' ~ *and' ek rjat* (RO-065), or *odā* and *adava* 'that' in Romungro and in Russian Romani, as in *ande odā kher/de adava kher* 'in that house' ~ *and' odā kher/d' adava kher* (HU-009; RUS-003, Yaroslavl, Russia). Naturally, the first word does not necessarily have to be a preposition, cf. *mange an štuba nāne jake but mēbeli* 'I do not have so much furniture in my room' ~ *mang' an* (LV-005), but deletion seems to occur more often when function words are involved.

Other items where the final vowel is frequently deleted to resolve a hiatus include, among others, the complementiser *te*, see, for example, before *avel* 'come' ~ *t' avel* (e.g. GR-002; HU-007; RO-004, Maglavit, Romania; UKR-008, Donetsk, Ukraine; YU-002, Deronje, Serbia), *ovel* 'become' ~ *t' ovel* (e.g. MK-002), *aštik* 'could' ~ *t' aštik* (e.g. RO-059), *ačas* 'he/she found' ~ *t' ačas* (RO-022); and the demonstrative pronoun, cf. o*va o murš* 'this man' ~ *ov' o murš* (GR-002). As noted by Boretzky (1993, p. 14), deletion also takes place in the future marker *ke/ka* in the Balkan dialects, but only optionally, cf. *na ke ovav* ~ *na k' avav* 'I will not be' (e.g. BG-013, Malo Konare, Bulgaria; BG-052, Dalgopol, Bulgaria; MK-002, Skopje, Macedonia), and not in all dialects. The deletion appears to be optional in the adverbial *avri*, too, for example Czech Vlax *āvr' o brišind del* 'it is raining outside' but *āvri angla kher* 'outside, in front of the house' (CZ-001).

One of two identical vowels may also be deleted, like in Romacilikanes. In such cases, the deleted vowel cannot be identified unambiguously; however, based on the fact that the last vowel of the first word is deleted when the vowels are different, we might presume that the same takes place when the vowels are identical, and the final vowel of the first word is deleted: *kana aljom* 'when I came' ~ *kan' aljom* (GR-002). The presumption that the word-final vowel of the first word is deleted is even more justified in the light of the fact that the word *avel* 'come, become' seems to trigger deletion more frequently; in Gurvari and in Čurari, for example, the final vowel of the preceding word is regularly deleted, as in the interrogative *ko* 'who', for example *ko avel* > *k' avel* (HU-007), or the complementiser *te*, for instance *te aves* > *t' aves*, even when other lexical items do not take part in the process: *ko adala roma* 'who are these people' and *te ašunav* 'so that I can hear' (MD-006).

Another strategy to resolve hiatus is the epenthesis of a /j/. This can happen in Romacilikanes, for example, at the boundary of two syllables within one word: *evreos* 'Jew' ~ [evˈrejos] (GR-002), as opposed to another variety spoken in Greece, Sofades, where it is [evˈreos] (GR-004). Complete reduction of the word-final consonant cluster in *grast* 'horse' can lead to inflected forms like *grajen*, which in turn yields the nominative form *graj* (EST-005).

5.3.5 Diphthongisation

Diphthongs of the forms /oi̯/, /ai̯/, /ui̯/, /ei̯/ and /ii̯/ are fairly difficult to distinguish from simple sequences of a vowel plus the glide /j/ (Matras 2002, p. 61). The most frequent of these are /oi̯/ and /ai̯/: *kaj* 'where', *roj* 'spoon' or the third person singular feminine personal pronoun *oj*, and in later developments, such as *paj* 'water' in Mexican Vlax (MX-001), or *džaj* 'you go' as a variant of *dža* in Sinti (RO-022), following the deletion of the word-final /s/ of the second person singular present tense concord marker. The diphthong /ui̯/ appears in only a few lexemes such as *muj* 'mouth' and *duj* 'two'.

The other two, /ei̯/ and /ii̯/, are typical of Vlax dialects, where /a/ shifted to /e/ in certain lexemes, such as *čhej/šej* < *čhaj* 'girl' or *dej* < *daj* 'mother', and where a large group of borrowed verbs, following the deletion of a loan-verb adaptation marker, are left with the sequence of /i/ and /j/ at the end of the third person singular form: *vorbij* 'speak', *musajij* 'make someone do something' (RUS-005, Moscow, Russia). The third person singular feminine personal pronoun shows umlaut in Lotfitka and Čuxny, thus rendering the diphthong /ei̯/: *jej* < *oj* (EST-005; EST-008, Pärnu, Estonia; LV-006, Riga, Latvia).

The diphthongs /ou̯/ and /au̯/ are also fairly common, replacing the sequences /ov/ and /av/ word-finally and also word-initially. Northwestern, Northeastern and Central varieties, like Finnish Romani, Čuxny, Lithuanian Romani, Sinti, Vend and Romungro, appear to be especially prone to this kind of diphthongisation: *au* 'I come' (FIN-008) or *jau* (EST-005, LT-005, LV-005), where the diphthong is retained in the past as well, as in *jaujom* 'I came', but Balkan and Vlax dialects, like Ursari and Kalderaš, may also be affected. A most conspicuous morphological position of this diphthong is the first person singular present tense personal concord marker *-av*: *sohajarav* 'I marry' ~ [sohajaˈrau̯] (SLO-001), *dikhav* 'I see' ~ [diˈkʰau̯] (RO-062, Ineu, Romania), *džinav* 'I know' ~ [d͡ʒɨˈnau̯] (PL-015, Mazury, Poland), *putrav* 'I open' [putˈrau̯] (RO-004), *kinav* 'I buy' ~ [kiˈnau̯] (RO-022), *sovav* 'I sleep' ~ [soˈau̯] (MD-001, Chișinău, Moldova). Diphthongisation may also be optional, like in Romanian Kalderaš, for instance: *žav* 'I go' ~ [ʒau̯]/[ʒav] (RO-008). The diphthong /ou̯/ frequently replaces the marker where it takes the form *-ov*: *hadov* 'I lift' ~ [ɣaˈdou̯] (LT-009, Vilnius, Lithuania), and it might also appear without the deletion of the /v/ in Molise Romani: *jouva* < *jov* 'he' (IT-010).

The diphthong /au̯/ can appear word-finally not only in varieties where the personal concord marker is affected, but also where it is not, in

132   M. A. Baló

lexical items like *alav/lav* 'word' ~ [aˈlau̯]/[lau̯], *gav* 'village' ~ [gau̯] (IT-011, Piacenza, Italy; SK-052), *biav* 'wedding' ~ [ˈbijau̯] (RO-004).[2] It can also occur word-initially: *auri* 'out' ~ [ˈau̯ri] in Finnish Romani and Čuxny, and word-medially in Finnish Romani, see *vauro* 'other' [ˈvau̯ro], as well as in Croatian varieties, for example *čhauro* 'little boy' ~ [t͡ʃʰau̯ˈro], probably following the deletion of the /o/: *čhavoro > čhavro > čhauro* (HR-001, Čakovec, Croatia; HR-002). In Prekmurski, as reported already by Boretzky and Igla (1993, p. 38), /au̯/ can occur optionally in stressed positions in place of /a/: *khelāhi* 'I was dancing', ~ [kʰeˈlau̯hi], *phagjom* 'I broke' ~ [ˈpʰau̯gʲom], *pāni* 'water' ~ [ˈpau̯nʲi], *ada* 'this' ~ [aˈdau̯] (SLO-001). In several Vlax dialects of Romania, /au̯/ appears as the first person singular concord marker: *žav* 'I go' ~ [ʒau̯]/[ʒav] either optionally, as in Kalderaš (RO-008, RO-065), or compulsorily, as in Ursari (RO-004). If diphthongised, the second component may also become lower: [ʒao̯] (RO-065).

The diphthongs /oa̯/ and /ea̯/ appear at the end of the demonstrative pronouns *kado/kade* 'this' and *kodo/kode* 'that', but also in other words following /k/: *koa* 'at', *škoala* 'school', and may also occur in other positions, like *seakovar* 'always' in Lingurari (RO-062); according to Boretzky (2003, p. 15), this is due to Romanian contact influence. Another dialect-specific process is in Molise Romani, where /u/ may become /ue̯/ and then further syllabified, occasionally accompanied by the addition of a word-final vowel: *džukel* 'dog' ~ [d͡ʒuguˈel]/[d͡ʒukuˈela] (IT-007, IT-011).

The /ov/ sequence in the third person singular masculine personal pronoun *jov/ov* also becomes a diphthong in several Northwestern and Northeastern dialects (e.g. EST-005, LV-005, FIN-008, LT-005, IT-011) and some Central dialects (e.g. SK-052), where the forms [jov], [jou̯] and [jo] vary. Diphthongisation of *ov* to [ou̯] also takes place in some Vlax dialects, like the Gurbet spoken in Croatia (HR-001) or Ursari (RO-004), where there is a variety of forms, including [vov], [vou̯], [voː], [ov], [ou̯] and [oːv], as well as in several Ukrainian dialects, where there is often variation between the diphthongised and the undiphthongised forms.

5.3.6   Fronting and Backing Processes

Individual dialects in certain lexemes show variation concerning vowels across the language (and even within the traditional dialect groups), cf. *čhaj* 'girl' ~ [t͡ʃʰaj] (BG-016) alongside [t͡ʃʰej] (BG-014) in Kalajdži, as well as Finnish Romani [t͡sej] (FIN-012), or Vlax [ʃej] (RO-058). Some dialects manifest a complete replacement of the /a/ with /e/ in other lexemes as well:

5 Romani Phonology   133

rašaj 'priest' is realised as [reˈʃej], *fejastra* 'window' as [feˈjestre], *mesaji* 'table' as [meseˈji] (RO-059, RO-072), *skamin* 'chair' as [skeˈmin] (RO-025, Deaj, Romania). In Finnish Romani, we see intra-speaker variation concerning the vowel of *daj* 'mother' ~ [daj]/[dej]/[dɛj].

Another lexeme where we see variation in the vowel quality within the Vlax and the Balkan dialect groups is *šero* 'head', where we find [ʃeˈro] (BG-024, Sofia, Bulgaria) alongside [ʃoˈro] (BG-052), with the former one being more typical of Northern Vlax, while the latter one more typical of Southern Vlax varieties (Boretzky 2003, p. 144). Matras (2002, p. 61) suggests that the form [ʃoˈro] represents a case of vowel harmony, with other items, such as the genitive suffix manifesting harmony as well (*-koro* for masculine and *-kiri* for the feminine). While this may be the case, it is worth noting that varieties are far from being uniform in this respect; in Arli, for instance, the genitive endings show vowel harmony, while *šero* remains [ʃeˈro] (MK-002). Occasionally, /e/ may be replaced by /o/ in Romungro, see *borš < berš* 'year' (RO-072), and the /e/ of the oblique may vary with /o/ in Finnish Romani, a vowel that is primarily used in the Layer I oblique ending of loan elements: *jēnes* alongside *jēnos* 'man.SG.ACC' (FIN-011).

The vowel of the first person singular present tense personal concord marker *-av*, accompanied by diphthongisation, may undergo backing in Lithuanian Romani and Polska Roma spoken in Lithuania, yielding forms like *džinov* 'I know' ~ [d͡ʒiˈnou̯] (LT-005) and *tirdov* 'I pull' ~ [tɨrˈdou̯] (LT-009). This may also take place word-finally in certain other lexemes when the sequence does not correspond to the personal concord marker: *lav* 'name' ~ [lou̯] or *bijav* 'wedding' [biˈjou̯], in free variation with [biˈjau̯] and [biˈjav] (LT-008).

5.3.7 The /o/ ~ /u/ Alternation

The back vowels /o/ and /u/ vary across dialects in the first person singular perfective marker, with some of the Northeastern and Balkan dialects manifesting /u/, rather than the /o/ of Central varieties, as a result of vowel raising[3]: *bikindžum* 'I sold' ~ [bikinˈd͡ʒum] (LV-005), *bikingjum* 'I sold' ~ [bikinˈɡʲum] (MK-002), *gjum* 'I went' ~ [ɡʲum] (MK-012, Skopje, Macedonia), *džudžum* 'I lived' ~ [d͡ʒuːˈd͡ʒum] (LV-006), *dikhjum/dikhlum* 'I saw' ~ [dikʰˈjum] (LV-005) and [dikʰˈlum] (MK-003, Skopje, Macedonia). The /u/ may be fronted after affricates in certain lexemes in Latvian Čuxny: *phendžum* 'I said' ~ [pʰenˈd͡ʒym], *kindžum* 'I bought' [kinˈd͡ʒym], but *javdžum* 'I came' ~ [javˈd͡ʒum], and there may also be variation, as in *džindžum* 'I knew' [d͡ʒinˈd͡ʒum]/[d͡ʒinˈd͡ʒym] (LV-005).

134 **M. A. Baló**

In Romani dialects spoken in Italy, the /u/ may only appear in certain verbs: *pindum* 'I said' (IT-011) but *šundom* 'I heard', etc. The /o/ ~ /u/ distinction is even more complex in Northwestern varieties, where the /o/ is often raised word-finally: *tino* 'small.ᴍ' ~ [tiˈnu] alongside [tiˈno] and *tikno* ~ [tikˈno] (IT-011), *varo* 'egg' ~ [vaˈru], as well as in the diminutive suffix *-or-*, as in *čavoro* 'little boy' ~ [t͡ʃavuˈro] and in certain other lexemes preceding /r/: *bori* 'bride' ~ [buˈri], *pori* 'tail' ~ [puˈri] (IT-007). Raising also takes place in Sinti genitive pronouns, for example *miro* 'my.ᴍ' ~ [ˈmiru] and *lesro* 'his.ᴍ' [ˈlesru] (RO-022), and in Latvian Romani, a Northeastern dialect, cf. *terno* 'young.ᴍ' ~ [terˈnu], as well as compound forms such as *po (pe + o)* 'to the' ~ [pu] alongside [po] (LV-006). The same can happen in Balkan dialects in inflectional endings in both stressed and unstressed positions, cf. the genitive of *manuš* 'man': [manuˈʃesko] (BG-009, Pčelnik, Bulgaria) alongside [manuˈʃusku] (BG-016), where the vowel of the oblique marker seems to assimilate to that of the genitive suffix. This is accompanied by possible intra-speaker variation: *romni* 'woman' ~ [rumˈni]/[romˈni] (BG-014). In Xoraxani, on the other hand, the /u/ may also be lowered, cf. **phuv > *phū > phō* 'earth' (BG-015).

5.4 Processes Affecting Consonants

5.4.1 Aspiration

Voiceless stops have aspirated counterparts in Romani: /pʰ/, /tʰ/, /kʰ/, and many dialects still preserve the distinctive quality (cf. Friedman 2001, p. 149): *ker-* 'do, make' ~ *kher* 'house' (RUS-005), *per-* 'fall' ~ *pher-* 'fill' (HU-007). Voiceless affricates may also be aspirated, especially /t͡ʃ/, for example *čhor-* 'pour' ~ *čhor* 'moustache' ~ *čor-* 'steal' (see the data in Bodnárová 2015), but also /t͡s/, although not in a distinctive function: *cǝr/cher* 'house' (UKR-004). In Servi, other phonological changes may lead to new minimal pairs: *puro* 'leg' ~ *phuro* 'old.ᴍ' (UKR-004). In Northeastern dialects, like North Russian, Lithuanian Romani and Polska Roma, the aspirated component of voiceless aspirated stops is velarised (cf. Matras 2002, p. 54), resulting in the clusters /px, tx, kx/ instead of /pʰ, tʰ, kʰ/: *pʰen* 'sister' ~ [pxən] (LT-005). Several dialects retain aspiration after affrication and palatalisation: *čher < kher* 'house' (MK-001, Skopje, Macedonia), *tjher < kher* (HR-003, Novigrad, Croatia), *dičhum < dikhlom* 'I saw' (YU-012, Beočin, Serbia).

Probably due to contact influence, loss of aspiration is not uncommon in varieties in contact with non-aspirating languages such as Hungarian,

Italian, Spanish, Romanian, Russian and Latvian. In Molise Romani, the process affects all aspirated consonants: *tou-< thov-* 'wash', *čauro < čhavoro* 'boy', *pen-< phen-* 'say', *kir< kher* (IT-010). In other varieties, de-aspiration is more selective, with aspirates in consonant clusters being more prone to it, see *dikljom/dikjom< dikhl(j)om* 'I saw' (RO-022; RO-058; SK-011, Krompachy, Slovakia; SK-059; UKR-001, Kharkiv, Ukraine) and *pral< phral* 'brother' (HU-009; MD-001; SK-059; YU-007, Čurug, Serbia). The velar stop and the post-alveolar affricate may also be de-aspirated: *kəl-< khel-* 'dance' (MD-006, YU-007), *čajori< čhajori* 'girl' (LV-005). Sinti is also claimed to have lost the aspiration in the affricate position (cf. Matras 2002, p. 54): *čao< čhavo* 'boy' (RO-022), but not in other positions. In some Vlax varieties, de-aspiration appears to be optional: *pral/phral* 'brother', *ker/kher* 'house' (RO-012, Gheorgheni, Romania; MX-001). In Finnish Romani, the aspirated stops may optionally lose their stop feature altogether, retaining the aspiration only, and thus may freely alternate with /h/, as in *phurano ~ hurano* 'old.ᴍ' (FIN-011), *hunn-~ khunn-* 'hear' (FIN-005), *thun ~ hunt* 'milk' (FIN-008). The aspirated stop /pʰ/ may also be replaced by /f/: *hunn-~ phunn-~ funn-* 'hear' (FIN-006), *fen ~ phen* 'sister', *fen-~ phen-* 'say' (FIN-005).

In the Xaladytka dialect spoken in north-eastern Poland, the aspirated component may undergo fortition, becoming a sibilant and rendering a consonant cluster (see also Sects. 5.5.1 and 5.5.3): *khil* 'butter' > *kšil ~* [kʃił], *phral* 'brother' > *phal > pšal ~* [pʃał]. This may take place optionally in Estonian Lotfitka: *phir-* 'walk' alongside *pšir-* (EST-009, Pärnu, Estonia).[4]

5.4.2 Voice

Voice as a distinctive feature is an overall characteristic of Romani, although some dialects lack certain voiced counterparts, most notably certain Vlax and Balkan varieties lack /d͡ʒ/ and replace it with /ʒ/, while /d͡z/ occurs mostly in certain Balkan and Northeastern dialects. In Xaladytka, a new instance of voice opposition emerges under Russian influence in the velar fricative position, with a voiced fricative before front vowels (cf. Matras 2002, p. 53): *heroj* 'leg' ~ [ɣeˈroj] (PL-014), although it can also be realised as a glottal /h/, just like the velar /x/, as in *xanjink* 'well' ~ [ˈhanʲiŋk], while in other Russian Romani varieties, under the influence of Russian, both can merge into /g/: [ˈgəroj] and [ˈganiŋk] (RUS-003). Voice alternation of a morphophonological nature between the singular and the plural is present in most Layer II case endings, e.g. dative *-ke/-ge* or locative *-te/-de* (cf. Matras 2002, p. 79).

136   M. A. Baló

Several varieties show tendencies of both voicing and devoicing. Heavy voicing, extending to all stop positions, is observable in dialects in contact with Italian, as part of the influence of a more general lenition process in Central and Southern Italian dialects (cf. e.g. Hualde and Nadeu 2011): *dado* < *tato* 'hot.ᴍ', *aga* < *aka* 'here', *džuguel* < *džukel* 'dog', *bor* < *por* 'feather', *bud* < *but* 'very, much' (IT-007, IT-010). Word-final /k/ may be voiced before a voiced consonant in Kalderaš: *ek meseli* 'a table' ~ [əg] as opposed to *ek pato* 'a bed' ~ [ək] (RO-065) and also word-internally in Gurvari: *cigno* < *tikno* 'small.ᴍ' (HU-007).

Devoicing often takes place word-finally in varieties in contact with languages where this is also common, thus Sinti *jop* < *job* 'he' and *džap* < **džab* < *džav* 'I go', alongside *džau* (RO-022), Polska Roma *jof* < *jov* 'he' (PL-003), *džinaf* < *džinav* 'I know' (PL-018), Russian Romani *jak* < *jag* 'fire' (RUS-008), *dat* < *dad* 'father' (BG-014, MK-012), *went* < *vend* 'winter' and *ajičč* 'yesterday' alternating with *ajiddž* (IT-010), *bryšint* < *brišind* 'rain', *tat* < *dad* 'father' (LT-007, LV-005). In Abruzzian Romani, /d/ is regularly devoiced after a stressed vowel: *thud* 'milk' ~ [ˈtuːtə], *vodro* 'bed' ~ [ˈvoːtərə] (Scala 2018, p. 179).

In several dialects, /v/ is devoiced as an instance of voice assimilation: *nasfalo* < *nasvalo* 'ill' (RO-066, Țăndărei, Romania; RO-072), *ratfalo* < *ratvalo* 'bloody.ᴍ' (Bodnárová 2015, p. 80), *butfar* < *butvar* 'often' (AL-001). In Finnish Romani, under the influence of Finnish, devoicing has an even wider scope, affecting most of the voiced consonants in initial and medial positions as well: *pūt putti* < *but buti* 'a lot of work', *cā* < *džā* 'I go' (FIN-005), *kau* < *gav* 'village', *cuklo* < *džuklo* 'dog' (FIN-006), although it may be optional, resulting in free variation: *dāt* ~ *tāt* 'father', *cau* ~ *čau* 'boy' (FIN-008), *touva dikjatas* ~ *douva tikjatas* 'he saw' (FIN-011), *bāl* ~ *pāl* 'hair' (FIN-012). In case of certain lexemes, the voiceless /k/ and /t/ may vary: *kraj* ~ *traj* 'horse' (FIN-002).

5.4.3 Reflexes of the Historical Cluster /ṇḍ/

The continuation of the historical retroflex cluster /ṇḍ/ is often a combination of the sonorants /n/ and /r/, occasionally containing the stops /d/ or /g/ as well. Thus, for example, Old Indo-Aryan *āṇḍá* 'egg' can have several different, present-day, dialect-specific forms; these possible forms include, among others, *jandro* in East Slovak Romani (SK-011), *vandro* in Sofades Romani (GR-004), *jaro/ jāro* in Arli, Čuxny, Polska Roma, Finnish Romani and Sinti (EST-005; YU-014, Zrenjanin, Serbia; FIN-006; LV-005; PL-018;

5 Romani Phonology   137

IT-011; RO-022), *anro* in some Romungro varieties (RO-001), *angro* in other Romungro varieties and certain Vlax dialects (RO-072, HR-001), *aro/arno* in some Balkan dialects such as Kalajdži (BG-014, BG-016) and Xoraxani (BG-015) or *vando* in Mečkari (AL-001). In certain dialects, these processes merge the words *aro* 'flour' and *aro* 'egg' (e.g. YU-012), while in other, Balkan and Northwestern varieties, a prothetic word-initial consonant helps maintain the distinction: *varo* 'flour' and *jaro* 'egg' (e.g. FIN-012, YU-011). In Molise Romani, the distinction is retained through gemination: *waro* 'egg' versus *warro* 'flour' (IT-010). We also have to note that the continuation of /ṇḍ/ is not regular within a variety and different dialects may contain different reflexes of the same cluster in different lexical items, or even for the same lexical item, cf. *mangro ~ manro* 'bread' (YU-002). There are several varieties where a uvular fricative /ʁ/ or a uvular trill /ʀ/ appears in place of the dental trill component, as the continuation of historical /ř/ (Matras 2002, pp. 50–51), see, for example, Kalderaš, Gurbet, Šanxajcy, Gabor and Lingurari *anřo* (RO-008; YU-004; UKR-011, Odesa, Ukraine; RO-009, Vălureni, Romania; RO-062).

5.4.4 Velarisation

The lateral /l/ may be velarised under contact influence, especially in dialects in contact with Polish and Russian: *balval* 'wind' ~ [baɫˈvaɫ] (LV-006, RUS-003), *luludʲi* 'flower' ~ [ɫuɫuˈdʲi] (RUS-005), *džuvel* 'live' ~ [d͡ʒuˈvəɫ] (UKR-004, UKR-008), *kinel* 'buy' ~ [kiˈneɫ] (PL-003). The velar /ɫ/ replaces the lateral /l/ following a vowel and is substituted by the semi-vowel /w/ word-initially or intervocalically in the Romani dialects of Poland: *zoralo* 'strong.M' ~ [zoraˈwo] (PL-003), *lel* 'take' ~ [wəɫ] (PL-019). While in some varieties, /l/ is not velarised after /i/ (Matras 2002, p. 52), for example *kolin* 'breast' ~ [koˈlin] versus *ilo* 'heart' ~ [iˈwo] (PL-015), in other dialects velarisation may spread to this position as well, at least intervocalically: *gili* 'song' ~ [giˈɫi] (LV-005), *milaj* 'summer' ~ [miˈɫaj] (UKR-015, Odesa, Ukraine). In loanwords containing a lateral /l/, the lateral feature is kept: *kolano* 'knee' ~ [kolaˈno], *palco* 'finger' ~ [ˈpal͡tso]. As Friedman (2001, p. 150) reports, the lateral /l/ is velarised only before back vowels in Macedonian Arli, just like in Macedonian: *bavlal* 'wind' ~ [bavˈɫaɫ] (MK-003); hence, the two are in complementary distribution: *gelo* 'he came' ~ [geˈɫo] and *geli* 'she came' ~ [geˈli] (MK-002). This distinction is also made in other dialects spoken in the Balkans, like Gurbet: [dʲeˈɫo] versus

138   M. A. Baló

[dʲeˈli] (YU-017), but not in all of them; in Kosovan Arli, for example, both forms contain a lateral /l/: [d͡ʒeˈlo] and [d͡ʒeˈli] (YU-016, Gnjilane, Kosovo).

5.4.5 Semi-Vowels

The semi-vowel /j/, although its status is marginal in the Romani phonological system (Matras 2002, p. 52), appears frequently in several positions in Romani: as the second element of diphthongs (see Sect. 5.3.5), as a prothetic consonant word-initially (see Sect. 5.5.2) and as a result of palatalisation processes (see Sect. 5.4.10). It may also replace the voiced post-alveolar affricate in Finnish Romani: *jēno* < *džēno* 'person', *jūvi* < *džūvi* 'lice', *jūli* < *džūli* 'woman' (see Granqvist 2007, p. 76) and the glottal fricative in Polska Roma: *jeruj* < *heruj* 'leg, foot' (PL-018). In Finnish Romani, the perfective marker *-d-* may be elided, especially in verb stems ending in /n/, leaving only /j/, but without any palatalisation on the /n/: *phenjom* 'I said' ~ [ˈpʰenjom], *činjal* 'you bought' ~ [ˈt͡ʃinjał] (FIN-002). In Arli, the omission of the final /n/ of verb stems (and also perfective stems) may also lead to the /j/ being the overt past tense marker: *šujum* 'I heard', *dijum* 'I gave', *phjum* 'I said' (YU-018, Prizren, Kosovo). These processes may result in forms that are even more contracted: Vend *phom* < *phendjom 'I said' (Bodnárová 2015, p. 86), Arli *pheam* < *phejam* < *phenjam < *phendjam 'we said' (YU-016). In Bugurdži (see also Boretzky 1993, p. 12), the /l/ of the feminine form of the participle is replaced by /j/: *gelo* 'he went' versus *geji* 'she went' (YU-012).

The presence of the velar approximant /w/ is a result of contact with languages whose sound inventories contain this phoneme. Thus, as mentioned in Sect. 5.4.4, dialects in contact with Polish often have /w/ in word-initial and intervocalic positions. This is also true for some Italian varieties, where /v/ can become a semi-vowel word-initially: *vast* 'hand' ~ [wast], *vend* 'winter' ~ [went]. Through Italian influence, it may also occur after /k/ and /g/, which leads to the merger of the demonstrative pronoun *kava* 'this' and the interrogative *ka* 'where' in [kwa]/[gwa] (IT-010).

Varieties in contact with Romanian/Moldovan, like Lingurari, Kangljari and Čurari, may also manifest the semi-vowel optionally in place of /v/ in word-initial or even syllable-initial position: *voj* 'she' ~ [voj]/[woj]/[wo] (MD-006, RO-066), *vazd-* 'lift' ~ [vazd]/[wazd] (RO-066), *balval* 'wind' ~ [balˈwal] (MD-006), *thovav* 'I wash' ~ [tʰoˈwau̯] (RO-062), and in the multiplicative suffix *-var*, see *butʲvar* 'often' ~ [ˈbutʲwar], *seakovar* 'always' ~ [ˈse̜akowar] (RO-062).

5.4.6 The Distribution of /h/ and /x/

There are varieties where /h/ and /x/ may merge into either of them, probably depending on the contact language; in the Balkan and Central dialects where they merge, /h/ is more common: *ha-* 'eat' (YU-011), *hovav-* 'lie' (HU-009), *hulav-* 'comb' (SK-059), although there are also examples for the spread of /x/ in East Slovak and Romungro: *kahnʲi* 'hen' ~ [ˈkaxnʲi], *ahaljol* 'understand' ~ [aˈxalʲoɫ] (SK-011), *hudav* 'I hold' ~ [ˈxudav] (RO-059).

In the Northeastern varieties, the velar fricative is more dominant, either voiced or voiceless: *haluvav* 'I understand' ~ [ɣaluˈvav], *xav* 'I eat' ~ [xav], (PL-014). The velarisation effect can extend to the aspirated component of aspirated stops, resulting in /px, tx, kx/ instead of /ph, th, kh/ in Lithuanian Romani and possibly leading to the emergence of a uvular fricative in place of the glottal fricative: *horoj* 'leg' [ʁoˈroj], *hajlovov* 'I understand' [ʁalʲoˈvov] (LT-005). In other varieties, it becomes a voiced velar fricative: [ɣoˈroj] and [ɣalʲoˈvov] (LT-007). A voiceless palatal fricative may emerge as a replacement for the aspirated velar stop: *dikhjom* 'I saw' ~ [diˈçom] (LT-008). The palatal fricative and the velar fricative are in complementary distribution in Finnish Romani, depending on the preceding vowel, replacing the voiceless post-alveolar sibilant word-finally, see *kax* 'wood, tree' ~ [kax] and *vex* 'forest' ~ [veç], and intervocalically, as in *raxal* 'priest' ~ [ˈrax:al] (FIN-005, FIN-012). This process is also encountered in Servi in the second person singular present tense concord marker, although without the palatal variant: *džas > džax* 'you go' (UKR-004). In the Southern Central dialects (Matras 2002, p. 52), a reverse process is observable, in which the voiceless alveolar sibilant replaces the velar fricative: *bast < baxt* 'fortune' (SK-059). The uvular fricative /χ/ is used instead of /x/ in Xoraxane Romane, a Vlax variety spoken in Greek Thrace, see, for example, *bax* 'fortune' ~ [baχ], although it may alternate with /x/ (Adamou and Arvaniti 2014, pp. 226–227).

5.4.7 Affrication and De-affrication

Affrication of alveolar stops frequently takes place in Romani, probably through an intermediary phase of palatalisation (Matras 2002, p. 53): *cikno < *tjikno < tikno* 'small.м' (BG-008, HR-001, UKR-010, YU-017) or *cigno/cino* in Gurvari (HU-007), *buci < buti* (YU-012), *cird- < *tjird- < tird-* 'pull' (HU-004, Győr, Hungary).

In several different dialects of the Balkans, as well as some Northwestern varieties, like Finnish Romani (see Granqvist 2007, p. 74), the velar /k/ as well

140　M. A. Baló

as its voiced and aspirated counterparts can undergo affrication[5] word-initially: *džino(v)-* < *gino(v)-* 'count' (MK-001), *čir* < *kir* 'ant', *činn-* < *kinn-* 'buy' (FIN-012), *čin-* < *kin-* 'buy' (YU-018), *dičum* < *dikh(j)um* 'I saw' in free variation (MK-012), *čher* < *kher* 'house', *čhelav* < *khelav* 'I play' (YU-002), *čermo* < *kermo* 'worm' (YU-015), *džučel* < *džukel* 'dog' (YU-016), *cer/čhər* < *kher* 'house' in several Ukrainian varieties, like Servi, Xandžari or Kubanska Vlaxurja (UKR-004, UKR-010, UKR-016).

These processes are interwoven with changes in the place of articulation of stops in lexical items such as *buti* 'work', which has forms such as *buci*, as mentioned above, but also *buki* (YU-004) and *buči* (YU-017), as well as palatalisation processes (see Sect. 5.4.10). The voiceless post-alveolar and alveolar affricates can both replace /t/ and /k/: *čiro* < *tiro* 'your.м' (YU-015), *cin-* < *kin-* 'buy' (BG-013), *ciri* < *kiri* 'ant' (YU-012), *cēr* < *kher* 'house' (FIN-012). Finnish Romani also shows the replacement of the palatalised alveolar stop and post-alveolar affricates by /t͡s/, as part of a devoicing process with a wider scope under Finnish influence (see Sect. 5.4.2), for instance *luluci* < *luludji* 'flower' (FIN-006), following earlier palatalisation from *luludi*.

The jotated perfective marker (see Sect. 5.4.10) in *-d-* is also prone to affrication: *bikindzum* < *bikindjom* 'I sold' (MK-012), *cindzom* < *cindjom* 'I bought' (BG-013). The affrication of the morphologically non-jotated feminine participle in Bugurdži should be noted as well: *kerdo* versus *kerdzi* 'done' (YU-012).

In certain Northeastern varieties, like Lotfitka, as well as in some Northern Central dialects, like Bergitka, the jotated perfective marker in *-d-* becomes a post-alveolar affricate: *šundžom* < *šundjom* 'I heard' (EST-010, Paide, Estonia; PL-007, Cracow, Poland; SK-011), as in *tadžo(v)-* < *tadjo(v)-* 'boil'. In Lithuanian Romani, palatalised and affricated forms vary and combine: *phendjom* 'I said' ~ [pxɐnˈdʲom]/[pxɐnˈd͡zʲom]/[pxɐnˈd͡ʒom] (LT-007). In Mečkari, palatalised and affricated consonants may also vary: *tjher/čher* < *kher* 'house' (AL-001). Free variation is also present among affricates and fricatives in Finnish Romani: *čūli/cūli* 'woman', alongside *džūli* and *jūli*, *cej/sej* 'girl' (FIN-011) and *sinn-/činn-* 'buy' (FIN-012).

De-affrication often results in alveolar sibilants; in certain Balkan and Northwestern varieties, the voiced alveolar sibilant can replace both the voiced and the voiceless alveolar affricates: *zis* < **dzis* < **dis* 'day' (BG-013), *zjes/zijes* < **djes* < **djives* < **dives* (MK-004, Kumanovo, Macedonia), *zau* < *cau* < *čau* 'boy' (FIN-011). In Crimean Romani, /s/ can replace /t͡s/ *sid-* < *cid-* 'pull' (UKR-001). De-affrication can also lead to the emergence of alveo-palatal sibilants instead of palato-alveolar sibilants in some Vlax varieties. This is perhaps most conspicuous in Russian Lovari, see, for example, *šavoro* 'little boy' ~ [ɕaˈvoːro] and *žav* 'I go' ~ [ʑav] (RUS-005).

5.4.8 Sibilants

The alveolar sibilant of the copula may be replaced by an alveo-palatal sibilant in some Greek varieties: *som* 'I am' ~ [ɕom] (GR-002). A shift from alveolar to post-alveolar sibilants is reported sporadically by Elšik et al. (1999, p. 303) in some Central varieties, for example *šo < so* 'what', which also takes place in some Italian dialects: *vašt < vast* 'hand' (IT-007), while a shift in the opposite direction is seen in certain Greek and Finnish Romani dialects: *naš- > nas-* 'run' (GR-004), *berš > bres* 'year' (GR-031), *štar > stār* 'four' (FIN-006); in the latter case, the sibilant may be deleted, rendering *tār*. In Sofades Romani, the shift may be optional: *murš/murs* 'man' (GR-004). In Finnish Romani, /ʃ/ may also be replaced by /h/, see *hēro* 'head', *hunn-* 'hear' (FIN-006).

5.4.9 Gemination

The existence of geminates in Romani is mostly triggered by contact influence and is restricted across the dialectal spectrum. An exception is the geminate trill, which emerges sporadically in certain lexemes intervocalically in some varieties without any apparent reason: *cerra/carra* 'a little' (YU-015, RO-072), *čorro* 'poor.M' (SK-016), *šaorri/šaorro* 'little girl/boy' (RO-065). Besides contact effects, another source of gemination might be assimilation: Southern Central *gullo < gudlo* 'sweet.M' (Elšík et al. 1999, p. 306), Hungarian Romungro *kello < kerlo* 'throat' (HU-009), although these might also be attributed to contact influence, as it is suggested by Matras (2002, p. 55) in connection with East Slovak *gaddžo < gadžo* 'non-Gypsy, farmer' (SK-011) and as it is supported by the gemination processes discussed below.

Čuxny, Finnish and Italian Romani varieties are the most affected by contact-related gemination, and they show similar processes as those presented above. We see gemination both intervocalically and word-finally in Molise Romani: *ajiddž < ajidž* 'yesterday' (IT-007), *gaddžo < gadžo* 'non-Gypsy, farmer', *dumen/tumen/dummen/tummen < tumen* 'you.PL' (IT-010). In Čuxny, intervocalic stops are geminated: *butti < buti* 'work', *džukkel < džukel* 'dog' (EST-005), *matto < mato* 'drunk.M', *sakko < sako* 'every' and even *zuppa* from Latvian *zupa* 'soup' (LV-005).

In Finnish Romani, virtually all consonants can be geminated: *putti < buti* 'work' (FIN-005), *dikk- < dikh-* 'see', *raxxal < raxal* 'priest', *kamm- < kam-* 'want', *činn- < kin-* 'buy', *kullipa < gullipe* 'sweets', *čerro < kerlo* 'throat' (FIN-011, FIN-012), although these latter two may be motivated by assimilation as well.

142 M. A. Baló

In Molise Romani, gemination may also take place at word boundaries; when the first word ends in a vowel, the initial consonant of the second word is geminated: *tere pen* 'your sister' ~ [ˌdereˈpːe], *ka džas* 'where are you going' ~ [ˌgwaˈd͡ʒːas] (IT-010). In Hungarian Romungro, this frequently happens to the copula: *čoro sa* '(he) was poor' [t͡ʃoˈroˌsːa] (HU-009).

As Romani originally lacks geminate consonants, degemination of loanwords is not uncommon. When words are borrowed from contact languages where there is gemination, like Hungarian, the consonant loses gemination, for example *čepo* 'a little' < Hungarian *csepp* 'drop' (SK-059) or *forin-* 'boil' < Hungarian *forr* 'boil' (HU-007).

5.4.10 Palatalisation and De-palatalisation

Various different palatalisation processes take place in several Romani dialects (cf. e.g. Boretzky 2001 for a detailed overview), which eventually lead to the emergence of palatalised or palatal consonants. Perhaps most prone to palatalisation are the alveolars /t, d, n, l/, but the velars /k/ and /g/ and the trill /r/ may also undergo it.

The term 'jotation' is also used in the literature concerning Romani linguistics, especially when referring to different processes of morphophonological palatalisation. These affect the copula; the derivation of mediopassive verbs; the inflection of feminine nouns ending in *-i*; and the perfective markers (Matras 2002, p. 67).

The intransitive marker *-(j)o(v)-*, used to form mediopassives, attaches to the perfective stem and may already contain /j/; hence, the outcome is a palatalised or palatal consonant: *puter-* 'open.TR' > puter-d- PERF. > puter-d-jo- 'open.ITR' ~ [ˈputerd͡ʲo]/[ˈputerɟo].

The diverse forms of the copula in Romani include one where the initial consonant of the copula in *s-* appears to be jotated, for example Xoraxani *sjom* 'I am' (BG-015), Kangljari *sjan* 'you are' (RO-064, Țăndărei, Romania). Although its origins are obscure, several Romani varieties contain traces of some form of palatalisation in the copula, especially ones where a perfective marker is more ostensible on it (accompanied by tense alteration and the reassignment of the marker, cf. Matras 2002, p. 143), for example *-l-* in some Ukrainian dialects: *sljom/sljan* (UKR-004; UKR-007, Kiev, Ukraine); *-in-* in Molise Romani: *sinjom/sinjan* (IT-010); and *-l-* or *-t-* in Central Romungro: *sljom/stjom* (SK-052). Another Xoraxani variety (BG-023, Šumen, Bulgaria) has the forms *sijom* and *sijan*, which suggests that the palatalisation of *s-* might be a secondary consequence of the loss of a

5 Romani Phonology   143

palatalised perfective marker. This is further supported by the existence of similar forms in other Balkan dialects, cf. *sijum/sijan* (MK-004, YU-012), and even on the copula in *h-*: *hijum/hijan* (YU-011).

Another source of palatalisation is the *-i* ending of feminine nouns. Whereas generally this is indeed a jotation effect, see *čhajōri* 'little girl' > plural *čhajōrja* (SK-059), for stems ending in consonants prone to palatalisation, this will yield palatal or palatalised consonants: **romni* 'Gypsy woman' > plural *romnja* ~ ['romɲa] (SK-052), **džuli* 'woman' > plural *džulja* ~ ['d͡ʒulʲa] (RO-059) or ['d͡ʒuʎa] (RO-072). In these Romungro varieties, palatalisation typically extends in effect to the singular form as well, rendering *romnji* ~ ['romɲi], *džuli* ~ ['d͡ʒulʲi] and ['d͡ʒuʎi]. The same happens to alveolars: *luludja* 'flower.PL' ~ [lulu'ja] > *luludji*, *butja* 'thing.PL' ~ [bu'ca] > *butji* (RO-072). In the Balkans, these processes lead to the affrication of alveolars: *luludi* 'flower' > *luludža* 'flower.PL', *buti* 'thing' > *buča* 'thing.PL' (YU-011). In Vlax varieties, particularly where the consonants remain palatalised, like [rom'nʲa] and [ʒuv'lʲa], the singular forms remain unaffected: [rom'ni] and [ʒuv'li] (RO-065),[6] similarly to certain Finnish Romani varieties: *jūja* 'woman.PL' but *jūli* 'woman' (FIN-006). The exact progress varies from dialect to dialect but appears to be uniform within a given dialect. For instance, in Hungarian Romungro, complete palatalisation takes place in the inflected forms, but the singular nominative forms are not palatalised: *būti* ~ ['buːti] > *būtja* ~ ['buːca], *romni* ~ ['romni] > *romnja* ['romɲa] (HU-009).[7] In individual dialects, palatalisation may take place selectively, not affecting every possible consonant or not affecting them to the same extent, and this may vary even within a dialect. In one variety of Xaladytka, for instance, most consonants are affected, and other positions besides the feminine inflection are involved as well, while in another one, palatalisation is much less extensive: *tiknji romnji* (PL-015) versus *tikni džuvli* (PL-014) 'little.F woman', although *panji* 'water' is palatalised in both. In Romanian Romungro, this may extend to other lexemes: *nane* > *nanji* 'is not' ~ [na'ɲi] (RO-072).

The jotation of the perfective marker is frequent and is possibly the result of a connecting particle containing /j/ (see Matras 2002, p. 67), as it is supported by the fact that all perfective markers take part in the process: *kin-d-* 'bought' > *kindj-* (YU-004), *beš-t-* 'sat' > *beštj-* (PL-014), *d-in-* 'gave' > *dinj-* (HU-009), *dikh-l-* 'saw' > *dikhlj-* (RO-025), even when the perfective marker undergoes affrication, as in Lithuanian Romani *phendjom* 'I said' ~ [pxɐn'd͡zʲom] (LT-007). They either surface as palatalised /dʲ, tʲ, nʲ, lʲ/ or palatal /ɟ, c, ɲ, ʎ/; the last one often merges with the palatal approximant /j/: *dikhjas* 'he/she saw', *mangjum* 'I wanted' (MK-012) or even

144   M. A. Baló

mandjum (MK-004). Individual dialects may show other processes, through which only /j/ is left as an overt perfective marker (see also Sect. 5.4.5).

A common process in several Romani dialects is the palatalisation of velars (also complemented by affrication, see Sect. 5.4.7), especially in positions preceding /i/ and /e/: *kermo > tjhermo* 'worm' (FIN-012), *kin->tjin-* 'buy' (PL-014), *gilom khere > djilom tjhere* 'I went home', *papinjake > papinjatje* 'goose.PL.DAT', *tuke > tutje* 'you.SG.DAT' (AL-001), *gili > djīli* 'song' (HU-009), *grastenge > grastendji* 'horse.PL.DAT' (UKR-004), *papinakir- > papinatjir-* 'goose.PL.GEN' (UKR-010), *gelem > djelem* 'I went' (HR-001), *kir > tjir* 'ant' (YU-017), *amendje* (MK-004) < *amengje* (MK-012) < *amenge* 'we.DAT'. Optionally, the palatalisation of velars may also affect the perfective forms, probably not independently of the retainment of /j/ as the sole perfective marker described above: **dikhlum > dikjum/ditjhum* 'I saw' (MK-012).

Alveolars are frequently palatalised in the Central, Northeastern and Vlax groups as well: *tikno > tjikno* 'small.M' ~ [cɨkˈno] (UKR-001), *dive > djivo* 'day' ~ [ɟɨˈvo] (UKR-008), *dives > djes* (RO-072), *tiro > tjiro* 'your.SG.M' (UKR-004). In some South Vlax dialects, the palatal stop may be substituted by a palatalised velar: **djes > gjes* 'day' (RO-065), **patja-> pakja* 'believe', **tjiro > kjo* 'your.SG.M' (RO-002). A palatal nasal emerges in certain, modified past forms in Romanian Romungro,[8] affecting the perfective markers *-d-* and *-in-*, possibly through elision and contraction: *xudinj-> xunj-* 'got', as in *xunjom* 'I got' ~ [xuˈɲom], *čhumidinj- > čhuminj-* 'kissed' (RO-072), *čhunj-* 'put.PFV', *runj-* 'cried' (RO-059).

Other consonants are not frequently palatalised, but there are occasional examples. Due to the optional elision of /i/, the voiced alveolar fricative may surface with additional palatalisation in Kovački, a Balkan dialect of Macedonia: *zijes ~ zjes* 'day', *bijanzijum ~ bijanzjum* 'I was born' (MK-004). In Polska Roma, the post-alveolar fricatives and affricates can be slightly palatalised: *berš* 'year' ~ [berɕ], *dža-* 'go' ~ [d͡ʑa], *čhaj* 'girl' ~ [t͡ɕaj], *žužo* 'clean.M' ~ [ʑuˈʑo] (PL-019). We find a palatalised /r/ in Kangljari: *rat* 'evening, night' ~ [rjat] (RO-066).

Palatalisation across word boundaries may also take place in Romungro, following the deletion of the word-initial /h/ in the copula: *pherdi hin* 'it is full.F' ~ [ˈpʰerjin] (RO-072).

Instances of de-palatalisation can be found in the perfective stems in some Balkan dialects: *diklum* 'I saw' (YU-014), *dželum* 'I went' (YU-018), *dinom* 'I gave' (GR-002), *asundom* 'I heard' (GR-004) and occasionally elsewhere: *tjindan* 'you bought' (UKR-004).

5.5 Other Phonological Processes

5.5.1 Elision

The consonants that are most prone to elision are /v/ and /j/ (see also Matras 2002, p. 65). The deletion of intervocalic /v/ is a general morphophonological reduction process in inflected forms of the mediopassive derivation in *-(j)o(v)-*, frequently accompanied by the deletion of the vocalic component of the personal concord marker, as in **barjoven > barjon* 'they grow' (BG-008, Sindel, Bulgaria), or less frequently, not, as in **maladjuvas > maladjuas* 'we meet' (RO-062). The elision of /v/ may extend to other morphologically significant, intervocalic positions, like the /v/ of the intransitive marker *-av-* in Ajia Varvara, e.g. *šilavav > šilaav* 'I am cold' (Igla 1996, p. 18). The process appears to have an even wider scope, taking place in morphologically neutral environments, in several Balkan, Vlax as well as Northeastern and Northwestern dialects: Ajia Varvara, Ursari and Finnish Romani **čhavo > čhao* 'boy' (Igla 1996, p. 18, as well as FIN-012, RO-004),[9] Xoraxani **čhavo > čhō* 'boy' (BG-015), Kalderaš **šavorro > šaorro* 'little boy' (RO-065), Laješa/Kišinevcy **šavoro > šaoro* (MD-001), Servi *čhavoro > čharo* (UKR-004). There are dialects where elision is optional, like Molise Romani: *čauro* 'little boy' alongside *čavoro* and *čaworo* with a semivowel (IT-007, IT-010), or Kərəmidarea Romani: *čhao/čhavo/čav* (RO-025). Diphthongisation and later monopthongisation are the results of the deletion of intervocalic /v/ in *-Vve-* sequences in Vend Romani: **tavel > *tael > tāl* 'he/she cooks' (Bodnárová 2015, pp. 84–85). The same sequence, *-ave-*, is reduced to /e/ in the second person singular future form of *jav-* 'come' in Lotfitka: **javesa > jesa* (LV-006).

In roughly the same cluster of dialects, intervocalic /j/ is frequently elided as well, for example Ajia Varvara *xajing > xaing* 'well', **čheja > čhea* 'girl.PL' (Igla 1996, p. 18) and also Laješa/Kišinevcy *šejori > šeori* (MD-001). There are varieties that show variation, like Gurbet: *pheja ~ phea* 'sister.PL' (MK-001), where the deletion of the /j/ is complemented by the loss of stem-final /i/: **čejori > čejor/čjor/čor* 'little girl' (YU-002).[10] In Polska Roma, on the other hand, /i/ is elided before /j/, see *bijav > bjaf* 'wedding' and *pijav > pjaf* 'I drink' (PL-018).

The change from /v/ to /j/ in Vend mentioned by Bodnárová (2015, p. 85) in derived nouns, such as *rojībe < *rovībe* 'crying', is somewhat analogous with the process described by Igla (1996, pp. 18–19) in Ajia Varvara, where the /v/ is elided in similar environments (**dukhavipe > dukhaipe* 'pain'), and might be a result of subsequent epenthesis to avoid the hiatus.

146   M. A. Baló

The elision of /l/ and /r/ in some Balkan and Northeastern varieties results in cluster reduction: *berš > beš* 'year' (YU-014), *balval > baval* 'wind' (YU-011, RUS-006), *phral > phal* 'brother' (RO-025), *phral > pšaɫ* (LT-005, LV-005, PL-003, RUS-006), accompanied by fortition. Cluster reduction as a form of simplification may also affect other consonants in the dialects of the Northwestern group, cf. Romanian Sinti **lesk(e)ro > lesru* 'his.M' (RO-022) or Finnish Romani *grej > rej* 'horse' (FIN-008).

Elision also affects the copula. The initial consonant[11] can optionally be reduced to zero, as in Romungro *hin/in* 'is' (RO-072) or as in Macedonian Arli, where it is elided after the 'intrusion' and reclassification of the perfective stem *-in-* (see Matras 2002, p. 230), resulting in forms like *inum/injum* 'I am' (MK-002, MK-003).

The /s/ may also be deleted in the singular instrumental suffix, yielding variation in Kosovan Arli, for example: *panjesa/panjea* 'water.INS' (YU-016). The elision of the consonantal component, which is itself the simplification of the consonant of the oblique marker and that of the instrumental suffix, may ultimately lead to the deletion of the vocalic component of the suffix: *thude* 'milk.INS' (RO-025).

Word-final deletion of /v/ is not uncommon, either. We find truncated forms of the third person pronoun *ov* 'he' in virtually all dialect groups: *o* (BG-052), *vo* (YU-017, MX-001, RO-065, HU-007, RO-059, UKR-015, RO-025), *jo* (SK-052, LT-007) and also of other lexemes: *ruv > ru* 'wolf', *žuv > žu* 'louse', *guruv > guru* 'bull', with the retention of the /v/ in inflected forms. In Northeastern dialects, the /v/ of the first person singular present tense concord marker of verbs can be deleted as well, see *džinov* 'I know' ~ [d͡ʒɨˈno] (LT-005), while also occurring as an alternative form of the lengthened or the diphthongised form: *pija/pijā* 'I drink', *dža/džau* 'I go' (EST-005).

The deletion of other word-final consonants partly affects consonant clusters: the nominative singular form of *grast* 'horse' might become *gras* (UKR-016) or even *gra* (HU-009); also *vast > vas* 'hand' (YU-014), *kast > kas* 'wood' (GR-031), *baxt > bax* 'luck' (PL-015), *brišind > brišin* 'rain' (AL-001). The nasal, in turn, may become labialised in some Greek varieties: *brisim* (GR-004, GR-031). The loss of the /r/ from the ablative ending is most conspicuous in Finnish Romani: *kāvesta* 'village.ABL', *phēnesta* 'sister.ABL'.

Another morphologically relevant instance of word-final deletion is the loss of the /s/ in the third person singular past tense concord marker *-as* in several Northeastern and Central dialects, as in *kindja < kindjas* 'he/she bought' (LT-008), *šundja < šundjas* 'he/she heard' (HU-009), which may be connected to a more general reduction of the /s/ in final position.

As for vowels, initial /a/ is deleted in Sinti, for example *avri > vri* 'out' (RO-022, cf. also Holzinger 1993). Northeastern dialects also have a tendency to avoid initial /a/, especially Polska Roma: *asa-* 'laugh' *> sa-* (PL-018).

5.5.2 Prothesis and Paragoge

Prothesis of /v/ and /j/ is a historically established strategy in Romani (cf. Matras 2002, p. 66), with common examples such as *vurdon* 'car, cart' from Ossetian *ordon*, the personal pronouns *ov, vov, jov* 'he' and their variants, as well as the words *andřo* 'egg' and *ařo* 'flour' (Matras 2002, p. 216). Various Romani dialects of Romania, where the form *urdon* 'car, cart' prevails, may contain additional word-initial elision of /v/ in *vudar > udar* 'door' (RO-025, RO-064, RO-065, RO-066, RO-059, RO-072), although this may take place alongside *vurdon*, for example in Gurvari (HU-007). Local processes, like the substitution of /v/ through /h/, might also affect this set of words: *hordon* 'cart' (RO-062).[12] In Northeastern dialects, the prothesis of /j/ exists alongside the deletion of word-initial /a/: *javen* (LV-005, RUS-008) versus *ven* (PL-018) 'you/they come'. The copula does not remain unaffected by prothesis, either: an /i/ may be added to both the short and the long forms: *isom* (EST-005), *isinom* (GR-032) 'I am'.

Paragoge can be seen in Romacilikanes and Gabor Romani, for example, see *brišind > brišindo* 'rain' (GR-002, RO-009), or in Kərəmidarea Romani: *urdonenca > urdonencar* 'cart.PL.INS' (RO-025). The word-final addition of a schwa in Abruzzian Romani is the result of the obligatory structure (C) CV in the prosodic skeleton of the last syllable of a word in co-territorial Romance dialects: *ker* 'house' ~ [ˈkeːrə], *rat* 'night' [ˈrattə] (Scala 2018, p. 171).

5.5.3 Metathesis

Although not common, there are some examples of metathesis in various Romani dialects: *dumar- < mudar-* 'kill' (EST-005), *tokor < kotor* 'slice' (IT-011), *bavłał < balval* 'wind' (MK-005), some of them leading to new consonant clusters: *bres < berš* 'year' (GR-031), *mruš < murš* 'man' (BG-014). Consonant clusters resulting from the fortition of the aspirated component of aspirated stops (see Sect. 5.4.1) in Latvian Lotfitka may also undergo metathesis: *phral* 'brother' *> phal > pšal > špal* and *phir-* 'walk' *> pšir-> špir-* (LV-006), *khil* 'butter' *> kšil > škil* (Anton Tenser, personal communication).

148   M. A. Baló

5.6   Dialect-Specific Processes

5.6.1 Labialisation in Sinti and Central Romani

The fricative /v/ may undergo labialisation as part of a later, more specific development, resulting in the emergence of a stop. Both the dialectal and the positional scopes of the process appear to be even broader than it was previously noted in relation to the Sinti group and fricatives in final position (Matras 2002, p. 50). Examples include Sinti, where this does not only take place word-finally, as in *biab* < *biav* 'wedding' and *lab* < *lav* 'word, name' (RO-022), but in other positions as well, cf. *koblo* < *kovlo* 'soft.M'; and Hungarian Romungro *sabi* < *savi* in *sabi džēne* 'everybody' (HU-009).

5.6.2 Morphophonological Processes in Northeastern and Finnish Romani

The /a/ vowel of the ablative case marker is realised as an /i/ in the Northeastern group: *thudestar* 'milk.ABL' ~ [thuˈdestɪr], *jarendar* 'egg.PL.ABL' [jaːˈrendɪr], *pšalestar* 'brother.ABL' [pʃaˈlestɪr] (EST-005), which may in turn be centralised in dialects where centralisation is common: *jagatar* 'fire.ABL' [jaːˈgatɨr], *papustar* 'grandfather.ABL' [paːˈpustɨr], *kapustendar* 'cabbage.PL. ABL' [kaːpusˈtendɨr] (LV-005), *phenjatar* 'sister.ABL' [pheˈɲatɨr], *pšalendar* 'brother.PL.ABL' ~ [pʃaˈłendɨr], *tumendar* 'you.PL.ABL' [tuˈmendɨr] (PL-003).

A salient archaism, the inherited synthetic comparative in *-eder* (Matras 2002, p. 234), is affected by a similar process, again only in the Northeastern dialect group: *terneder* 'younger' ~ [terneˈdɪr] (LV-006), *phureder* 'older' [pʰurəˈdɪr] (LT-005), *bliskeder* 'closer' [blɪsˈkədɪr] (PL-014).

The open central /a/ of the first person singular present tense concord marker is replaced by /o/ in Lithuanian Romani, *haľovav* 'I understand' ~ [ɣaljoˈvov] (LT-008), while in Finnish Romani, the /e/ of the nominal suffix *-ipe* changes to /a/: *čōripa* < *čoripe* 'poverty' (FIN-012).

5.7   Syllable Structure

There are no particular restrictions on syllable types in Romani. We encounter words with syllables containing only a single vowel, and individual words may have a CCVCC pattern. Depending on the dialect, the nucleus of a syllable can take the form VV, comprising a diphthong or a long vowel, but under Slavic influence, there are examples of lexemes with a syllabic /r/, too.

As for consonant clusters in onsets and codas, they generally conform to the sonority sequencing principle, which may be overridden by cross-linguistically common exceptions, such as a sibilant plus stop sequence in the onset (*štar* 'four', *skamin* 'chair'). Later borrowings may contain consonant clusters of the form CCC, with the first consonant being a sibilant: *strax* 'fear' (EST-005, RUS-003). Both initial and final consonant clusters can undergo reduction.

5.8 Stress

In the inherited component of Romani, stress tends to be attracted to the final positions of a word. Although this is somewhat ambiguous, if inflection, derivation and the lexicon are considered from a historical linguistic aspect, word-final stress seems to have been the dominant pattern, which is still preserved in many dialects, as we can see on root words from various word classes: *brišín* 'rain', *othár* 'from there', *romní* 'woman', *šošój* 'rabbit', *rikonó* 'dog', *avdivé* 'today'; on derived nominative forms and adjectives, see *xolajpé* 'anger', *rikonoró* 'puppy', *londó* 'salty.M', *khandinó* 'stinking' *balanó* 'of pig/pork.M'; and on inflected forms: *grastén* 'horse.PL.ACC', *kamél* 'he/she wants', *šunáv* 'I hear', *phendóm* 'I said'. Stressed inflectional affixes include the oblique marker for nouns and the personal concord markers for verbs, including mediopassive verbs in most dialects[13]; they operate on borrowed items, as well, for example *veruizáv* 'I believe' and *šišés* 'bottle.ACC' from Macedonian *veruva* 'believe' and *šiše* 'bottle', respectively (MK-012). Adjective derivational suffixes also retain stress when attached to borrowed items: *rēgikó* 'old' from Hungarian *régi* (HU-007). Personal concord markers override any possible stress on verb derivational markers, as well.

This is slightly complicated by a set of additional, unstressed affixes, both nominal and verbal, that are attached to word endings stressed in accordance with those above. These unstressed affixes include nominal case markers (cf. e.g. Friedman 1991 for their evolvement) and the verbal suffixes expressing future (*-a*) and remoteness (*-as/-ahi*). Their unstressed nature and the shift of stress to the oblique marker and the personal concord marker are retained in the whole lexicon, including the borrowed component, cf. e.g. *vikendéske* 'for the weekend' from Macedonian *vikend* 'weekend' (MK-012).

The treatment of the stress of the nominative form of loan words is somewhat more problematic, and there are several possible strategies. The strategy used when the word is borrowed without any adaptation marker is that the original stress is retained, as in *fóro(s)* 'town' < Greek *foros* 'tax' (Matras 2002, p. 63), *limóri* 'grave' < Greek *limori* 'starvation' (Boretzky 1994; Igla 1996), but the different stress pattern is then neutralised in the inflected forms (see above). Early borrowings may also manifest shift of stress to the word-final syllable: *simadjí* 'pawn' < Greek *sīmadi* 'mark'.

In the case of later borrowings, the adaptation markers *-o(s)*, *-u(s)*, *-i(s)* and *-a,* borrowed from Greek, are employed (Matras 2002, p. 81; Elšík 2000, p. 18). As they do not originally belong to the set of stressed suffixes, they do not attract stress by default. For disyllabic words, that is, for words with two syllables including the adaptation marker, this will evidently lead to initial stress: *drúgo* 'friend' < Russian *drug* 'friend' (LT-007), *móros* 'sea' < Russian *more* (EST-005). For trisyllabic words, however, there is no ready-made strategy for placing the stress unambiguously on the first or the second syllable, so it is prone to fluctuation, see *żołnjéžo* 'soldier' < Polish *żołnierz* (PL-018), *údvara* 'yard' < Hungarian *udvar* (RO-072). In addition to that, assimilation to the inherited stress pattern through shift of stress to the final syllable is also possible: *pijací* 'market' < Hungarian *piac* (HU-009), *motorí* 'car' < Czech/Slovak/Hungarian *motor* 'engine' (CZ-001).

A correlation between vowel length and stress is not obvious, see *āláto* 'animal' < Hungarian *állat* (HU-009) or *káštēli* 'castle' < Hungarian *kastély* (SK-059), but there are varieties where lengthened vowels may attract stress, even in the inherited component: *šavóro* 'little boy' (HU-004), *mesáji* 'table' (CZ-001). Stress patterns are further confused in dialects in contact with languages where initial or penultimate stress dominates, which can also extend to the inherited vocabulary, see for example *khángēri* 'church' (SK-052), where stress shifts to the first syllable, while the vowel of the second syllable is lengthened.

Acknowledgement The support of the Hungarian National Research, Development and Innovation Fund (grants K 111961 and K 125596, principal investigator: László Kálmán) is gratefully acknowledged.

Notes

1. A sample number in the Romani Morpho-Syntax Database consists of a numerical code assigned to each sample obtained from a single speaker, preceded by a country code representing the respective country where the recording was made.
2. In some Vlax dialects, like Moldovan Čurari, the second component of the diphthong is lowered: *gav* 'village' ~ [gaọ], *kamav* 'I love' ~ [kaˈmaọ], *anav* 'name' ~ [aˈnaọ], etc. (MD-006). In some Romanian Kalderaš varieties, lowering takes place in the first person singular present tense personal concord

marker, for example, *dikhav* ' I see' [di'kʰaǫ], but not elsewhere: *gav* 'village' [gav] (RO-065).

3. In Vlax dialects, the first person singular perfective marker underwent loss of palatalisation and a subsequent umlaut: *-em* < *-j-om* (Matras 2002, p. 139).

4. As Anton Tenser noted through personal communication, the Lotfitka and Xaladytka varieties spoken in Latvia also exhibit this kind of fortition, with forms containing both the post-alveolar /ʃ/ and the alveolar /s/: *khil* 'butter' > *ksil*, *phir-* 'walk' > *psir-*, *dikh* 'see' > *diks-*.

5. Most probably in accordance with the consonants used in the contact language, they are pronounced as either alveo-palatal [t͡ɕ, d͡ʑ], as in South Slavic, or palato-alveolar [d͡ʒ, t͡ʃ], as in North Slavic, Hungarian, Romanian, etc.

6. According to Boretzky (2001), palatalisation might be behind the disappearance of /n/ from the singular form of such lexical items as *paj* 'water' and *phej* 'sister' in Kalderaš.

7. Although even here, there are exceptions: *pānji* 'water' ~ ['pa:ɲi] (HU-009).

8. These dialects show signs that are often considered as characteristics of 'transitional' varieties, like Gurvari.

9. The /v/ in the inflected forms is usually retained: *čhaves* (RO-004)/*cāves* (FIN-012) 'boy' ACC., but see Kangljari and Xoraxani *čhajes* (RO-064, BG-023), where it is replaced by a glide.

10. See also the optional deletion of the stem-final /j/ in Hungarian Romungro: *čhaj* alongside *čha* (HU-009).

11. The alternation between /s/ and /h/ in grammatical paradigms affecting the copula, the remoteness marker *-as/-ahi*, interrogatives and determiners, the second person singular and first person plural future forms, as well as the singular instrumental suffix is discussed in detail by Matras (1999).

12. The fluctuation of /h/ is not unusual, cf. *atjar-* (RUS-005), *ačar-* (YU-015) and *hačar-* (HU-004) 'understand'.

13. In the contracted third person singular present tense form, stress may shift to the stem in a few dialects, perhaps as a result of the contraction, see *bárol* 'he/she grows' instead of *bāról* (RUS-005); see also Matras (2002, p. 63).

References

Adamou, Evangelia, and Amalia Arvaniti. 2014. Greek Thrace Xoraxane Romane (illustrations of the IPA). *Journal of the International Phonetic Association* 44 (2): 223–231.

Ariste, Paul. 1978. On two intonations in a Romani dialect. *Estonian Papers in Phonetics* 1978: 5–7.

Arvaniti, Amalia. 2016. Analytical decisions in intonation research and the role of representations: Lessons from Romani. *Laboratory Phonology: Journal of the Association for Laboratory Phonology* 7 (1): 1–43.

152   M. A. Baló

Arvaniti, Amalia, and Evangelia Adamou. 2011. Focus expression in Romani. In *Proceedings of the 28th West Coast conference on formal linguistics*, ed. Mary Byram Washburn, Katherine McKinney-Bock, Erika Varis, Ann Sawyer, and Barbara Tomaszewicz, 240–248. Somerville, MA: Cascadilla Proceedings Project.

Bodnárová, Zuzana. 2015. Vend Romani: Grammatical description and socio-linguistic situation of the so-called Vend dialects of Romani. PhD dissertation, Charles University, Prague.

Boretzky, Norbert. 1991. Contact induced sound change. *Diachronica* 8: 1–16.

Boretzky, Norbert. 1993. *Bugurdži: deskriptiver und historischer Abriß eines Romani-Dialekts*. Wiesbaden: Harrassowitz.

Boretzky, Norbert. 1994. *Romani. Grammatik des Kalderaš-Dialekts mit Texten und Glossar*. Wiesbaden: Harrassowitz.

Boretzky, Norbert. 2001. Palatalisation and depalatalisation in Romani. *Sprachtypologie Und Universalienforschung* 54 (2): 108–125.

Boretzky, Norbert. 2003. *Die Vlach-Dialekte des Romani*. Wiesbaden: Harrassowitz.

Boretzky, Norbert, and Birgit Igla. 1993. *Lautwandel und Natürlichkeit. Kontaktbedingter und endogener Wandel im Romani* (Arbeitspapiere des Projekts 'Prinzipien der Sprachwandels' 15). Essen: Universität GH Essen, Fachbereich Sprach- und Literaturwissenschaften.

Boretzky, Norbert, and Birgit Igla. 2004. *Kommentierter Dialektatlas des Romani*. Wiesbaden: Harrassowitz.

Elšík, Viktor. 2000. Romani nominal paradigms. In *Grammatical relations in Romani: The noun phrase*, ed. Viktor Elšík and Yaron Matras, 9–30. Amsterdam: John Benjamins.

Elšík, Viktor, Milena Hübschmannová, and Hana Šebková. 1999. The Southern Central (ahi-imperfect) Romani dialects of Slovakia and Northern Hungary. In *Die Sprache der Roma. Perspektiven der Romani-Forschung in Österreich im interdisziplinären und internazionalen Kontext*, ed. Dieter W. Halwachs and Florian Menz, 277–390. Klagenfurt: Drava.

Friedman, Victor A. 1991. Case in Romani: Old grammar in new affixes. *Journal of the Gypsy Lore Society*, 5th Ser., 1 (1):85–102.

Friedman, Victor A. 2001. Romani multilingualism in its Balkan context. *Sprachtypologie Und Universalienforschung* 54 (2): 148–161.

Gardner, David J., and Sarolta A. Gardner. 2008. A provisional phonology of Romani. *Romani Studies* 18 (2): 155–199.

Granqvist, Kimmo. 2007. *Suomen romanin äänne- ja muotorakenne* (Suomen itämaisen seuran suomenkielisiä julkaisuja 36; Kotimaisten kielten tutkimuskeskuksen julkaisuja 145). Helsinki: Suomen itämainen seura & Kotimaisten kielten tutkimuskeskus.

Granqvist, Kimmo. 2009. Two hundred years of Romani linguistics. *Studia Orientalia* 108: 245–265.

Grigorova, Evelina. 2001. Intonatorische Formula im Kalderaš und Sofia-Erli. In *Was ich noch sagen wollte – a multilingual Festschrift for Norbert Boretzky on occasion of his 65th birthday*, ed. Birgit Igla and Thomas Stolz, 369–388. Berlin: Akademie Verlag.

Harris, Alice C. 2017. *Multiple exponence*. Oxford: Oxford University Press.

Holzinger, Daniel. 1993. *Das Romanes: Grammatik un Diskursanalyse der Sprache der Sinte* (Innsbrucker Beiträge zur Kulturwissenschaft 85). Innsbruck: Verlag des Instituts für Sprachwissenschaft der Universität Innsbruck.

Hualde, José Ignacio, and Marianna Nadeu. 2011. Lenition and phonemic overlap in Rome Italian. *Phonetica* 68: 215–242.

Igla, Birgit. 1996. *Das Romani von Ajia Varvara*. Wiesbaden: Harrassowitz.

Matras, Yaron. 1999. s/h alternation in Romani: An historical and functional interpretation. *Grazer Linguistische Studien* 51: 99–129.

Matras, Yaron. 2002. *Romani: A linguistic introduction*. Cambridge: Cambridge University Press.

Miklosich, Franz. 1872–1880. *Über die Mundarten und Wanderungen der Zigeuner Europas*. Vienna: Karl Gerold's Sohn.

Scala, Andrea. 2018. Italo-Romance phonological rules and Indo-Aryan lexicon: The case of Abruzzian Romani. In *Advances in Italian dialectology: Sketches of Italo-Romance grammars*, ed. Roberta D'Alessandro and Diego Pescarini, 165–187. Brill: Leiden.

Vekerdi, József. 1985. *Cigány nyelvjárási népmesék*. Debrecen: Kossuth Lajos Tudományegyetem.

6

Romani Morphology

Viktor Elšík

6.1 Introduction

The chapter presents a concise overview of the morphological structure of words in the Romani language. While it focuses on the morphology of the major word classes, viz. verbs, nouns, adjectives, and adverbs, which are well distinguished in Romani in terms of their inflectional behaviour, morphology of minor words classes, such as the copula, the article, pro-words, and quantifiers, is also considered whenever relevant. I draw on data from numerous grammatical descriptions of different Romani dialects[1] and numerous studies on Romani morphology, as well as on mostly unpublished fieldwork data on varieties of Central Romani (cf. Elšík et al., in prep.).[2] Dialect-specific examples of morphological structures are identified as such, while examples without a dialect specification represent conservative and/or cross-dialectally widespread structures.

Section 6.2 presents a brief overview of research on Romani morphology. Section 6.3 outlines the typological aspects of Romani morphology. Sections 6.4 and 6.6 are devoted, respectively, to inflection and morphological word-formation (i.e. derivation, compounding, and conversion) in

---

This chapter was supported by the Charles University project Progres Q10, *Language in the shiftings of time, space, and culture*

V. Elšík (✉)
Charles University, Prague, Czech Republic
e-mail: viktor.elsik@ff.cuni.cz

© The Author(s) 2020
Y. Matras and A. Tenser (eds.), *The Palgrave Handbook of Romani Language and Linguistics*, https://doi.org/10.1007/978-3-030-28105-2_6

different word classes, and Sect. 6.5 discusses morphological integration of lexical borrowings. Inflectional and derivational classes are discussed in Sect. 6.7. The final part of the chapter (Sect. 6.8) highlights salient and cross-linguistically interesting morphological features of Romani and outlines the prospects for further research in Romani morphology.

6.2 Research on Romani Morphology

Romani morphology is mainly described, in different degrees of detail, in numerous grammatical descriptions of individual Romani varieties, including descriptions dedicated to morphology (e.g. Miltner 1965). In addition, there are several detailed synchronic studies of specific morphological structures and their functions in a single dialect (e.g. Ariste [1973] on aktionsart prefixes in Latvian Romani, Hübschmannová [1984] on word-formation in Slovak Romani, Cech [1996] on the inflectional vs. derivational status of valency morphology in Sepečides, Holzinger [1996] on the role of the category of aspect in the thematic organization of narrative texts in German Sinti, Rusakov [2001] on imperatives in Russian Romani, or Pirttisaari [2005] on participle marking in Finnish Romani).

Numerous morphological studies on Romani assume a comparative perspective, providing overviews of a morphological topic across Romani dialects (e.g. Matras [2001] on TAM categories or Schrammel [2005] on aktionsart prefixes), often accompanied by a reconstruction of the relevant Proto-Romani structures (e.g. Boretzky [1995] on copula inflection, Boretzky [2000] on the inflection of the definite article, or Elšík [2000b] and Matras [2000] on the morphology of personal and demonstrative pronouns, respectively). Several papers research the Indo-Aryan sources of Romani morphological structures (e.g. Woolner [1924] and Bloch [1932] on the copula, Schmid [1963] on the suffix of abstract nominalizations, Beníšek [2009] on two denominal adverbial markers, or Beníšek [2010] on several non-finite verb forms). A general cross-dialectal and diachronic overview of Romani morphology can be found especially in the introduction to Romani linguistics by Matras (2002, pp. 42–45, 72–164) and in the textual part of the Romani dialect atlas by Boretzky and Igla (2004, pp. 65–207).

Many studies on Romani focus on borrowing in the morphological domain (e.g. Bakker [1997] on borrowing of loanword adaptation markers and patterns, Rusakov and Abramenko [1998] on interference in the case system, Boretzky [2013] on loanword gender assignment, or Friedman [2013] on borrowing and morphological integration of Turkish verbs), including several overviews of morphological borrowings (esp. Eloeva and Rusakov 1990; Boretzky and Igla 1991; Boretzky 1998, 1999). In addition, Romani morphological structures are also discussed in numerous general works on aspects of language contact (e.g. Comrie 2008, pp. 19–21 on borrowing of inflectional morphology or Wohlgemut 2009, pp. 98, 119–120, 224–225 on adaptation of loanverbs). Aspects of Romani morphology are often analysed in a broader typological and theoretical context (e.g. Friedman [1991] on the suffix status of Romani case markers or Koptjevskaja-Tamm [2000] on the typological properties of Romani genitives) and Romani morphological data are discussed in several general works in linguistic typology (e.g. Plank 1995, pp. 11–13 on double case marking) and morphological theory (e.g. Stump 1993, pp. 450–451 on rules of referral and syncretisms in Welsh Romani verb inflection).

6.3   Morphological Typology

Romani is a language with rich inflectional and derivational morphology and a relatively high degree of synthesis. Inflections may consist of up to three suffixes and one prefix and there are often several derivational affixes in a word. Polysynthetic word forms are well attested in several dialects, e.g. Welsh Romani *muter-im-aŋ-er-īa-ker-es-k-ō* [micturate-NOUN-OBL.PL-GEN-OBL.SG.F-GEN-OBL.SG.M-GEN-NOM.SG.M] 'of a tea-hawker', which is an inflectional genitive of a double onomasiological genitive (cf. *muter-im-aŋ-er-ī* 'tea', literally 'one of micturation'), or Selice Romani *bi-basť-āz-atat-in-av-ker-ď-om-ahi*   [PRIV-luck-VERB-CAUS-LOAN-CAUS-FREQ-PFV-1SG.PFV-REM] 'I would have often made [so.] call for misfortune', which is an inflectional counterfactual conditional form of a frequentative of a causative of a denominal verb; however, they do not occur frequently in discourse.

Affixation is the prevailing morphological operation, as non-concatenative morphology is absent or marginal, depending on dialect. Different types of reduplication have developed in some dialects. For example, Sepečides, partly as a borrowing from Turkish, has instances of exact full root reduplication, e.g. *dum-dum-es-te* [back~back-OBL.SG.M-LOC] 'back on back' (← *dum-o* 'back'), inexact full form reduplication, e.g. *čhave-mave* 'children and the like' (← *čhav-e* [child-NOM.PL] 'children') or *zurano-murano* 'strong and the like' (← *zur-an-o* [strength-ADJ-NOM.SG.M] 'strong'), and inexact partial root reduplication, e.g. *lop-lol-o* 'intensely red, scarlet' (← *lol-o* 'red') or *pap-parn-o* 'snow-white' (← *parn-o* 'white'). Some of the reduplications may be inherited from Proto-Romani, cf. *dum-dum-e-sa* [back~back-OBL.SG.M-SOC] 'back on back' also in Austrian Lovari. Modification (i.e. phonological alternation independent of affixation) is only attested as a marginal morphological means in a few dialects. In Selice Romani, for example, some adjectives encode their attributive dependency by means of a shortening of their lexical vowel, e.g. *kōl-o* 'soft' → attributive *kol-o*.

Most affixes are external to roots and continuous, while discontinuous affixes or roots seem to be unattested. Prefixes are more restricted than suffixes, both paradigmatically and syntagmatically. Although a single prefix may be reconstructed for Proto-Romani, viz. privative *bi-* in adjective derivation, e.g. *bi-čač-o* 'untrue' (← *čač-o* 'true'), numerous dialects have borrowed prefixes from, or grammaticalized prefixes on the model of, their L2s in functions such as the superlative degree, e.g. *neg-bar-eder* 'the biggest' (← *bar-eder* [big-NPOS] 'bigger'); pronominal indefiniteness and/or negation, e.g. *vare-kon* 'somebody' and *ni-kon* 'nobody' (← *kon* 'who'); aktionsart, e.g. *do-ker-* 'to finish doing' (← *ker-* 'to do'); and more. Instances of several prefixes in a word form are rare, e.g. Selice Romani *leg-bi-bast-al-eder* [SUP-PRIV-luck-ADJ-NPOS] 'the least lucky', which is the superlative of a privative derivation. Suffixes, on the other hand, are numerous and functionally much more varied in all dialects and there are often several suffixes per word (see the polysynthetic word forms above).

While most affixes are separative or monoexponential, some inflectional suffixes are cumulative or polyexponential in that they express values of several inflectional categories simultaneously, viz. case and number in nouns, e.g. vocative plural *-ale(n)*; case, number, and gender in adjectives, e.g. nominative singular feminine *-i*; and person, number, and aspect in verbs, e.g. perfective first person plural *-jam-*. Affixes with a different type of exponence frequently combine within an inflectional formant, e.g. dative plural *-en-ge* [-OBL.PL-DAT] (i.e. cumulative plus separative) in nouns; oblique singular feminine comparative *-eder-a* [-NPOS-OBL.SG.F] (i.e. separative plus cumulative) in adjectives; and first person plural irrealis *-d-jam-asi* [-PFV-1PL.PFV-REM] (i.e. separative plus cumulative plus separative) in verbs.

Many affixes display suppletive alternations, which contribute to the existence of relatively numerous morphological, i.e. inflectional and derivational, classes (see Sect. 6.7). Root suppletion, on the other hand, is relatively rare, widespread examples being: case suppletion in third person pronouns, e.g. nominative *o-n* [3.NOM-NOM.PL] 'they' vs. oblique *(o)l-en-* [3.OBL-OBL.PL-] 'them'; aspect suppletion in a few verbs, e.g. non-perfective *dža-* 'to go' vs. perfective *ge-l-* [go.PFV-PFV-]; and degree suppletion in a few adjectives, e.g. positive *lačh-o* 'good' vs. non-positive *f-eder* [good.NPOS-NPOS] 'better, the best'. Morphophonological allomorphy may affect both affixes and roots, e.g. Zargari *dikh-es-°* [see-2SG-SBJV] 'you see' vs. *dukh-āv-°* [see-1SG-SBJV] 'I see' with regressive vowel harmony, and *māng-us-°* [want-2SG-SBJV] 'you want' with a progressive one.

6.4 Inflectional Morphology

6.4.1 Verbal Inflection

Both lexical verbs and the copula inflect for tense–mood. Lexical verbs also inflect for aspect and, in some dialects, mirativity and/or evidentiality. All verbs cross-reference the categories of the grammatical subject (person, number and, in some dialects and structural contexts, also gender) in finite forms. Pronominal direct objects may be cliticized to transitive verbs and a few dialects have developed irregular object enclitics, e.g. Epiros Romani *dikhav= i* 'I see her' (cf. full *ola* 'her'), or even fused the object enclitics with subject-inflected verb forms, e.g. Abruzzian Romani *dikkašt < *dikhas tut* 'we see you' (cf. Elšík and Matras 2006, p. 212). Valency morphology is usually treated as derivational, although it is very productive in some dialects (see Sect. 6.6.2). Negation is mostly analytical, though third person negative copula forms may be synthetic and irregular, e.g. affirmative *si* 'is', *sas* 'was' vs. negative *naj* 'is not' and *nās* 'was not' in Slovak Lovari. The only inherited non-finite form is the perfective participle, which has adjectival inflection and which may also be used finitely (see below). The Proto-Romani non-perfective participle and converb in *-(i)nd-* as well as the perfective converb in *-i* (cf. Beníšek 2010, pp. 71–79) are no longer productive and must be considered to be deverbal derivations synchronically (see Sects. 6.6.4–6.6.5). While the Indo-Aryan infinitive has been refunctionalized in Romani (cf. Beníšek 2010, pp. 53–71), some dialects have developed a novel infinitive through fossilization of a finite subjunctive form (cf. Boretzky 1996).

The categories of tense–mood and aspect combine into several TAM values (and sets of forms). Proto-Romani lexical verbs may be reconstructed (cf. Matras 2001) to have possessed the imperative (e.g. *ker* 'do!'), the subjunctive (e.g. *keres* '[that] you do'), the present–future (e.g. *keresa* 'you do, will do'), the imperfect (e.g. *keresasi* 'you were doing, would do'), the aorist / preterite / perfective (e.g. *kerdjal* 'you did, have done, will have done'), and the pluperfect (e.g. *kerdjalasi* 'you had been doing, would have done'). The aorist and the pluperfect have been analysed as expressing the perfective aspect, while the other TAM values may be interpreted as non-perfective (cf. Matras 2001, p. 165). The imperfect and the pluperfect have been analysed as expressing 'remoteness' or contextual inaccessibility, which accounts for their various past, conditional, and other uses (cf. Matras 2001, pp. 165–166).

The remote forms have been lost in some dialects (e.g. imperfect in some Gurbet varieties and the pluperfect in some varieties of North Central Romani) and some dialects only retain their modal uses: in Finnish Romani, for example, the non-perfective remote form has no past uses (e.g. *čērehas* 'you would do' < **keresasi*). In other dialects, the remote forms have been renewed through grammaticalization of periphrastic copular constructions (e.g. Skopje Arli *kerejaine* < **keresa(s) sine*). In the non-remote non-perfective domain, the originally subjunctive ('short') form has, in some dialects, taken over the present functions of the original present–future ('long') form, so that there is now a distinction between a present and a future but no indicative vs. subjunctive opposition (e.g. Podunajské Biskupice Romani *keres* 'you do' vs. *keresa* 'you will do'). Independent of this development, the future has been innovated through grammaticalization of various (e.g. de-volitive, de-necessitative, and de-venitive) periphrastic constructions in some dialects and there are now some dialects that differentiate the subjunctive, the present, and the future (e.g. Ajios Athanasios Romani *keres* '[that] you do' vs. *kerea* < **keresa* 'you do' vs. *ke* = *keres* 'you will do'). Less commonly, de-volitive marking may also renew the conditional mood (e.g. Kaspichan Romani *kan* = *keresa* 'you would do' and *kan* = *keresas* 'you would have done', in addition to the future *kan* = *keres* 'you will do'). The 'long' form may also be specialized for declarative or prospective conditional uses (cf. Matras 2001, pp. 174–175). Some Sinti dialects differentiate the subjunctive and two sets of present–future forms (e.g. *keres* '[that] you do' vs. *kerē* and *kerehə* < **keresa* 'you do, will do'). Several dialects have developed periphrastic perfects and pluperfects (e.g. Finnish Romani *som čerdom* 'I have done' and *sommas čerdom* 'I had done').

The inflection for the person and number of the grammatical subject results in six category combinations per TAM value (e.g. aorist *kerdjom* 'I did', *kerdjal* 'you did', *kerdjas* 's/he did', *kerdjam* 'we did', *kerdjan* 'you's did', *kerde* 'they did'). Proto-Romani had a general syncretism of the second and third persons in the non-perfective plural forms, which has been extended to perfective and/or singular contexts as well in some dialects (cf. Elšík and Matras 2006, pp. 121–124), e.g. *soven* 'you's slept, they sleep', *sovēs* 'you were sleeping, s/he was sleeping', and *sovals* 'you slept, s/he slept' in German Sinti. In some Romani varieties of Ukraine, person is completely neutralized in plural perfective forms, e.g. *sute* 'we, you's, they slept' (cf. Elšík and

6 Romani Morphology   161

Matras 2006, p. 124). In the imperative mood, only the second person singular form is morphologically dedicated, while all the other imperative (–hortative) forms are syncretic with the subjunctive. Those dialects that retain the so-called active participles in the third person singular of perfective intransitives also cross-reference the gender of the subject in these forms (e.g. aorist *gelo* 'he went' vs. *geli* 'she went'). In a few dialects, the gender-marking forms contrast with gender-indifferent forms (e.g. aorist *geljas* 's/he went') and encode surprise, unexpectedness, or inference, and so the category of mirativity and/or evidentiality (cf. Matras 1995).

In the inherited system, all verb inflection markers are suffixes. Closest to the inflectional stem are aspect suffixes, followed by person–number suffixes (which are differentiated for aspect, e.g. non-perfective *-es-* vs. perfective *-al-* in the second person singular), followed by tense–mood suffixes. (See Sect. 6.7 for further segmentation of the person–number markers.) The most complex are the perfective forms, with all three types of suffixes in the inflectional formant, e.g. pluperfect *ker-d-jal-asi* [do-PFV-2SG.PFV-REM]; the final, tense–mood, suffix has a zero realization in the aorist, e.g. *ker-d-jal-°* [do-PFV-2SG.PFV-NREM]. (The inflectional stem plus the perfective suffix constitute the perfective stem, e.g. *ker-d-* ← *ker-* 'to do', though several verbs have irregular (or even suppletive, see Sect. 6.3) perfective stems in most dialects, e.g. *su-t-* ← *sov-* 'to sleep'.) Most non-perfective forms do not contain any aspect marking, and so the inflectional formant consists of two suffixes only, e.g. imperfect *ker-es-asi* [do-2SG.NPFV-REM] and present (or future, etc., in some dialects) *ker-es-a* [do-2SG.NPFV-NREM]; the final suffix has a zero realization in the subjunctive (or present, in some dialects), e.g. *ker-es-°* [do-2SG.NPFV-SBJV]. Only the so-called middle verbs (see Sect. 6.6.2) show overt non-perfective marking, e.g. *mat-jov-es-°* [drunk-MID.NPFV-2SG.NPFV-SBJV] '[that] you get drunk' (vs. perfective *mat-il-jal-°* [drunk-PFV-2SG.PFV-NREM] 'you got drunk'). Finally, in the second person singular imperative form, there is a single suffix that marks all the inflectional categories cumulatively, e.g. *phurd-e* [breathe-IMP.2SG] 'breathe!'; the suffix has a zero realization with most verbs, e.g. *ker-°* [do-IMP.2SG] 'do!'. The perfective participles mostly contain the perfective suffix and an adjectival inflection, e.g. *ker-d-o* [do-PFV-NOM.SG.M] 'done', though the participial marker may also be distinct from the perfective suffix.

While renewed imperfects retain the inherited structure, e.g. Skopje Arli *ker-ej-aine* [do-2SG.NPFV-REM], de-volitive futures and conditionals involve a proclitic marker, e.g. Ajios Athanasios Romani *ke=ker-es-°* [FUT=do-2SG.NPFV-SBJV] 'you will do', which is described as a prefix in some sources. In a few dialects, the perfective forms have undergone a major

162   V. Elšík

restructuring: the perfective stem is now identical to the inflectional stem (i.e. it does not contain an aspect suffix and does not involve any irregularities), and the perfective aspect is marked exclusively by the perfective person–number suffixes, e.g. *sov-al-°* [sleep-2SG.PFV-NREM] in Manuš, replacing older *su-t-al-°* [sleep-PFV-2SG.PFV-NREM].

A sample Proto-Romani inflectional paradigm of a verb (*ker-* 'to do, to make') is shown in Table 6.1; only the dedicated (2SG) imperative form is shown and the perfective participle is represented by its stem:

The copula shows numerous inflectional irregularities *vis-à-vis* lexical verbs. It does not encode aspect, and tense–mood distinctions tend to be more numerous than those in lexical verbs. In Podunajské Biskupice Romani, for example, there are eight tense–mood values in the copula (as against six TAM values in lexical verbs): the imperative (e.g. *ov* 'be!'), the present indicative (e.g. *ssal* 'you are'), the preterite indicative (e.g. *ssaláj* 'you were'), the present subjunctive (e.g. *oves* '[that] you are'), the preterite subjunctive (e.g. *ūñal* '[that] you were'), the future (e.g. *ovesa* 'you will be'), the hypothetical conditional (e.g. *ovesáj* 'you would be'), and the counterfactual conditional (e.g. *ūñaláj* 'you would have been'). The copula has several suppletive roots, with non-indicative (including future) forms provided by verbs indicating a change of state (e.g. *ov-* 'to become', perfective stem *ū-ň-*, in the above example). The non-third person indicative copula forms show deponency, in that they parallel the *perfective* forms of lexical verbs in their person–number marking, e.g. the present *h-al-°* [COP.IND-2SG-NREM] 'you are' and the preterite *h-al-s* [COP.IND-2SG-REM] 'you were' in German Sinti

Table 6.1   Proto-Romani inflectional paradigm of the verb *ker-*

IMP	*k̍er-°*		
1SG	*ker-ˈav-°*	*ker-ˈav-a*	*ker-ˈav-asi*
2SG	*ker-ˈes-°*	*ker-ˈes-a*	*ker-ˈes-asi*
3SG	*ker-ˈel-°*	*ker-ˈel-a*	*ker-ˈel-asi*
1PL	*ker-ˈas-°*	*ker-ˈas-a*	*ker-ˈas-asi*
2PL	*ker-ˈen-°*	*ker-ˈen-a*	*ker-ˈen-asi*
3PL	*ker-ˈen-°*	*ker-ˈen-a*	*ker-ˈen-asi*
	SUBJ	PFUT	IMPF
PTC	*ker-d–ˈ*		
1SG	*ker-d-ˈjom-°*		*ker-d-ˈjom-asi*
2SG	*ker-d-ˈjal-°*		*ker-d-ˈjal-asi*
3SG	*ker-d-ˈjas-°*		*ker-d-ˈjas-asi*
1PL	*ker-d-ˈjam-°*		*ker-d-ˈjam-asi*
2PL	*ker-d-ˈjan-°*		*ker-d-ˈjan-asi*
3PL	*ker-d-ˈe-°*		*ker-d-ˈes-asi*
	AOR		PLPF

paralleling, respectively, the aorist *sov-al-°* [sleep-2sg.pfv-nrem] 'you slept' and the pluperfect *sov-al-s* [sleep-2sg.pfv-rem], and may even show (quasi-) perfective suffixes in some dialects, e.g. the preterite *s-t'-al-ahi* [cop.ind-pfv-2sg-rem] 'you were' paralleling the counterfactual *res-t'-al-ahi* [reach-pfv-2sg.pfv-rem] 'you would have reached' in Klenovec Romani.

6.4.2 Nominal Inflection

Lexical nouns inflect for the paradigmatic categories of nominal case and number and have an inherent gender, masculine vs. feminine, which surfaces in forms agreeing with nouns. Though animacy is indirectly relevant for noun inflection, it is not an inflectional category in a strict sense (see below and cf. Elšík 2000a, pp. 10–12). A few dialects have developed the category of associative plurality in names of persons and nouns denoting professions (cf. Elšík and Matras 2006, pp. 322–323). Several dialects have lost case inflection in lexical nouns (and some even in pronouns), with lexically restricted remnants of non-nominative cases analysable as denominal derivations (cf. Elšík and Matras 2006, pp. 317–318). Gender dissolution in nouns is only attested in the non-native varieties of Finnish Romani, where dedicated masculine markers optionally extend to the inflection of the original feminines (e.g. Granqvist 2012, p. 36).

The category of nominal case has eight values (usually termed nominative, vocative, accusative, dative, locative, ablative, sociative/instrumental, and genitive) in most dialects, though several dialects have lost the vocative and there are several dialect-specific instances of case mergers. For example, the ablative has taken over the functions of the locative in Polish Romani, completely replacing its forms, and in Zargari the ablative took over the sociative and the dative merged with the genitive. Although the genitives typically agree in adjectival case, number, and gender with their head nouns, displaying *Suffixaufnahme*, they are better analysed as inflectional (sets of) forms of nouns rather than denominal possessive adjectives (cf. Koptjevskaja-Tamm 2000). In several dialects, the genitive has developed two phonologically distinct and functionally specialized variants (e.g. predicative vs. attributive genitives in Welsh Romani, or postposed vs. preposed genitives in Slovak Lovari). Novel case values, such as the illative (e.g. Vysoká Romani illative *Požombu* 'to Bratislava' vs. locative *Požombate* 'in Bratislava'), are rare and semantically restricted. Inanimate nouns usually do not form the accusative, as inanimate direct objects are mostly marked by the nominative; nevertheless, inanimate accusatives do occur in certain structural contexts in

164   V. Elšík

some dialects (cf. Lípa 1967; Elšík 2000a, pp. 10–12). Case syncretism is restricted to nominative–accusative homonymy in some inflectional classes in a few dialects (cf. Elšík and Matras 2006, pp. 92–93). The category of number differentiates two values, the singular and the plural, which are consistently distinguished in all cases. A single exception is the nominative, where some dialects exhibit number syncretism in one masculine inflectional class (e.g. *murš* 'man, men').

All nominal inflection markers are suffixes. Closest to the inflectional stem are cumulative case–number (or Layer I or internal case) suffixes, followed by separative case (or Layer II or external case) suffixes (whose status as suffixes rather than enclitic postpositions has been clearly established by Friedman 1991), followed by adjectival agreement suffixes. (See Sect. 6.7 for further segmentation of the case–number markers.) The marking of nominal case thus has a layered character (e.g. Matras 1997). The nominative (and vocative) forms contain the cumulative case–number suffix alone, e.g. nominative singular *gadž-o* [nonRom-NOM.SG] 'non-Rom' and nominative plural *gadž-e* [nonRom-NOM.PL] 'non-Roms'; the suffix has a zero realization in some inflection classes in the nominative (only singular in some dialects), e.g. *murš-°* [man-NOM(.SG)] 'man, (men)'. In most of the other case forms, the inflectional formant consists of two suffixes: one that marks the oblique (i.e. the set of oblique cases) and number cumulatively and a separative case suffix, e.g. dative singular *gadž-es-ke* [nonRom-OBL.SG-DAT] and dative plural *gadž-en-ge* [nonRom-OBL.PL-DAT]. In other words, the oblique forms are based on oblique stems, which consist of the inflectional stem plus an oblique suffix, e.g. *gadž-es-* and *gadž-en-*. In most dialects, the separative case suffix has a zero realization in the accusative, e.g. singular *gadž-es-°* [nonRom-OBL.SG-ACC] and plural *gadž-en-°* [nonRom -OBL.PL-ACC], though in some dialects the accusative singular of masculines must be derived from the oblique singular stem by an elision of the final phoneme, e.g. OBL *gadž-es-* → ACC *gadž-e*, which makes its structure less transparent (cf. Elšík 2000a, p. 13). Overt accusative marking is exceptional, e.g. Gemerská Hôrka Romani *gādž-e-t* [nonRom-OBL.SG-ACC]. Finally, the most complex are the genitive forms, which contain three suffixes: an oblique suffix and the genitive suffix are part of genitive stems, e.g. singular *gadž-es-ker-* [nonRom-OBL.SG-GEN-] 'of a non-Rom' and plural *gadž-en-ger-* [nonRom-OBL.PL-GEN-] 'of non-Roms', and the final suffix marks adjectival agreement, e.g. *gadž-es-ker-e* [nonRom-OBL.SG-GEN-NOM.PL] '(they) of a non-Rom'.

A sample Proto-Romani inflectional paradigm of a noun (*gadžo* M 'non-Rom') is shown in Table 6.2; the genitive is represented by genitive stems:

6 Romani Morphology 165

Table 6.2 Proto-Romani inflectional paradigm of the noun *gadžo*

	SG	PL
NOM	gadž-ʹo	gadž-ʹe
VOC	gadž-ʹeja	gadž-ʹale
ACC	gadž-ʹes-	gadž-ʹen-
DAT	gadž-ʹes-ke	gadž-ʹen-ge
LOC	gadž-ʹes-te	gadž-ʹen-de
ABL	gadž-ʹes-tar	gadž-ʹen-dar
SOC	gadž-ʹes-sa	gadž-ʹen-sa
GEN	gadž-ʹes-ker-	gadž-ʹen-ger-

Pronouns (i.e. nominal pro-words) show various inflectional irregularities *vis-à-vis* lexical nouns. Of all pronouns, only the singular third person pronouns encode gender (cf. *ov* 'he' vs. *oj* 'she'), though some dialects have lost the distinction in the nominative due to convergence with genderless languages (cf. Elšík and Matras 2006, p. 142). Number is generally encoded in personal pronouns and, in some dialects, also in reflexives, while interrogatives, indefinites, etc., are number-indifferent in most dialects. Personal pronouns may, in some dialects, be the only nominals to retain case inflection and may have more case distinctions than nouns, such as a special prepositional case form (e.g. *ma* distinct from the accusative *man* 'me') or two sets of nominative forms (e.g. the independent *ov* and the enclitic *lo* 'he'). There are numerous marking irregularities in pronouns, including case suppletion in third person pronouns (see Sect. 6.3) or irregular marking of genitives of non-third person and some reflexive pronouns (cf. Elšík 2000b, pp. 78–80).

6.4.3 Adjectival Inflection

Adjectivals, a word class centred around lexical adjectives, typically agree with their heads in adjectival case, number, and gender, though many dialects also have a class of uninflected adjectivals. Case agreement of adjectivals may be suspended with inanimate head nouns and several dialects now lack case agreement in general (cf. Elšík 2000a, pp. 25–26). Also, in some dialects, number and gender agreement is lost in predicative adjectivals (cf. Matras 2002, p. 95). A few dialects have developed an inflectional distinction between attributive and predicative forms of adjectivals.

The category of adjectival case has only two values, the nominative and the oblique, and thus differs from nominal case. While the adjectival nominative is used in agreement with nominative head nouns, the adjectival oblique case is used with any of the several oblique cases (see Sect. 6.4.2) of the head noun, e.g. *lače gadžeske* [good.OBL.SG.M # nonRom(M).DAT.SG] 'to a good non-Rom' and *lače gadžestar* [good.OBL.SG.M # nonRom(M).ABL.SG] 'from a good non-Rom'. In other words, adjectivals only index the distinction between the internal (Layer I) case suffixes of nouns and may be said to show deflected case agreement. Nevertheless, adjectivals are generally nominalized and inflected for nominal case when they are employed as heads of noun phrases, either in postposition to nouns, e.g. *gadžeske lačheske* [nonRom(M).DAT.SG # good.DAT.SG.M] 'to a non-Rom, the good one', or when the nominal head is elided, e.g. *lačheske* 'to a good one' [good.DAT.SG.M]. In some dialects in contact with Slavic, adjectivals have developed full case agreement, inflecting for nominal case even when preposed, e.g. *lačheske gadžeske* [good.DAT.SG.M # nonRom(M).DAT.SG] 'to a good non-Rom'. Gender is generally neutralized in the plural and most dialects neutralize both gender and number in the oblique case (while a minority of dialects retain a distinct form for the feminine singular oblique). Case may be neutralized in some inflectional classes of adjectives (cf. Elšík 2000a, p. 25).

The categories of adjectival agreement are mostly marked cumulatively, within a single suffix, e.g. *lač-o* [good-NOM.SG.M], which may have a zero realization in the base form, e.g. Sepečides *šukar-°* [nice-NOM] contrasting with *šukar-e* [nice-OBL]. In some inflectional classes of adjectives, however, the cumulative suffix may be preceded by a separative case suffix in the oblique case, e.g. *ungrik-on-a* [Hungarian.ADJ-OBL-OBL.SG.F] in Eastern Uzh Romani.

A sample Proto-Romani inflectional paradigm of an adjective (*lačho* 'good') is shown in Table 6.3:

In addition to lexical adjectives, the class of adjectivals includes: articles; adnominal demonstratives; deictic, interrogative, indefinite, universal, etc., pro-words of identity, quality, and quantity; and cardinal and ordinal numerals and quantifiers. Adjectival agreement also occurs in genitive forms of nouns and pronouns (see Sect. 6.4.2) and in most perfective participles of verbs (see Sect. 6.4.1). Unlike the other adjectivals, the definite article and, where they exist, also non-emphatic variants of demonstratives

Table 6.3 Proto-Romani inflectional paradigm of the adjective *lačho*

	SG.M	SG.F	PL
NOM	*lač-ˈo*	*lač-ˈi*	*lač-ˈe*
OBL	*lač-ˈe*	*lač-ˈa*	*lač-ˈe*

and pronominal genitives cannot be nominalized and may be indeclinable in some dialects (cf. Elšík and Matras 2006, p. 319). While cardinals, at least the lower ones, show case agreement in most dialects, higher numerals may be, and quantity pro-words always are, uninflected (cf. Elšík and Matras 2006, p. 319), unless nominalized, e.g. *keti džen-en-sa* [how_many person-OBL.PL-SOC] 'with how many people' vs. *ket-en-sa* [how_many-OBL.PL-SOC] 'with how many ones'. The adjectival inflection of nominal genitives may encode fewer distinctions than that of adjectives in some dialects (cf. Elšík and Matras 2006, p. 228). Demonstratives mostly retain specific inflectional suffixes (cf. Matras 2002, pp. 107–108) and (at least some) forms of the definite article (cf. Boretzky 2000) cumulate inflectional categories with the lexical meaning of definiteness, e.g. the nominative masculine singular *o*. At least in some dialects, prepositions that have obligatorily fused with (nominative) forms of the definite article may be analysed as agreeing in number and gender with their noun complement (cf. Matras 2002, p. 96), e.g. *andr-i bar-°* [in-SG.F # garden(F)-NOM.SG] 'in the garden'.

6.4.4 Degree Inflection

Many dialects have inherited from Proto-Romani morphological marking of degree in gradable adjectives and adverbs by means of a non-positive suffix, cf. *bar-eder* 'bigger, the biggest; more greatly, the most greatly' (← *bar-o* 'big' and *bar-es* 'greatly'). Some dialects have further differentiated the non-positive degree into a comparative and a superlative, through borrowing or grammaticalization of superlative affixes, mostly prefixes, e.g. *jek-bareder* 'the biggest' vs. *bareder* 'bigger', though analytic means of marking the superlative are also attested (Elšík and Matras 2006, p. 147). Many dialects, nevertheless, have lost morphological degree marking and developed analytical means to mark degree (cf. Elšík and Matras 2006, pp. 145–155 for a detailed overview). In Slovene Romani, some lexemes have retained morphological marking, e.g. *kal-ede* 'blacker' while others have developed analytic marking, e.g. *hede lolo* 'redder', literally 'better red'. At least one dialect, Zargari, has lost the category of degree altogether. While the distinction between adjectives and deadjectival adverbs is mostly neutralized in non-positive degree forms, a few dialects do differentiate adjectival and adverbial degrees, e.g. Selice Romani *gullikan-eder* 'more sweetish' (← *gullikān-o* 'sweetish') vs. *gullikāšš-abban* 'in a more sweetish way' (← *gullikāšš-on* 'in a sweetish way').

6.5 Morphological Integration of Loanwords

There are several types of morphological integration in Romani of loanwords of the major inflected word classes. Which of the types of morphological integration (or non-integration) applies depends on the word class and the diachronic layer of the loanword and may show cross-dialectal variation.

Inflected loanwords from pre-Greek L2s (as well as some, presumably early, Hellenisms) were fully integrated through assignment to existing Proto-Romani inflectional classes, and so they are, as a rule, indistinguishable from indigenous, i.e. Indo-Aryan, vocabulary on morphological grounds. Prolonged intensive contact with Byzantine Greek has resulted in the borrowing of frequent forms of Greek loanwords together with their inflectional and derivational markers (e.g. nominative markers in nouns and adjectives), and thus a development of morphological classes specific to late Hellenisms. In the next stage, the numerous Greek morphological markers had been abstracted from their source forms and applied to loanwords from post-Greek L2s as well. As a result of this development (and of its re-iterations in later, dialect-specific, contact situations), some Greek and most post-Greek loanwords typically possess the so-called *xenoclitic* (formerly called *athematic*) morphology, i.e. marked morphology that explicitly signals their foreign origin in Romani (see Elšík and Matras 2006, p. 325 for details). Given the contrast with xenoclisis, the morphology typical of indigenous vocabulary and pre-Greek loanwords may be termed *oikoclitic* (formerly called *thematic*) morphology. From a synchronic point of view, there are two basic types of xenoclitic integration of loanwords:

First, some classes of inflected loanwords are morphologically integrated by means of overt suffixes that precede inflections, i.e. by means of pre-inflectional adaptation markers. In Latvian Romani, for example, borrowed verbs are adapted by means of the suffix -*in*-, e.g. *beidz-in-* 'to finish' (< Latvian 3SG *beidz*), which is mostly followed by oikoclitic inflections, although the xenoclitic -*i* suffix is an option in the third person singular, e.g. *beidz-in-el ~ beidz-in-i* 's/he finishes'. While the adaptation marker may be, and mostly is, followed by oikoclitic inflections, its very presence is a sign of xenoclisis. Pre-inflectional adaptation is typical of borrowed verbs, well attested with borrowed adjectives (e.g. Versend Romani *vad-n-o* 'wild', *somorū-mn-o* 'sad', *ďeng-av-o* 'weak' < Hungarian *vad, szomorú, gyenge*, respectively) but rare with borrowed nouns, where it is restricted to at most a few lexemes within a variety (e.g. Selice Romani *lāngoš-kiň-a* 'lángos' < Hungarian *lángos*). Many dialects possess several verb adaptation markers, whose distribution may reflect aspect, diathesis and transitivity, and the loanverb's diachronic layer.

For example, in Epiros Romani, the transitive verb 'to ask' (< Greek *rot-ó*) has the non-perfective stem *rot-**iz**-* vs. the perfective stem *rot-**in**-d-*, and the intransitive verb 'to get married' (< Greek *pandr-ev-ó*) has the non-perfective stem *pandr-**ez**-* vs. the perfective stem *pandr-**esá**-jl-*. And in Ajios Athanasios Romani, recent Hellenisms are adapted by means of productive complex markers, which are differentiated for diatheses, e.g. active *aravonj-**as-ker**-* 'to engage [so.]' (< Greek *arravonj-áz-o*) and middle *aravonj-**as-á**-o-* 'to get engaged' (< Greek *arravonj-áz-ome*), while Turcisms and older Hellenisms contain vocalic adaptation suffixes (-*a*-, -*e*-, -*i*-, or -*o*-), undifferentiated for diathesis in their non-perfective forms. An adaptation marker may be a dedicated means of loanword integration, or have, in addition, other, derivational, functions. For example, the verb adapting suffixes in Finnish Romani, -*av*- and -*uv*-, are primarily derivational valency markers.

Second, some classes of inflected loanwords are morphologically integrated without any pre-inflectional adaptation, through an immediate assignment to a xenoclitic inflectional class, i.e. xenoclitic inflectional integration. For example, the loan-noun *iškolāš-i* 'schoolchild' (< Hungarian *iskolás*) in Selice Romani is assigned to a xenoclitic masculine class and adapted, in its base form, by suffixation of the nominative singular -*i*; and the loan-noun *iškol-a* 'school' (< Hungarian *iskola*) is assigned to a xenoclitic feminine class and adapted, in its base form, by re-analysis of the final /a/ of the source form as the nominative singular suffix -*a*. Integration into xenoclitic inflectional classes is typical of borrowed nouns and adjectives. Due to interparadigmatic levelling, some classes of Greek or post-Greek loanwords have lost their xenoclitic inflection in some dialects and may be synchronically analysed as exhibiting oikoclitic inflectional integration (cf. Elšík 2000a, pp. 23–26). Also, oikoclitic inflectional integration is sometimes attested with lexical exceptions, such as the oikoclitic noun *moz-i* 'cinema' in East Slovak Romani (< Hungarian *mozi* 'movie, cinema'); or the oikoclitic verb *gir*- 'to enter, to get in' in Prilep Romani (< Turkish *gir*-), which is the only Turkish-origin verb without pre-inflectional adaptation.

In some dialects, there are also individual instances or even classes of morphologically unintegrated loanwords. The lack of morphological integration may be of different types. First, inflectional forms of a source word may be borrowed without any morphological integration and function as uninflected base forms, e.g. Vend *šlek(t)* 'bad, evil' (< German *schlecht*). Second, some inflectional forms of a loanword may be non-integrated borrowings of inflectional forms of the source word, while other inflectional forms of the loanword show inflectional integration. For example, Kisbajom Romani borrows nominative singular and nominative plural forms of nouns

170   V. Elšík

from Hungarian without any morphological (or phonological) integration, whereas most other case forms are regularly inflected, e.g. nominative *serb* 'Serb' (<*szerb*) and *serb-ek* 'Serbs' (<*szerb-ek*) but dative *serb-os-ke* [Serb-OBL.SG-DAT] and *serb-en-ge* [Serb-OBL.PL-DAT] (see Bodnárová 2014 for further complexities). Finally, loanwords may be borrowed together with their inflectional paradigms (cf. Matras 2002, pp. 134–135; Elšík and Matras 2006, pp. 135–137), as is the case of Turkish-inflected verbs in some Romani dialects in the Balkans, Crimean Tatar-inflected verbs in Crimean Romani, or Russian-inflected verbs in Russian and Lithuanian Romani.

It is sometimes the case that a dialect systematically borrows a certain type of morphologically complex forms from a L2 rather than deriving category-equivalent forms internally. For example, while some dialects derive adverbs from borrowed adjectives internally, e.g. Hucín Romani *ros-n-**on-e*** 'in a bad way' (← *ros-n-o* 'bad' < Hungarian *rosz*), and possess internally formed degree forms of adverbs (identical to those of adjectives), e.g. Hucín Romani *ros-n-eder* 'worse; in a worse way', other dialects systematically borrow deadjectival adverbs and their degree forms, alongside adjectives, e.g. Selice Romani *ďoršan* 'quickly' (< Hungarian *gyors-an*) and *ďoršabban* 'more quickly' (< Hungarian *gyors-abb-an*), alongside *ďorš-n-o* 'quick' (< Hungarian *gyors*).

6.6 Morphological Word-Formation

6.6.1 General Remarks

The most common type of morphological word-formation in Romani is derivational morphology, with suffixation clearly prevailing over prefixation; derivational reduplication is only attested in a few dialects (see Sect. 6.3). Further morphologically relevant types of word-formation include the much less common compounding (see Sect. 6.6.7 for a detailed discussion) and different types of processes that may be subsumed under the term conversion (see Sect. 6.6.8 for details).

While most derivational markers are word-class specific, a few are indiscriminate in that they may apply to derivational bases of different word classes and/or derive lexemes of different word classes. For example, the suffix *-ipe* in Sepečides derives nouns from verbs (e.g. *l-**ipe*** 'taking' ← *l-* 'to take'), nouns from adjectives (e.g. *xulan-**ipe*** 'richness' ← *xulan-o* 'rich'), and nouns from nouns (e.g. *amal-**ipe*** 'friendship' ← *amal* 'friend'); and the diminutive suffix *-ōr-* in Selice Romani derives nouns from nouns (e.g. *vodr-ōr-o* 'nice little bed' ← *vodr-o* 'bed'), adjectives from adjectives (e.g. *šudr-ōr-o* 'nice and cool' ← *šudr-o* 'cool'), and adverbs from adverbs (e.g. *polōk-ōr-e* 'nice and slowly' ← *polōk-e* 'slowly'). Some derivations maintain the word class of their derivational base, while others do not. Productive or at least numerous are, in most dialects, deverbal and deadjectival verbs and nouns, denominal and deadverbial adjectives, and deadjectival adverbs.

Productivity of a word-formation process in a dialect often seems to be restricted due to the systematic presence, in this dialect, of loanwords in the relevant semantic category. In Central Romani varieties of North Slavic bilinguals, for example, if masculine human nouns are borrowed from the current contact language, so are the corresponding feminine human nouns, e.g. both *rextor-is* '(male) teacher' and *rextork-a* 'female teacher' (< Slovak *rechtor* and *rechtork-a*, respectively), and so there is no space for a productive derivation of feminines. This contrasts with the extremely productive derivation of nouns denoting females in most Central varieties of Hungarian bilinguals, e.g. *tanītō-**kiň**-a* 'female teacher' (← *tanītō* '(male) teacher' < Hungarian *tanító*), since these varieties do not borrow such nouns from Hungarian (where nouns specifically denoting females are mostly compounds with the noun *nő* 'woman', cf. *tanító+nő*).

6.6.2 Verb Derivation

Valency-changing verb morphology is partly inherited from Proto-Romani. The middle suffix **-jov-* commonly derives inchoative verbs from adjectives, e.g. *mat-**jov**-* 'to get drunk' (← *mat-o* 'drunk'), and anticausative verbs from transitive verbs, e.g. *tav-d-**jov**-* 'to cook ITR' (← *tav-* 'to cook TR') or *dikh-**jov**-* 'to be seen, to seem' (← *dikh-* 'to see'), and competes with the middle suffix *-áv-*, probably more recently grammaticalized from the verb *av-* 'to come', in some dialects (cf. Matras 2002, pp. 126–127). Anticausatives derived from intransitive verbs, if they exist, mostly convey a lower degree of agentivity, e.g. Selice Romani *asa-ň-**ov**-* or *asa-**saj-ov**-* 'to smile unconsciously or spontaneously' (← *asa-* 'to smile, to laugh'). As in the intransitive domain, there is a partial marking overlap in some dialects in the transitivizing domain as well, viz. between deadjectival factitives and deverbal causatives. In Selice Romani, for example, the markers *-(j)ar-* and *-(j)aj-ār-* are typical of factitives, e.g. *māṭ-**ar**-* or *maṭ-**aj-ār**-* 'to make [so.] drunk' (← *māṭ-o* 'drunk'), but also apply to some verb bases, e.g. *sojv-**ar**-* 'to make [so.] sleep' (← *sov-* 'to sleep') and *ruš-**aj-ār**-* 'to make [so.] be on bad terms' (← *ruš-* 'to be on bad terms'), while the marker *-(a)v-* is specifically causative. In Sepečides, on the other hand, all of the numerous causative markers (e.g. *-av-*, *-ar-*, *-ker-*, *-av-ker-*, and *-ar-ker-*) are synchronically distinct from the factitive suffix *-jar-*, e.g. *xurd-jar-* 'to make small(er)' (← *xurd-o* 'small'), which is only diachronically related to the causative suffix *-ar-*, e.g. *mar-d-ar-* 'to make [so.] hit' (← *mar-* 'to hit'). Causatives are especially productive in dialects in contact with Turkish and Hungarian, in some varieties possessing second causatives of intransitive or lexicalized transitive verbs, e.g. Selice Romani *dara-v-av-* 'to make [so.] frighten [so.]' ← *dara-v-* 'to frighten [so.]' ← *dara-* 'to fear' (cf. Hübschmannová and Bubeník 1997), and borrowed causative markers, e.g. Selice Romani *poť-atat-in-av-* 'to make [so.] pay' ← *poť(-)in-* 'to pay' (cf. Elšík 2007).

On the other hand, lexical-aspectual (aktionsart) verb derivations are mostly dialect-specific. Some dialects possess deverbal verbs, usually termed frequentatives or iteratives, which express meanings such as repeated or frequent occurrence of an event, its intensity, or its distribution among several participants. Frequentatives are very productive in some varieties and double frequentatives are well attested, e.g. Uzhhorod Romani *čovr-ker-ker-* 'to steal repeatedly multiple things' (← *čovr-* 'to steal'). Further, many dialects derive deverbal verbs by means of (mostly borrowed) prefixes that encode spatial and/or aktionsart modifications, e.g. Latvian Romani *aiz-kēr-* 'to shut, to close' (← *kēr-* 'to do, to make'), *naie-dikh-* 'to hate, to dislike' (← *dikh-* 'to see'), or *pie-rakir-* 'to persuade' (← *rakir-* 'to speak'). (Lexicalized modification of verbs through syntactically free adverbs is not discussed in this chapter, as it is not morphological in nature.)

Denominal verbs are few in most dialects (cf. Matras 2002, pp. 119–128) and their marking is often cross-dialectally varied, e.g. *gil-jab-*, *gil-jav-*, *ďij-āz-in-*, etc. 'to sing' (← *gil-i*, *ďil-i*, etc. 'song'). Relatively common is marking by means of deadjectival morphology, e.g. quasi-inchoative *mel-áv-o-* 'to get dirty' and quasi-factitive *mel-ar-* (← *mel* 'dirt') in Ajia Varvara Romani. Numerous or productive denominal verb derivations are only attested in a few dialects. For example, in Welsh Romani, the factitive suffix *-(j)er-* applies to numerous noun bases, e.g. *dud-jer-* 'to illuminate' (← *dud* 'light'), *krafnī-er-* 'to nail' (← *krafnī* 'nail'), and *vaŋušt-er-* 'to finger' (← *vaŋušt-ō* 'finger'). And in Selice Romani, the denominal verb derivation by means of the marker *-āz-in-*, which contains the Hungarian-origin suffix *-āz-*, is fully productive, e.g. *mostar-āz-in-* 'to slap [so.] in the face' (← *mostar* 'slap in the face'), *repaň-āz-in-* 'to be fond of eating carrot' (← *repaň-i* 'carrot'), or *somsīdkiň-āz-in-* 'to be after a female neighbour' (← *somsīdkiň-a* 'female neighbour'). Deadverbial verbs are marginal, though attested in some dialects, e.g. Central Romani *siď-an-*, *siď-ar-*, *siď-ov-* 'to hasten' (← *sig* 'quickly, fast') or Welsh Romani *mask-er-* 'to come between, to separate' (← *mask-al* 'between').

6.6.3 Noun Derivation

The most productive among deverbal and deadjectival noun derivations are nominalizations (sometimes called abstract noun derivations) that primarily serve as a means of word-class transposition, e.g. Selice Romani *iringer-ibe* 'repeated turning around' (← *iringer-* 'to turn around repeatedly') or *kora-jārd-ipe* 'blindedness' (← *korajārd-o* 'blinded'). Nevertheless, such nominalizations often acquire more concrete meanings through lexicalization, e.g. Welsh Romani *star-iben* 'arrest, prison' (← *stār-* 'to seize'), Sepečides *xorax-an-ipe* 'Turkey' (← *xaraxan-o* 'Turkish'), or Selice Romani *zelen-ipe* 'plant' (← *zelen-o* 'green'). Abstract nouns may also be derived from other word classes, such as nouns or pronouns, e.g. Ajia Varvara Romani *thagar-ipe* 'kingdom' (← *thagar* 'king') or Selice Romani *ništ-ipe* 'trifle, triviality, pettiness' (← *ništ(a)* 'nothing'), and even from inflected word forms, e.g. Selice Romani *buter-ipe* 'being more numerous' (← *but-er* 'more', a comparative form) alongside *but-ipe* 'numerousness' (← *but* 'many, much') or Prilep Romani *si-pe* 'being' (← *si* 'is, are') and *nane-pe* 'not being' (← *nane* 'is not, are not'). While Proto-Romani possessed several complementary markers of abstract nominalizations, viz. deadjectival *-ipen*, oikoclitic deverbal *-(i)b-o* (Beníšek 2010, pp. 53–54), and xenoclitic deverbal *-(i)mo* of Greek origin (Matras 2002, pp. 74–75), most dialects have lost some of the inherited distinctions (e.g. conflating the deadjectival and the deverbal marking). On the other hand, many dialects have borrowed additional nominalizers from their L2s, e.g. Austrian Lovari *roman-šag-o* 'Romani way of life' (← *roman-o* 'Romani ADJ', Hungarian-origin suffix).

Though mostly unproductive (and sometimes even non-transparent due to loss of derivational bases), deverbal agentive nouns in *-(av)n-* are widely attested, e.g. Ajia Varvara Romani *khel-avn-o* 'dancer' (← *khel-* 'to dance'), Welsh Romani *båš-n-ō* 'cock, rooster' (← *båš-* 'to cry as an animal'), or Slovak Lovari *pir(-)āmn-o* 'boyfriend, lover' (← **pir-* 'to be in love'). Agentives may also be derived by borrowed suffixes, e.g. Ajia Varvara Romani *xoxam-dži-o(s)* 'lier' (← *xoxav-* 'to lie', Turkish-origin suffix) or Selice Romani *māťov-āš-i* 'drunkard' (← *māťov-* 'to get drunk', Hungarian-origin suffix). Other kinds of deverbal noun derivations are mostly marginal. In Selice Romani, for example, there is a single instrument derivation, viz. *lavav-ō* 'photographic camera' (← *lavav-* 'to have [sth.] taken, to photograph', Hungarian-origin suffix).

Denominal nouns are varied in their category semantics. A widespread category is the so-called motion, i.e. the derivation of nouns denoting females from those denoting males. Most Romani dialects retain some derivations by means of the, no longer productive, suffix *-n-* (see Sect. 6.6.8 for a semantically identical inflectional derivation), e.g. *manuš-**n**-i* 'female human' (← *manuš* 'human') and *grast-**n**-i* 'mare' (← *grast* 'horse'), and many dialects have borrowed, often highly productive, motion markers, e.g. Zargari *qahreman-**is**-a* 'heroine' (← *qahreman-i* 'hero'), Sepečides *kujum-dž-**ik**-a* 'female goldsmith' (← *kujumdž-us* 'goldsmith'), Austrian Lovari *sint-**ojk**-a* 'Sintica, Sinto woman' (← *sint-o* 'Sinto'), Selice Romani *kaňhāl-**kiň**-a* 'cutie, a good-looking female' (← *kaňhāl-o* 'dandy, looker'), or German Sinti *sikəpaskr-**ec**-a* 'female teacher' (← *sikəpaskr-o* 'teacher'). Also widespread are diminutives, which may be derived by both indigenous (*-oṛ-* and *-ičh-*) and borrowed suffixes, e.g. Divín Romani *bāl-**ōr**-o* 'piglet' (← *bāl-o* 'pig'), *verd-**at**-i* 'little cart' (← *verd-a* 'cart'), or *lavuť-**ic**-a* 'little violin' (← *lavut-a* 'violin'). Many Romani dialects retain some inherited names of trees derived from the names of their fruits, e.g. *ambrol-**in*** 'pear tree' (← *ambrol* 'pear') or *phabal-**in*** 'apple tree' (← *phabaj* 'apple'). While the derivation is still productive in some dialects, e.g. Slovak Lovari *kireš-**in*** 'cherry tree' (← *kireš-a* 'cherry', a loanword from Romanian) or Sepečides *šeftal-**ilin*** 'peach tree' (← *šeftal-ij-a* 'peach', a loanword from Turkish), other dialects have replaced it with analytic collocations.

Usually unproductive but cross-dialectally common are privative and negative prefixal derivations, e.g. Selice Romani ***bi**-bast* 'misfortune' and ***na**-bast* 'bad luck' (← *bast* 'good luck'). Often similar in marking to deverbal agentives (see above) are denominal agentives, e.g. Selice Romani *mas-**āš**-i* 'meat lover' (← *mas* 'meat'), and occupation nouns, e.g. Welsh Romani *čaml-**ār**-ī* 'butcher' (← *čaml-ī* 'slaughterhouse'). Many dialects retain isolated remnants of several obsolete derivations, e.g. Welsh Romani *pīr-**and*** 'foot [of the bed etc.]' (← *pīr-ō* 'foot'), *men-**r**-ī* 'necklace' (← *men* 'neck'), *mum-**al**-ī* 'candle' (← *mum* 'wax'), or *mar-**ikl**-ī* 'cake' (← *mār-ō* 'bread'). Dialect-specific denominal noun derivations include, for example, pejorative human nouns, e.g. Selice Romani *khul-**ajc**-i* 'a person smelling of excrements' (← *khul* 'excrement') or *mutr-**iš**-i* 'person suffering from urinary incontinence, pants-pisser' (← *muter* 'urine'), or nouns denoting artificial counterparts to natural objects, e.g. Selice Romani ***mī**-kašt* 'plastic tree' (← *kašt* 'wood, tree') or ***mī**-čūč-i* 'fake breast' (← *čūč-i* 'breast').

6.6.4 Adjective Derivation

Denominal adjectives are varied in their marking, with most dialects possessing reflexes of several indigenous, oikoclitic, suffixes, and one or two suffixes of Greek or later origin. The latter are mostly used with xenoclitic

6 Romani Morphology   175

bases, e.g. Vend *lah-itik-o* 'Vlax Romani ADJ' (← *lah-o* 'Vlax Rom'), though they may extend to oikoclitic ones in some dialects, e.g. Russian Kalderaš *bibold-ick-o* 'Jewish' (← *bibold-o* 'Jew'). Productive indigenous suffixes, on the other hand, may also extend to xenoclitic bases in some dialects, e.g. Selice Romani *krušk-āl-o* 'pear ADJ' (← *krušk-a* 'pear', a loanword from South Slavic). Some of the derivations show consistent marking across most dialects and must have been inherited from Proto-Romani, e.g. *ṛom-an-o* 'Romani' (← *ṛom* 'Rom') and *kašt-un-o* 'wooden' (← *kašt* 'wood'), though dialect-specific innovations may affect such derivations: cf. Pavlovce Romani *rom-adun-o* 'Romani' and Welsh Romani *kåšt-an-ō* (through merger of **-un-* with *-an-*) or Prilep Romani *kašt-un-an-o* (through reinforcement by *-an-*). The individual oikoclitic denominal suffixes show certain semantic tendencies: adjectives in *-(j)al-* often describe physical (bodily, meteorological, etc.) properties or states, e.g. *zor-al-o* 'strong' (← *zor* 'strength, force'), *jag-al-o* 'fiery' (← *jag* 'fire'), or *phumb-al-o* 'pusy' (← *phumb* 'pus'), and various ethical or behavioural characteristics, e.g. *čhib-al-o* 'talkative, cheeky' (← *čhib* 'tongue, language') or *pativ-al-o* 'esteemed, honest, faithful' (← *pativ* 'honour, respect'); adjectives in *-val-* are mostly derived from body-part nouns, e.g. *dand-val-o* 'toothy' (← *dand* 'tooth'); adjectives in *-an-* are mostly derived from names of animals, e.g. *šošoj-an-o* 'hare, rabbit ADJ' (← *šošoj* 'hare, rabbit'), and ethnic groups, e.g. *balam-an-o* 'Greek' (← *balam-o* 'Greek'); adjectives in *-un-* are mostly derived from names of materials, e.g. *phanṛ-un-o* 'silken' (← *phanṛ* 'silk'); and adjectives in *-ikan-* are often derived from nouns denoting humans, e.g. *džuvl-ikan-o* 'feminine, female' (← *džuvl-i* 'woman, female'), including ethnic or religious groups, e.g. *das-ikan-o* 'Slavic, Orthodox' (← *das* 'Slav, Orthodox'). Different suffixes applied to identical bases may convey different derivational meanings. In Selice Romani, for example, there is a contrast between plain relational *serv-ik-o* 'Slovak' and similative *serv-ikān-o* 'Slovak-like' (← *serv-o* 'Slovak').

Deadverbial adjectives, which are mostly derived from spatial and temporal adverbs, seem to have contained a specific marker in Proto-Romani (probably **-utn-*), as reflected, for example, in Latvian Romani *opr-atun-o* 'upper' (← *opr-e* 'up, upwards') and *taša-tun-o* 'yesterday's, tomorrow's' (← *taša* 'yesterday, tomorrow'). Nevertheless, in numerous dialects, the deadverbial suffix **-utn-* merged with denominal *-un-* in, some or all, deadverbial derivations, e.g. Versend Romani *andr-ūn-o* 'internal' (← *ānd-e* 'inside, inwards'), and Welsh Romani reflects the merger of **-un-* with *-an-* (see above) in most deadverbial adjectives, too, e.g. *pal-an-ō* 'hindmost' (← *pāl-ē* 'behind'). Synchronically, there may be several deadverbial adjective suffixes in a dialect (e.g. *-utn-*, *-ukn-*, and *-un-* in Selice Romani),

176   **V. Elšík**

differentiating spatial vs. temporal bases or bases of different spatial dimensions. In many dialects, the deadverbial adjective suffixes also occur in those denominal derivations that have a clearly spatial or temporal semantics, e.g. Sepečides *veš-**utn**-o* 'forest-dwelling, mountain-dwelling' (← *veš* 'forest, mountain') and *kurk-**un**-o* 'weekly' (← *kurk-o* 'Sunday, week'). Adjectives derived from manner adverbs are marginal, e.g. Selice Romani *polōk-**un**-o* 'slow' (← *polōk-e* 'slowly').

Deverbal adjectives, too, may rely on the primarily deadverbial adjective suffixes, e.g. Prilep *pindžar-**utn**-o* 'acquainted, known' (← *pindžar-* 'to be acquainted, to know [so.]'), or specific variants thereof, e.g. Seredne Romani *ašar-**gutn**-o* 'boastful' (← *ašar-* 'to praise'). While indigenous specific deverbal derivations are rare and unproductive, e.g. Selice Romani *asa-**nd**-o* 'smiley, riant' (← *asa-* 'to laugh, to smile'), a few dialects possess productive borrowed deverbal suffixes, e.g. Selice Romani *asav-ōš-**n**-o* 'ridiculous' (← *asav-* 'to make laugh', Hungarian-origin suffix). Adjectives derived from verbal participles are rare but attested, e.g. Sepečides *mang-l-**un**-o* 'beloved' (← *mang-l-o* 'loved, wished, wanted') or *kin-d-**ikan**-o* 'acquired, bought' (← *kin-d-o* 'bought').

Several semantically well-defined derivational categories of deadjectival adjectives are attested in different dialects, including privatives (e.g. ***bi**-londo* 'saltless' ← *londo* 'salty'), frequentatives (e.g. Uzhhorod Romani *nasval-**ker-d**-o* 'frequently ill, sickly' ← *nasval-o* 'ill'), diminutives (e.g. Slovene Romani *bokhal-**or**-o* ← *bokhal-o* 'hungry'), attenuatives (e.g. Russian Kalderaš *nasval-**ičos**-o* 'sickly, sickish' ← *nasval-o* 'ill'), and similatives (e.g. Selice Romani *roman-**ikān**-o* 'Romani-like' ← *romān-o* 'Romani'). In addition, numerous deadjectival adjectives have idiosyncratic meanings and do not represent a well-defined category, e.g. Welsh Romani *ruč-**an**-ō* 'tall' (← *ruč-ō* 'high'), Versend Romani *kuč-**āl**-o* 'valuable' (← *kuč* 'expensive'), Serbian Kalderaš *čač-**un**-o* 'real, veracious, actual' (← *čač-o* 'true, right'), or Ajia Varvara Romani *phirn-**ikan**-o* 'sly, cunning' (← *phirn-o* 'clever, smart').

6.6.5   Adverb Derivation

Manner adverbs are regularly derived from adjectives (and, in some dialects, also from participles) by means of the indigenous suffix **-es*, e.g. Welsh Romani *duman-es* 'gloomily' (← *duman-ō* 'gloomy'), *xuïïmen-es* 'filthily' (← *xuïïmen* 'filthy'), or *garad-es* 'secretly' (← *garad-ō* 'hidden, secret'). The manner marker may be complex and contain (originally) xenoclitic extensions in some dialects, e.g. Vend *nāng-ōn* 'nakedly' < **nang-on-es* (← *nāng-o* 'naked'). In many dialects, manner adverbs derived from ethnic adjectives that contain Greek-origin adjective-deriving suffixes retain the Greek-origin adverb suffix *-a*, e.g. Vend *ungr-ik-a* 'in Hungarian' (← *ungr-ik-o* 'Hungarian ADJ'), *kopaná-ck-a* 'in Beash' (← *kopaná-ck-o* 'Beash ADJ'), and *lah-itik-a* 'in Vlax Romani' (← *lah-itik-o* 'Vlax Romani ADJ'). Manner markers borrowed from post-Greek L2s are also attested. In Selice Romani, for example, adverbs from attenuative and similative adjectives in *-ikān-* are derived by means of Hungarian-origin markers, e.g. *phur-ikā-šš-on* 'anciently' (← *phur-ikān-o* 'ancient, archaic').

Denominal adverbs have spatial, temporal, and only rarely other meanings, e.g. Welsh Romani *kher-ē* 'at home, (to) home' (← *khēr* 'house, home'), *rāt-ī* 'at night' (← *rat* 'night'), *dives-āra* 'by day' (← *dives* 'day'), and *pīr-al* 'on foot' (← *pīr-ō* 'foot'). In some dialects, the indigenous adverbial suffix *-e*, usually with xenoclitic extensions, remains productive as a marker of temporal simultaneity with days of week, e.g. Serbian Kalderaš *žoj-in-e* 'on Thursday' (← *žoj-a* 'Thursday', a loanword from Romanian). Borrowed denominal adverbial suffixes are also attested, e.g. Selice Romani *masek-ātū* 'since many months ago' (← *masek* 'month', Hungarian-origin suffix). Deadverbial adverbs mark spatial orientation, e.g. Ajia Varvara Romani *mamuj-al* 'from the opposite side' (← *mamuj* 'on/to the opposite side'), or various temporal specifications, e.g. Serbian Kalderaš *d-agjes-ara* 'from today on' (← *agjes* 'today') or Selice Romani *idž-al-tū* 'since yesterday' (← *īdž* 'yesterday'), and often draw on a similar set of markers as denominal adverbs. Non-perfective and perfective converbs, e.g. Sepečides *phir-indos* 'while walking, on foot' (← *phir-* 'to walk') and Russian Romani *sov-i* 'having slept' (← *sov-* 'to sleep'), are lexically restricted and thus may be analysed as deverbal adverb derivations.

6.6.6 Other Derivations

Cardinal numerals are the bases for the derivation of other types of numerals. Ordinals are mostly derived from cardinals by the Greek-origin xenoclitic suffix *-t-*, e.g. *šov-t-o* 'sixth' (← *šov* 'six'), though lower numerals often show irregularities and a few dialects have innovative markers, e.g. Zargari *šov-edin-o* 'sixth' (← *šov* 'six'). The Proto-Romani multiplicative suffix *-var* is retained in multiplicative numerals in many dialects, e.g. Versend Romani *štār-val* 'four times' (← *štār* 'four'), and some dialects also employ it in newly developed ordinal–multiplicative numerals, e.g. Versend Romani *štār-to-var* 'for the fourth time' (← *štārto* 'fourth'). Many dialects have developed

178   V. Elšík

de-interrogative indefinite, negative, and/or universal pro-words (cf. Elšík and Matras 2006, pp. 286–290), often derived by means of borrowed or grammaticalized prefixes, e.g. Podunajské Biskupice Romani *vala-kāj* 'somewhere', *ikār-kāj* 'anywhere whatsoever', *ni-khāj* 'nowhere', *sa-khāj* 'everywhere' (← *kāj* 'where'). Similarly, morphological relations between different deictic pro-words may also be analysed as derivational in some dialects, e.g. Selice Romani *am-avka* 'in a contrasting way' (← *avka* 'so').

6.6.7 Compounding

Word-formation by compounding is much less common than derivation (e.g. Matras 2002, p. 119) and is rarely productive. Most dialects possess reflexes, often no longer transparent, of several Proto-Romani compounds. Inherited verbal compounds consist of a light verb head and a preceding nominal root or a perfective converb in *-i*. The former usually contain the light verb 'to give', e.g. *kan+d-* 'to obey' (← *kan* 'ear' + *d-* 'to give'), and show varying degrees of internal coherence. The light verbs compounded with converbs are more varied and may show cross-dialect variation, e.g. *lidža-*, *ledž-* etc. < *le-i+dža-* 'to carry' (← *l-* 'to take' + *dža-* 'to go'; cf. Beníšek 2013) and *xud-*, *uštid-* etc. < *uxt-i+d-* vs. *xtyl-*, *štil-* etc. < *uxt-i+l-* 'to grasp, catch' (← *uxt-* 'to jump' + *d-* 'to give' vs. *l-* 'to take'). Also of ultimate compound origin are the middle verbs, which consist of the verb *ov-* 'to become' and a preceding adjective, participle, or verb stem (see Sect. 6.6.2). Inherited adjectival compounds consist of an adjective head and a preceding nominal root, e.g. *pinṛang-o* < *pinṛ+nang-o* 'barefoot' (← *pinṛ-o* 'foot' + *nang-o* 'naked'). Other types of Proto-Romani compounds are rare, e.g. *balevas* 'bacon' < *bal-e+mas* (← *bal-o* 'pig' + *mas* 'meat, flesh') or *budžand-o*, *bužangl-o* (etc.) 'sly, cunning' < *but+džand(l)-o* (← *but* 'much' + *džand(l)-o* 'knowing', a participle of the verb *džan-* 'to know').

Dialect-specific compounds have developed from univerbation of multi-word collocations, e.g. Krosno Romani *ada+g'ives* 'today' (← *ada* 'this' + *g'ives* 'day'), or through structural borrowing from L2s. For example, Vend *gra+verd-a* 'coach, horse-drawn carriage' (← *gra* 'horse' + *verd-a* 'carriage') is calqued on German *Pferd-e+kutsche* and Selice Romani *fẽ+fŏr-o* 'capital' (← *fẽ* 'main' + *fŏr-o* 'town, city') is a semicalque of Hungarian *fő+város*. Contact-induced compounding also occurs in function words, as in the inessive adverbs *edej+ānde* 'inside' (← *edej* 'here' + *ānde* 'to inside') in Vend, which calques Hungarian *ide+benn*.

Different compounds have various degrees of internal coherence, with some coming close to (the less coherent) multi-word collocations. One coherence criterion, among many, is the lack of internal morphology, as in Moldava Romani *adā+ďives-es-ker-o* [this+day-OBL.SG-GEN-NOM.SG.M] 'today's', where the deictic element does not inflect (cf. *ale*, the oblique singular masculine form of *adā*). In other instances, there is a fuzzy boundary between compounding and derivation. For example, while privative adjectives such as *bi-lačh-o* 'bad' (← *lačh-o* 'good') are usually analysed as derivations by means of a privative prefix, privative nominal genitives such as *bi+god-ja-ker-o* [PRIV+brain-OBL.SG-GEN-NOM.SG.M] 'brainless, mindless' are mostly analysed as compounds (i.e. ← *bi* 'without' + *god-i* 'brain, mind'). Compounds often lose transparency due to matter erosion and loss of segmentability of their components, as in Uzh Romani *žoďiv* 'wheat' < *žuž-o+ďiv* (← *žuž-o* 'clean' + *ďiv* 'cereal, corn') or Latvian Romani *param-o* 'roll, bun' < *parn-o+mār-o* (← *parn-o* 'white' + *mār-o* 'bread'). Transparency may also be reduced due to a lexical loss of some of the components. For example, *kaňh-a+jār-o* 'egg' (cf. *kaňh-i* 'chicken, hen') in Selice Romani is no longer fully transparent, since the noun *jār-o* 'egg' only occurs within this quasi-compound.

Productive compound patterns are most common in complex numerals, where they may compete with multi-word collocations. In Serednie Romani, for example, the additive compounds such as *deš-u-trīn* [ten-ADD-three] '13' and *biš-thaj-trīn* [twenty-ADD-three] '23', which contain two distinct additive numeral connectors, contrast with additive collocations such as *tranda the trīn* [ten and three] '33', which contain the regular conjunctive coordinator ('and'). One dialect-specific example of productive compounding is the formation of adjectives designating a composite colour pattern in Selice Romani: they are coordinative compounds consisting of an attenuative adjective and a plain adjective, e.g. *lōl-ast-o+pārn-o* 'red-and-white', literally 'reddish white'.

6.6.8 Conversion

There are several distinct types of morphological processes that may be subsumed under the term conversion: first, some lexemes are formed by what may be termed inflectional derivation, i.e. change of inflection, including in the base form, without the employment of any derivational marker (since the inflectional stems of both lexemes are identical, this morphological relation lacks directionality). Like derivation proper, inflectional derivation may or may not involve a change in word class. No change in word class is involved in the inflectional derivation of gender counterparts in nouns, e.g. *gadž-o* 'non-Romani man' ↔ *gadž-i* 'non-Romani woman', *rakl-o* 'non-Romani lad' ↔ *rakl-i* 'non-Romani girl', *čovaxan-o* 'wizzard' ↔ *čovaxan-i* 'witch', etc. Word-class changing inflectional derivation may be illustrated, for example, by the noun–adjective pair *čiken* 'fat, lard' ↔ *čikn-o* 'fat, lardy' or the noun–verb pair *čor* 'thief' ↔ *čor-el* 's/he steals'.

Another type of conversion, which will be termed word-class conversion, is the change of word class (and hence inflection) without any overt modification of the base form of the lexeme. Onomasiological nominalization of adjectives appears to be the most common kind of word-class conversion, e.g. Selice Romani *kaňhālo* 'relating to hen' → 'dandy, looker', *šilāli* 'cold F' → 'cold sore', *serviko* 'Slovak ADJ' → *serviko* 'Slovakia', and some dialects may also nominalize adverbs, e.g. Selice Romani *tāha* 'tomorrow' → '(the day of) tomorrow', and even multi-word adverbials, e.g. *pal o dīlo* 'after the noon, in the afternoon' → *palodīlo* '(the) afternoon'. The nominalized lexemes show nominal inflection, e.g. *tāha-s-ke* [tomorrow-OBL.SG-DAT] 'for tomorrow' or *palodīl-i* [afternoon-NOM.PL] 'afternoons'. Well attested is also adjectivization of nouns, which acquire adjectival inflection in the attributive position, e.g. Selice Romani *kotor* 'piece' → 'hefty', as in *kotor-e murš-es-ke* [hefty-OBL.SG.M man(M)-OBL.SG-DAT] 'to a hefty man'. Rarely attested is the conversion of a noun into a predicative adverb, e.g. Selice Romani *tatipe* 'warmth' → 'warm', as in *tatipeder hi adaj* 'it is warmer here', with a comparative form of the adverb.

Word-class change is also involved in the onomasiological nominalization of genitives, which are adjectival case forms of nouns (see Sect. 6.4.2), e.g. Bohemian Romani *kašt-es-ker-o* [wood-OBL.SG-GEN-NOM.SG.M] '(he) of the wood' → 'carpenter' or German Sinti *kan-en-gər-i* [ear-OBL.PL-GEN-NOM.SG.F] '(she) of the ears' → 'earring'. In several dialects, the onomasiological genitives are synchronically distinct from attributive genitives, in that the former retain phonologically more complex variants of the genitive suffix. In Welsh Romani, for example, onomasiological genitives contain the 'longer' genitive suffix *-ker- ~ -ger-*, which also occurs in predicative uses of grammatical (i.e. non-onomasiological) genitives, while the 'shorter' genitive suffix *-k- ~ -g-* occurs in attributive genitives, e.g. *īv-es-ker-ō* [snow-OBL.SG-GEN-NOM.SG.M] 'January', literally '(he) of the snow', vs. *īv-es-k-ō dives* 'snowy day'. A similar formal split sometimes occurs in onomasiological uses of further inflectional categories. In Selice Romani, for example, the lexeme *gād-a* 'clothes', an onomasiological plural of the noun *gad* 'shirt', is distinct both semantically and formally from the latter's regular plural *gad-a* 'shirts' (there is no singular form **gād* 'a piece of clothing').

6.7 Inflectional and Derivational Classes

Affixes that are synonymous and, at the same time, formally unrelated through morphophonological alternations may be considered to be suppletive. The presence of affix suppletion in inflectional morphology results in inflectional classes, i.e. verb conjugations and noun and adjective declensions; derivational classes are the analogical phenomenon in derivational morphology. Within inflectional morphology, cumulative suffixes (cf. Sect. 6.3) are more likely to be sensitive to, i.e. to encode, inflectional classification, though separative suffixes, both inflectional and derivational, may also be suppletive. While chronological compartmentalization of the lexicon into oikoclitic and xenoclitic classes (cf. Sect. 6.5) is an important aspect of morphologically encoded classification, there are also classes and markers that are neutral with regard to chronological compartmentalization.

In nouns, inflectional classes differ exclusively in the case–number suffixes. In Selice Romani, for example, there are six suppletive markers of the nominative singular (viz. -°, -o, -i, -e, -a, and -ja), four of the nominative plural (viz. -e, -a, -ja, and -i), eight of the oblique singular (viz. -s-, -es-, -is-, -as-, -nas-, -a-, -ja-, and -i-), and five of the oblique plural (viz. -n-, -en-, -jen-, -nen-, and -on-). Especially, the oblique markers allow further morphological segmentation (cf. Elšík 1997, p. 36; 2000a, pp. 18–19): for example, the oblique plural markers in Selice Romani may be analysed as bimorphemic markers consisting of a classification suffix (viz. none, -e-, -je-, -ne-, and -o-) and a categorial suffix (viz. the actual oblique plural suffix -n-). Some of the case–number suffixes are exclusive to nouns of a certain gender (e.g. the oblique singular markers that contain categorial -s- are always masculine) and nouns that differ in gender always differ in their inflectional class as well, i.e. never inflect alike. Separative case suffixes are identical across inflectional classes of nouns (exceptions are only found in the inflection of pronouns), as are some marginal case–number suffixes (e.g. the vocative plural suffix in most dialects). In adjectives, inflectional classes differ especially in the agreement (i.e. case–number–gender) suffixes. Morphological degree marking, on the other hand, is mostly uniform across classes, with the exception of a few irregular adjectives (and adverbs).

182 V. Elšík

In verb inflection, one may distinguish non-perfective, perfective, and imperative classes. The existence of L2-inflected verbs in some Romani dialects (cf. Sect. 6.5) naturally also contributes to inflectional classification of verbs. Mostly uniform across inflectional classes are tense–mood suffixes and perfective person–number suffixes, with the exception of the perfective third person singular: the Proto-Romani distinction between participle-like gender-marking forms of transitive verbs and dedicated gender-neutral forms of intransitive verbs (cf. Elšík and Matras 2006, pp. 81–82), which has been levelled in numerous dialects, does contribute to verb classification. The classification into perfective verb classes is the most elaborate: most dialects have around half a dozen distinct perfective suffixes (e.g. *-d- ~ -ď-, -t- ~ -ť-, -l- ~ -j-, -īl- ~ -īj-, -n- ~ -ň-, -in- ~ -iň-*, and *-ind- ~ -inď-* in Selice Romani) and several verbs with irregular perfectives. The membership of a verb in a perfective class is mostly determined by a combination of phonological, derivational, and semantic factors (cf. Elšík and Matras 2006, pp. 80–81). Although participle suffixes are mostly identical to perfective suffixes, participle classes need not fully coincide with perfective classes. In some South Central dialects, for example, the verbs *ťin-* 'to buy' and *poťin-* 'to pay' share the perfective class but have distinct participle marking (cf. *ťin-d-o* 'bought' vs. *poť-ime* 'paid'). The classification into non-perfective (or present) verb classes is encoded in the non-perfective person–number suffixes. Proto-Romani possessed a distinction between the regular first singular suffix *-(a)v-* and the suffix *-am-*, which was retained in loanwords from Iranian, e.g. *kam-am* 'I want' (cf. Beníšek 2010, p. 68); and between the regular third person singular suffix *-(e)l-* and the suffix *-i*, which was, perhaps optionally, retained in loanwords from Greek (cf. Elšík and Matras 2006, p. 81). While most dialects have replaced the borrowed non-perfective suffixes through analogy, some have developed novel non-perfective classes through phonological developments, especially contractions in middle verbs. Ajia Varvara Romani, for example, has three sets of non-perfective person–number suffixes, e.g. 1SG *-v-, -av-*, and *-iav-* (< *-ov-av-*), 2SG *-s-, -es-*, and *-os-* (< *-ov-es-*), and 3SG *-l-, -el-*, and *-ol-* (< *-ov-el-*), which may be analysed as bimorphemic markers consisting of a classification suffix (viz. none, *-a- ~ -e-*, and *-ia- ~ -o-*) and a categorial suffix (viz. the actual person–number suffixes *-v-, -s-*, and *-l-*).

Derivational classes, i.e. formally unrelated derivational markers within a single, semantically defined, derivational category, are also well attested. Many dialects, for example, possess several markers for nominal diminutives, whose selection is determined by the inflectional class of the base noun, e.g. *bar-ōr-o ← bar* M 'stone', *bār-ōr-i ← bār* F 'garden' vs. *feld-ic-a ← feld-a* F 'field', *for-ic-os ← for-os* M 'city' vs. *savār-īt-is ← savār-is* M 'bridle' in Latvian Romani.

6.8 Highlights and Prospects

Romani is a language with rich inflectional and derivational morphology. It exhibits a number of typologically interesting features, such as the layered system of case marking in nouns and the distinction between nominal vs. adjectival case (Sects. 6.4.2–6.4.3); the adjectival character of the nominal genitive (Sects. 6.4.2–6.4.3) and the possibility of its further nominalization (Sect. 6.6.8); tense–mood marking in verbs in a more external position than person–number marking (Sect. 6.4.1); productive xenoclitic inflectional and derivational classes and markers, i.e. those that explicitly signal foreign origin of lexemes and derivational bases, to which they apply (Sect. 6.5); the possibility of borrowing of lexemes together with their inflectional paradigms (Sect. 6.5); and more. Romani shows a significant degree of cross-dialect variation in its morphological categories and their marking, partly due to structural and material borrowing from different L2s.

While major aspects of Romani morphology are well described, both in the numerous dialect-specific descriptions and from a cross-dialectal and diachronic perspective (see Sect. 6.2), there certainly is space for further research. Grammars of individual dialects frequently lack any discussion of allomorphy, sufficient detail in the description of inflectional and derivational classes, or a comprehensive description of word-formation categories and markers, including a detailed account of their productivity, and numerous aspects of Romani morphology (e.g. semantics of inflectional cases, adjective derivation, onomasiological nominalizations of genitives, to name just a few) still lack a detailed cross-dialectal account.

Notes

1. The chapter contains published examples from the following Romani dialects (and dialect groups): Skopje Arli, Prilep, Ajios Athanasios, Sepečides, Epiros, and Zargari (South Balkan); Kaspichan (North Balkan); Abruzzian (Apennine); Slovene (Slovene); Versend and Vend (incl. Kisbajom) (South Central); Bohemian and Eastern Uzh (incl. Uzhhorod and Serednie) (North Central); Russian and Serbian Kalderaš, Austrian and Slovak Lovari, and Ajia Varvara (Vlax); Russian, Latvian, and Polish (Northeastern); and German Sinti, Manuš, Finnish, and Welsh (Northwestern). See the overview of dialect groups and the sources in the chapter on Romani dialectology in this volume.
2. The chapter contains unpublished examples from the following local varieties of Central Romani: Divín, Klenovec, Podunajské Biskupice, and Selice (South Central); and Gemerská Hôrka, Hucín, Krosno, Moldava [nad Bodvou], Pavlovce [nad Uhom], Vysoká [nad Kysucou] (North Central).

References

Ariste, Paul. 1973. Lettische Verbalpräfixe in einer Zigeunermundart. *Baltistica* 9 (1): 79–81.

Bakker, Peter. 1997. Athematic morphology in Romani: The borrowing of a borrowing pattern. In *The typology and dialectology of Romani*, ed. Yaron Matras, Peter Bakker, and Hristo Kyuchukov, 1–21. Amsterdam: John Benjamins.

Beníšek, Michael. 2009. Middle Indo-Aryan ablative and locative markers in Romani. *Indo-Iranian Journal* 52 (4): 335–362.

Beníšek, Michael. 2010. The quest for a Proto-Romani infinitive. *Romani Studies*, 5th ser., 20 (1): 47–86.

Beníšek, Michael. 2013. Central Romani *lidža-/ ledž-*: A vestige of an Indo-Aryan compound verb and its cross-dialectal variability. *Acta Orientalia Academiae Scientiarum Hungaricae* 66: 471–486.

Bloch, Jules. 1932. Le présent du verbe "être" en tsigane. *Indian Linguistics* 2: 309–316.

Bodnárová, Zuzana. 2014. Loanword integration: A case study of Kisbajom Romani. *Romani Studies*, 5th ser., 24 (1): 71–91.

Boretzky, Norbert. 1995. Die Entwicklung der Kopula im Romani. *Grazer Linguistische Studien* 43: 1–50.

Boretzky, Norbert. 1996. The "new" infinitive in Romani. *Journal of the Gypsy Lore Society*, 5th ser., 6: 1–51.

Boretzky, Norbert. 1998. Interference in Romani: Functional change in inherited grammatical categories. *Journal of the Gypsy Lore Society*, 5th ser., 8 (1): 19–46.

Boretzky, Norbert. 1999. Grammatical interference in Romani: Loan formations for foreign categories. *Acta Linguistica Hungarica* 46 (3): 169–200.

Boretzky, Norbert. 2000. The definite article in Romani dialects. In *Grammatical relations in Romani: The noun phrase*, ed. Viktor Elšík and Yaron Matras, 31–63. Amsterdam: John Benjamins.

Boretzky, Norbert. 2013. Gender adaptation in loan layers of Romani. *STUF—Language Typology and Universals* 66 (4): 404–424.

Boretzky, Norbert, and Birgit Igla. 1991. *Morphologische Entlehnung in den Romani-Dialekten*. Essen: Universität GH Essen.

Boretzky, Norbert, and Birgit Igla. 2004. *Kommentierter Dialektatlas des Romani. Teil 1: Vergleich der Dialekte. Teil 2: Dialektkarten mit einer CD Rom*. Wiesbaden: Harrassowitz.

Cech, Petra. 1996. Inflection/derivation in Sepečides-Romani. *Acta Linguistica Hungarica* 43: 67–91.

Comrie, Bernard. 2008. Inflectional morphology and language contact, with special reference to mixed languages. In *Language contact and contact languages*, ed. Peter Siemund and Noemi Kintana, 15–32. Amsterdam: Benjamins.

Eloeva, Fatima A., and Aleksandr Ju. Rusakov. 1990. *Problemy jazykovoj interferencii (cyganskie dialekty Evropy): Učebnoe posobie*. Leningrad: Leningradskij gosudarstvennyj universitet.

Elšík, Viktor. 1997. Towards a morphology-based typology of Romani. In *The typology and dialectology of Romani*, ed. Yaron Matras, Peter Bakker, and Hristo Kyuchukov, 23–59. Amsterdam: John Benjamins.

Elšík, Viktor. 2000a. Romani nominal paradigms: Their structure, diversity and development. In *Grammatical relations in Romani: The noun phrase*, ed. Viktor Elšík and Yaron Matras, 9–30. Amsterdam: John Benjamins.

Elšík, Viktor. 2000b. Dialect variation in Romani personal pronouns. In *Grammatical relations in Romani: The noun phrase*, ed. Viktor Elšík and Yaron Matras, 65–94. Amsterdam: John Benjamins.

Elšík, Viktor. 2007. Affix extraction: A case study on Hungarian Romani. PhD thesis. Prague: Charles University.

Elšík, Viktor, and Yaron Matras. 2006. *Markedness and language change: The Romani sample*. Berlin: Mouton De Gruyter.

Elšík, Viktor, Michael Beníšek, and Zuzana Bodnárová. In preparation. The linguistic atlas of Central Romani. Manuscript. Prague: Charles University.

Friedman, Victor A. 1991. Case in Romani: Old grammar in new affixes. *Journal of the Gypsy Lore Society*, 5th ser., 1: 85–102.

Friedman, Victor A. 2013. Compartmentalized grammar: The variable (non-) integration of Turkish verbal conjugation in Romani dialects. *Romani Studies*, 5th ser., 23 (1): 107–120.

Granqvist, Kimmo. 2012. *Lyhyt Suomen romanikielen kielioppi*. Helsinki: Kotimaisten kielten keskus.

Holzinger, Daniel. 1996. Verbal aspect and thematic organisation of Sinte narrative discourse. *Grazer Linguistische Studien* 46: 111–126.

Hübschmannová, Milena. 1984. Nominalization in Slovak Romani. *Quaderni Del Siculorum Gymnasium, Rassegna Della Facoltà Di Lettere E Filosofia Dell'Università Di Catania* 14: 27–70.

Hübschmannová, Milena, and Vít Bubeník. 1997. Causatives in Slovak and Hungarian Romani. In *The typology and dialectology of Romani*, ed. Yaron Matras, Peter Bakker, and Hristo Kyuchukov, 133–145. Amsterdam: John Benjamins.

Koptjevskaja-Tamm, Maria. 2000. Romani genitives in cross-linguistic perspective. In *Grammatical relations in Romani: The noun phrase*, ed. Viktor Elšík and Yaron Matras, 123–149. Amsterdam: John Benjamins.

Lípa, Jiří. 1967. Ke skloňování v cikánštině. *Slovo a Slovesnost* 28 (4): 406–410.

Matras, Yaron. 1995. Verb evidentials and their discourse function in Vlax Romani narratives. In *Romani in contact: The history, structure, and sociology of a language*, ed. Yaron Matras, 95–123. Amsterdam: Benjamins.

Matras, Yaron. 1997. The typology of case relations and case layer distribution in Romani. In *The typology and dialectology of Romani*, ed. Yaron Matras, Peter Bakker, and Hristo Kyuchukov, 61–93. Amsterdam: John Benjamins.

Matras, Yaron. 2000. The structural and functional composition of Romani demonstratives. In *Grammatical relations in Romani: The noun phrase*, ed. Viktor Elšík and Yaron Matras, 95–122. Amsterdam: John Benjamins.

Matras, Yaron. 2001. Tense, aspect, and modality categories in Romani. *Sprachtypologie Und Universalienforschung* 53 (4): 162–180.

Matras, Yaron. 2002. *Romani: A linguistic introduction*. Cambridge: Cambridge University Press.

Miltner, Vladimír. 1965. The morphologic structure of a new Indo-Aryan language of Czechoslovakia: A key to the Gypsy morphology. *Indian Linguistics* 26: 106–131.

Pirttisaari, Helena. 2005. A functional approach to the distribution of participle suffixes in Romani. In *General and applied Romani linguistics. Proceedings from the 6th international conference on Romani linguistics*, ed. Barbara Schrammel, Dieter W. Halwachs, and Gerd Ambrosch, 114–127. Munich: Lincom Europa.

Plank, Frans. 1995. (Re-)Introducing Suffixaufnahme. In *Double case: Agreement by Suffixaufnahme*, ed. Frans Plank, 3–110. New York: Oxford University Press.

Rusakov, Alexandr Ju. 2001. Imperative in North Russian Romani. In *Typology of imperative constructions*, ed. Victor S. Xrakovskij, 268–299. München: Lincom.

Rusakov, Alexandr Ju., and Olga Abramenko. 1998. North Russian Romani dialect: Interference in case system. *Grazer Linguistische Studien* 50: 109–133.

Schmid, Wolfgang P. 1963. Das Zigeunerische Abstraktsuffix *–ben/–pen*. *Indogermanische Forschungen* 68: 276–283.

Schrammel, Barbara. 2005. Borrowed verbal particles and prefixes in Romani: A comparative approach. In *General and applied Romani linguistics. Proceedings from the 6th international conference on Romani linguistics*, ed. Barbara Schrammel, Dieter W. Halwachs, and Gerd Ambrosch, 99–113. Munich: Lincom Europa.

Stump, Gregory. 1993. On rules of referral. *Language* 69: 449–479.

Wohlgemuth, Jan. 2009. *A typology of verbal borrowings*. Berlin: De Gruyter Mouton.

Woolner, Alfred C. 1924. Studies in Romani philology III: The verb substantive. *Journal of the Gypsy Lore Society*, 5th ser., 3: 180–184.

7

Romani Syntactic Typology

Evangelia Adamou and Yaron Matras

7.1 State of the Art

This chapter presents an overview of the principal syntactic-typological features of Romani dialects. It draws on the discussion in Matras (2002, chapter 7) while taking into consideration more recent studies. In particular, we draw on the wealth of morpho-syntactic data that have since become available via the Romani Morpho-Syntax (RMS) database.[1] The RMS data are based on responses to the Romani Morpho-Syntax questionnaire recorded from Romani-speaking communities across Europe and beyond. We try to take into account a representative sample. We also take into consideration data from free-speech recordings available in the RMS database and the Pangloss Collection. In addition, our chapter is informed by cross-linguistic studies in syntactic typology, as represented by the entries of the World Atlas of Language Structures (WALS), and other selected typological work.

Matras (2002, chapter 7) covers in comparative perspective prominent features of Romani syntactic typology, including linear order in the

---

E. Adamou (✉)
National Centre for Scientific Research in France (CNRS), Villejuif, France
e-mail: evangelia.adamou@cnrs.fr

Y. Matras
School of Arts, Languages, and Cultures,
University of Manchester, Manchester, UK
e-mail: yaron.matras@manchester.ac.uk

© The Author(s) 2020
Y. Matras and A. Tenser (eds.), *The Palgrave Handbook of Romani Language and Linguistics*, https://doi.org/10.1007/978-3-030-28105-2_7

187

noun phrase, constituent order in the verb phrase, possession and external possession, and complex clauses. Since then, only a small number of studies have considered specific topics in Romani syntactic typology in comparative perspective: Elšík and Matras (2006) devote chapters to modality (morphological) case roles and localization (the lexico-grammatical expression of spatial relations). Elšík and Matras (2009) discuss modality categories, while Matras and Tenser (2016) provide an overview of complementation. Tenser's (2016) discussion of semantic map borrowing in Northeastern Romani dialects is perhaps an isolated study of a syntactic-typological topic in a particular dialect group. In addition, consideration is given to syntactic-typological categories in a number of descriptive studies of individual dialects that have followed Matras (2002), among them Tenser (2005) on Lithuanian Romani; Tenser (2008) on the Northeastern dialects; Leggio (2011) on Mitrovica Romani; Arvaniti and Adamou (2011) and Adamou (2016) on Greek Thrace Romani; Adamou (2013) on Mexican Vlax; Bodnárová (2015) on Vend Romani; Leggio and Matras (2017) on Kangljari Romani; and Benišek (2017) on a North Central Romani 'diaspora' variety spoken in Ukraine.

7.2   The Noun

In this section, we discuss linear order in the noun phrase, the prepositional phrase and the possessive noun phrase, as well as agreement.

7.2.1 The Noun Phrase

The Romani noun phrase (NP) has four prenominal slots. Quantifiers such as 'all' and 'every' occupy the first slot. A number of determiners that typically do not combine with one another occupy the second slot: demonstratives, definite and indefinite articles, and possessive determiners such as 'my'. Numerals occupy the third slot, and descriptive adjectives the fourth, immediately preceding the noun. Demonstratives, possessive determiners and descriptive adjectives can (in some dialects) optionally follow the noun. Figure 7.1 illustrates the linear order within the Romani NP (adapted from Matras 2002).

[quantifier] + [determiner] + [numeral] + [adjective] + NOUN + [options]

Fig. 7.1   Linear order in the NP

7 Romani Syntactic Typology   189

Most Romani dialects have a four-term system of demonstratives which distinguishes reference to the discourse context vs. the speech situation (a distinction that only partly corresponds to proximal vs. distal in physical space), and +specific vs. −specific (Matras 2002, pp. 103–104). Some dialects exhibit a reduced two-term system (e.g. Sinti Romani) (for reference of dialect names, see Elšík and Beníšek, this volume). Demonstratives generally inflect for gender, number and case and typically precede the noun (DEM-N). The prenominal position is illustrated in (1) from Czech Vlax.

(1) Czech Vlax, Czech Republic (RMS, CZ-001, 386)[2]

kadi	angrustji	anda	somnakaj-i
this.NOM.F	ring	from	gold-is

'This ring is made of gold'.

In addition, demonstratives may follow the noun (N-DEM). This option is reported for some RMS dialects from Romania such as Ursari, Spoitori, Kurturare and Kangljari/Peptenari. In this case, however, the definite article is required (the article remains in the prenominal position), e.g. Spoitori *o skaunos kaka* (the chair this) 'this chair'; or Sofades Romani (Greece) *i romni adaja* (the woman this) 'this woman' (example 3 below).

The definite article always precedes the noun (ART-N), as in (2a) from Sofades Romani. Some dialects show reduction or a loss of the definite articles as a result of contact with languages that have no definite articles, as in (2b) from the Polska Roma dialect spoken in Poland, (2c) from a Lovari variety spoken in Russia and (2d) from Finnish Romani:

(2) 'I couldn't open the door'.
(a) Sofades, Greece (RMS, GR-004, 419)

nasti	putravas	i	porta
cannot	open.1SG.REM	DEF.OBL.F	door

(b) Polska Roma, Poland (RMS, PL-003, 419)

me	na	mogindžom	te	phiravel	vudara
I	NEG	can.PFTV.1SG	COMP	open.INF	door

(c) Lovari Čokeši, Russia (RMS, RUS-005, 419)

mə	naštyk	putros	udar
I	cannot	open.1SG.REM	door

(d) East Finnish Romani, Finland (RMS, FIN-002, 419)

me	na	vojuvā	firavel	fūtar
I	NEG	can.1SG	open.INF	door

In most Romani dialects, demonstratives and definite articles cannot form combinations. However, in Romani dialects of Greece, combinations are possible, under Greek influence (Igla 1996, p. 165). In (3) from Sofades, a demonstrative precedes the article (DEM-ART-N), and another follows the noun (ART-N-DEM).

(3) Sofades, Greece (RMS, GR-004, 422)

adaj	i	čhaj
this.NOM.F	DEF.NOM.F	girl

i	romni	adaja
DEF.NOM.F	woman	this.NOM.F

therela	trine	čhaven
has.3SG	three.OBL	children.OBL.PL
'This girl, this woman, has three children'.		

Romani shows an indefinite article, used with singular nouns, derived from the numeral *jek/ekh/ek* 'one', grammaticalized to various degrees (Matras 1994; Friedman 2001). Example in (4) shows the indefinite article in Vlax Romani from Greece accompanying the presentation of a new participant. Example (5) illustrates the indefinite article with a non-referential noun. Adamou (2016, p. 158) notes that in this Romani variety, the indefinite article is not used with generic nouns, representing the highest level of grammaticalization.

(4) Xoraxane, Greece (Pangloss Collection, https://doi.org/10.24397/pangloss-0000297#S1)

ek	xoraxni	sas	kxamni
INDF	Turkish_woman	was.3SG	pregnant
'A Turkish woman was pregnant'.			

(5) Xoraxane, Greece (Pangloss Collection, https://doi.org/10.24397/pangloss-0000297#S10)

mangav	phenel	ek	romni
want.1SG	says.3SG	INDF	woman
'He says: I want a woman'.			

7 Romani Syntactic Typology   **191**

Like definite articles, indefinite articles too are lost in some dialects (such as Polish and Russian Romani) due to contact.

Romani numerals and quantifiers precede nouns (NUM-N, QNT-N). This order is illustrated in (6) for the numeral 'two' and in (7) for the quantifier 'many'.

(6) Kalderaš, Romania (RMS, RO-065, 477)

si	ma	duj	peha
is	me.OBL	two	sisters

'I have two sisters'.

(7) Mečkari, Albania (RMS, AL-001, Txt)

ka	tə	aven	but	manuša	andre
COMP	COMP	come.3PL	many	men	inside

'So that many people can get in'.

Adjectives that express a descriptive property, such as 'big', 'good' or 'red', precede the nouns (ADJ-N). This is illustrated in (8) for the adjective 'big' in Mexican Vlax. However, speakers can also postpose adjectives (Matras 2002, p. 167), though the precise motivations in terms of information structure and correlation with prosodic features are not yet fully understood. This is the case in various RMS samples from Romania, including Vlax, Sinti and Romungro, as well as in Vlax dialects in other countries (Czech Republic, Mexico and Ukraine), Lombard Sinti, as well as in some samples from the Balkans, including Albania, Macedonia and Serbia. The N-ADJ order is illustrated in (9) for Mexican Vlax, using the same adjective, 'big'. (Note that variation in the placement of the adjective is also found in the current contact language, Spanish, associated with differences in meaning or in the degree of evaluation.)

(8) Mexican Vlax, Mexico (RMS, MX-001, 593)

o	dat	katar	šavořo	sas	les	ek	bari	šoro
DEF	father	from	boy	was	him.OBL	INDF	big	beard

'The boy's father had such a big beard'.

(9) Mexican Vlax, Mexico (RMS, MX-001, 908)

jek	žukel	baro	daravel	le	cinořen
INDF	dog	big	frighten.3SG	DEF	children.OBL.PL

'A big dog frightens the children'.

Unlike in Mexican Vlax, in some dialects postnominal adjectives only occur with doubling of the definite article, e.g. in Agia Varvara Vlax in Greece: *i čhej i bari* (the girl the big) 'the big girl', replicating the Greek model (Igla 1996, p. 166). Whereas in Romani determiner spreading requires a post-nominal adjective, in Modern Greek it can occur with both a prenominal and postnominal adjective (Kolliakou 2004).

7.2.2 Prepositional Phrase

Romani has prepositions, as commonly found in other Indo-European languages spoken in Europe, whereas postpositions are dominant in Modern Indo-Aryan languages of the Indian subcontinent:

(10) Sofia Erli, Bulgaria (RMS, BG-024, 644)

o	lil	si	upral	i	masa
DEF	letter	is	on	DEF	table

'The letter is on the table'.

7.2.3 Possessive Noun Phrase

The locus of marking in the possessive noun phrase is on the dependent (possessor), not on the head of the phrase (possessed noun). The order of the genitive adnominal (possessor) in relation to the head noun (possessed) is typically GEN-N, the genitive preceding the noun it modifies. Romani adnominal genitives can serve to identify the referent that is expressed by the head noun; they are dubbed 'anchoring' genitive adnominals (Koptjevskaja-Tamm 2000, p. 126). Anchoring genitive adnominals are used among others for kinship, as illustrated in (11), body parts, as in (12), and ownership, as in (13). Genitive adnominals in Romani can also serve to qualify the head noun, for example, to express quality, age, duration or material, as illustrated in (14). These are the so-called non-anchoring genitive adnominals. Koptjevskaja-Tamm (2000, p. 145) stresses that anchoring genitive adnominals are closer to nouns, as they involve reference, whereas non-anchoring genitive adnominals show lower degrees of similarity with nouns as they are non-referential.

(11) Czech Vlax, Czech Republic (RMS, CZ-001, 594)

koda-j	šāv-esk-i	dej
this.NOM.F-DEF.NOM.F	boy-GEN.M-NOM.F	mother

sas	lāši	taj	kamaratska
was	nice.F	and	friendly

'The boy's mother was nice and friendly'.

(12) Czech Vlax, Czech Republic (RMS, CZ-001, 600)

e	rom-esk-o	šejro
DEF.OBL.M	man-GEN.M-NOM.M	head

sas	tejle	šaradoj	kolopo-sa
was	down	cover.GER	hat-INS

'The man's head was covered with a hat'.

(13) Czech Vlax, Czech Republic (RMS, CZ-001, 511)

jekhe	šāv-esk-o	gad	sas	šingerdo
one.OBL	boy-GEN.M-NOM.M	shirt	was	cut

'One boy's shirt was torn'.

(14) Kalajdži, Bulgaria (RMS, BG-007, 841)

kindem	galben-osk-o	koro
buy.PFTV.1SG	gold-GEN.M-NOM.M	bracelet

thaj	ka	dav	les	məndrə	dija-ke
and	FUT	give.1SG	it.OBL	my.OBL	mother.OBL.F-DAT

'I bought a golden bracelet that I will give to my mother'.

As these examples show, possessors in the genitive case agree with the possessed head noun in number, gender, as well as in case, here in the nominative. Romani thus offers a typologically interesting example of 'double case' or 'Suffixaufhname' (Payne 1995; Plank 1995). These examples further illustrate that determiners, such as articles, demonstratives and numerals, can determine the possessor. For example, the definite article *e* in (12) is in the oblique case, agreeing with the genitive case of the possessor 'man'. In (11), however, the demonstrative, *kodaj* 'this', agrees with the possessed head noun in gender and case, a type of agreement noted by Koptjevskaja-Tamm (2000, p. 130) as a breakdown of the traditional system.

In some Romani dialects, the genitive may appear in the postnominal position (N-GEN) with more or less high frequency (this option is reported in RMS samples from the Balkans, including Albania, Bulgaria, Greece, Macedonia, Romania and in some samples from Serbia, but also in Molise Romani, Crimean Romani, Eastern Rumungro and two samples

194   E. Adamou and Y. Matras

from Ukraine). In this case, a definite article determines both the head noun and the genitive. This is illustrated in (15) with an example from Sofades Romani, a variety in contact with Greek that shares a similar pattern, i.e. *o pateras tu ayorju* (DEF.NOM.SG.M father.NOM.SG.M DEF.GEN.SG.N boy.GEN.SG.N) 'the boy's father'.

(15) Sofades, Greece (RMS, GR-004, 593)

o	dat	i	čhav-esk-o
DEF.M	father	DEF.OBL.M	boy-GEN.M-NOM.M

thelas	but	bare	čhora
had.3SG.REM	very	big.PL	beard

'The boy's father had such a big beard'.

In some dialects, the postnominal order is preferred for compounds in non-anchoring function, e.g. in Lovari *kher le dil-eng-o* (house DEF.OBL. PL crazy-GEN.PL-NOM.M) 'mental institution'. These kinds of genitive adnominals are compatible with definite articles, e.g. *o kher le dilengo* (DEF.NOM.M house DEF.OBL.PL crazy-GEN.PL-NOM.M) 'the mental institution'.

7.2.4 Agreement

Romani nominals inflect for case, gender and number. Definite articles, demonstratives, adjectives and genitive adnominals inflect for case, gender and number, whereas indefinite articles only inflect for case. Romani has a relatively large case inventory, with 6–7 case types in the sense of Iggesen (2013, WALS 49): it has an (unmarked) nominative, an independent oblique, as well as dative, ablative, locative, genitive and instrumental, which attach to the oblique case (see Elšík, this volume). A vocative suffix is also integrated into the nominal paradigm and has potential effect on agreement. As many other Indo-European languages, Romani is a language with two genders; following Corbett (2013, WALS 30), we consider a language to have a gender system when there are different agreement patterns with the verb, adjective, numeral or determiner:

(16) Arli, Macedonia (RMS, MK-003, 593)

bari	brada
big.NOM.F	beard

'a big beard'

(17) Arli, Macedonia (RMS, MK-003, 908)

baro   džukeł
big.NOM.M   dog
'a big dog'

Gender agreement is neutralized in the plural of adjectives. Gender loss is ongoing in some Romani dialects due to contact with languages with no gender distinction, as in Finnish Romani. In (18), genitive *caiesko* in *-o* (originally masculine) accompanies the head noun 'father' (masculine), while in (19), the same form appears with 'mother' (feminine):

(18) Finnish Romani, Finland (RMS, FIN-002, 596)

cai-esko	tāt	cinjas	ta	peres	nevo	pēres
girl-GEN	father	buy.PFTV.3SG	this	year	new	car

'The girl's father bought a new car this year'.

(19) Finnish Romani, Finland (RMS, FIN-002, 597)

cai-esko	taieha	sas	hyök	sonatiko	angrusti
girl-GEN	mother	was	beautiful	golden	ring

'The girl's mother had a beautiful gold necklace'.

7.3   The Verb

7.3.1 Alignment

Following Malchukov, Haspelmath and Comrie (2010), we distinguish three types of constructions involving a verb: intransitive constructions comprise a single argument (S). Monotransitive constructions comprise an agent or agent-like argument (A) and a patient or patient-like argument (P), traditionally referred to as an object. Ditransitive constructions consist of a (ditransitive) verb, an agent argument (A), a recipient-like argument (R) and a theme argument (T). At the notional level, the R argument would correspond to what is traditionally known as an indirect object, and the T argument to a direct object.

Most Romani dialects display what Malchukov, Haspelmath and Comrie (2010) identify as neutral alignment $(A = S = P)$ in most clauses, alongside what is identified as accusative alignment $(A = S \neq P)$ in 'indexing' (agreement or person cross-reference) and 'flagging' (adpositional marking) with animates, see more details in Sect. 7.6. In ditransitive constructions, alignment is neutral when considering 'ordering' (word order) and 'indexing' (T = P = R), though it is indirective in 'flagging' (T = P ≠ R). In sum, Romani does not rely on word order to encode the functions of core arguments. Rather, information structuring determines word order in the verb phrase.

7.3.2 Word Order in Main Clauses

Most Romani dialects exhibit what can be classified as a thetic-categorical distinction in word order patterns (cf. Sasse 1995; Matras 1995): categorical predications, or those that pick up a topical category as the perspective of the utterance, tend to show the subject in pre-verbal position. This is exemplified in (20), where Speaker A introduces the topical entity 'The Bajaša' (the Beash people) in a question. Speaker B then picks up the same as a topic entity to answer the question in the following turn in an adjacency pair:

(20) Kurturare, Romania (RMS, RO-015, Txt)
Speaker A:

Vi	e	Bajaša	žan	po	kris?
also	DEF.PL	Bajaša	go.PL	to.DEF.M	court

Speaker B:

Le	Bajaša	či	žan,	le	Bajaša	marən	pe
DEF.PL	Bajaša	NEG	go.PL	DEF.PL	Bajaša	fight.PL	REFL

Speaker A: 'Do the Bajaša also go to kris [Romani court]?'

Speaker B: 'The Bajaša do not go, the Bajaša fight'.

Thetic constructions, on the other hand, do not rely on picking up a single argument as a predication base but instead on the situation as a whole. This is indicated through verb-subject (VS) word order. VS order is often used in presentational constructions to introduce new topics into a narrative setting.

(21) Nea Smirni, Greece (RMS, GR-032, Txt)

aviljo	othe	lako	čhavo	kata	xorafi
came.3SG.M	there	her.M	boy	from	field

'Her boy came there from the fields'.

Another frequent function of VS order is consecutive, where the predication is introduced as an immediate consequence of the preceding one:

(22) Lovari (Matras 1994, p. 117)

(a)

Vi	mure	papos	avile	line	anda
also	my.OBL	grandfather.OBL	come.PFTV.3PL	took.PFTV.3PL	from

o	kher,	marde	les.
DEF.OBL.M	house	beat.PFTV.3PL	him.OBL

'They came and picked up my grandfather too, they beat him'.

(b)

Taj	gelas	lesko	káko	taj	počindas	vareso	bare	bare
and	went.3SG	his.M	uncle	and	pay. PFTV.3SG	something	big.PL	big.PL

love	taj	kindas	les	avri.
money	and	buy.PFTV.3SG	him.OBL	out

'And (so) his uncle went and paid a lot of money and bought him free'.

(c)

Taj	muri	mami	garádžulas
and	my.F	grandmother	hide.3SG.REM

ande	veša	mure	dadesa.
in.PL	woods	my.OBL.M	father.INS

'And my grandmother was hiding in the woods with my father'.

The event portrayed in (22b) is presented as the outcome of the preceding state of affairs; this is indicated through VS order. In (22c), we then have a new perspective, introduced by anchoring the predication around a different topical entity. Here, SV order occurs.

These discourse-pragmatic functions allow making some general predictions about the occurrences of SV and VS, which relativize the impression of free or extremely flexible word order rules. Arguably, there are also additional factors that play a role in the choice of word order, most notably the choice of particular types of predicates and subjects. Igla (1996, p. 153) suggests that VS is the unmarked word order when the subject is inanimate, non-determined and a non-agent, the variant SV being restricted to a (contrastive) emphasis of S. On the other hand, maximum variation is found with subjects that are animate, determined, and which figure as agents. The constraints on variability are thus understood as a continuum (non-agentive animate subjects figuring in between). Predicates that are more likely to trigger VS are those involved in presentative constructions, such as existentials and some verbs of motion, particularly those expressing arrival. Igla (1996, p. 151) lists in this connection statements about time and nature (*nakhlas ekh berš* 'a year passed').

In Romani monotransitive clauses, P-like arguments generally follow the verb, whether they are new or given in the discourse:

(23) Xoraxane, Greece (Adamou 2016, p. 176)

lav	e	lastika
take.1SG	DEF.OBL.F	hose

'I take the hose'.

P-like arguments may precede the verb for topicalization and focus, generally combining with prosodic marking (Arvaniti and Adamou 2011), as in (24), where the focused constituent, 'pills', combines with de-accenting of the postfocal material, in this case the verb.

(24) Xoraxane, Greece (Arvaniti and Adamou 2011, p. 243)

me	apora	peradom
my	pills	lost.1SG

'I lost my PILLS'.

Fronting of P arguments is possible in a variety of dialects (reported for RMS samples from Bulgaria, Czech Vlax, Romungro, Finnish Romani, Macedonian Arli, Gabor and Šušuwaje in Romania).

Universally, A arguments are rarely expressed by full NPs in natural discourse, as noted for several corpora from a variety of languages (Haig and Schnell 2016). In Romani, when A arguments are expressed by an NP and co-occur with P pronominal arguments, the pronominal P argument follows the verb:

(25) Erli (Boretzky 1998, p. 147)

pale	dikhel	la	o	thagar
again	see.3SG	her.OBL	DEF.NOM.M	king

'The king saw her again'.

(26) Welsh Romani (Sampson 1926, p. 226)

kamdias	les	ī	raklī
love.PFTV.3SG	him.OBL	DEF.NOM.F	girl

'The girl loved him'.

The typical Balkan 'pronominal object doubling' construction is found in the Balkan and Vlax dialects of Romani (RMS samples from Bulgaria, Moldavia, Romania, Ukraine, as well as in Nea Smirni in Greece, Molise in Italy, and some samples in Serbia and Kosovo). Pronominal object doubling involves exposition of a topical patient, with a co-referential resumptive pronoun in the position following the verb (cf. Bubeník 1997, p. 100; see also Friedman 2000):

(27) Sepeči, Turkey (Cech and Heinschink 1999, p. 142)

adaja	gili	da	but	gilavelas	la
this.F	song	too	much	sing.3SG.REM	her.OBL

'She used to often sing this song too'.

(28) Bugurdži (Boretzky 1993a, p. 95)

patózel	les	o	divi	e	romes
squeeze.3SG	him.OBL	DEF.NOM.M	giant	DEF.OBL.M	man.OBL

'The giant squeezes the man'.

There is agreement that the construction is not grammaticalized in Romani, but represents a facultative structure triggered at the discourse level (see Boretzky 1993a, pp. 94–96; Bubeník 1997, p. 102; Friedman 2000, p. 197). Friedman (2000) points out that unlike the other Balkan languages, Romani preserves a rather complex case declension and does not have a clear opposition between clitic and non-clitic object pronouns. Both the motivation for object doubling and the structural resources employed in the construction therefore differ.

In Romani ditransitive constructions, with verbs such as 'to give', 'to sell', 'to lend', 'to tell', recipient-like arguments (cf. indirect objects) and theme-like arguments (cf. direct objects) typically follow the verb. In several dialects, nominal R arguments may precede or follow nominal T arguments; thus, in most RMS samples from Romania, the two orders are equally frequent. TR (or DO-IO) order is possible in Ukraine, possible but not preferred in Sofia Erli and Spoitori, while it is the preferred option in Nea Smirni in Greece. The two word order patterns are exemplified in (29a) and (29b). Similar options are available for pronominal arguments.

(29) 'The priest gives the godmother the baby'.
AVRT
(a) Kalderaš, Serbia (RMS, YU-010, 965)

o	rašaj	del	e	čjirv-ja-ke
DEF.NOM.M	priest	give.3SG	DEF.OBL.F	godmother-OBL.F-DAT

e				cinor-es
DEF.OBL.F				baby-OBL.M

AVTR
(b) Lithuanian Romani, Lithuania (RMS, LT-005/LT-008, 965)

rašaj	del	čhavor-es	bold-e	da-ke
priest	give.3SG	boy-OBL.M	baptized-OBL.M	mother.OBL.F-DAT

Definite and indefinite animate T arguments can be fronted or topicalized in a number of dialects, but this is more rarely the case for inanimate T arguments (coding indicates this possibility in four RMS samples for definite inanimate objects in the accusative; none when they are indefinite). T arguments can precede verbs when focused, as can be seen in the example in (30). Here, the T argument, 'swipes', combines with the focus-sensitive particle *em*. The R argument, the dative pronoun *tuke* 'to you', remains in the postverbal position.

TVR
(30) Xoraxane, Greece (Adamou 2016, p. 179)

em	birindʒi	moromandila	aas	tuke
FOC	first_class	swipes	give.1SG.REM	you.DAT

'I was giving you first-class swipes!'

In the Northeastern dialects, non-topical R arguments appear before the verb, as in example (31) where the dative pronoun *tuke* 'to you' precedes the verb 'to tell' (see Boretzky 1996b, p. 102; Rusakov and Abramenko 1998, p. 128).

TARV
(31) Russian Roma, Russia (RMS, RUS-003, 963)

im'ej	v	vidu	odova	so	me	tuke	rakirav
have	in	mind	that.M	what	I	you.DAT	tell.1SG

'You should keep in mind what I tell you'.

7.3.3 Word Order in Interrogative and Subordinate Clauses

In wh-questions, the wh-word appears in clause initial position:

(32) 'What did he give you? Nothing'.
(a) Romungro, Hungary (RMS, HU-009, 385)

so	tut	dinja?		ništa
what	you.OBL	give.PFTV.3SG		nothing

(b) Lovari, Serbia (RMS, YU-015, 385)

so	das	tu	vo?	khanči
what	give.PFTV.3SG	you	he.NOM	nothing

In yes/no questions, a VS order is illustrated for Romungro in (33). Variation between a VS and an SV order is recorded in RMS samples from Velingrad Yerli in Bulgaria, Romungro in Hungary, Molise and Kylmyš in Ukraine, and Katolikurja in Serbia, Gabor, Šušuwaje, Piculesči and Spoitari from Romania, among other. VS dominant order in yes/no clauses is reported in the RMS samples from Nea Smirni in Greece, Lombard Sinti in Italy, Mexican Vlax, and in most dialects of Romania.

(33) 'Is the water boiling?'
Romungro, Hungary (RMS, HU-009, 887)

tatjol	o	pānji?
boil.3SG	DEF.M	water

In non-factual subordinations, such as purpose clauses, modal complements and conditional clauses introduced by *te*, the verb immediately follows the conjunction *te*. In some dialects, the verb may occupy the final sentence position, in particular through influence from Slavic contact languages. Such uses are reported in the RMS samples from the Balkans (Bulgaria, Greece, Macedonia and Serbia) but also Austrian Sinti, Romungro in Hungary, Molise in Italy, Crimean in Russia, Laeši Kurtej in Moldavia, Kubanska Vlaxurja in Ukraine and Eastern Rumungro in Slovakia. Examples (34) and (35) illustrate the variation in the position of the verb in a subordinate clause in Romungro, occurring within the same elicitation context.

(34) Romungro, Hungary (RMS, HU-009, 345b)

na	kamav	ando	gav	te	džan
NEG	want.1SG	in.DEF.M	village	COMP	go.INF

'I do not want to go to town'.

(35) Romungro, Hungary (RMS, HU-009, 346b)

na	kames	te	džan	ando	gav
NEG	want.2SG	COMP	go.INF	in.DEF.M	village

'You do not want to go to town'.

Sinti varieties show various degrees of convergence with German word order rules. In the most extreme cases, the German distinction between main clause (verb in second position), subordinate clause (verb in final position) and interrogative clause (verb in initial position) is adopted consistently (see Matras 1999b).

Non-factual complement clauses and conditional clauses, both introduced by *te*, show an overwhelming, if not absolute, tendency towards VS order.

(36) Lovari (Matras 1994, p. 225)

amende	akana	te	merel	varekon
us.LOC	now	COMP	die.3SG	somebody

'Among us, now, if somebody dies ...'

(37) Sinti, Germany (Holzinger 1993, p. 163)

me	kamoms	te	vals	tu
I	want.1SG.REM	COMP	come.2SG.REM	you

'I would have liked you to have come'.

(38) Sinti, Germany (Holzinger 1993, p. 156)

te	krel	miri	čaj	kova,	dan	leli	daba
COMP	do.3SG	my.F	daughter	this	then	get.3SG.F	blows

'If my daughter does this, she will get blows'.

This rule is not compromised even in those varieties of German Sinti that have adopted German word order and that have the verb in final position in all other subordinate clauses (Matras 1999b). Isolated exceptions to the rule are found however in some of the Central dialects (Boretzky 1996b, p. 107) and most systematically in Roman as shown in (39).

(39) Roman (Wogg and Halwachs 1998, p. 53)

te	me	valakaj	gejom
COMP	I	somewhere	went.1SG

'If I went somewhere...'

For Sepeči, Cech and Heinschink (1999, p. 144) suggest that tendencies towards VS in temporal adverbial clauses, as in (40), may be overridden when S is focused, resulting in SV, as in (41). Example in (42) illustrates SV order with a pronoun.

(40) Sepeči, Turkey (Cech and Heinschink 1999, p. 144)

kana	isine	o	roma	ko	balanipe
when	was	DEF.M	Rom.PL	in	Greece

'When the Rom were in Greece...'

(41) Sepeči, Turkey (Cech and Heinschink 1999, p. 144)

kana				čhaj	isinomas
when				girl	was.1SG

'When I was a young girl ...'

(42) Xoraxani, Bulgaria (RMS, BG-015, 869)

kana	odva	asala	bütüj	kvartal	može	te
when	DEM.M	laugh.3SG	everyone	neighbour	can	COMP

šunel						les
hear.3SG						him.OBL

'When he laughs, the whole neighbourhood can hear him'.

Some Central European dialects show tendencies towards what Boretzky refers to as a 'split verb frame' (Boretzky 1996b, pp.104–105). This involves the fronting of constituents of the modal quasi-infinitive verb in *te*-clauses, see examples in (43) from Roman and from Polska Roma in (44).

(43) Roman (Wogg and Halwachs 1998, p. 48)

ada	berš	kezdinčom	andi	iškola	te	džal
this	year	begin.PFTV.1SG	in.F	school	COMP	go.INF

'That year I began to go to school'.

(44) Polska Roma (Matras 1999a, p. 19)

taša	džasam	sare	dro	veš	kašta	te	čhineł
tomorrow	go.1PL.FUT	all	in	forest	wood.PL	COMP	cut.INF

'Tomorrow we will all go to the forest to cut wood'.

7.4 Complex Clauses

7.4.1 Relative Clauses

In this chapter, we rely on the definition of relative clauses as subordinate clauses that are used to delimit the reference of a NP (Andrews 2007). Almost all Romani dialects in the RMS sample introduce relative clauses with the uninflected complementizers *kaj* (from *kaj* 'where'). Most also use the uninflected complementizer *so/hoj* 'what' to relativize nouns referring to non-humans, but some dialects additionally use them for humans. Some dialects also use the relative pronouns *savo* 'which' (inflecting for case, gender and number) and *kon* 'who' (inflecting for case). As seen in (45), Romani relative clauses are externally headed and postnominal; that is, the relative clause follows the head noun (NRel). Subject relativizers can follow two 'primary' relativization strategies (Keenan and Comrie 1977): the 'gap strategy' shows a complementizer without explicit coreferentiality with the head noun (45a), while the inflected relative pronoun (45b) shows agreement with the head noun:

(45) 'The man who came to the wedding has many new cars/a new car'.
(a) Nea Smirni Romani, Greece (RMS, GR-032, 590)

oduua	rom	ka	avilo	ko	bjav
that.M	man	COMP	come.PFTV.3SG	to.M	wedding

isineh	but	nava	amakši
was	many	new	car

(b) Kaldaraš, Romania (RMS, RO-008, 590)

o	murš	savo	avilo	kaj	nunta
DEF.NOM.M	man	who	come.PFTV.3SG	to.F	wedding

si	les	mašina	nevi
is.3SG	him.OBL	car	new.F

Pronominal resumption in relative clauses may have developed in Early Romani through contact with Greek (Matras 1994, pp. 206–210); it is also available in Modern Greek (Alexopoulou 2006). Case, animacy and definiteness may condition the resumptive strategy, which in many dialects is obligatory with non-nominative subjects.

Examples in (46) and (47) illustrate optional resumption in restrictive relatives. In (46a), the resumptive pronoun carries the case marking for the direct object relative clause. In (46b), there is no resumption, but the head is marked for the oblique (direct object) case.

(46) 'The man that I/we saw yesterday is here (again)'.
(a) Kaldaraš, Romania (RMS, RO-008, 809)

o	manuš	savo	dikhljam	les	arači
DEF.NOM.M	man	REL	see.PFTV.1PL	him.OBL	yesterday

sy	pale	kače
is	again	here

(b) Nea Smirni Romani, Greece (RMS, GR-032, 809)

i	muršes	kaj	dikhlom	i rat	isi	athe
DEF.OBL.M	man.OBL.M	COMP	see.PFTV.1SG	yesterday	is	here

Similarly, in (47a), no resumption appears where the relative pronoun *saveske* inflects for case, while in (47b) resumption carrying case marking accompanies the uninflected complementiser *ka*:

(47) 'This is the boy who I gave the money to'.
(a) Kaldaraš, Romania (RMS, RO-008, 813)

kadoa	sy	o	raklo	saves-ke	dem	love
this.M	is	DEF.NOM.M	boy	REL.OBL-DAT	gave.1SG	money

(b) Nea Smirni Romani, Greece (RMS, GR-032, 813)

oduva	o	čhavo	ka	dinom	leh	o	love
this.M	DEF.NOM.M	boy	COMP	gave.1SG	him.OBL	DEF.M	money

7.4.2 Complement Clauses

A complement clause functions as a core argument of the matrix verb instead of a NP (Dixon 2010, pp. 370, 380). Typical matrix verbs with complement clauses are epistemic verbs, such as 'say', 'see', 'know', and manipulation verbs, such as 'want', 'ask', 'tell'. Modal verbs of a 'secondary semantic type', such as 'begin', verbs expressing mental states, like 'fear', and the impersonal modals of ability 'can', 'cannot' and necessity 'must', also introduce complement clauses. In typological perspective, Romani complement

206 E. Adamou and Y. Matras

clauses are finite and 'balanced'; that is, the verb form follows that of the independent declarative (Cristofaro 2013, WALS 128). Romani complement clauses are introduced by complementizers of the types KAJ and TE (see Matras and Tenser 2016 for a recent overview). KAJ (from 'where') is also used for relative clauses. TE can probably be linked to an Old Indo-Aryan correlative function (Matras 2002, p. 180) and also introduces conditional clauses. KAJ introduces complements portraying factual events, with an independent truth-value, whereas TE introduces non-factual or modal events, with no independent truth-value. This mirrors a distinction found in the Balkan languages. Friedman (1985) discusses *te* in the context of what he calls the 'Dental Modal Subordinator' of the Balkan languages whose primary function is to denote ontologically non-real events (Balkan Slavic *da*, Albanian *të*, Romanian *să*, Greek *na*).

In several dialects, the complementizer KAJ has been replaced by borrowed functional equivalents: Vlax *kə/ke* from Romanian; Arli and Greek Vlax *oti* from Greek; and Central Romani *hod/hodž/hod'/hot/hoj* from Hungarian. By contrast, TE is stable, with rare exceptions; for example, Bulgarian Xoraxani borrows *da* from Bulgarian. In some dialects, the complementizer is omitted with uninflected impersonal modals of positive and negative ability 'can' and 'cannot' (see Elšík and Matras 2006, p. 206; Matras and Tenser 2016 for more details). Welsh Romani and Istrian/Slovene Romani are the only dialects that have not retained the factuality distinction, but generalize *te*.

Examples in (48) illustrate the use of KAJ:

(48) 'They (probably) thought that I was in the pub'.
Arli, Macedonia (RMS, MK-003, 460)

ola	najverojatno	mislinde	kaj	injum	me	ko	bari
they	probably	think.PFTV.3PL	COMP	was.1SG	I	to.M	bar

Kalderaš, Serbia (RMS, YU-010, 460)

von	gndosardine	kaj	sem	me	ando	birto
they	think.PFTV.3PL	COMP	was.1SG	I	in.M	bar

East Slovak, Slovakia (RMS, SK-011, 460)

mišljinde	peske	hoj	som	and(r)e	karčma
think.PFTV.3PL	REFL.DAT	COMP	is.1SG	in.M	bar

TE is used for non-factual events. Agent control and manipulative intent of the agent are relevant aspects in manipulation clauses involving a manipulator (the agent of the modal verb) and a manipulee (the agent of the complement verb) (see Matras 2002; Matras and Tenser 2016). On the hierarchy of control, we find in some dialects a split between the plain use of TE and a combination of TE and a 'reinforcer', often KAJ, in the combination *kaj te*, etc. (see Matras and Tenser 2016), especially with different-subject manipulation or weak manipulative power or intent:

(49) 'I want him/her to go away/home'.
(a) Arli, Macedonia (RMS, MK-003, 436)

mangava	le	te	džal	peske
want.1SG	him.OBL	COMP	go.3SG	REFL.DAT

(b) Kalderaš, Serbia (RMS, YU-010, 436)

me	kamav	te	voj	žaltar
I	want.1SG	COMP	she	go_away.3SG

(c) East Slovak Romani, Slovakia (RMS, SK-011, 436)

kamav	hoj	te	džal	khere
want.1SG	COMP	COMP	go.INF	home

(d) Polska Roma, Poland (RMS, PL-018, 436)

kamdomys	kej	te	otdžał	juv
wan.PFTV.1SG.REM	COMP	COMP	go.INF	he

(e) Sinti, Romania (RMS, RO-022, 436)

kamau	ti	džal	u	vek
want.1SG	COMP	go.3SG	to	away

(50) 'I told her to buy mushrooms, onions and cabbage'.
(a) Arli, Macedonia (RMS, MK-003, 438)

vakerdum	łake	te	kineł	pečurke	purum	hem	armin
tell.PFTV.1SG	her.DAT	COMP	buy.3SG	mushrooms	onions	and	cabbage

(b) Kalderaš, Serbia (RMS, YU-010, 438)

me	lake	phendem	te	čjinol	gljive	purum
I	her.DAT	tell.PFTV.1SG	COMP	buy.3SG	mushrooms	onions

taj	šax
and	cabbage

(c) East Slovak, Slovakia (RMS, SK-011, 438)

phendžom	lake	hoj	te	cinel	hubi
tell.PFTV.1SG	her.DAT	COMP	COMP	buy.INF	mushrooms

cibulja	he	jarmin
onions	and	cabbage

(d) Polska Roma, Poland (RMS, PL-018, 438)

phendom	łake	te	kineł	gžyby	purom	i	armen
tell.PFTV.1SG	her.DAT	COMP	buy.INF	mushrooms	onions	and	cabbage

(e) Sinti, Romania (RMS, RO-022, 438)

phindžjom	laki	te	kinel	i	šfami
tell.PFTV.1SG	her.DAT	COMP	buy.3SG	DEF.NOM.PL	mushrooms

puruma	ti	šaxa
onions	and	cabbage

Manipulation and purpose clauses in Romani generally show similar complementation strategies (see Sect. 7.4.3).

7.4.3 Adverbial Clauses

Romani adverbial clauses are generally finite; that is, the verbs in the subordinate clause are marked for person and number. They are introduced by various adverbial subordinators, which derive from grammaticalized inherited items as well as borrowings, and occupy the initial position in the subordinating clause. Table 7.1 presents an overview of the Romani adverbial subordinators.

Boretzky (1993b) notes that Romani dialects distinguish conditional clauses based on the truth-value of the proposition, in particular, between realis and irrealis, similar to other Balkan languages (cf. Friedman 1985). Examples in (51) illustrate the conditional clauses for realis from the main dialectal groups in the RMS samples. Most conditional clauses are introduced by the subordinator TE. Some dialects exhibit variation with borrowed subordinators such as *ako* (from Slavic), as in (51b) from the Kalderaš variety, while Polska Roma shows *ho* 'what', which has been generalized as an adverbial subordinator, in (51d).

7 Romani Syntactic Typology   209

Table 7.1 Adverbial subordinators in Romani

conditional	condition (realis and irrealis)	te, bi/by, ako, -se, kana, kada, an te
	potential condition ('whether')	te, ob te, či/čy, dali, li, mi
	concessive condition ('even if')	vi te, nina te, kajk te
	irrealis concession ('as if')	har/sar te, hata kaj
temporal	simultaneity	kana, kada/keda, sar/har/syr, kaj, so, afu
	anteriority	sar/syr/har, angla sar, angla kodo ke, bi te na, prin te
	posteriority	kana, kada/keda, sar/har/syr, kaj, so, posle, čim, pala kodo ke, akana, jekh kaj, jekh ta
causal relations	cause, reason, explanation	kaj, kə/ke, vajl, anda kodo ke, sostar, soske, sar, adake sar, sebepi kaj, afu, jati, zere, bo, mer, jer, lebo, pošto
purpose		te/ti, kaj te, hot te, kə te, ja te, či te
other	negative circumstance ('without')	bi te, oni te

(51) 'If I drink a lot of milk, I will be strong'.
(a) Arli, Macedonia (RMS, MK-003, 423)

te	pilum	but	thud	k	ovav	but	silno
COMP	drink.PFTV.1SG	much	milk	FUT	become.1SG	much	strong.M

(b) Kalderaš, Serbia (RMS, YU-010, 423)

ako	pjav	but	thud	avava		zuralo
if	drink.1SG	many	milk	become.FUT.1SG		strong.M

(c) East Slovak, Slovakia (RMS, SK-011, 423)

te	pijava	but	thud	avava		zoralji
COMP	drink.FUT.1SG	many	milk	become.FUT.1SG		strong.F

(d) Polska Roma, Poland (RMS, PL-018, 423)

ho	pjava	but	thud	to	vava	zurało
COMP	drink.FUT.1SG	much	milk	CORR	become.FUT.1SG	strong.M

Examples in (52) illustrate that TE shows greater stability in irrealis conditional clauses, supplemented in some dialects by borrowed conditional particles, as in Eastern Slovak Romani *bi* in (52c):

210 E. Adamou and Y. Matras

(52) 'If you had come yesterday, you would have seen her'.
(a) Arli, Macedonia (RMS, MK-003, 411)

te	avinje	erati	ka	dikhejne	ła
COMP	come.PFTV.2SG.REM	yesterday	FUT	see.PFTV.2SG.REM	her.OBL

(b) Kalderaš, Serbia (RMS, YU-010, 411)

te	avilanas	arači	dikhlanas	la
COMP	come.PFTV.2SG.REM	yesterday	see.PFTV.2SG.REM	her.OBL

(c) East Slovak, Slovakia (RMS, SK-011, 411)

te	bi	avehas	tajsa	ta	bi	la
COMP	COND	come.2SG.REM	yesterday	CORR	COND	her.OBL

dikhehas
see.2SG.REM

(d) Polska Roma, Poland (RMS, PL-018, 411)

te	vjanas	tejsa	to	ła	dyktanas
COMP	come.PFTV.2SG.REM	yesterday	CORR	her.OBL	see.PFTV.SG.REM

Potential condition ('whether') is often expressed by TE, as in (53c) for Sinti, though as the other examples in (53) show there is a strong tendency to use borrowed particles in this function:

(53) 'I asked the male teacher whether he is coming to the wedding'.
(a) Arli, Macedonia (RMS, MK-003, 429)

pučhlum	e	učitele	dali	ka	avol	ko	bijav
ask.PFTV.1SG	DEF.OBL.M	teacher	whether	FUT	come.3SG	to.M	wedding

(b) East Slovak, Slovakia (RMS, SK-011, 429)

phučljom	mire	učiteljostar	či	avela	pro
ask.PFTV.1SG	my.OBL.M	teacher.ABL	whether	come.3SG.FUT	to.M

bijav
wedding

(c) Sinti, Romania (RMS, RO-022, 429)

bučom	o	profesares	te	vela	pe	bijap
ask.PFTV.1SG	DEF.M	teacher.OBL.M	COMP	come.3SG	to.OBL.M	wedding

7 Romani Syntactic Typology   211

General simultaneity 'when' is usually expressed by the subordinator *kana*, which can also be used for more precise temporal relations such as immediate anteriority ('as soon as') or parallel duration ('while', 'as long as'). In some dialects, specific simultaneity, 'just as', is expressed through a different subordinator, for example *sar* in (54c) from East Slovak Romani and *syr* in (54d) from Polska Roma. The temporal domain shows extensive borrowing as can be seen in (54a) for Arli using the Slavic *koga*.

(54) 'When I was young, I lived in a big house in a town'.
(a) Arli, Macedonia (RMS, MK-003, 623)

koga	injumine	terno	živindum	ko	baro	kher	ki	dis
when	was.1SG	young.M	live.PFTV.1SG	in.M	big.M	house	in.F	town

(b) Kalderaš, Serbia (RMS, YU-010, 623)

kana	semas	terno	traisardem	ande	jekh	baro	kher
when	was.1SG	young.M	live.PFTV.1SG	in.OBL.M	INDF	big.M	house

ande	jekh	foro
in.OBL.M	INDF	town

(c) East Slovak, Slovakia (RMS, SK-011, 623)

sar	somas	cikno	bešavas	andro	jekh	baro	kher
how	was.1SG	young.M	live.PFTV.1SG	in.M	INDF	big.M	house

andro	foros
in.M	town

(d) Polska Roma, Poland (RMS, PL-018, 623)

hyr	homys	terno	to	homys	andre	baro	khir
how	was.1SG	young.M	CORR	was.1SG	in.OBL.M	big.M	house

bešjto	andre	furo
live.PTCP.M	in.OBL.M	town

Some dialects show two separate conjunctions for anteriority, corresponding to the degree of presupposition: e.g. in Lovari *angla kodo ke avilo* 'before he arrived' and *angla kodo te avel* 'before he arrives'.

Cause and reason are expressed with the complementizer KAJ, as in (55b) for Kalderaš, or with case-marked interrogatives, usually in the dative or

212   E. Adamou and Y. Matras

ablative, such as *soske* 'because' (lit. 'for-what') in (55a) for Arli, or else with a borrowed conjunction and calquing.

(55) 'I went home because I was tired'.
(a) Arli, Macedonia (RMS, MK-003, 462)

gelum	khere	soske	injumine	umorno
went.1SG	home	what.DAT	was.1SG	tired.M

(b) Kalderaš, Serbia (RMS, YU-010, 462)

me	gelem	khere	kaj	semas	hičjino
I	went.1SG	home	COMP	was.1SG	tired.M

For purpose clauses, most dialects use the complementizer TE. Some dialects combine KAJ or a borrowed functional equivalent with TE as can be seen in East Slovak Romani in (56c) and Polska Roma in (56d). This is often sensitive to degree of control and subject identity across the two clauses:

(56) 'I opened the window so that I can hear you'.
(a) Arli, Macedonia (RMS, MK-003, 443)

phadum	o	žami	te	šaj	te	havav	tu
open.PFTV.1SG	DEF.NOM.M	window	COMP	can	COMP	hear.1SG	you

(b) Kalderaš, Serbia (RMS, YU-010, 443)

me	putardem	e	feljastra
I	open.PFTV.1SG	DEF.OBL.F	window

te	šaj	te	ašunav	tu
COMP	can	COMP	hear.1SG	you

(c) East Slovak, Slovakia (RMS, SK-011, 443)

phundradžom	e	bloka	hoj	tut	te	šunav
open.PFTV.1SG	DEF.OBL.F	window	COMP	you.OBL	COMP	hear.1SG

(d) Polska Roma, Poland (RMS, PL-018, 443)

phiradom	okna	kej	tot	te	šjonav
open.PFTV.1SG	window	COMP	you.OBL	COMP	hear.1SG

7.4.4 Non-finite Forms

As illustrated in the previous section, Romani subordinate clauses are predominantly finite. Indeed, an inherited infinitive was most likely lost through contact with Iranian languages and, in particular, through contact with Greek and other Balkan languages, which all exhibit loss of the infinitive. The so-called new infinitive (Boretzky 1996a) that can be noted in several dialects probably emerged after the migration from the Balkans to Northern and Western Europe under the influence of infinitives in the contact languages. New infinitives are found in Sinti, Finnish Romani, Romungro and Romani spoken in Poland, Ukraine and Slovakia. The new infinitive developed from the historical present tense personal markers following loss of person agreement, see (57) for a generalized second person singular form in *-(e)s* and in (58) for the third-person singular in *-(e)l*.

(57) East Finnish Romani, Finland (RMS, FIN-008, 754)

jou	pyrjylä	ceer-es	putti
he	begins	do-INF	work

'He begins to work'.

(58) East Slovak, Slovakia (RMS, SK-002, 345b)

na	kamav	te	dža-l	andro	foros
NEG	want.1SG	COMP	go-INF	in.M	town

'I do not want to go to town'.

In a Romani variety from Ukraine, the infinitive has the form of a present subjunctive without the final consonant:

(59) Servi, Ukraine (RMS, UKR-004, 754)

vov	ačhel	te	tire	buti
he	begin.3SG	COMP	do.INF	work

'He begins to work'.

Romani makes use of gerunds as converbs in *-indoj* for simultaneity or cause:

(60) Mexican Vlax, Mexico (RMS, MX-001, 961)

rovindoj	bešli	paša	amende
cry.GER	sat.F	next	us.LOC

'Crying she sat down next to us'.

7.5 Negation

Clausal negation in Romani is expressed through verb negators and negative indefinites. The most distinctive feature of Romani verb negators is that they are sensitive to the mood of the verb. Most Romani dialects have separate negators for indicative and non-indicative, while some dialects also have distinct negators for indicative, subjunctive and imperative clauses.

Most dialects use the negator *na* for the indicative, as can be seen for Arli in (61a), East Slovak Romani in (61c) and Polish Romani in (61d). Innovative negators are found in some dialects; for example, in the Sinti sample in (61e), we note the use of the postposed negator *nit* (also *nicht*) from German, and the use of the negator *či* in the Kalderaš sample in (61b). The independent negator *či* is generally used in Northern Vlax. It probably started as a negative scalar focus particle 'neither, nor, not even' deriving from the indefinite *či*, and then became a marker of negative clause coordination, in all likelihood under the influence of Romanian *nici … nici* (see Elšík 2000). The negator *in* is used in Southeastern Vlax (possibly a reduced form of the original negator, later modified through an initial vowel) and *ni* for Southwestern Vlax (possibly a Southern Vlax innovation, which may have merged with the Slavic negators of the surrounding languages *ne/nie*).

(61) 'I don't know'.
(a) Arli, Macedonia (RMS, MK-003, 344b)

na	džanava
NEG	know.1SG

(b) Kalderaš, Serbia (RMS, YU-010, 344b)

me	či	žanav
I	NEG	know.1SG

(c) East Slovak, Slovakia (RMS, SK-011, 344b)

na	džanav
NEG	know.1SG

(d) Polska Roma, Poland (RMS, PL-018, 344b)

na	džinav
NEG	know.1SG

7 Romani Syntactic Typology   215

(e) Sinti, Romania (RMS, RO-022, 344b)

džinau	nit
know.1SG	NEG

In the imperative, most dialects use *ma*, as shown in (62), for Arli, East Slovak Romani, Polish Romani and Sinti. In some dialects, as in several Vlax dialects illustrated through the Kalderaš sample in (62b), the negator *na* has been extended to the imperative, most likely before its replacement by an innovative negator in the indicative, or has been generalized independent of the mood of the verb, e.g. in Ukrainian Central Romani (Benišek 2017, p. 397).

(62) 'Friends, don't get angry (at me)'.
(a) Arli, Macedonia (RMS, MK-003, 367)

amałalen	ma	hołanen
friends.VOC	NEG	be_upset.IMP.PL

(b) Kalderaš, Serbia (RMS, YU-010, 367)

xanamika	na	len	xoli	pe	mande
friends	NEG	take.IMP.PL	anger	on	me.LOC

(c) East Slovak, Slovakia (RMS, SK-011, 367)

čhavale	ma	javen	xoljamen
friends.VOC	NEG	become.IMP.PL	angry

(d) Polska Roma, Poland (RMS, PL-018, 367)

mire	čhave	ma	denervinen	tomenge
my	children	NEG	be_angry.IMP.PL	you.2PL.DAT

(e) Sinti, Romania (RMS, RO-022, 367)

mra	māla	ma	aven	xojmen
my.PL	friends	NEG	become.IMP.PL	angry

In the subjunctive, the negator can be the same as either the indicative or the imperative negator:

(63) 'I (will) shut the window so that he can't hear us'.
(a) Arli, Macedonia (RMS, MK-003, 444)

ka	phandavo	o	žami	te	na	havol	amen	ov
FUT	shut.1SG	DEF.M	window	COMP	NEG	hear.3SG	us	he

216   E. Adamou and Y. Matras

(b) Sinti, Romania (RMS, RO-022, 444)

kerjom	cu	i	fenstra	ma	ti	šunel	u	men
do.PFTV.1SG	shut	DEF.F	window	NEG	COMP	hear.3SG	he	us.OBL

Many dialects have a unique negator for the third-person copula. In the Arli (MK-003) and East Slovak (SK-011) samples, for example, one finds the use of *nani/nane*. In the Kalderaš sample from Serbia, one can observe the more general Vlax negative copula *naj*< *na hi* (NEG is.3SG) (Elšík and Matras 2009).

In Welsh Romani and in some Sinti/Manuš varieties, the indefinite marker *kek* 'nothing' (<*ka-jekh*) is occasionally used as an independent, postposed indicative negator, e.g. *kamelas kek* 'he didn't want' (Elšík 2000). In German Sinti, the German particle *gar* undergoes a similar development, and in some varieties, it serves as the principal indicative negator, e.g. *kamom gar* 'I didn't want'.

Negative indefinites are prone to renewal processes through internal grammaticalization and borrowing. Their specialization as negatives is recent and dialect-specific (Elšík 2000). Negative indefinite expressions in Romani are generally related to indefinites with a positive meaning, though in some cases traces of positive readings appear only marginally (e.g. general Vlax *khanči* 'nothing', but Agia Varvara Vlax *kajši* 'something'). One can therefore assume that clause negation relied originally primarily on the verb negator rather than on an indefinite negative. This state of affairs is generally continued in Romani irrespective of the subsequent specialization of some of the indefinite expressions as negative indefinites.

(64) Polska Roma, Poland (RMS, PL-018, 385)

so	jov	tu	dyja?	Čhi
what	he	you	give.PFTV.3SG	nothing

'What did he give you? Nothing'.

(65) Polska Roma, Poland (RMS, PL-018, 740)

čhi	pe	na	kerdža
nothing	REFL	NEG	do.PFTV.3SG

'Nothing happened'.

7.6 Case Representation

7.6.1 Semantic Roles

Alignment in 'flagging' is nominative-accusative (of the standard type) for the animate arguments. This means that the single argument of an intransitive clause (S) and the agent-like argument (A) of a monotransitive clause are marked with the same case (i.e. nominative), whereas the animate patient-like argument of a monotransitive clause (P) takes a different case, which is more marked than the nominative case. Different authors refer to this case as an 'accusative' or as an 'independent oblique' (see Matras 2002). In contrast, the inanimate P argument has the same marking as the S and A arguments; that is, it exhibits neutral case marking. The different case marking patterns observed in Romani depending on the types of full NP are quite common cross-linguistically (Comrie 2013, WALS 98).

In Romani, the recipient-like (R) argument of verbs such as 'to give' and 'to show' is expressed through the dative case marker, see (66a). However, the independent oblique case may also be used, as exemplified in (66b).

(66) 'People give the priest some food'.
(a) Lithuanian Romani (RMS, LT-007, 966)

manuša	den	rašaske	nabut	xaben
man.PL	give.3PL	priest.OBL.M.DAT	some	food

(b) Sinti, Romania (RMS, RO-022, 966)

o	manuša	den	o	rašajes	xaben
DEF.PL	man.PL	give.3PL	DEF.M	priest.OBL.M	food

The recipient-like (R) argument for the 'benefactive' and 'goal' roles is expressed mainly through the dative case marker and a preposition, as in the Sinti sample in (67a), and more rarely through the locative case, as in the example from Kalderaš in (67b).

(67) 'He left this food for you (sg) and your brothers'.
(a) Sinti, Romania (RMS, RO-022, 851)

jop	mukjas	kao	xaben	vaš	tuke	ti	vaš	te
he	leave.PFTV.3SG	this.M	food	for	2SG.DAT	and	for	your.PL

phralenge
brother.OBL.PL.DAT

(b) Kalderaš, Serbia (RMS, YU-010, 851)

vo	mekla	kado	xabe	pala	tute
he	leave.PFTV.3SG	this.M	food	for	2SG.LOC
thaj	pala	čjire	phrala		
and	for	your.PL	brother.PL		

In most dialects, the R-like argument used for source is generally expressed with the ablative case, see example in (68a). Lithuanian Romani is an exception: the locative case is used, as in (68b), sometimes in variation with the ablative which is currently being replaced by the locative more generally (see Tenser 2005 for more details; see Matras 1999a on a comparable development in the Polska Roma dialect).

(68) 'I got these flowers from my sister'.
(a) Sinti, Romania (RMS, RO-065, 479)

kae	bluma	jom	fun	mr	phenjatar
DEM.PL	flower.PL	take.PFTV.1SG	from	my	sister.OBL.F.ABL

(b) Lithuanian Romani, Lithuania (RMS, LT-005, 479)

mɔ	lyjom	da	kvjaty	mre	pxenjate
I	take.PFTV.1SG	DEM	flower.PL	my.OBL	sister.OBL.F.LOC

The Romani comitative marker, encoding accompaniment, and the instrumental marker, encoding the instrument used for an action, are the same, as in other European languages (see Stolz et al. 2013, WALS 52). Example in (69) illustrates the use of a comitative, relying on the instrumental case marker -ca, and example in (70) illustrates the use of an instrumental, with the same case.

(69) Central Slovak Romani, Slovakia (RMS, SK-031, 483)

geljom	ando	foro	mire	duje	phralenca
went.1SG	in.M	town	my.OBL.PL	two.OBL	brother.OBL.PL.INS

'I went to town with my two brothers'.

(70) Central Slovak Romani, Slovakia (RMS, SK-031, 777)

murdardža	kaxnja	čuraha
kill.PFTV.3SG	chicken.OBL.F	knife.OBL.F.INS

'He killed the chicken with a knife'.

7 Romani Syntactic Typology 219

For clausal possession, Romani uses the verb 'to be' and encodes the possessor in the oblique, see examples in (71) (for adnominal possession see Sect. 7.2). This is most likely a relic of the genitive origin of the oblique case in Middle Indo-Aryan. In Balkan dialects of Romani, the possessor in the oblique case may be reduplicated, see an example from Arli in (71a).

(71) 'She has a brother'.
(a) Arli, Macedonia (RMS, MK-003, 976)

ła	isi	ła	phrał
she.OBL	is	she.OBL	brother

(b) Kalderaš, Serbia (RMS, YU-010, 976)

la	si	phral
she.OBL	is	brother

(c) East Slovak, Slovakia (RMS, SK-011, 976)

la	hin	phral
she.OBL	is	brother

(d) Polska Roma, Poland (RMS, PL-018, 976)

ła	hi	phal
she.OBL	is	brother

'External possession' refers to cases where the possessor is external to the noun phrase that contains the possessed. Proto-Romani most likely had an external possessor construction marked by the independent oblique. This construction has been preserved in most Romani dialects, as can be seen in the examples of inalienable possession in the samples from Kalderaš, Slovak Romani, Polish Romani and Sinti from Romania, in (72). Crevels and Bakker (2000) note that some dialects follow case marking from their contact languages. For example, Russian Roma use the locative case and Latvian Romani uses the dative, see (72f) and (72g), respectively. Finally, Arli illustrates a case of so-called internal possession (72a).

(72) 'My nose hurts'.
Arli, Macedonia (RMS, MK-002, 982)

mo	nak	dukhala
my.M	nose	hurt.3SG

220 E. Adamou and Y. Matras

(b) Kalderaš, Serbia (RMS, YU-010, 982)

man	dukhal	o	nak
me.OBL	hurt.3SG	DEF.NOM.M	nose

(c) East Slovak, Slovakia (RMS, SK-011, 982)

dukhal	man	o	nakh
hurt.3SG	me.OBL	DEF.NOM.M	nose

(d) Polska Roma, Poland (RMS, PL-018, 982)

man	dukhał	nakh
me.OBL	hurt.3SG	nose

(e) Sinti, Romania (RMS, RO-022, 982)

dukhal	man	u	nak
hurt.3SG	me.OBL	DEF.NOM.M	nose

(f) Russian Roma, Russia (RMS, RUS-003, 982)

mande	dukxal	o	nak
me.LOC	hurt.3SG	DEF.NOM.M	nose

(g) Latvian Romani, Latvia (RMS, LV-006, 982)

mange	dukxala	nakx
me.DAT	hurt.3SG	nose

Experiencer verbs frequently function differently to other transitive verbs (see Verhoeven 2010). Example (73) illustrates the coding of an experiencer as an indirect object with a dative.

(73) East Slovak, Slovakia (RMS, SK-011, 993)

kampol	mange	mire	kamaraden
like.3SG	me.DAT	my.PL	friends.OBL.PL

'I like my friends'.

Stative predicates are marked in the nominative case:

(74) Kalderaš, Serbia (RMS, YU-010, 988)

vo	si	rašaj
he.NOM	is.3SG	priest.NOM.SG.M

'He is a priest'.

In sum, nominative case is the least complex case and serves to encode subjects, inanimate patient-like arguments (objects), possessees and stative predicatives. Possessors, clausal and external, and animate patient-like arguments are marked by the independent oblique (or accusative) case. The independent oblique can also be used in some dialects for recipient-like arguments, in variation with the dative. Dative case is also used for the experiencer, together with the oblique case. Genitive case is used for adnominal possessors. The comitative and instrumental roles are coded by the instrumental case, without any adpositions. Source is encoded by the ablative case, sometimes in combination with an adposition. The benefactive role is generally encoded by an adposition and dative case.

7.6.2 Local Relations

Localization may be encoded in adpositional NPs or on locational NPs, without the use of an adposition, through case marking on the noun. The factors that determine this choice depend on prominence hierarchies involving animacy, definiteness, referentiality, lexicality, etc. Non-separative inessive localization ('in, into') is coded by the nominative and the locative case, see example in (75). Locative case may also code non-separative contact relations ('on').

(75) Sofia Erli, Bulgaria (RMS, BG-024, 917)

oj	phiravel	e	čhaves	vastende
she	carries.3SG	DEF.OBL.M	child.OBL.M	arm.OBL.PL.LOC

'She carries the child in her arms'.

In contrast, the ablative case codes separative localizations, e.g. 'out of', 'from', 'from the top of', and a number of peripheral localizations, e.g. 'across, over', 'around', 'through' and 'by'.

The dative case encodes the directive adessive, 'to, toward'. The instrumental case encodes the perlative, 'through', in particular in dialects that are in contact with Slavic. In the Central Romani dialects, instrumental may also code the sequentive 'along'.

In most adpositional NPs, we note variation between the use of nominative case and oblique cases such as locative, accusative or ablative case (for further details on 'nominative vs. oblique split', see Elšík and Matras 2006, p. 247). The choice between these cases depends on prominence hierarchies: oblique cases are preferred with pronouns.

222   E. Adamou and Y. Matras

Several South Balkan dialects have developed a general local adposition from the adessive *ke/te* that combines with a more specialized adposition. These complex adpositions generally combine with the nominative case, whereas the simple adpositions combine with the oblique cases.

7.6.3 Temporal Relations

Simultaneous temporal relations are coded through a variety of means depending on individual dialects; for example, for clock time, locative case is used in Kalajdži *efta saxatende* 'at 7 o'clock' (RMS, BG-007), the ablative case in East Slovak Romani *efta orendar* 'at 7 o'clock' (RMS, SK-011) and the adessive *ke/te* adposition with nominative case in Sofia Erli *ko efta o sahati* 'at 7 o'clock' (RMS, BG-024).

Posterior-durative relations, 'since', are coded through ablative case in Finnish Romani, e.g. *niijalko čhoones-ta* 'since June' (RMS, FIN-008, 458) as well as in the Northeastern Romani dialects and most Central dialects, whereas several other dialects rely on the adposition *katar/tar* 'from', e.g. *tar o juni* 'since June', in Arli (RMS, MK-003, 458).

Anterior-durative relations, 'until', are coded by the adessive *ke/te*, e.g. *ko lynaj* 'until the summer' in Russian Romani (RMS, RUS-003, 453), or by *ke/te* in combination with a limitative particle, e.g. *ži ko nilaj* 'until the summer' in Romungro from Romania (RMS, RO-001, 453). More rarely, the inessive may be used, e.g. *ži ando verano* 'until the summer' in Mexican Vlax (RMS, MX-001, 453), *dži andro ljinaj* 'until the summer' in East Slovak Romani (RMS, SK-011, 453).

Finally, anterior and posterior sequence relations, 'before' and 'after', are coded through the spatial adpositions *angle/anglal* and *pal/palal*, respectively.

7.7   Conclusion

In this chapter, we presented an overview of selected syntactic-typological features of Romani. We showed that Romani, an Indic language, exhibits a number of features that have been shaped through contact with non-Indic languages during the past millennium. For example, Romani exhibits nominative-accusative and neutral case alignment, whereas morphological ergative alignment is found in many Indic languages and can be reconstructed for Proto-Romani (Bubeník 2000; Matras 2002).

Innovations of the Early Romani period, through intensive contact with Byzantine Greek, include grammaticalization of a definite article (a unique feature among New Indo-Aryan languages); use of the resumptive relativization strategy and of interrogatives as relativizers; factuality distinction in subordinate clauses; changes in word order, i.e. VS used as a connective-narrative order, and SV as a contrastive-thematic order; emergence of a dominant VO order following a change from a dominant OV order (OV order is still encountered in Indic languages, see Dryer 2013a, WALS 83).

In accordance with cross-linguistic tendencies associated with a VO order, Romani dialects have prepositions (an innovative feature from a New Indo-Aryan perspective where postpositions are common) and a dominant ADJ-N order in NPs, the adjective preceding the noun (an order that is more frequently associated with OV languages) (Dryer 2013d, e, f, WALS 95, 96, 97). In addition, relative clauses are postnominal (NREL), a feature which is cross-linguistically common, but tends to be absent in Indic languages where the relative clause precedes the noun (RELN) (Dryer 2013c, WALS 90). Interestingly, Romani has kept dependent marking in possessive noun phrases, a dominant feature of the languages of India (Nichols and Bickel 2013, WALS 24). The Romani genitive noun phrase precedes the head noun, an order that is rare in European languages but predominant in India (Dryer 2013b, WALS 86).

The migration of the Romani-speaking populations beyond the Balkans led to the split of Romani into contemporary dialects. Contact with a number of different languages shaped the typological features of particular Romani varieties, leading, for example, to the emergence of new infinitives in some dialects, and the loss of definite articles or gender distinction in others.

Romani is of interest to typologists as it illustrates the significance of the geographical distribution of typological features over genetic affiliation at two levels: first, through the emergence of a number of shared innovations in contact with Byzantine Greek, which changed the typological profile of Romani in comparison with the other Indo-Aryan languages and, second, through dialect-specific innovations which emerged following contact with different European languages.

Notes

1. Accessed at http://romani.humanities.manchester.ac.uk/rms/. Viktor Elšík and Yaron Matras 2001–present.
2. Glosses following the Leipzig Glossing Rules as expanded within the project 'Designing Spoken corpora for Cross-linguistic Research' (funded by the French National Research Agency).

References

Adamou, Evangelia. 2013. Replicating Spanish *estar* in Mexican Romani. *Linguistics* 51 (6): 1075–1105.

Adamou, Evangelia. 2016. *A corpus-driven approach to language contact: Endangered languages in a comparative perspective*. Boston and Berlin: Mouton de Gruyter.

Alexopoulou, Theodora. 2006. Resumption in relative clauses. *Natural Language & Linguistic Theory* 24 (1): 57–111.

Andrews, Avery D. 2007. Relative clauses. In *Language typology and syntactic description*, ed. Timothy Shopen, 206–236. Cambridge: Cambridge University Press.

Arvaniti, Amalia, and Evangelia Adamou. 2011. Focus expression in Romani. In *Proceedings of the 28th west coast conference on formal linguistics*, ed. Mary Byram Washburn, Katherine McKinney-Bock, Erika Varis, Ann Sawyer, and Barbara Tomaszewicz, 240–248. Somerville, MA: Cascadilla Proceedings Project.

Benišek, Michael. 2017. Eastern Uzh varieties of North Central Romani. Unpublished PhD thesis, Charles University of Prague.

Bodnárová, Zuzana. 2015. Vend Romani: A grammatical description and sociolinguistic situation of the so-called Vend dialects of Hungary. Unpublished PhD thesis, Charles University of Prague.

Boretzky, Norbert. 1993a. *Bugurdži. Deskriptiver und historischer Abriß eines Romani Dialekts*. Wiesbaden: Harrassowitz.

Boretzky, Norbert. 1993b. Conditional sentences in Romani. *Sprachtypologie und Universalienforschung* 46: 83–99.

Boretzky, Norbert. 1996a. The 'new infinitive' in Romani. *Journal of the Gypsy Lore Society*, 5th ser., 6: 1–51.

Boretzky, Norbert. 1996b. Entlehnte Wortstellungssyntax im Romani. In *Beiträge zum 10*, ed. Norbert Boretzky, Werner Enninger, and Thomas Stolz, 95–121. Bochum: Brockmeyer.

Boretzky, Norbert. 1998. Erli. Eine Bestandsaufnahme nach den Texte von Gilliat-Smith. *Studii Romani* 5–6: 122–160.

Bubeník, Vít. 1997. Object doubling in Romani and the Balkan languages. In *The typology and dialectology of Romani*, ed. Yaron Matras, Peter Bakker, and Hristo Kyuchukov, 95–106. Amsterdam: John Benjamins.

Bubeník, Vít. 2000. Was Proto-Romani an ergative language? In *Grammatical relations in Romani: The noun phrase*, ed. Yaron Matras and Viktor Elšík, 205–227. Amsterdam: John Benjamins.

Cech, Petra, and Mozes F. Heinschink. 1999. *Sepečides-Romani. Grammatik, Texte und Glossar eines türkischen Romani-Dialekts*. Wiesbaden: Harrassowitz.

Comrie, Bernard. 2013. Alignment of case marking of full noun phrases. In *The world atlas of language structures online*, ed. Matthew S. Dryer and Martin Haspelmath. Leipzig: Max Planck Institute for Evolutionary Anthropology. Available at http://wals.info/chapter/98. Accessed on 25 July 2017.

Corbett, Greville G. 2013. Number of genders. In *world atlas of language structures online*, ed. Matthew S. Dryer and Martin Haspelmath. Leipzig: Max Planck Institute for Evolutionary Anthropology. Available at http://wals.info/chapter/30. Accessed on 25 July 2017.

Crevels, Mily, and Peter Bakker. 2000. External possession in Romani. In *Grammatical relations in Romani: The noun phrase*, ed. Yaron Matras and Viktor Elšík, 151–185. Amsterdam: John Benjamins.

Cristofaro, Sonia. 2013. Utterance complement clauses. In *The world atlas of language structures online*, ed. Matthew S. Dryer and Martin Haspelmath. Leipzig: Max Planck Institute for Evolutionary Anthropology. Available at http://wals.info/chapter/128. Accessed on 25 July 2017.

Dixon, Robert M.W. 2010. *Basic linguistic theory*. Oxford: Oxford University Press.

Dryer, Matthew S. 2013a. Order of object and verb. In *The world atlas of language structures online*, ed. Matthew S. Dryer and Martin Haspelmath. Leipzig: Max Planck Institute for Evolutionary Anthropology. Available at http://wals.info/chapter/83. Accessed on 25 July 2017.

Dryer, Matthew S. 2013b. Order of genitive and noun. In *The world atlas of language structures online*, ed. Matthew S. Dryer and Martin Haspelmath. Leipzig: Max Planck Institute for Evolutionary Anthropology. Available at http://wals.info/chapter/86. Accessed on 25 July 2017.

Dryer, Matthew S. 2013c. Order of relative clause and noun. In *The world atlas of language structures online*, ed. Matthew S. Dryer and Martin Haspelmath. Leipzig: Max Planck Institute for Evolutionary Anthropology. Available at http://wals.info/chapter/90. Accessed on 25 July 2017.

Dryer, Matthew S. 2013d. Relationship between the order of object and verb and the order of adposition and noun phrase. In *The world atlas of language structures online*, ed. Matthew S. Dryer and Martin Haspelmath. Leipzig: Max Planck Institute for Evolutionary Anthropology. Available at http://wals.info/chapter/95. Accessed on 25 July 2017.

Dryer, Matthew S. 2013e. Relationship between the order of object and verb and the order of relative clause and noun. In *The world atlas of language structures online*, ed. Matthew S. Dryer and Martin Haspelmath. Leipzig: Max Planck Institute for Evolutionary Anthropology. Available at http://wals.info/chapter/96. Accessed on 25 July 2017.

Dryer, Matthew S. 2013f. Relationship between the order of object and verb and the order of adjective and noun. In *The world atlas of language structures online*, ed. Matthew S. Dryer and Martin Haspelmath. Leipzig: Max Planck Institute for Evolutionary Anthropology. Available at http://wals.info/chapter/97. Accessed on 25 July 2017.

Elšík, Viktor. 2000. Inherited indefinites in Romani. Paper presented at the Fifth International Conference on Romani Linguistics, Sofia, 14–17 September 2000.

Elšík, Viktor, and Yaron Matras. 2006. *Markedness and language change*. Berlin: Mouton de Gruyter.

Elšík, Viktor, and Yaron Matras. 2009. Modality in Romani. In *Modals in the languages of Europe*, ed. Björn Hansen and Ferdinand de Haan, 267–324. Berlin: Mouton de Gruyter.

Friedman, Victor A. 1985. Balkan Romani modality and other Balkan languages. *Folia Slavica* 7: 381–389.

Friedman, Victor A. 2000. Proleptic and resumptive object pronouns in Romani: A Balkan noun phrase perspective. In *Grammatical relations in Romani: The noun phrase*, ed. Yaron Matras and Viktor Elšík, 187–204. Amsterdam: John Benjamins.

Friedman, Victor A. 2001. The Romani indefinite article in its historical and areal context. In *Was ich noch sagen wollte... A multilingual festschrift for Norbert Boretzky. Sprachtypologie und Universalienforschung, Beihefte, Studia typologica 2*, ed. Birgit Igla, and Thomas Stolz, 287–301. Berlin: Akademie Verlag.

Haig, Geoffrey, and Stefan Schnell. 2016. The discourse basis of ergativity revisited. *Language* 92 (3): 591–618.

Holzinger, Daniel. 1993. Das *Rómanes. Grammatik und Diskursanalyse der Sprache der Sinte*. Innsbruck: Verlag des Instituts für Sprachwissenschaft der Universität Innsbruck.

Iggesen, Oliver A. 2013. Number of cases. In *The world atlas of language structures online*, ed. Matthew S. Dryer and Martin Haspelmath. Leipzig: Max Planck Institute for Evolutionary Anthropology. Available at http://wals.info/chapter/49. Accessed on 25 July 2017.

Igla, Birgit. 1996. *Das Romani von Ajia Varvara. Deskriptive und historisch-vergleichende Darstellung eines Zigeunerdialekts*. Wiesbaden: Harrassowitz.

Keenan, Edward, and Bernard Comrie. 1977. Noun phrase accessibility and universal grammar. *Linguistic Inquiry* 8: 63–99.

Kolliakou, Dimitra. 2004. Monadic definites and polydefinites: Their form, meaning and use. *Journal of Linguistics* 40: 263–333.

Koptjevskaja-Tamm, Maria. 2000. Romani genitives in cross-linguistic perspective. In *Grammatical relations in Romani: The noun phrase*, ed. Yaron Matras and Viktor Elšík, 123–149. Amsterdam: John Benjamins.

Leggio, Viktor D. 2011. The dialect of the Mitrovica Roma. *Romani Studies*, 5th ser., 21 (1): 57–113.

Leggio, Viktor D., and Yaron Matras. 2017. Variation and dialect levelling in the Romani dialect of Ţăndărei. *Romani Studies*, 5th ser., 27(2):173–209.

Malchukov, Andrej, Martin Haspelmath, and Bernard Comrie. 2010. Ditransitive constructions: A typological overview. In *Studies in ditransitive constructions: A comparative handbook*, ed. Andrej Malchukov, Martin Haspelmath, and Bernard Comrie, 1–64. Berlin and New York: Mouton de Gruyter.

Matras, Yaron. 1994. *Untersuchungen zu Grammatik und Diskurs des Romanes. Dialekt der Kelderaša/Lovara*. Wiesbaden: Harrassowitz.

Matras, Yaron. 1995. Connective (VS) word order in Romani. *Sprachtypologie und Universalienforschung*. 48: 189–203.

Matras, Yaron. 1999a. The speech of the Polska Roma: Some highlighted features and their implications for Romani dialectology. *Journal of the Gypsy Lore Society*, Fifth ser., 9(1): 1–28.

Matras, Yaron. 1999b. Subject clitics in Sinti. *Acta Linguistica Academiae Scientiarum Hungaricae* 46: 147–169.

Matras, Yaron. 2002. *Romani: A linguistic introduction*. Cambridge: Cambridge University Press.

Matras, Yaron, and Anton Tenser. 2016. Complementizers in Romani. In *Complementizer semantics in European languages*, ed. Kasper Boye and Petar Kehayov, 341–375. Berlin: Mouton de Gruyter.

Nichols, Johanna, and Bickel, Balthasar. 2013. Locus of marking in possessive noun phrases. In *The world atlas of language structures online*, ed. Matthew S. Dryer and Martin Haspelmath. Leipzig: Max Planck Institute for Evolutionary Anthropology. Available at http://wals.info/chapter/24. Accessed on 25 July 2017.

Payne, John. 1995. Inflecting postpositions in Indic and Kashmiri. In *Double case: Agreement by Suffixaufnahme*, ed. Frans Plank, 283–298. New York and Oxford: Oxford University Press.

Plank, Frans. 1995. (Re-)introducing Suffixaufnahme. In *Double case: Agreement by Suffixaufnahme*, ed. Frans Plank, 3–110. New York and Oxford: Oxford University Press.

Rusakov, Alexandr, and Olga Abramenko. 1998. North Russian Romani dialect: Interference in case system. *Grazer Linguistische Studien* 50: 109–133.

Sampson, John. 1926 (1968). *The dialect of the Gypsies of Wales, being the older form of British Romani preserved in the speech of the clan of Abram Wood*. Oxford: Clarendon Press.

Sasse, Hans-Jürgen. 1995. 'Theticity' and VS order: A case study. *Sprachtypologie und Universalienforschung*. 48: 3–31.

Stolz, Thomas, Cornelia Stroh, and Aina Urdze. 2013. Comitatives and instrumentals In *The world atlas of language structures online*, ed. Matthew S. Dryer and Martin Haspelmath. Leipzig: Max Planck Institute for Evolutionary Anthropology. Available at http://wals.info/chapter/52. Accessed on 25 July 2017.

Tenser, Anton. 2005. *Lithuanian Romani*. Munich: Lincom Europa.

Tenser, Anton. 2008. Northeastern group of Romani dialects. Unpublished PhD thesis. University of Manchester.

Tenser, Anton. 2016. Semantic map borrowing—Case representation in Northeastern Romani dialects. *Journal of Language Contact* 9: 211–245.

Verhoeven, Elisabeth. 2010. Agentivity and stativity in experiencer verbs: Implications for a typology of verb classes. *Linguistic Typology* 14: 213–251.

Wogg, Michael, and Dieter W. Halwachs. 1998. *Syntax des Roman*. Oberwart: Verein Roma.

Part III

Contact

8

The Impact of Turkish on Romani

Victor A. Friedman

8.1 Introduction

The impact of Turkish on Romani is, in many respects, comparable to the impact of Turkish on the other Balkan languages, although in certain respects there are some remarkable differences between Romani and its co-territorial languages. As a 'Balkanized Indic language' (Matras 1994), all the Romani dialects show what Friedman (1985a) calls the *Dental Modal Subordinator* (DMS), *te*, whose usage is functionally equivalent to that of Balkan Slavic *da*, Balkan Romance *să, si, s'*, Albanian *të*, and Greek *na* (cf. also Friedman and Joseph, forthcoming). However, only the dialects of the Balkans show a future marking particle based on etymological 'want,' usually *ka* (see Boretzky and Igla 2004, vol. I, pp. 172–174, vol. II, pp. 63, 244 for details), another Balkanism that, like the DMS, uses native material to express convergent grammar. It is, for the most part, the dialects with the Balkan future that show an impact of Turkish comparable to Turkish influence on the other Balkan languages. In general, it can be observed that while the effect of Byzantine Greek on the structure of Romani was profound and is found throughout Romani (Elšík and Matras 2006, pp. 68–84),

V. A. Friedman (✉)
University of Chicago, Chicago, IL, USA
e-mail: vfriedm@uchicago.edu

La Trobe University, Melbourne, VIC, Australia

© The Author(s) 2020
Y. Matras and A. Tenser (eds.), *The Palgrave Handbook of Romani Language and Linguistics*, https://doi.org/10.1007/978-3-030-28105-2_8

232   V. A. Friedman

the impact of Turkish more or less coincides with the boundaries of the Ottoman Empire. And just as the shifting of these boundaries over the centuries is reflected in relative degrees of Turkish influence (and Balkan convergences in general), so, too, those dialects spoken where that influence remained longest show the more profound impact. In some of these areas, Turkish continues to be a contact language, while in others it does not, and this, too, has ongoing relevance.

8.2   Lexicon and Phonology

The lexical impact of Turkish on Romani can be described as pervasive but relatively localized and at present in a process of retreat in certain areas. Within Europe as a whole, Romani dialects pattern to some extent with their co-territorial languages in terms of Turkish lexical influence. This means that the farther the dialect is from the boundaries of the Ottoman Empire, the fewer Turkisms occur. While there is evidence of Roms in Southeastern Europe prior to the Ottoman invasion of the fourteenth century, the general dispersal of Roms throughout Europe coincides with the Ottoman expansion, and it is striking that while Slavic lexicon appears as far afield as Caló and Catalonian Romani, e.g., *zamba* 'frog,' *kralitsa* 'queen' (Friedman 1988, p. 19; Ackerley 1914/1915, p. 131), significant amounts of lexicon of Turkish origin appear to be limited to the Balkans. In general, words of Turkish origin appear to be totally lacking in North Romani (e.g., Sampson 1926; Bhatia 1963), while in Central dialects, the occasional Turkism was undoubtedly mediated by some other Balkan language (Balkan Slavic and/or Balkan Romance) with which the dialect was in contact at some point in its history, or perhaps, even by another Romani dialect. Thus, for example, the word for 'kidney,' Turkish *böbrek*, which remains the only word for that organ in Macedonian (*bubreg*), Bulgarian (*băbrek*), and the former Serbo-Croatian (*bubreg*) and is, *mutatis mutandis*, the normal word in Balkan and South Vlax Romani throughout the former Ottoman Balkans, occurs as far afield as Veršend (Versend) Romani (*bobreško*), Burgenland Romani and East Slovak Romani (*bubreška*), Prekmurski Romani and Lovara (*bubreško*), Kalderaš (*bobereško/ bobriško*) as well as Dolenjski Romani (*bubrego*) (ROMLEX).[1] Its occurrence in regions that were never, or only briefly, under Ottoman control is the result of lexical spread mediated by other languages, rather than of direct contact with Turkish.[2]

In the Balkans itself, it is likely that the number of Turkisms historically in Romani was comparable to the number found in other Balkan languages.

8 The Impact of Turkish on Romani   233

Thus, for example, out of c. 350 Turkisms in Messing (1988), Škaljić (1966) has about 300 (Friedman 1989). Considering that Šklajić's (1966) dictionary of Turkisms has 6878 headwords for the former Serbo-Croatian, and Grannes et al. (2002) have 7427 for Bulgarian, it is not unfair to assume that, historically, Romani did not differ significantly.[3] As with the other Balkan languages, so, too, in Romani, loanwords can be found in all parts of speech and all types of vocabulary. Particularly noteworthy are those types identified by Friedman and Joseph (2014 and forthcoming) as E.R.I.C. loans, i.e., Essentially Rooted In Conversation. Such loanwords are typified as being closed class and generally borrowing-resistant items such as kinship terms, numerals, pronouns and bound morphology, as well as conversationally based elements such as taboo expressions, idioms, and phraseology, and also discourse elements such as connectives and interjections (cf. the Leipzig–Jakarta list in Tadmor et al. 2010, pp. 238–241). In Friedman and Joseph (2014 and forthcoming), we argue that such shared vocabulary is diagnostic of *Sprachbund* formation, and the Turkish elements in Romani are consistent with the fact that the Romani dialects of the Balkans are part of the Balkan *Sprachbund*.

Thus, for example, the use of Turkish kinship terms such as *teyze* (*teze*) 'aunt' and *dayı* (*dajo*) '[maternal] uncle' as well as *baba* 'father' (especially as a vocative) is characteristic of Albanian, Bosnian, Pomak, as well as various Romani dialects. One can also adduce here the use of Turkish numerals, e.g., as reported by Gilliat-Smith (1944, p. 19) for Varna (Xoraxane) Kalajdži and in Elšík and Matras (2006, p. 170) for Kaspičan, and (Varna) Gadžikano, where numerals above 'three' have been replaced by Turkish. Similarly, in Pomak villages in present-day Greece, Turkish numerals are used for 'five' and above (Theokharidēs 1996, p. 53), and Šiškov (1936, p. 11) reports that in Dovan-Hisar, in the Dedeagach (Greek Alexandroupolis) region, all the numerals were Turkish for both Christian and Muslim Bulgarian speakers. The borrowed Turkish pronoun *onlar* 'they' (sometimes realized as *onnar* or *onna*) occurs in various Romani dialects of eastern Bulgaria (Elšík and Matras 2006, p. 101; Gilliat-Smith 1944, p. 19) as well as of eastern Macedonia (Friedman field notes). Here it is worth noting that the native Romani 3PL pronoun in this region is generally *on*, and it is therefore possible that the Turkish plural marker was added to the native Romani pronoun. This particular example appears to be unique to Romani, although the productive borrowing of Turkish plural markers (-*lar/-ler*), i.e., their addition to non-Turkish words, occurs in dialectal Albanian and Macedonian, and Turkish words with Turkish plurals also occur in Aromanian, Bulgarian, and the former Serbo-Croatian. Such spread of the Turkish plural into Romani does not, however, seem to be the case, despite the adoption of Greek, Romanian, and Balkan Slavic plural markers in various

234   V. A. Friedman

dialects (cf. Elšík and Matras 2006, p. 234). Examples of Turkish loanwords can be adduced for Romani as for the other Balkan languages for all the other classes identified as E.R.I.C. loans.

One aspect of Turkisms in Romani that until recently differentiated it from co-territorial Balkan languages was the fact that since Romani remained for a longer time strictly in the realm of oral communication. Turkisms that in the other Balkan languages were marginalized by processes of standardization, either by being rendered archaic, historical, or stylistically lowered, remained the neutral everyday terms (cf. Kazazis 1972; Friedman 1996a). Thus, Romani *askeri* (Turkish *asker*) is still the unmarked term for 'soldier' in many dialects of the Balkans, as it still is in Turkish. The various co-territorial nation-state languages have replaced *asker* with other terms, so that *asker* means specifically 'Turkish soldier (during the Ottoman period).' Similarly, Turkish *sokak*, Romani *sokako/sokaki* is the normal word for 'street' in both languages, but in all the Balkan nation-state languages, it means 'alley' (cf. Kazazis 1973, 1975; Adamou 2010).

A striking example comes from the 1994 extraordinary census in the Republic of Macedonia. In accordance with the Census Law, all the documents were translated into all the languages mentioned in the 1991 Constitution—Macedonian, Albanian, Turkish, Romani, Aromanian, and Serbian—as well as English (for the sake of the international observers, see Friedman 1996b for details). This represented one of the first uses of Romani (and Aromanian) as an official language in Macedonia (and more or less anywhere else in Europe at that time). For Romani (and Aromanian), the fact that a literary norm was (and is) still in the process of elaboration meant that the census documents themselves were connected to processes of standardization. Among the items to be enumerated in the census was the number of baths and toilets in each dwelling. All those languages with established, elaborated norms used euphemistic neologisms or recent borrowings as their official terminology on the census forms (P-2, VI.8 and 9 in Antonovska et al. 1994): Macedonian *banja, klozet*, Albanian *banjo, nevojtore*, Turkish *banyo, banyo-ayakyolu*, Serbian *kupatilo, klozet*. Except for the Serbian deverbal noun meaning 'bathing place,' all the words for 'bath' are Latinate borrowings. The Macedonian and Serbian words for 'toilet' are from the British [*water*]*closet*, while the Albanian and Turkish are neologisms that can be glossed as 'necessarium' and 'bath-footplace,' respectively. The Romani documents, however, used the Turkisms *hamami* and *kenefi*, respectively.[4] *Hamam* is the standard Turkish word for 'bath' but has come to mean 'Turkish bath' or 'public bath,' while the *kenef* is considered vulgar in Turkish as well as in the other Balkan standard languages, although in Aegean Macedonian dialects it is still the normal word, and it has even become archaic in some regions in the Republic of Macedonia. More recent data from ROMLEX, however, which gives *toalet* for Kosovo Arli and *toaleto* for Macedonian Arli, indicate that in this sphere, as in others, the practices of current contact languages are replacing Turkisms, although some items, e.g., *avazi* 'vote' (Turkish *avaz* 'voice, shout' < Persian *āwāz* 'voice'), a calque on Macedonian *glas* meaning both 'voice' and 'vote,' still seem to be the preferred lexical item in Romani-language news reports.

The replacement just alluded to is an ongoing process in some parts of the Balkans, as growing numbers of Romani speakers have increasing contact with respective Balkan nation-state languages. Igla's (1996, pp. 236–237) observation with respect to Agia Varvara Romani (Athens), made a decade or so after Messing (1988) collected the material for his glossary, is that the number of Turkisms in that dialect has declined significantly (but see Sect. 8.3 on Turkish conjugation). In those Balkan regions where Turkish remains a significant everyday language, e.g., Western Thrace (Greece), and parts of eastern Bulgaria, of eastern Macedonia, and of Kosovo (and, of course, Turkey itself), continued knowledge of Turkish correlates with continued use of Turkish lexicon. In some regions where knowledge of Turkish has declined relatively recently, or where some speakers take pride in the specificity of their dialect vis-à-vis the standard (e.g., Bitola for Macedonian, Kosovo for Albanian, and Romani in general), speakers view many Turkisms as distinctive parts of their speech. From the 1980s to the 2000s in Macedonia, there were competing ideologies concerning vocabulary enrichment for what was projected to be the Romani standard in Macedonia: some favored the use of Turkisms as a distinctive part of colloquial Romani while others favored neologisms or the importation of words from other Indic languages (e.g., Jusuf and Kepeski 1980; cf. Friedman 1985b; Abercrombie 2018). It is worth noting that precisely, the same discussion took place during the earliest years of the codification of Macedonian in the late 1940s, with Slavic taking the place of Indic. As it so happened, in the case of Macedonian, the opposition to Turkisms was explicit and vigorous and resulted in the types of marginalization found in other Balkan standard languages as described above (Friedman 1996a; Adamou 2010). In the case of Romani, it also appears that Turkisms are generally not being deployed in contexts such as news outlets and government documents. In Macedonian towns, Turkish remained the primary language associated with urban life in general, and among Muslims in particular, into the 1970s, while during the 1980s the effects of rural-to-urban migration and the crises associated with Kosovo resulted in the replacement of Turkish with Albanian among many Muslims (a trend that has its basic origins in the Albanian occupation of western Macedonia during World War II, cf. Ellis 2003).[5] In general, however, the rise of Albanian has not affected Romani-speaking Muslims in Macedonia (cf. Adamou 2010; but see also Sect. 8.6).

One aspect of the lexicon that could also be treated in the section on morphology relates to derivation. Owing both to the significance of Turkish inflectional morphology in Romani and to the fact that derivation is itself a bridge between lexicon and morphology, the derivational elements will be treated here (cf. Friedman and Joseph, forthcoming). At issue are the derivational suffixes that in Turkish can be represented as *-CI, -lIk,* and *-lI,* where the vowel represents any of the Turkish high vowels (*i, ı, ü, u*) and *C* represents voiced and voiceless realizations of the palatal affricate.[6] All of these suffixes are highly productive in all the Balkan languages, i.e., occurring on various non-Turkish words and new formations, e.g., Slavic *lov-* 'hunt' > Balkan Slavic *lovdžija* 'hunter,' *pubertet* 'puberty' > *pubertetlija* 'adolescent' [colloquial or pejorative],' etc. Of these, the respective realizations of the agentive suffix *-CI* in the various Balkan languages are the most productive. It is striking, therefore, that none of these suffixes is particularly common or productive in the Romani dialects of the Balkans, although occasional formations are attested, e.g., Bugurdži *limordžija* 'grave-digger' (*limori* 'grave'), *asjavdžis* 'miller' (*asjav* 'mill'), Sepeči *mindžardžis* 'womanizer' (*mindž* 'vagina'), *xoxamdžis* 'cheater' (*xoxavel* 'cheat'), Sofia Erli *vurdondžis* 'cart-driver' (*vurdon* 'cart'). In Slavic, the suffix is *-džija/–čija*, since final *-i* was impermissible for singular nouns until relatively recently. In some Romani dialects, the suffix has been nativized by the addition of the masculine nominative suffix *-s*, which then effects borrowings from Slavic, e.g., Burgudži *lovdžis* 'hunter' < *lovdžija*, but in the same dialect, *limordžija* indicates that the suffix itself was mediated by Slavic.

In general, Turkish has not had much impact on Romani phonology other than the importation of /ü/ or the frequency of schwa (from Turkish high back unrounded vowel), mainly in Turkish loanwords (cf. Paspati 1870, p. 38). In this, it does not differ from other local dialects of various Balkan languages (Friedman 2006).

8.3   Inflectional Morphology

The impact of Turkish on Romani inflectional morphology is significant in those dialects where it occurs. Five features can be identified as especially significant: (1) adjectival gradation, (2) case affixes, (3) agglutinative possessive markers, (4) preterite person markers, and (5) Turkish conjugation (including but not always limited to tense/aspect/mood markers).

8.3.1 Adjectival Gradation

Elšík and Matras (2006, pp. 146–155) provide a detailed account of adjectival gradation in a large sample of Romani dialects, and the account here is based largely on that with additional material from Friedman and Joseph (forthcoming) and my own fieldwork in Macedonia. Romani has a synthetic comparative marker—suffixed *-eder*—which can be reconstructed as such for Early Romani. This remains the only comparative in some Northern dialects, and it is preserved to varying degrees in a variety of other dialects, sometimes accompanied by an analytic marker and sometimes occurring alone in selected lexical items. Thus, for example, even in the Balkan dialects, which generally show strong convergences with their co-territorial languages in analytic gradation via borrowing and calquing, individual lexical items sometimes preserve the older synthetic comparative, e.g., *but* 'many, very' > *buteder* 'more' or *pobuter*. This occurs in Macedonia and Bulgaria, where the respective nation-state language has a suppletive comparative (inherited from an older synthetic comparative) in the same lexical item: *mnogu/mnogo* 'many, very' versus *povekje/poveče* 'more.' Turkish completely lacks synthetic comparatives and uses the particles *daha* 'more' and *en* 'most' for comparative and superlative, respectively. These are both borrowed into many Balkan and South Vlax Romani dialects, sometimes in competition with particles from other Balkan languages, sometimes not. The West Rumelian variants *daa* and *em* sometimes occur in Romani dialects of Macedonia, and Elšík and Matras (2006, p. 151) also cite variants *taa/thaa* and *xen*. Balkan Slavic, like Turkish, preserves an inherited differentiation between comparative and superlative using distinct morphemes (in Slavic, *po* and *naj*), whereas Albanian, Balkan Romance, and Greek all use the definite of the comparative as the superlative. Romani dialects tend to follow the pattern of the current co-territorial nation-state language in this respect, although some dialects do not; for example, Agia Varvara near Athens still uses the Turkish or Slavic form of the comparative in forming the superlative, e.g., *daha/po baro* 'bigger,' *o daha/po baro* 'the biggest.' An exception is Karditsa Arli, where older Macedonian *po* is retained for the comparative but Greek *pio* 'more' is borrowed to mark the superlative (versus definite + *pio* in Greek).

8.3.2 Case Marking

Romani dialects in general are quite conservative in preserving the case system of Early Romani. According to Elšík and Matras (2006, p. 234), borrowed oblique case markers do not substitute for inherited case markers, although some nouns may be borrowed with their foreign case forms. For

238 V. A. Friedman

example, in Kaspičan and (Varna) Gadžikano, the Turkish locative and ablative case markers, *-DA*, and *-DAn*, respectively, are used with some toponyms, e.g., *Sofijada* 'in Sofia,' *Rusijadan* 'in Russia' (Elšík and Matras 2006, p. 235) and Kaspičan also uses the Turkish dative, *-(y)A* with toponyms, e.g., *Indijaja* 'to India' (RMS, KX 628).[7] The ablative and locative case affixes are also borrowed into other Balkan languages, e.g., Albanian (from Turkish) *hava* 'air, weather' has both native *në hava* (literally 'in air') and Turkish ablative *havadan* to mean 'in the open, up in the air.' Similarly, Salonica Judezmo *dunyade* 'in the world' (Turkish *dünya* 'world' + locative), although with the wrong vowel harmony (correct would be *-da*), shows a Turkish locative on a Turkish word (Bunis 1999, p. 91).

We can include here some adverbial Turkish expressions that involve case-like postpositions, some of which are shared with other Balkan languages, e.g., Romani and Macedonian *sabajle*, colloquial or dialectal Albanian *sabahile* 'in the morning' from Turkish *sabah* 'morning' + *ile* 'with' (also *sabahleyin*). We can also note here that there is some calquing of Turkish case functions in dialects that borrow Turkish postpositions, to be discussed in Sect. 8.5 (cf. also Elšík and Matras 2006, pp. 232, 234–238).

Finally, we can note that although Romani tends to be quite conservative in preserving the inherited case system of Early Romani, some erosions are occurring in the Balkans such as dative-locative merger and the replacement of the dative-locative, as well as ablative, with prepositional constructions, e.g., Skopje Arli *me ka džav ko gav* 'I will go to the village,' *me ka bešav ko gav* 'I will live in the village,' *aljum taro gav* 'I came from the village.' Such tendencies are especially strong in some of the dialects of Macedonia and Bulgaria, where co-territorial nation-state languages have precisely these kinds of phenomena. West Rumelian Turkish occasionally shows similar dative-locative confusion (Friedman 2006, p. 664).

8.3.3 Agglutinative Possession Markers

A number of Romani dialects in contact with Turkish, which has personal possessive suffixes, sometimes borrow these suffixes, at least in the first person. Thus, for example, Sepeči and other dialects in contact with Turkish have *Devlam!* 'O my God!' from the vocative *Devla* and the Turkish 1SG possessive *-m* (Cech and Heinschink 1999). Similarly, the form *Fatmam* 'my Fatma' occurs as a vocative in a Skopje Arli tale (Cech et al. 2003, p. 68). Sechidou (2011) cites the form *sarimiz* 'all of us' from Ajios Athanasios (Serres), which consists of Romani *sar-* 'all (oblique stem)' and the Turkish 1PL possessive *-imiz*.

8.3.4 Preterite Person Markers

In certain Romani dialects that have Turkish conjugation (see Sect. 8.3.5), mostly in eastern Bulgaria, but also elsewhere, the Turkish 2PL marker -nIz is copied (with phonological adaptation) to the native Romani 2PL preterite marker, and, in some cases, it is extended to the 1PL preterite. The relevant Romani dialects devoice, and sometimes lose, the final -z of Turkish, and the -I-, which in Turkish is realized as -ı-, -i-, -u-, -ü- according to the rules of vowel harmony, is fixed as either -u- or schwa. The evidence that this extension is a Romani-internal innovation is the fact that the Turkish dialects with which these Romani dialects are in contact have the 1PL preterite (*DI*-past) ending -k (Elšík and Matras 2006, pp. 135–136; Dallı 1976, pp. 119–124). Table 8.1, based on that in Elšík and Matras (2006, p. 136), gives the 1PL and 2PL preterite endings for the relevant Romani dialects. As can be seen from Table 8.1, Kaspičan has completely replaced both 1PL and 2PL preterites with Turkish-influenced forms. (Varna) Gadžikano has variation in 1PL, Vălči Dol and Agia Varvara have variation in both 1PL and 2PL, and Kalburdžu and Crimean Romani (whether from earlier contact with Turkish or later contact with Tatar) have the extension only in the 2PL.

In terms of motivation for this development, Early Romani distinguished 2SG preterite -al from 2PL preterite -an, but in the Balkan and Vlax dialects, the -l of the 2SG preterite was replaced by -n, which led to homonymy in the 2SG and 2PL preterite. In some dialects, the homonymy was eliminated by extending the -e of the 3PL preterite to the 2PL (-en) and sometimes even to the 1PL preterite (-am>-em). The alternation in Agia Varvara Romani here is especially clear: either the innovative 2PL preterite in -en or the older -an with homonymy with the 2SG eliminated by the addition of -Vs, which in a sense exactly parallels the Turkish *DI*-past (2SG -n 2PL -nIz; cf. Elšík and Matras 2006, pp. 113–115, 122–124). In general linguistic terms, it is worth noting that this example is a solid contradiction to the twenty-first-century revival of the claim that morphology is never

Table 8.1 Romani 12PL person markers (Balkan and Vlax dialects)

Dialect	1PL	2PL
Kaspičan	-am-əs	-an-əs
(Varna) Gadžikano	-am~-am-əs	-an-əs
Vălči Dol	-am~-am-ə(s)	-an~-an-ə(s)
Agia Varvara	-am~-am-us	-en~-an-us
Crimean Romani	-am	-an-us
Kalburdžu	-am	-an-ə(s)

240   V. A. Friedman

borrowed (e.g., Labov 2007, pp. 348–349; but see also Matras 2014 on why the borrowing of inflectional morphology is dispreferred).

8.3.5 Turkish Conjugation

The conjugation of verbs of Turkish origin using Turkish inflection is arguably the most striking feature of the impact of Turkish on Romani dialects. While other Balkan languages have taken the *-di-* of the Turkish *DI*-past as a morpheme for adapting verbs of Turkish origin (usually followed by the *-s-* of the Greek sigmatic aorist, e.g., Turkish *dokun-* 'touch' > Rhodopian Bulgarian *dokun-di-s-a* 'offend'), some of the Romani dialects of the Balkans are unique among the Balkan languages in having incorporated Turkish conjugational paradigms wholesale, to varying degrees.[8] Especially significant in this respect are dialects like that of Agia Varvara, where there has been no contact with Turkish since the exchange of populations with Greece in 1923, but where Turkish conjugation is still a vital part of the dialect. This fact contributes to the argument that while in some languages the verb signals the language in a code-switching context (e.g., Domari; cf. Matras 2012, pp. 384–390), the generalization cannot be applied in a blanket fashion to all linguistic situations (see also Matras 2014, p. 69). The following account is based largely on Friedman (2013a).

Turkish conjugations occur in North and South Balkan and South Vlax dialects in regions where there was close contact with Turkish throughout the Ottoman period.[9] The phenomenon, however, is not present in all such dialects. The specific dialects that are adduced here are given in Table 8.2 (SEB = Southeast Bulgaria, NEB = Northeast Bulgaria). Unless otherwise specified, data are drawn from RMS. **Se**peči is based on Cech and Heinschink (1999), **Fu**tadži is based on Ivanov (2000), and **A**gia **V**arvara is based on Igla (1996). Materials from Kaspičan, Haskovo, Tsarevo, and Stefan Karadzhovo are taken from Draganova (2005) and Komotini (Turkish Gümülcine) from Adamou (2006, 2010).[10] Dialects in angled brackets are not specified in RMS as having Turkish conjugations, but examples appear in the database. Bold-faced letters are those used for the abbreviations in Table 8.3 and the examples.

With regard to the Turkish categories taken into Romani, at the maximal level there are eight Turkish tense/aspect/mood (TAM) markers in Lewis' (1967, p. 136) terms, or eight of the nine position-three inflections in Göksel and Kerslake's (2005, pp. 79–83), and, in addition to these, the verbal negator, the infinitive marker, and clitic copular forms. Of the TAM markers, the simple preterite in *-DI* is the most common, this is followed by the two

8 The Impact of Turkish on Romani 241

Table 8.2 Romani dialects with Turkish conjugation

South Balkan	North Balkan	South Vlax
Crimean	Futadži (Haskovo SEB)	Agia Varvara (Athens)
Florina Arli (Greece)	Kaspičan Xoraxani [Sevlievo] (NEB)	Komotini (Greece)
Prizren (Kosovo)	<Pazardžik Malo Konare> (SEB)	Sindel Kalburdži (NEB)
Sepeči (Turkey)	Sliven Muzikanti (SEB)	Vălči Dol (= Laxo, NEB)
	Sliven Nange[Gradeški](SEB)	Varna Kalajdži (= Trakijski Kalajdži, Vlaxorja NEB)
	Spoitori (=SE Romania Kalajdži)	
	Šumen Xoraxane (NEB)	
	<Varna Burgudži> (=Parpulii, NEB)	
	Varna Gadžikano (NEB)	

Note There is considerable fluidity with regard to exonymic and endonymic practices among Romani-speaking groups in the Balkans. A given term may apply to groups speaking very different dialects, a single town may be home to more than one Romani dialect, and a term used a century ago may no longer be in use by speakers today. Moreover, in some cases shift from Romani to a non-Romani language has occurred in the course of the past century. Gilliat-Smith (1944) reports Turkish conjugation from a dialect called Kalajdži that he recorded in Varna that is North Balkan. Strictly speaking, Crimean Romani was in contact with Crimean Tatar more recently than with Turkish, but we include it here as part of the general pattern. The speakers recorded do not know Crimean Tatar and speak a South Balkan Romani dialect. Prizren Turkish conjugation is limited to code-switches

presents, the progressive or imperfective in *-(I)yor* and the so-called aorist or *geniş zaman* 'broad tense' in *-(A/I)r/-z* (henceforth *r*-present). Next in order of frequency is the optative (also called 'subjunctive') in *-(y)A*. Next in the hierarchy is the *mIş*-past, which occurs in two usages, one participial and the other finite. The participial use is not of interest to us here, although it will be noted, but the finite use has important implications for the systems of the relevant dialects. Finally, the Turkish future in *-AcAk*, the verbal negator *-mA-*, the infinitive marker *-mAk*, and the conditional marker *-sA* occur in a very limited number of dialects.[11] These last raise issues of differentiating what Friedman (2013a) identifies as compartmentalization from code-switching and code-mixing.[12] The necessitative or obligative in *-mAlI* and the locative infinitive (*–mAktA*) that Göksel and Kerslake's (2005, p. 83) label *imperfective*—excluded by Lewis from this level of marker and limited to formal contexts in Turkish—are absent. The preterite clitic copula *idi* also occurs.

All dialects with Turkish conjugation have at least the *DI*-past, which is the TAM category (and marker, insofar as Romani also uses a dental that is sometimes realized as a stop) closest to the Romani simple preterite:[13]

242 V. A. Friedman

(1) phenel   ke   rome   **bejen-di-k**
     say.PRS.3SG   that   husband.ACC   like-PST-1PL
     'he says we liked your husband' (Ko)

Next in order of occurrence and frequency is some form of the present tense. Turkish has two TAM markers that can correspond to the Romani present: the *yor*-present, which is described as progressive or imperfective, and the *r*-present, which is gnomic and can also function in Turkish as a future.[14] Among the dialects that have only the Turkish present in addition to the Turkish *DI*-past, some have only the *r*-present (Sp, AV), some have only the *yor*-present (SM), and some have both (SK, perhaps FA). In general, dialects with additional TAM categories have both presents, although sometimes these dialects lack the *yor*-present (Fu). In those dialects with both presents, the *r*-present occurs in future and subjunctive clauses with *ka* and *te*, respectively, although *yor*-presents can also occur in these environments.

(2) Voj   ačelas   paš   lende   taj   **konušur**   lenge.
     she   stand.IMPF.3SG   by   them.LOC   and   speak.PRS.3SG   them.DAT
     'She was standing between them and talking to them.' (VD 649)[15]

(3) Vov   **konuš-ujor**   gadibor   but   ta   kerda   man   te
     he   talk-PRS.PROG   so.much   very   and   made.PST.3SG   me.ACC   SBJV
     bristarav   so   mangav.
     forget.PRS.1SG   what   want.PRS.1SG
     'He talked so much, he made me forget what I wanted.' (VD 785)

(4) Naj   man   kančik   <u>protiv</u>   te   **jardəmn-ar-əm**   tuke.
     not.is   me.ACC   nothing   against   SBJV   help-PRS-1SG   you.DAT
     'I don't mind helping you.' (SK 710)

(5) Odova   aela   mere   kerete   <u>za</u> <u>da</u>   te   **konuš-u-i**   mansa.
     he   come.IMPF.3SG   my.OBL   house.LOC   for   SBJV   SBJV   speak-PRS.PROG   me.INS
     'He came to my house in order to speak with me.' (SK 440)[16]

(6) Kan   **bekl-er-im**   tut   angli   cərkva.
     FUT   wait-PRS-1SG   you.ACC   before.F   church
     'I will wait for you in front of the church.' (SK1009)

(7) Kan   **bekl-ior-um**   tut   andi   kangiri.
     FUT   wait-PRS.PROG-1SG   you.ACC   on.F   church
     'I will wait for you in front of the church.' (VD 1009)

Among those dialects with both present and preterite Turkish inflection, we can distinguish those that also have cliticized *idi* and those that do not. Dialects without cliticized *idi* such as AV and Sp form imperfects and pluperfects using Romani agglutinative material:

(8) ou deža **ček-ti**-sas anglal te resas ame ote
he already go.out-PST-REM before SBJV arrive.PRS.1PL we there
'he had already gone before we got there.' (Sp 389)

Those dialects with cliticized *idi* suffix it to the *r*-present to form an imperfect. Draganova (2005, p. 94) writes that *idi* does not occur with the *yor*-present in Romani, and indeed, no examples have turned up. Examples (9) and (10), however, show that both *r*-present plus *idi* and *DI*-past alone can have imperfect meaning:

(9) But manuša sa kaj kupono, samo odova manuš ani **tan-ər-də**
many person.PL were at party only that.M person which knew-PRS-PST
meri dade odova **konuš-ur-di** mansa.
my.ACC father he talk-PRS-PST me.INS
'There were many people at the party, but only the man who knew my father, talked to me.' (SK 389)

(10) Diklem o ker **ani** savjatar **konuš-tu-nus**.
see.PST.1SG the house which what.ABL speak-PST-2PL
'I saw the house that you were talking about.' (SK 610)

While the two presents of Turkish represent a relatively small deviation from the single present of Romani, and the cliticization of Turkish *idi* parallels the use of the Romani remoteness marker *-as* or *sine*, the Turkish optative-subjunctive represents a major challenge to the Romani system insofar as the Turkish optative-subjunctive is synthetic, whereas the Romani optative-subjunctive is constructed analytically using the particle *te* and the present tense.[17] Example (11) shows an optative with *te*, while Example (12) shows an optative without *te*.

(11) Ov avijas me kereste te **konuš-sun** mansa.
he come.IMPF my.OBL house.LOC SBJV speak-OPT.3SG me.INS
'He came to my house to talk to me.' (SN 440)

(12) Odia ep bisterla **kapa-sən** o dar.
she always forget.3SG.PRS close-OPT.3SG the door
'She always forgets to close the door.' (SK 907)

244   **V. A. Friedman**

The expression of futurity with Turkish verbs in Romani has three possibilities: Romani future marker + Turkish present as seen in Examples (6) and (7) above, Romani future marker + Turkish optative as in (13) and Turkish future as in (14).

(13) Kidal   kam   **diištir-elim**   e   dasengo   dišinmenki   e
     thus   FUT   change-OPT.1PL   the   Bulgarian.PL.GEN   thinking   the
     romenge   askal.
     Rom.PL.DAT   about
     'Thus we will change Bulgarian thinking about Roms.' (Fu)

(14) Ame   naši   **dön-dže-s**   ži   kana   **doorul-ma-jə**   odia.
     we   can't return-FUT-1PL   until   when   get.well-NEG-PRS   she
     'We cannot go back, until she gets well.' (VG 384)

The use of the future marker with an optative is likely a calque on the older form of the Balkan future, which uses an analytic subjunctive clause, i.e., future particle plus subjunctive marker plus finite verb.

Example (15) has a dative infinitive where a Romani verb would require a *te*-clause. It can be argued that the preceding Turkish word precipitated a code-switch; however, in the case of (16), the presence or Romani *te* does not permit such an explanation. It would appear, rather, that as in some other Romani dialects outside the Balkans (Boretzky 1996a), a new infinitive is arising in some Romani dialects in eastern Bulgaria under Turkish influence. It is worth noting that this is the opposite of what happens in Turkish dialects in the western Balkans (e.g., Macedonia), where the optative replaces the infinitive on the model of the Indo-European Balkan languages (Friedman 1982, pp. 31–32; Friedman 2006, pp. 664–666).

(15) Mi   phen   **bašla-də**   **baar-ma-a**   kana   tharde   amaro   kher
     my.F sister begin-PST scream-INF-DAT   when   burn.PST.3PL our.M   house
     'My sister began to scream when they burned down our house.' (VG 759)

(16) Rači   lijom   o   grastis   gijom   te   **ajda-ma-a**.
     yesterday take.PST.SG the horse.ACC   go.PST.1SG   SBJV   ride-INF-DAT
     'Yesterday I took my horse and went for a ride.' (ŠX 1000)

Turkish verbal forms in *-mIş* can be either perfect participles or evidential forms. Insofar as they are implicated in evidentiality, *-mIş*-forms will be discussed in Sect. 8.4 with examples. For the purposes of this section, it is sufficient simply to note their presence or absence in a given dialect.

8 The Impact of Turkish on Romani 245

Table 8.3 Turkish conjugations occurring in Romani dialects

	VB	Se	SM	Sp	AV	FA	VD	SK	VK	SN	Fu	Ts	Ko	Ks	VG	ŠX
di	+	+	+	+	+	+	+	+	+	+	+	+	+	+	+	+
r	−	(−)	−	+	+	+	+	+	+	+	+	+	+	+	+	+
y[or]	−	(−)	+	−	−	+?	+	+	+	+	−	+	+	+	+	+
idi	−	−	−	−	−	−	−	+	+	+	+	+	+	+	+	+
OPT	−	−	−	−	−	−	−	−	te+	te+	te+	te+	ø+	(te)+	ø+	(te)+
miş	(pt)	−	−	−	−	−	−	(pt)	−	−	+	?	−	+	+	+
FUT	−	−	−	−	−	−	−	−	−	−	k+opt	k+opt	+	+	+	+
NEG	−	−	−	−	−	−	−	−	−	−	−	−	+	+	+	+
INF	−	−	−	−	−	−	−	−	−	−	−	−	−	+	+	+

(Cr & PMK=VB) Sepeči presents occur only in code-switches

Note Tsarevo can use both the *r*-present and the optative with *ka*. According to Draganova (2005, pp. 92–93), Kaspičan can use the Turkish future with and without the Romani future marker *kan* and with either Romani or Turkish negation. Only the Turkish type appears in RMS. The form *bejnoer* 'he likes' in FA looks like it might be from a *yor*-present, but that data are inadequate for certainty. The verb *azetme-* 'hate' (SK 1003) contains the Turkish negative marker but appears to be simply lexicalized. Elsewhere in this dialect, Turkish verbs are negated with Romani *in* (e.g., SK 384)

246   V. A. Friedman

Table 8.3 summarizes the types of Turkish paradigms that occur in the Romani dialects given in Table 8.2. Turkish present tense forms in Sepeči appear to be code-switches rather than conjugated forms. The designation (pt) for *mIş*-forms indicates that they are only used as perfect participles; ø + indicates that *te + indicative* is an alternative to plain optative while (*te*) + indicates that the optative can occur with or without *te*.[18] The dialects in bold letters are North Balkan, underlined bold are South Balkan, and italics are South Vlax.[19]

Based on this material, we can identify the following implicational hierarchy of copying of Turkish conjugations in Romani:

preterite < present [*-r ~ -yor*] < clitic *idi* <optative < fut. & neg.<inf.

The finite *mIş*-past is problematic insofar as Komotini (and perhaps Tsarevo) does not have it while having the future, and negative markers are missing from Futadži.[20]

From a Romani dialectological viewpoint, North Balkan Romani shows the heaviest copying, Southern Vlax shows the next highest degree, while lesser degrees of copying are to be found in representatives of all the three Romani dialect groups of the entire region. While it is true that the heaviest copying is concentrated in eastern Bulgaria, where Turks are also heavily concentrated, dialects such as Florina Arli have been cut off from contact with Turkish since 1923 while Sepeči is spoken by Muslims in Izmir, i.e., in constant contact with Turkish. A sociolinguistic factor may well be the relative status of Turkish as a contact language in the larger environment. In eastern Bulgaria, where Turks and Roms were similarly persecuted as Muslims and non-Bulgarians by the communist state during the 1980s and at various times before that, Turkish has shared a certain prestige of resistance with Romani while also exerting an assimilatory pressure on it. In Turkey itself, however, as the socially dominant language in every respect, pressures for linguistic segregation are more obvious. It is clear from the data, however, that knowledge of Turkish by itself does not account for the presence of Turkish conjugation, except, perhaps, in the heaviest cases of copying. Even in those dialects, however, proficiency in Turkish is not always present.

In terms of the hierarchy of copying, as indicated above, Romani is most receptive to the Turkish *di*-past, which not only corresponds most readily to the Romani simple preterite, but also bears a superficial resemblance to it in the use of a suffixal dental stop, as well as final *-m* to mark first person singular and *-n* for second singular. Although the present is normally less marked than the past, this preference for copying or preserving copies of the Turkish preterite is consistent with the various factors involved. Next in order is the present, although different dialects take different paradigms. Then comes the optative, which may or may not be integrated into the Romani analytic pattern of subjunctive subordination. The optative seems to represent a significant boundary in the copying of Turkish inflection. Insofar as some Romani dialects in the Balkans distinguish an indicative in -*a* from a subjunctive without -*a*, there is a formal distinction corresponding to a functional or notional one in native grammar. Whereas the optative integration with or replacement of *te* constructions is consistent with Romani grammar in the Balkans—as noted above, West Rumelian Turkish dialects under heavy Indo-European Balkan influence use the optative to replace the infinitive on the model of the Balkan analytic subjunctive—the *mIş*-past, which is next in the hierarchy of copying, introduces new grammatical distinctions for Romani.[21] In Futadži Romani, this significantly affects the morphosyntax of native verbs (see Sect. 8.4 below). Finally, there is a correlation between synthetic future, negative, and infinitive marking. Unlike the optative, the synthetic nature of the Turkish future is alien to the structure of Romani in the Balkans, which is distinguished by a Balkan type of future using an invariant particle derived from lexical 'want,' and once the Turkish future is integrated, the way is open for infixal negation and even the infinitive as well. It is worth noting that heavily Balkanized West Rumelian Turkish moves in the opposite direction, substituting the optative for the future (see Friedman 2006 for details). Although these last features are characteristic of dialects whose speakers are still actively bilingual in Turkish, such bilingualism is also found among speakers of dialects that do not have such a deep penetration (heavy copying) from Turkish.

The compartmentalization of Turkish conjugation within Romani grammar, in certain respects, resembles the affect of Greek on Romani declension, insofar as the distinction between oikoclitic and xenoclitic declension, which dates from the period of Early Romani contact with Greek, also involves a compartmentalization based on language(s) of origin. However, the Turkish phenomenon is not as widespread and shows varying degrees of pervasiveness. Nonetheless, Turkish verbs in Romani constitute a unique paradigmatic class—in some instances, long after contact with Turkish has ceased. The hierarchy of integration follows expectable structural lines modified, however, by formal, pragmatic, and sociolinguistic factors. Although the phenomenon as a whole crosses Romani dialectological lines, i.e., it is found in North Balkan, South Balkan, and South Vlax, heavier degrees of copying are concentrated in

248 V. A. Friedman

the eastern Balkans. Nonetheless, mere geography and/or knowledge of Turkish cannot account for the dialectal differences. It is likely that sociolinguistic factors are relevant in classifying and explaining Romani dialect typology in the context of contact with Turkish, particularly the prestige of Turkish during the Ottoman period, but possibly also prestige factors related to Romani intergroup dynamics or attitudes.

8.4 Evidentiality

Since the eleventh century, Turkish has been described as having a distinction between a witnessed (*-DI*) and unwitnessed (*-mIş*) past. Moreover, the oldest Turkic documents (eighth-century inscriptions on stone) give evidence of having such a distinction (Dankoff 1982; Tekin 1968). For Balkan Slavic and Albanian, the documentation makes it clear that evidential strategies have their origins in the Ottoman period, most likely owing to contact with Turkish, and the evidentials of Gorna Belica (Bela di suprã) Frasheriote Aromanian and Meglenoromanian result from contact with Albanian and Macedonian, respectively (Friedman 1994, 2010, 2018). Turkish has had both direct and indirect influences on the incorporation of evidential distinctions into Romani in the Balkans. The direct influence involves the incorporation of the Turkish *mIş*-past with or without additional modifications. The indirect influence involves the deployment of interrogative marking as an evidential strategy resulting from contact with Balkan Slavic.

8.4.1 Turkish *mIş*-Past and Related Phenomena

According to Kyuchukov (2012), *-mIş* is borrowed as an evidential particle in some Romani dialects of Bulgaria, a situation similar to that observed by Kappler and Tsiplakou (2018) for Cypriot Greek. Moreover, in Skopje Arli, *imiš* can be used as a particle marking evidentiality (Friedman 2019). However, the incorporation of the *mIş*-past in connection with Turkish conjugation is specific to Romani, as are certain additional particles.

Example (17) shows a contrast between the finite *DI*- and *mIş*-pasts of the type that would occur in Turkish. Here the *mIş*-past is referring to an unwitnessed action:

(17) Odia   artəkən   **git-miš**   ame   kana   **git-ti-k**   kaj   kher.
      they   already   go-PST.*mIş*   we   when   go-PST.*DI*-1PL   at   house
      'He had already gone before we got there.' (VG 389)

In Example (18), taken from a folk tale, the *mIş*-past is used with Turkish verbs in contexts where it would be expected in Turkish, while with native Romani verbs in the same contexts, the particle *berim* is normally placed immediately after the verb or its pronominal object if that follows the verb.[22]

(18)	Oda	kana	dikljas	la	*berim*	**don-muš**	pe	taneste.
	he	when	see.PST.3SG	her.ACC	berim	freeze-PST. *mIş*	in	place.LOC
	'When he saw her [berim], he froze in his tracks [lit. 'place']' (Fu)							

On rare occasion, *berim* occurs after a temporal expression in the verb phrase (5 out of 85 in a 7000 word corpus), three times after a present tense (but always when used with historical present meaning), once each after a subject and a locative expression. Norbert Boretzky (2018, pp. 37–42) considers the particle to come from Turkish *belli* 'sure, known,' but I propose the postposition *berin* 'according to this' to be another possible candidate, as it is phonologically closer and semantically could carry a notion of secondary attribution appropriate to the evidential-like meanings of the *mIş*-past. The Futadži phenomenon is unique in that—unlike the repurposing of interrogatives (see Sect. 8.4.2) and the evidential-like opposition between gender and person agreement in third singular intransitive preterites in some Romani dialects (Matras 1995)—it is a native development co-occurring with an integrated foreign (Turkish) category.

8.4.2 Interrogative Markers as an Evidential Strategy

The Turkish interrogative marker *mi* and the Slavic interrogative marker *li* are both borrowed into Romani dialects in the Balkans as interrogative markers, but in some dialects, they have also developed extended uses as types of evidential markers. The Turkish marker *mi* and the Slavic marker *li* serve identical dubitative marking functions in Skopje Barutči and Kriva Palanka Arli, respectively.[23] Dubitativity is the active refusal to commit to the truth of a statement, i.e., an expression of doubt, disbelief, sarcasm, etc. The statement itself is normally based on a previous real or presumed statement or report. Dubitativity, like admirativity—the expression of surprised realization and acceptance of an unexpected state of affairs—is a part of what I have called the *confirmative/nonconfirmative complex*.[24] Both the Turkish *mIş*-past and the Macedonian *l*-past have dubitative usages of their respective forms, and the Romani use of interrogative particles to express this meaning is arguably an expressive calque on that usage. Example (19a) gives a Macedonian dubitative, which involves the use of an *l*-form, which is the unmarked past.[25] The context is two people conversing on the telephone. Speaker A claims that he is in (calling from) America. Speaker B, convinced or knowing full well that Speaker A is lying, retorts with Speaker A's original statement, but using a dubitative, which in Macedonian involves repeating the statement and shifting the tense into a paradigm using the verbal *l*-form. Example (19b) is the equivalent in Kriva Palanka Arli, and Example (19c) is the equivalent of Speaker B's dubitative in Skopje Barutči.

(19a) A: | *Jas* | *sum* | *vo* | *Amerika.* | | | |
|---|---|---|---|---|---|---|
| | I | am | in | America | | | |
| B: | *Abe* | *ti* | *si* | *bil* | *vo* | *Amerika!* | *Lažeš!* |
| | VOC | you | are | L.M | in | America! | lie.2SG.PRS |
| A: | 'I am in America.' | | | | | | |
| B: | 'Oh, sure, you're in America! You're lying!' | | | | | | |

(19b) A: | *Me* | *sijum* | *ki* | *Amerika.* | | | |
|---|---|---|---|---|---|---|
| | I | am | in | America | | | |
| B: | *Abe* | *tu* | *hinjan* | *li* | *t-i* | *Amerika!* | *Hohavea* |
| | VOC | you | are | li | in-F.DEF | America | lie.2SG.PRS |
| A: | 'I am in America.' | | | | | | |
| B: | 'Oh, sure, you're in America! You're lying!' | | | | | | |

(19c) B: | *Abe* | *tu* | *injan* | *mi* | *ki* | *Amerika.* | *Hohavea!* |
|---|---|---|---|---|---|---|
| | VOC | you | are | *mi* | in | America. | lie.2SG.PRS |
| | 'Oh sure, you are in America! You're lying!' | | | | | | |

The Macedonian use of *bil* and the Romani usages of 'be' + *mi/li* correspond to the Turkish use of *imiş* in the same context. As an example of Turkish influence on Romani, this usage is arguably one that could involve indirect rather than direct influence. Both Turkic and Slavic use their respective interrogative markers as types of emphatic particles, so in principle either language or both could have been the possible source in Romani, although the Macedonian usage is itself the result of Turkish influence (Friedman 2013b, 2018).

However, Slavic *li* is also used as an evidential marker in the North Balkan dialect of Sliven, Bulgaria, where it has the same full range of meanings as in the Bulgarian evidential system and can be affixed to any preterite verb (Kostov 1963, pp. 123,132–133, 1973, pp. 107–108).[26] Kostov speculates that the origin of this *li* is the Bulgarian resultative participle in -*l*, the evidential use of which is itself, as in Macedonian, a calque on Turkish (Friedman 2018). Igla (2004, 2006) reinvestigated the situation in Sliven and argues that the Sliven Romani *li* as evidential has its origins in the Slavic interrogative marker, which finds a typological parallel with the usages I recorded for Skopje Barutči and Kriva Palanka Arli. Thus, the use of borrowed interrogative markers as evidential markers in Romani, while ultimately connected to Turkish influence, is in at least some cases only indirectly so.

8.5   Syntax

The most significant impact of Turkish on Romani syntax is in those dialects that have either borrowed Turkish postpositions as postpositions—rather than transforming them into prepositions, as happens in other Romani dialects of the Balkans and in other Balkan languages in general—or transformed some native prepositions into postpositions. Turkish has also influenced the choice of case marking even when actual word order is not affected. For example, Agia Varvara Romani maintains prepositional structure but calques Turkish case agreement, e.g., *sona duj čonendar* 'after two months.ABL' (Messing 1988, p. 114) (cf. Turkish *iki aydan sonra* '2 months. ABL after') but *pala i Patrigi* (Messing 1988, p. 97) 'after Easter.NOM.' Kaspičan (RMS 1018, 627, 525, 756, respectively) has postpositions, e.g., *paraske ičin* 'for money.DAT' *Erdelezi ičin* 'for St. George's Day.NOM' (Turkish *için* 'for'), *xəzmečestar sora* 'after work.ABL' but also plain case or prepositional structures, e.g., *me tudeske džava* 'I go for milk.DAT,' *pala ek kašteste* 'behind a tree.LOC.' Sliven Nange (RMS 426, 513, respectively) has both postpositional and prepositional uses of the native *pala[l]* 'after' *štar zisendar palal* 'after four days.ABL,' but *palal eke brešestar* 'after one year. ABL' where the ablative calques the Turkish usage with *sonra*. In most dialects of the Balkans, *pala* takes a nominative or locative, as in the examples with 'tree' and 'Easter' just cited or *pala mande* 'after me.' Cf. also Example (13) above from Futadži, *e romenge askal* 'about the Roms,' where *askal* is a native form and other dialects would have a plain dative, or preposed *askal*.

8.6   Turkish and Language Shift

One other impact of Turkish on Romani is language shift. While the shift of Romani speakers to Turkish in Turkey itself is unremarkable, it is worth noting that some Romani communities (or communities of Romani origin)

252   V. A. Friedman

have shifted to Turkish in Bulgaria and Macedonia as well. In Bulgaria, some Turkish speakers of Romani origin identify as a separate ethnic group, calling themselves *Millet* which is Turkish for 'nation' (Atanasov 2004). These can be compared to the *Egipkjani* 'Egyptians' (formerly *Gjupci*, now 'Balkan Egyptians'; same etymon as English *Gypsy*) and *Ashakli* (literally 'charcoal burner 'from Albanian *eshkë* 'charcoal'), who are Albanian-speaking Muslims of Romani origin (which, however, they deny) in Macedonia and Kosovo.[27] In parts of eastern Macedonia, some Roms have shifted to Turkish but retain their Romani identity (Friedman 2003, pp. 109–113).

8.7   Conclusion

In certain respects, the Romani dialects of the Balkans are typical of Balkan languages in terms of the impact of Turkish, and it is significant that it is precisely those dialects spoken in the Balkans that show this impact. In this sense, the distribution of Romani dialects actually helps define a northern linguistic boundary for the Balkan Peninsula. As with Balkan Slavic and Balkan Romance, so, too, with the Romani dialects of the Balkans, the impact of Turkish is one of the effects and results of the linguistic convergence that produced the Balkan *Sprachbund*. Thus, for example, the overall lexical impact of Turkish does not differ significantly from the impact on other Balkan languages. Similarly, analytic comparison of adjectives is typically Balkan, albeit in some Romani dialects more specifically influenced by Turkish. In the case of Romani, however, there are some unique features not found in the other Balkan languages. Most notable among these are the presence of Turkish conjugation in some Romani dialects and also the relative absence of the productivity of Turkish derivational morphemes that are productive in the other Balkan languages. Thus, in a sense, Matras' (1994) statement that Romani is a Balkanized Indic language, cited at the beginning of this article, can be nuanced further by saying that those dialects of the Balkans are especially close to their co-territorial neighbors precisely because of the shared contact with Turkish. At the same time, however, Romani differs from its co-territorial neighbors in the features it incorporates or does not incorporate. This in turn can be attributed to the specific nature of Romani multilingualism in the Balkans, but also to the relatively conservative nature of the relationship of Romani to Turkish in the context of the post-Ottoman nation-states.

Notes

1. Albanian *bubrek* is now archaic, while the word is not listed in Greek and Romanian sources.
2. In the case of this particular lexical item, we should note that according to Skok (1971, p. 224), the form *bubrik* in Istria and other dialects points to an original *jat*, which supports the claim that this is a pre-Ottoman Turkic loan in Slavic. The Romani forms in -*ško*, etc., are from a BCSM diminutive *bubrežak* (genitive singular *bubreška*). Cf. also the point made by Kazazis (1972, p. 95), that in various languages of the Balkans, Turkisms spread to regions outside Ottoman control after the establishment of nation-states whose standard languages were based on dialects that were in contact with Turkish, e.g., Muntenia for Romanian and eastern Herzegovina for Serbo-Croatian.
3. See also Adamou and Shen (2017) and Adamou and Granqvist (2015), who note that approximately 15% of all words in normal conversation in the speech of trilingual Romani-Turkish-Greek speakers in Xanthi (Greek Thrace) are Turkish. While such analyses are lacking for other regions in the Balkans, and especially for the nineteenth century, before the spread of literacy and the establishment of nation-state standard languages, it is fair to speculate that similar figures would have occurred elsewhere in the region.
4. Aromanian likewise used colloquial Turkisms: *hàmami* and *hale,* respectively. In the 2002 census forms, for which the same six languages were defined as official, the words were the same except that the Romani variants were spelled *amami* and *khenefi*—reflecting local variations in pronunciation. The Turkish replaced *banyo-ayakyolu* with *tualet*, and Albanian had *banjë* for *banjo*. For political reasons, as of this writing (2018), Macedonia has not held a census since 2002, although one is scheduled for 2020.
5. The exception to this generalization is Debar, where for centuries Albanian and Macedonian were the respective town languages of the Muslim and Christian townspeople, all townspeople were bilingual, and Turkish was associated with the surrounding villages rather than the town. While the raising of the status of Albanian—like that of all the other Balkan languages—has its origins in the nineteenth century (Skendi 1967), such developments had little to no effect on Macedonian towns until World War II.
6. In fact, all Turkish high vowels neutralize to [i] in final position in West Rumelian Turkish (i.e., the dialects of Albania and former Yugoslavia as well as adjacent parts of Greece and Bulgaria).
7. RMS is the Romani Morpho-Syntactic Database. See RMS in the bibliography for the URL. KX refers to the Kaspičan Xoraxani dialect in RMS, and 627 refers to the number of the question where the datum appears. Henceforth, only the names of the respective dialects followed by the question reference will be given for citations for RMS. For a complete explanation of the abbreviations referring to dialects, see the explanation in Table 8.2.

8. Some Romani dialects in contact with other languages, e.g., Russian, Croatian, and Greek, also have borrowed inflected verbs (Matras 2002, pp. 134–135), but none of these dialects change the basic quadripartite inherited Romani tense-aspect system (perfective/non-perfective and remote/non-remote). The integration of Turkish conjugation, however, shows far more variability both in terms of the number of paradigms that integrate and in terms of the dialects into which the paradigms are integrated.

9. The terms 'North' and 'South' serve as a convenient shorthand for the fact that within the Vlax group, the basic division is between those dialects whose northernmost groups are to the north of all those designated as 'south.' In the case of the Balkan dialect group, the term 'south' is used because the southernmost South Balkan dialects are south of any north Balkan, also known as *zis*-dialect or Balkan II dialects.

10. Gilliat-Smith (1944) reports and gives examples of Turkish conjugation for Varna Kalajdži.

11. Draganova (2005, pp. 95–96) reports the conditional in *-sA* for Tsarevo, Haskovo, and Kaspičan, but it does not occur in the RMS or Futadži materials.

12. *Code compartmentalization*, unlike *code-switching* or *code-mixing*, is a situation in which material from a contact language or languages is integrated into the grammatical system of the receiving language, but is also segregated. The oikoclitic versus xenoclitic declensions of Romani are a prime example, but, as Friedman (2013a) argues, Turkish conjugation is a similar one.

13. Turkish verbs are given in bold face; words in languages other than Romani are underlined only if they are part of the verb phrase. Examples from RMS are given with reference numbers to the entries in the database.

14. See Göksel and Kerslake (2005) for a comprehensive account of Turkish TAM markers.

15. See note 7 for explanation of notation.

16. The SK and VG dialects both have progressive presents that resemble the *y*-present characteristic of West Rumelian Turkish. However, forms such as *šišijo* 'it swells' and *doorulmajə* 'she does not get well' indicate that this is simply a surface similarity caused by erosion in the Romani dialects. In the other dialects, the *yor*-present is readily recognizable, but we cannot rule out the possibility that some dialects now in eastern Bulgaria might have acquired their Turkish present conjugations in Western Rumelia. The *r*-present also occurs with *te* and *ka*.

17. In some Romani dialects, the distinction between the Romani long present ending in *-a* and the short-present lacking this final vowel is one of non-subjunctive/subjunctive, such that the latter occurs after modal markers such as subjunctive *te* and future *ka*. This distinction is not made in various Arli dialects, however (Cech and Heinschink 2002; Friedman field notes). Outside the Balkans, the long form in *-a* sometimes develops into a future, sometimes into a formal oratory style.

8   The Impact of Turkish on Romani   255

18. Additional factors such as the use of clitic forms of 'be' (especially *idi*) seem to correlate with the presence of the present/past opposition.
19. For Tsarevo, Draganova (2005) does not give a classification and the data are insufficient to suggest one.
20. Note that the category *imperative* is not included here, since the 2SG imperative is -Ø in both Turkish and Romani, and the 2PL ends in -*n* for both languages.
21. The *mIş*-participle itself does not introduce anything grammatically new, and as a non-finite type, it has many corresponding copies from other contact languages in Europe.
22. As of this writing (2018), this usage has not been attested in any other dialect of Romani other than the Futadži of Haskovo.
23. See Friedman (2017) and Boretzky (1996b) for more on Skopje Barutči Arli.
24. See Friedman (2012a, b) and the references therein. The term *admirative* precedes the currently popular term *mirative* by more than a century, and the latter has a more dubious status (Hill 2012).
25. In Standard Macedonian and the dialects on which it is based, the inherited synthetic aorist and imperfect are marked for confirmativity, while the old inherited perfect using the auxiliary 'be' with what used to be a resultative participle, in -*l*, has become the unmarked past. This unmarked past, by virtue of its contrast to a marked confirmative, can be deployed in various (nonconfirmative) evidential strategies. In the southwestern dialects, a new perfect using the auxiliary 'have' and what used to be the past passive participle (now a verbal adjective) has restricted the old perfect entirely to nonconfirmative uses. This is an ongoing process that is spreading north and east (Friedman 2014 and field notes).
26. I have argued elsewhere (Friedman 2002, 2012a) that evidential strategies in Balkan Slavic always have some sort of past reference (either to a previous state of affairs or real or putative statement), since they cannot be used felicitously with genuine present or future meaning, e.g., one cannot look at the sky, see it suddenly cloud over, and exclaim 'It's going to rain!' with an admirative *l*-form in Balkan Slavic. Further research is needed, however, to determine whether these same restrictions apply to the Romani phenomena discussed here.
27. The Ashkali live in Kosovo and speak Geg, while the Egipkjani live mainly in southwestern Macedonia and speak Tosk. When I first met Egipkjani in Ohrid in 1976, they informed me (in Macedonian): *Nie sme Gjupci. Ne znaeme od kaj sme.* 'We are Gjupci, we don't know where we come from.' By 1981, however, they had developed the identity of *Egipkjani* 'Egyptians' and registered as such in the 1981 census, although they were classed as 'Other' and not enumerated separately. They were recognized as a separate nationality in the 1991 Yugoslav census and the 1994 Macedonian census, but were included again with 'Others' in the 2002 Macedonian census (see Friedman 2012b, pp. 271–272). There are also Christian Gjupci in southwestern Macedonia who speak Macedonian.

References

Abercrombie, Amelia. 2018. Language purism and social hierarchies: Making Romani standard in Prizren. *Language in Society* 47 (1): 1–21.

Ackerley, Frederick George. 1914/1915. The Romani speech of Catalonia. *Journal of the Gypsy Lore Society*, n.s., 8: 99–140.

Adamou, Evangelia. 2006. Field notes on Komotini Romani. Research funded by CNRS–Lacito.

Adamou, Evangelia. 2010. Bilingual speech and language ecology in Greece: Romani and Pomak in contact with Turkish. *Language in Society* 39 (2): 147–171.

Adamou, Evangelia, and Kimmo Granqvist. 2015. Unevenly mixed Romani languages. *International Journal of Bilingualism* 19 (5): 525–547.

Adamou, Evangelia, and Rachel Xingjia Shen. 2017. There are no language switching costs when codeswitching is frequent. *International Journal of Bilingualism* 20 (1): 1–18.

Antonovska, Svetlana, et al. 1994. *The 1994 census: Data for the present and the future*. Skopje: Republički zavod za statistika.

Atanasov, Ivan (ed.). 2004. *Millet: Meždu Cila i Haribda*. Veliko Tărnovo: Amalipe. Film.

Bhatia, Rishi Gopal. 1963. A Gypsy grammar. PhD dissertation, University of Pennsylvania, Philadelphia.

Boretzky, Norbert. 1996a. The 'new infinitive' in Romani. *Journal of the Gypsy Lore Society*, 5th ser., 6: 1–51.

Boretzky, Norbert. 1996b. Arli: Materialen zu EIeinemNEM südbalkanischen Romani-Dialekt. *Grazer Linguistische Studien* 46: 1–31.

Boretzky, Norbert. 2018. *Der Romani-Dialekt der Futadžides von Chaskovo/Bulgarien*. Graz: Grazer Linguistische Monographien.

Boretzky, Norbert, and Birgit Igla. 2004. *Komentierter Dialektatlas des Romani. Teil 1: Vergleich der Dialekte. Teil 2: Dialektkarten mit einer CD Rom*. Wiesbaden: Harrassowitz.

Bunis, David M. 1999. *Voices from Jewish Salonika*. Jerusalem–Thessaloniki: Misgav Yerushalayim, National Authority for Ladino Culture, Ets Ahaim Foundation of Thessaloniki.

Cech, Petra, and Mozes F. Heinschink. 1999. *Sepečides–Romani: Grammatik, Texte und Glossar einestürkischen Romani-Dialekts*. Wiesbaden: Harrassowitz.

Cech, Petra, and Mozes F. Heinschink. 2002. The Arli dialect of Priština and other Arli varieties spoken in Serbia and Macedonia. Paper presented at the 6th international conference on Romani linguistics, center for the study of modern European languages and the University of Graz, September 12–14, Austria.

Cech, Petra, Christiane Fennesz-Juhasz, Dieter W. Halwachs, and Mozes F. Heinschink. 2003. *E bengali Romni. So Roma phenen taj gilaben – Die schlaue Romni. Märchen und Lieder der Roma*. Klagenfurt/Celovec: Drava.

8 The Impact of Turkish on Romani   257

Dallı, Hüseyin. 1976. *Kuzeydoğu Bulgaristan türk ağızları üzerine araştırmalar*. Ankara: Türk Dil Kurumu.

Dankoff, R. (ed. and trans. with J. Kelly). 1982. *Mahmud al-Kāšğarī, Compendium of the Turkic Dialects (Dīwān luğāt at-Turk)*, Part I. Cambridge: Tekin.

Draganova, Desislava. 2005. Turkish verbs in Bulgarian Romani. In *General and applied Romani linguistics: Proceedings of the sixth international conference on Romani linguistics*, ed. Barbara Schrammel, Dieter Halwachs, and Gerd Ambrosch, 90–97. Munich: LinCom Europa.

Ellis, Burcu Akan. 2003. *Shadow genealogies: Memory and identity among urban Muslims in Macedonia*. Boulder, CO: East European Monographs.

Elšík, Viktor, and Yaron Matras. 2006. *Markedness and language change: The Romani sample*. Empirical Approaches to Language Typology 32. Berlin: Mouton de Gruyter.

Friedman, Victor A. 1982. Balkanology and Turcology: West Rumelian Turkish in Yugoslavia as reflected in prescriptive grammar. In *Studies in Slavic and general linguistics, vol. 2, South Slavic and Balkan Linguistics*, ed. A.A. Barensten, R. Sprenger, and M.G.M. Tielemans, 1–77. Amsterdam: Rodopi.

Friedman, Victor A. 1985a. Balkan Romani modality and other Balkan languages. *Folia Slavica* 7 (3): 381–389.

Friedman, Victor A. 1985b. Problems in the codification of a standard Romani literary language. In *Papers from the fourth and fifth annual meetings: Gypsy Lore Society, North American Chapter*, ed. Joanne Grumet, 56–75. New York: Gypsy Lore Society.

Friedman, Victor A. 1988. A Caucasian loanword in Romani. In *Papers from the eighth and ninth meetings: Gypsy Lore Society, North American Chapter*, ed. Cara DeSilva, Joanne Grumet, and David J. Nemeth, 18–20. New York: Gypsy Lore Society.

Friedman, Victor A. 1989. Toward defining the position of Turkisms in Romani. In *Jezik i kultura Roma*, ed. Milan Šipka, 251–267. Sarajevo: Institut za proučavanje nacionalnih odnosa.

Friedman, Victor A. 1994. Surprise! Surprise! Arumanian has had an admirative! *Indiana Slavic Studies* 7: 79–89.

Friedman, Victor A. 1996a. The Turkish lexical element in the languages of the Republic of Macedonia from the Ottoman period to independence. *Zeitschrift für Balkanologie* 32 (2): 133–150.

Friedman, Victor A. 1996b. Observing the observers: Language, ethnicity, and power in the 1994 Macedonian census and beyond. In *Toward comprehensive peace in Southeastern Europe: Conflict prevention in the South Balkans*, ed. Barnett R. Rubin, 81–105, 119–126. New York: Council on Foreign Relations/ Twentieth Century Fund.

Friedman, Victor A. 2002. Hunting the elusive evidential: The third-person auxiliary as a Boojum in Bulgarian. In *Of all the slavs my favorites: Studies in honor of howard I aronson on the occasion of his 66th Birthday*, ed. Victor A. Friedman and Donald L. Dyer, 203–230. Bloomington, IN: Slavica.

Friedman, Victor A. 2003. Romani as a minority language, as a standard language, and as a contact language: Comparative legal, sociolinguistic, and structural approaches. In *Multilingualism in global and local perspectives: Selected papers from the Eighth Nordic Conference on Bilingualism*, ed. Kari Fraurud and Kenneth Hyltenstam, 103–133. Stockholm: Stockholm University.

Friedman, Victor A. 2006. The Balkans as a linguistic area. In *Elsevier encyclopedia of language and linguistics*, vol. 1, chief ed. Keith Brown, 657–672. Oxford: Elsevier.

Friedman, Victor A. 2010. The Age of the Albanian admirative: A problem in historical semantics In *Ex Anatolia Lux: Anatolian and Indo-European studies in honor of H. Craig Melchert*, ed. Ronald Kim, Norbert Oettinger, Elisabeth Rieken, and Michael Weiss, 31–39. Ann Arbor: Beech Stave Press.

Friedman, Victor A. 2012a. Perhaps mirativity is phlogiston, but admirativity is perfect. *Linguistic Typology* 16 (2): 505–527.

Friedman, Victor A. 2012b. *Macedonian studies 2*. Skopje: Macedonian Academy of Sciences and Arts.

Friedman, Victor A. 2013a. Compartmentalized grammar: The variable (non)-integration of Turkish verbal conjugation in Romani dialects. *Romani Studies* 23 (1): 107–120.

Friedman, Victor A. 2013b. The use of *li* as a marker of evidential strategy in Romani. *Contrastive Linguistics* 38 (2–3): 253–261.

Friedman, Victor A. 2014. *The grammatical categories of the Macedonian indicative*, 2nd ed. Bloomington, IN: Slavica.

Friedman, Victor A. 2017. Seven varieties of Arli: Skopje as a center of convergence and divergence of Romani dialects. *Romani Studies*, 5th ser., 27 (1): 29–45.

Friedman, Victor A. 2018. Where do evidentials come from? In *The Oxford handbook of evidentiality*, ed. Alexandra Y. Aikhenvald, 124–147. Oxford: Oxford University Press.

Friedman, Victor A. 2019. Evidentiality in South Balkan (Arli) Romani: The use of *imiš*. In *Festschrift for Mozes Heinschink*, ed. Dieter W. Halwachs and Petra Cech, 105-114. Graz: University of Graz.

Friedman, Victor A., and Brian D. Joseph. 2014. Lessons from Judezmo about the Balkan Sprachbund and contact linguistics. *International Journal of the Sociology of Language* 226: 3–23.

Friedman, Victor A., and Brian D. Joseph. Forthcoming. *The Balkan languages*. Cambridge: Cambridge University Press.

Göksel, Aslı, and Celia Kerslake. 2005. *Turkish: A comprehensive grammar*. London: Routledge.

Gilliat-Smith, Bernard. 1944. A Bulgarian Gypsy tale. *Journal of the Gypsy Lore Society*, 3rd ser., 23: 15–21.

Grannes, Alf, Kjetil Rå Hauge, and Hayriye Süleymenoğlu. 2002. *A dictionary of Turkisms in Bulgarian*. Oslo: Novus.

Hill, Nathan W. 2012. "Mirativity" does not exist: *ḥdug* in "Lhasa" Tibetan and other suspects. *Linguistic Typology* 16: 389–433.

8 The Impact of Turkish on Romani 259

Igla, Birgit. 1996. *Das Romani von Ajia Varvara – Deskriptive und historisch vergleichende Darstellung eines Zigeunerdialekts.* Balkanologisches Veröffentlichungen 29. Wiesbaden: Harrassowitz.

Igla, Birgit. 2004. Spreženie na glagola v Slivenskija romski dialekt. *Andral* 35–36: 19–50.

Igla, Birgit. 2006. Zur Renarrative im slivener Romani. *Balkansko ezikoznanie* 40 (1): 55–63.

Ivanov, Ivan 2000. *Futadžiite. The Futadjides. Futadžides.* Haskovo: Fondacia Tolerantnost i vzaimopomošt.

Jusuf, Šaip, and Krume Kepeski. 1980. *Romani gramatika—Romska gramatika.* Skopje: Naša kniga.

Kappler, Matthias, and Stavroula Tsiplakou. 2018. Miş and miʃimu: An instance of language contact in Cyprus. In *Linguistic minorities in Turkey and Turkic speaking minorities in the periphery*, ed. Christiane Bulut, 275–282. Wiesbaden: Harrassowitz.

Kazazis, Kostas. 1972. The status of Turkisms in present-day Balkan languages. In *Aspects of the Balkans*, ed. Henrik Birnbaum and Spiros Vryonis, 87–116. The Hague: Mouton.

Kazazis, Kostas. 1973. ΤΑΚΥΔΡΟΜΣ's 'Turkish lessons'. In *Issues in linguistics: Papers in honor of Henry and Renée Kahane*, ed. Braj B. Kachru et al., 394–408. Urbana: University of Illinois Press.

Kazazis, Kostas. 1975. Greek reactions to an Ancient Greek primer for Turks. *Modern Philology* 73 (2): 162–165.

Kostov, Kiril. 1963. Grammatik der Zigeunersprache Bulgariens: Phonetik und Morphologie. PhD dissertation, Humboldt University of Berlin.

Kostov, Kiril. 1973. Zur Bedeutung des Zigeunerischen für die Erforschung Grammatischer Interferenzerscheinungen. *Balkansko ezikoznanie* 16: 99–113.

Kyuchukov, Hristo. 2012. The use of evidentiality as a language devise. Paper presented at the 10th international conference on Romani linguistics, September 5–7, University of Barcelon.

Labov, William. 2007. Transmission and diffusion. *Language* 83 (2): 344–387.

Lewis, G. 1967. *Turkish grammar.* Oxford: Oxford University Press.

Matras, Yaron. 1994. Structural Balkanisms in Romani. In *Sprachlicher Standard und Substandard in Südosteuropa und Osteuropa*, ed. Norbert Reiter, 195–210. Wiesbaden: Harrassowitz.

Matras, Yaron. 1995. Verb evidentials and their discourse function in Vlach Romani narratives. In *Romani in contact: The history, structure and sociology of a language*, ed. Yaron Matras, 95–123. Amsterdam: John Benjamins.

Matras, Yaron. 2002. *Romani: A linguistic introduction.* Cambridge: Cambridge University Press.

Matras, Yaron. 2012. *A Grammar of Domari.* Berlin: De Gruyter Mouton.

Matras, Yaron. 2014. Why is the borrowing of inflectional morphology dispreferred? In *Borrowed morphology*, ed. Francesco Gardani, Peter Arkadiev, and Nino Amiridze, 45–80. Berlin: De Gruyter Mouton.

Messing, Gordon M. 1988. *A glossary of Greek Romany: As spoken in Agia Varvara (Athens)*. Columbus: Slavica.

Paspati, A. 1870. *Études sur les Tchinghianés ou Bohémiens de l'Empire Ottoman*. Constantinople: A. Korméla. Reprinted 1973, Osnabrück: Biblio Verlag.

ROMLEX = Halwachs, Dieter, Barbara Schrammel, and Astrid Rader. 2006. Romani Lexical Database. University of Graz. http://romani.uni-graz.at/romlex/.

RMS = Yaron Matras, and Viktor Elšík. 2001–2005, 2008. Romani Morpho-Syntactic Database. University of Manchester. http://romani.humanities. manchester.ac.uk/rms/.

Sampson, John. 1926. *The dialect of the Gypsies of Wales*. Oxford: Oxford University Press. Reprinted 1968.

Sechidou, Irene. 2011. *Balkan Romani: The Dialect of Ajios Athanasios/Greece*. Munich: LinCom Europa.

Šiškov, Stoju N. 1936. *Bǎlgaro-mohamedanite (pomaci): istoriko-zemepisen i naro-doučen pregled s obrazi*. Plovdiv: Tǎrgovska pečatnica.

Škaljić, Abdulah. 1966. *Turcizmi u srpskohrvatskom jeziku*. Sarajevo: Svjetlost.

Skok, Petar. 1971. *Etimologijski rječnik hrvatskoga ili srpskoga jezika*. Zagreb: Jugoslavenska akademija znanosti i umjetnosti.

Skendi, Stavro. 1967. *The Albanian national awakening: 1878–1912*. Princeton: Princeton University Press.

Tadmor, Uri, Martin Haspelmath, and Bradley Taylor. 2010. Borrowability and the notion of basic vocabulary. *Diachronica* 27 (2): 226–246.

Tekin, Talat. 1968. *A grammar of Orkhon Turkic*. Bloomington, IN: Indiana University Press.

Theokharidēs, Petros D. 1996. *Grammatikē tēs Pomakikēs Glōssas*. Thessaloniki: Aigeiros.

9

The Impact of Slavic Languages on Romani

Anna-Maria Meyer

9.1 Introduction

After the arrival of the Roma on the European continent, they very quickly came into contact with speakers of Slavic languages. The first evidence for the presence of Roma in Southeastern Europe dates back to the middle of the fourteenth century. Around the year 1400, they reached Poland, Bohemia and other regions of Central Europe, and the first document proving the presence of Roma in Russia dates to 1733 (Samer 2003; Demeter et al. 2000, p. 187). Today, Slovakia, Macedonia and Bulgaria have the highest percentage of Roma among the countries with a Slavic-speaking majority (numbers according to Grienig 2010), and, with very few exceptions, all speakers of Romani are at least bilingual.

It is clear against this historical background that the Slavic languages will have served as both old and recent donor languages for Romani. For instance, the Roma in Russia have been in contact not only with Russian, but, before that, also with West and South Slavic languages and have kept linguistic features from these earlier contact situations to different degrees. All Romani dialects in Europe have been influenced by the South Slavic languages in the Balkans, but most strongly balkanised are, of course, the dialects of the speakers that have stayed in this region until today. With respect

---

A.-M. Meyer (✉)
Department of Slavic Studies, University of Cologne, Cologne, Germany
e-mail: anna-maria.meyer@uni-koeln.de

© The Author(s) 2020
Y. Matras and A. Tenser (eds.), *The Palgrave Handbook of Romani Language and Linguistics*, https://doi.org/10.1007/978-3-030-28105-2_9

261

to the Balkans, it would not be right to state that only the Slavic Balkan languages (Macedonian, Bulgarian and the Serbian Torlak dialects) have acted as donor languages for Romani; rather, they have to be seen as a part of the larger Balkan *Sprachbund*, a linguistically very complex entity which often makes it impossible to identify one single donor language.

Bearing in mind the long history of language contact between Slavic and Romani as well as the similarities between the Slavic languages, it is not always possible to tell from which Slavic language a contact feature was borrowed. Moreover, due to the fact that communication between the Slavic and Roma populations has for centuries been characterised by face-to-face encounters, spoken forms of Slavic languages and dialects have played a larger role in contact scenarios than have the Slavic standard languages. The influence of Slavic standard varieties is growing, however, along with growing rates of school attendance and literacy among the Roma.

The dialect groups of Romani that have been influenced by Slavic are mainly the Northeastern, Northern Central, Southern Central and South Balkan I as well as different Vlax dialects (for an overview, cf. the maps in Matras 2002, pp. 11–12), but Slavic influence can be found in Romani varieties all over the world (cf., e.g., Hancock 1983 for Texan Romani). The extent of Slavic influence on different Romani dialects can vary considerably and depends on several factors, such as the respective population's way of life, its degree of integration into the majority population and for how long it has been sedentary; an illustration of such differences based on the example of the Polska and Bergitka Roma varieties in Poland can be found in Meyer (2016). Vlax dialects generally exhibit less influence from Slavic languages than do non-Vlax dialects, but there are exceptions, such as the variety of the Kišinyovcy in Ukraine and South Russia, described by Čerenkov (2008, p. 493).

The present article relies on the available research literature and language data from the Romani Morpho-Syntax (RMS) database of the University of Manchester (Elšík and Matras 2001). It aims to give an overview of the topic, although it has to be kept in mind that the picture cannot be complete due to the summary nature of the present publication and the fact that not all Romani dialects in question have been investigated to a sufficient degree. Most of the available research literature pertains to the Balkan varieties, North Russian Romani and the Northern Central dialect in Slovakia. This alone is not sufficient for a complete picture of Romani, but, complemented by the limited information available for other Romani varieties, does enable us to give a fair representation of the effects of contact with South, East and West Slavic languages. Of course, Slavic lexical and structural borrowings do not stop at the borders of the Slavic countries, but very often migrate further, together with their speaker communities, for example from Slovenia to Italy. In the course of such migrations, layers of loans can replace each other, and by far not all lexical and structural borrowings keep their place in the respective Romani variety forever.

The indisputable pioneer among researchers of this language contact was Franz Miklosich (1813–1891), as seen especially in his treatise *Die slavischen Elemente in den Mundarten der Zigeuner* 'The Slavic elements in the vernaculars of the Gypsies' (1872). This seminal work has been extended in many later publications.

The present contribution is organised according to the various levels of linguistic structure that have been affected by language contact in the following order: lexicon, phonetics and phonology, nominal morphology, verbal morphology and syntax.

9.2   Lexical Borrowing

The impact of Slavic languages on Romani is most obvious in the lexicon (cf. the comprehensive compilation of lexical borrowings from Slavic into Romani in Boretzky 2013). Lexical borrowings also reflect the domains of life that have been affected by contact with the respective surrounding Slavic-speaking population.

In studying these borrowings, there are (at least) two problems the researcher has to face: First, it is not always possible to decide whether one is dealing with an established or a nonce borrowing (see Poplack et al. 1988, p. 52 for terminology), because one requires a sufficiently large data source to answer this question, and this is not always the case. Second, it can be difficult to tell whether a lexeme was taken from a recent or an earlier Slavic contact language, which is especially problematic in the case of closely related Slavic languages, for example Croatian and Slovene in the case of Doljenski in Slovenia (Cech and Heinschink 2002, p. 2). In such cases, there is nothing for it but to label the borrowing more generally as 'Slavic' or 'South Slavic'.

As mentioned above, there are different layers of loans in the Romani languages and their analysis sheds some light on the historical migration routes of the Roma through Europe. For example, the Lotfitka dialect contains, alongside recent Russian borrowings, also loans from Polish as a recent contact language, e.g. *breza* < *brzoza* 'birch tree', *venka* < *wędka* 'fishing pole', etc. (Tenser 2016, p. 220). North Russian Romani has *blato* < Bulgarian *blato* 'dirt, mud' and *praxo* < Serbian / Croatian / Bosnian *prah* 'dust, ashes' from its Balkan past, *vendzlo* < Polish *węzeł* 'knot' from earlier contact with Polish and, of course, many borrowings from the recent contact language, Russian (Wentzel 1980, pp. 31–32; Gilliat-Smith 1922, p. 156). Furthermore, Slavic words are not restricted to Romani dialects in Slavic-speaking countries; for example, Matras (2010, p. 64) and Hancock (1983, p. 118) enumerate *dosta* 'enough', *kralis* 'king', *vodros* 'bed', *dzhamba* 'toad', *mačka* 'cat' and many other early Slavic loans that can be found in Angloromani, Welsh Romani or Texan Romani.

An example of a shift in meaning by analogy to a contact language is found in *šukipe* from Bulgarian Romani: this lexeme has adopted the meaning 'mainland' in addition to 'drought' due to the influence of Bulgarian *suša* (from a Slavic root meaning 'dry'), which also has both meanings (Kostov 1963, p. 161). Furthermore, numerous examples clearly show that spoken varieties of Slavic rather than the Slavic standard languages were the sources of borrowing, e.g. *dripes* 'clothes' and *polena* 'fields' (Standard Bulgarian *drexi* and *poljana*) taken from a Southeastern Bulgarian Rup dialect and found in the Romani dialect of the Rhodopes, Bulgaria (Igla 1997, pp. 148–149).

Slavic languages have served not only as direct donor languages for lexical units, but also as intermediary languages. Thus, for instance, many German words like *biglajs* < *Bügeleisen* 'pressing iron' have entered East Slovak Romani via Slovak (Rácová 1997, p. 85). Occasionally, Romani words disappear due to Slavic influence; as an early example, Gilliat-Smith characterised the case of *musi* 'arm', from the Romani dialect of St. Petersburg as follows: '*Musí* always disappears in dialects subject to Slavic influence owing to most Slavic languages using only one word to express 'arm' and 'hand'' (Gilliat-Smith 1922, p. 155). On the other hand, sometimes, several parallel words from different languages coexist, e.g. in East Slovak Romani *svetos* < Slovak *svet*, *vilagos* < Hungarian *világ* and *luma* < Romanian *lume*, all meaning 'world' (Rácová 1995, p. 13). Furthermore, some pairs of originally synonymous words are now used with slight differences in meaning, creating variation in speech; for instance, in Serbian Kalderaš, *mlada* (a South Slavic loan) exclusively means 'bride' and *bori* (inherited Romani) means 'daughter-in-law; newly-married woman' (Boretzky 1994, pp. 181–182).

As for parts of speech, nouns are borrowed more often than verbs and verbs more often than adjectives. A precise count can be found in Meyer (to appear) for the Polska and Bergitka dialects in Poland and in Boretzky (1994, p. 179) for Kalderaš in Northern Serbia. The counts reveal the following (rounded) ratios of nouns to verbs to adjectives: 7:4:1 (Kalderaš), 6:1:1 (Polska) and 6:2:1 (Bergitka).

9 The Impact of Slavic Languages on Romani 265

Romani has not only borrowed Slavic lexemes for new items and phenomena which have no inherited equivalents in Romani, such as *škola* 'school', but also replaced inherited words, e.g. East Slovak Romani *myšos* < Slovak *myš* 'mouse', *stromos* < *strom* 'tree' (Kralčák 1999, p. 180). In North Russian Romani, especially the younger generation of speakers frequently replaces Romani words with Russian equivalents: *guruv* is replaced with *byko* < Russian *byk* 'ox', *ryč'* with *medvedyo* < *medved'* 'bear' and *buzno* with *kozyol* 'billy-goat' (Toropov 2005, p. 364). The question as to which semantic fields have been affected by Slavic borrowings is most elaborately treated in Meyer (to appear) for the Polska and Bergitka dialects in Poland and by Boretzky (1993, pp. 117–124) for Kosovan Bugurdži. Both studies show that the semantic fields of nature (animals, plants, weather, landscape, etc.) and dwelling (buildings, furniture, household articles) have been most strongly influenced by the Slavic contact languages (Polish and Serbocroatian, respectively); additionally, the fields of politics and military, education, economy, the human body, religion and food have been affected in Polska and Bergitka, while Boretzky lists tools and people for Bugurdži.

Lastly, speakers' attitudes towards loan words can differ. Rácová (2000, p. 45) refers to Slovak Romani speakers with a high language consciousness who refuse to use Slovak words and rather rely on inherited elements to enlarge their vocabulary. Consequently, they prefer *dikhado* (< inherited *dikh-* 'to see') to *d'ivadlos* (< Slovak *divadlo* 'theater'), *l'il'ali* (< *lil* 'leaf; page') to *kñižka* (< *knižka* 'book.DIM') or *sikhad'i* (< *sikh-* 'to learn') to *škola* 'school'; they furthermore use such mixed collocations as *vladno avrikidno manuš* 'representative of government', derived on the basis of Slovak *vládny* 'governmental', Romani *te khidel avri* 'to elect' and Romani *manuš* 'man' (Rácová and Horecký 2000, p. 14; Rácová 2007, p. 131). Other speakers of Romani insert Slavic words into their speech freely and regard them as a natural part of their language.

9.2.1 Nouns

There is great variation with respect to whether and how borrowed Slavic nouns are adapted to Romani grammar. Unlike nonce borrowings, established borrowings are adapted to the gender system of Romani, which recognises only two genders, in contrast to the three found in Slavic languages. Slavic masculine and neuter nouns receive—with some variance across dialects—the Greek-derived endings *-os* / *-o*, *-as*, *-is* / *-i* or *-e* and are assigned to the class of Romani athematic masculines: *fermer-o* < Russian *fermer*.M 'farmer', *vagon-o* < Russian *vagon*.M 'waggon' and *kridl-os* < Slovak *krídl-o*.NEUT 'wing' (Semiletko 2008, p. 361; Čerenkov and Demeter 1990, p. 291). Of special interest are masculine nouns ending in *-a*, such as Bulgarian *sǎdij-a* 'judge'. They are adapted to Bulgarian Romani in their original form with the feminine definite article *i*, such that the resulting form is *i sǎdij-a* by analogy to Bulgarian *sǎdij-a-ta*.ART.F 'the judge', but morphosyntactically, they are treated as masculines: *i sǎdija si lačh-o*.M 'the judge is good' (Kostov 1989, p. 121). Feminine nouns receive or keep the ending *-a*, e.g. in North Russian Romani *pušk-a* < Russian *pušk-a*.F 'cannon' (Čerenkov and Demeter 1990, p. 292). As a basic principle, what applies to loans in Romani in general also applies to loans from Slavic: 'Loans may be assigned gender based on the natural sex of the animate noun, on the grammatical gender of the loan in the source language or the grammatical gender of the original noun which it replaces, or else on the phonological shape (usually the ending) of the loan' (Matras 2002, p. 72). Borrowed word stems can be very productive in terms of word formation, e.g. Russian *žar* 'heat, blaze' and the adjective *žarkij* 'hot' have served as a basis for *žar-o* 'hot. ADJ', *žar-k-es* 'hot.ADV, *žar-inela* 'he heats', *žar-k-itko* 'hot-headed' and many more derivations in North Russian Romani (Toropov 2005, p. 363).

9.2.2 Verbs

The adaptation of Slavic verbs is also based on Greek endings that were taken over in the period of Early Romani and have stayed productive ever since (Matras 2002, p. 128). The most frequent suffix used for this purpose outside the Balkans is *-in-*. Moreover, there are individual deviations; for instance, nonce borrowings from Czech and Slovak in South Slovak Romani get an additional Hungarian suffix *-ál-*: *sledov-ál-inel* 'to follow; obey' < Slovak *sledovat'* / Czech *sledovat* 'to follow, observe' (Elšík 2007, p. 26). The situation in the Balkans is more complex; there is great variation in the adaptation of loan verbs. The most widespread markers there are *-in-* / *-an-* / *-on-*, *-iz-* / *-az-* / *-oz-* and *-is-* / *-as-* / *-os-* (Matras 2002, p. 128). Vlax dialects use *-is-*, to which *-ar-* is attached for transitive verbs; most non-Vlax dialects use *-in-* and some Bulgarian and the Bugurdži/Kovač dialects in Macedonia use *-iz-* (Igla 1991, p. 51). In North Russian Romani, there is a strong tendency not to adapt Russian loan verbs (Rusakov and Abramenko 1998, p. 110). However, it depends on the verb; for the adapted forms *te xodines* < *xodit'* 'to go', *te dumines* < *dumat'* 'to think' and *te kupines* < *kupit'* 'to buy' are more common than their non-adapted alternatives, probably because these verbs are particularly frequent and have been existing in the

9 The Impact of Slavic Languages on Romani 267

dialect for a long time (Eloeva and Rusakov 1990, p. 28). Cf. also Boretzky (1993, pp. 124–127) for an overview of the semantic fields associated with (South) Slavic loan verbs in Serbian Bugurdži.

9.2.3 Adjectives

Boretzky (1994, p. 175; 1993, pp. 116–117) notes that only very few adjectives have been borrowed into the Balkan Romani dialects that he investigated. Nor is a preference for certain semantic groups noticeable, except that three colour terms have been borrowed from South Slavic: *kafeno* 'brown', *zeleno* 'green' and *zlatno* 'gold'. One of the most frequently borrowed Slavic adjectives in Romani is *drugo < drugi* 'another, the other', replacing inherited *(j)aver* (Boretzky 1999, p. 69). A widespread adaptation pattern for both masculine and feminine adjectives is the ending *-o*; this is recorded, e.g. for East Slovak Romani (Rácová 2015, p. 88), North Russian Romani (Eloeva and Rusakov 1990, p. 21), Arli in Macedonia (Friedman 2001a, p. 153) and West Bulgarian Romani (Minkov 1997, p. 74). The plural and oblique endings also seem to be largely uniform (*-a* and/or *-on(e)-*; see, e.g., Boretzky 1993, p. 117 on Kosovan Bugurdži). A frequently used strategy is to retain inflection on adjectives from the contact language, as in Serbian Kalderaš *but dosadn-i si le* 'they are very bothersome' (Matras 2002, p. 95; Boretzky 1994, p. 48) where the Serbian plural inflectional ending *-i* is kept.

9.2.4 Adverbs and Particles

The majority of adverbs and particles in Romani have been taken from contact languages. The following diagram shows the wide variety of Slavic temporal and phase adverbs in Romani. 86 Romani varieties from the RMS database that have all been in contact with Slavic languages have been analysed for each of several types of temporal or phasal adverbial determination to discover how many of them use a Slavic loan or a Slavic-Romani mixed form to express these categories (Fig. 9.1).

On top of the frequency scale are 'always' (*vinagi / uvek / zawsze / vsegda*, etc.), 'already' (*veče / već / juž / uže*, etc.), 'often' (*često / często / často / stalno*, etc.) and 'never' (*nikoga / nikad / nigdy / nikda*, etc.). Adverbs for 'today' and 'tomorrow' are almost never borrowed from Slavic.

The range of local adverbs acquired from Slavic is much smaller; it consists only of 'left' (*naljavo / nal(j)evo / (v)levo,* etc.), 'direct' (*(na)pravo / preko / direktno / rovno / prosto / bezpośrednio / prjamo*, etc.), 'nowhere' (*njakăde*

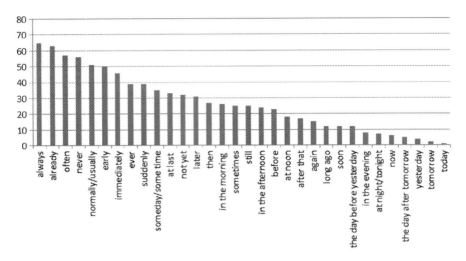

Fig. 9.1 Borrowing of Slavic temporal and phasal adverbs in Romani

/ *nigde* / *nigdzie*, etc.), 'somewhere' (*negde* / *gde-nibud'*, etc.) and 'outside' (*na zewnątrz* and the contamination *pe ulica* < Russian *na ulice*). Adverbs with the meanings 'back', 'here' and 'there' are never borrowed from Slavic (Fig. 9.2).

Among the focus particles and intensifiers, 'neither' (usually in contaminations with inherited *na*: *ni na* / *tože na* / *is-to na* / *też na*, etc.), 'also / too / as well' (*sášto* / *tože* / *isto* / *t(i)eż*, etc.), 'enough' (*dostatäčno* / *dost(a)* / *dość* / *dovoljno*, etc.) and 'only' (*samo* / *tol'ko* / *tylko*) have most frequently been borrowed from Slavic; 'little', 'much / a lot' and 'so' bring up the rear end of the scale (Fig. 9.3).

Another interesting form noted by Elšík et al. (1999, p. 339) is *inakšie* 'else, otherwise' in East Slovak Romani. The suffix -*š*- is a comparative marker in Slovak; thus, *inakšie* is a sham comparative because it is synonymous with non-comparative *inak*. Interrogative sentences are introduced by the Slavic particle *či* / *čy*, which introduces polar (or yes-no) questions, e.g. East Slovak Romani *Či na oj odi ehas so mange il'as ka romňa?* 'Was it not her who took my wife away?' (Rácová 2015, p. 92). For further examples of adverbs and particles cf. Cech and Heinschink (2001b, p. 353) for Doljenski in Slovenia, Rácová (2015, p. 92) for East Slovak Romani, Boretzky (1993, p. 115; 1994, p. 174) for Kalderaš and Bugurdži in Kosovo and Serbia and Meyer (to appear) for the dialect of the Polska Roma in Poland.

When adverbs are derived from Slavic adjectives, they receive their own suffixes, usually the Romani adverb derivational suffix -*es* (Lithuanian Romani *ran-es* < Polish *rano* 'early', LT-005, 770) or -*ones* (East Slovak Romani

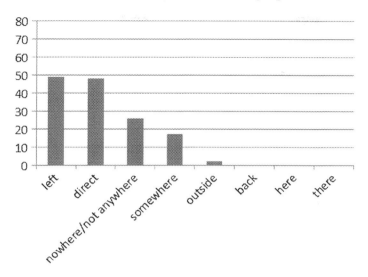

Fig. 9.2 Borrowing of Slavic local adverbs in Romani

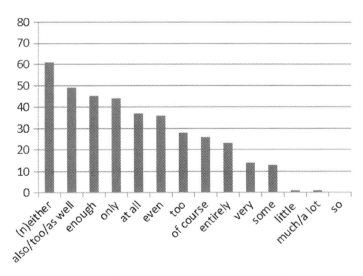

Fig. 9.3 Borrowing of Slavic focus particles and intensifiers in Romani

všeobecn-ones 'omnipresent' < Slovak *všeobecne*); the latter goes back to the oblique suffix of the athematic sub-class of adjectives, *-on-* (Rácová 2015, p. 91). A related phenomenon is found in adverbs expressing the day of the week, which, in East Slovak and Northeastern Romani, also often get the marker *-on-* + *-e* as in *vtork-one* 'on Tuesday', *piatk-one* 'on Friday' (Tenser 2005, p. 14).

9.2.5 Quantifiers and Numerals

Popular Slavic quantifiers are *celo* 'whole', *dosta* 'enough', *para* 'a couple of' and *s(v)ako* 'every' (Beníšek 2013, p. 52; Boretzky 1993, pp. 111–112). Of special interest is the idiom *svako drom* 'every time', which is composed of Slavic *svako* and Romani *drom* 'way; time' (Leggio 2011, p. 83). South Slovak Romani has the pronoun *sogodi* 'every, each, all' instead of *savoro*, containing the Slovak suffix *-god* and the Romani variety in the West Ukrainian Carpathians uses *kapka*, lit. 'drop(let)', to express 'a bit', the diminutive being *kapkica* 'a little bit' (Beníšek 2013, p. 52). The most frequently borrowed Slavic numeral is 'thousand', e.g. *tysjača* in Lithuanian Romani (LT-005, 476; LT-007, 476) and North Russian Romani (RUS-008, 476), *tysiące* in Lithuanian Romani and the dialect of the Polska Roma (LT-008, 476; LT-009, 476) and *tišic* in East Slovak Romani (SK-002, 476).

9.2.6 Calques

Another method used to create new words and phrases on the basis of Slavic contact languages is calquing. Among the earliest evidence of calques in Romani are attestations recorded in Petulengro's (1915, p. 68) notes on Drindari in Northeastern Bulgaria, but it is for East Slovak Romani that they have been researched most thoroughly. Written texts by Romani writers and activists include forms like *maškarthemutno* < Slovak *medzinárodný* 'international' or *bikherengro* < Slovak *bezdomovec* 'homeless' (Rácová and Horecký 2000, p. 14; Rácová 2007, p. 133). Similar phenomena are documented for North Russian Romani: *vybut'aker'iben* < Russian *vyrabotka* 'elaboration' or *dorak'ir'iben* < *dogovor* 'contract' (Wentzel 1980, p. 32); these are hybrid formations between calqued and directly borrowed language material. Slovak influence in East Slovak Romani is also visible in the copying of reduplicative constructions, which are used to mark duration or intensity. Reduplication takes place in different ways, among others in combination with *sar* 'how' (*marel sar marel* < Slovak *bije ako bije* 'he beats for a long time'; Rácová 2015, p. 84) or *so* 'what' (*berš so berš* < *rok čo rok* 'year after year'; Rácová and Samko 2015, p. 177). Adjectives are rarely reduplicated, but constructions like *šukar prešukar* < *krásny prekrásny* 'extremely beautiful' are possible (Rácová and Samko 2015, p. 170).

There are countless further instances of calques from Slavic constructions, but only a few shall be named here: the inherited syntactic model for 'What is your name?' is the structurally New Indo-Aryan construction *Sar*

9 The Impact of Slavic Languages on Romani 271

hin tiro lav? Among the new constructions that have developed under Slavic influence is *Sar pes vičines?*:

(1) 'What is your name?'

Romani	*Sar pes*	*vičines?*
Czech	*Jak se*	*jmenuješ?*
Slovak	*Ako sa*	*menuješ /voláš?*
Polish	*Jak się*	*nazywasz?*
	how REFL	call.2SG.PRS

A very similar case is that of *Keci ori?* 'What time is it?' (cf. Miltner 1965, p. 107; Rácová 2015, pp. 92–93). In addition, a few very characteristic Russian constructions have been calqued in North Russian Romani, among them the construction for 'to marry':

(2) 'The second sister has married a fellow'.
   (a) North Russian Romani   (Rusakov and Abramenko 1998, p. 129)
     Sr'edn'e pxen vygeja   pale   rakleste   pale   rom.
     second   sister went.out behind fellow.LOC behind man
   (b) Russian
     Drugaja sestra vyšla   za   muž za   molodogo čeloveka.
     second   sister went.out behind man behind young.ACC man.ACC

9.3 Phonetics and Phonology

The Slavic languages have also left their mark on Romani phonetics and phonology.

A widespread phonetic contact phenomenon is the devoicing of stops in word-final position as in Russian, Polish, Czech and Slovak—for example the pronunciation of *dad* as [dat] or *pandž* as [panč]. This is a tendency that can be found in many Romani dialects influenced by European languages (Matras 2002, p. 54; Puscher 2005, p. 17; Meyer 2016, p. 148). In Southeastern Europe, dialects in contact with Romanian and Serbian / Croatian / Bosnian have kept their final voiced consonants, whereas dialects in contact with Bulgarian and Macedonian have not (Boretzky and Igla 1999, p. 713; Minkov 1997, p. 60).

A very characteristic phonetic feature of Russian is vowel reduction in unstressed position, which has, however, been transferred into native Romani words only in very rare cases, such as Lovari Čokeši (Moscow) *žjuvalo* [ʒʲuˈvalə] 'full of fleas' (RUS-005, 38) or *varekoti* [ˈvarɪkatʲi] 'some'

272   **A.-M. Meyer**

(RUS-005, 400). Of course, it regularly appears in Russian loans such as North Russian Romani *pogoda* [pa'godə] 'weather' (RUS-006, 79).

Among the Slavic standard languages, Czech, Slovak, Serbian / Croatian / Bosnian and partially also Slovene maintain a phonological difference between long and short vowels. As a consequence, distinctive vowel length—independent of stress—has become an areal contact phenomenon for Romani dialects as well, sometimes merely phonetical, as in Czech Vlax (cf. CZ-001, 23, 98, 131, etc.), sometimes phonological, as Beníšek (2013, p. 48) attests for Serednye Romani in Western Ukraine. He gives the example *bar* 'stone' vs. *bār* 'fence'. (For East and West Slovak Romani, cf. Kalina 1882, p. 8; Rácová and Horecký 2000, p. 23; Elšík et al. 1999, p. 309.)

As Barannikov (1931, p. 21) has already noted, 'the influence of Ukrain[ian] and Russian phonetics accounts […] for the extensive use of palatal sounds which occur not only in recent borrowings, but also in ancient Gypsy words'. The palatalisation of consonants before front vowels with phonemic status is typical of Russian, but to a lesser extent also of other Slavic languages. This has been transferred to the Northeastern dialects of Romani; North Russian Romani for instance contains 17 palatalised consonant phonemes (Matras 2002, p. 58; cf. also Eloeva and Rusakov 1990, pp. 11–13), and also Romani dialects in contact with Ukrainian are affected (Barannikov 1931, p. 3; Semiletko 2008, p. 362; Beníšek 2013, p. 48; Toropov and Gumeroglyj 2013, p. 210). In the Central dialects, palatalisation is restricted to /n/ and /l/ (Matras 2002, p. 50). The affricates /č/ and /dž/, on the other hand, have a palatal pronunciation in all Romani dialects of the Baltic group, triggered by Russian, but under Belarusian influence, they are non-palatal in all positions except before front vowels, e.g. Belarusian-Lithuanian Romani *čororó* vs. North Russian Romani *č'ororó* 'poor'. A second peculiarity is the shift from the palatal dentals /d'/ and /t'/ to /dz'/ and /c'/, which also corresponds to Belarusian (Čarankoŭ 1974, pp. 38–39). Jotation has also been contact-induced, affecting especially verbs in the past and the mediopassive in most dialects in contact with palatalising languages: **kerdjom > kerd'om > kerdžom* 'I did', **dikhtjom > dikht'om > dikhćom* 'I saw' (Matras 2002, p. 68). Genuine palatals are a recent phenomenon and have been acquired through contact, as in Macedonian and Montenegrin Arli and Gurbet: *kher > ćher* 'house', *kin- > ćin-* 'to buy' (Matras 2002, p. 49).

One of the most striking contact-induced changes is the shift of stress to the penultimate or initial syllable in Western and Central European dialects (Matras 2002, p. 205). A hub of this development is found in the varieties influenced by Slovak and its surrounding languages, because

9 The Impact of Slavic Languages on Romani

Standard Slovak has initial and the Eastern Slovak dialects as well as Polish have penultimate stress (Matras 2002, p. 64; Elšík et al. 1999, p. 307). This affects not only borrowed, but also inherited words, such as *čiriklo* 'bird' in West Slovak Romani (Kalina 1882, p. 8). However, many dialects have kept their conservative stress pattern even under Slavic influence, for example Kosovan Gurbet (Leggio 2011, p. 61), dialects in Bulgaria (BG-001-052), Macedonia (MK-001-012) and Slovenia (SLO-001), or exhibit considerable variation, as in Prilep Arli in Macedonia (Boretzky 1999, p. 36). In loan words, usually the stress pattern of the Slavic donor language is adopted.

Furthermore, several sounds characteristic of the Slavic contact languages have been adopted into Romani, of which only a selection can be presented here. Of course, numerous foreign sounds have been taken over through lexical borrowings, like /š':/ from Russian into Crimean Romani: *ščaveli* < *ščavel'* 'sorrel', *boršči* < *boršč* 'borscht' (Toropov and Gumeroglyj 2013, p. 218). More interesting are those sounds that spread beyond loan words into the inherited lexicon. For example, in Poland, /l/ has been substituted by the semi-vowel /w/ in the environment before all vowels except /i/, e.g. *love* > *łowe* [woˈvɛ] 'money' (Matras 2002, p. 50; Meyer 2016, p. 148). In some dialects such as Croatian Gurbet (HR-001) and the dialect of the Ruska Roma (RUS-003), /l/ has undergone strong velarisation. The alternation of /x/ and /h/ is also a contact phenomenon: in Kosovan and Macedonian Arli and Bugurdži, they merge into /h/ due to South Slavic, Albanian and Turkish influence, whereas in Romani dialects under Polish and Russian influence they merge into /x/ (Matras 2002, p. 52; Elšík et al. 1999, p. 296). In Northeastern dialects, we also find that /i/ or /e/ has been replaced by the central vowel /i/ as a result of contact with Russian, Ukrainian and Polish (Matras 2002, p. 59; Barannikov 1931, p. 4; 1933, p. 37). In Gurbet, Bohemian Romani and other dialects, a syllabic /r/ has developed by analogy to the same sound in Serbian and Czech, e.g. *berš* > *brš* (Kopernicki 1889, p. 125; Matras 2002, p. 60). Syllabics /r/ and /l/ are also frequently found in Croatia and Macedonia, e.g. in the dialect of the Manuša Čurjarja (HR-003) and Arli (MK-002). In the Balkans, the vowel phonemes have not been noticeably modified with the exception of the spread of the central vowel /ə/, which exists in Bulgarian, Albanian and Turkish, into the regional Romani dialects and even beyond loan words, e.g. *aver* > *javər* (Boretzky and Igla 1999, p. 712). The RMS database contains numerous examples of a stressed central vowel in Romani dialects in Bulgaria (BG-001, BG-007, BG-008, etc.), e.g. [brəˈʃənt] 'rain' in Rešitari / Čergari, spoken in Velingrad (BG-012, 91).

9.4 Nominal Morphology

The influence of Slavic languages upon Romani nominal morphology is found to varying degrees in word formation affixes and inflectional endings, the case system, the definite article, the category of comparison and pronouns. While matter replication is predominant in the lexicon, phonetics and phonology, morphology and syntax are mostly characterised by pattern replication.

9.4.1 Word Formation Affixes and Inflectional Endings

Individual Romani dialects have continuously borrowed plural endings for nouns ever since the time of Early Romani, among them *-ovi*, *-i* and *-e* (Matras 2002, p. 85). The plural ending *-o(v)ja* derives from Bulgarian *-ove* or Serbian *-ovi*, plus the indigenous plural marker *-a*. The plural ending *-ja* is possibly a contracted form of *-o(v)ja* (Boretzky et al. 2008, p. 13), whereas *-ovia* / *-ovja* in East Slovak Romani is said to have been adapted from Slovak (Červenka 2004, p. 184). Bulgarian Romani frequently uses the Bulgarian vocative ending (Kostov 1963, p. 69).

Furthermore, Slavic diminutive affixes as well as affixes marking feminine gender have been frequently borrowed. The diminutive suffixes *-ic(a)* and *-ka* are widely used in the Balkans and seem to be restricted to European loans (Matras 2002, p. 76). Ješina (1886, pp. 18, 25) identified *-ica* already in the nineteenth century for Bohemian Romani as a marker of female gender: *lurd-ica* 'wife of a soldier' < *lurdo* 'soldier', *čor-ica* 'female thief' < *čor* 'thief', as diminutive affixes he names *-ičkos*, *-ička* and *-inka*. In Romani dialects spoken in Russia, *-ka* serves as a suffix for female persons: *khelitor-ka* 'female dancer' < *khelitori* 'dancer', while *-ica* can be used as both a diminutive and a feminine marker: *rrot-ica* 'little skirt' < *rrotja* 'skirt', *sebev-ica* 'female tailor' < *sebevo* 'tailor' (Čerenkov and Demeter 1990, p. 288; Tcherenkov 1999, p. 136). North Russian Romani additionally has *-uško* from Russian to generate affectionate forms (Wentzel 1980, p. 58).

Further Slavic affixes in Romani are *-izmo*, *-isto*, *-ato* and *-cija* < Russian *-izm*, *-ist*, *-at*, *-cija* for internationalisms (Wentzel 1980, p. 58) and—as an exceptional example of prefixation—*pra-* 'great' from Slovak in East Slovak Romani: *pra-papus* 'great-grandfather' (Červenka 2004, p. 179). Semiletko (2008, p. 361) notes that the Servy and Lovari in Ukraine have the endings *-no*, *-kosko*, *-koske* and *-koski* which probably go back to earlier contact, because similar endings were used in Ukrainian in the sixteenth and seventeenth centuries; however, he does not name any examples, and there is no evidence of these in the RMS database.

9.4.2 Case

In the Balkans, Romani has kept its relatively complex case system, in contrast to the other Balkan languages. Both the structure and the inventory have stayed almost untouched in the conservative Balkan dialects; only a few cases have taken over functions that are characteristic of their equivalents in other Balkan languages (Boretzky and Igla 1999, p. 715). A visible influence from Bulgarian is the increased use of prepositional constructions. Igla (1999, pp. 210–212) shows for Sofia Erli that, e.g. with respect to constructions with the preposition 'without', the original case government became destabilised historically and was then overridden when the Bulgarian preposition *bez* 'without' was borrowed together with its own governmental properties.

In addition, Bulgarian Erli has a genitive periphrasis according to the Slavic model, as in the following example:

(3) Genitive periphrasis ('the boy's father', inherited construction *o čhaveskoro dat*)

   (a) Bulgarian   (b) Bulgarian Erli
      bašta-ta na momče-to   *o dat k-o čhavo*
      father-ART to boy-ART   ART father to-ART boy

The preposition *ko* 'to' takes over the function of a genitive, analogous to Bulgarian *na* (Boretzky and Igla 1999, p. 716).

Another interesting phenomenon is the reflexive dative, which is documented, e.g., for Serbian Kalderaš (Boretzky 1994, p. 167), Kosovan Bugurdži (Boretzky 1993, p. 109) and Arli in Macedonia, Kosovo and Southern Serbia (Boretzky 1996b, p. 21). Boretzky (1994, p. 167) calls it a 'dative of inner involvement', and, according to Matras (2002, p. 88), it 'entails a benefactive reading': *džava mange* (go.1SG.PRS myself.DAT) 'I am going', *sovelas peskə* (sleep.3SG.PRF himself.DAT) 'he slept', *pijava mange kafava* (drink.1SG.PRS myself.DAT coffee.ACC) 'I am drinking coffee', and even with the copula *ine peske jek phuri* 'there once was an old woman' (see below). This is probably triggered by Bulgarian and Macedonian, because a similar phenomenon is found in these Slavic languages:

(4) Dativus ethicus

   (a) Macedonian (Mišeska-Tomic 2009,   (b) Arli (Macedonia, Boretzky 1996b, p. 21)
      p. 105)
      Kako mi ste?   *ine peske jek phuri*
      how me.DAT be.2PL   be.3SG.PRF her.DAT one old.woman
      'how are you, my dear ones?'   'there once was an old woman'

Several dialects from the RMS database (Russian and North Russian Romani in Russia; Servi, Xandžari, Kubansa Vlaxurja, Kubanski Servi, Plaščuny and Gimpeny in Ukraine) copy from Russian the split between the marking of positive and negative possession, e.g.

(5) Positive possession ('she has a brother')
    (a) Russian
        u neyo   est'   brat
        at she.GEN be.3SG brother

    (b) North Russian Romani (Russia, RUS-006, 976)
        late   sy   o   pšal
        she.LOC be.3SG ART brother

(6) Negative possession ('she does not have a brother')
    (a) Russian
        u neyo   net brat-a
        at she.GEN NEG brother-GEN

    (b) North Russian Romani (RUS-006, 973)
        late   nane   pšal-es
        she.LOC be.3SG.NEG brother-OBL

Also of interest is the frequent copying of the Russian instrumental into North Russian Romani. Tenser (2016, pp. 213–214) mentions two kinds of constructions:

(7) Instrumental construction ('to work with a hammer')
    (a) Russian
        rabotat' molotk-om
        work.INF hammer-INS

    (b) North Russian Romani (RUS-008, 693)
        te   keres buty čukane-sa
        COMP do.2SG work hammer.INS

(8) Promotion of state construction ('I become a director')
    (a) Russian
        ja stanovlj-us'   direktor-om
        I   become-1SG.REFL director-INS

    (b) N. Russian Romani (RUS-008, 354a)
        me ker-av pe   dir'ektoro-sa
        I   do-1SG REFL director-INS

(cf. also Wentzel 1980, p. 64; Gilliat-Smith 1932, p. 76; Sergievskij 1931, p. 35; Rusakov and Abramenko 1998, p. 119). Tenser (2005, pp. 40–47; 2016) describes the re-organisation of the case system in Lithuanian Romani under Russian and Polish influence.

Among the evidence of Slavic influence upon the case system of Romani are also constructions with verbs of removal plus dative (cf. Boretzky 1994, p. 167 on Serbian Kalderaš), depletion of the partitive genitive in favour of the nominative (Boretzky 1993, p. 109) or disappearance of the genitive in favour of ablative constructions in Arli and Prilep in Macedonia. The latter are triggered by Macedonian dialects that do not construct the old Slavic genitive with the preposition *na*, but also with *ot*. This *ot* is taken over into Romani as an ablative or as a construction with the inherited preposition *katar* 'where from' (Boretzky 1999, p. 126).

9.4.3 Articles

Among the Slavic languages, only Macedonian, Bulgarian and partly the Torlak dialects of Serbian have a definite article. The marking of indefiniteness with the numeral 'one' is optional in Romani as well as in the Balkan Slavic languages and very restricted in Romani dialects outside the Balkans (Friedman 2001b, p. 288). The Romani dialects under the influence of the Slavic languages without an article are in the process of losing their own definite article (Boretzky 1999, p. 176; Matras 2002, p. 96), e.g. Polska Roma *piravav dudali* instead of *piravav e dudali* 'I am opening the window' (Matras 1999, p. 10). Uhlik (1951, p. 53) noted this loss for Bosnian Gurbet already in 1951; however, there is no evidence of this in the RMS database. Under the influence of languages without articles, like Serbian in the Balkans, there is often uncertainty with respect to the use of the definite article, insofar as it is sometimes used where it is not justified semantically (Boretzky and Igla 1999, p. 714). An analysis of the RMS database shows that in the Romani dialects in contact with Bulgarian and Macedonian, the inherited use of the definite article has remained untouched, whereas the dialects in contact with the East and West Slavic languages have partially lost it. No Romani dialect from the database shows a complete loss of the definite article, but very strong reduction can be found in Lithuania, Latvia and Poland. In these dialects, the definite article is more likely to be maintained when it is a part of a preposition like *ando / andi, pašo / paši, ko / ki, telo, palo, pro* or *anglo.* Some samples of these dialects, like the Polska Roma (PL-003), Bergitka (PL-007) and East Slovak (SK-002), make frequent use of demonstrative pronouns and deictic expressions like *dava / da, kada / kaja / kała / kole / kola,* etc., instead of a definite article, which is very probably triggered by their Slavic contact languages.

9.4.4 Comparison

As Romani originally expressed comparative and superlative meaning through a single form (*-eder*), it can be said that the whole category of comparison has expanded under Slavic influence (Boretzky 1993, p. 106). In the Romani dialects of the Balkans, the inherited comparative form *-eder* has been largely replaced by an analytical form with the Slavic prefix *po-*, a late Balkanism, e.g. Velingrad Yerli (Bulgaria) *but* 'much' > *po-but* 'more' instead of *buteder*. Even the only suppletive comparative in Romani, *lačho* 'good' > *feder* 'better' can be replaced by the form *po-lačho* (Kostov 1963, p. 86; Boretzky 1993, p. 107;

278   A.-M. Meyer

1999, p. 55; Cech and Heinschink 2001b, p. 355). Boretzky and Igla (1999, p. 717) explain this early and fundamental change in relation to the morphological transparency of the Balkanic comparative formation. In some dialects in the Balkans, *po-* has both comparative and superlative meaning: *i potikni* 'the smallest'. Where the formation of the comparative follows more complex and less transparent synthetic rules, such as in the East, West and some South Slavic languages, the Romani dialects have kept the old form *-eder* (Boretzky 1999, p. 55). North Russian Romani in some cases even borrows the Russian comparative marker *-š-*: *miro ternedyr-š-o pšal* < Russian *moj mlad-š-yj brat* 'my younger brother' (RUS-006, 621).

Since the settlement in the Balkans, Romani languages have adopted the Slavic prefix *naj-* to express superlative meaning, with either the positive or comparative form of the adjective, cf. *naj-baro* (Kosovan Arli, Kosovo, YU-016, 615) and *naj-baredyr* (Polska Roma, Poland, PL-003, 615) 'the biggest' (cf. also Kalina 1882, p. 8; Ješina 1886, p. 28; Rácová 2015, p. 89). According to the inherited pattern as exemplified by Kalajdži *xen o phuro manuš* 'the oldest man' (Bulgaria, BG-007, 995), the order of elements in a construction with *naj-* can vary, e.g. *naj o phuro manuš* instead of *o naj-phuro manuš* (Velingrad Yerli, Bulgaria, BG-001, 995). There are also some interesting particular forms like Doljenski (Slovenia) *najrajš* 'most gladly' < Slovenian *rado* 'gladly' (Cech and Heinschink 2001b, p. 355). In the Vlax varieties, Romanian *maj-* is used to form the superlative instead of *naj-*. Some dialects in contact with Russian in Russia and Ukraine use the Russian superlative marker *samyj* or modified *samo*, which can be combined with both a positive (*samo baro*, Russian Roma, RUS-003, 615) and a comparative form (*samo feder*, Servi, Ukraine, UKR-004, 829), in rare cases even with an additional superlative marker as in Gimpeny *samo najbaro* (Ukraine, UKR-020, 615; cf. also Boretzky 1999, p. 55; Eloeva and Rusakov 1990, p. 17). The prefix *pre-* to construct an elative, e.g. *prelačho* 'extremely good', is also of Slavic origin; in the Vlax dialects, it has been transmitted by Romanian (Matras 2002, p. 203).

9.4.5 Indefinites

Especially in the Eastern and Southeastern dialects of Romani, the system of indefinites ('any, some') has been renewed through borrowings as a recent contact development (Matras 2002, p. 115). An analysis of the RMS data shows that the richest inventories can be found in Servy / Nakhale

9 The Impact of Slavic Languages on Romani   279

(UKR-018) and Servi (UKR-004) in Ukraine, consisting of the East Slavic forms *-to*, *-nibud'*, *-tos*, *-s*, *čut'* and *ljubo*. Dialects in contact with Polish borrow *-ś*, *-kolwiek* and *byle*, e.g. Polish Xaladytka (PL-014) and Polska Roma (PL-018). Czech and Slovak influence is comparatively weak in this regard (cf. Elšík et al. 1999, p. 350), though Rácová (2015, p. 90) and Lípa (1965, p. 34) mention *choč-* / *choc-* < *hoci-*, *malo* < *málo*, *šeli* < *šeljako*, *-si* and *ňekero* as having been borrowed into Romani dialects in contact with Slovak. In addition, there is an interesting contamination of Romani *vare-* and Slovak *da-* to form *dare-* in some East Slovak varieties (Elšík et al. 1999, p. 349). The most common forms from South Slavic are *ne-*, *-bilo* and *svako*, as for example in Bačkačke (Serbia, YU-007) and Arli (Macedonia, MK-002). Boretzky and Igla (1999, p. 726) also mention *i-*, *ma-* and *-godi* / *god(er)*. In Arli, Prilep and Erli, there are new formations with *di-* / *de-* / *da-* which have either been borrowed from Bulgarian *edi-* or Serbian *eda-* 'any-' (Boretzky et al. 2008, p. 20) or derived from *gde* / *kəde* 'where' (Boretzky 1999, p. 177). Kosovan Gurbet has developed the determiner *disave* 'some' through the combination with the interrogative *sav-* 'which' and *disar* 'somehow' through the combination with *sar* 'how'. The free-choice determiner *bilosafar* 'any' is composed of Slavic *bilo-*, inherited *sa* and Albanian *-far* (Leggio 2011, p. 83).

Very common in Romani are negative indefinite pronouns with the Slavic negative prefix *ni-* / *n'i-*, which is added to an inherited interrogative pronoun: *n'iko(n)* / *nikoj* 'nobody', *n'iso* 'nothing', *n'ik(h)aj* 'nowhere', *n'isavo* / *nijek(h)* / *n'ič'i* 'nobody', *n'išar* / *nisar* 'by no means' or *nikaring* 'nowhere (directional)' (Rácová 2015, p. 90; Pančenko 2013, p. 15; Boretzky 1999, pp. 68–69; on older forms cf. Kalina 1882, p. 60; Ješina 1886, pp. 61–62; Kostov 1963, p. 155). Romani has also frequently taken over whole Slavic negative pronouns in numerous regional varieties, for example *nic* / *n'ic* / *nič* / *n'ič* / *n'iš(t)* / *ništa* / *ništo* 'nothing', *nikdy* / *nigdy* / *n'igda* / *nikoga* / *nikəde* / *nikad* 'never', *nigde* 'nowhere', *niko* 'nobody', *nikako* 'in no way' (Lípa 1965, p. 34; Rácová 2015, p. 90; Beníšek 2013, p. 52; Boretzky 1994, p. 171; 1999, pp. 68–69). The strongest Slavic influence affects the pronouns meaning 'nothing' and 'nobody', for which there are practically no inherited forms left, only in Kalderaš are *khonik* and *khanči* still in use (Boretzky 1993, p. 112; 1994, p. 171). The versions with dental *n-* are from Serbian / Croatian / Bosnian, those with palatal *n'-* from later contact languages such as Slovak or Russian. North Russian Romani (RUS-006, 701 and others) *-nito* is an interesting mixed form consisting of the two Slavic constituents *ni-* and *-to*.

9.4.6 Interrogatives

The most stable interrogative pronouns in Romani are *so* 'what' and *sar* 'how'. Due to South Slavic influence, inherited *kana* 'when' has often been replaced by *kad(a)* / *ked(a)* / *koga* (Boretzky 1999, p. 67; Cech and Heinschink 2001b, p. 352); in Russian, Ukrainian and Polish Romani dialects, one can also find *k(i)edy* < Polish *kiedy*. The pronoun *ko(n)* 'who' is also relatively stable; only in Arli and Prilep, Macedonian *koj* is also widespread. The reduced form *ko* in numerous Romani dialects might have developed under the influence of Slavic *k(t)o* (Boretzky 1999, p. 67). In Romani, interrogatives also generally serve as relatives; only in some Bulgarian varieties, they get an additional suffix *-to*, modelled on Bulgarian: *kon-to* 'who', *koga-to* 'when', *soske-to* 'because' (Boretzky 1999, p. 68; Kostov 1963, p. 97; Minkov 1997, p. 82).

9.4.7 Possessives

Cech and Heinschink (2001b, p. 352) observe that, in Doljenski, the 3PL of the reflexive possessive pronoun 'his / her own' tends to be extended to all grammatical persons, a development modelled on Slovene *svoj*. Arli, spoken in the Southern Balkans, shows that unstressed, postposed pronouns can be used possessively as in Macedonian: *ko dad laki*, cf. Macedonian *kaj tatko-i* 'to her father' (Boretzky 1996b, p. 13). Furthermore, Boretzky (1999, p. 61)—unfortunately without providing examples—notes that the Romani dialects in the Southern Balkans have developed two rows of possessive constructions, as have Bulgarian and Macedonian: *moj(a)ta kniga* with possessive pronoun vs. *knigata mi* with enclitic personal pronoun, both meaning 'my book'.

9.4.8 Personals and Demonstratives

Language contact has hardly affected personal and demonstrative pronouns in Romani, with only a few known examples: in Hravati / Doljenski (Slovenia) and the variety of Kumanovo (Macedonia), the personal pronoun *oni* 'they' has been 'modelled on Slavic, but drawing on inherited *on*' (Matras 2002, p. 209; cf. also Cech and Heinschink 2001a, p. 156; Boretzky et al. 2008, p. 16).

9.5 Verbal Morphology

Probably, the most striking Slavic contact feature in Romani is the presence of aspect prefixes, for which reason they will be addressed here first. Other important contact-affected areas of verbal morphology are tense, the infinitive, voice and reflexivity, modality, the conditional, renarrativity / evidentiality and the imperative.

9.5.1 Slavic Aspect

The category of verbal aspect with its two grammatical meanings of 'perfective' and 'imperfective' is a hallmark characteristic of the Slavic languages. The principal method of deriving a perfective verb form from an imperfective stem is through prefixation, e.g. Russian *pisat'*.IMPF > *na-pisat'*.PFV 'to write'. In many cases, this entails the introduction of so-called actionality (Ger. *Aktionsart*) to the verbal semantics, characterising the activity either phasally or in terms of quantification (Gvozdanović 2011, pp. 782–784). These aspectual prefixes have been borrowed into Romani dialects to various degrees, as will be shown below, and it seems that a relatively long period of contact was necessary for this development to have occurred (Elšík et al. 1999, p. 371; Lípa 1965, pp. 123–124). An elaborate study of this contact phenomenon in Southeastern Europe can be found in Igla (1998) with respect to Bulgarian Romani and an interesting early investigation on the languages of Bosnia in Ackerley (1941, p. 83).

In the Balkans, the borrowing of Slavic aspectual prefixes into Romani has been much more restricted than elsewhere. The most frequently borrowed prefixes are *po-* and *do-*, but also *iz-*, *za-* and others can be found. Sometimes the verb's actionality is modified by the prefix by analogy to the Slavic contact language as in the example from Rhodope Erli *dikhles* 'he looked at' > *po-dikhles* 'he briefly looked at' (Igla 1997, p. 149; cf. also the examples in Igla 1998, p. 68). In Doljenski (Slovenia), the Slavic aspectual prefixes mark a punctual action in the past, so they carry grammatical meaning (Cech and Heinschink 2001b, p. 361). However, in many cases, prefixation does not bring about a change in meaning, as in Doljenski *bistrav* > *za-bistrav* 'to forget' (Cech and Heinschink 2001b, p. 69) or Arli *kinel* > *po-kinel* 'to buy' (Friedman 2001a, p. 152). There are also numerous cases in which prefixation seems rather arbitrary, compare for example *Ax mamo! So tu kerdjan.*IMPF? 'O mother! What have you done?' (RUS-003,

487) and *Ax dado! So tu skerdjan*.PFV? 'O father! What have you done?' (RUS-003, 488). Cech and Heinschink (2001b, p. 348) show for Doljenski that, in some cases, only the prefixed verb form has survived, as the initial unprefixed form has become lost, as in **bisteri > po-bisteri* 'to forget'.

The borrowing of Slavic aspectual prefixes is most distinctive in the Northern Central dialects in contact with the East and West Slavic languages, which can be ascertained from many investigations, such as Barannikov (1931, p. 21), Čarankaŭ (1974, p. 37) or Rácová (2015, p. 79). Exceptions are the conservative Vlax dialects, such as Russian Kalderaš (Čerenkov and Demeter 1990, p. 300). The inventory of Slavic aspectual prefixes is much larger in these dialects than in the Balkans; the dialect of the Russian Roma (RUS-003), for example, has *za-, roz- / roz-, ot-, u-, pere-, po-, do-, pod-, s- / z-, vy-* and *pri*. The prefixes can specify the actionality expressed by the verb, as in East Slovak Romani, such as completion: *do-xal < *Slovak *do-jest'* 'to eat up', suddenness: *z-vičinel < z-volat'* 'to call out' or spatial relations: *pre-bešel < pre-sadnut'* 'to change seats'. Prefixed verbs have become an integral component of East Slovak Romani and have usually kept the meaning they had in the donor language (Rácová 2015, pp. 79–80). Prefixed verbs also often serve as a basis for the formation of abstract nouns: *thovel* 'to put' > *pre-thovel* 'translate' > *pre-thoviben* 'translation' by analogy to Slovak *pre-klad* (Rácová 2015, p. 81; cf. also the detailed description by Rácová and Horecký 2000). Beníšek (2013, p. 54) gives an interesting example from Serednye Romani for an extension of meaning triggered by Slavic aspectual prefixes: *othov-* results from the combination of *thov-* 'to put' and Slavic *od-* 'away'. The basic meaning 'to put aside' has been extended to mean 'to hide' at the expense of inherited *garuv-*, which has become obsolete. For examples from Poland, cf. Meyer (2016, p. 149), for Belarus, cf. Čarankaŭ (1974, p. 37). Some conscientious speakers consider the use of Slavic prefixes to render their language 'impure' (Rácová 1999, p. 65) and try to avoid them; for example, in Slovak Romani, the Slavic aspectual prefix *vy-* can be replaced by inherited *avri* as in *dičhol avri* vs. *vyzerat'* 'to look like' (Rácová 2015, p. 81). Gilliat-Smith (1922, p. 161) and Rusakov (2001a, p. 320), however, take account of the fact that such originally Slavic prefixes have somewhat paradoxically also been preventing certain Romani verb stems from dying out.

One method of forming an imperfective verb from a perfective stem in the Slavic languages is suffixation, e.g. Russian *dat'*.PFV > *da-va-t'*.IMPF 'to give'. In such cases, the verbal semantics, including actionality, remain unchanged. This strategy has also been copied into Romani, although to a much lesser extent than prefixation. In the Northern Central dialects, the inherited transitivising affix -*av*- has changed its meaning by analogy to Slavic imperfectivising suffixation, e.g. Bohemian Romani *čhiv*- 'to throw' > *čhiv-av*- 'to throw repeatedly' (Matras 2002, p. 123).

With respect to whether the complete Slavic aspect system has been transferred into the Romani dialects in contact with West and East Slavic languages, Friedman (1985, p. 387) and Boretzky (1989, p. 368) argue that it has not; on the other hand, Eloeva and Rusakov (1990, p. 16) come to the conclusion that North Russian Romani is in the process of crossing over from its old tense system to a tense-aspect system very similar to that of Russian. Matras (2002, p. 159) speaks of a 'wholesale borrowing of the Slavic aktionsart [i.e. actionality] prefix system (or Slavic aspect)' but argues that this is merely a strategy for word derivation introducing lexical actionality.

9.5.2 Tense

A contact-induced innovation in the tense system of Romani is the formation of an analytic perfect. In some Arli varieties, a new perfect construction has developed under Macedonian influence, linking the past participle with the auxiliary 'to be':

(9) Perfect formation ('I have told you')

Arli:	*sinum tumenge vakerdo*	
Macedonian:	*sum ti*	*rekov*
	I.am you.DAT	say.1SG.PTCP (Matras 2002, p. 157)

For a few situative verbs, comparable constructions can denote the present, e.g. Polska Roma and West Slovak Romani *me som bešto* 'I sit / am seated' (Matras 2002, p. 157). In Arli, there is a tendency to form the perfect with the auxiliary 'to be', which can lead to confusion with passive forms: *sigo sinum bisterdo* 'I have quickly forgotten' or 'I was quickly forgotten'. These forms are modelled on the intransitive verbs of movement in Macedonian like *sum dojden* 'I have come' (Boretzky 1994, pp. 163–164). In North Russian Romani, the opposition imperfect-aorist has disappeared under Russian influence. The old aorist now serves as a general past and the imperfect as a special, rarely used aspect form with iterative meaning, e.g. *bagand'a* 'he / she sang' (Rusakov 2001a, p. 314).

Apart from these developments, Slavic influence mainly affects the future and this, again, mainly in the Balkan varieties. Sepeči, Arli and Bugurdži

284 A.-M. Meyer

have developed an analytic future marker *ka* (Matras 2002, p. 157), and practically all Romani dialects have a typical Balkan future based on *kam-* 'to love, want' or, more marginally, *mang-* 'to want, demand' (Boretzky and Igla 1999, p. 719; Friedman 2001a, p. 154). According to Boretzky and Igla (1999, p. 718), the diversity of forms suggests that this feature has developed separately in the individual dialects. The negated form is *na / naj ka / naj te / nanaj / nane te*, modelled on Bulgarian and Macedonian *njama / nema da* (Boretzky et al. 2008, p. 29; Minkov 1997, p. 83). North Russian Romani and Ukrainian dialects have an analytic future with an auxiliary based on the Romani verb stems *l-* 'to take' or *(j)av-* 'to be, become; come': *me l-ava te bagav* or *me av-ava te bagav* < Russian *ja budu / stanu pet'* 'I will sing' (Rusakov 2001b, pp. 297–298; Matras 2002, p. 158). The simple future in North Russian Romani is also taken from Russian and involves aspect prefixes: *s-bagala* < Russian *on s-poyot* 'he will sing.PF' instead of inherited *bagala* (Rusakov 2001a, p. 314). An interesting feature of all Romani dialects in contact with Ukrainian (and Russian) is a syncretism of all plural forms of the perfective past: *ame / tume / vone tjerde* < *my / vy / vony zrobyly* 'we / you.PL / they did', which is a recent pan-Ukrainian development (Tenser 2012, p. 44).

9.5.3 The 'New Infinitive'

Romani does not have an inherited infinitive; the early and very restricted use of an infinitive in modal constructions got lost completely due to contact with Iranian and the Balkan languages and was replaced by a non-factual 'that' construction. In later contact with infinitive languages like Slovenian, Czech, Slovak and Polish, Romani has adapted a new infinitive. This new infinitive, which can be called a 'debalkanisation-effect', is very elaborately described in Boretzky (1996a), and already Puchmayer (1821, p. 18) mentioned this development for Bohemian Romani in contact with Czech. In Bohemian Romani, the infinitive is mainly used in less integrated clauses, such as in the case of serialisation (10), but not in modal sentences (11):

(10) Serialisation in Bohemian Romani (Matras 2002, p. 162)
    De   mange te pijel!
    give.2SG.IMP me.DAT drink.INF
    'Give me (something) to drink!'

9 The Impact of Slavic Languages on Romani   285

(11) Modality in Bohemian Romani (Matras 2002, p. 162)

> *Me les   kamav   te mukav te terd'ol.*
> I   it.OBL want.1SG.PRS leave.INF stand.INF
> 'I want to leave it standing'.

Interestingly, not all Romani varieties in contact with West and East Slavic have developed a new infinitive; above all, the Vlax dialects have not, while Eastern Europe shows a rather mixed picture (Boretzky 1996a, p. 6).

The new infinitival form is usually introduced by the non-factual complementiser *te* (apart from in modal constructions such as *me ladžu vakeri* 'I am ashamed to say', Matras 2002, p. 162), followed by the 3SG Present, e.g. *te šunel* 'to hear'. Thus, the functionality of finite forms has been extended from subjunctive constructions into the domain of an infinitive. In East Slovak Romani, the 2 or 3PL has been generalised for this purpose. According to Matras (2002, p. 161), '[t]he boundaries of this isogloss are defined by the neighbouring dialects of the North Russian Roma to the north, Welsh Romani to the west, and Piedmontese Sinti to the south, which do not show new infinitives'. Consequently, the new infinitive has indeed developed only under the influence of infinitive languages, but not in all dialects in contact with such languages.

Concerning its functions, the new infinitive follows the respective contact languages. Among them is quasi-nominalisation of the verb: Northern Central *te vakerel hi rup, te na vakerel somnakaj* 'to talk is silver, not to talk is gold' (Boretzky 1996a, p. 19) and use as a converb of simultaneity: West Slovak Romani *pale dikhle oda moxtore te džal tele pan'eha* 'again they saw those chests drifting down the river' (von Sowa 1887, p. 165; Matras 2002, p. 162).

A special case found in Doljenski in Slovenia and Istria, where the infinitive form ends in *-i*, is a recent innovation possibly triggered by the Croatian and Slovene infinitive ending *-ti* (Cech and Heinschink 2001a, p. 166; Boretzky 1996a, p. 11; Matras 2002, pp. 161–162). These forms are morphologically distinct from any finite forms and thus suggest a development of a true infinitive.

9.5.4 Voice and Reflexivity

Early Romani had a construction made up of copula auxiliary and past participle to form passives, in which both transitive and intransitive verbs could be used, for example *si kerdo* 'is done' (Matras 2002, p. 128). According to Boretzky (1986, p. 207; 1994, p. 165), the passive developed only on

European soil. The older form uses the reflexive pronoun with different personal forms: *man* 'me, myself', *tut* 'you, yourself', *pe(s)* 'he / she, himself / herself', etc., but under Slavic influence, *pe(s)* has become generalised to occur with all grammatical persons (Boretzky 1996b, p. 21).

For example, Romani dialects in the Balkans have three means of expressing passive meaning, but, as the adaptation of Bulgarian and Macedonian reflexive verbs proceeds, they are being replaced by the reflexive form (Igla 2001, pp. 406–409). Igla and Sechidou (2012) demonstrate very elaborately how these dialects replicate the reflexive and passive verbs of Bulgarian and Greek. The fact that a construction with the particle *se* in Bulgarian can have both passive and reflexive meaning, but a construction with *pes* in Bulgarian Romani is exclusively reflexive, creates an asymmetry with the consequence that *pes* is extended to new contexts and acquires passive meaning as well. Thus, the Bulgarian analytic passive has served as a model for the creation of an analytic passive in Bulgarian Romani. The new construction (intransitive verb plus *pes*, e.g. *margjovel pes* 'he is beaten') has spread and is replacing the old synthetic form and the old reflexive pattern. Romani dialects under Slavic influence outside the Balkans, however, use the transitive marker plus *pes*: *marel pes* 'he is beaten' (Igla and Sechidou 2012, pp. 169, 172).

Reflexive constructions and the generalisation of *pes* triggered by Slavic are also on the rise outside the Balkans. Rácová (2015, p. 82) gives the following examples for East Slovak Romani: *me pes khosav* < Slovak *ja se utieram* 'I am cleaning myself', *jon pes khosen* < *oni sa utierajú* 'they are cleaning themselves'. Also, under Slovak influence, some non-reflexive verbs have become reflexive: *ladžal pes* < *han'bit sa* 'to be ashamed' instead of *ladžal*. Evidence for Ukrainian Romani can be found in Barannikov (1931, p. 21, e.g. *dikhe-pe* < Ukr. *dyvyty-sja* 'to see'), for North Russian Romani in Sergievskij (1931, p. 57, e.g. *morava-pe* < Russ. *moju-sj* 'I am washing myself') and Rusakov (2001a, p. 321).

In practically all European Romani dialects, a kind of medialis construction composed of an active verb and a reflexive dative pronoun is known, which expresses that the agent fulfils an action willingly and in his own interest (cf. Sect. 4.2 on the dativus ethicus). The word *peske / penge* in such constructions shows a tendency towards generalisation to other grammatical persons just like *pes* (Šebková 1999, p. 159; Rácová 2015, p. 90).

The reflexive form can also have a modal function in impersonal dative constructions, which conforms to Balkan Slavic, Albanian and Romanian and is also contact-induced: *Na xal pes mange* < Serbian *ne jede mi se*, Bulgarian *ne mi se jade* 'I don't feel like eating' (Boretzky and Igla 1999, p. 722).

Lastly, Hübschmannová and Bubeník (1997, pp. 136–144) mention the so-called second causative, i.e. the pattern 'to make X do Y' or 'to have Y done by X'. This feature has been lost in Slovak Romani due to Slovak influence and is now expressed periphrastically as in Czech and Slovak (the inherited form is represented by Hungarian Romani here):

(12) Loss of the second causative

(a) Inherited form: *I sasuj (...)* *maravlahi* *la pre čhaveha*
the mother-in-law beat.CAUS.3SG.IMPF she her.ACC boy.INS

(b) Slovak Romani: *E sasvi (...)* *kerlas upre peskere čhas,* *kaj la te marel*
the mother-in-law do.PST on her.ACC son.ACC that her.DAT beat.INF

(c) Slovak: *Machocha (...) vyvolala* *syna,* *aby ju* *zbil*
Mother-in-law order.3SG.PFV son.ACC that her.DAT beat.3SG.PFV
'The mother-in-law made her son beat her [=the daughter-in-law]'

9.5.5 Modality

The most stable modal expression in Romani is 'want', usually expressed by *kam-*, in the Balkans also *mang-* 'to want, demand' (Matras 2002, p. 163), with some exceptions: in Romani dialects in Croatia, a construction with Croatian *želi-* or *voli-* 'to want, love, wish' can be found: *uvek želisardam te žav ande Indija* or *uvek volisardem te džav ande Indija* 'I have always wanted to go to India' (Čurarja Arlije HR-002, 628 and Manuša Čurjarja, HR-003, 628). In Doljenski, Slovene *hoči* has been borrowed: *Hočemo da lam duj phabaja* 'We want to take two apples' (Cech and Heinschink 2001b, p. 357).

Negative ability ('cannot') is also relatively stable and usually constructed with inherited *našti* (Matras 2002, p. 163). One exception is North Russian Romani, which adapts Russian *ne (s)moč'* and inflects it as in Russian: *me ni smog te urakirav la te džal manca* 'I couldn't convince her to come with me' (RUS-003, 713).

Positive ability is more open to borrowing. All dialects in contact with Slavic languages use Slavic *može* or the verbal stem *mog-* / *mož-* instead of inherited *šaj* (Boretzky 1999, p. 112). Doljenski also has *lako* < Slovene *lahko*: *I brzo lende lako živinamo* 'we can also live without them' (Cech and Heinschink 2001b, p. 357). Moreover, there is a tendency to differentiate

288   A.-M. Meyer

between a general and a situative ability by analogy to Slavic and Greek: *šaj / ašti* vs. *džan-*, cf. Bulgarian *znaja* vs. *moga*, Russian *umet'* vs. *moč'*, Polish *potrafić* vs. *móc,* etc. However, Boretzky and Igla (1999, p. 721) are undecided as to whether this phenomenon is inherited or due to interference.

Stems with the meaning 'to like, love' are also prone to borrowing, for example *obič-* < Bulgarian *običam, voli-* < Croatian *voljeti, lub-* < Polish *lubić* and *ljub-* < Russian *ljubit'*. Most innovations and variations are, however, found in the area of necessity (Matras 2002, pp. 162–163). The most frequently borrowed Slavic modal stems are *treb-* and *mus-* 'must', but also *mora-* 'ibid.' and the modal particles *valjazla / valjani* < Serbian *valja* 'it is necessary' and *nek(a)* 'may, shall' (Boretzky and Igla 1999, pp. 720–721; Boretzky et al. 2008, p. 83), for example: East Slovak Romani *mušinav te džal* 'I must go' (Rácová 2015, p. 83), Kosovan Gurbet *mora te džav* 'ibid.' (Leggio 2011, p. 94), Bulgarian Romani *trebinen tuke pare?* 'do you need money?' (Kostov 1963, p. 133). The inflection of the Slavic contact language is retained only in the Romani dialects that borrow Serbian or Macedonian *mora-,* i.e. *moram.*1SG*, moraš.*2SG, etc. (Elšík and Matras 2009, p. 295). For a detailed description of expressions of necessity in East Slovak Romani, cf. Rácová (2015, p. 83). She also observes the adoption of Slovak *mat'* 'to have' for modal constructions: *So majinav te kerel?* < *čo mám robit'?* 'what shall I do?' (Some Romani dialects in contact with Slovak and Polish also borrow 'to have' in possessive constructions, e.g. *me majinav duj phenja* 'I have two sisters', PL-014, 477. The borrowing of Slavic *mat-* 'to have' in modal constructions is always accompanied by the borrowing of Slavic *mat-* in regular possessive constructions.)

9.5.6 The Conditional

In most European Romani dialects, the inherited conditional conjunction *te / ti* is stable, but a number of dialects (cf. table in Matras 2002, pp. 156, 187) have borrowed the Slavic conditional particle *bi / by* or South Slavic *ako.* Matras (2002, p. 158) explains this as follows: 'Where a solid factual basis for an assertion is missing, speakers are inclined to devise new strategies to reinforce their assertive authority'. Doljenski in Slovenia and Istria, for example, has copied the Slavic pattern with the result of a mixed construction of Romani *te / ti* and Slavic elements. The particle *bi* is used as a marker of unreal circumstances, followed by a truncated Romani verb: *Rado bi pe khel tuha* 'I would like to play with you' (for an elaborate description on this phenomenon in Doljenski cf. Cech and Heinschink 2001a, pp. 168–170; 2001b, pp. 358–360). In addition, Macedonian Arli reflects the four-fold conditional subdivision of Macedonian (hypothetical vs. expectative and within these fulfillable vs. unfulfillable; Friedman 2001a, p. 154). For syntactic peculiarities of the conditional cf. Sect. 9.6.3.

9.5.7 Renarrative and Evidentiality

In some Romani dialects in Bulgaria, e.g. in Sliven, a speaker can mark an action he or she has not witnessed personally by using the perfect form of the verb with the suffix *-li*: *Oda vakerjas mangi, či tu phirsas-li* 'he told me that you were going' (Kostov 1963, p. 133). This must have been influenced by the Bulgarian renarrative, a special verb form which signals that a speaker is repeating someone else's statement; however, the Bulgarian renarrative is not constructed with *li* (cf. Bulgarian *toj mi kaza če ti si hodel*). As Friedman (1999, p. 520) puts it, the dialect in Sliven 'has borrowed the evidential category of Bulgarian by reinterpreting the /l/ of the *l*-participle as a particle, viz. *li*'. Cf. also the general discussion about evidentiality in Romani in Matras (2002, p. 156) and Boretzky (1999, p. 85).

9.5.8 Imperative

The imperative in Romani has gone through various changes, depending on the respective Slavic contact language. In the inherited construction, the verb stem (if necessary expanded by an integration marker) serves as the imperative form: *dža!* 'go.SG!', *džan!* 'go.PL!', *ma dža!* 'don't go.SG!'. In contact with South Slavic, *nek(a)* has been borrowed: *nek avel!* 'he shall come!' (Boretzky 1996b, p. 22). Boretzky (1993, p. 107) sees a possible South Slavic influence in a second, more attenuated negative imperative: *ma te džas!* < Serbian *nemoj da ideš!* 'don't go!'. The imperative in North Russian Romani is described in detail by Rusakov (2001b, pp. 290–297). This dialect borrows from Russian the analytic imperative formation along with the particles *davaj*, *-ka* and *že*: *davaj sbagas!* 'let us sing!' and transfers the Russian use of indicative forms into its own imperative paradigm: *džasa!* < *pojdyom!* 'let's go!'. Sometimes, inherited and borrowed forms are combined as in *džan'ti!* 'come.PL in!', in which *-n-* (palatalised in the example due to regressive assimilation) is an element from Romani and *ti* (*-te*) an element from Russian (Eloeva and Rusakov 1990, p. 18).

9.6 Syntax

The field of syntax seems to have received the least attention from researchers in the context of Slavic-Romani language contact. In the following, I discuss prepositions and conjunctions as well as object doubling, conditional sentences and negation.

9.6.1 Prepositions and Conjunctions

All Romani dialects in contact with Slavic languages have borrowed Slavic prepositions to varying degrees. An analysis of borrowed Slavic prepositions in 86 dialects from the RMS database reveals the following picture (Fig. 9.4).

According to this analysis, 'except' (*osven / osim / oprócz / krome / okrem*, etc.) and 'after' (*sled / posle / pošle / čerez*, etc.) are the most frequently borrowed Slavic prepositions. Other relatively frequent Slavic prepositions in Romani are 'around' (*okolo / dookoła / vokrug*, etc.) as well as 'through' and 'across' (*kroz / prez / przez / čerez / preko*, etc.). 'About', 'from', 'in', 'to', 'into', 'by' and 'under' have never been borrowed from Slavic contact languages, 'above', 'on' and 'out' only once. Boretzky (1994, p. 168) also notes *po* 'each' in use with numbers. Contaminations of Slavic and Romani are also counted here, for example *dre kierunko / pre kierunko / dre strona / smerom*

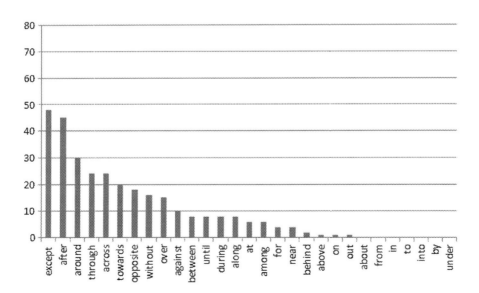

Fig. 9.4 Borrowing of Slavic prepositions into Romani

ke 'towards', *preko drom (ki)* / *preko puta*, etc., 'opposite' and *bizo* 'without', which consists of Romani *bi* 'without', Slavic *bez* 'ibid.' and the definite article *o*. Another interesting instance of contamination mentioned in the literature is *prekal* 'beyond', which is composed of Slavic *preko* 'through' and Romani *-al* < *perdal* 'ibid.' (Boretzky 1999, p. 118). East Slovak Romani borrows Slovak *o* to express the meaning 'after': *o duj kurke* < Slovak *o dva týždne* 'after two weeks' (Rácová and Horecký 2000, p. 74), while in Bergitka (Poland), there is a construction with *o* bearing spatial meaning, e.g. *buxlikano o duj metri* < Polish *poszerzony o dwa metry* 'two metres longer' (Meyer 2016, p. 149). Rácová and Horecký (2000, p. 55) also mention the adoption of Slovak *po* into East Slovak Romani with several different meanings. To what extent the case government of the Slavic languages has been incorporated into Romani along with the borrowed prepositions seems to vary (Elšík et al. 1999, p. 375), but requires further investigation.

Conjunctions are borrowed from Slavic into Romani more frequently than are prepositions, as reflected in the data below (Fig. 9.5).

The three conjunctions most frequently borrowed from Slavic are 'neither…nor…' (*ni…ni…* / *nito…nito…* / *ani…ani…*, etc.), 'but' (*no* / *ale*

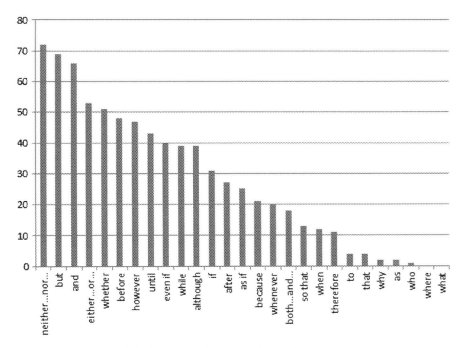

Fig. 9.5 Borrowing of Slavic conjunctions into Romani

/ *ali* / *a* / *ama*) and 'and' (*a* / *i*). Almost two-thirds of the Romani dialects that have borrowed Slavic 'and' have also adopted the differentiation between adversative *a* and copulative *i*. Further frequently borrowed Slavic conjunctions in Romani are 'either…or…' (*ili…ili…* / *albo…albo…* / *alebo…alebo…*), 'whether' (*da li* / *czy*, etc.) and 'before' (*pred(i)* / *poka* / *zanim*, etc.). Contaminations are also possible, e.g. *kana-to* / *xoc-kana* 'whenever', *daže kana* / *daže syr* / *esli dava*, etc., 'even if', *syr by* / *syr budto* / *sar bi*, etc., 'as if' or *sled kana* / *posle kaj* / *sled kaj*, etc., 'after'. An interesting case is Croatian *nek*, which was originally an optative particle, but has been transformed into a conjunction (Elšík 2008, pp. 270–271). The constructions *adake syr* < Russian *tak kak* 'because' and *pal adava so* < Russian *potomu čto* / *iz-za togo, čto*, 'ibid.' are calques (Sergievskij 1931, p. 81). In South Slavic languages, *da* is a widespread factual complementiser and has been borrowed as such into Romani, for example in Doljenski *džanu, da mro čhavo ma rado imini* 'I know that my son loves me'. Cech and Heinschink (2001a, p. 172) assume that the conjunction *kaj* for factual complements first has merged with non-factual *te* / *ti* and was then replaced by Slavic *da*. Subordinate clauses with 'if' are introduced either by inherited *te* or, under South Slavic influence, by *li*: *pušlem e maestro de li avol ko abav* 'I asked the teacher if he would come to the wedding' (Leggio 2011, p. 107), and, under West Slavic influence, by *či* / *čy*: *Kampel te phučel, či pes manuša prindžaren* 'it is necessary to ask if the people know each other' (Rácová 2015, p. 91; Matras 2002, p. 187).

9.6.2 Object Doubling

Pronominal object doubling is a characteristic Balkan phenomenon found in Romani dialects in the Balkans and in Vlax varieties, although with different manifestations depending on the respective contact language. Object doubling is most distinctive in Macedonian, e.g. *go vidov bratot*, literally 'I saw him the brother'; consequently, Romani dialects in contact with Macedonian are most strongly affected. However, the feature is not grammaticalised but optional and generally less widespread in Romani than in the other Balkan languages. An example from Arli (Macedonia) is: *i kniga.o halja la.o o her*, literally 'the donkey ate it the book'. Object doubling is very often used in possessive constructions with the auxiliary *si* plus accusative: *i daj.o si la.o duj čhave* 'the mother has two children' (Boretzky 1999, p. 125; Boretzky and Igla 1999, p. 727; Friedman 2001a, p. 158; Matras 2002, pp. 173–174).

9.6.3 Conditional Sentences

As mentioned above, the Slavic conditional particle *bi / by* has frequently been borrowed into Romani dialects. In Bulgarian Romani, for example, *bi* can stand in front of or after the verb in a conditional sentence: *Te na pheng-janasbi mange, sar bidžanavas meda?* 'if you hadn't told me, how should I have known?' (Kostov 1963, p. 138). East Slovak Romani only inserts *bi* if it is not clear from the context that we are dealing with a conditional (Rácová 2015, p. 83); for North Russian Romani cf. Wentzel (1980, p. 137). In the Balkans, inherited *te* can be replaced by *ako* or *bi*, but there is also a construction with *ka* as in *ka dikhelas* 'would see, would have seen' modelled on Greek or Macedonian (*k'e gledaše* 'ibid.') (Boretzky 1999, p. 107). In Doljenski, conditional sentences are introduced by *ako* or *da* as in South Slavic: *Ako bi ma ov love, me bi av but pute* 'if I had money, I would come often' or *da bi džan, kon hi li doja romni, phenave tuke* 'if I had known who that woman is, I would have told you' (Cech and Heinschink 2001b, p. 360).

9.6.4 Negation

Apart from the negative particle, more complex negative constructions in Romani have also been influenced by the Slavic contact languages. Already Ackerley (1941, p. 83), who investigated Bosnian Romani, noticed that Romani dialects have tended to adopt Slavic double negation, as did Kostov (1963, p. 155) for Bulgarian Romani and Cech and Heinschink (2001a, p. 170) for Doljenski in Slovenia and Istria, for example: *Nije Rajko nič mothav*, literally 'Rajko did not say nothing'. Thus, the preterite in Doljenski is negated with the Slavic copula *nije* 'is not', in combination with the Romani verb stem; instead of the participle, Romani uses the truncated verb. In the variety of Sliven (Bulgaria), *nanaj / nama* is used for negation, which usually appears in combination with *te* and reflects the Bulgarian construction *njama da* (Kostov 1963, p. 155). Southwestern Vlax varieties have *ni* as a negator, 'perhaps an original Southern Vlax innovation, which may have merged with the Slavic negators of the surrounding languages (*ne/nie*)' (Matras 2002, p. 189). In *ne*-dialects—most dialects in Ukraine, among others—the separate imperative marker *ma* has been lost in favour of *na* for all kinds of negation (Anton Tenser, personal correspondence). However, as with other syntactic contact phenomena, negation in Romani requires further research.

9.7 Conclusion

Since the arrival of the Roma in Europe, Romani has been influenced by Slavic contact languages not only in lexicon, but also in phonetics and phonology, morphology and syntax. The affected dialect groups are mainly the Northeastern, Northern Central, Southern Central and South Balkan I as well as different Vlax dialects, but Slavic influence can be found in Romani varieties all over the world. The influence is most obvious in the lexicon, and early Slavic loans like *kralis* 'king' or *dzhamba* 'toad' can be found in Romani dialects worldwide. Most strongly influenced are the semantic fields of nature and dwelling. The largest groups of loans are nouns, but also verbs, temporal and phasal adverbs and quantifiers have frequently been borrowed from Slavic.

Probably, the most widespread contact phenomena in the field of phonetics and phonology is the devoicing of stops in word-final position (in all Romani dialects except those in contact with Serbian / Croatian / Bosnian) and the shift of stress to the penultimate or initial syllable in the Central European dialects. East Slavic palatalisation of front vowels has been widely transferred to the Northeastern group. Furthermore, several characteristic sounds of the respective Slavic contact language(s) have been adopted into Romani, e.g. /ł/ from Polish, /ə/ from Bulgarian, /ɨ/ from Russian, Ukrainian and Polish, syllabic /r/ from South Slavic and Czech as well as velarised /l/ from East Slavic.

In Romani nominal morphology, the category of comparison has generally expanded under Slavic influence and those dialects in contact with Slavic languages without an article (i.e. all but Macedonian and Bulgarian) are in the process of losing their own definite article. An interesting novelty in the Romani case system is the use of a reflexive dative, especially in the Balkan varieties in contact with South Slavic. Russian, Ukrainian and Polish have had a significant influence on the case system of Romani dialects in Russia, Ukraine and Lithuania.

Central to verbal morphology is Slavic aspect: aspectual prefixes have been adapted in all Romani varieties in contact with Slavic, but the size of the inventories varies a lot from very restricted on the Balkans to very distinctive in the Northern Central dialects. However, the grammatical category of Slavic aspect as a whole has not been taken over into Romani. In the tense system, most Slavic influence can be found in the future; on the Balkans, we can also witness the development of an analytic perfect. Boretzky (1996a) has introduced the term of a 'new infinitive' that has developed in many (but not all) Romani dialects in contact with infinitive languages like Slovenian, Czech, Slovak and Polish. Also, under Slavic influence the reflexive pronoun *pe(s)* has become generalised to occur with all grammatical persons, most widespread in the Balkans. The most stable Romani modal expressions are 'want' and 'cannot', whereas 'can', 'like / love' and especially 'must' are very open to borrowings from Slavic. A large number of Romani dialects have borrowed Slavic conditional particles.

In Romani syntax, especially Slavic conjunctions and prepositions have been frequently borrowed. The field of syntax requires more research in the future, at which especially negation is a promising field of study. Generally, it is remarkable that the Romani language has survived and kept a stable core of vocabulary and grammatical structures until the present day, in spite of the strong influence exerted upon it by Slavic (and other) majority languages surrounding them since the eleventh century.

References

Ackerley, Frederick George. 1941. Bosnian Romani: Prolegomena. *Journal of the Gypsy Lore Society*, 3rd ser., 20: 78–84.

Barannikov, Aleksei Petrovič. 1931. Songs of the Ukrainian gypsies. *Journal of the Gypsy Lore Society*, 3rd ser., 10 (1): 1–53.

Barannikov, Aleksei Petrovič. 1933. *The Ukrainian and South Russian Gypsy dialects*. Leningrad: Izdatel'stvo Akademii Nauk SSSR.

Beníšek, Michael. 2013. Sered.nye Romani: A North Central Romani variety of Transcarpathian Ukraine. In *Romani V. Papers from the annual meeting of the Gypsy Lore Society. Graz 2011*, 2, ed. Barbara Schrammel-Leber and Barbara Tiefenbacher, 42–59. Graz: Grazer Romani Publikationen.

Boretzky, Norbert. 1986. Zur Sprache der Gurbet von Priština (Jugoslawien). *Giessener Hefte für Tsiganologie* 3 (1–4): 195–217.

Boretzky, Norbert. 1989. Zum Interferenzverhalten des Romani (Verbreitete und ungewöhnliche Phänomene). *Zeitschrift für Phonetik, Sprachwissenschaft und Kommunikationsforschung* 42 (3): 357–374.

Boretzky, Norbert. 1993. *Bugurdži. Deskriptiver und historischer Abriß eines Romani-Dialekts*. Berlin: Harrassowitz (Osteuropa-Institut der Freien Universität Berlin, Balkanologische Veröffentlichungen 21).

Boretzky, Norbert. 1994. *Romani. Grammatik des Kalderaš-Dialekts mit Texten und Glossar*. Berlin: Harrassowitz (Osteuropa-Institut der Freien Universität Berlin, Balkanologische Veröffentlichungen 24).

Boretzky, Norbert. 1996a. The 'new' infinitive in Romani. *Journal of the Gypsy Lore Society* 6 (1): 1–51.

Boretzky, Norbert. 1996b. Arli. Materialien zu einem südbalkanischen Romani-Dialekt. *Grazer Linguistische Studien* 46: 1–30.

Boretzky, Norbert. 1999. *Die Verwandtschaftsbeziehungen zwischen den südbalkanischen Romani-Dialekten. Mit einem Kartenanhang.* Frankfurt am Main etc.: Peter Lang (Studien zur Tsiganologie und Folkloristik 27).

Boretzky, Norbert. 2013. Lexikalische Slavismen im Romani. *Zeitschrift für Balkanologie.* 49 (1): 10–46.

Boretzky, Norbert, and Birgit Igla. 1999. Balkanische (südosteuropäische) Einflüsse im Romani. In *Handbuch der Südosteuropa-Linguistik*, ed. Uwe Hinrichs, 709–731. Wiesbaden: Harrassowitz.

Boretzky, Norbert, Petra Cech, and Birgit Igla. 2008. *Die südbalkanischen Dialekte (SB I) des Romani und ihre innere Gliederung. Analyse und Karten.* Graz: Universität Graz, Institut für Sprachwissenschaften.

Cech, Petra, and Mozes F. Heinschink. 2001a. A dialect with seven names. *Romani Studies* 11: 137–184.

Cech, Petra, and Mozes Heinschink. 2001b. Sinti Istriani, Lički Šijaci, Gopti und Cigani Brajdiči. Die Doljenski Roma in Slovenien. In *"Was ich noch sagen wollte…"—A multilingual Festschrift for Norbert Boretzky on occasion of his 65th birthday*, ed. Birgit Igla and Thomas Stolz, 341–368. Berlin: Akademie Verlag.

Cech, Petra, and Mozes F. Heinschink. 2002. Vokabular der Dolenjski Roma aus Novo Mesto und Bela Krajina, Slowenien. In *Romani IV. Special issue of Grazer Linguistische Studien*, 58, ed. Dieter W. Halwachs and Gerd Ambrosch, 1–42.

Čarankoŭ, Lev N. 1974. Cyhanski dyjalekt u belaruskim moŭnym asjaroddzi. *Belaruskaja Lingvistyka* 6: 34–40.

Čerenkov, Lev Nikolaevič. 2008. Cyganskaja dialektologija v Ukraine. Istorija i sovremennoe sostojanie. In *Romy Ukraïny: Iz mynuloho v majbutnje (do Roms'koï Dekady Jevropy 2005–2015)*, 489–503. Kyïv: Inst. Ukraïns'koï Archeografi ta Džereloznavstva im. M.S. Hruševs'koho.

Čerenkov, Lev Nikolaevič, and Roman Stepanovič Demeter. 1990. Kratkij grammatičeskij očerk kelderarskogo dialekta cyganskogo jazyka. In *Cygansko-russkij i russko-cyganskij slovar' (kėldėrarskij dia-lekt)*, ed. Roman Stepanovič Demeter, Pyotr Stepanovič Demeter, and Lev Nikolaevič Čerenkov, 285–306. Russkij jazyk: Moskva.

Červenka, Jan. 2004. Některá specifika morfologie substantiv v subdialektech severocentrální romštiny ve slovenských regionech Kysuce, Turiec a Liptov. *Romano džaniben* 14 (jevend): 177–185.

Demeter, Nadezhda Georgievna, Nikolay Vladislavovič Bessonov, and Vladimir Konstantinovič Kutenkov. 2000. *Istorija cygan: Novyj vzgljad.* Voronež: IPF "Voronež".

Eloeva, Fatima Abisalovna, and Aleksandr Yur'evič Rusakov. 1990. *Problemy jazykovoj interferencii. Učebnoe posobie.* Leningrad: Leningradskij Gosudarstvennyj Universitet.

Elšík, Viktor. 2007. Loanwords in Selice Romani, an Indo-Aryan language of Slovakia. http://ulug.ff.cuni.cz/lingvistika/elsik/Elsik_Loanwords-in-Selice-Romani_071104.pdf. Date Accessed 13 October 2017.

9 The Impact of Slavic Languages on Romani   297

Elšík, Viktor. 2008. Grammatical borrowing in Hungarian Rumungro. In *Grammatical borrowing in cross-linguistic perspective*, ed. Yaron Matras and Jeanette Sakel, 261–282. Berlin, New York: Mouton de Gruyter.

Elšík, Viktor, Milena Hübschmannová, and Hana Šebková. 1999. The Southern Central (*ahi*-imperfect) Romani dialects of Slovakia and northern Hungary. In *Die Sprache der Roma. Perspektiven der Romani-Forschung in Österreich im interdisziplinären und internationalen Kontext*, ed. Dieter Halwachs and Florian Menz, 277–390. Klagenfurt, Celovec: Wieser.

Elšík, Viktor, and Yaron Matras. 2001. RMS database. romani.humanities.manchester.ac.uk/rms/. Date Accessed 20 November 2018.

Elšík, Viktor, and Yaron Matras. 2009. Modality in Romani. In *Modals in the languages of Europe. A reference work*, ed. Björn Hansen and Ferdinand de Haan, 267–322. Berlin: Mouton de Gruyter.

Friedman, Victor A. 1985. Balkan Romani Modality and Other Balkan Languages. *Folia Slavica 7*: 381–389.

Friedman, Victor A. 1999. Evidentiality in the Balkans. In *Handbuch der Südosteuropa-Linguistik*, ed. Uwe Hinrichs, 519–544. Wiesbaden: Harrassowitz.

Friedman, Victor A. 2000. Romani in the Balkan Linguistic League – Synchrony and Diachrony. In *Valkanikē Glossología: Synkhronía kai diakhronía. Balkanlinguistik: Synchronie und Diachronie*, ed. Christos Tzitzilis and Charalampos Symeonidés, 95–105. Thessaloniki: University of Thessaloniki.

Friedman, Victor A. 2001a. Romani multilingualism in its Balkan context. *Sprachtypologie und Universalienforschung* 54: 46–159.

Friedman, Victor A. 2001b. The Romani indefinite article in its historical and areal context. In *"Was ich noch sagen wollte…" A multilingual Festschrift for Norbert Boretzky on occasion of his 65th birthday*, ed. Birgit Igla and Thomas Stolz, 287–301. Berlin: Akademie Verlag.

Gilliat-Smith, Bernard Joseph. 1922. The language of the St. Petersbourg Gypsy singers. *Journal of the Gypsy Lore Society*, 3rd ser., 1: 153–162.

Gilliat-Smith, Bernard Joseph. 1932. The dialect of the Gypsies of Northern Russia (Being a review of Professor M. V. Sergievski's Cyganski Jazyk). *Journal of the Gypsy Lore Society*, 3rd ser., 11 (1): 71–88.

Grienig, Gregor. 2010. Roma in Europa. In *Berlin Institut für Bevölkerung und Entwicklung*. www.berlin-institut.org/online-handbuchdemografie/bevoelkerungsdynamik/regionale-dynamik/roma-in-europa.html. Date Accessed 31 October 2017.

Gvozdanović, Jadranka. 2011. Perfective and Imperfective aspect. In *The Oxford handbook of tense and aspect*, ed. Robert I. Binnick, 781–802. Oxford: OUP.

Hancock, Ian. 1983. Slavic influence on Texan Romani. *Southwest Journal of Linguistics* 6 (2): 115–132.

Hübschmannová, Milena, and Vít Bubeník. 1997. Causatives in Slovak and Hungarian Romani. In *The typology and dialectology of Romani*, ed. Yaron Matras, Peter Bakker, and Hristo Kyuchukov, 133–145. Amsterdam: John Benjamins.

Igla, Birgit. 1991. On the treatment of foreign verbs in Romani. In *In the Margin of Romani. Gypsy languages in Contact*, ed. Peter Bakker and Marcel Cortiade, 50–55. Amsterdam: University of Amsterdam, Institute for General Linguistics (Studies in language contact 1).

Igla, Birgit. 1997. The Romani dialect of the Rhodopes. In *The typology and dialectology of Romani*, ed. Yaron Matras, Peter Bakker, and Hristo Kyuchukov, 147–158. Amsterdam: John Benjamins (Current issues in linguistic theory 156).

Igla, Birgit. 1998. Zum Verbalaspekt in bulgarischen Romani-Dialekten. *Grazer Linguistische Studien* 50: 65–79.

Igla, Birgit. 1999. Disturbances and innovations in the case system in Bulgarian Romani dialects. *Acta Linguistica Academiae Scientiarum Hungaricae* 46: 201–214.

Igla, Birgit. 2001. Zur Entwicklung der Diathese in bulgarischen Romani-Dialekten. In *"Was ich noch sagen wollte..." A multilingual Festschrift for Norbert Boretzky on occasion of his 65th birthday*, ed. Birgit Igla and Thomas Stolz, 405–422. Berlin: Akademie Verlag.

Igla, Birgit, and Irene Sechidou. 2012. Romani in contact with Bulgarian and Greek: Replication in verbal morphology. In *Morphologies in contact*, ed. Martine Vanhove, Thomas Stolz, Aina Urdze, and Hitomi Otsuka, 163–176. Berlin: Akademie Verlag. (Studia typologica, Beihefte 10).

Ješina, Josef. 1886. *Romáňi čib oder die Zigeuner-Sprache. Grammatik, Wörterbuch, Chrestomathie*. Leipzig: List & Francke.

Kalina, Antoine. 1882. *La langue des Tziganes slovaques*. Posen: J.K. Zupański.

Kopernicki, Isidore. 1889. Notes on the dialect of the Bosnian gypsies. *Journal of the Gypsy Lore Society* 1 (3): 125–131.

Kostov, Kiril. 1963. Grammatik der Zigeunersprache Bulgariens: Phonetik und Morphologie. Unpublished doctoral dissertation, Humboldt University, Berlin.

Kostov, Kiril. 1989. Zur Determination der a-stämmigen entlehnten Maskulina in der Zigeunersprache Bulgariens. *Balkansko ezikoznanie/Linguistique balkanique* 32 (2): 119–122.

Kralčák, Ľubomír. 1999. Slovenčina v kontakte s rómčinou. In *Slovenčina v kontaktoch a konfliktoch s inými jazykmi*, ed. Slavomír Ondrejovič, 178–185. Special issue of Sociolinguistica Slovaca 4.

Leggio, Daniele Viktor. 2011. The dialect of the Mitrovica Roma. *Romani Studies* 21 (1): 57–113.

Lípa, Jiří. 1965. *Cikánština v jazykovém prostředí slovenském a českém: k otázkám, starých a novejších složek v její gramatice a lexiku*. Praha: Nakl. Československé akademie věd.

Matras, Yaron. 1999. The speech of the Polska Roma: Some highlighted features and their implications for Romani dialectology. *Journal of the Gypsy Lore Society*, 5th ser., 9: 1–28.

Matras, Yaron. 2002. *Romani. A linguistic introduction*. Cambridge: CUP.

9 The Impact of Slavic Languages on Romani

Matras, Yaron. 2010. *Romani in Britain: The afterlife of a language.* Edinburgh: EUP.

Meyer, Anna-Maria. 2016. Wielojęzyczna Polska – język romski w kontakcie z polszczyzną. *Postscriptum polonistyczne* 2 (18): 145–155.

Meyer, Anna Maria. To appear. Lexical borrowings and one-word codeswitches: Polish-Romani and Romani-Polish. *Anzeiger für slavische Philologie.* XLVI: 9–28.

Miklosich, Franz. 1872. *Die slavischen Elemente in den Mundarten der Zigeuner.* Wien: Karl Gerold's Sohn (Über die Mundarten und die Wanderungen der Zigeuner Europas. Separatabdruck aus dem XXI. Bande der Denkschriften der philosophisch-historischen Classe der kaiserlichen Akademie der Wissenschaften 1).

Miltner, Vladimír. 1965. The morphologic structure of a New Indo-Aryan language in Czechoslovakia. *Indian Linguistics* 26: 106–131.

Minkov, Michael. 1997. A concise grammar of West Bulgarian Romani. *Journal of the Gypsy Lore Society*, 5th ser., 7: 55–95.

Mišeska-Tomić, Olga. 2009. Clitic and non-clitic possessive pronouns in Macedonian and Bulgarian. In *Investigations in the Bulgarian and Macedonian nominal expression*, ed. Olga Dimitrova-Vulchanova and Olga Mišeska-Tomić, 95–120. Trondheim.

Pančenko, Januš Aleksandrovič. 2013. *Izučenie vlašskogo dialekta romskogo jazyka: poiski i nachodki.* Kiev: Naučno-issledovatel'skij centr orientalistiki imeni Omel'jana Pricaka NaUKMA.

Petulengro. 1915. Report on the Gypsy tribes of North-East Bulgaria. *Journal of the Gypsy Lore Society*, n.s., 9: 65–109.

Poplack, Shana, David Sankoff, and Christopher Miller. 1988. The social correlates and linguistic processes of lexical borrowing and assimilation. *Linguistics* 26: 47–104.

Puchmayer, Anton. 1821. *Románi čib: das ist, Grammatik und Wörterbuch der Zigeuner Sprache.* Prag: Fürst-erzbischöfliche Buchdruckerey.

Puscher, Wilfried. 2005. Romani und Russisch in Kontakt. Novation und Tradition. Graz (diploma thesis).

Rácová, Anna. 1995. The lexicon of 'Slovak' Romany language. *Asian and African Studies* 4 (1): 8–14.

Rácová, Anna. 1997. Romani in contact with Slovak language. In *Intercultural contacts between East and West*, ed. Viktor Krupa, 83–87. Bratislava: Slovak Academic Press.

Rácová, Anna. 1999. On the category of aspectuality in Slovak Romani. *Asian and African Studies* 8 (1): 62–66.

Rácová, Anna. 2000. Rómske základy ako zdroj neologizácie v slovenskej karpatskej rómčine. In *Človek a jeho jazyk. 1. Jazyk ako fenomén kultúry*, ed. Klára Buzássyová, 45–51. Bratislava: Veda.

Rácová, Anna. 2007. Romany word-formation bases as a source of neologization in the Slovak Carpathian Romany language. *SKASE Journal of Theoretical Linguistics* 4 (1): 127–131.

300 A.-M. Meyer

Rácová, Anna. 2015. Slovak language and Slovak Romani. In *Romani studies: Contemporary trends*, ed. Christo Kyuchukov, Lukasz Kwadrans, and Ladislav Fizik, 79–95. München: LINCOM.

Rácová, Anna, and Milan Samko. 2015. Structural patterns and functions of reduplicative constructions in Slovak Romani. *Asian and African Studies* 2: 165–189.

Rácová, Anna, and Ján Horecký. 2000. *Slovenská karpatská Rómčina. Opis systému.* Bratislava: Veda.

Rusakov, Aleksandr Yur'evič. 2001a. The North Russian Romani dialect. Interference and code switching. In *The Circum-Baltic languages. Typology and contact*, ed. Östen Dahl and Maria Koptjevskaja-Tamm, 313–337. Amsterdam, Philadelphia: John Benjamins.

Rusakov, Aleksandr Yur'evič. 2001b. Imperative in North Russian Romani dialect. In *Typology of imperative constructions*, ed. Viktor Samuilovič Chrakovskij, 287–299. München: Lincom.

Rusakov, Alexandr, and Olga Abramenko. 1998. North Russian Romani dialect: Interference in case system. *Grazer Linguistische Studien* 50: 109–133.

Samer, Helmut. 2003. Arrival in Europe. In *Rombase. Didactically edited information on Roma*. rombase.uni-graz.at. Date Accessed 31 October 2017.

Šebková, Hana. 1999. *Romaňi čhib. Klíč k učebnici slovenské romštiny*. Praha: Fortuna.

Semiletko, V'jačeslav. 2008. Do pytannja pro leksyčni osoblyvosti sjervits'koho dialektu movy romiv Ukraïny. In *Romy Ukraïny: Iz mynuloho v majbutnje (do Roms'koï Dekady Jevropy 2005–2015)*, 359–363. Kyïv: Inst. Ukraïns'koï Archeografiï ta Džereloznavstva im. M.S. Hruševs'koho.

Sergievskij, Maksim Vladimirovič. 1931. *Cyganskij jazyk. Kratkoe rukovodstvo po grammatike i pravopisaniju*. Moskva: Central'noe Izdatel'stvo Narodov SSSR.

Tcherenkov, Lev Nikolaevič. 1999. Eine kurzgefasste Grammatik des russischen Kalderaš-Dialekts des Romani. *Grazer Linguistische Studien.* 51: 131–166.

Tenser, Anton. 2005. *Lithuanian Romani*. Munich: Lincom Europa.

Tenser, Anton. 2012. A report on Romani dialects in Ukraine: Reconciling linguistic and ethnographic data. *Romani Studies* 22 (1): 35–47.

Tenser, Anton. 2016. Semantic map borrowing—Case representation in Northeastern Romani dialects. *Journal of Language Contact* 9 (2): 211–245.

Toropov, Vadim Germanovič. 2005. Cyganskie dialekty. In *Jazyki Rossijskoj Federacii i sosednych gosudarstv*, 354–365. T. III. Moskva.

Toropov, Vadim Germanovič, and Viktor Borisovič Gumeroglyj. 2013. Opyt sostavlenija alfavita dlja zapisi ustnoj reči krymskich cygan. In *Cyganskij jazyk v Rossii. Sbornik materialov rabočego soveščanija po cyganskomu jazyku v Rossii. Sankt-Peterburg, 5 oktjabrja 2012g*, ed. Kirill Aleksandrovič Kožanov, Sof'a Alekseevna Oskol'skaya, and Aleksandr Yur'evič Rusakov. Sankt-Peterburg: Nestor-Istorija.

Uhlik, Rade. 1951. *Prepozitivni i postpozitivni član u gurbetskom.* Sarajevo: Orijentalni Institut.

von Sowa, Rudolf. 1887. *Die Mundart der slovakischen Zigeuner.* Göttingen: Vandenhoeck und Ruprecht.

Wentzel, Tatjana Wladimirowna. 1980. *Die Zigeunersprache (Nordrussischer Dialekt).* Leipzig: Verlag Enzyklopädie.

10

The Impact of Hungarian on Romani

Zuzana Bodnárová and Jakob Wiedner

10.1 Introduction

The Hungarian language occupies a particular position in Central Europe: unlike all other neighbouring languages, which belong to the Indo-European language family, Hungarian is a Finno-Ugric language and thus differs substantially from the surrounding languages both lexically and structurally. Despite the influence of Slavic languages and German, the structural particularity of Hungarian has been preserved throughout the centuries.

Hungarian is spoken today mainly in Hungary as well as in the adjacent territories of all its neighbouring countries—namely in southern Slovakia, in the Austrian state of Burgenland, in the Slovenian region of Prekmurje, in the Croatian county of Osijek-Baranja, in the Serbian province of Vojvodina, and in the historical regions of Transylvania in Romania and Carpathian Ruthenia in Ukraine. All these areas were under the rule of the Kingdom of Hungary until 1918. In the nineteenth century, the Hungarian authorities followed a strict Magyarisation policy, which aimed at the linguistic and cultural assimilation of minorities in the country. This policy is what probably accounts for the fact that numerous Romani communities in the Kingdom of Hungary, especially in the Hungarian-speaking areas, gradually shifted to Hungarian. Today, the majority of Roma in Hungary do not speak Romani.

Z. Bodnárová (✉) · J. Wiedner
University of Graz, Graz, Austria

© The Author(s) 2020
Y. Matras and A. Tenser (eds.), *The Palgrave Handbook of Romani Language and Linguistics*, https://doi.org/10.1007/978-3-030-28105-2_10

From a geopolitical point of view, Hungarian has been spoken in the Carpathian basin since it was conquered by the Hungarians at the turn of the tenth century, when the Kingdom of Hungary was established in the year 1000. Since then, Hungary has been an important political factor in Central Europe, even though it lost its independence when the Ottoman Empire occupied the country in 1526 and annexed it. After the expulsion of the Ottomans, Hungary became a part of the Habsburg Empire. Modern Hungary regained full independence only after World War I.

The first recorded appearance of Roma in the Hungarian-ruled territories dates back to the beginning of the fifteenth century. This was the time when Romani groups began to migrate to various regions of Europe from the Byzantine Empire, which was defeated by the Ottomans in 1453. Those Roma who either migrated to or passed through the Carpathian basin came into contact with speakers of Hungarian. Other Romani groups chose different migration routes or did not leave the territory of the former Byzantine Empire, and therefore, the Romani dialects spoken by them show no Hungarian influence.

Due to the historical and political changes during the past centuries, and especially the political re-ordering of Central Europe after the two world wars, it is necessary to differentiate between an ongoing and a former impact of Hungarian on Romani. In the former case, Hungarian was, and remains, the most important or even only contact language of the local Romani groups, while in the latter case, the new, dominant, contact language has either entirely replaced Hungarian or diminished its influence. For instance, German became the official and dominant language of the Burgenland Roma after Burgenland had been unified with Austria after World War I, and Slovak became the only contact language for most Slovak Roma after the formation of Czechoslovakia. There are also Romani speakers who migrated to Hungarian-speaking areas only in the last few centuries. The Romani dialects that they speak therefore show greater influences from European languages other than Hungarian. An example of such a group is the Sinti who moved from Germany and Austria to Hungary only at the beginning of the twentieth century and whose Romani dialect consequently shows more German influence than Hungarian.

Hungarian-induced linguistic features are distributed unevenly across the Romani dialects, depending on the intensity and length of contact. The Romani dialects that have been exposed to the longest Hungarian influence are South Central Romani and some varieties of North Vlax Romani. The former is spoken in a few non-contiguous areas of Hungary as well as in

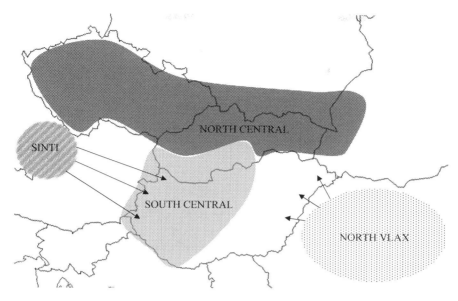

Fig. 10.1 Romani dialect groups influenced by Hungarian

southern Slovakia, in the Austrian Burgenland and the Slovenian Prekmurje. The latter is spoken in Romania, Hungary and, due to the extensive migration of speakers, in several other European and non-European countries. The Hungarian impact on Romani is less prominent in North Central Romani (except for varieties in the Hungarian-speaking regions of Slovakia) and, even less, in Hungarian Sinti Romani, which represents a sub-dialect of Northwestern Romani. The speakers of North Central Romani live in Slovakia and in the adjacent regions of Poland and Ukraine as well as in the Czech Republic. Hungarian Sinti is almost extinct by now (Fig. 10.1).

When identifying the linguistic changes in Romani that were triggered by Hungarian, one should keep in mind that Romani dialects are primarily influenced by dialectal and colloquial Hungarian. For instance, in some South Central Romani varieties in Slovakia the long open back vowel /á/ [ɒ:] is rounded while the phonologically distinct short /a/ [a] is unrounded (see Sect. 10.2.2). This phonological feature is conditioned by the local Hungarian dialect, since in standard Hungarian the rounding is reversed: the long vowel /á/ [a:] is unrounded and the corresponding short /a/ [a] is rounded.

Furthermore, owing to some features that Hungarian shares with its neighbouring languages, it is not always possible to determine which

306 Z. Bodnárová and J. Wiedner

contact language is the source of a linguistic change in Romani. Examples of such unclear instances are the emergence of verbal particles in the Vend sub-dialect of South Central Romani (henceforth Vend Romani, see Sect. 10.3.1) or the introduction of infinitive constructions to North Central Romani (see Sect. 10.3.2). Vend Romani has been exposed to contact with Hungarian and German, both of which have a rich system of verbal particles. Infinitive constructions are used in both Slovak and Hungarian, which are the present and former contact languages, respectively, of most North Central Romani varieties.

The impact of Hungarian on Romani has been discussed or mentioned mainly within grammatical descriptions of Romani dialects (see, e.g., Hutterer and Mészáros 1967, Elšík et al. 1999, Halwachs and Wogg 2002, Bodnárová 2015) and comparative studies (see, e.g., Boretzky 1996, Hübschmannová and Bubeník 1997, Elšík 2000). Only some recent studies focus directly on particular linguistic changes triggered by Hungarian (see, e.g., Elšík 2006). Elšík's (2007) study is the first of its kind to account for the overall impact of Hungarian on South Central Romani varieties spoken in Slovakia and northern Hungary. The present chapter intends to summarise the impact of Hungarian on various Romani dialects, drawing largely on Elšík (2007), and referring the reader to other literature for further details.

The impact of Hungarian on Romani is discussed within the sections Phonology, Morphology, Syntax and Lexicon. Each section begins with a brief overview of some relevant linguistic features of both Early Romani, a reconstructed variety of Romani representing the period prior to the outward migration of Roma from the Byzantine Empire (see Matras 2002, pp. 18–20), and Hungarian in order to outline the initial linguistic situation at the arrival of Romani speakers to Hungarian-speaking territory. We will then show how the linguistic structures of Romani were influenced by Hungarian in the relevant Romani dialects.

10.2 Phonology

10.2.1 Consonants

The phonemic inventories of Hungarian and Early Romani (see Matras 2002, p. 56; Baló, this volume) show certain similarities but also significant differences. Both Hungarian and Early Romani are characterised by the existence of a relatively rich set of alveolar and post-alveolar fricatives and affricates: /s/, /z/, /š/, /ž/ and /c/, /dz/, /č/, /dž/. Hungarian differs from

10 The Impact of Hungarian on Romani 307

Early Romani in that it has distinctive consonant length and possesses the palatalised consonants /ľ/ (merged with /j/ in most Hungarian dialects), /ň/, /ď/ and /ť/. The latter two consonants are treated in Early Romani as allophonic variants of the non-palatalised dentals. Early Romani retains, in contrast to Hungarian, a phonologically distinct aspiration in the series of voiceless stops /ph/, /th/ and /kh/ as well as in the post-alveolar affricate /čh/. It also maintains a phonemic distinction between the glottal /h/ and the velar /x/ as well as between the alveolar /r/ and the uvular /ř/ [ʀ], the latter sound being a continuation of the original retroflex stop /ḍ/ [ɖ]. The velar /x/, the uvular /ř/ and the aspirated consonant phonemes are absent in Hungarian.

In general, Hungarian enriched the consonant inventory of Romani. It has brought to Romani a series of palatalised consonants and the distinctive consonant length whereas all Romani dialects influenced by Hungarian preserved at least some of the original aspirated sounds. The phonemic distinction between /h/ and /x/ as well as between /r/ and /ř/ has been in some form affected by Hungarian.

Elšík et al. (1999, pp. 288–295) discuss the emergence of palatal consonants in Central Romani. These include the non-aspirated stops /ť/ and /ď/, the nasal /ň/, the lateral /ľ/ and, in addition, the aspirated stop /ťh/ which emerged due to palatalisation of the velar /kh/, e.g. *makhin* > *máťhin* 'fly', *díkhjol* > *díťhol* 'to appear, seem'. With the exception of /ťh/, Hungarian has or, in case of the palatal lateral, used to have the same palatal consonants. Thus, it is clear that Hungarian played a primary role in the formation of palatals in South Central Romani. For the palatals in North Central Romani, we can assume an influence of both Hungarian and Slovak (palatals in Slovak are /ň/, /ť/, /ď/ and /ľ/). The same series of palatals, namely /ň/, /ť/, /ď/ and /ľ/, developed also in North Vlax Romani under the influence of Hungarian (Hutterer and Mészáros 1967, p. 9).

Palatal consonants in Central Romani arose through palatalisation of dental and velar stops preceding the phoneme /i/ (e.g. *burnik* > *burňik* 'palm', *kinel* > *ťinel* 'to buy') as well as through jotation (e.g. *tatjarel* > *taťarel* 'to warm', *phagjol* > *phaďol* 'to break'). In Hungarian Vend Romani, as described by Bodnárová (2015, p. 82), the palatals /ď/ and /ť/ may also arise through the fortition of /j/ in post-consonantal position. The palatal /ď/ is employed after voiced and the palatal /ť/ after voiceless consonants, e.g. *čhipja* > *čhipťa* 'languages; tongues', *hevjálo* > *hevďálo* 'leaky'. To a lesser extent, the initial /j/ also underwent fortition to /ď/ in the same Romani dialect, e.g. *jakh* > *ďakh* 'eye', *jiv* > *ďiv* 'snow' (for the further development of this sound change involving affrication in Austrian Vend Romani see Halwachs and Wogg

308   Z. Bodnárová and J. Wiedner

2002, p. 5). Both processes are modelled on the Western Transdanubian dialect of Hungarian, e.g. *kalaptya* < standard Hungarian *kalapja* 'his/her hat', *borgyu* < standard Hungarian *borjú* 'calf', *gyég* < standard Hungarian *jég* 'ice', *gyün* < standard Hungarian *jön* 'comes'.

A further development in most Central Romani varieties influenced by Hungarian is the merger of /ʎ/ and /j/ (e.g. *géljom* > *géjom* 'I went') which occurs in most Hungarian dialects too (e.g. *lyuk* /ʎuk/ > /juk/ 'hole'). Elšík (2007, p. 263) notes in this regard that the loss of /ʎ/ represents a rare case of Hungarian-induced phoneme loss in South Central Romani. Furthermore, Elšík et al. (1999, pp. 294–295) observe that the de-lateralisation of /ʎ/ to /j/ did not necessarily happen simultaneously with the same development in the surrounding Hungarian dialects. From a diachronic perspective, the disappearance of /ʎ/ in some varieties of South Central Romani appears to be a later, more recent phenomenon. As reported by Cech and Heinschink (1999, pp. 10–11), a similar sound change is ongoing in several North Vlax varieties under Hungarian influence. Here, /l/ changes to /j/ when followed by /i/, or, in certain instances, also when followed by another vowel, e.g. **rakli* 'non-Romani girl' > *rakji* and *rakja* in the oblique case. As reported by Hutterer and Mészáros (1967, p. 12), the palatal /ʎ/ is in free variation with /j/ (but also with /l/), which seems to reflect the loss of /ʎ/ in favour of /j/ in Hungarian, e.g. *foľovo ~ fojovo ~ folovo* 'river' (< Hungarian *folyó*).

Distinctive consonant length in relevant Romani dialects was also triggered by Hungarian. This is especially the case for the South Central Romani varieties in present contact with Hungarian (see Elšík et al. 1999, pp. 304–306, Elšík 2007, p. 263, Bodnárová 2015, pp. 76–78). For instance, in the South Central variety spoken in the Hungarian village Versend, we find minimal pairs like *ola* (oblique feminine definite article) vs. *olla* 'those' and *idegeno* 'foreign (noun)' vs. *idegenno* 'foreign (adjective)'. The development of long, geminated, consonants is, however, not uniform in the individual South Central varieties. Most varieties preserve geminates only in Hungarian loanwords (e.g. *cigaretta* from Hungarian *cigaretta* 'cigarette'), while others have extended the use of geminates to indigenous words. In the respective Romani dialects, geminates often emerge due to assimilation of consonant clusters, *kerlo* > *kello* 'throat', *upre* > *uppe* 'on'. They also result from the lengthening of consonants preceding /j/, which conforms to the lengthening rule of Hungarian, e.g. *bútja* > *búťťa* 'works', *paramisja* > *paramissa* 'tales'. Vowel syncope is another process which leads to the emergence of long consonants, e.g. *erďavisajijum* > *erďavisajjum* 'I worsened', *khelelahi* > *khellahi* 's/he was dancing', *phenenahi* > *phennahi* 'they were saying'. In some South Central varieties, the vowel syncope is optionally followed by an assimilatory change between morpheme boundaries, e.g. *perla > pella* 's/ he will fall', *genlahi > gellahi* 's/he was reading'. The source of this change is certainly Hungarian, a language that exhibits a broad variety of assimilatory changes. Elšík et al. (1999, p. 306) report on an interesting case of gemination found between word boundaries where the copula undergoes gemination when preceded by a word with final vowel, e.g. *na ssine odoj* 'they were not there' vs. *odoj sine* 'they were there'.

Gemination seems to be maintained only as long as the Romani dialect is in contact with Hungarian. Boretzky and Igla (1993, p. 41) mention, moreover, that gemination in Romani triggered by contact with Hungarian occurs only to a limited degree in comparison with Finnish Romani where Finnish contact-induced geminates are more frequent. North Central and North Vlax Romani do not distinguish consonant length and, accordingly, in these Romani dialects the Hungarian loanwords have undergone de-gemination, e.g. Hungarian *akkor > North Central Romani akor* 'then', Hungarian *villa > North Vlax Romani vila* 'fork'. Similarly, de-gemination is seen in the South Central variety spoken in Burgenland where the Hungarian contact language has been recently replaced by German, e.g. Hungarian *akkor > Burgenland Romani akor* 'then', Hungarian *villa > Burgenland Romani vila* 'fork'.

Due to Hungarian influence, in South Central Romani the velar fricative /x/ and the glottal fricative /h/ merged into the glottal /h/. Since both fricatives are preserved in North Vlax and North Central Romani, despite the fact that these dialects have also been influenced by Hungarian, Elšík et al. (1999, pp. 295–297) assume that the loss of the uvular /x/ in South Central Romani is triggered by Serbo-Croatian rather than Hungarian. Nevertheless, in a later study, Elšík (2007, p. 263) refers to Hungarian as the source of this sound change. Hutterer and Mészáros (1967, p. 12) note that in North Vlax Romani /x/ is sometimes replaced by /h/ due to the intensive Hungarian influence.

Hungarian influence also triggered the merger of the Early Romani uvular /řr/ with /r/ in most varieties of South Central Romani, e.g. *řom > rom* 'Romani man', *čořo > čoro* 'poor'. Less commonly, the uvular continues in the form of a geminate /rr/, merely as an allophonic variant of /r/, e.g. *řom > rrom* 'Romani man', *čořo > čorro* 'poor'. This is typical for some North Vlax varieties (Hutterer and Mészáros 1967, p. 13). The occurrence of the geminate is, however, limited to a few lexemes and its distribution is not uniform across the varieties. The development of /rr/ from /ř/ was probably motivated by the existence of consonant length in Hungarian.

10.2.2 Vowels

Like other languages of the Finno-Ugric family, Hungarian has a relatively large set of distinctive vocalic phonemes that form a set of back and front vowel pairs: /a/ – /e/, /o/ – /ö/, /u/ – /ü/. The phoneme /i/ is considered 'neutral' and therefore does not form a pair with another vowel. The distinction between back and front vowels is connected to the rule of vowel harmony. Inherited words—if they are not compounds—and suffixes can only contain either front or back vowels, e.g. *öröm* 'joy, delight' vs. *állat* 'animal'. Consequently, 'with pleasure' appears in Hungarian as *öröm-mel* while 'with (an) animal' appears as *állat-tal*. The neutral vowel /i/ can occur with both back and front vowels, e.g. *isz-om* 'I drink, drink-1SG' vs. *víz-ben* 'in water, lit. water-in'. Another specific feature of Hungarian is the existence of vowel length, which is phonologically distinctive: each vowel has both a short form and a long form.

Early Romani has no phonemic vowel length, since the historical, Old Indo-Aryan, vowel length distinction had been lost by the time the Roma migrated to Europe and the modern Romani dialects were formed (see Matras 2002, p. 34). In contrast to Hungarian, the inventory of vowel phonemes in Early Romani only includes /a/, /e/, /i/, /o/ and /u/ (see Matras 2002, p. 58).

Looking at the vowel qualities of Hungarian-influenced Romani dialects, we can conclude that contact with Hungarian enriched the Romani vowel inventory. South Central and North Vlax Romani, for instance, retain the short and long front rounded vowels /ö(:)/ and /ü(:)/ in some recent Hungarian loanwords (see Hutterer and Mészáros 1967, p. 7; Elšík et al. 1999, p. 309; Elšík 2007, p. 263; Bodnárová 2015, p. 89), e.g. Hungarian *csütörtök* > South Central Romani *čütörtök* 'Thursday', Hungarian *történet* > North Vlax Romani *törtineto* 'story'. However, as pointed out by Elšík et al. (1999, p. 309) and Cech and Heinschink (1999, p. 1), Hungarian loanwords are adapted to Romani through de-labialisation of the front rounded vowels, e.g. Hungarian *kökény* 'clackthorn' > Romani *kekéňi*. Cech and Heinschink (1999, p. 2) also note that front rounded vowels in North Vlax Romani are mostly preserved in initial position, while usually de-labialised in other positions. Sometimes the long /ö:/ in final position changes to /o:/ (Elšík et al. 1999, p. 35). This sound change is found in both South Central and North Vlax Romani, e.g. Hungarian *festő* > South Central Romani *feštó* 'painter', Hungarian *gyeplő* > North Vlax Romani *ďiplova* 'reins'.

Due to contact with dialectal Hungarian, several South Central and North Central Romani varieties contrast two short mid vowels: /e/ and /ɛ/ (or /æ/). For instance, Elšík (2007, p. 263) reports on the open-mid front

10 The Impact of Hungarian on Romani 311

vowels /æ/ and /æː/ in the South Central variety of Selice that occur mostly in loanwords. They are phonologically distinct to their closed-mid counterparts, as illustrated by the minimal pair comprising the Hungarian loanword /dæ/ 'but' and the inherited verb /de/ 'give!'. In case of some Vend Romani varieties in Hungary, Bodnárová (2015, pp. 90–91) observes three different realisations: mid [e], open-mid [ɛ] and near-open [æ]. The first realisation is in complementary distribution to the latter two, which are free variants. Also here, the phonetic realisation corresponds to the one found in the neighbouring Hungarian dialect. The three variants occur, however, not only in Hungarian loanwords but also in inherited words in which there is a tendency to use the mid vowel in the last syllable and the open vowels in all other positions. Gardner and Gardner (2008, p. 167) assume for the North Vlax Gábor Romani dialect that the existence of the distinct open-mid [ɛ] and closed-mid [e] front vowels is the result of Hungarian influence since in Hungarian they are distinct phonemes too: the short [ɛ] and the long [eː]. Gábor Romani does not, in contrast to Hungarian, have distinctive vowel length, and so the difference lies only in vowel quality. According to Cech and Heinschink (1999, p. 3), in the North Vlax Romani dialect of the Austrian Lovara the pronunciation of /e/ as open-mid [ɛ] is also influenced by Hungarian. Interestingly, only some of those persons who still speak Hungarian, the earlier contact language, pronounce the phoneme /e/ in this way. Younger speakers who have no knowledge of Hungarian have adopted the local German pronunciation of this phoneme.

Elšík (2007, p. 263) mentions another influence of dialectal Hungarian on the inventory of vowel qualities in the South Central Romani variety of the Slovak village Selice, namely the realisation of long /aː/ as [ɒː] and the short /a/ as [a]. In standard Hungarian, the long and the short sounds are pronounced the opposite way. Bodnárová (2015, p. 90) observes a similar development in the South Central Romani variety of Kisbajom. Here, the phonemes /a/ and /aː/ are both pronounced in two different ways: In inherited words or older Hungarian loanwords, the short-long phoneme pair is realised as [a] and [ɑː], while in recent Hungarian loanwords it is pronounced as [ɒ] and [aː]. The former pair of phonemes is taken from dialectal Hungarian and the realisation of the latter phoneme pair agrees with that in standard Hungarian. Bodnárová concludes that the quality of the open back vowel reflects an ongoing change in the local Hungarian dialect, which is nowadays being replaced by standard Hungarian. Indigenous Romani words and older loanwords thus follow the older, Hungarian dialectal pronunciation while recent Hungarian loanwords conform to the standard Hungarian pronunciation.

Distinctive vowel length has developed in both South Central and Vlax Romani due to Hungarian influence, e.g. in the minimal pair *sapano* 'wet' vs. *sápano* 'snake's, of snake' in Vend Romani. In case of North Central Romani, the influence of Hungarian could also have played a role in the development of distinctive vowel length in the past alongside Slovak. According to Elšík et al. (1999, pp. 309–310), long vowels in Central Romani are, similarly to Hungarian and also to Czech and Slovak, independent of the position of stress. The main processes that gave rise to long vowels in Romani are contraction and compensatory lengthening (see, e.g., Matras 2002, p. 60), e.g. *dives > dí* 'day'. For South Central Romani, Elšík et al. (1999, pp. 309–313) observe that long vowels in inherited words usually emerged in stressed syllables. They observe that long vowels may become lexicalised as well as functionalised. As a result of the former process, the lexicalised length may occur also in an irregular position (such as in closed syllables). This is illustrated by the case of adjectives where a long stem-vowel developed in predicative adjectives in contrast to the attributive adjectives where the stem-vowel remains short. Similarly, Bodnárová and Wiedner (2015a, pp. 166–168) observe that in Vend Romani the vowel length has become functionally distinctive in the imperfect suffix *-ahi* as opposed to the irrealis suffix *-áhi* (originally both marked by short *-ahi*). They explain the development of the long vowel in this case through the process of analogical extension. This process also accounts for the emergence of long vowel forms of the monosyllabic possessive pronouns, *mro/i/e* 'my', *tro/i/e* 'your.SG' and *pro/i/e* 'one's own' which are used only in connection with the words *daj* 'mother' and *dad* 'father'. Despite the similar processes that lead to the emergence of distinctive vowel length, long vowels are not distributed evenly across the dialects, nor across individual varieties of a dialect.

In the North Vlax dialect of Lovara Romani, but not in Gábor Romani, there is also distinctive vowel length in both inherited words and loanwords. Hutterer and Mészáros (1967, p. 7) and Boretzky and Igla (1993, p. 35) remark that in North Vlax Romani, similarly to Hungarian, vowels can be short or long irrespective of the stress.

Finally, the influence of Hungarian led to the introduction of vowel harmony, a linguistic feature that is highly uncommon in Indo-European languages, in the South Central Romani variety spoken in Selice. Elšík (2007, p. 263) remarks, however, that this feature is restricted to a few indigenous affixes in combination with certain Hungarian loanwords, e.g. *farkašš-a* [farkaʃːa] 'wolves' vs. *kémívešš-e* [kæːmiːvæʃːæ] 'bricklayers', *bika-ha* [bikaha] 'with a bull' vs. *kečke-he* [kætʃkæhæ] 'with a goat'. Also Boretzky and Igla (1993, p. 42 based on Vekerdi 1971) report on the existence of

10 The Impact of Hungarian on Romani — 313

limited vowel harmony in the Central-Vlax transitional variety of Gurvari in the instrumental suffix *-(e)hel-(a)ha* and the second person singular future marker *-(e)he* based on the original *-(e)ha*.

10.2.3 Stress

The stress patterns of Early Romani and Hungarian are substantially different. Early Romani had word-level grammatical stress in which either the final syllable of a lexical root or, in case an inflectional suffix is added, the suffix is stressed (see Matras 2002, pp. 62–64 for a detailed overview). In Hungarian, by contrast, the stress lies always on the first syllable. In case a verbal particle is prefixed to a verb, the particle takes the stress.

Romani dialects influenced by Hungarian differ significantly in their stress patterns. In general, a single dialect may use a mix of initial, penultimate and ultimate stress, but with a clear dominance for one pattern. North Vlax Romani, for instance, retains the conservative, final, stress. Despite the dominance of this pattern, due to contact with Hungarian the stress may also shift to the initial syllable especially in Hungarian loanwords (Hutterer and Mészáros 1967, p. 18; see also Boretzky and Igla 1993, p. 31), e.g. *furčavo* (< Hungarian *furcsa*) 'strange', *galbeno* (< Romanian *galben*) 'yellow'. In the Central Romani dialects, the stress patterns of various sub-dialects are not uniform. Elšík et al. (1999, p. 306) conclude that there is no Central Romani dialect spoken in Slovakia that shows the conservative stress pattern. The Romani dialects of western and central Slovakia exhibit initial stress, like Hungarian and Slovak. In this case, it cannot be determined to what extent the change of stress pattern was motivated by Hungarian. Elšík (2007, p. 264) mentions that stress generally shifted to the initial syllable also in some South Central Romani varieties of Slovakia and northern Hungary, a change that had been undoubtedly triggered by Hungarian. Elšík states, furthermore, that the intonation pattern of these Romani varieties is identical to that of the local Hungarian dialect. In Vend Romani, as described by Bodnárová (2015, pp. 108–109), the most common position of the stress is the penultimate syllable, while the recent, morphologically non-adapted, Hungarian loanwords are borrowed together with the Hungarian stress pattern, e.g. *felvonuláš* (< Hungarian *felvonulás*) 'procession'.

For Sinti Romani in general, Boretzky and Igla (1993, p. 33) suggest that the partial shift of stress to early positions is a change that was probably initiated by contact with South Slavic and perhaps Hungarian before the speakers came into contact with German.

10.3 Morphology

Hungarian is a Finno-Ugric language and has an agglutinative morphological structure, which is substantially different from that of the surrounding fusional or inflecting Indo-European languages, including Romani. However, due to the fact that Romani shows certain agglutinative features in its morphology, the two languages exhibit structural similarities to some extent.

In both Early Romani and Hungarian, nouns and adjectives are derived through suffixation (for Early Romani, see Matras 2002, pp. 74–76, 113–116, 119–128). In Early Romani, the formation of new verbs is also carried out by means of suffixes that are appended to the root of the verb and that precede inflectional suffixes. These suffixes are used for both denominal derivations and valency alternation. Hungarian verbal derivation affixes match the Romani pattern in both function and position. In addition, Hungarian derives new verbs by means of verbal particles, which are, on the other hand, absent from Early Romani. Additionally, Hungarian uses suffixes and verbal particles to add aktionsart marking to verbs. In Early Romani, aktionsart was not marked morphologically (see Matras 2002, pp. 117, 152, 155, 161). In the case of indefinites, Early Romani makes use of both prefixes and suffixes while in Hungarian only prefixes are used.

With regard to inflection, Early Romani nominal inflection distinguishes between a masculine and a feminine gender, singular and plural number and shows a three-layer case system typical of the New Indo-Aryan languages (Matras 2002, pp. 72, 78–94). Hungarian, on the other hand, does not have grammatical gender but also distinguishes between singular and plural. Case is marked by either case suffixes or postpositions. In contrast to Hungarian, Early Romani is not believed to have distinguished morphologically between the comparative and the superlative of adjectives. Both are marked by the suffix *-eder* (see Elšík and Matras 2006, p. 146). The inherited verbal inflection of Romani consists of a present stem and a perfect stem that are followed by the respective sets of inflectional suffixes (see Matras 2002, pp. 117–118, 135–136). In Hungarian, verbs are also inflected by means of suffixation but a verb has only one stem. Unlike Early Romani, Hungarian uses infinitive constructions and an analytical construction to express future tense, formed with the verb *fog-* and the infinitive verb. Early Romani has no infinitive and future tense is not morphologically distinct from present tense.

10.3.1 Derivational Morphology

The vast majority of Hungarian derivational markers were borrowed into Romani merely as part of lexical loans and have not become extended to the inherited lexicon. Nevertheless, Romani also borrowed some derivational morphemes from Hungarian which are either productive or, more frequently, lexically limited in the respective Romani dialects.

The most frequently borrowed derivational suffix is the abstract nominaliser *-(i)šag-* which originates in Hungarian *-ság-/(-ség-)*, while the morpheme *-i-* represents a remnant of the regular adaptation marker of verbs, *-in-*. In North Central Romani, the suffix *-išag-* is employed in both inherited and borrowed verbs, e.g. *xiň-išag-os* 'diarrhoea' from Romani *xinel* 'to defecate', or *pis-išag-os* 'writing, script' from the Slavic-origin *pisinel* 'to write' (Elšík et al. 1999, p. 330). Interestingly, however, it has not gained (full) productivity in South Central and North Vlax Romani where the pre-Hungarian derivational suffixes (i.e. the inherited *-ipe/-ibe* or the Greek-origin *-imo*) are used instead. Vend Romani varieties are exceptional in that the Hungarian-borrowed suffix *-išág-* is attested in the pre-Hungarian lexicon too, such as in *phur-išág-o* 'old age' (<*phúro* 'old') (see Bodnárová 2015, pp. 124–125). In North Vlax Romani, the suffix *-šag-* in combination with inherited roots is attested but very rare, e.g. *roman-šag-o* 'Romani way of living'<*romano* 'Romani' (Cech and Heinschink 1999, p. 90).

In some South Central Romani varieties, the derivational suffix *-áš-*, rarely *-éš-/-íš-* (cf. Hungarian *-ás-*, *-és-*), gave rise to a few action nouns, e.g. *muk-áš-i* 'divorce, separation'<*muken* 'to leave, let' or *pelin-éš-i* 'quarrel'<*pelínen* 'to quarrel' (cf. Elšík 2007, p. 265). Agentive nouns are exceptionally derived with the Hungarian-borrowed suffixes *-áš-/-oš-* in some South Central varieties, e.g. *džuvj-áš-i* 'womanizer'<*džuvli* 'woman' (Elšík 2006, pp. 53–54). In Vend Romani, the suffix derives nouns denoting ethnic or kin groups, e.g. *kopan-áš-i* 'trough-maker Roma' (<Slavic *kopana* 'trough') or *bob-oš-i* 'name of a Romani sub-group' (<Slavic *bob* 'bean').

Regarding adjectival derivation, the Hungarian-borrowed suffix *-oš-*, or rarely *-eš-* or *-áš-*, (cf. Hungarian *-(V)s*) is attested in a few adjectives in some South and North Central Romani varieties (see Boretzky and Igla 1991, p. 13; Elšík et al. 1999, pp. 338–339; Bodnárová 2015, pp. 146–147), e.g. *kiral-oš-no* 'of cottage cheese'<*kíral* 'cottage cheese', *bríg-áš-no* 'sad'<*bríga* 'sorrow'.

The influence of Hungarian is also apparent in the formation of indefinite pronouns and adverbs. For instance, the free-choice marker *akár-* (<Hungarian *akár-*) '-ever' is attested in South Central, North Vlax (see

also Boretzky and Igla 1991, p. 22) and Hungarian Sinti Romani but not in North Central Romani. In addition, South Central Romani borrowed the specific marker *vala-* (<Hungarian *vala-*) 'any-', and some varieties use the free-choice marker *bár-* (<Hungarian *bár-*) '-ever' instead of *akár-*. Universal markers, as pointed out by Elšík and Matras (2006, p. 290), are rarely borrowed in Romani in general. A noteworthy exception is the Hungarian-borrowed marker *minden-* 'every-' in the South Central variety of Selice (e.g. *minden-káj* 'everywhere') as well as in the transitional dialect of Gurvari Romani (e.g. *minden-ko* 'everyone'). The Hungarian prefix *se-* 'no-' for negative indefinites has not been borrowed into Romani. Further Hungarian prefixes borrowed into South Central Romani are *am-* (deictic contrast) and *uďan-* (deictic identity), the latter being attested also in North Vlax. They are used to translate Hungarian expressions, such as in *am-odá* (cf. Hungarian *am-az*) 'that other one' and *uďan-odoj* (cf. Hungarian *ugyan-ott*) 'on the same place'.

In Vend Romani, the Hungarian-borrowed derivational marker of manner adverbs, *-ón/-on*, is productive and competes with the original marker *-e* (Halwachs 1998, pp. 77–78; Bodnárová 2015, p. 159), e.g. *phár-ón* (cf. *phár-e*) 'hardly' < *phár-o* 'hard'. Some South Central varieties of Slovakia borrowed the Hungarian adverb-deriving suffix *-kor* denoting a certain point in time (Elšík et al. 1999, p. 314) but use it only with a few inherited Romani words, e.g. *epašrat-kor* 'at midnight'. Furthermore, Elšík and Matras (2006, p. 235) observe that the dialectal Hungarian ablative suffix *-tú* (standard Hungarian *-tól/-től*) was introduced into South Central Romani via ablative borrowings from Hungarian. This suffix, however, is not a productive case marker in Romani as it is merely used to derive adverbs with ablative meaning from a few inherited adverbs, e.g. *khéral-tú* 'from home'.

The impact of Hungarian on Romani verb formation consists of the borrowing of a few Hungarian derivational suffixes, the internal re-analyses of Romani suffixes according to the Hungarian pattern and the emergence of verbal particles in Romani.

Most commonly borrowed is the Hungarian denominal derivational suffix *-(V)z-*. In Romani, the suffix has the form *-az-/-áz-* which is followed by the Greek-origin adaptation marker *-i(n)-*. This became a productive means to derive new verbs only in some South Central Romani varieties (see Elšík et al. 1999, p. 365; Elšík 2006, pp. 33–35), e.g. Versend Romani *lavut-áz-ínen* 'to play violin' < *lavut-a* 'violin'. In North Vlax Romani, the suffix is only rarely attested with pre-Hungarian nouns, e.g. *buť-az-ij* 'to work' < *buť-i* 'work' (Cech and Heinschink 1999, p. 93). Vend Romani uses, in contrast to other South Central varieties, a different denominal marker borrowed from Hungarian, namely *-ál-* (from Hungarian *-(V)l-*), e.g. *máčh-ál-ín-el* 'to fish' < *máčh-o* 'fish' (see, e.g., Bodnárová 2015, p. 185).

The original, Romani, transitive marker *-av-* has been re-analysed and is used in Central and North Vlax Romani as a causative marker. Elšík (2007, p. 269) suggests, based on dialect comparison, that the retention and productivity of causative marking in South Central Romani are motivated by the Hungarian pattern. The influence of contact languages on the usage and function of the Romani causatives has been observed earlier by Hübschmannová and Bubeník (1997) based on the dialect comparison of South Central and North Central Romani. They show that in South Central Romani the marker *-av-*, like the corresponding derivational marker in Hungarian causatives, forms both first ('to make someone do') and second causatives ('to make someone make someone else do'), while in the Slovak-influenced North Central Romani it is employed only in first causatives and is not productive, thus conforming to the Slovak pattern.

South Central Romani often borrows the Hungarian causative suffix (*-tat-/-tet-/-at-/-et-*) together with the verb root and marks additionally the causation by the Romani suffix *-av-*, e.g. *táncol-tat-ináv-en* (< Hungarian *táncol-tat*) 'to make someone dance'. Despite the double marking, these formations express single causation. Elšík (2006, pp. 35–38; also Elšík 2007, p. 269) reports on the analogical extension of double causative marking (the Hungarian *-tat-* and the Romani *-av-*) to some inherited and internally derived verbs in the South Central Romani variety spoken in Selice, e.g. *ďijáz-(a)tat-in-av-en* 'to make someone sing' < *ďijáz-in-en* 'to sing'.

Another Hungarian-induced contact feature in Romani is the emergence of iterative or frequentative de-verbal derivations. According to Elšík (2006, pp. 26–27; 2007, p. 269), contact with Hungarian led to the re-analysis of the inherited Romani transitive suffix *-ker-* as a valency-neutral iterative suffix. Iterative derivations are fully productive in Romani dialects influenced by Hungarian (see, e.g., Cech and Heinschink 1999, pp. 92–93; Elšík et al. 1999, pp. 370–371), with the exception of Hungarian Sinti, which has not developed iteratives. A voiced variant of the iterative suffix, i.e. *-ger-*, has emerged in South Central Romani. The iterative suffix is sometimes extended by a preposed morpheme such as *-el-* or *-er-* in North Central Romani and *-in-* in South Central Romani (Elšík et al. 1999, p. 371). The use of the extended suffix is conditioned either on the quality of the stem-final consonant, the origin of the verb or the number of syllables in the verb (see Bodnárová 2015, p. 186).

Bodnárová and Wiedner (2015b, p. 205) report on an ongoing change in some Vend Romani varieties where the dialectal German-origin prefix

318   Z. Bodnárová and J. Wiedner

um- competes with the inherited suffix *-ker-/-ger-* in order to express the iterative meaning. Since contact with German was lost and Hungarian became again the only contact language of these Romani varieties, the prefix marking modelled on dialectal German is decreasing in favour of the suffix marking that is promoted by the Hungarian pattern.

The most striking influence of Hungarian with regard to verb derivation is the development of verbal particles in South Central and North Vlax Romani (see Kiefer 2010, pp. 158–160; Schrammel 2005; Bodnárová and Wiedner 2015b). Elšík et al. (1999, p. 373) remark that verbal particles are also found in North Central Romani, but their distribution is limited because they functionally compete with the well-established aktionsart prefixes that are modelled on Slovak, the recent contact language of North Central Romani. Verbal particles in Hungarian Sinti are, judging by the examples given in Mészáros (1980, p. 12), apparently of German origin. Nevertheless, the recent influence of Hungarian on the further development of verbal particles in Hungarian Sinti should not be disregarded. Other Romani dialects that have been in contact with both German and Hungarian include Austrian Lovara (North Vlax) and Vend Romani (South Central). In Austrian Lovara Romani, as noted by Cech and Heinschink (1999, p. 85), verbal particles most likely emerged under the earlier Hungarian influence and have been further shaped by later German influence. The development of verbal particles in Vend Romani, as mentioned by Bodnárová and Wiedner (2015b), is a more complex issue, since some varieties show significant influence from German (e.g. German-borrowed particles) while others do not. Owing to the fact that the Vend Roma were simultaneously in contact with both German and Hungarian while residing in the Austro-Hungarian border region, it is difficult to determine which of the two languages played the initial role in the development of verbal particles in these Romani varieties.

As observed by Elšík et al. (1999, p. 373), verbal particles are generally translated into South Central Romani based on the Hungarian model (e.g. *ánde čukinel* < Hungarian *be-csuk* 'to close, lock up, lit. into-close') and are only borrowed exceptionally (e.g. *síja džal* < Hungarian *széjjel-megy* 'to dissolve, lit. apart-go'). Kiefer (2010, p. 159) points out a similar process in North Vlax Romani where the verbal particles are exact translations of the corresponding Hungarian particles when the meaning is transparent to the speakers; otherwise, the particle is borrowed. Some Vend Romani varieties in Hungary differ from other South Central varieties in that they tend to borrow verbal particles directly from German and Hungarian even though their

10   The Impact of Hungarian on Romani   319

meaning is not transparent, such as the resultative particle *el* < Hungarian *el* (Bodnárová and Wiedner 2015b, p. 210).

The overwhelming majority of Romani particle verbs are direct translations of the respective Hungarian particle verbs (see, e.g., Elšík 2007, p. 269). Thus, verbal particles are not a productive means to derive new verbs independently using the particle verbs of the contact language. Elšík (2007, p. 269) notes, however, that a few exceptions of internal word formations are attested in South Central Romani, such as *ánde sov-* 'fall asleep, lit. inward sleep' vs. *el-alsz-* 'fall asleep, lit. away sleep'. Bodnárová and Wiedner (2015b, pp. 205–207) consider such exceptions to be the result of a process where either the verb component of the particle verb is substituted by a light verb or the German-origin particle verb is being synchronised with the corresponding Hungarian expression.

As hinted above, verbal particles emerged in Romani through various processes including grammaticalisation of Romani spatial adverbs, loan translations and direct lexical borrowings from Hungarian. Bodnárová and Wiedner (2015b, p. 201) discuss an additional process found in Hungarian Vend Romani which involves the grammaticalisation of some German expressions as verbal particles. For instance, the German-borrowed prefix *ver-* was re-interpreted under Hungarian influence as verbal particle (i.e. *fer*, resultative aktionsart), in accordance with the corresponding Hungarian verbal particle *el-*.

10.3.2 Inflectional Morphology

The impact of Hungarian on the inflectional morphology of Romani is much less significant than on derivational morphology (see also Matras and Adamou, this volume, for the general trend in Romani). The distribution of the majority of features discussed in this section is limited to a couple, or even to a single variety, of South Central Romani. The only Hungarian-induced features that are widespread inter-dialectally or intra-dialectally include gender neutralisation in the third person singular pronoun, the emergence of infinitive constructions and superlative formations that are morphologically distinct from comparatives.

South Central Romani varieties in northern Hungary mark the inherited third person plural pronoun *ón* 'they' additionally by the Hungarian plural marker *-k*, resulting in *ónk* 'they'. Elšík (2000, p. 77) assumes that the development of *ónk* 'they' (cf. *ój* 'he, she, it') was triggered by its phonological similarity to the corresponding Hungarian pronoun *ők* 'they' (cf. *ő* 'he, she, it'). Within the area of this innovation, namely in the Romani variety spoken in the Hungarian village Mátraverebély, the Hungarian plural marker has also been extended to the past third person plural forms of verbs, irrespective of their origin, e.g. *kerd'-ék* (< *kerd'-e*) 'they made', *lüvind'-ék* (< *lüvind'-e*) 'they shot', as well as the copula *siň-ék* (< *siň-e*) 'they were'. Furthermore, the Hungarian plural marker has also infiltrated some varieties of Vend Romani (Bodnárová 2014, pp. 130–135). Here, the Hungarian plural suffix *-(V)k* is employed in the morphologically non-adapted consonant-final nouns borrowed from Hungarian, e.g. both Romani and Hungarian *rák* (plural *rák-ok*) 'crab'. The Hungarian plural marker is also employed in the accusative (e.g. *rák-ok* 'crab (ACC)'), which does not correspond to either the Hungarian (cf. *rák-ok-at* 'crab (ACC)') or the expected Romani form (cf. *rák-en* 'crab (ACC)'). Therefore, these plural forms are best seen as situated somewhere on the imaginary line between code-switching and borrowing.

A further contact-induced feature in the domain of plural marking is reported by Elšík (2007, pp. 266–267), namely the development of associative plurals in the South Central Romani variety of Selice, which replicates the Hungarian pattern. Associative plural forms denote a person and other people who are associated with this person, e.g. *kémíveš-ingere* (cf. Hungarian *kőműves-ék*) 'bricklayer and his work team' vs. *kémíveš-e* (cf. Hungarian *kőműves-ek*) 'bricklayers'.

Synthetic case marking is rarely borrowed into Romani and is lexically restricted. The only well-attested example is the Hungarian accusative marker *-t* which is employed with the inherited reflexive pronoun *pe(s)* 'oneself', resulting in *pet* (exceptionally *pest*), in several South Central Romani varieties of the Hungarian-Slovak border region. Elšík et al. (1999, p. 342) see this form as a result of an analogy with the original second person form *tu-t* 'yourself' that comprises the irregular accusative suffix *-t*. Contrary to Elšík et al., Bodnárová (2015, pp. 168–169) assumes that the suffix *-t* is borrowed from Hungarian, cf. Hungarian *magá-t* 'oneself-ACC'. Recent data[1] support the latter claim by showing the expansion of the Hungarian accusative suffix *-t* to the relative (*ak-ast* 'who-ACC'), indefinite (*valak-ast* 'someone-ACC') and interrogative pronouns (*k-ast* 'who-ACC').

The influence of Hungarian resulted in the loss of morphological gender distinction in the third person singular pronoun in some varieties of South Central and North Vlax Romani (Elšík 2000, p. 76). These dialects and even their varieties are not consistent as to whether the original feminine (i.e. *ój*, *voj*) or masculine form (i.e. *óv*, *vov*) is generalised as the

10 The Impact of Hungarian on Romani

gender-neutral third person pronoun of the meaning 'he, she, it'. Furthermore, Bodnárová (2015, p. 115) attributes the increase of feminine nouns in Vend Romani to both German and Hungarian influence. In South Central Romani, the majority of consonant-final nouns are adapted by the adaptation suffixes *-o/-i* into the masculine class, e.g. *eďetem-o* (masc.) < Hungarian *egyetem* 'university'. At the time when Vend Romani was in contact with German, it borrowed several consonant-final German nouns without any adaptation suffixes and assigned to them the gender value found in the source language, e.g. *ampós* (masc.) < German *Amboss* (masc.) 'anvil', *mašin* (fem.) < dialectal German *Maschin* (fem.) 'machine'. Following this pattern, Vend Romani is currently borrowing extensively Hungarian consonant-final nouns, which are morphologically not adapted, e.g. *eďetem* < Hungarian *egyetem* 'university'. As Hungarian has no grammatical gender, these loan nouns are randomly assigned either masculine or feminine gender when borrowed into Romani. Thus, unlike in other South Central Romani varieties, there is a considerable increase in the number of feminine loan nouns in Vend Romani at the expense of masculine nouns.

The overt marking of superlative forms through prefixation has developed, to some extent, in all Romani dialects in contact with Hungarian. South Central Romani directly borrowed the Hungarian prefix *leg-* (> Romani *leg-* or *lek-*) 'the most' which precedes the comparative form of adjectives (*bar-eder* 'bigger' > *leg-bar-eder* 'the biggest') thus replicating the Hungarian pattern (*nagy-obb* 'bigger' > *leg-nagy-obb* 'the biggest'). The fact that both Romani and Hungarian form comparatives by suffixation leads Elšík (2007, p. 266) to suggest that the survival of the Romani comparative suffix is also an outcome of contact with Hungarian. Hungarian Sinti uses the prefix *leg-* or its de-voiced variant *lek-* as in *lek-šuk-eder* 'the most beautiful' (Mészáros 1980, p. 13). Most North Central Romani varieties express the superlative degree with the prefixes *jeg-*, *neg-* or *meg-*. According to Elšík et al. (1999, p. 336, also Elšík and Matras 2006, p. 154), the former two prefixes may have resulted from the contamination of the Hungarian *leg-* by the Romani numeral *jekh* 'one' and the Slovak superlative prefix *naj-*, respectively. The latter prefix, though it is phonetically similar to *leg-*, seems to be a grammaticalised form of the particle *mek/meg* (< Hungarian *még*) 'still'. The Hungarian prefix is also attested in some North Vlax varieties as well as in the transitional Cerhari dialect (Elšík and Matras 2006, p. 151). Here, the prefix *leg-* is preposed to the Romanian-origin comparative particle *maj* which is followed by the base, non-comparative, form of the adjective, e.g. *leg-maj baro* 'the biggest'.

322   Z. Bodnárová and J. Wiedner

There is no doubt that the introduction of the infinitive to South Central Romani is modelled on Hungarian (Boretzky 1996, p. 5) while in case of Vend Romani German influence should also be taken into account. Considering the fact that infinitive constructions are also well established in North Central Romani, the influence of Hungarian must have played an initial role in the emergence of infinitives in this Romani dialect as well. Infinitives are also present in Hungarian Sinti but, based on the comparison with German Sinti, they are most likely to have emerged under German influence. Infinitive constructions are absent in North Vlax Romani. However, Hutterer and Mészáros (1967, p. 26; also Boretzky 1996, p. 5–6) mention direct borrowing of Hungarian infinitives into North Vlax Romani, especially with less established Hungarian loan verbs, e.g. *žalas sórakozni* (cf. Hungarian *járt szórakozni*) 's/he was going to have fun'. A similar process is described by Elšík and Matras (2006, p. 179) for the South Central variety of Selice. Here, the Hungarian infinitive suffix *-ni* (*-ňi* in Romani) may be added to Hungarian roots or even to inherited roots with Hungarian-origin derivational markers, e.g. *huhuráz-ňi* (cf. Hungarian *gombáz-ni*) 'to collect mushrooms'. This innovative form, which does not require the complementiser *te*, competes with the Hungarian-replicated infinitive described above.

Regarding TAM marking, direct borrowing of Hungarian morphemes into Romani is insignificant. An example is given for Vend Romani in Bodnárová (2015, pp. 197–198) where the Romani future marker *-a* competes with an analytic construction which comprises the borrowed auxiliary *fogín-el* (< Hungarian *fog*) 'will' and the infinitive verb, e.g. *foginá t' užárel* 'I will wait'. The future is double marked since the auxiliary *fogín-el* is inflected for future tense, i.e. by the suffix *-a*.

10.4 Syntax

Due to the fact that Hungarian marks all grammatical cases except the nominative by means of suffixation, word order in the language is relatively free. Within noun phrases, however, word order is fixed. Here, the first position is reserved for the article, the demonstrative or the indefinite pronoun. Attributive adjectives, which unlike predicative adjectives are not inflected, follow the determiner and immediately precede the noun they describe.

Following the 'conservative' syntactic pattern (see Matras 2002, pp. 166–167), the object in Romani is usually placed after the verb (VO).

The subject may occur both before and after the verb (SV and VS). The first position of a noun phrase is usually reserved in Romani for a determiner, followed by an attributive adjective. The final position is occupied by the actual noun. Here, Romani and Hungarian share a similar word order pattern without having influenced each other at an earlier point in time.

Elšík (2007, p. 272) points out some clause-level features of South Central Romani that originate in Hungarian. These include (1) the preverbal position of focused constituents, (2) the fully grammaticalised word order in noun phrases in which the modifiers obligatorily precede the noun and (3) postposed Hungarian-origin adpositions and the focus particle *iš* (< Hungarian *is*) 'also, too'. The latter two contrast with the adpositions of pre-Hungarian origin and the inherited focus particle *te* 'also, too' both of which are preposed. Postpositions are also attested but are rare in North Vlax Romani (see Hutterer and Mészáros 1967, p. 65). Examples are *tar* 'from' (e.g. *opral tar* 'from above'), *vorta* 'opposite' (e.g. *e khéres vorta* 'opposite the house') and *fele* '-wards' (e.g. *opre fele* 'upwards').

The linear order of verbal particles and verbs in South Central Romani roughly agrees with that of Hungarian (see, e.g., Bodnárová and Wiedner 2015b, p. 201). In sentences without a focused constituent, the verbal particle directly precedes the verb, e.g. *fer bujinďa* 's/he hid; lit. (resultative verbal particle) s/he hid' in *Fer bujinďa pal ék kašt.* 'S/he hid behind a tree'. On the other hand, the verbal particle is placed after the verb in sentences with a focused constituent, since the immediate preverbal position is occupied by this focused constituent, e.g. *Pal ék kašt bujinďa fer* 'S/he hid behind a tree (and not somewhere else)'. Pronominal direct objects take the position between the verbal particle and the verb while in Hungarian they are placed after the particle verb (cf. Wogg and Halwachs 1998, pp. 18–19). The position of verbal particles in North Vlax Romani differs from that described above in that verbal particles, unlike in Hungarian, take the post-verbal position also in sentences without a focused constituent (Hutterer and Mészáros 1967, p. 22, Vekerdi and Mészáros 1974, p. 159), e.g. *bešel téle* 's/he sits down, lit. sits-down', cf. South Central Romani *téle bešel* or Hungarian *le-ül* 's/he sits down, lit. down-sits'. Vekerdi and Mészáros (1974, p. 160) further remark that verbal particles only sometimes precede the verb, especially in subordinated clauses.

The most salient Hungarian influence on Romani syntax manifests itself in the extensive borrowing of coordinators and subordinators. Both South Central and North Vlax Romani borrowed the disjunctive coordinator *vaď*/*vaj* (cf. Hungarian *vagy*) 'or' and *vaď – vaď* 'either – or' as well as the adversative *de* (cf. Hungarian *de*) 'but', but not the conjunctive coordinator 'and' (cf. Elšík 2007, p. 273; Vekerdi and Mészáros 1974, p. 104). As recent data suggest, some South Central Romani dialects even borrow the conjunctive *ost* from dialectal Hungarian *oszt* 'and'. Modelled on Hungarian, several South Central and North Vlax varieties distinguish two adversative coordinators, *de* 'but' and *hanem* 'but rather', and two disjunctive coordinators, *taj/haj* 'and' and *meg/pedig/pale/pa* 'in turn'.

The most commonly borrowed subordinator is *hoď/hot/hoj* (< Hungarian *hogy*) 'that', which has a function of introducing complement clauses. It occurs not only in South Central and North Vlax but also in North Central Romani. There is a tendency in Romani to borrow adverbial subordinators from Hungarian which introduce causal and temporal clauses, e.g. *mërt* and *mivël* 'since, because', *mire* and *miëlét* 'before', *még/míg* 'until' and *mióta/miúta* 'since' (see, e.g., Vekerdi and Mészáros 1974, p. 150; Elšík 2007, p. 273).

Some South Central varieties borrowed the Hungarian relativising prefix *a-*, e.g. *a-kija* (cf. Hungarian *a-hová*) 'where (relative adverb)' vs. *kija* (cf. Hungarian *hová*) 'where (interrogative adverb)' (Elšík et al. 1999, p. 348). Other South Central varieties copy the function of relativisers in Hungarian, such as the relativiser 'who' that is used with nouns denoting humans, while the relativiser 'what' refers to non-human head nouns (see Elšík 2007, p. 275).

Traces of Hungarian influence are also found in the case system. Some inherited cases of Romani are re-interpreted to express syntactic roles according to the Hungarian model. For instance, the dative case is now used in South Central Romani to mark predicate complements as well as the directive meaning 'to move against something', following thus the Hungarian pattern, e.g. *géli bótoškiňa-ke* (cf. Hungarian *elment boltosnő-nek*) 'she started to work as a saleswoman', or *le kaštes-ke man múkav* (cf. Hungarian *a fá-nak dőlök*) 'I lean against the tree'. The case system of North Vlax Romani also changed under Hungarian influence, resulting, for example, in the use of the instrumental case in temporal function *angla kodo šele beršen-ca* (cf. Hungarian *száz év-vel ezelőtt*) 'hundred years ago'. Some prepositions are also used in accordance with the Hungarian pattern; an example is the usage of the adposition *tel* 'under' in South Central and North Vlax Romani to express future distance ('in X's time') and telic extent ('in') relations (Elšík and Matras 2006, p. 264).

One of the outstanding features of Hungarian is that nouns preceded by a quantifier are usually marked as singular, e.g. *sok fa* 'many trees; lit. many tree'. As a result of Hungarian influence, in the South Central Romani varieties spoken in the Hungarian Nógrád County nouns following a quantifier are optionally marked as singular. This concerns especially Hungarian-borrowed nouns, e.g. *dú čaládo* (cf. Hungarian *két család*) 'two families; lit. two family'. Number agreement between the verb and the subject that includes a quantifier also conforms to the Hungarian rule, according to which both constituents are marked for singular, e.g. *dú čaládo bešel* 'two families live; lit. two family lives'.

Contact with Hungarian has not only enriched the Romani system, but sometimes led to its simplification. One example is the loss of case agreement between adnominal cardinal numbers and the noun, *dúj* (*dúj-e*) *muršenca* 'with two men', as reported by Elšík (2007, p. 271) for South Central Romani.

10.5 Lexicon

Of all linguistic domains addressed in the present chapter, the impact of Hungarian is strongest in the area of the lexicon, be it in the form of loan translations or direct lexical borrowings. Loan translations are very common in Romani. Examples were discussed in the respective sections. Regarding lexical borrowings, Elšík (2009, pp. 276–277) and Bodnárová (2015, p. 278) each attempted to enumerate Hungarian loanwords in one variety of South Central Romani with roughly the same result: the highest number of Hungarian loanwords in South Central Romani is represented by nouns (roughly 60% of all nouns in Elšík's corpus of 1536 lexemes and Bodnárová's corpus of 4129 dictionary headwords) and is followed by that of verbs, adjectives and adverbs, each amounting to between 40 and 50%. Function words are less prone to borrowing (ca. 20%) but, on the other hand, they often replicate the Hungarian pattern (see, e.g., the case of verbal particles in Sect. 10.3.1). Vekerdi (1980) compared the amount of Hungarian loans in various Romani dialects spoken in Hungary based on the analysis of short text data. He comes to the conclusion that the amount of Hungarian loans increases with the time the Romani dialect has been influenced by Hungarian. Thus, the highest number of Hungarian loanwords can be found in South Central Romani, followed by Gurvari Romani and, subsequently, by Vlax Romani. The number of Hungarian loans in Sinti Romani is insignificant. Vekerdi (1980, p. 367) notes, however, that the amount of Hungarian loans depends mostly on the topic of actual speech.

10.6 Conclusion

Romani dialects that are characterised by long-lasting intensive contact with Hungarian exhibit the influence of this contact language in all linguistic areas. Although some Hungarian-origin features are widespread inter-dialectally, the distribution of most features discussed here is limited to either a sub-dialect or a group of closely related varieties. Other features have developed only in certain varieties of different Romani dialects.

The impact of Hungarian, or any other post-Greek contact language, on Romani attracted the focus of researchers only in recent years, lagging behind growing interest since the 1980s in the study of language contact phenomena. The influence of Hungarian on Romani has been most thoroughly described for the case of South Central Romani, which is in fact the Romani dialect influenced to the greatest extent by Hungarian. The Hungarian layer is less striking in North Central and North Vlax Romani, since these dialects are, or have been, also influenced by other contact languages, namely by West or East Slavic dialects in the former and Romanian and other post-Hungarian contact languages in the latter case. Hungarian Sinti has not been studied with regard to the Hungarian impact, most probably due to the small size of this community and the fact that this Romani dialect is almost extinct by now.

The impact of Hungarian is most noticeable in the lexicon of the Romani dialects under Hungarian influence. A significant amount of content words are either loanwords or loan translations from Hungarian, whereas Romani function words turn out to be more persistent. Following the lexicon, the impact of Hungarian is the second strongest in the area of phonology. Hungarian-induced linguistic changes include the emergence of distinctive vowel and consonant length as well as the introduction of rounded front vowels and Hungarian stress pattern, thus enriching, simplifying or replacing the Romani phonological system. To a lesser extent, Hungarian has also had an impact on Romani morphology. Here, Hungarian influenced the derivational morphology of Romani more strongly than the inflectional morphology. Noteworthy in this respect are the internal re-analysis of inherited suffixes according to the Hungarian model and the introduction of verbal particles into Romani. In syntax, the impact of Hungarian is perceptible as well. Besides changes in word order and in the usage of grammatical cases corresponding to the Hungarian patterns, Hungarian influence in syntax is evident in the extensive borrowing of Hungarian coordinators and subordinators.

Note

1. The recent data on South Central Romani come from the project Linguistic Atlas of Central Romani (Czech Science Foundation) 2011–2013.

References

Bodnárová, Zuzana. 2014. Loanword integration: A case study of Kisbajom Romani. *Romani Studies* 24 (1): 71–91.

Bodnárová, Zuzana. 2015. Vend Romani: A grammatical description and sociolinguistic situation of the so-called Vend dialects of Romani. PhD thesis. Charles University, Prague.

Bodnárová, Zuzana, and Jakob Wiedner. 2015a. Analogical extension of vowel length in Vend Romani. *Acta Linguistica Hungarica* 62 (2): 157–170.

Bodnárová, Zuzana, and Jakob Wiedner. 2015b. A comparative study of verbal particles in varieties of Vend Romani. *Romani Studies* 25 (2): 197–216.

Boretzky, Norbert. 1996. The new infinitive in Romani. *Journal of the Gypsy Lore Society*, 5th ser., 6 (1): 1–51.

Boretzky, Norbert, and Birgit Igla. 1991. Morphologische Entlehnung in den Romani-Dialekten. Arbeitspapiere des Projektes „Prinzipien des Sprachwandels", 4. Universität GH Essen, Fachbereich Sprach- und Literaturwissenschaften, Essen.

Boretzky, Norbert, and Birgit Igla. 1993. Lautwandel und Natürlichkeit. Kontaktbedingter und endogener Wandel im Romani. Arbeitspapiere des Projekts „Prinzipien des Sprachwandels", 15. Universität GH Essen, Fachbereich Sprach- und Literaturwissenschaften, Essen.

Cech, Petra, and Mozes Heinschink. 1999. *Basisgrammatik. Arbeitsbericht 1A des Projekts Kodifizierung der Romanes-Variante der österreichischen Lovara hrsgg*, v. Dieter W. Halwach. Wien: Verein Romano Centro.

Elšík, Viktor. 2000. Dialect variation in Romani personal pronouns. In *Grammatical relations in Romani* (Current issues in linguistic theory 211), ed. Viktor Elšík and Yaron Matras, 65–94. Amsterdam and Philadelphia: John Benjamins.

Elšík, Viktor. 2006. Affix extraction: A case study on Hungarian Romani. PhD thesis, Charles University, Prague.

Elšík, Viktor. 2007. Grammatical borrowing in Hungarian Rumungro. In *Grammatical borrowing in cross-linguistic perspective* (Empirical approaches to language typology, 38), ed. Yaron Matras and Jeanette Sakel, 261–282. Berlin and New York: Mouton de Gruyter.

Elšík, Viktor. 2009. Loanwords in Selice Romani, an Indo-Aryan language of Slovakia. In *Loanwords in the world's languages: A comparative handbook*, ed. Martin Haspelmath and Uri Tadmor, 260–303. Berlin: Mouton De Gruyter.

Elšík, Viktor, and Yaron Matras. 2006. *Markedness and language change: The Romani sample* (Empirical approaches to language typology, 32). Berlin and New York: Mouton de Gruyter.

Elšík, Viktor, Milena Hübschmannová, and Hana Šebková. 1999. The Southern Central (ahi-imperfect) Romani dialects of Slovakia and northern Hungary. In *Das österreichische Romani im europäischen Kontext*, ed. Dieter Halwachs and Florian Menz, 277–391. Klagenfurt: Drava.

Gardner, David J., and Sari A. Gardner. 2008. A provisional phonology of Gabor Romani. *Romani Studies* 18 (2): 155–199.

Halwachs, Dieter W. 1998. *Morphologie des Roman. Basisgrammatik der Romani-Variante der Burgenland-Roma. Arbeitsbericht 3a des Projekts Kodifizierung und Didaktisierung des Roman*. Graz: Romani-Projekt.

Halwachs, Dieter W., and Michael Wogg. 2002. *Burgenland-Romani*. Munich and Newcastle: Lincom.

Hübschmannová, Milena, and Vít Bubeník. 1997. Causatives in Slovak and Hungarian Romani. In *The typology and dialectology of Romani* (Current issues in linguistic theory, 156), ed. Yaron Matras, Peter Bakker, and Hristo Kyuchukov, 133–145. Amsterdam and Philadelphia: John Benjamins.

Hutterer, Miklós, and György Mészáros. 1967. *A lovári cigány dialektus leíró nyelvtana*. Budapest: Magyar Nyelvtudományi Társaság.

Kiefer, Ferenc. 2010. Areal-typological aspects of word-formation. The case of aktionsart-formation in German, Hungarian, Slavic, Baltic, Romani and Yiddish. In *Negation in Uralic languages*, ed. Matti Miestamo, Anne Tamm, and Beáta Wagner-Nagy, 601–614. Amsterdam and Philadelphia: Benjamins.

Matras, Yaron. 2002. *Romani: A linguistic introduction*. Cambridge: Cambridge University Press.

Mészáros, György. 1980. *A Magyarországi szinto cigányok: Történetük és nyelvük*. Budapest: Magyar nyelvtudományi társaság.

Schrammel, Barbara. 2005. Borrowed verbal particles and prefixes in Romani: a comparative approach. In *General and applied Romani linguistics*, ed. Dieter Halwachs, Barbara Schrammel, and Gerd Ambrosch, 99–113. Munich: Lincom Europa.

Vekerdi, József. 1971. The Gurvari Gypsy dialect in Hungary. *Acta Orientalia Academiae Scientiarum Hungaricae* 24 (3): 381–389.

Vekerdi, József. 1980. Numerical data on loan words in Gypsy. *Acta Linguistica Academiae Scientiarum Hungaricae* 30 (3–4): 367–373.

Vekerdi, József, and György Mészáros. 1974. *A magyarországi oláh cigány nyelvjárás mondattana*. Budapest: Magyar nyelvtudományi társaság.

Wogg, Michael, and Dieter W. Halwachs. 1998. *Syntax des Roman. Arbeitsbericht 6 des Projekts Kodifizierung und Didaktisierung des Roman*. Oberwart: Verein Roma.

11

Romani and Contact Linguistics

Yaron Matras and Evangelia Adamou

11.1 Introduction

Romani is a language that is permanently in contact: there isn't a single monolingual Romani-speaking community, and probably no adult individual is monolingual in Romani. Bilingualism almost always starts at an early age, often in the family. As a minority community, often socially marginalized and dependent on contacts with the majority population for their livelihood, Roma always acquire the language of the surrounding majority population, and often that of regional minority groups as well, in a situation where bilingualism is unidirectional; that is, Roma acquire other languages but members of neighbouring populations only very seldom acquire Romani. This sociolinguistic asymmetry in power relations makes Romani the recipient of contact influences from neighbouring languages. Since Romani populations are geographically dispersed but show very similar sociolinguistic relations with their respective neighbouring populations, Romani dialects exhibit a range of contact influences from different

Y. Matras (✉)
School of Arts, Languages, and Cultures,
University of Manchester, Manchester, UK
e-mail: yaron.matras@manchester.ac.uk

E. Adamou
National Centre for Scientific Research in France (CNRS), Villejuif, France
e-mail: evangelia.adamou@cnrs.fr

© The Author(s) 2020
Y. Matras and A. Tenser (eds.), *The Palgrave Handbook of Romani Language and Linguistics*, https://doi.org/10.1007/978-3-030-28105-2_11

languages. All this makes Romani a fascinating 'laboratory' for the study of bilingualism and contact-induced language change. Not only does Romani offer an opportunity to compare the impact of diverse contact languages on a rather homogeneous stock of inherited structures, the historical migrations of Romani populations have led to changing contact constellations, resulting in successive layers of contact influences within individual dialects. This enables us to correlate the historical depth of contact with patterns of contact-induced change in particular areas of structure (see Matras 2002, Chapter 8; and see Elšík and Matras 2006).

Our aim in this chapter is to review the contribution that the study of contact-induced change in Romani has had to developing concepts, methods and theory in contact linguistics, as well as to present a bird's-eye view of structural contact phenomena that are assumed to have affected Romani as a whole and thus to be constitutive of the language, and those that characterize contact-induced changes in contemporary Romani dialects. We draw on descriptive work in Romani linguistics as well as on a large body of studies that have been devoted specifically to contact phenomena in Romani. We also refer in some instances to data from the online Romani Morpho-Syntax Database (RMS). Not only is this the largest and most comprehensive online resource that documents the dialects of Romani (and indeed the dialects of any language, as far as we are aware), it is also the only descriptive-typological language documentation resource that systematically tags items (including word forms and grammatical morphemes, and in some instances entire categories) for borrowing and historical depth of borrowing (see below). As a language documentation resource, RMS itself thus demonstrates important advances in the study of contact linguistics.

11.2 Approaches to Contact in Romani Linguistics

11.2.1 Topics

Contact influences have figured prominently in the dialectological study of Romani since its early beginnings. Miklosich's (1872–1880) seminal work on the dialects of Romani gave much consideration to loanwords and used them to trace the migrations of Romani-speaking populations across Europe and to propose a classification of the dialects of Romani based on the constitutive impact of the respective contact languages on individual dialect groups. On the basis of the shared Greek component in all Romani dialects,

Miklosich asserted that a Greek-speaking area had been the 'European homeland of the Gypsies' and the point of departure for subsequent migrations across the European continent.

The Indo-Aryan genealogical heritage of Romani had been well established since the appearance of Pott's (1844–1845) work. Nonetheless, many early discussions continued to group together the Indo-Aryan dialects of Romani with speech variants attributed to various itinerant populations. Of the latter, those that were characterized by a Romani-derived lexicon received attention as distinct contact varieties. Haugen (1949) described the use of Romani vocabulary embedded into Norwegian as an identity marker, questioning the 'languageness' of such stylistic hybrids, while Hancock (1970) and Boretzky (1985) both drew parallels between such so-called mixed varieties (vernacular forms of the majority language with a Romani lexical component) and creoles as in-group vernaculars that owed their emergence to a blend of structures of different origins. Thomason and Kaufman (1988) discussed Angloromani (the 'mixed' variety of English Romani Gypsies, which embeds Romani vocabulary into vernacular English), based on constructed examples from the literature, as one of the examples of what they called 'broken transmission' of languages across generations. They proposed that Angloromani was a 'mixed language' that had emerged as a result of a wholesale replacement of Romani grammar by that of the contact language, English, a scenario that is disputed (see Matras 2010). The presence of Romani-derived core lexicon along with, in some cases, traces of grammatical formation (especially in word derivation), in several different attested varieties in itinerant communities led to the emergence of a comparative discussion context and the postulation of a language type now commonly referred to as 'Para-Romani' (see Bakker and Courtiade 1991; and see Bakker, this volume). From a purely structural viewpoint, such varieties have been defined as blends of Romani lexicon with non-Romani grammar, which emerged following the abandonment of Romani as an everyday, all-purpose community language, coupled with the motivation to flag group identity as well as to have a group-internal means of communication. Usage-based studies have since defined this as an 'emotive mode' of speech whereby scattered group-internal, usually Romani-derived lexical items are used to evoke solidarity and the processing of a turn, utterance or discourse portion from the perspective of a particular set of shared values (see Matras et al. 2007; Matras 2010).

Not unrelated is the contribution of Romani vocabulary to other languages, in particular slang varieties. Lists of slang items of Romani etymology have been provided in both early and more recent studies (for an overview see Matras 2002, p. 249), with a number of contributions addressing theoretical implications including the association of Romani with anti-establishment defiance which makes it a prestige variety in the social periphery (cf. Leschber 1995; Matras 1998a; see also contributions to Matras 1998b).

The wealth of contact phenomena attested in Romani prompted a series of works aimed at compiling a comprehensive overview of borrowed structures across Romani dialects for particular categories (cf. Friedman 1985; Boretzky and Igla 1991, 1993; Matras 1994b, 1996; Elšík 2001). Drawing on the RMS Database, Elšík and Matras (2006) postulate borrowing hierarchies for Romani dialects, while Matras (1998b, 2009, 2015) draws on Romani examples to propose generalizations and universal predictions on the borrowability of structural categories. Modern descriptive discussions of Romani (e.g. Igla 1989; Matras 1994a) generally give prominent attention to contact phenomena, and many case studies are devoted to contact phenomena in individual dialects, such as Elšík's (2009) discussion of lexical loans in Selice Romani of Slovakia.

Surprisingly little attention has been devoted to sociolinguistic and discourse-related aspects of contact in Romani. In what is a rather isolated case study, Réger (1979) discusses second language acquisition, while Matras (2009) draws on Romani examples in his discussion of code-switching. Halwachs (1993) introduces patterns of language maintenance and language shift in the multilingual repertoires of Romani migrants, while Adamou and Granqvist (2015) and Adamou (2016) introduce a corpus-based evaluation of Romani switching patterns with a focus on inter-speaker variation. Leggio (2015) discusses the use of multilingual language resources in a Romani online forum, Leggio and Matras (2017) discuss the impact of contact on the use of orthographic variants in social media, and Abercrombie (2018) shows how a multilingual repertoire shapes attitudes to language and standardization.

11.2.2 Concepts

Alongside the many descriptive contributions, discussions of contact phenomena in Romani have given rise to a number of novel concepts that have enriched the field of contact linguistics more generally. All Romani dialects display a split in the assignment of lexicon (nouns, verbs and adjectives) to two distinct types of inflection, the first continuing early Modern Indo-Aryan (with traces of late Middle Indo-Aryan) while the second relies on inflectional markers adopted from Byzantine Greek. Generally, pre-European lexicon is assigned to the first, while European loans, including most (but not all) Greek loans, are assigned to the second, which is thus the more productive for new vocabulary except for internal derivations. This split had been coined, using a term borrowed from Indo-European linguistics, 'thematic' (i.e. pre-European) vs. 'athematic' (i.e. European) grammar, by Kaufman (1979), though the terminology is often attributed to Hancock (1995 and earlier manuscripts). Bakker (1997) demonstrates that Greek-derived so-called athematic morphology replicates a pattern used in Greek to adopt loanwords from other languages, while Elšík (2000) introduces etymology systematically as one of the dimensions of the Romani nominal paradigm, adopting in later work the more bespoke terms 'oiko-clitic' (indigenous, i.e. pre-European) and 'xenoclitic' (used for loans, i.e. European) (cf. Elšík and Matras 2006; see also Elšík, this volume).

Controversial is the notion of Romani as a 'deficient language', proposed by Boretzky (1989) in an early attempt to provide an overview of contact behaviour in the language. Boretzky's claim that the wholesale borrowing of entire categories into Romani (notably in the domain of particles, especially adversatives) might point to the absence of those structural categories in the pre-European forerunner or 'Proto-Romani' is refuted by Matras (1998b), who links the wholesale adoption of certain categories to their discourse functionality as markers of 'monitoring-and-directing' of hearer participation and therefore the bearers of a cognitive load linked to the speaker's degree of assertive authority when dealing with propositions that challenge or are not directly inferable from a shared presupposition domain. Matras (1996, 1998b) introduces the term 'fusion' to account for such wholesale replacement and demonstrates that the process observed in Romani can also be found in other languages in contact. Hinting at that observation, Auer (1999) introduces the term 'fused lect' with reference to examples taken from Holzinger's (1993) description of Sinti Romani. Opinions have since been split, with some accepting Auer's position that the high rate of German lexical and grammatical borrowings appearing alongside spontaneous lexical insertions from German in the speech of the Romani-German bilingual Sinti Romani community offers an example of an in-between stage that could link 'borrowing' in the plain sense and the formation of a 'mixed language'. Others regard Sinti Romani, much like all other Romani dialects and indeed countless minority or indigenous languages in contact with a powerful majority language, as a case of far-reaching borrowing which nevertheless demonstrates notable constraints and does not, in fact, offer any pathway for a gradual transition to the kind of languages that have been labelled 'mixed languages' (as defined in Bakker and Mous 1994; Matras and Bakker 2003, and elsewhere) and which combine predication grammar from one source with core lexicon and/or nominal grammar from another.

Above we already mentioned the term 'Para-Romani' (Bakker and Courtiade 1991), widely used to describe the replication of a sizeable structural component, primarily lexical and some grammatical relics, following language shift from Romani to the majority or regional language. For some authors (cf. Matras 2010), the concept entails a notion of post-vernacular language use that is associated on the one hand with language death and so-called afterlife, and on the other hand with the need to maintain a distinct in-group mode of communication akin to the functionality of secret lexicons, widely found among various itinerant populations, whether of Romani or other backgrounds. Other authors have argued for a distinction between Para-Romani varieties and secret languages (cf. Bakker 1998), regarding the former as part of a class of 'intertwined' languages that owe their emergence to a pre-determined combination of lexicon and grammar from distinct sources, as part of the process of new identity-building. Other explanations offered for Romani 'mixed dialects' (Boretzky and Igla 1994) suggest a more volatile process of identity renegotiation, possibly as part of a process of partial assimilation into indigenous itinerant populations (cf. Hancock 1992). Noteworthy is thus the widespread adoption in Romani linguistics of the notion of a 'Para-' language as one that is historically related but functionally and structurally confined. With a focus on this constrained and specialized functionality, some authors have associated Para-Romani with wholesale euphemism/dysphemism (Burridge and Allen 1998) or bystander-oriented deixis (Rijkhoff 1998), and more recently with an 'emotive mode' of communication (Matras et al. 2007; Matras 2010).

Shifting contact languages in the history of Romani as a whole and its individual varieties have inspired a model that distinguishes historical layers of contact. First introduced by Matras (1998b) and then adopted as a category in the RMS Database and subsequently in discussions of borrowing hierarchies in Romani (Matras 2002; Elšík and Matras 2006), the model identifies, for each variety of the language, an older, recent and current contact language (or languages). The Older L2 is one that has had considerable, prolonged impact on the forerunner of a particular dialect. Speakers, especially elderly speakers, are often aware of this impact, even if that L2 is no longer spoken by members of the community. The Recent L2 is the contact language that is no longer used by the entire community of speakers of a particular Romani dialect as their everyday language outside the home, but which may still be used by the parent or grandparent generation (or by the first generation of immigrants, in migrant communities) and to which the younger generation may still be exposed, at least occasionally. The Current L2 is the principal contact language used by the community for everyday interaction with the non-Romani majority, and often as a family language alongside Romani. For example, Lovari Romani as spoken in Germany (Maras 1994a) has Romanian as Older L2, Polish as Recent L2 and German as Current L2, while Ajia Varvara Vlax (Igla 1989) has Romanian as Older L2, Turkish as Recent L2 and Greek as Current L2. Contact languages change, however, not only as a consequence of the migration of Roma, but sometimes as a result of shifting power relations among languages in situ. Thus, in some areas of southern Slovakia, Hungarian has shifted from Current to Recent L2 as Romani-speaking communities adopted Slovak as Current L2. The method of stratifying contact influences in diachronic depth has made it possible to assess the susceptibility of individual structural categories to borrowing and often to repeated, 'replacive' borrowing and convergence, laying the foundations for a model of implicational hierarchies of grammatical borrowing (Matras 1998b, 2009) as well as repositioning the discussion of borrowing within a model of markedness (Elšík and Matras 2006).

In regard to the latter, Elšík and Matras (2006) describe borrowing, in its incipience, as a strategy that supports bilingual speakers in successfully managing language choices in interaction: it reduces the need for choices to be made among word forms or morphemes of equivalent function, and so it increases communicative efficiency without compromising the separation of languages and language contexts and the potential for flagging identity that this separation entails (see also Matras 2009, pp. 159–160). For that reason, there is no single correlation between borrowing and 'markedness', as defined by criteria such as complexity and internal differentiation. Discussing implicational borrowing hierarchies as evidenced by a sample of Romani dialects, Elšík and Matras (2006, p. 371) show how different hierarchies align themselves in different ways with respect to the features 'complexity' and 'differentiation', respectively. For example, the value 'plural' is more prone to borrowing than the value 'singular' and is at the same time 'marked' as showing higher complexity and lower differentiation than singularity. By contrast, the value 'nominative' (in nominal case paradigms) shows higher borrowability than the value 'oblique', but is unmarked through lower complexity and greater internal differentiation.

Work on Romani has also had an impact on our understanding of convergent processes or 'pattern replication' (Matras 2009). Friedman's (1985) discussion of particular structures of Romani in the Balkan context was followed by Matras's (1994b) attribution of wholesale syntactic-typological convergence in the Balkans to Early Romani, coining the concept of a 'Balkanised New Indo-Aryan language'. The concept of 'contact-induced functionalisation' of categories (Matras 1994a, 1998d) as applied to Romani played a role in inspiring Heine and Kuteva's (2005) much-cited model of contact-induced grammaticalization. Case-specific discussions on the overall theme of convergence have been devoted to the re-functionalization of inherited subject clitics in Romani as a means of adopting typological distinctions from the contact language, such as German verb–subject inversion (Matras 1999) or the split among attributive predications in Spanish (Adamou 2013), as well as the functionalization of Romani location expressions to replicate German aktionsart particles (Igla 1992), among others. Tenser (2016) introduces the concept of 'semantic map borrowing' in connection with the re-functionalization of case markers in Northeastern Romani dialects in contact with Russian, Polish and Latvian.

A number of Romani dialects show exceptional contact behaviour in their replication of verb conjugation paradigms with borrowed lexical verbs. Igla (1989) first pointed out the survival of Turkish paradigms with Turkish lexical verbs in the Ajia Varvara dialects of Greece. This phenomenon, since attested in various Romani dialects of the Balkans (and incipiently, in other regions as well), has been described as a form of 'compartmentalized' grammar (Friedman 2013; Matras 2015) or as a stage in an interrupted process of mixed language creation (Adamou 2010; Adamou and Granqvist 2015). Introducing methods from experimental psycholinguistics to the study of Romani, Adamou and Shen (2019) demonstrate that among Romani populations that also speak Turkish, language mixing is a dynamic process. Their experimental results show that cognitive cost in sentence processing depends on whether Turkish verbs have a more frequent Romani counterpart variant.

Finally, while the focus on contact behaviour in lexicon has tended to be on the rate of retention of pre-European (Indo-Aryan) words (cf. Boretzky 1992), viewed from the perspective of lexical borrowability Romani has since been presented as the reference point for 'heavy borrowing', showing a staggering borrowing rate of 62.7% on the comparative measure introduced by Haspelmath and Tadmor (2009) (cf. Elšík 2009). When comparing rates of contact words in natural speech (all word-classes considered), Adamou (2016) also finds that the Romani corpora are on the upper side of a language mixing scale, showing 20–35% tokens from the current contact language(s).

11.3 Proto-Romani and Early Romani as Languages in Contact

The pre-European forerunner of Romani ('Proto-Romani') demonstrates a number of traits that point to convergent developments with the so-called Dardic or northwestern frontier languages of the Indian sub-continent into what will have been a Central Indo-Aryan language (see Matras 2002). In particular, the evidence is apparent in the presence of agglutinated case affixes and the renewal of the past tense conjugation. The transitivizing suffix *-ar-* may have been a direct borrowing from the northwestern languages. Pre-European lexical loans point to contact with Iranian languages and Armenian (see Scala, this volume), and it appears that some grammatical items, such as the adjectival comparative marker *-eder*, the adjectival prefix *bi-* 'without', the indefinite marker *či* and the modal *šaj* 'can', may have been Iranian borrowings, while the nominal derivation marker in *-ik* is shared with Iranian and Armenian. Several syntactic-typological properties of Romani, such as the prepositioning of local relation adverbs (i.e. the development of prepositions), the emergence of external ('remote') tense markers that follow person affixes (*s-om-as* be-1SG-REM 'I was'), the reduction of the infinitive in modal constructions, the use of resumptive pronouns with head nouns in non-subject roles in relative clauses and the loss of Middle Indo-Aryan relativizers in *y-/j-* and reliance instead on conjunctions derived from interrogatives, could have emerged in Proto-Romani in contact with Iranian languages.

Constitutive of 'Early Romani'—the term used to designate the common European or Anatolian ancestor of present-day Romani dialects for which individual forms can be reconstructed drawing directly on material that is continued in contemporary dialects—was contact with Byzantine Greek. Apart from several dozen lexical items of Greek origin that tend to be retained by Romani dialects today, as well as grammatical lexicon such as the adverbs *pale* 'again', *palpale/parpale/papale* 'back', and *komi* 'still', the word for 'tomorrow' (*tasja/tajsa/taha-*), and the numerals *efta* '7', *oxto* '8', and *enja* '9' as well as higher numerals, Greek has had a striking influence on Romani morphology, both derivational and inflectional. In derivation, we find the suffix for ordinal numerals *-to* (as in *duj-to* 'second'), the nominalizer *-imo(s)* pl. *-imata*, indefinite *-moni*, participial *-imen* and the adjectival derivational suffixes *-itik-/-itk-/-ick-/-ik-*, among others. In inflection, Romani adopts nominal class markers *-o(s)*, *-i(s)* and *-a*, plural *-i* from Greek and adjectival endings *-o* and *-a*. With verbs, Greek tense/aspect endings, present

-iz-/-az-/-in-, etc., and aorist *-s-*, are adopted. These inflectional configurations constitute the 'athematic' or 'xenoclitic' grammar paradigms that serve to integrate loan vocabulary from subsequent contact languages in the individual dialects. With nouns, the Greek inflection template figures in the nominative case and serves as a basis to which inherited non-nominative case markers are added (see Elšík, this volume). With verbs, the Greek aspectual markers serve as derivational morphemes that identify the verb stem as a loan, often in combination with inherited valency markers, and are followed by inherited person markers. Some Romani dialects maintain a Greek 3SG present tense person marker *-i* with loan verbs.

It is plausible that many of the Balkan properties of Romani morpho-syntactic typology emerged in contact with Greek. This appears to be most obvious in the development of a pre-posed definite article from inherited deictic elements (cf. Matras 2002), as well as the grammaticalization of oblique pronouns from demonstratives. The distinction between factual and non-factual clauses and complementizers (see Adamou and Matras, this volume) may also owe its history to convergence with Greek, like the shift to VO word order and the variable position of subject and verb in the sentence. The structure of adverbial and relative clauses tends to be compatible with Greek, though it may have its origin in pre-European (Western Asian) contacts.

11.4 Contact in Contemporary Romani Dialects

Detailed discussions of the impact of principal contact languages and language groups appear in this volume in the contributions by Meyer (on Slavic), Friedman (on Turkish) and Bodnárová and Wiedner (on Hungarian). Individual Romani dialects have absorbed influences also from most other European languages including Modern Greek, Romanian, Italian, French, Spanish, Basque and Finnish. In the following, we provide a brief sketch of typical influences in individual areas of structure.

11.4.1 Phonology

Although there is a lack of studies on this particular area, it is evident that prosody is particularly susceptible to contact influences and Romani dialects are often recognizable by their distinct prosody patterns which mirror elements of their current contact languages. Arvaniti and Adamou (2011) draw attention to the similar intonation patterns in wh- and polar questions as realized in Greek Thrace Romani and Modern Greek (see Adamou 2016 for more details and Grigorova 1998 for a similar study on Romani and Bulgarian prosodic convergence). Stress patterns remain conservative in many dialects, with accentuation falling on root or particular grammatical affixes (see Baló, this volume), but some Romani dialects of Western Europe have, by and large, shifted to word-initial stress, in contact with English and German, while the dialect of Prizren shows, in contact with Albanian, penultimate stress. Stress shifting patterns have been noted in individual dialects, where stress occasionally shifts to an earlier syllable than the one habitually carrying stress. The reasons for this phenomenon are not entirely clear; they could be related to speakers' mixed dialect background, with focus marking replicating the contact language's model, or to metrical reasons (see Adamou and Arvaniti 2014). Northwestern and Central European dialects of Romani often adopt distinctive vowel length in contact with English, German, Finnish and Hungarian. The inventory of phonemes is, as a rule, enriched by the incorporation of lexicon from the current and often earlier contact languages, but borrowed phonemes are often restricted to borrowed lexicon. The phonemes /f/ and /ts/ are present primarily in loanwords but entered the language during the period of pre-European contacts. Loan phonemes from contemporary contact languages include rounded and central vowels, diphthongs and palatals. There is a discernible adoption of phonetic values (points and mode of articulation) which tends to affect the inherited component and is thus subject to 'backwards diffusion' (Matras 2009). Examples are the articulation of /r/ as uvular [ʀ] in contact with German or the realization of /a/ as [ɑ] reported for British Romani. In many cases, such shifts in articulation may lead to changes in the phonemic system; such is the tendency towards merger of /s/ and /š/ in Greek dialects of Romani, the velarization of /l/ to /ł/ in contact with Polish, the differentiation of /e/ and /ə/ in contact with Romanian, consonant gemination in contact with Finnish and Italian, the merger of the glottal /h/ with velar /x/ in contact with Russian and Greek, and the adoption of palatalization of dental and velar consonants in many Romani dialects of Eastern Europe.

11.4.2 Morphology

Borrowed nominal derivational morphology from contemporary contact languages, including agentive, diminutive and feminine markers, typically accompanies borrowed nouns but does not always diffuse to the pre-European lexical component (but, e.g. of such diffusion; see, e.g. Meyer, this volume). There is, however, a widespread tendency to rely on borrowed derivational markers for indefinite expressions. These include Romanian-derived *vare-,-godi*, *i-*, *bilo-*, *de-*, and *se-* (South Slavic), *-far* (Albanian), *vala-*, *akar-* (Hungarian), *nibud'-* (Russian) and more. Romani dialects in contact with Polish, Russian, Ukrainian and Slovak and to a lesser extent those in contact with Lithuanian, Bulgarian and Greek, borrow productive aktionsart prefixes to modify inherited verb stems. Polish Romani, for example, shows almost wholesale borrowing of the full set of aktionsart (Slavic aspect) prefixes, leading to derivations like *za-pindžkirel* 'to introduce' from *pindžkirel* 'to recognize' (Polish *za-poznać* and *poznać*), *do-resel* 'to obtain' from *resel* 'to arrive' (Polish *do-stąpić* and *stąpić*), *pše-džal* 'to cross, climb over' from *džal* 'to go' (Polish *prze-chodzić* and *chodzić*). An attestation of productive borrowing of word-changing morphology is British Romani *ladj-fully* 'shamefully', while in Romani dialects in contact with Hungarian, the nominalizing suffix *-išág-* is adopted (see Bodnárová and Wiedner, this volume, also for additional borrowed derivational affixes of Hungarian origin). Alongside the borrowing of morphological forms, Romani dialects in contact with strongly agglutinative languages, notably Hungarian and Turkish, show an increase in the productivity of inherited valency morphology (causative and passive) (see Elšík, this volume).

Borrowed inflectional morphology is relatively widespread in nominative plural markers, such as *-urj-/uri* of Romanian origin in Vlax, *-e* of Southern Slavic origin in the (predominantly Western) Balkan dialects and *-ides* of Greek origin in the eastern Balkan dialects. All these attach to borrowed European nouns, not just from the source language of the markers themselves, and Vlax *-urj-* even attaches to some Greek loans that entered the language prior to the period at which the suffix itself was acquired (e.g. *for-uri* 'towns', from Greek *foros*). It is also common in the inflection of adjectives to form comparative and superlative markers, where those are inflected morphemes in the contact languages, as in Hungarian (see Bodnárová and Wiedner, this volume). Both nominal plurals, and comparative and superlative markers on adjectives, can in fact be considered as borderline items between inflection (which relates to a constituent's position in the sentence or discourse) and derivation (which affects standalone meaning).

A number of curious instances of morphological borrowing can be found across the dialects. The first is the borrowing of plural inflectional endings that attach to personal pronouns, where the shape of the pronouns in the contact language is similar, leading to an outcome where Romani adopted plural third person pronouns that are identical or near-identical to those of the contact language: the original Romani third person pronouns are *ov/oj* 'he/she' and *on* 'they'; they appear in most Romani dialects, sometimes with minor phonological stem modifications. The form of the third person plural pronoun in some varieties of Hungarian Romani (Romungro) is *on-k*, which replicates the plural ending of the Hungarian third person pronoun (singular *ő*, plural *ő-k*). In Slovenian Romani, the form is *on-i*, replicating the pronominal form in Slovene (singular *on*, plural *on-i*), and in some varieties of Thracian Romani that are or were in contact with Turkish, the form is *on-nar*, replicating the Turkish structure (singular nominative *o*, singular oblique *on-*, plural *on-lar*). In all three contact languages, the ending that is used to indicate plurality on the pronoun is also the ending that is used to indicate plurality on nouns.

A somewhat comparable example is found in the past tense verb conjugation paradigm of a number of Romani dialects of Bulgaria in historical contact with Turkish. The inherited Romani past tense concord markers contain the consonant *-m* in the first person (singular *-om/-em/-im*, depending on dialect, plural *-am*) and a consonant *-n* in the second person (singular *-an*, plural *-en*). They resemble the corresponding Turkish singular forms 1sg *-Vm* and 2sg *-Vn* (with variation subject to vowel harmony). The Turkish plural pronouns are augmented forms of the singular morphemes: 1PL *-VmVz*, 2PL *-VnVz*. By analogy, these Romani dialects form a past tense 1PL concord marker *-amus* and a past tense 2PL marker *-enus*. Here too, the agglutinative marking of plurality in the contact language makes the marker *-us* analysable. It is replicated in Romani with inherited verbs, replacing the original marker (which is preserved in other dialects of the language). A similar process is found in Slovene Romani. Here, the original Romani past tense 1PL marker *-am* has been replaced by the corresponding Slovene affix *-amo* on the basis of the formal resemblance between the two. The analogy is then extended to the Romani 2PL (originally *-an* or *-en*), for which the Slovene affix *-ate* is adopted (which has no formal resemblance to the original Romani form).

A 'genuine' borrowing of a pronominal form is found in Molisean Romani. Here, inherited object pronouns are cliticized, replicating the structure in the regional Italian vernacular. But for the 1PL and the reflexive pronoun, the Italian form *čə* is adopted: *dikkajom-čə* 'I hurt myself'. English Romani, now extinct but documented in a series of amateur notes spanning two centuries (cf. Matras 2010), shows the borrowing of the English genitive *-s* in word compositions with inherited material, as in *daval's tem* 'heaven' (literally 'God's country'), as well as the English gerundial marker *-in(g)*, as in *mandi sas wel'in keri* 'I was comin' home'. For the most part, borrowed

342   **Y. Matras and E. Adamou**

inflectional endings on verbs are confined to borrowed lexicon. As mentioned above, many Balkan Romani dialects show systematic compartmentalization whereby Turkish verb inflection accompanies Turkish derived lexical verbs:

Kalburdžu Romani dialect of Sindel in Northeastern Bulgaria (RMS, BG-008)

(1) pandž-e   daka-en-da   sona   bašla-də   te   konušu-i
     five-OBL   minute-OBL.PL-ABL   after begin-PAST.3SG   COMP   talk-3SG
     'After five minutes he started to talk'.

Here, in fact, the Turkish-derived verb 'begin' takes the Turkish-derived conjugation ending of the 3SG in the preterite, while the equally Turkish-derived verb 'talk' in the subjunctive takes the Greek-derived 3SG ending -*i* that is reserved for loan verbs in various other Romani dialects. It is not uncommon for borrowed modal verbs to retain the inflectional ending of the source language. Particularly common are frozen impersonal forms in the 3SG, such as *može* 'it is possible', from South Slavic, used as an impersonal expression 'can', but occasional person-inflected forms are also found, such as Serbian Romani *mora-m* 'I must', which retains the Serbian 1SG ending. The following example from the Romani dialect of Parakalamos in Greece shows three distinct layers of Greek-derived verb inflection: the impersonal form in the 3SG in *prepi* 'must, it is necessary', the person-inflected form *bor-o* 'I can' and the incipient use of the Greek person inflection in the Greek-derived lexical verb *diavaz-o* 'I read', contrasting with the integration into Romani inflection of another Greek-derived verb, *vojt-iz-av* 'I help' (drawing on the loan verb integration marker -*iz*- borrowed from Greek into Early Romani):

Parakalamos in the northwestern Greek province of Epirus (RMS, GR-002)

(2) na   *bor-o*   te   *diavaz-o*   soske   *prepi* te   vojt-iz-av
     NEG   can-1SG   COMP   study-1SG   because   must   COMP   help-LOAN-
                                                                          1SG

     me   daj-a
     my.OBL   mother-OBL
     'I cannot study because I have to help my mother'.

11.4.3 Syntax and Morpho-Syntactic Convergence

Various areas of structure show examples of 'pattern replication' (Matras 2009) or restructuring of form-meaning alignment. In nominal typology, we find tendencies towards loss of definite and indefinite articles under the

11 Romani and Contact Linguistics   343

influence of Polish and Russian and of loss of gender agreement and gender distinctions under the influence of Finnish and Hungarian. While word order in the noun phrase generally remains intact, dialects in the Balkans, especially those in contact with Romanian and Greek, show optional stylistic postpositioning of demonstratives and adjectives (see Adamou and Matras, this volume). In contact with Russian, Romani shows some significant changes to case alignment (see Tenser 2016), as can be seen in the following example:

Russian Romani, Ekaterinburg (RMS, RUS-008)

(3) man   na   sys   kxere
    I.OBL   NEG   was.3SG   at.home
    'I was not at home'.

cf. Russian:

menya   ne   bylo   doma
I.ACC   NEG   was.3SG   at.home

cf. Polish Romani (RMS, PL-003)

me   na   somys   khere
I.NOM   NEG   was.1SG   at.home

In the verb phrase, dialects in contact with German and Hungarian show a tendency to calque aktionsart particles drawing on location expressions, as in Sinti Romani (Germany) *kerau pre* 'I open' (lit. 'I.make up'), based on German *ich mache auf*. In contact with German, there is a tendency to formalize verb–subject inversion when the first sentence position is occupied by another constituent (see Matras 1999), while in contact with Hungarian there is a tendency for the copula to appear in final position in declarative clauses. Romani dialects in contact with Western Slavonic languages tend to bring forward the pronominal object to pre-verbal position:

Bergitka Roma, Krakow (RMS, PL-007)

(4) jov   łes   na   dikhla
    he.NOM   him.OBL   NEG   see.PAST.3SG
    'He didn't see him'.

cf. Macedonian Arli, Skopje (RMS, MK-002)

ov   na   dikhlja   ole
he.NOM   NEG   see.PAST.3SG   him.OBL

In the Romani dialects of Central Europe and Ukraine, subject agreement in modal complement clauses is neutralized and the subordinate verb takes on a uniform inflection, derived in most cases from either the 3SG or 2SG, leading in effect to the emergence of a 'new infinitive' (see Adamou and Matras, this volume). Calquing also leads to the emergence of auxiliary verbs in some dialects, as in the emergence of a perfect auxiliary based on the verb 'to have' (itself derived from the inherited verb 'to hold') in contact with Greek—*therav kerdo* 'I have done'—or based on the verb 'to be' in dialects in contact with Macedonian and of a progressing auxiliary from the verb 'to be' in English Romani: *shum to jaw* 'I am going to walk'.

Adamou (2013) reports that Mexican Romani speakers developed a distinction between attributive predications using the copula *si* 'to be' and the third person subject clitic pronouns in *l-*. She argues that this innovation aims to replicate the Spanish *ser* vs. *estar* 'to be' copula variation, a claim that has since been confirmed by quantitative evidence (Padureet al. 2018). This increase in complexity in Mexican Romani also offers an interesting counter-example to the hypothesis of simplification of alternatives among bilinguals as a strategy to reduce cognitive load. However, when Adamou et al. (2019) compare the Romani–Spanish copula preferences to those of Mexican Spanish monolinguals, they find that simplification of alternatives is currently taking place among bilinguals, with the generalization of the Romani clitics in third person affirmative clauses driving the generalization of the Spanish copula *estar*. The diachronic and synchronic Mexican Romani data therefore support bidirectional processes of conceptual transfer.

11.4.4 Grammatical Vocabulary

As noted above, Romani has served as a model for the postulation of borrowing hierarchies in the domain of grammar and especially grammatical function words (Matras 1998b, 2009), allowing a significant step in the revision of Thomason and Kaufman's (1988) somewhat crude borrowing hierarchy in which 'function words' were treated as a wholesale, uniform category on the borrowing scale.

All Romani dialects borrow the adversative conjunction 'but' from the current or recent contact language, a testimony to its particular susceptibility to borrowing. The borrowing hierarchy 'but' > 'or' > 'and' was demonstrated for Romani dialects, with reference to the historical stratification of contact languages (Older, Recent and Current L2). The same hierarchy has been identified in a number of other cross-linguistic samples, prompting the suggestion that long-term borrowing is triggered by cognitive factors that relate to the processing of interrupted presuppositional chains, leading to 'interference' or spontaneous innovation and, if duly propagated, to structural change (Matras 1998b). Romani discourse markers such as fillers and tags are invariably those of the current contact language, demonstrating the 'fusion' of so-called monitoring and directing operations across speakers' repertoire of linguistic resources; this suggests that speakers have all linguistic resources available to them at all times, but also that Romani speech norms lack impediments on conformity to a distinctive set in these particular areas of structure, contrasting with what is otherwise an overall strong sense of language loyalty and cross-generation language transmission. Similarly, all phasal adverbs ('still', 'already', 'no longer'), focus particles ('even', 'only', 'every', 'also/too') and sequential discourse markers (of the type 'and then', 'and so') are borrowed from recent or older contact languages.

Exclusively of European origin are the focal quantifiers 'every' (*svako/sako* from Slavic, *her/er* from Turkish), 'entire/whole' (*celo* from Slavic, *intrego* from Romanian, *-lauter* from German, *kre(j)t* from Albanian), 'same' (*isto* from South Slavic) and frequently also the ordinal 'first' (*pervo* from Slavic, *eršto* from German). In Balkan dialects in direct contact with Turkish, the Turkish numeral classifier *tane* is frequently replicated for the contrastive focus of a numeral (Adamou 2016). In the numeral system, '1000' is usually a European loan: Sinti and Central dialects *ezero(s)* (Hungarian), Northeastern *tisač* (Slavic), Vlax *mija* (Romanian) and Balkan *hilja* (Greek). Expressions for days of the week, time adverbs and qualifying sentential adverbs (e.g. 'probably', 'exactly') also tend to be borrowed.

When it comes to other domains of function words, the picture is more mixed. Indefinite expressions are certainly among the categories with very high 'matter' replication, both of full indefinite expressions (such as, in respective dialects, Slavic *ništa* 'something/nothing', Romanian *uni* 'some', Hungarian *šoha* 'never', Greek *tipota* 'nothing', Turkish *hič* 'none' and more) and of indefinite markers to which inherited ontological morphemes are added (such as Vlax Romani *vare-so* 'something, *vare-kon* 'somebody' with *vare-* from Romanian).

Based on RMS data, we can also identify adpositions that are most prone to borrowing from contemporary (older, recent or current) contact languages:

(5) Frequently borrowed adpositions by meaning:
opposite, between, against, among, around, through, without, instead of, except for
beyond, since, during, towards, with, from

As discussed by Elšík and Matras (2006, pp. 267–269), the general semantic hierarchy that emerges from this pattern is one in which peripheral relations (those involving more than one reference point, or movement) show greater borrowability than core relations. In addition, we encounter once again the semantics of contrast and discontinuity (and thus breaking of presuppositional inference) as a factor supporting borrowability (see Matras 2009). The final two positions on the list, 'with' and 'from', represent relations that are usually encoded in Romani by case relations but represented in individual dialects by borrowing of the preposition 'with' from German, Greek, Spanish or Italian and of 'from' from German or Slavic. Borrowed adverbial subordinators are common especially for simultaneity ('while'), cause and result ('because'), concession ('although') and negative circumstance ('without'), with a number of dialects borrowing conditional conjunctions, respectively, from Turkish, Finnish, Italian, Russian and Romanian. In contact with Slavic, Romani dialects tend to borrow the conditional particle that attaches to the verb phrase, *by*, *li* or *dali*. A number of interrogatives also show frequent borrowing, notably 'how much' and (less frequently) 'when'.

The factual complementizer (inherited *kaj*) is replaced by loans from Hungarian, Italian, Greek, Bulgarian, (Balkan) Turkish and Romanian in the respective dialects. Among modality expressions, 'must' shows high borrowability from recent or older contact languages (meaning that as a borrowing, it remains relatively stable and not susceptible to short-term change of contact language). The potential modal 'can' is borrowed in some dialects, while 'cannot' is more rarely borrowed (see Elšík and Matras 2006, pp. 209–210).

11.4.5 Content Lexicon

Surprisingly, for a language that is permanently in contact, and indeed has been described by some specialists as 'deficient' (cf. Boretzky 1989) in that it is inherently dependent on material from neighbouring languages, very few studies have been devoted to lexical borrowing in Romani. As noted above, most studies on Romani lexicon tend to focus on the retention rate and etymological sources of pre-European vocabulary (cf. Scala, this volume). At the same time, it is noteworthy that modern studies on lexical borrowing are generally few, and the field was given a boost only fairly recently through the comparative study of Haspelmath and Tadmor (2009). Part of that enterprise is Elšík's (2009) work on a dialect of Slovak (Selice) Romani, which has become the benchmark for 'heavy lexical borrowing'. Applying Haspelmath and Tadmor's (2009) list of some 1400 categorized meaning entries to Selice Romani, Elšík finds that borrowings make up over 90% of items in the domain 'household, modern world, agriculture', over 80% in the domain 'clothing, warfare', over 70% of words for 'animals, social and political relations, and the physical world', over 60% in 'religion and belief, speech and language, law, technology, food and drink', over 50% for 'time, the body, motion, perception, emotion, cognition, values', over 40% for 'spatial relations' and over 30% for 'quantity, and kinship'. It is noteworthy, however, that 'borrowing' in the sense applied in the comparative study covers all items that are identified as having a non-core etymology, and thus for Romani, it includes pre-European and Medieval Greek loans, and not just contemporary loans (older, recent and current European contact language).

The RMS Database tends to confirm these findings, as far as the comparison allows, for Romani as a whole. It also allows us a more nuanced comparative examination among the dialects for individual expressions within the contact-susceptible categories. We find that in the RMS category 'human beings', frequent borrowings include the terms for 'soldier' and 'friend'. For 'animals', the word 'cat' is usually borrowed. Among 'body parts', 'fur' and 'skin' are more likely to be borrowed, while in the domain 'nature' frequently borrowed items are 'sea', 'weather', 'sky' and 'dust'. Frequently borrowed core verbs include 'speak', 'pay' and 'love'.

Lexical semantic convergence is common, though this too is an area that has so far seen few if any dedicated studies. From the now extinct English Romani (cf. Matras 2010), we can mention collocations such as *ke divous* 'today', combining the Romani preposition *ke* 'to' with **dives* 'day', and expressions such as *sår o čeros* 'all the time', where Romani **sa*, a plurality quantifier, shifts to become a determiner.

11.5 Conclusion

This chapter has outlined research and critical questions in contact linguistics involving Romani. In sum, it appears that language contact is to a great extent constitutive of Romani. In particular, Romani is associated with some cross-linguistically rare outcomes as it exhibits 'heavy' borrowing in both lexicon and grammar. Over the past decades, exploration of Romani dialects has given rise to new concepts, especially in the search for explanations for the emergence of mixed languages, either through substantial replication of paradigms leading to compartmentalization or through near wholesale retention of lexicon after language shift.

An important goal for current and future research in Romani linguistics remains the understanding of abandonment of Romani and the transition to Para-Romani as well as of the continuum of borrowing and code-switching as noted in some mixed dialects. In addition, comparison of contact behaviour in Romani and other languages can help refine borrowing hierarchies and offer an explanatory account (see Matras 2009), including by linking contact outcomes to their anchoring in language ecology (Adamou 2010). Lastly, we believe that the management of complex linguistic repertoires offers an avenue for future research in the study of Romani, with potential impact on the field of critical sociolinguistics. Such sociolinguistic and discourse-based studies are still missing in the context of Romani linguistics and will hopefully become a priority for new researchers entering the field.

References

Abercrombie, Amelia. 2018. Language purism and social hierarchies: Making a Romani standard in Prizren. *Language in Society* 47 (5): 741–761.

Adamou, Evangelia. 2010. Bilingual speech and language ecology in Greece: Romani and Pomak in contact with Turkish. *Language in Society* 39 (2): 147–171.

Adamou, Evangelia. 2013. Replicating Spanish *estar* in Mexican Romani. *Linguistics* 51 (6): 1075–1105.

Adamou, Evangelia. 2016. *A corpus-driven approach to language contact: Endangered language in a comparative perspective*. Berlin: De Gruyter Mouton.

Adamou, Evangelia, and Amalia Arvaniti. 2014. Greek Thrace Xoraxane Romane. *Journal of the International Phonetic Association* 44: 223–231.

Adamou, Evangelia, and Kimmo Granqvist. 2015. Unevenly mixed Romani languages. *International Journal of Bilingualism* 19 (5): 525–547.

Adamou, Evangelia, Stefano De Pascale, Yekaterina Garcia-Markina, and Cristian Padure. 2019. Do bilinguals generalize *estar* more than monolinguals and what is the role of conceptual transfer? *International Journal of Bilingualism* 23 (6): 1549–1580. https://doi.org/10.1177/1367006918812175.

Adamou, Evangelia, and Rachel X. Shen. 2019. There are no language switching costs when codeswitching is frequent. *International Journal of Bilingualism* 23 (1): 53–70.

Arvaniti, Amalia, and Evangelia Adamou. 2011. Focus expression in Romani. In *Proceedings of the 28th west coast conference on formal linguistics*, ed. Mary Byram Washburn, Katherine McKinney-Bock, Erika Varis, Ann Sawyer, and Barbara Tomaszewicz, 240–248. Somerville, MA: Cascadilla Proceedings Project.

Auer, Peter. 1999. From codeswitching via language mixing to fused lects: Toward a dynamic typology of bilingual speech. *International Journal of Bilingualism* 3: 309–332.

Bakker, Peter. 1997. Athematic morphology in Romani: The borrowing of a borrowing pattern. In *The typology and dialectology of Romani*, ed. Yaron Matras, Peter Bakker, and Hristo Kyuchukov, 1–21. Amsterdam: Benjamins.

Bakker, Peter. 1998. Para-Romani language versus secret languages: Differences in origin, structure, and use. In *The Romani element in non-standard speech*, ed. Yaron Matras, 69–96. Wiesbaden: Harrassowitz.

Bakker, Peter, and Marcel Cortiade (eds.). 1991. *In the margin of Romani. Gypsy languages in contact*. Amsterdam: Institute for General Linguistics.

Bakker, Peter, and Maarten Mous (eds.). 1994. *Mixed languages: 15 case studies in language intertwining*. Amsterdam: IFOTT.

Boretzky, Norbert. 1985. Sind Zigeunersprachen Kreols? In *Akten des 1 Essener Kolloquiums über Kreolsprachen und Sprachkontakte*, ed. Norbert Boretzky, Werner Enninger, and Thomas Stolz, 43–70. Bochum: Verlag N. Brockmeyer.

Boretzky, Norbert. 1989. Zum Interferenzverhalten des Romani (Verbreitete und ungewöhn-liche Phänomene). *Zeitschrift Für Phonetik, Sprachwissenschaft Und Kommunikationsforschung* 42: 357–374.

Boretzky, Norbert. 1992. Zum Erbwortschatz des Romani. *Zeitschrift Für Phonetik, Sprachwissenschaft Und Kommunikationsforschung* 45: 227–251.

Boretzky, Norbert, and Birgit Igla. 1991. *Morphologische Entlehnung in den Romani-Dialekten (Arbeitspapiere des Projektes "Prinzipien des Sprachwandels" 4)*. Essen: Universität GH Essen, Fachbereich Sprach- und Literaturwissenschaften.

Boretzky, Norbert, and Birgit Igla. 1993. *Lautwandel und Natürlichkeit. Kontaktbedingter und endogener Wandel im Romani (Arbeitspapiere des Projekts "Prinzipien des Sprachwandels" 15)*. Essen: Universität GH Essen, Fachbereich Sprach- und Literaturwissenschaften.

Boretzky, Norbert, and Birgit Igla. 1994. Romani mixed dialects. In *Mixed languages: 15 case studies in language intertwining*, ed. Peter Bakker and Maarten Mous, 35–68. Amsterdam: IFOTT.

Bubeník, Vít. 1995. On typological changes and structural borrowing in the history of European Romani. In *Romani in contact: The history, structure, and sociology of a language*, ed. Yaron Matras, 1–23. Amsterdam: Benjamins.

Burridge, Kate (with Keith Allan). 1998. The X-phemistic value of Romani in non-standard speech. In *The Romani element in non-standard speech*, ed. Yaron Matras, 29–49. Wiesbaden: Harrassowitz.

Elšík, Viktor. 2000. Romani nominal paradigms: Their structure, diversity, and development. In *Grammatical relations in Romani: The noun phrase*, ed. Viktor Elšík and Yaron Matras, 9–30. Amsterdam: Benjamins.

Elšík, Viktor. 2001. Word-form borrowing in indefinites: Romani evidence. *Sprachtypologie Und Universalienforschung* 54 (2): 126–147.

Elšík, Viktor. 2009. Loanwords in Selice Romani, an Indo-Aryan language of Slovakia. In *Loanwords in the world's languages. A comparative handbook*, ed. Martin Haspelmath and Uri Tadmor, 260–303. Berlin: Mouton de Gruyter.

Elšík, Viktor, and Yaron Matras. 2006. *Markedness and language change: The Romani sample*. Berlin: Mouton de Gruyter.

Friedman, Victor A. 1985. Balkan Romani modality and other Balkan languages. *Folia Slavica* 7: 381–389.

Friedman, Victor A. 2013. Compartmentalized grammar: The variable (non)–integration of Turkish verbal conjugation in Romani dialects. *Romani Studies* 23 (1): 107–120.

Grigorova, Evelina. 1998. Interrogative intonation of two Bulgarian Romani dialects: Sofia Erli and Kalderaš. *Grazer Linguistische Studien* 50: 45–63.

Halwachs, Dieter W. 1993. Polysystem, Repertoire und Identität. *Grazer Linguistische Studien* 39–40: 71–90.

Hancock, Ian F. 1970. Is Anglo-Romanes a creole? *JGLS*, 3rd ser., 49: 41–44.

Hancock, Ian F. 1992. The social and linguistic development of Scandoromani. In *Language contact: Theoretical and empirical studies*, ed. Ernst Håkon Jahr, 37–52. Berlin: Mouton de Gruyter.

Hancock, Ian F. 1995. *A handbook of Vlax Romani*. Columbus: Slavica.

Haspelmath, Martin and Uri Tadmor (eds.). (2009). *Loanwords in the world's languages: A comparative handbook*. Berlin: Mouton de Gruyter.

Haugen, Einar. 1949. A note on the Romany "language". *Norsk Tidskrift for Sprogvidenskap* 7: 388–391.

Heine, Bernd, and Tania Kuteva. 2005. *Language contact and grammatical change*. Cambridge: Cambridge University Press.

Holzinger, Daniel. 1993. *Das Rómanes. Grammatik und Diskursanalyse der Sprache der Sinte*. Innsbruck: Verlag des Instituts für Sprachwissenschaft der Universität Innsbruck.

Igla, Birgit. 1989. Kontakt-induzierte Sprachwandelphänomene im Romani von Ajia Varvara (Athen). In *Vielfalt der Kontakte*, ed. Norbert Boretzky, Werner Enninger, and Thomas Stolz, 67–80. Bochum: Verlag N. Brockmeyer.

Igla, Birgit. 1992. Entlehnung und Lehnübersetzung deutscher Präfixverben im Sinti. In *Prinzipien des Sprachwandels I: Vorbereitung*, ed. Jürgen Erfurt, Benedikt Jeßing, and Matthias Perl, 38–56. Bochum: Verlag N. Brockmeyer.

Kaufman, Terrence. 1979. Review of Weer Rajendra Rishi, Multilingual Romani Dictionary. *International Journal of the Sociology of Language* 19: 131–144.

Leggio, D. Viktor. 2015. Radio Romani Mahala: Romani identities and languages in a virtual space. In *Virtual citizenship? Roma communities, inclusion policies, participation and ICT tools*, ed. Alfredo Alietti, Martin Olivera, and Veronica Riniolo, 97–114. Milan: McGraw-Hill Education.

Leggio, D. Viktor, and Yaron Matras. 2017. Orthography development on the Internet: Romani on YouTube. In *Creating orthographies for endangered languages*, ed. Mari C. Jones and Damien Mooney, 254–275. Cambridge: Cambridge University Press.

Leschber, Corinna. 1995. Romani lexical items in colloquial Rumanian. In *Romani in contact: The history and sociology of a language*, ed. Yaron Matras, 151–176. Amsterdam: Benjamins.

Matras, Yaron. 1994a. *Untersuchungen zu Grammatik und Diskurs des Romanes. Dialekt der Kelderaša/Lovara*. Wiesbaden: Harrassowitz.

Matras, Yaron. 1994b. Structural Balkanisms in Romani. In *Sprachlicher Standard und Substandard in Südosteuropa und Osteuropa*, ed. Reiter, Norbert, Uwe Hinrichs, and Jefiina van Leeuwen-Turnocová, 195–210. Wiesbaden: Harrassowitz.

Matras, Yaron (ed.). 1995. *Romani in contact: The history and sociology of a language*. Amsterdam: Benjamins.

Matras, Yaron. 1996. Prozedurale Fusion: Grammatische Interferenzschichten im Romanes. *Sprachtypologie Und Universalienforschung* 49: 60–78.

Matras, Yaron. 1998a. The Romani element in Jenisch and Rotwelsch. In *The Romani element in non-standard speech*, ed. Yaron Matras, 193–230. Wiesbaden: Harrassowitz.

Matras, Yaron. 1998b. Utterance modifiers and universals of grammatical borrowing. *Linguistics* 36: 281–331.

Matras, Yaron (ed.). 1998c. *The Romani element in non-standard speech*. Wiesbaden: Harrassowitz.

Matras, Yaron. 1998d. Convergent development, grammaticalization, and the problem of 'mutual isomorphism'. In *Sprache in Raum und Zeit*, ed. Winfried Boeder, Christoph Schroeder, and Karl-Heinz Wagner, 89–103. Narr: Tübingen.

Matras, Yaron. 1999. Subject clitics in Sinti. *Acta Linguistica Academiae Scientiarum Hungaricae* 46: 147–169.

Matras, Yaron. 2002. *Romani: A linguistic introduction*. Cambridge: Cambridge University Press.

Matras, Yaron. 2009. *Language contact*. Cambridge: Cambridge University Press.

Matras, Yaron. 2010. *Romani in Britain: The afterlife of a language*. Edinburgh: Edinburgh University Press.

Matras, Yaron. 2015. Why is the borrowing of inflection morphology dispreferred? In *Borrowed morphology*, ed. Francesco Gardani, Peter Arkadiev, and Nino Amiridze, 47–80. Berlin: De Gruyter Mouton.

Matras, Yaron, and Peter Bakker (eds.). 2003. *The mixed language debate: Theoretical and empirical advances*. Berlin: Mouton de Gruyter.

Matras, Yaron, Hazel Gardner, Charlotte Jones, and Veronica Schulman. 2007. Angloromani: A different kind of language? *Anthropological Linguistics* 49 (2): 142–164.

Miklosich, Franz. 1872–1880. *Über die Mundarten und Wanderungen der Zigeuner Europas X–XII*. Wien: Karl Gerold's Sohn.

Padure, Cristian, Stefano De Pascale, and Evangelia Adamou. 2018. Variation between the copula *si* 'to be' and the *l*-clitics in Romani spoken in Mexico. *Romani Studies* 28 (2): 263–292.

Pott, August. 1844–1845. *Die Zigeuner in Europa und Asien. Ethnographisch-linguistische Untersuchung vornehmlich ihrer Herkunft und Sprache*. Halle: Heynemann.

Réger, Zita. 1979. Bilingual Gypsy children in Hungary: Explorations in "natural" second-language acquisition. *International Journal of the Sociology of Language* 19: 59–82.

Rijkhoff, Jan. 1998. Bystander deixis. In *The Romani element in non-standard speech*, ed. Yaron Matras, 51–67. Wiesbaden: Harrassowitz.

Tenser, Anton. 2016. Semantic map borrowing—Case representation in Northeastern Romani dialects. *Journal of Language Contact* 9: 211–245.

Thomason, Sarah G., and Terrence Kaufman. 1988. *Language contact, creolization and genetic linguistics*. Berkeley: University of California Press.

12

Para-Romani Varieties

Peter Bakker

12.1 Introduction

Para-Romani does not refer to a single variety of Romani, but a set of varieties. Another term used for the phenomenon is 'Romani mixed dialects' (Boretzky and Igla 1994). As the prefix *Para-* in the name suggests, Para-Romani (hence, PR) varieties are distinguishable from Romani in the strict sense. Romani in the strict sense has a Romani lexicon and a Romani grammatical system, both of which go back to an Indic core. PR varieties, however, have a Romani vocabulary, but the original grammatical system of Romani is virtually completely lost. Instead, an existing grammatical frame, typically that of the co-territorial language, is used. Thus, PR varieties share with each other a continuation of much of the lexicon, as well as a loss of the Romani grammatical system.

Here is an example from a text in the Para-Romani variety called Angloromani that speaker Cornelius Price shared with John Sampson in 1897 (Sampson 1930, p. 57):

(1) *yeka divés* there was a *muš* *jal*-in' on the *drom* *dik*-in' for *būti* (Angloromani PR)
    one   day   there was a man go-ing on the road look-ing for work

---

P. Bakker (✉)
Aarhus University, Aarhus, Denmark
e-mail: linpb@cc.au.dk

© The Author(s) 2020
Y. Matras and A. Tenser (eds.), *The Palgrave Handbook of Romani Language and Linguistics*, https://doi.org/10.1007/978-3-030-28105-2_12

354   P. Bakker

This sentence, randomly chosen from a longer narrative, can be said to have the grammatical frame of English (phonology, morphology, syntax), but the content words are from Romani. The numeral *yeka* 'one' is the same as Welsh Romani *jekh*, with the final *-a* either a remnant of the lost aspiration (Sampson 1930, p. 50) or a remnant of attributive numeral inflection *-e* (cf. Matras 2002, p. 96). The content words are all shared with Welsh Romani (Sampson 1926). The word *divés* is the same as the Welsh Romani word *dives* 'day', with a stress mark. Then *muš* is Romani *murš* 'man', *jal-* is derived from the third person form *džal* '(s)he goes' used as a base form, *dik-* is from the Romani root *dikh-* 'to see, to look' and *būti* is the Romani word for 'work'. Note that English idioms are also translated directly, such as 'one day' and 'to look for'. Romani roots have English inflections and have been adjusted to English phonology.

This looks superficially like lexical borrowing: loanwords are inserted into English. Yet, the scale of it is exceptional: in this narrative, 94% of content words are Romani, and some 81% of the function words and bound morphemes are from English. A rough count of the story from which this sentence was taken shows that 117 function words are from English and 27 from Romani, whereas four of the content words are from English and 98 from Romani. When such a huge dichotomy between content words and grammatical forms is found, specialists assume that this is the result of a special process of language mixing, and not of a process of lexical borrowing for filling gaps in the lexicon. It is not code-switching either, as the speakers do not know the original Romani grammar. A special socio-historical process is assumed for specific purposes. Most agree that such languages are conscious creations. For a discussion, see the papers in Bakker and Mous (1994), Matras (1998a, b), and Matras and Bakker (2003).

Strictly on the basis of linguistic data, it is easy to distinguish these Para-Romani varieties from the Romani language and its dialects. Whereas Romani has verb inflection, overt case marking and adjectival inflection for gender, number and case, these endings are not used at all in any of the Para-Romani varieties (cf. Hancock [1984a] for a comparison between Indic-inflected Romani and Angloromani). In the Para-Romani varieties, morphology (and syntax and phonology) is not like Romani, but identical to the co-territorial language, English in the case of the example above.

The opposite does not exist: there are no languages with a Romani grammatical system and a non-Romani lexicon. Romani populations are always bi- or multilingual; hence, lexical influences of contact languages can be extreme in Romani. Romani is subject to more than average lexical and grammatical borrowing. Elšík (2009) studied loanwords in a Slovak Romani dialect. In a cross-linguistic comparison, Tadmor (2009, p. 56) counted 62% lexical borrowings for Selice Romani in a specific list of cultural vocabulary, which was the highest percentage of all 41 languages in the sample.

The number of mixed Romani dialects about which at least some information is now available is about a dozen. The mixed varieties are marginal to Romani proper, both geographically and in terms of numbers of speakers. Romani is spoken by at least 3.5 million people (Matras 2002, p. 238), and all the Para-Romani varieties together probably by no more than 100,000 people. The number of Romani speakers is thus thirty times higher than the number of all PR speakers together. Geographically, almost all varieties have emerged in the westernmost fringe of Europe, not in the east: Spain, France, Britain, Scandinavia, and in addition some more isolated cases in Greece, Hungary and Turkey, close the south-eastern fringe of Europe. PR varieties seem to be absent in regions where Romani is stronger, either in terms of numbers of speakers or in transmission to younger generations. Yet, one cannot say that Romani and PR varieties are or were in complementary distribution, as both Romani and PR varieties are found in Hungary, Greece and Turkey.

In order to distinguish between Romani proper and the mixed varieties, the term Para-Romani has been proposed (first by Cortiade 1991). The prefix *para-* indicates that some forms of Romani have undergone such radical changes in the direction of another language, that the resulting PR varieties should be considered new varieties, each with a different grammatical system, and these grammatical systems are virtually identical with those of the corresponding languages the speakers are in contact with. Their Romani component links them to Romani and Romani dialectology, and as such, they are studied in connection with other varieties of Romani. They are included in the Romani linguistics bibliography (Bakker and Matras 2003). Their mixed nature justifies their study also in the context of mixed languages and language contact: they are central to the discussion of language contact and especially the study of mixed languages (Bakker and Mous 1994; Matras 2000, 2010; Bakker 2013). Their exceptional nature in communication also affords the phenomenon a special place in sociolinguistics.

The study of mixed languages commenced, after a few false starts, in the 1990s, after which the existence of mixed languages as a distinct category had become recognized, and since then, different types of mixed languages have been established (see Matras [2000] for a discussion of the processes, and Meakins [2013, 2016] and Bakker [2017a] for recent overviews). It should be mentioned that this body of work has not convinced all linguists of the existence of a separate category of mixed languages, for different reasons: Greenberg (1999), Dimmendaal (1995; 2011, pp. 238–245) and

Versteegh (2017) reject the notion of mixed language. In addition, not all researchers include PR varieties among the prototypical mixed languages as they are not native tongues. The discussion of the existence of a special category of mixed languages relates mainly to two points. Some authors doubt whether the processes that lead to so-called mixed languages are categorically or quantitatively different from what has been observed in other processes of language change, e.g. code-switching, lexical borrowing, extreme borrowing, gradual language shift (see, e.g., Myers-Scotton 1998; Thomason 1995; Matras 2010). Others believe, thinking in terms of historical linguistics, that mixed languages can always be comfortably classified in a family with one of the component languages, which could be the language of the verb, of the inflectional morphology, of the function words, or of the lexicon or the bulk of the lexicon. They may also consider them unexceptional from a developmental point of view, taking the lexicon language or the grammar language as the original language of the community, before the mixture took place, and then the rest is borrowed. For an overview of the debate, see also Matras and Bakker (2003).

I take the position that only languages with two overt genealogical affiliations in about the same degree can be considered mixed. For instance, genealogical ambiguity is present if 80% of one basic component (e.g. lexicon) and 80% of another basic component (e.g. inflectional morphemes) from another language. That would include Para-Romani varieties, at least in the stages before massive lexical loss, as can be experienced in Angloromani in Britain (Matras et al. 2007) and Caló in Spain (McLane 1977; Gamella et al. 2015). Angloromani and Caló as documented after 1900 would thus not fall within these criteria. Based on the research on twenty-first-century Angloromani, Matras (2010) fittingly called the results 'the afterlife of a language' and Gamella et al. (2015) use the metaphor of a 'long agony' with regard to Caló.

One issue that needs to be discussed is the status of PR varieties as languages in their own right. In assessing this, one has to distinguish between earlier stages in which a much greater deal of Romani lexicon, up to 800 words, was inserted on the one hand, and on the other the period after 1900 for Caló and Angloromani, when individuals might know no more than a few dozen Romani words. It has been claimed that such sources are fabricated and the number of reported Romani elements has been increased artificially. Against such a claim, one can argue that it is unlikely that researchers in a dozen countries would create the same type of artificial language, even when the researchers knew neither Romani nor the host language, as in the case of Basque Romani. As for the modern attestations, based on fieldwork, it is clear that such a speech form could not be considered an independent and full-fledged language. In this vein, Matras (2002, p. 246) calls PR varieties registers or styles of the respective majority languages.

The issue of sources is fundamental in the discussion of the history and the function of PR varieties. On the basis of tape recordings and surveys in the twenty-first century or the late twentieth century, the range of functions as well as the knowledge of the Romani lexicon is remarkably limited. In contrast, virtually all written sources from the 1600s to the mid-1900s show a much higher density of Romani lexemes in PR varieties. The main question is whether these early sources provide inauthentic, or even fabricated, samples of speech, or whether there was a diachronic development with a decrease in language use and hence a decline in lexical knowledge. This controversy also relates to the domains of use, from a potential everyday language (for which there is no unambiguous documentation) to a situation-related, communicatively motivated, strategic insertion of Romani elements in the discourse of the host language. Bakker (e.g. 1995) and Adiego (e.g. 2002, 2019) tend to take the earlier sources at face value, whereas Matras (2010) projects his detailed modern observations to having been the case in the past as well. This chapter tends to rely on the older material.

12.2 Definition, Terminology and Overview of Para-Romani Varieties

12.2.1 Overview of Para-Romani Varieties

Thus far, around a dozen Para-Romani varieties have been identified in the literature. The following Indo-European languages have combined with a Romani lexicon: the Romance languages Spanish, Catalan, Portuguese and probably French; the Germanic languages Low German, Swedish, Norwegian and English; Greek, in two distinct independent varieties Dortika (Igla 1991) and Finikas (Sechidou 2005). Further, there are Para-Romani varieties with a non-Indo-European grammatical base: Hungarian (Finno-Ugric family), Turkish (Turkic) and Basque (isolate). In addition, there are Gypsy varieties in Armenia (Lomavren) that are similarly mixed, and possibly also in the Middle East (Qirishmal, see Boretzky and Igla 1994). I will give a number of examples.

Bakker and Van der Voort (1991) provided the first comparative study, and some case studies were included in Bakker and Cortiade (1991), soon followed by Boretzky and Igla (1994). From the recent literature, several additional ideas about the genesis emerge.

358   P. Bakker

Basque is a non-Indo-European language with a complex verbal inflection, including affixes indicating subject, object and indirect object, as well as a dozen or so case endings. Here is an example, with Romani elements underlined (Bakker 1991, p. 68):

(2)	Xau-a,	goli keau-zak,	mol	but-er-ago	akhin-en	d-u-k	(Basque Romani)
	child-DEF	song make- IMP	wine	much-COMP- COMP have-FUT	it-have- you		
	haurr-a,	kanta-zak,	arno	gehi-ago	ukan-en	d-u-k	(Basque)
	child-DEF	sing-IMP	wine	much-COMP	have-FUT	it-have- you	

'Child, sing, you will have more wine'
(Romani *čavo* 'boy', *gili* 'song', *ker-av* 'I do', *mol* 'wine', *but* 'much', *buter* 'more', *ač-* 'to stay, have, be', or cf. *assin* 'to be' in Sentmenat's Catalan Romani; Adiego 2002, p. 62)

The next example of Danish/Low German Para-Romani as documented in Denmark (Miskow and Brøndal 1923, p. 117).

(3)	dik	de	bar-e	sjukri	kakni	(Sindi)
	See	the	big-AGR	beautiful	hen	
	Seht	die	große,	schöne	Henne!	(High German)
	Se	den	store,	kønne	høne	(Danish)

'Look at the big, beautiful hen'
(Romani *dikh-* 'to see', *bar-* 'big', *šukar* 'beautiful', *kahni* 'hen')

The speakers of Dortika in Greece call themselves Romis, pl. Romiðes (Greek endings) in their own language and their language Romika (Triandaphyllidis 1924, p. 19; Igla 1991, p. 95). In this language, the nouns are inflected like Greek but the verbs do not get Greek verbal inflection.

(4)	pinela	tu	balam-u	posa	stal-e	θa	dela	(Dortika)
	say	DEF	Greek-DAT	how.much	money-PL	FUT	give	
	pes	tu	anθropu	posa	xrim-ata	θa (su)	disi	(Greek)

'ask the man how much money he will give'
(Romani *phenela* '(s)he says', *balamo* 'Greek', *astale* 'money' (PL), *dela* '(s)he gives')

Turkish is a language with agglutinative morphology, with concatenating suffixes. It has vowel harmony, which entails that the vowel of affixes will adjust to the vowel of the root. Caferoğlu (1943) documented a Turkish PR variety and called it the language of the Geygel Yürüks (Caferoğlu 1943, p. 196, quoted in Bakker 2001, p. 314).

(5)   Dav-*alım-mı*   *gacı-yı*   *naş-tır-alım-mı*   (Geygel)
         give-1PL.SUBJ-Q   girl-O   flee-CAUS-1PL.SUBJ-Q
         Ver-elim-mi   çocuğ-a   ver-mi-yelim-mi   (Turkish)
         'Shall we give the girl [to him or] shall we put [the stranger] to flight'
         (the PR and Turkish phrases are from the original, with hyphens added; the English translation is given in Lewis 1950–1955, pp. 219–220; he remarks that *naş-tır* means 'to flee' (rather: 'to chase'), not 'to give' as in the Turkish phrase; an alternative translation would be: 'Should we give it to the stranger or should we chase him away')
         (Romani *dav* 'I give', *gadži* '(non-Gypsy) woman,' *naš-* 'to flee')

Hungarian is a language with vowel harmony, rich case marking and an article system. The PR variety is, to the extent that we know, not documented except for a few phrases (Réger 1995, p. 88, note 6).

(6)   nagyon   kamel-om   a   romnyi-t   (Hungarian
                                                             Para-Romani)
         very.much   love-1SG   DEF   Gypsy.woman-ACC
         nagyon   szeret-em   az   asszony-t   (Hungarian)
         'I love the woman very much'
         (Romani *kam-* 'to want, love', *romnji* 'Romani woman')

These examples show that the patterns of distribution of lexical and functional elements between Romani and non-Romani are quite similar in all varieties, in that Romani lexical items are inserted in the same way in the different languages. In all cases, all or almost all of the content morphemes, especially the more basic ones, are from Romani, whereas all or almost all productive morphology is from the local language. Constituent order is also from the local language. We find variation in the free grammatical morphemes, such as demonstratives, personal pronouns, question words and prepositions.

One of the first extensive sources of a Para-Romani variety is a study of Caló by the Spanish orientalist José Antonio Condé (1766–1820), cf. Adiego (2004). It has been dated at 1809 (Charnon-Deutsch 2004), and the material was probably collected in or around Sevilla. Most likely, it is a copy of a late eighteenth-century manuscript (Adiego 2019). In its 32 chapters, most of them not exceeding one page, he provides a vocabulary, basic grammatical information and around 150 example sentences. These sentences contain 648 words (tokens) and 236 of these are unique roots.

360   P. Bakker

A calculation of etymological origins of roots, endings and grammatical morphemes gives the following results as in Table 12.1. Percentages of types and tokens do not differ dramatically.

The numbers in Table 12.1 show that the lexicon is overwhelmingly Romani (87%), whereas verbal inflection is completely Spanish. Nominal plural marking is roughly equally indicated with a Spanish suffix (40%) as with a Romani suffix (48%), thus going against a strict grammar-lexicon dichotomy. Possessive pronouns, articles and conjunctions are overwhelmingly Spanish, and adverbs, numerals and the copula are overwhelming Romani. The two Spanish verb roots (*mandizarar* 'to send', Spanish *mandar*) and *rabizar* (Sp. *rabiar* 'to rage') both contain the *-izar-* element known from other Romani dialects (Vlax and Welsh Romani) to integrate verbal loans (Matras 2002, p. 133).

Assuming that only a very limited number of speakers were interviewed, perhaps only one female, by the compiler of the document, these numbers contrast with the knowledge of Caló words in Andalusia in the 2010s. Most of the 290–360 'most common and widespread' Caló words that people were asked about were known only by a small minority of speakers. The average person knew 129 of them, passively or actively. The authors add: 'It is very rare to hear spontaneous conversations in Caló beyond a few phrases' (Gamella et al. 2016, p. 113). Claiming a language status for such cases is not justified.

12.2.2 Generalizations and Contrasts

These Para-Romani varieties are clearly distinct from Romani as it is spoken in large parts of Europe. Sometimes the term 'inflected Romani' is used for varieties that inherited the Indic grammatical system, but that term is misleading in that the Para-Romani varieties are inflected as well, albeit using the inflectional system of the language of the host country. Sometimes 'conservative Romani' is also used for the varieties with Indic inflection, which is also somewhat misleading in that some PR varieties have preserved a number of lexical and grammatical words that have been lost in Central and Eastern European varieties. In this paper, I will use the term 'Indic-inflected' to indicate Romani in contrast to Para-Romani. These terms are not ideal either, because inflection is only one of the affected domains. In addition, some of the Romani inflection suffixes, notably those used with loanwords, have been borrowed from or influenced by Greek (Matras 2000, p. 74).

12 Para-Romani Varieties   361

Table 12.1 Frequency of categories by language etymology in Conde's 150 sentences

	Romani	Spanish	Unknown	Ambiguous
All lexical roots	*144 Types (87%)*	*4 Types (2%)*	*7 types (4%)*	*1 type (1%)*
Nouns	71 types (96%) 117 tokens (97%)	0	2 types (3%) 2 tokens (2%)	1 (1%) 1 (1%)
Verb roots	65 types (90%) 157 tokens (95%)	2 types (3%) 3 tokens (2%)	5 types (7%) 5 tokens (3%)	
Adjectives	8 types (80%) 16 tokens (89%)	2 types (20%) 2 tokens (11%)	0	0
Function words	*30 types*	*31 types*	*1 type*	*3 types*
Adverbs	12 types (85%) 21 tokens (84%)	2 types (15%) 4 tokens (16%)	0	0
Numerals	1 type (100%) 1 token (100%)	0	0	0
'to be'	6 types (100%) 12 tokens (100%)	0	0	0
Personal pronouns	4 types (66%) 43 tokens (83%)	2 types (33%) 9 tokens (17%)	0	3 types (37%) 45 tokens (51%)
Possessive pronouns	1 type (14%) 1 token (12%)	6 types (86%) 7 types (87%)	0	0
Articles, definite and indefinite	0	5 types (100%) 52 tokens (100%)	0	0
Conjunctions	1 type (17%) 3 tokens (17%)	5 types (83%) 15 tokens (83%)	0	0
Question words	2 types (50%) 16 tokens (84%)	2 types (50%) 3 tokens (16%)	0	0
Negators	1 type (33%) 7 tokens (44%)	1 type (33%) 7 tokens (44%)	1 type (33%) 2 tokens (12%)	0
Prepositions	2 types (20%) 2 tokens (0.3%)	8 types (80%) 70 tokens (97%)	0	0
Morphology				
Inflectional verb morphemes and clitics	0	100% Spanish	0	0
Nominal morphology: plural	11 types (48%) 13 tokens (57%)	9 types (40%) 10 tokens (43%)		3 types (13%)

Modern varieties of, e.g., Caló and Angloromani display considerably fewer Romani words than older sources. It is sometimes said, on the basis of modern forms of speech, that older sources were made as 'Romani' as possible (Acton and Kenrick 1984, pp. 10, 11), and therefore not authentic (e.g. Kenrick 1971, p. 6). That is unlikely, however, for two main reasons. First, in several sources, Romani and non-Romani roots and function words are used frequently for the same meanings, e.g. personal pronouns or demonstratives; the non-Romani ones would have been filtered out if speakers or researchers had wanted to eliminate non-Romani elements. Second, the striking similarities between the PR varieties based on different language pairs make it unlikely that a similar form of purism was prevalent with all those researchers, or speakers who worked with students of the language (for a discussion of purism in mixed languages, see Bakker 2003b).

The fact that Romani became mixed with languages belonging to completely different branches of Indo-European and three non-Indo-European languages is an indication that typological and structural differences between Romani and the languages in contact do not hinder the mixture of languages. The languages that were sources of PR varieties belong to various types, ranging from relatively isolating types like French, through modestly and strongly inflecting languages like Swedish and Basque, and on to agglutinative languages like Turkish and Hungarian. There are clearly no morphological constraints against mixture. Similarly, when we look at word order typology, we find SOV languages involved such as Turkish, SVO languages like English and languages which base their word order on pragmatic principles (sometimes called 'free word order languages') such as Hungarian, and mixed types such as Basque. We also find different orders of nouns and adjectives.

Most of the PR varieties are spoken in the westernmost parts of Europe, probably by the descendants of people who arrived in those parts in the fifteenth or early sixteenth century, hence the descendants of the first wave of immigration of Gypsies into Europe from the Balkans. The PR varieties seem to share some lexicon and a number of shared strategies that are not found among speakers of Vlach, Central and Balkan dialects (see Bakker 1999; Matras 2002, ch. 9, 2005; Tcherenkov and Laederich 2004).

The self-designation as a group among speakers of the western PR varieties is often not 'Rom', but a different ethnic label is used, e.g. *Kalo* (from Romani *kalo* 'black, dark'), *Manuš/Manouche* (R. *manuš* 'human'), *Sinto* (of contested origin) and *Romanitšel* (of contested origin). Note that some of these terms are also used in Romani-speaking groups, e.g. Finland, France and Germany.

No terms for clans and subgroups based on professions are used, like 'Coppersmith', even though that is very common in other Romani societies. The word *Rom* in PR varieties often only means 'husband', and the language is called *Romanes*, preserving the old meaning of 'relating to Gypsies'. This is also the case for some non-PR speakers in Western Europe (Bakker 1999).

Perhaps only a few dozen lexical items are used in PR and adjacent varieties. Examples are *prasar-/plasar-/ples-* 'to pay' (Wales, England, Spain, Finland, Scandinavia, Germany, Russia, Baltics), *konitsa* 'basket' (Basque Country, Catalonia, Spain, Norway, Sinti, England) and *stanja* 'stable' (Catalonia, England, Norway, Finland, Denmark, Sweden, Sinti, Baltic, Wales). This set of words appears of diverse origin, particularly Slavonic, German and Greek. The presence of these words suggests a common past, perhaps due to encounters and liaisons on the road in Western Europe.

Further, a small set of coin names from Bohemia are continued for local currencies in Wales, England, Sweden, Norway, Finland, Germany, Spain and the Basque Country, but not elsewhere, except of course in regions where the coins with these names were still being used in recent times (Bakker 2017b, and below).

Para-Romani varieties have been documented from the early seventeenth century. In a 1616 word list from England (McGowan 1996; Bakker 2002), two phrases/sentences are presented that show structures typical for Para-Romani: *coore the gorife*, translated as 'go beat the cow' (Romani *kūr-* 'to hit'; *guruv* 'cattle'), and *shwist with a saister in the end* 'staff with a pike' (*shwist* of uncertain origin, perhaps a misreading for *kasht* 'wood', *saster/sastri* 'iron'). These phrases are the oldest PR phrases we are aware of. But a reflection by language scholars on the genesis started first in the late 1800s, and the comparative study only in the 1990s.

12.2.3 Para-Romani as a Mirror Image of Lexical Borrowing

There are no direct witnesses to the genesis of PR varieties. The process is to be reconstructed on the basis of socio-historical and longitudinal linguistic data. There are several grounds to consider the process of the genesis of these mixed languages as different from normal transmission and language change. More commonly, each new generation modifies the previous generation's speech slightly. PR varieties, however, cannot have come about through slow generational transmission. This does not mean that the whole transformation from Romani bilingualism has taken place at the same time.

First, we can mention the sheer quantity of Romani lexical elements in PR varieties. Even in quite extreme circumstances like Italian and English in Maltese, Spanish in Chamorro and French in English, the everyday lexicon is much less affected than more peripheral lexicon, i.e. more frequent words are borrowed rather than less frequently used ones. Everyday and high-frequency words like 'man', 'work', 'sleep' are more likely to be from Romani than technical terms like 'dentist', 'accountancy' or 'hypnosis', however. In PR, it is thus first and foremost the everyday vocabulary that is not from the local language, as was clear in all of the examples above. In secret languages, it is special vocabulary that is adjusted, and in the usual cases of borrowing, cultural words and words for new concepts are borrowed.

Second, the concepts that are most typically borrowed from one language into another are less frequently used words and cultural innovations. That is the general pattern, also for Romani. There is a tendency in PR varieties, however, to coin new terms for them. For instance, Angloromani speakers may create forms like *rokkermengri* 'telephone', from *raker-* '*to talk*' (Matras 2010, p. 74), also as a playful creation. In modern times, however, this process is not prevalent in the spoken language, but more limited to language challenges and play (see, e.g., Kenrick 1979).

Third, place names are usually among the first to be used in processes of borrowing, including Romani. Normally, people who visit or immigrate to a new society with a different language will use the existing local place names. In PR varieties, however, speakers tend to create new names for cities (Bakker 1995, pp. 133–134). Sometimes these toponyms are translations of place names, sometimes they are descriptions, or they are based on geographical characterizations. Matras (2010, pp. 109–110) lists a.o. *apreytem* ('above-country') for Scotland and *kawlagav* ('black-town') for Blackpool.

Fourth, there is something special about coin names in PR—a trait also found in other Romani varieties of Western Europe. Speakers normally take over the terms for coins from the country of residence, but PR speakers adjust coin names from a previous country of residence (e.g. Bohemia) in the new country (e.g. Sweden), adapting the relative values of the old monetary system to the ones of the new places of residence. Four coin names in PR varieties go back to a set of currencies once common in continental Europe: *xara* 'small coin' goes back to Czech Haler, *kuruna* is a coin named 'crown', *guruša* goes back to a coin named *Grosso* and *tromin* is cognate with the former Greek currency *drachme*, and Arabic *dirham*. These four terms, or a subset of them, are found in Romani varieties of Wales, Scandinavia, Finland, Germany, Spain, Basque Romani, but not in Central, Balkan and Vlax varieties of Romani (Bakker 2017b).

Thus, in a sense, the 'borrowing' process in PR varieties is a mirror image of what is found in common cases of borrowing. This lexical borrowing hierarchy is valid for all cases of normal borrowing, but in PR varieties it is the exact opposite:

Place names > coin names > newly introduced items > everyday vocabulary.

The use of Romani (and occasionally other) elements in PR varieties is clearly not instigated by gap-filling in the lexicon, but for 'symbolising group membership and flagging shared values and a particular pool of experiences' (Matras 2010, p. 172). The Romani elements are insertions into the frame of the host languages, and the combination of these insertions from one language source within the frame of another language can be seen as resulting in a mixed language.

This offers some evidence against the claim that there is nothing special in the genesis of mixed languages and PR, especially the quantity and the nature of 'borrowings' (e.g. Versteegh 2017).

12.2.4 Romani Lexicon in PR

It is of interest to study how much of the Romani vocabulary is actually present in PR varieties.

One can make a calculation on the basis of the common inherited lexicon from Early Romani, i.e. the vocabulary items from Indian languages and the borrowings from Iranian, Armenian and Greek that are present in all branches of Romani. Matras (2002, p. 21) made an informed estimate of 1000 lexical roots that are pre-European, the so-called Early Romani roots, which includes 800 shared pre-European items (see also Scala, this volume). Of these pre-European words, some 70 are Iranian borrowings and perhaps 40 are from Armenian. In addition, there are between 200 and 250 roots of Greek origin. The Indo-Aryan component amounts to some 650–700 roots. No Romani dialect preserved all of them; Finnish Romani preserved up to 450 Indic roots, and other dialects under 600.

In historical linguistics, researchers often use the Swadesh lists in order to compare languages, in order to establish how similar they are, and sometimes even to estimate when two varieties split off from one another. Boretzky (1998) investigated both the 100 item word list (in practice 97) and the 200 item word list (in practice 211) for Romani and PR. For 70 of 97 words (over 70%), a root inherited from Early Romani is in use in Spanish PR, which made Boretzky conclude that the lexical retention rate in Caló is particularly high (Boretzky 1998, p. 104). It must be said that there are relatively many words in Caló sources that are of obscure origins, sometimes due to falsifications (see, e.g., Adiego [2005b] for the origin of fake vocabulary and Adiego and Martin [2006, p. 23], who identified 115 words that were not genuine words in one Caló word list alone). Angloromani (AR), on the other hand, has not been subject to much invention of words. The retention numbers for AR are comparable to those of Caló, namely 80%, and also 80% for Norwegian Para-Romani and 70% for Swedish Para-Romani (Boretzky 1998, pp. 109, 112). Boretzky (1998, p. 108) counts 520 Early Romani roots in Smart and Crofton's (1875) material and 450 in Borrow's Caló (1841). These numbers are quite high, but not as high as for Romani varieties like Bugurdži (150 of 750 lost, i.e. 80% retention) and North Serbian Kalderash (76% retention; 180 roots lost) (Boretzky 1998, p. 114). On the other hand, Boretzky (1998, p. 114) remarks that the mixed varieties preserve many words that have disappeared from other varieties of Romani. In short, the loss of vocabulary for PR was hardly more than for varieties of Romani in the Balkans or Central Europe. The current knowledge of Romani words among speakers of PR, however, is usually much lower, perhaps as low as a few dozen (cf. McLane 1977).

Matras (2010, pp. 124–125) reached similar conclusions. His fieldwork in England yielded around 500 Romani-derived roots ('predecessors') plus 60 from other sources. He measured a rate of loss of around 10% compared to earlier published sources. Note that this refers to the collective knowledge of previous generations, not individuals. The individuals with the highest number of unique expressions knew around 200 on average, most of them of Romani origin. Similarly, Gamella et al. (2015) found that Gitanos in Spain in the 2010s understood only around 129 words on average, out of a list of 355 words, and younger people even fewer. The state of knowledge of Caló appears much lower than that of Angloromani (Gamella et al. 2015, p. 89).

12.3 Theories of Genesis

Several theories have been proposed to explain the phenomenon of Para-Romani varieties, pre-empted by Coelho and Schuchardt in the 1800s. Virtually, all researchers acknowledge that a special process has taken place that led to these mixed languages. Some researchers have linked the varieties with other types of special languages or contact phenomena (cf. contributions in Matras 1998c). In discussing these theories, we have to keep the linguistic procedure of creating new language structures separate from the socio-historical processes that gave rise to the acts of identities that are connected to the creation of the new language.

The first debate about the origin of individual Para-Romani varieties emerged in the 1970s, when Hancock (e.g. 1970, 1976) and Kenrick (1971, 1979) discussed the genesis of Angloromani (see Acton and Kenrick 1984; Hancock 1984b; Bakker 2000 for a summary), and argued for both sudden (Hancock) and slow emergence (Kenrick), and different social and historical processes, without reaching a consensus.

An early idea on the genesis of Angloromani is **gradual grammatical borrowing**. Researchers suggested that the original language was Romani and speakers started to borrow more and more words from English, followed by more and more morphology, syntax and phonology, with the end result of Angloromani (Thomason and Kaufman 1988, p. 6; Kenrick 1979). This was also suggested for other mixed languages by Myers-Scotton (1998), who relates the genesis of mixed languages to code-switching and a shift in matrix language, roughly the language of the grammatical frame. A major problem with this idea is that it does not explain why especially the most frequent and colloquial words in Angloromani are from Romani: What happened to the lexical borrowings from English into Romani, which started the whole process? It is also refuted in Matras (2010) drawing on historical attestations of British Romani.

Thomason and Kaufman (1988) included Angloromani in their seminal book on contact-induced language change. They believed that the grammar of English was borrowed: 'the lexicon is that of the English Gypsies' ethnic heritage, while the entire grammar has been borrowed (in effect) from English' (p. 7) and 'AngloRomani is the product of two entirely distinct historical processes: inherited vocabulary, borrowed grammar' (see also Thomason and Kaufman 1988, pp. 49, 88, 201). The process for Angloromani would, according to them, have been parallel to the genesis of Ma'a, where lexical borrowing from Bantu into a Cushitic language was intensified by grammatical borrowing, in the end leading to a mixed language with Cushitic lexicon and Bantu grammar. This view has been criticized in Bakker (2003a) as untenable: if first lexicon and then morphology and syntax were borrowed, then a Bantu language would have been the result, not the mixed language as it is. In the PR case, mutatis mutandis, English rather than Angloromani would have been the result. Coelho (1892) pre-empted this when he suggested morphological borrowing. Coelho discussed PR in Portugal, with its roots in Spain. He believed that Portuguese and Spanish had taken over the lost Romani grammar: 'In [Portugal PR], the Romani vestiges are almost exclusively limited to words and some derivational processes: Spanish and still Portuguese occupy the space left by Romani grammar. In this way, through successive mixtures, the Romance element was eliminating the Romani' (1892, p. 45). Already few years earlier, historical linguist Hermann Paul believed that morphological borrowing played a major role: 'The most extensive adoption of flectional endings took place in the Romani language. Therefore there is a Spanish Romani and an English Romani' (Paul 1886, p. 347).

Hugo Schuchardt (1884, pp. 8–10) briefly discussed Caló and Angloromani in the context of morphological borrowing, as examples of 'languages whose grammar does not stop at the reception of isolated foreign elements'. He identified Spanish plural morphemes and Spanish verbal conjugations. He showed that Caló still had quite a few Romani grammatical elements, and suggested that Caló was the result of taking over grammatical elements from Spanish, but probably not as individual morphemes, but as whole sets. He seems to consider it a gradual process, as he expected further absorption of Spanish elements into Caló. Schuchardt also wrote that he had no criteria to consider a language like Caló as still Romani or already Spanish at specific points in its development. Many researchers today do not consider PR as a transitory stage, but as endpoints of a special process (after which, of course, the languages keep developing). After their genesis, they may have merged with the local languages.

Ian Hancock linked Angloromani with **creoles** (1970) and **pidgins** (1976) (see also Hancock 1984b). Para-Romani varieties were also included in the *Bibliography of Pidgin and Creole Languages* (Reinecke et al. 1975). Hancock summarizes a sixteenth-century source in which the union between newly arrived Romani speakers in the British Isles would have formed one group with local English vagrants. Neither group could learn the language of the other, and thus, they resorted to the creation of a pidgin. 'In time, however, the Romanes-English pidgin gained greater currency over the original Romanes, giving rise to the now creolized Anglo-Romanes dialect' (Hancock 1970, p. 43). Previous pidginization would be observable in the fact that non-English phonemes were lost as well as Romani morphology. There are important structural differences between creoles and Para-Romani varieties, however, which force us to reject the idea (cf. also the critical evaluation in Matras 2010, p. 169). In creoles, virtually all morphemes, lexical and grammatical, are from one language, the so-called lexifier, and the grammatical system differs substantially from that of the lexifiers and other contributing languages (see, e.g., Daval-Markussen et al. 2017). In Angloromani, however, the bound morphemes and the meanings of these morphemes are identical to those of (colloquial) English—and that is never the case in pidgins or creoles, where such bound morphemes are not part of the language. Hancock gives the example of 'the kettle is boiling' and 'I saw that place' as Romani *kekávi kerióla* (stem *ker-*, detransitivizing suffix – *io-*, third person *–l* and present *–a*) and Angloromani *de kekaubie's kerrivin'*, as well as Romani *me dikhóm odóva than* and Angloromani *mandi dicked 'duvva tan*. In an English-lexifier creole, these sentences could be something like *kedel stand boil* and *mi bin lukim dati plesi*. English morphology in pidgins and creoles is almost always completely lost, and new grammatical structures are formed, incl. here a transitive morpheme *–im*. There is no documentation of a pidgin stage for PR, but in the socio-historical scenario sketched, it could have been possible. Even so, Angloromani has not subsequently developed into anything like a creole, as no new grammatical system was developed; instead, an intertwining of Romani and English took place (cf. Bakker and Mous 1994 for the term). In all other PR varieties, the situation is exactly parallel with Angloromani. Boretzky (1985) likewise disagrees with the view of PR varieties as creoles.

A second suggestion for the genesis of PR is the process of **relexification**. The term relexification has several meanings, all having to do with the replacement of a lexicon. In the case of Angloromani, the English lexicon would have been replaced with a Romani lexicon (see, e.g., Boretzky and Igla 1994).

Some researchers have suggested that there was an ongoing shift in a speech community, and younger generations prevented the shift by preserving what was recoverable, namely the lexicon (e.g. Boretzky and Igla 1994; see also Brenzinger 1987; Sasse 1992). This is the so-called **U-turn hypothesis**. Boretzky (1985) was an early comparative study of Para-Romani varieties, involving Angloromani, Caló and a structurally comparable variety spoken in Armenia, Lomavren. Boretzky suggested that these PR varieties were formed when young people no longer had access to the full system of the language and were only able to insert the most conspicuous elements (lexical items) from the language of their parents or grandparents into the local language (e.g. English) that had become their mother tongue.

Kenrick (1979, p. 113) compared earlier data of Angloromani with contemporary Romani data from Finland and concluded that Angloromani had undergone a parallel development earlier, where the phonology had converged with that of English, and increased mixing would have led to the PR. The documentary evidence was scarce, however.

Matras (2000) proposed a holistic or **compartmentalization approach** to mixed languages. Lexical reorientation, selective replication, convergence and categorial fusion are processes that account for the wide diversity of the properties of mixed languages in different combinations. The different functions of mixed languages are linked to a compartmentalization of processes. A functional turnover, in the form of a shift from Romani to English, combined with a process of selective replication, i.e. the insertion of Romani into host language frames, led to the PR varieties.

Adamou and Granqvist (2015, p. 537) compared two Romani varieties, from Greece and from Finland, which they called 'unevenly mixed languages' and which they suggested could be a stage in the development of a mixed language. These display basically Romani lexicon and grammar but with a relatively high (ca. 10%) proportion of Turkish- and Finnish-inflected verbs, respectively. Here are two examples (Romani underlined):

(7) <u>liːjas</u>   kokonaːn   <u>maːn</u>   oma-ksi   ja   <u>deːvel</u>   täytt-i
    take-PST.3SG entirely   me   own-TRN   and   God   fill-PST.3SG
    '<u>God took me</u> wholly unto himself and filled me.' (Adamou and Granqvist 2015, p. 526)

<u>(8)</u>   <u>dʒan-es</u>   <u>kasa</u>   konuʃ-ijor-sun   <u>akana</u>   (Thrace Romani)
      know-2SG   who.INS   talk-PROG-2SG   now
      '<u>Do you know</u> <u>who</u> you're talking to <u>now</u>?'   (Adamou and Granqvist 2015, p. 537)

Similar patterns have been observed in North Russian Romani, where Russian verbs are frequently used (Adamou and Granqvist 2015, p. 542; Rusakov 2001) and in at least 18 Romani varieties under (former) influence of Turkish in which some Turkish-inflected verbs are used (Friedman 2010, 2013; Adamou 2012). The authors 'suggest that this type of Romani language mixing illustrates an early stage of mixed language formation that did not develop into an independent mixed language'. The authors think that an 'arrested matrix language turnover analysis is plausible' (a process proposed by Myers-Scotton 1998) for both the Thrace case and the Finland case. This would mean that an ongoing process of shift to Finnish and Turkish, respectively, was stopped at a point where only some items (notably verbs) had been taken over. The unevenly mixed languages would be 'the result of an interrupted process of mixed language formation' (p. 544).

Matras (2010) provides a detailed scenario for the development of Angloromani. Whereas previously Romani was used in the homes and in contact with other Roma, and English was used for contacts outside the community, increasing numbers of English speakers, including travellers of non-Romani origin, joined the Romani-speaking communities, causing a language shift towards English within a few decades, between the late eighteenth century and the middle of the nineteenth century. In the mid-nineteenth century, there were still people who could speak both Romani and Angloromani (besides English), as is witnessed by Smart and Crofton (1875), probably as extremes on a continuum (Matras 2010, p. 93). The Romani elements were maintained for emotional reasons as an emblematic badge of Romani-ness. Indic-inflected Romani was abandoned rather abruptly (except in Wales), and Romani grammatical elements disappeared within a few generations (Matras 2010, pp. 89–94, 168–171), due to a functional turnover from Romani to English as a home language, resulting in a 'Romani component that is hosted within the utterance and discourse framework of English' (Matras 2010, p. 91).

12.4 Functions of Para-Romani Varieties

The functional range of uses of PR varieties is quite limited in modern times. The language is not, at least today, used in longer narratives or conversations. Nineteenth-century sources from the UK do provide narratives in PR (e.g. Smart and Crofton 1875), but recent texts seem contrived and are not examples of spontaneous speech (e.g. in Carling et al. 2014). Where spontaneous speech has been recorded on tape, the density of Romani words was not extensive (e.g. Leigh [1998] for Caló, Matras [2010] for Angloromani). Earlier documentation suggests a fuller range of use (see, for example, Bakker 1998, 2000).

PR varieties are not, at least in the observable past, learned by children (but see Bakker [1998, pp. 87–88] for quotes from the nineteenth century on children speaking Angloromani), and today, they are used only sporadically by adults on special occasions, and are thus 'a different kind of language' (Matras et al. 2007), facilitated by its necessary coexistence with a local language.

Kenrick (1979) listed a number of functions for the use of Angloromani: self-identification; identification by checking whether the interlocutor understands you; internal trading jargon; songs; wordplay and lexical challenges; as a secret language and in oaths and endearments.

PR varieties are used in specific situations, sometimes associated with secrecy (so that bystanders could not understand), sometimes associated with internal group values, which means that the language should not be used in the presence of outsiders. The use of PR today is triggered by situations ripe with emotive value (Matras 2010).

It appears almost impossible for speakers to engage in everyday conversation in Angloromani (Matras 2010, pp. 96–97). The reason is simple: it is not used for daily information exchange, but rather to elicit the hearer's solidarity. Matras (2010) argues that the use of Angloromani (AR) is triggered by a complex set of interactional strategies, such as directives, warnings, the circumference of cultural taboos, and the inclusion and exclusion of certain bystanders and interlocutors. Thus, 'the choice of AR elicits the hearer's identification with the speaker's emotional involvement - a sense of solidarity that has its base in the activation of an exclusive presuppositional domain of experiences, attitudes and interests that are shared by group members' (Matras 2010, p. 134). The restricted use also leads to loosening of grammatical norms (e.g. omission of English articles) and changes of meanings.

12.5 Similar Phenomena: Secret Languages Among Non-Romani Groups

In many societies in the Old World, there are groups that use special vocabulary as a badge of group identity and a convenient way of communicating with each other without bystanders interfering, often referred to as cryptolects. These groups often consist of people who engage in itinerant economic activities and are thus more mobile than the members of the surrounding society that they interact with. Para-Romani varieties have some sociolinguistic and linguistic traits in common with such languages, but they almost in all cases can clearly be distinguished on social and linguistic grounds (Bakker 1998). PR varieties make less use of camouflaging strategies by altering the shape of words taken from the local language. Likewise, PR lexicon covers especially everyday vocabulary, whereas such secret languages as used among specialized groups like beggars, drug users or traders mostly cover meanings in the realm of authorities, professional activities and the like, often with several words for the same tabooed concept. Often forms or meanings of part of the vocabulary are distorted in such languages, e.g. the use of 'carrots' meaning 'fingers', the employment of metaphors (e.g. 'sparker' for 'horse') or the addition of syllables to make words less recognizable. Such processes are either unknown in PR or quite marginal, obviously because the foreign vocabulary makes such processes unnecessary. This further suggests that the processes behind the genesis of PR and cryptolects are different (Bakker 1998).

Already in medieval Europe, similar types of languages existed in which everyday words were replaced with foreign words or with creative cryptolectal formations. Rotwelsch had been documented from the Middle Ages in

German-speaking regions (Kluge 1901). The earliest sources of Rotwelsch showed mainly German-derived vocabulary and some Romance roots, but this core was supplemented later with Hebrew and Romani words. This has led to the characterization of Rotwelsch as a (lexical) mixture of German, Hebrew/Yiddish and Romani, embedded in German (see Matras [1998b] and Kluge [1901] for sources). In the Middle East in medieval times, peripatetic groups were reported to use secret words (Bosworth 1976) in their Arabic. The language of the Banū Sāsān in the Middle East between the fourth and thirteenth century was basically Arabic with at most a few hundred non-Arabic words, some of which have been identified as Persian, and some as Jewish.

Matras (2010) also discusses similarities and contrasts between secret languages and PR. He takes an intermediate position: there was a slow process of loss of Romani inflectional grammar and a sudden process of shift of the predication grammar to that of the host language.

12.6 Historical Developments

Thanks to the diligence of aficionados and researchers in Spain, the UK and Scandinavia, we have data from Basque PR (assembled in Bakker 1991), Spanish PR (Adiego 2002; Montoya and Gabarri 2010; Krinková 2015), Catalan PR (Adiego 2012), Swedish PR (Gjerdman 1950) and Angloromani PR (Smart and Crofton 1875), and more, covering several centuries, which could make it possible to track longitudinal developments. Documentation could also allow us to exclude certain theories of origin.

There are virtually no utterances in historical documents that mix Romani and Para-Romani in the same text (but cf. Matras 2010, pp. 93–94), which suggests that the transition from Romani to Para-Romani was a fairly sudden process rather than one that took place over many centuries. Smart and Crofton (1875) have material in both Indic-inflected Angloromani and PR, which shows that they coexisted in the same community. On the other hand, a slow process has been suggested several times (e.g. Kenrick 1971; Thomason and Kaufman 1988 for Angloromani, Adiego 2019 for Caló), which would not align very well with the observation that the first attestations of Para-Romani are old. The first documentation of English sentences in which Romani words were embedded, reminiscent of Angloromani dates from 1616, less than a century after the arrival of Gypsies in Britain, and more than three centuries before Romani, was still attested in the UK (Bakker 2002).

374 P. Bakker

A late seventeenth-century word list of the 'Gypsy Jargon' from Spain likewise already contains some traces that suggest that it was a Para-Romani variety, with forms like *chor-ar* 'to steal', *naj-ar-se* 'to leave' *cocal-es* 'male sex' (originally 'bone') and *gurrav-ador* 'barber', with Spanish verbal and nominal endings indicated in bold (Adiego 1998).

The earliest data for Scandoromani are much more recent. The oldest sentence recorded in Scandinavia was a phrase uttered in a court case in 1709, and it is Indic-inflected Romani, not Para-Romani (Bakker et al. 2017), but the speaker may have been a Sinti woman from Germany. A 1764 phrase was identified as 'perfect Scandoromani' (Carling et al. 2014, p. 8), ca. 250 years after the arrival of Gypsies in Sweden:

(10) beng-an   der   lingero   truppo
      devil-DEF   in   3PL.POSS   body
      'the devil in their body'

The PR nature of this phrase can be contested, however, especially if it is read as *beng ander lingero truppo*. Sources from the 1840s are more extensive, and clearly Para-Romani, e.g. Andersson's materials from the 1840s (Gjerdman 1950). In example (11), *–ar* is the Swedish present tense marker, *ejn* the Swedish indefinite article, *eler* the word for 'or', and constituent order is also conspicuously Swedish (Gjerdman 1950, p. 113).

(11) dova   atj-ar   ejn   Bang   Buro   eler   latju — tjavo   (Scando-
                                                                                         Romani 1847)
      3SG   BE-PRES   INDEF   devil   farmer   or   INDEF   good   boy
      Dender   er   en   satans   bonde   eler   en   bra   karl   (Swedish)
      'He is a devilish farmer or a good guy'
      (Romani *odova* 'this', sometimes also used for third person singular pronoun; *beng* 'devil',
          buro 'farmer' in some dialects only, *lačo* 'good', *čhavo* 'boy')

In order to study the development of Para-Romani varieties through time, I will discuss Basque Romani, Catalan Romani, Caló and Angloromani, as I have most extensive sources for these.

Bakker (1991) discussed a few dozen sources of language use of the Gypsies in the Basque Country. A 1715 source with two words does not shed light on the language; an 1833 source shows a form of Indic-inflected Romani rather than PR. However, from 1848 onwards, all documentation shows a clear form of Basque PR. Michel (1848, p. 10r. ff.) provided only a word list, but as virtually all nouns and adjectives end in *–a* (singular) or *–ak* (plural) as in Basque in the citation forms, and the verbs end in *–tzea* (<*tcia*>), a Basque nominalizing suffix, the presence of a Basque grammatical system is beyond any doubt. From that time, all sources are clearly PR in the region.

The sources for Catalan Romani are quite interesting. Catalan Romani as documented in the early twentieth century was a typical PR variety, with basically no traces of Indic morphology or syntax (Adiego 2012, p. 317). The oldest source is Sentmenat's vocabulary between 1728 and 1762, which also contains some phrases, and these show a mostly Indic-inflected Romani, e.g.:

---

(12) | Bro | baró | dabel | te | del | amen-di | o | cielos
| 1SG.M | big.M | God | to | give-3SG | 1PL-DAT | DEF.M | heaven
'Let my great God give us the heaven' (Adiego [2002, p. 64], who translates as 'Mi gran Dios nos dé el cielo', i.e. 'Our great God gave us (the) heaven') (Romani *miro* 'my' (M), *baro* 'big', *Devel* 'God', *te* '(hope) that' *del* 'he gives' *amende* 'to us' *o* DEF.ART, Spanish *cielo* 'heaven', Romani masculine noun adaptation marker *-os*)

Sentmenat's materials display a fairly conservative dialect with Indic nominal inflection, distinguishing also between loan strata (e.g. the ending *–os* in the Spanish word for 'heaven', *cielo*) and pre-European strata. Personal pronouns are Romani, definite articles as well (with one exception **la** *piri* 'the chicken').

After that, sources showed more Catalan influence. Adiego (2012, p. 317) characterized Catalan Romani of the 1840s as follows: it 'was not yet a mixed language, insofar as it retained Romani verb inflections and pronouns and Romani endings to express the number and gender of nouns and adjectives, while only the oblique cases of the nominal declension had been completely replaced by the use of (mostly) Catalan prepositions'. The following illustrates the overall Romani structure but with a Catalan preposition (here: *da*) that replaced all case marking:

---

(13) | Pi-as | paigmin | da | lacri | gamik
| Drink-1PL | water | of | 3SG.F.POSS | source
'We drink water from their fountain/well' ('boire de l'eau de leur fontaine.') (Catalan Romani in 1837, quoted in Ackerley 1914/1915, p. 119) (*Pi-as* drink-1PL 'we drink', *pani* 'water', *lakri* (3SG.F.POSS) 'her', but translated as 'their', *hanik/xeni* 'well, source')

Around 1900, the Catalan author Juli Vallmitjana wrote several works of fiction in which speakers of Catalan PR were quoted (e.g. 1908). Adiego (2012) analysed the PR used there. Catalan PR preserved the Romani plural endings, including the inherited-loan word distinction, but otherwise its grammatical system was Catalan. Here is an example:

(14) Aixís   un   <u>juquel</u>   rabiós   els   busquini   les   <u>ger-à</u>
     let's.hope   INDF-M dog   rabid   DEF.PL   bite   DEF.PL   leg-PL
     'Let's hope a rabid dog bites their legs!' (Adiego 2012, p. 311)
     (*džukel* 'dog', *her-a* 'legs')

The verbs follow Catalan inflection, and many stems are based on the Romani third person forms, e.g. *pən-él-u* 'I say', based on Romani *phen-el* 'he/she says' and Catalan *–u* 1SG.PRS. Personal pronouns are always Catalan, with one exception, *manguis* for first person singular. The plural marker is Romani.

On the basis of these data, Adiego suggests that the transition from Indic-inflected Romani to the PR variety was a relatively slow process, which he reconstructs as follows: 'first, loss of oblique cases, replaced by prepositions (prior to first attestations), then, loss of verbal inflection (between 1850 and 1900) and then, loss of noun plural inflection (after 1900)'. Thus, Adiego concludes that the 'Para-Romani dialect Catalan Gypsies was the result of a gradual borrowing of inflectional endings and function words from Catalan, rather than a sudden relexification of Catalan through Romani loanwords' (Adiego 2012, p. 317). This can also be argued for Caló, where Romani plural endings and adjectival morphology were still in use, when verbal morphology had completely become Spanish (cf. Adiego 2019).

As the sources for Angloromani are the most extensive, I will survey the development of that variety in more detail. Matras (2010, p. 58) mentions, as the earliest sources from the UK, documents from 1542 (Indic Romani), 1615 (Angloromani) and 1776/1785 (Indic Romani). In Table 12.2, I provide an overview based on my own study (Bakker 2000) of the early materials in chronological order (skipping some that are so limited that one cannot draw conclusions about the grammatical system), indicating whether phonology, morphology, functional/grammatical markers and constituent order are like Romani (R), English (E), or roughly equally Romani and English (R,E) or more Romani or English (R > E, E > R), i.e. more than half. PHO = phonology, MOR = morphology, FGM = Free grammatical morphemes, SYN = syntax. After the name of the collector/author, an indication of the amount of material is provided in the form of the number of phrases/sentences in parentheses.

12 Para-Romani Varieties   377

Table 12.2 Romani and English in early sources of Romani in England

	PHO	MOR	FGM	SYN
1776 Bryant	E > R	R	R	?
1790s Whiter (ca. 150)	E	R > 0	R	R
1798 N.N. (40)	R,E	R > E,0	R > E	R > E
1805 Lee/Irvine (15)	E	R	E	E?
1818 Copsey/Axon (17)	E	R > E	R,E	R
1818 Bright (42)	E	R > 0	R > E	E > R
1832–1833 Fox (18+)	E	R	R,E	E
1836 Roberts (7)	E > R	R > E	R > E	E > R?
1850s Taylor	E	E	R,E	E
1859 Norwood/Cooper	E	E,R	?	E > R
1860 Norwood/Bluett	E	E	E,R	E
1863 Norwood/Buckland	E	R	R > E	E > R
1865 Sinclair	E	R,E,0	R > E	E
1872 Sanderson	E	E > R	E,R	E

The few sentences that Bryant quotes in his material collected in 1776 make clear that it is a non-Anglicized form of Romani: it contains pronominal clitics, verb agreement, case markers, plural endings, articles with correct gender and non-English word order. However, gender concord is sometimes violated (e.g. *bauro charrie* 'sword', *baro* (M) *čuri* (F) 'big knife'), combining masculine and feminine (Bryant 1785, p. 391). Irvine (1817), who had his data from the Lee family, displays unambiguous PR, with a sentence like this:

(15)   Can you <u>roku</u> Roomus and play upon the <u>bosh</u>?

(cf. Welsh Romani *raker-* 'to speak', *båšimangeri* 'fiddle', from the verb *båšavel* 'play an instrument', with a nominalizing suffix). This material also displays Romani plural markers.

The results are somewhat ambiguous: one can interpret this as a sudden genesis slightly different from location to location, or as a gradual development: there seems to be a transition between 1818 and 1836 to greater English dominance. Also, the Catalonian data suggest a gradual development, with a precedence of loss of nominal inflection.

12.7 Conclusions

In this chapter, we have discussed what PR varieties are, how they may have come into being and what their functions are in the speaker communities.

PR varieties can be described as speech strategies in which lexical items, sometimes also grammatical elements such as copulas and pronouns, overwhelmingly come from Romani and are inserted into a frame of a host language, where the host language is not only used as the language of communication with outsiders, but also commonly within the PR speech community. The use of Romani items is connected with an emotive mode, in which cultural values and taboos as well as group demarcation trigger insertion. PR varieties are clearly forms of speech that are unmistakably distinguishable from Indic-inflected Romani and structurally similar to types of mixed languages combining lexicon and grammatical system documented elsewhere in the world.

Many early studies considered the PR varieties as languages in their own right, but recent data collected by Matras and his team in England and Gamella and his team in Spain cast doubt on this. Both studies mention the shared perception of the speakers that the original language is lost and only remnants are known by them, and neither Caló nor Angloromani (and by implication other PR varieties) are full-fledged languages. Even Carling et al. (2014) mention 'remnants of a language', even though they consider Scandoromani a full-fledged language. PR varieties are not used in the full range of domains as minority languages in bilingual societies, and linguistic norms have been relaxed considerably, partly due to their limited use.

There are several theories about their genesis. We can exclude, on both socio-historical and linguistic grounds, that PR varieties are the result of pidginization or creolization. Unlike in the case of pidgins, there were no longer-lasting situations where Gypsies and non-Gypsies lacked a common language, as both Romani (internally) and the host language (for external communication) were widely available. Neither do PR varieties display regularization and reduction as is commonly observed in pidgins and creoles. Also not plausible is a scenario of relexification in the sense of Muysken (1981). In his model, based on his case study of Media Lengua, the inserted lexical items adopt the meaning(s) of the replaced lexical items (in Angloromani English meanings for Romani items), but there is no evidence for such semantic transfer in PR. A scenario of gradual replacement of a Romani grammatical system by one of the host languages over a few generations seems compatible with the linguistic and socio-historical data, as shown on the basis of diachronic data from Spain and Catalonia, according to a recent study by Adiego (2019).

The most likely model is one related to what has been called the U-turn model. Matras (2010) suggested that once the increased presence of host language speakers in an otherwise tight-knit community caused a shift from Romani to the host language, a conscious act of identity triggered a link with the ancestral language through insertion. This may have happened quickly, over one or several generations, as suggested by Bakker (2000, 2002) and Matras (2010, pp. 168–172) on the basis of Angloromani data.

Some of the controversies in connection with PR varieties are connected to the data collection. It is only in recent decades that fieldwork tools have enabled researchers to undertake surveys of language knowledge, perception and conversational practices. Data from the twenty-first century suggest infrequent insertion of Romani items in the host languages, contrasting with earlier, dictated sentences, translated narratives and data transmitted through writing (e.g. in letters) in which close to the complete lexicon consisted of Romani insertions. The question is whether twenty-first-century speech practices have existed for one or two centuries, in which case such earlier texts are fabricated, or whether the early texts are authentic samples of speech, in which case the modern recordings would constitute a case of advanced language obsolescence, as the data in Matras (2010) and Gamella et al. (2015) suggest, or contrived by speakers or researchers (as suggested by Matras [2015] for the texts in Carling et al. [2014]).

PR varieties have been studied in the theoretical frameworks of Romani dialectology, contact-induced language change and the study of mixed languages. In Romani dialectology, they have a special place in that they do not constitute full-fledged dialects: only the lexicon can be studied, and some few remnants of the grammatical systems, as most of the language is identical to the host language. The quantity of studies of PR within language contact studies is limited and revolves mostly around the role of code-switching, pidginization/creolization, the connections with lexical borrowing and whether maintenance, shift or a third process plays the major role. PR varieties are sometimes included in studies of mixed languages, and sometimes they are not, mainly because of the question of their stability and their languageness.

The fact that no fewer than five full-length monographs were devoted to PR varieties in recent years is an indication of the continued interest in the phenomenon (Matras 2010 on Angloromani; Montoya and Gabarri 2010 on Caló; Carling et al. 2014 on Swedish Romani; Krinková 2015 on PR varieties of the Iberian peninsula; Andersson 2016 on Andalusian youngsters' attitudes towards Caló). An increasing number of sociolinguistic and lexicographic documentation projects as well as in-depth diachronic and synchronic documentation of lexicon and more or less spontaneous utterances, by both community members and academics, has enabled a huge leap forward in our understanding of the phenomena.

Despite intensive research, the exact circumstances of genesis are uncertain: data from longer time ranges could be interpreted as either a sudden genesis or a slow process, and the social and linguistic processes could have a different timeline, such as a sudden shift of the predication grammar and a slow process of the loss of Romani inflection, as suggested by Matras (2010).

Today, the use of most PR varieties is limited to special interactional situations flagging a Romani world contrasting with outsiders. In the past, they may have been used in a broader range of functions, including narratives and daily interaction within the community (Adiego 2005a; Matras 2010).

References

Ackerley, Frederick George. 1914/1915. The Romani speech of Catalonia. *Journal of the Gypsy Lore Society*, n.s., 8: 99–140.

Acton, Thomas, and Donald Kenrick (eds). 1984. *Romani rokkeripen to divvus: The English Romani Dialect and its contemporary social, educational and linguistic standing*. London: Romanestan Publications.

Adamou, Evangelia. 2012. Verb morphologies in contact: Evidence from the Balkan area. In *Morphologies in contact*, ed. Martine Vanhove, 143–162. Berlin: De Gruyter.

Adamou, Evangelia, and Kimmo Granqvist. 2015. Unevenly mixed Romani languages. *The International Journal of Bilingualism* 19 (5): 525–547.

Adiego, Ignasi-Xavier. 1998. The Spanish Gypsy vocabulary of manuscript 3929, Biblioteca Nacional de Madrid (18th Century): A rereading. *Journal of the Gypsy Lore Society*, 5th ser., 8 (1): 1–18.

Adiego, Ignasi-Xavier. 2002. *Un vocabulario español-gitano del Marqués de Sentmenat (1697–1762). Edición y estudio lingüístico*. Barcelona: Universitat de Barcelona.

Adiego, Ignasi-Xavier. 2004. Lengua Ethigitana o de gitanos por José Antonio Conde (1866–1820). Tercera edición crítica tras autopsia del manuscrito. Barcelona: Universitat de Barcelona (working paper).

Adiego, Ignasi-Xavier. 2005a. The vestiges of Caló today. In *General and applied Romani linguistics: Proceedings from the 6th International Conference on Romani linguistics*, ed. Barbara Schrammel, Dieter Halwachs, and Gerd Ambrosch, 60–78. Munich: Lincom Europa.

Adiego, Ignasi-Xavier. 2005b. The first Caló dictionary ever published in Spain (Trujillo 1844): An analysis of its sources. *Romani Studies* 15: 125–143.

Adiego, Ignasi-Xavier. 2012. Catalan Romani (caló català) in the work of Juli Vallmitjana: An initial appraisal. *Zeitschrift für Katalanistik* 25: 305–320.

Adiego, Ignasi-Xavier. 2019. Para una historia de la lengua gitana española: realidad y artificio. Presentación, Simposio XLVIII Sociedad Española de Lingüística, Madrid.

Adiego, Ignasi-Xavier, and Ana Isabel Martín. 2006. George Borrow, Luis de Usoz y sus respectivos vocabularios Gitanos. *Revista De Filología Española* 86 (1): 7–30.

Andersson, Pierre. 2016. Actitudes hacia la variedad Caló y sus hablantes. Un estudio sociolingüístico de las opinions de adolescentes andaluces. Romanica Gothoburgensia LXXII. Göteborg: Universitet. http://hdl.handle.net/2077/42006.

Bakker, Peter. 1991. Basque Romani—A preliminary grammatical sketch of a mixed language. In *In the margin of Romani: Gypsy languages in contact*, ed. Peter Bakker and Marcel Cortiade, 56–90. Amsterdam: Publikaties van het Instituut voor Algemene Taalwetenschap 58. Studies in Language Contact I.

Bakker, Peter. 1995. Notes on the genesis of Caló and other Iberian Para-Romani varieties. In *Romani in contact: The history, structure and sociology of a language*, ed. Yaron Matras, 125–150. Amsterdam: John Benjamins.

Bakker, Peter. 1998. Para-Romani languages versus secret languages: Differences in origin, structure, and use. In *The Romani element in non-standard speech*, ed. Yaron Matras, 69–96. Wiesbaden: Harrassowitz.

Bakker, Peter. 1999. The Northern branch of Romani: Mixed and non-mixed varieties. In *Die Sprache der Roma. Perspektiven der Romani-Forschung in Österreich im interdisziplinären und internazionalen Kontext*, ed. Dieter Halwachs and Florian Menz, 172–209. Klagenfurt: Drava.

Bakker, Peter. 2000. The genesis of Angloromani. In *Scholarship and the Gypsy struggle: Commitment in Romani studies*, ed. Thomas Acton, 14–31. Hatfield: University of Hertfordshire Press.

Bakker, Peter. 2001. Romani and Turkish. In *Was ich noch sagen wollte: A Multilingual Festschrift for Norbert Boretzky on occasion of his 65th birthday*, ed. Birgit Igla and Thomas Stolz, 303–326. Berlin: Akademie Verlag (Studia Typologica Band 2).

Bakker, Peter. 2002. An early vocabulary of British Romani (1616): A linguistic analysis. *Romani Studies*, 5th ser., 12 (2): 75–101.

Bakker, Peter. 2003a. Mixed languages as autonomous systems. In *The mixed language debate*, ed. Yaron Matras and Peter Bakker, 107–150. Berlin: Mouton de Gruyter.

Bakker, Peter. 2003b. Purism and mixed languages. In *Purism in minor languages, endangered languages, regional languages, mixed languages: Papers from the conference on 'Purism in the age of globalisation', Bremen, September 2001*, ed. Joseph Brincat, Winfried Boeder, and Thomas Stolz, 98–139. Bochum: Universitätsverlag Dr. N. Brockmeyer (Diversitas Linguarum 2).

Bakker, Peter. 2013. *Mixed languages*. Oxford Bibliographies online. Oxford University Press. www.oxfordbibliographies.com.

Bakker, Peter. 2017a. Typology of mixed languages. In *The Cambridge handbook of linguistic typology*, ed. Alexandra Y. Aikhenvald and Robert M.W. Dixon, 217–253. Cambridge: Cambridge University Press.

Bakker, Peter. 2017b. Romani coin names. In *Languages of resistance: Ian Hancock's contribution to Romani studies*, ed. Hristo Kyuchukov and William New, 91–100. München: LINCOM.

Bakker, Peter, and Hein Van der Voort. 1991. Para-Romani languages: An overview and some speculations on their genesis. In *In the margin of Romani: Gypsy languages in contact*, ed. Peter Bakker and Marcel Cortiade, 16–44. Amsterdam: Publikaties van het Instituut voor Algemene Taalwetenschap 58. Studies in Language Contact I.

Bakker, Peter, and Marcel Cortiade, eds. 1991. *In the margin of Romani: Gypsy languages in contact*. Amsterdam: Publikaties van het Instituut voor Algemene Taalwetenschap 58. Studies in Language Contact I.

Bakker, Peter, and Yaron Matras. 2003. *Bibliography of modern Romani linguistics: Including a guide to Romani linguistics*. Amsterdam: John Benjamins.

Bakker, Peter, and Maarten Mous (eds.). 1994. *Mixed languages. 15 case studies in language intertwining*. Amsterdam: IFOTT.

Bakker, Peter, Sebastian Casinge, and Jon Pettersson. 2017. Anna Maria Adamsdotter: Her life and her language. Paper presented at Baltic Sea Conference on Romani Studies, 19–21 April, Södertörn University, Stockholm, Sweden.

Boretzky, Norbert. 1985. Sind Zigeunersprachen Kreols? In *Akten des 1. Essener Kolloquiums über Kreolsprachen und Sprachkontakt*, ed. Thomas Stolz, Norbert Boretzky, and Werner Enninger, 43–70. Bochum: Brockmeyer.

Boretzky, Norbert. 1998. Der Romani-Wortschatz in den Romani-Misch-Dialekten. In *The Romani element in non-standard speech*, ed. Yaron Matras, 97–132. Wiesbaden: Harrassowitz.

Boretzky, Norbert, and Birgit Igla. 1994. Romani mixed dialects. In *Mixed languages: 15 case studies in language intertwining*, ed. Peter Bakker and Maarten Mous, 36–68. Amsterdam: IFOTT.

Borrow, George. 1841. *The Zincali: An account of the Gypsies of Spain*. London: Murray.

Bosworth, Clifford Edmund. 1976. *The Mediaeval Islamic underworld: The Banū Sāsān in Arabic society and literature*. Leiden: E. J. Brill.

Brenzinger, Mathias. 1987. Die Sprachliche und Kulturelle Stellung der Mbugu (Ma'a). MA thesis, University of Cologne, Cologne.

Bryant, Jacob. 1785. Collections on the Zingara, or Gypsey language. *Archaeologia* 7: 387–394.

Caferoğlu, Ahmet. 1943. Geygeli Yürüklerinin kullandıkları gizli dili [The secret language used by the Geygel nomads]. In *Anadolo Ağizlarindan Toplamalar*, ed. Ahmet Caferoğlu, 196–198. Istanbul: Bürhaneddin Basimevi [reprinted in 1994: Türk Dil Kurumu Yayınları].

Carling, Gerd, Lenny Lindell, and Gilbert Ambrazaitis. 2014. *Scandoromani. Remnants of a mixed language*. Leiden, Netherlands: Brill.

Charnon-Deutsch, Lou. 2014. *The Spanish Gypsy: The history of a European obsession*. Philadelphia: Penn State University Press.

Coelho, F. Adolpho. 1892. *Os Ciganos de Portugal. Com um Estudo sobre o Calão*. Lisboa: Imprensa Nacional.

Conde, José Antonio. Ca. 1810. Lengua Ethigitana o de Gitanos. Madrid, Real Academia de la Historia, Manuscript 9–5969 (237–92).

Cortiade, Marcel. 1991. Romani versus Para-Romani. In *In the margin of Romani: Gypsy languages in contact*, ed. Peter Bakker and Marcel Cortiade, 1–15. Amsterdam: Publikaties van het Instituut voor Algemene Taalwetenschap 58. Studies in Language Contact I.

Daval-Markussen, Aymeric, Kristoffer Friis Bøegh, and Peter Bakker. 2017. West African languages and creoles worldwide. In *Creole studies—Phylogenetic approaches*, ed. Peter Bakker, Finn Borchsenius, Carsten Levisen, and Eeva Sippola, 141–174. Amsterdam: John Benjamins.

Dimmendaal, Gerrit J. 1995. Do some languages have a multi-genetic or non-genetic origin? An exercise in taxonomy. In *Proceedings of the Fifth Nilo-Saharan Conference, Nice, 1992*, ed. Robert Nicolai and Franz Rottland, 354–369. Cologne: Rüdiger Köppe.

Dimmendaal, Gerrit J. 2011. *Historical linguistics and the comparative study of African languages*. Amsterdam: John Benjamins.

Elšík, Viktor. 2009. Loanwords in Selice Romani, an Indo-Aryan language of Slovakia. In *Loanwords in the world's languages: A comparative handbook*, ed. Martin Haspelmath and Uri Tadmor, 260–303. Berlin: De Gruyter Mouton.

Friedman, Victor. 2010. Turkish grammar in Balkan Romani: Hierarchies of markedness in Balkan linguistics. *Balkanistica* 23: 107–124.

Friedman, Victor. 2013. Compartmentalized grammar: The variable (non)-integration of Turkish verbal conjugation in Romani dialects. *Romani Studies* 23 (1): 107–120.

Gamella, Juan F., Cayetano Fernández Ortega, and Ignasi-Xavier Adiego. 2015. The long agony of Hispanoromani: The remains of Caló in the speech of Spanish Gitanos. *Romani Studies* 25 (1): 53–93.

Gamella, Juan F., Ignasi-Xavier Adiego, and Cayetano Fernández Ortega. 2016. A Caló Lexicon with data about its knowledge by a group of Spanish Gitanos or Calé. In *Interacciones entre el caló y el español. Historia, relaciones y fuentes*, ed. Iva Buzek, 113–135. Brno: Masarykova Univerzita.

Gjerdman, Olof. 1950. Djos Per Anderssons ordlista i original. *Dialektstudier tillägnade Gunnar Hedström*, 85–126. Uppsala: Landsmål- och Folkminnesarkivet.

Greenberg, Joseph H. 1999. Are there mixed languages? In *Essays in poetics, literary history and linguistics presented to Viacheslav Vsevolodovich Ivanov on the occasion of his seventieth birthday*, ed. Lazar S. Fleischman et al., 626–633. Moscow: OGI.

Hancock, Ian F. 1970. Is Anglo-Romanes a creole? *Journal of the Gypsy Lore Society*, 3rd ser., 49 (1–2): 41–44.

384 P. Bakker

Hancock, Ian F. 1976. The pidginization of Angloromani. In *New directions in Creole studies*, ed. George Cave, 1–23. Georgetown: University of Guyana.

Hancock, Ian F. 1984a. Romani and Angloromani. In *Languages in the British Isles*, ed. Peter Trudgill, 367–383. Cambridge: Cambridge University Press.

Hancock, Ian F. 1984b. The social and linguistic development of Angloromani. In *Romani rokkeripen to divvus: The English Romani dialect and its contemporary social, educational and linguistic standing*, ed. Thomas Acton and Donald Kenrick, 89–134. London: Romanestan Publications.

Igla, Birgit. 1991. Dortika: A Greek variety of a Romani mixed dialect. In *In the margin of Romani: Gypsy languages in contact*, ed. Peter Bakker and Marcel Cortiade, 91–101. Amsterdam: Publikaties van het Instituut voor Algemene Taalwetenschap 58. Studies in Language Contact I.

Irvine, Francis. 1817. On the similitude between the Gipsy and Hindostanee languages. *Transactions of the Literary Society of Bombay* 1: 57–70.

Kenrick, Donald. 1971. Anglo-Romani today (sociolinguistics). In *Current changes amongst British Gypsies and their place in international patterns of development: Proceedings of the Research and policy conference of the National Gypsy Education Council*, ed. Thomas Acton, 5–14. Oxford: National Gypsy Education Council.

Kenrick, Donald. 1979. Romani English. *International Journal of Sociology of Language* 19: 111–120.

Kluge, Friedrich. 1901. *Rotwelsch: Quellen und Wortschatz der Gaunersprache und der verwandten Geheimsprachen*. Strassburg: Karl Trübner.

Krinková, Zuzana. 2015. *From Iberian Romani to Iberian Para-Romani varieties*. Prague: Karolinum and Nakladatelstvi Univerzity Karlovy.

Leigh, Kate. 1998. Romani elements in present-day Caló. In *The Romani element in non-standard speech*, ed. Yaron Matras, 243–282. Wiesbaden: Harrassowitz.

Matras, Yaron. 1998a. Para-Romani revisited. In *The Romani element in non-standard speech*, ed. Yaron Matras, 1–27. Wiesbaden: Harrassowitz.

Matras, Yaron. 1998b. The Romani element in German secret languages: Jenisch and Rotwelsch. In *The Romani element in non-standard speech*, ed. Yaron Matras, 193–230. Wiesbaden: Harrassowitz.

Matras, Yaron. 1998c. *The Romani element in non-standard speech*. Wiesbaden: Harrassowitz.

Matras, Yaron. 2000. Mixed languages: A functional-communicative approach. *Bilingualism: Language and Cognition* 3 (2): 79–99.

Matras, Yaron. 2002. *Romani: A linguistic introduction*. Cambridge: Cambridge University Press.

Matras, Yaron. 2005. The classification of Romani dialects: A geographic-historical perspective. In *General and applied Romani linguistics*, ed. Dieter Halwachs and Barbara Schrammel, 7–26. Munich: Lincom Europa.

Matras, Yaron. 2007. Grammatical borrowing in Domari. In *Grammatical borrowing in cross-linguistic perspective*, ed. Yaron Matras and Jeanette Sakel, 151–164. Berlin: Mouton de Gruyter.

Matras, Yaron. 2010. *Romani in Britain: The afterlife of a language*. Edinburgh: Edinburgh University Press.

Matras, Yaron. 2015. Review of Scandoromani: Remnants of a mixed language by Gerd Carling, Lenny Lindell, Gilbert Ambrazaitis. *Romani Studies* 25 (2): 225–229.

Matras, Yaron, and Peter Bakker (eds.). 2003. *The mixed language debate: Theoretical and empirical advances*. Berlin: Mouton de Gruyter.

Matras, Yaron, Hazel Gardner, Charlotte Jones, and Veronica Schulman. 2007. Angloromani: A different kind of language? *Anthropological Linguistics* 49 (2): 142–184.

McGowan, Alan. 1996. *The Winchester confessions 1615–1616: Depositions of travellers, Gypsies, fraudsters, and makers of counterfeit documents, including a vocabulary of the Romany language*. South Chailey, East Sussex: Romany and Traveller Family History Society.

McLane, Merrill F. 1977. The Calo of Guadix: A surviving Romany lexicon. *Anthropological Linguistics* 19: 303–319.

Meakins, Felicity. 2013. Mixed languages. In *Contact languages: A comprehensive guide*, ed. Peter Bakker and Yaron Matras, 159–228. Berlin: De Gruyter Mouton.

Meakins, Felicity. 2016. Mixed languages. *Oxford Research Encyclopedia of Linguistics*. https://doi.org/10.1093/acrefore/9780199384655.013.151.

Michel, Francisque. 1848. Bohémiens, Mendiants, Gueux, Cours des miracles. In *Le Moyen Age et la Renaissance, Tome 1, chapître 9*, ed. P. Lacroix. Paris: N.P.

Miskow, Johan, and Viggo Brøndal. 1923. Sigøjnersprog i Danmark. *Danske Studier* 20: 97–145.

Montoya, Juan Ramón, and Israel Gabarri. 2010. *La lengua romaní en España desde el siglo XVIII hasta nuestros días*. Madrid and Logroño: Private Publication.

Muysken, Pieter. 1981. Halfway between Quechua and Spanish: The case for relexification. In *Historicity and variation in creole studies*, ed. Arnold Highfield and Albert Valdman, 52–78. Ann Arbor: Karoma.

Myers-Scotton, Carol. 1998. A way to dusty death: The matrix language turnover hypothesis. In *Endangered languages: Language loss and community response*, ed. Lenore A. Grenoble and Lindsay J. Whaley, 289–316. Cambridge: Cambridge University Press.

Paul, Hermann. 1886. *Prinzipien der Sprachgeschichte*, 2. Ausg. Halle: Niemeyer.

Réger, Zita. 1995. The language of Gypsies in Hungary: An overview of research. *International Journal of the Sociology of Language* 111: 79–91.

Reinecke, John E., et al. 1975. *A Bibliography of Pidgin and Creole languages*. Honolulu: University Press of Hawaii.

Rusakov, Aleksandr. 2001. The North Russian Romani dialect: Interference and code switching. In *Circum-Baltic languages*, ed. Östen Dahl and Maria Koptjevskaja-Tamm, 313–338. Amsterdam and Philadelphia: John Benjamins.

Sampson, John. 1926. *The Dialect of the Gypsies of Wales: Being the older form of British Romani preserved in the speech of the clan of Abram Wood*. Oxford: Clarendon Press.

Sampson, John. 1930. Two stories of Cornelius Price. *Journal of the Gypsy Lore Society*, 3rd ser., 9 (3): 49–57.

Sasse, Hans Jürgen. 1992. Theory of language death. In *Language death: Factual and theoretical explorations with special references to East Africa*, ed. Mathias Brenzinger, 7–30. Berlin: Mouton de Gruyter.

Schuchardt, Hugo. 1884. Dem Herrn Franz von Miklosich zum 20. November 1883. *Slawo-deutsches und Slawo-italienisches*. Graz: Leuschner & Lubensky.

Sechidou, Irene. 2005. Finikas Romika: A Greek Para-Romani variety. *Romani Studies* 15 (1): 51–79.

Smart, Bath C., and Henry T. Crofton. 1875. *The dialect of the English Gypsies*, 2nd ed. London: Asher & Co.

Tadmor, Uri. 2009. Loanwords in the world's languages: Findings and results. In *Loanwords in the world's languages: A comparative handbook*, ed. Martin Haspelmath and Uri Tadmor, 55–75. Berlin: De Gruyter Mouton.

Tcherenkov, Lev, and Stéphane Laederich. 2004. The Rroma. Otherwise known as Gypsies, Gitanos, Jifti, Tsiganes, Țigani, Çingene, Zigeuner, Bohémiens, Travellers, Fahrende, etc. Vol. I: *History, language and groups*. Vol. II: *Traditions and texts*. Basel: Schwabe.

Thomason, Sarah Grey. 1995. Language mixture: Ordinary processes, extraordinary results. In *Spanish in four continents: Studies in language contact and bilingualism*, ed. Carmen Silva-Corvalán, 15–33. Washington, DC: Georgetown University Press.

Thomason, Sarah Grey, and Terrence Kaufman. 1988. *Language contact, creolization and genetic linguistics*. Berkeley: University of California Press.

Triandaphyllidis, Manolis A. 1924. Eine zigeunerisch-griechische Geheimsprache. *Zeitschrift für vergleichende Sprachforschung auf dem Gebiete der Indogermanischen Sprachen* 52 (1/2): 1–42.

Vallmitjana, Juli. 1908. *Sota Montjuic*. Barcelona: L'Avenç.

Versteegh, Kees. 2017. The myth of the mixed languages. In *Advances in Maltese linguistics*, ed. Benjamin Saade and Mauro Tosco, 245–266. Berlin: De Gruyter.

Part IV

Variation

13

Romani Dialectology

Viktor Elšík and Michael Beníšek

13.1 Introduction

Romani, a prevailingly oral language of a diaspora minority, which, moreover, lacks a widely accepted standard, exhibits a remarkable degree of cross-dialect variation. While this chapter does not aim to present a full account of Romani cross-dialect variation, we do intend to address major issues of Romani dialectology. After a brief discussion of the extent and parameters of cross-dialect variation in Romani (Sect. 13.2), we outline the criteria and history of dialect classification and present an up-to-date overview of Romani dialect groups (Sect. 13.3). The synchronic patterns of cross-dialect variation within Romani as well as the nature of Romani dialect groups have been subject to different diachronic interpretations, depending especially on what importance is ascribed to different diachronic sources of cross-dialect variation. Two competing diachronic models of Romani

---

This chapter was supported by the Charles University project Progres Q10, Language in the shiftings of time, space, and culture.

V. Elšík (✉) · M. Beníšek
Charles University, Prague, Czech Republic
e-mail: viktor.elsik@ff.cuni.cz

M. Beníšek
e-mail: michael.benisek@ff.cuni.cz

© The Author(s) 2020
Y. Matras and A. Tenser (eds.), *The Palgrave Handbook of Romani Language and Linguistics*, https://doi.org/10.1007/978-3-030-28105-2_13

cross-dialect variation, the genealogical model and the diffusion model, have emerged in recent decades in a fruitful academic debate, the main points and arguments of which will be summarized and evaluated (Sect. 13.4). The final part of the chapter (Sect. 13.5) concludes and outlines the prospects for further research in Romani dialectology.

13.2 Cross-Dialect Variation

13.2.1 Extent of Variation

Romani shows a remarkable degree of cross-dialect variation, which manifests itself at all levels of linguistic structure. There are, first of all, innumerable cross-dialect differences in the formal identity and origin of semantically equivalent words and morphemes. For example, the Proto-Romani adjective *tikno* 'small, little' has been, in some dialects, replaced by: its former diminutive *tiknoṛo*; *xurdo*, originally 'tiny, minute', of Persian origin; *buka*, originally 'mouthful', of Greek origin; *besko* and *bita*, originally 'a bit', of Low German and English origin, respectively; *čepo*, originally 'a drop of', of Hungarian origin; and more. There are also countless cross-dialect differences in the phonological shape of cognate words and morphemes (e.g. **tikno > tiknu, tino, tinjo, ťikno, čikno, čikono, cikno, cəkno, cigno, cino, sikno*, and more) and in the meanings of cognates (e.g. *buka* *'mouthful' > 'a piece of', 'a little, a few', 'tiny', 'small, little'). Finally, there are numerous differences between Romani dialects in the structure of their sound system, grammar, and the lexicon from a typological point of view. To name just a few examples, some dialects—but not others—possess: vowel harmony; a definite article; postpositions; vigesimal numerals; the T–V distinction in reference to the addressee; polysemy of the meanings 'yesterday' and 'tomorrow'; and many more.

Despite cross-dialect differences, all Romani dialects share a structural core, which, apart from linguistic universals, consists of a number of language-specific typological features, such as the existence of velar plosives, inflectional classes in nouns, subject cross-reference on verbs, as well as of at most several dozen cognate words and morphemes, such as reflexes of the etymon *dikh-* 'to see; to look'. On the other hand, numerous structural linguistic features are widespread but not universal within Romani, as they are lacking in a few dialects. For example, whereas almost all Romani dialects inflect nouns for case, possess the complementizer *te* or its reflexes, and use the noun *ŗom* or its reflexes in the meaning of 'husband', Apennine dialects have lost case inflection in nouns, only retaining it in pronouns (cf. Elšík 2000, p. 67; Elšík and Matras 2006, pp. 317–318); Dolenjska Slovene Romani has replaced the complementizer *te* with a loanword *da* (Cech and Heinschink 2001, p. 167; Cech 2006, p. 60; Matras 2002, p. 210; Elšík and Matras 2006, p. 186); and the Vend dialects of Hungary only retain *rom* as an ethnonym, employing *murš*, originally 'man, male', in the meaning of 'husband' (Bodnárová 2015, pp. 281–282). The universal and near universal features of Romani, the overwhelming majority of which have been inherited from Proto-Romani, may be summarily described as Common Romani (cf. Matras 2002, p. 20).

It is certainly not the case that all Romani dialects are inherently mutually intelligible, though we are unaware of any empirical studies on this issue. Consider, for example, such a basic sentence as 'all my children are still small': Can a speaker from Kaspichan, Bulgaria, who says *epci me xurde thaa čikone*, possibly understand a speaker from Helsinki, Finland, who says *sāre mo kenti āxena panna peska*, and vice versa? Despite this, it has hardly been considered in Romani linguistics to conceive of Romani as a subgroup of closely related languages, rather than as a single language, and to reserve the term *dialects* for those Romani varieties that have a reasonable degree of structural similarity and mutual intelligibility. (Nevertheless, the plural term Romani *languages* is often encountered outside of specialist circles.) The mutual intelligibility of Romani dialects is restricted especially due to lexical borrowing (cf. Boretzky 1995, p. 71) from different contact languages (e.g. *epci* 'all' and *thaa* 'still' from Turkish in the Kaspichan example vs. *panna* 'still' from Greek and *kenti* 'children' and *peska* 'small' from Low German in the Helsinki example) and reductive sound changes in some dialects (e.g. *zabəj < *giljabani* 'she sang' in a Bulgarian variety of Romani, cf. Angǎčev 2008, p. 75; Elšík 2008, p. 214), though other types of innovations, too, certainly play a role.

Nevertheless, regular or prolonged exposure to a non-native Romani dialect may enhance its intelligibility to a speaker of another dialect and, given the appropriate social conditions, result in bidialectism, with demographic asymmetry being an important factor in developing asymmetrical bidialectism (cf. Boretzky 1995, p. 72). For example, in addition to their native dialect, the Vlax Roms of Selice, a village in Slovakia, learn (an ethnolectal variety of) the very different dialect of the much more numerous Hungarian Roms of Selice, who, on the other hand, hardly understand the dialect of the Vlax Roms (Elšík 2009, p. 273; cf. also Lípa 1979, pp. 55–56).

13.2.2 Parameters of Variation

Like other languages, Romani shows structural linguistic variation depending on various external, non-linguistic, parameters. There are differences between Romani varieties of different countries, regions, localities, and neighbourhoods (i.e. geographical dialects); between varieties of different sub-ethnic and large kinship (e.g. clan) groups (i.e. subethnolects and clanolects); between varieties of speakers of different generations, genders, type of residence (urban vs. rural, cf. Friedman 2017a), and other social variables (i.e. sociolects); and between varieties of different families (i.e. familiolects) and individual speakers (i.e. idiolects). Romani dialectology has largely focused on the geographical and the sub-ethnic dimensions of variation, while structural linguistic variation due to social factors and kinship is much less researched (but see Matras 2004 ; Leggio and Matras 2017) and there are hardly any variationist studies on Romani. However, variation due to social factors is sometimes described in passing in descriptions of geographically defined dialects. For example, the grammar of Eastern Uzh Romani by Beníšek (2017) contains numerous notes on generational variation within individual local varieties (e.g. on the use of reflexives on pp. 193–195).

Despite the fact that Romani is a diaspora language, i.e. a language not spoken in a contiguous area, the geographical dimension of variation is as essential in Romani as in areal languages, since its structural linguistic variation clearly reflects geographical factors. Numerous patterns of synchronic variation within Romani are best accounted for diachronically in terms of gradual geographical diffusion of linguistic innovations, which has occurred among both sedentary and regionally itinerant or semi-itinerant Romani populations (cf. Matras 2005, p. 20; 2010, pp. 42–43) and which, additionally, may have been bolstered by gradual short-distance diffusion of speakers, whose demographic growth compelled them to search for new markets for their services (cf. Elšík 2003, p. 55). Numerous clusters of Romani varieties display areal patterns of variation, forming dialect continua, with geographical distance between Romani varieties correlating, to a considerable extent, with the degree of their structural difference (cf. Matras 2005, p. 7).

Nevertheless, the areal patterns of variation have often been disturbed by long-distance migrations of Romani speakers. Numerous times throughout the Roms' European history, migration brought speakers of divergent Romani dialects, i.e. of dialects that had previously undergone divergent developments in separate areas, to live within a single country, region, and—not at all unusually—even within a single locality or neighbourhood (e.g.

Lípa 1979; Boretzky 1995, p. 69; 1998, p. 4; Matras 2002, p. 214; Elšík 2003, p. 56). The speakers of the new co-territorial dialects had mostly developed distinct sub-ethnic identities, which often indirectly limit the amount of linguistic interaction among the groups (e.g. as a result of group endogamy) and may impose ideological restrictions on diffusion of linguistic innovations (cf. Boretzky 1995, pp. 70–71). On the other hand, likewise due to long-distance migration, speakers of closely related Romani varieties now often reside in geographically distant regions, sometimes losing any social and linguistic contact with other members of their sub-ethnic group and sometimes retaining varying degrees of contact (cf. Marushiakova and Popov 2004; Matras 2013). Thus, due to the complex migration histories of the Roms, the geographical and the migration-induced (sub-ethnic) dimensions of structural linguistic variation of Romani are intertwined in a complex way.

A dialectological landscape consisting, exclusively or prevalently, of varieties that show no or weak areal patterning of their structural linguistic variation has been characterized as consisting of so-called insular dialects (Boretzky 1998). Such dialects are said to lack gradual geographical transitions and not to form dialect continua, with geographical distance being a poor predictor of the degree of their structural linguistic difference. An insular dialect landscape is most likely to have resulted from multifarious migrations in different times of different groups of Romani speakers from different and often unknown locations. While Boretzky (1998) acknowledges that some clusters of Romani varieties exhibit more insular characteristics than others, referring to the Balkan group of Romani (see Sect. 13.3) as a prime example, he nevertheless goes as far as claiming that Romani dialects *in general* are insular rather than areal (cf. also Boretzky 2007, p. 314). However, Boretzky's (1998, p. 17) scepticism regarding the areality of some clusters of Romani varieties, such as the Central groups of Romani (see Sect. 13.3.3), can be shown to derive from his lack of access to geographically detailed data (cf. Elšík 2003, p. 55).

The geographical distribution of structural linguistic variants in Romani can be, and has been, represented in dialectological maps, with different variants of a structural feature represented by distinct graphical symbols and/or separated by isoglosses (e.g. Boretzky 1999a, b, 2000, 2003; Boretzky and Igla 2004; Boretzky et al. 2008; Matras 2002, 2004, 2005; Granqvist 2017; Elšík et al., in preparation.). Nevertheless, the migration-induced dimension of structural linguistic variation does complicate the mapping in several respects:

Recent migrations are often disregarded in mapping, in that the migrants' linguistic variety is put back in space and time, so to speak, i.e. geographically represented in its traditional, pre-migration, location (cf. Matras 2005, p. 7; 2010, pp. 47–48), and so in effect conceived as a displaced areal variety (cf. Elšík 2003, p. 56). The assumption is that the localization of a structural linguistic variant in its pre-migration geographical context is more revealing with regard to the diachrony of the mapped structural linguistic feature than its localization in the post-migration geographical context. Nevertheless, different linguistic features and variants of a relocated variety may require differing treatment (cf. Boretzky 1998, p. 4). It makes little sense, for example, to map a recent loanword from a post-migration contact language into the pre-migration location of a Romani variety. Disregarding speaker migration in geographical representation of structural linguistic variation becomes problematic as soon as there has been sufficient time to develop post-migration linguistic innovations and the migrants' variety has begun to integrate linguistically into the post-migration areal context. What is more, the pre-migration location of a migrants' variety may be unknown or may only be possible to reconstruct from linguistic evidence, which makes a pre-migration geographical representation of a structural linguistic variant impossible, or methodologically problematic, respectively.

Co-territorial dialects of distinct sub-ethnic groups may require distinct layers of geographical representation, i.e. distinct dialectological maps (cf. Boretzky 1998, pp. 4–5). To mention one of many cases, the geographical representation of numerous linguistic variants in the Romani varieties of Slovakia only makes sense if one maps separately variation within the Central dialects, whose speakers have been settled there for several centuries, and variation within the Vlax dialects, whose speakers are later, though not recent, immigrants into the area. Consider, for example, the development, in Romani of Slovakia, of the Proto-Romani cluster /nr̩/ within the lexeme *manr̩o 'bread'. The cluster is reflected as simplified /r/ in the Central dialects in the whole country, with the exception of the extreme northeast, where /ndr/ has developed through excrescence (Elšík et al., in preparation; cf. also Matras 2002, pp. 226–227); and as metathesized /rn/ in the Vlax dialects of western and central Slovakia but conservative /nr/, which may be simplified to /r/ in casual speech, in the Vlax dialects of eastern Slovakia. In other words, the two isoglosses, viz. Central /r :: ndr/ and Vlax /rn :: nr ~ r/, are distinct both in their geographical localization and in their linguistic content, and thus must be indexed to the distinct sub-ethnic and dialect groups.

13.3 Dialect Classification and Overview of Dialect Groups

13.3.1 Criteria for Dialect Classification

Perceptual dialectology, i.e. the study of how non-linguist speakers perceive variation in their language, has just begun to be explored in the Romani context (cf. Friedman 2017b) and is far from being able to present any systematic evidence. As for expert linguistic views, there is no single classification of Romani varieties into dialect groups, as different authors may use, and have used, differing criteria for classification, often in connection with their differing objectives and methodologies. Presently, there appears to be a general consensus that dialectological (as against, for example, sociolinguistic or cultural anthropological) classification of linguistic varieties should be based exclusively on their linguistic structure (cf. Boretzky 1995, p. 73) and *not* on any external characteristics of the speakers of these varieties and their speech communities, such as their present-day or traditional place of residence, 'way of life' (e.g. itinerant vs. sedentary), profession, religion, ethnonymy, bilingualism patterns and contact languages, and the like. To be sure, structural linguistic variation between dialects, and so dialectological classification, may sometimes correlate with some of the external characteristics (see also Sect. 13.2.2), especially at a local level. For example, there is often a correlation between structural linguistic features of a dialect and speakers' ethnonyms within a certain region; thus, almost every Romani-speaking group of *Romungri* in Transylvania retains the affricate /čh/, whereas every group of *Korturari* has changed it to a fricative (cf. Urech and Heuvel 2011, p. 154; Heuvel and Urech 2014, pp. 48–49). Especially present-day or past contact languages of Romani speech communities are often indirectly linked to structural linguistic classification of their dialects, as contact-induced innovations, such as the borrowing of *vodro* 'bed' from South Slavic (cf. Bakker 1999) or the contact-induced development of the 'new' infinitive (cf. Boretzky 1996b), are of structural linguistic nature, and thus constitute valid classification criteria. Despite such potential correlations, the external criteria per se cannot be considered definitional for dialectological classification.

In principle, Romani dialects may be classified for various synchronic purposes and by means of various methods, including typological comparison in selected features, dialectometric assessment of overall structural similarity, or experimental assessment of inherent intelligibility (see Sect. 13.2.1). Nevertheless, in practice, Romani dialects have mostly been classified from a diachronic, historical linguistic, perspective, i.e. in terms of the origin and development of the present-day patterns of cross-dialect structural linguistic variation. Two models of diachronic interpretation of the synchronic variation, a genealogical one and a diffusion one, differ in their theoretical conception of what dialect classification amounts to and which structural linguistic features represent the appropriate classification criteria (see Sect. 13.4 for an extensive discussion), though they converge on a concrete taxonomy of primary dialect groups of Romani (which we survey in Sect. 13.3.3).

The diachronic dialect classification, especially (though not exclusively) as pursued within the genealogical model, often makes use of hierarchical taxonomy. For example, the Romani idiolect of a speaker (A. K.) from the village of Selice, Slovakia, may be classified on several hierarchical levels as a variety of the *Domák* clanolect of the Selice local variety within the Eastern Podunajsko dialect region of the Northwestern subgroup of the non-Vendic dialect zone of the South Central dialect group, which may perhaps be subsumed under the Central dialect supergroup. (There is little terminological consensus with regard to the different levels of classification.) The issue of dialect classification and its hierarchical taxonomy is closely linked to a question that sometimes arises in popular discussions about Romani: 'How many dialects does Romani have?' An appropriate answer, of course, must take into account the semantic vagueness of the term *dialect* and cannot be more definitive than something along the lines of: 'Romani has X dialects at hierarchical level H according to the classification by author A, who uses classification criteria C'. A concrete example of such a quantitative statement is the following: Elšík et al. (in preparation) classify their sample of over 400 local varieties of Central Romani into two dialect groups, 12 dialect subgroups and 70 dialect regions on the basis of a complex of structural linguistic (i.e. phonological, grammatical, and lexical) criteria.

13.3.2 A Brief History of Dialect Classification

Attempts at dividing Romani into a number of more or less discrete groups of closely related dialects have a history that goes back almost 150 years (see Hancock 1988; Bakker 1999, pp. 173–180; Matras 2002, pp. 218–225; 2013, pp. 201–206 for more information). An example of an early division that was based on socio-cultural rather than linguistic criteria is Paspati (1870), who studied Romani in Thrace and drew a distinction between the dialects of sedentary Roms and those of itinerant Roms. While his specimens of the sedentary variety, presumably acquired from Roms settled in the vicinity of Istanbul, are quite homogeneous, what Paspati presents under the variety of nomads seems to be a conglomerate of diverse dialects with no exclusive common trait (see Boretzky 1999b, pp. 17–19). The first attempt to classify all known Romani dialects throughout Europe was that by Miklosich (1873), who established 13 groups on the basis of the major surrounding linguistic groups rather than on internal linguistic criteria. Miklosich referred to dialects of: (i) the Greek Gypsies, (ii) the Romanian Gypsies, (iii) the Hungarian Gypsies, (iv) the Bohemian and Moravian Gypsies, (v) the German Gypsies, (vi) the Polish and Lithuanian Gypsies, (vii) the Russian Gypsies, (viii) the Finnish Gypsies, (ix) the Scandinavian Gypsies, (x) the South Italian Gypsies, (xi) the Basque Gypsies, (xii) the English and Scottish Gypsies, and (xiii) the Spanish Gypsies. Miklosich's main interest was to analyse various layers of lexical borrowings from European languages in the individual dialects and then to trace the historical migration routes of their speakers within Europe, often with the help of historical documents.

The first purely linguistic classification, which later became quite influential, was presented by Gilliat-Smith (1915–1916), who introduced into Romani dialectology the term *Vlax* Romani and established a twofold division of Romani into the Vlax dialects and the *non-Vlax* dialects. Although his scheme was primarily meant to describe the dialect situation in northeastern Bulgaria, he suggested (p. 66) that these two units may constitute primary branches from which any Romani dialect could be derived, at least in the Balkans. Gilliat-Smith discussed various lexical, phonological, and grammatical features differentiating the two branches of Bulgarian Romani, while, at the same time, taking into account cross-dialect diversity within each branch. While Gilliat-Smith's assumption of a common non-Vlax branch was later abandoned, his claim that Vlax constitutes a distinct dialect group became firmly established in subsequent discussions (cf. Boretzky 2003). Kochanowski (1963) proposed a further division of the non-Vlax branch into four sub-branches: *Balkan* Romani; *Carpathian* Romani, containing dialects now referred to as Central Romani; *German* Romani, consisting of the Sinti–Manuš dialects; and finally *Northern* Romani, corresponding to the group later referred to as Northeastern Romani (see Sect. 13.3.3). Kochanowski's classification was further elaborated in a taxonomic overview by Vencel' and Čerenkov (1976), who classified Romani dialects into eight primary groups on the basis of selected structural criteria (their relation to the taxonomy presented in Sect. 13.3.3 is given in square brackets): I Dialects of the northern parts of the USSR and Poland [= Northeastern], II Sinti [= part of Northwestern], III Dialects of Slovakia and Hungary [=Central], IV Dialects of the Erlides in Bulgaria, Macedonia and Serbia, Ursari of Romania and Moldova, Crimean Roms, and Drindari of Bulgaria [=South Balkan and North Balkan], V Kalderari and Lovari dialects of Romania and Gurbet dialects of Yugoslavia [=Vlax], VI dialects of Ukraine [=Ukrainian and partly also Vlax], VII Finnish dialect [=part of Northwestern], and VIII Welsh dialect [=part of Northwestern].

An alternative classification was presented by Kaufman (1979; cf. also Hancock 1988, pp. 202–203), who recognized three divisions in the network of twenty Romani dialect groups, viz. the *Balkan* division, the *Northern* division, and the *Vlax* division, plus three groups unaligned with any of these divisions, such as *Greek* Romani (presumably Paspati's dialect of sedentary Gypsies), *Zargari* (a Balkan Romani dialect spoken in Iran), and *Iberian* Romani. He did not establish a separate division of the Central (or Carpathian) dialects; instead, he considered the dialects now called South Central Romani to be part of the Balkan division, while the dialects now referred to as North Central Romani were relegated to the Northern division. Kaufman (1979, p. 134) claimed to have based his classification on unique innovations and features shared within the respective divisions, without, however, specifying any of them. An entirely different attempt at a classification was that of Courthiade (1998; also Cortiade 1991), who divided Romani dialects into three basic layers: *Balkan–Carpathian–Baltic* (comprising virtually all non-Vlax dialects), *Gurbet–Ćergar* [=South Vlax, see Sect. 13.3.3], and *Kelderar–Lovari* [=North Vlax]. Courthiade's classification, which is based on just two phonological innovations, combines Miklosich's model of Romani migration waves and Gilliat-Smith's dichotomization between Vlax and non-Vlax.

The 1990s witnessed a boom of scholarly interest in Romani linguistics that also gave rise to vivid discussions on Romani dialect classification. On the basis of previous discussions, Bakker and Matras (1997, pp. xvii–xx) outlined a division of Romani into four main groups: *Balkan*, *Vlax*, *Central*, and *Northern* and pointed to what they called *generic* traits of the groups. Bakker (1999, p. 178) called this division into four units the *consensus* branching and argued for a genealogical ('genetic') nature of the most diverse Northern branch of dialects. He analysed a number of shared lexical, grammatical, and phonological features in various dialects spoken on the northeastern, northern, western, and southwestern fringes of Europe to indicate that these dialects must have developed from a common ancestor spoken by the first emigration wave of Roms from the Balkans. As Matras (2002, pp. 222–223) demonstrates, most of the features listed by Bakker are either conservative or common traits and are therefore not indicative of a genealogical nature of the group, while others are shared sociolinguistic strategies that reflect social and cultural specifics of the Romani groups in northern and western Europe (cf. also Matras 1999, pp. 1–3). Instead, Matras (2002, p. 10) divides Bakker's Northern branch into the independent groups of the *Northwestern*, the *Northeastern*, the *British*, and the *Iberian* dialects, accompanied by isolated groups of dialects in southern Italy and in Slovenia. Later, Matras (2010, pp. 82–88) revised the position of British Romani as an independent group and pointed out the tight affinities of the British dialects with Northwestern Romani.

In a series of publications, Boretzky divided the Central, Balkan, and Vlax branches into two subordinate units each: North Central vs. South Central (Boretzky 1999a), South Balkan I vs. South Balkan II (Boretzky 2000, *South Balkan* being the author's term for the Balkan dialects), and North Vlax vs. South Vlax (Boretzky 2003). Especially in the case of the Central and the Balkan dialects, the differences between the two subgroups are deemed to be great enough to grant the subgroups the status of distinct branches (cf. also Boretzky 2007). The dialect atlas by Boretzky and Igla (2004) divides Romani into seven major units (their relation to the taxonomy presented in Sect. 13.3.3 is given in square brackets): I *Northern* conglomeration [= Northwestern and Iberian], II *Northeastern* family [id.], III *North Central* group [id.], IV *South Central* group [id.], V *Vlax* family [id.], VI *South Balkan* I conglomeration [= South Balkan], and VII *South Balkan* II family [= North Balkan]. A transitional character is ascribed to the I/VI *Abruzzian* [= Apennine] dialects, which are placed between the Northern and the South Balkan I dialects, and to the IV/VI *Gopti* dialect [= Slovenian], which is placed between the South Central and the South Balkan I dialects. The *East Ukrainian and South Russian* [= Ukrainian] dialects are considered by Boretzky and Igla (2004) to be dialects of Northeastern origin that have acquired a massive Vlax admixture. In later works, Boretzky (e.g. 2007; 2012, pp. 95–96) took into consideration the lesser known *Transylvanian* [id.] dialects and linked them to North Central Romani.

13.3.3 Overview of Dialect Groups

In this section, we outline the taxonomy of Romani dialect groups that has emerged over recent decades (see Sect. 13.3.2). We differentiate 12 dialect groups, classifying as separate taxons both well-established groups and several groups (viz. Apennine, Transylvanian, and Ukrainian Romani) that have sometimes been considered to be transitional between, or form part of, the

400 V. Elšík and M. Beníšek

well-established groups. We provide a basic characterization of each dialect group, including information on the geographical distribution of speakers, the internal divisions of the group, and an overview of dialects that have been described in scholarly literature. The survey of descriptive works is restricted to major sources and is far from exhaustive (see also Matras 2002, pp. 6–12; Boretzky and Igla 2004, pp. 26–31 for lists of further sources).[1] The presentation also includes a brief survey of selected structural features characteristic of each group, with a focus on diagnostic innovations.

South Balkan Romani

South Balkan Romani, called South Balkan I in the works of Boretzky (e.g. 2007) and Boretzky and Igla (2004), is a cluster of relatively diverse Romani dialects that have developed in the southern Balkans after the Medieval Romani migrations to the other parts of Europe. The oldest reliable description of South Balkan dialects is Paspati's (1870) account of the Romani dialects in Thrace (inappropriately called *Rumelian Romani* in Romani linguistics), while the closely related dialect of the Ajios Athanasios neighbourhood of Serres has recently been described by Sechidou (2011). Other South Balkan dialects of Greece include a variety of the *Romacel* musicians in the village of Parakalamos of the Epirus region (Matras 2004), a variety spoken in Sofades of the central Greek region of Thessaly (Schulman 2010), and a dialect formerly spoken around Thessaloniki by the *Sepečides* 'Basket-weavers' (Cech and Heinschink 1996, 1999). In the centre of the Balkan area, we find Romani dialects spoken by communities that are often referred to by variants of the Turkish word *yerli* 'settled'. These include Arli-type dialects in Serbia, Kosovo, Macedonia, and northern Greece (Boretzky 1996a), including the dialect of Prilep, Macedonia (Boretzky and Cech 2016); Erli in Sofia, Bulgaria (Calvet 1982; Minkov 1997), and in the Rhodopes (Igla 1997); and Yerli in southwestern Bulgaria. The South Balkan dialects are also spoken by communities that departed from the southern Balkans in various times, such as the dialect of the *Ursarja* 'Bear-leaders' in Romania and Moldova (Matras 2013) and the dialect of Crimean Roms now spoken in Ukraine, Russia, and Georgia (Toropov 2009). Outlying South Balkan varieties are also spoken in Iran by communities whose ancestors migrated from the Balkans eastwards (Windfuhr 1970; Djonedi 1996; Baghbidi 2003). General surveys of South Balkan Romani are Boretzky (1999b) and Boretzky et al. (2008).

There are hardly any shared South Balkan Romani innovations that are exclusive to the group. The majority of features enumerated by Boretzky and

Igla (2004, pp. 263–264) as typical of the 'South Balkan I conglomerate' are retentions and the few internal innovations (e.g. short forms of possessive adjectives *mo* 'my' and *to* 'your') are also attested in other dialects. Moreover, many of the innovations shared by all South Balkan dialects are contact-induced features of the Balkan linguistic area, a typical example being the analytic formation of the future tense by a devolitive particle (e.g. *ka* < *kam-* 'to want'). Distinctive innovations can be identified for different dialect subgroups within South Balkan Romani (cf. Boretzky 1999b; Boretzky and Igla 2004, pp. 266–277; Boretzky et al. 2008).

North Balkan Romani
North Balkan Romani, which is referred to as South Balkan II by Boretzky (2000), Drindari–Kalajdži–Bugurdži by Matras (2002, p. 7), or Balkan *zis*-dialects by Elšík and Matras (2006, p. 415), is a fairly homogeneous group of dialects spoken in parts of Bulgaria, Macedonia, Kosovo, and Romania, with the core area in northern and eastern Bulgaria. The group's alternative name Drindari–Kalajdži–Bugurdži is motivated by some of the speakers' profession-based ethnonyms, viz. *Drindarja* (from Bulgarian *drăndar* 'carder'), *Bugurdžides* 'Drill-makers' (from Turkish *burgucu*), and *Kalajdžides* 'Tinners' (from Turkish *kalaycı*). The most detailed description exists for the Bugurdži dialect in Kosovo (Boretzky 1993). Drindari-type dialects spoken in Bulgaria were studied especially by Gilliat-Smith (1913–1914, 1915–1916) and by Kenrick (1967, 1969). A North Balkan dialect is also spoken by the *Spoitorja* 'Tinners' of Wallachia (e.g. Sarău 1998).

North Balkan Romani is characterized by a series of palatalizations (and further developments) of velar, dental, and lateral consonants before /i/ and /j/, which have produced the distinctive word forms such as *z(j)ab-* or *zeb-* 'to sing' (< **giljab-*), *zis* or *zes* 'day' (< **dives*), and *il* 'paper' (< **lil*). Typical morphological features are the plural marker *-oja* of loan masculines in *-os*, deictic expressions beginning in *ki-* (e.g. *kikiso* 'such'), the copula stem in *s(i)j-*, and zero perfective stems with some verbs (e.g. *ker-om* [do-1SG.PFV] 'I did'). See Boretzky (2000) for details.

Apennine Romani
Apennine Romani, also called South Italian Romani (e.g. Bakker 1999), is a cluster of dialects spoken in the southern Italian regions of Abruzzo, Molise, and Calabria. They are described, along with other Romani dialects of Italy, in Soravia (1977) and in the comparative dictionary by Soravia and Fochi (1995), while an older source for the Molisean dialect is Ascoli (1865).

402 V. Elšík and M. Benišek

Apennine Romani has been influenced by Italian to a considerable extent and has developed numerous dialect-specific idiosyncrasies. Typical phonological features include the reduction of mid vowels to /ə/ in unstressed syllables (e.g. *leskərə* 'his' < **leskero*), the paragoge of /ə/ after consonants (e.g. *dandə* 'tooth' < **dand*), and the gemination of some consonants between short vowels (e.g. *akkana* 'now' < **akana*, *avijommə* 'I came' < **aviljom*). Innovations in morphology include the renewal of the imperfect through grammaticalization of a periphrastic copular construction (e.g. *suvasənə* 'I was sleeping' < **sovava(s) sine*) and the presence of pronominal object suffixes, including reflexive suffixes, in verbs (e.g. *dikkallə* 'I see him' and *kareppə* 's/he is called'). Apennine Romani also stands out in having no case inflection in nouns.

Slovene Romani

Slovene Romani is spoken in the Dolenjska region of southeastern Slovenia (*Dolenjski Roma*) and, as a result of migrations during World War II, also in several locations in northern Italy. In the past, related dialects were also spoken in Croatia, whence ancestors of the current Slovene Romani speakers emigrated in the nineteenth century (cf. Uhlik 1973, where they are referred to as *Gopti*). There are thorough descriptions of the Dolenjska dialect (Cech and Heinschink 2001, 2002; Cech 2006), while the dialect spoken in Italy (confusingly called *Istrian Sinti*) is briefly outlined by Soravia (1977, pp. 66–74).

Slovene Romani is transitional between the Arli dialects of the South Balkan group and the South Central dialects in some respects (see Boretzky and Igla 2004, p. 262). They show a strong influence of Slovene and Croatian and numerous idiosyncratic innovations, e.g. the development of the penultimate stress pattern, peculiar person–number suffixes in verbs (1SG *-u*, 2SG *-e*, 3SG *-i*, 1PL *-amo/-an*, 2/3PL *-en*), the remoteness suffix *-e*, copular forms in *h-*, the absence of the definite article, the full case agreement of adjectives with nominal heads, and no complementizer in the infinitive construction.

South Central Romani

South Central Romani is a group of dialects spoken in parts of Slovakia, Hungary, Austria, and Slovenia as well as by post-war migrants from Slovakia to Czechia. Two divisions of South Central Romani are usually distinguished, the Vendic and the non-Vendic subgroup. Vendic Romani is spoken in southwestern Hungary (the Vend dialect proper; Vekerdi 1984;

Bodnárová 2015), the Burgenland region of eastern Austria (e.g. Halwachs 2002), and the northeastern Slovenian region of Prekmurje (e.g. Baranja 2013). The more heterogeneous non-Vendic subgroup (sometimes imprecisely referred to as *Romungro*) is spoken in southwestern and south central Slovakia, in northern Hungary (Elšík et al. 1999), and in the village of Versend in southern Hungary (Bodnárová 2009).

South Central Romani shares numerous features with both Slovene Romani and Arli to the south and the adjacent North Central dialects to the north (see Boretzky 1999a and the discussion in Sect. 13.4). Characteristic of the whole group is the replacement of the original stress pattern by either initial or penultimate stress, the sound change /x > h/, debuccalization in *tāha* 'tomorrow', the loss of /v/ in consonant clusters involving a liquid (e.g. *āri* < **avri* 'out', *āl-* < **avl-* 'to come PFV'), the remoteness marker *-ahi* (< **asi*), the sociative form *kasaha* 'with whom', borrowing of the Hungarian indefinite prefix *vala-*, and the development of an infinitive.

North Central Romani
North Central Romani is a group of dialects that historically emerged in the northern parts of the Kingdom of Hungary. Nowadays, North Central dialects are spoken in most of Slovakia, in Czechia, in southeastern Poland, and in a few localities in westernmost Ukraine (Transcarpathia and Galicia). The original Central dialects of Czechia are extinct due mainly to extermination of most of their speakers during World War II, the most detailed description of Czech Romani being the work by Puchmayer (1821) on Bohemian Romani. A closely related dialect in western Slovakia is described by Sowa (1887), while Lípa (1963) is a description of a small cluster of Romani varieties spoken in eastern Slovakia. The vocabulary of East Slovak Romani varieties is documented by the dictionary of Hübschmannová et al. (1991). Owing to post-war migrations, Slovak dialects are now also spoken in Czechia. The Polish varieties of North Central Romani (sometimes referred to as the dialect of the *Bergitka* Roms) are documented by the texts in Kopernicki (1930) and described in the dictionary by Rozwadowski (1936), while the varieties of Transcarpathian Ukraine are described in detail by Beníšek (2017).

All North Central dialects share a conspicuous influence of Hungarian and North Slavic. Innovations typical of North Central Romani are the loss of iotation in verbal and nominal forms (e.g. *barar-* < **barjar-* 'to make grow', *suva* < **suvja* 'needles'), alveolar affrication in *keci* (< **keti*) 'how much' and *ciral* (< **kiral*) 'cheese', the lexical form *žužo* (< **šužo*) 'clean', and the third-person present copula in *h-* but *s-* in the other persons. Numerous features, such as the loss of the original stress pattern, debuccalization of /s/ in grammatical morphemes (e.g. *tuha* < **tusa* 'with you'), and the development of an infinitive, are shared with the neighbouring South Central dialects, whereas others, e.g. the replacement of the non-indicative non-perfective copula root *ov-* by *av-* (< 'to come'), are shared with other neighbouring dialect groups. There are also non-trivial commonalities with the Transylvanian dialects.

In addition, the dialect of the *Plaščuny*, who inhabit a vast area of eastern Ukraine and Russia, was suggested to be closely related to North Central Romani (Cherenkov 2005; Čerenkov 2008, pp. 497–498), although it also shares some features with the other dialects of Ukraine (Northeastern, Ukrainian, and Vlax). Boretzky and Igla (2004, p. 300) describe the *Plaščuno* dialect as a mixed dialect.

Transylvanian Romani
The Transylvanian Romani dialects are spoken in Romanian Transylvania, except for its southernmost counties, and in some locations of eastern and southern Hungary. They are mostly associated with Romani populations that have a secondary Hungarian ethnic identification and who are often referred to as *Romungri* 'Roms [who are] Hungarians' by Vlax Romani groups (cf. Urech and Heuvel 2011). Transylvanian Romani belongs to the least studied Romani dialects even though there are specimens of the dialect going back to the eighteenth century (Vekerdi 2006). The work of Wlislocki (1884) on Transylvanian Romani has been accused of plagiarism and data fabrication (Lípa 1968; Grant 1995, pp. 56–57). Recently, the Transylvanian dialects have been researched by Heuvel and Urech (2014), who refer to them as *North Transylvanian* dialects in order to distinguish them from the *South Transylvanian* dialects of unambiguous (North) Vlax affiliation (cf. also Matras 2013). Isolated Transylvanian dialects in Hungary are sketched by Vekerdi (1971) and Mészáros (1976).

Although the area of Transylvanian Romani partly overlaps with the North Vlax area, the Transylvanian dialects do not participate in some typical North Vlax innovations such as /čh > ś/. The fact that the Transylvanian dialects share several innovations with North Central Romani (e.g. the devolitive necessity modal *kamp-*) has led Boretzky (2007) to view Transylvanian Romani as part of the North Central group. However, there are also numerous Transylvanian Romani features that occur in neither of the two neighbouring groups, e.g. the copula forms in *h-* in all persons and the negative pronouns *khaj-či*, etc., 'nothing' (cf. Heuvel and Urech 2014).

Vlax Romani

Vlax Romani originated in the Romanian-speaking territory, but it is now the most widespread Romani dialect group around the world due to several migration waves of Roms from Wallachia and Moldavia during the past centuries. It is generally agreed that it consists of two divisions: North Vlax and South Vlax. An important comparative work on Vlax Romani is Boretzky (2003).

North Vlax Romani is a relatively coherent group. A major division is between the Lovari(-type) varieties of the *Lovāra* 'Horse dealers' (from Hungarian *ló* 'horse') and related populations, which form the dominant Vlax dialect in Central Europe (e.g. Pobożniak 1964; Hutterer and Mészáros 1967; Cech and Heinschink 1998; Wagner 2012) and those of the *Kalderaša, Kelderaša, Kelderara*, etc., 'Coppersmiths' (from Romanian *căldăraş* or *căldărar*) and related populations. The latter are still widely spoken in Romania (cf. Matras 2013), though the most detailed descriptions of Kalderaš(-type) Romani are on out-migrant varieties spoken in Sweden (Gjerdman and Ljungberg 1963), Serbia (Boretzky 1994; Sabaini et al. 2015), the USA (Hancock 1995), and Russia (Tcherenkov 1999; Oslon 2018). Further North Vlax dialects are those spoken by various groups in Ukraine and Russia; the dialects of the *Vlaxurja* are referred to as *Right-bank ('B')* dialects in Barannikov (1934).

South Vlax Romani, which appears to be more heterogeneous than North Vlax Romani, encompasses varieties spoken especially in the southern Balkans and Turkey as well as by recent migrants in western Europe. The most thoroughly described variety is that of Ajia Varvara in Athens (Igla 1996), which is spoken by Roms who were part of a Christian population resettled from Turkey in the 1920s. South Vlax dialects that have been substantially influenced by Turkish are known from Greece (Adamou 2010; Adamou and Arvaniti 2014) and Bulgaria (cf. Friedman 2013). South Vlax varieties that are often referred to as Gurbet-type dialects are spoken in the countries of the former Yugoslavia (e.g. Ackerley 1941; Boretzky 1986) and in Albania (Mann 1933, 1935) and also by more or less recent migrants from this region to Italy (Soravia 1983; Franzese 1986; Leggio 2011). Leggio and Matras (2017) describe a variety of the *Kangljari* of Ţăndărei in southeastern Romania, which combines northern and southern Vlax features due to recent inter-dialect levelling.

Vlax Romani is characterized by a layer of Romanian borrowings and by a number of common phonological developments, such as velarization in the consonant clusters */tl > kl/ (e.g. *šutlo > *šuklo* 'sour') and */dl > gl/ (e.g. *gudlo > *guglo* 'sweet'), the development of */ni/ to a palatal approximant (e.g. **pani > paj(i)* 'water'), palatalization and further developments of dentals before /i/ and /j/ (e.g. **tiro > t'iro*, *t'o*, *kiro*, etc., 'your'), umlaut in **daj > dej* 'mother', or idiosyncratic sound changes in *milaj* 'summer' (< *nilaj), *kha(j)ni* 'chicken' (< *kaxni), or *kher* 'boot' (< *tirax). Vlax Romani also displays, for example, the Romanian-origin plural suffix *-uri(a)* in xenoclitic masculines and the verb *hatjar-* or *haljar-* 'to understand'. A typical North Vlax innovation is the fricativization of the aspirated affricate */čh/ > /š/. Numerous features that distinguish North vs South Vlax Romani are morphological or morphosyntactic, e.g. the indicative negator *či* in North Vlax vs *ni* or *in* in South Vlax. See Boretzky (2003) for details.

Ukrainian Romani

Ukrainian Romani is spoken in Ukraine and southwestern Russia by Roms who often refer to themselves as *Servy*. The traditional homeland of the Servy was in the Left-bank Ukraine, Donbas, and Slobozhanshchyna, though their current distribution stretches from Lviv in western Ukraine to the Volga River in Russia (Čerenkov 2008, p. 491). A linguistic description of Ukrainian Romani is provided by Barannikov (1934), who uses the term *Left-bank ('A')* dialects to refer to this dialect group.

Ukrainian Romani contains layers of older Romanian influence and more recent Ukrainian and Russian influence. It is characterized by debuccalization of intervocalic /s/, large-scale apocope of /s/ but its lenition to /x/ in present verb inflection (2SG **-es > -ex*, 1PL **-as > -ax*), the past copula stem in *sl'-* (e.g. 1SG *sl'om* 'I was', 3SG *sl'a* 's/he was'), peculiar word forms such as *t'ev* 'where', and an infinitive based on the historical 2SG (e.g. *t'ere* 'to do' and *dža* 'to go'). It also exhibits palatalization and affrication of velars (e.g. **ker- > t'er-* 'to do', **kher > cxer* 'house'), which are shared with several other Romani dialects of Ukraine, particularly with the North Vlax varieties of the *Vlaxurja* (cf. Tenser 2012).

Northeastern Romani

Northeastern Romani is spoken by dispersed communities over a large area stretching from Poland via Belarus, Ukraine, and the Baltic countries to

Russia. Most thoroughly described is the (North) Russian Romani dialect (Sergievskij and Barannikov 1938; Wentzel 1988), also called *Xaladytka*, although the latter term is a self-appellation for a small part of Russian Roms and may be considered derogatory by others. Varieties of Russian Romani are spoken not only in Russia, but also in other post-Soviet countries and in Poland (Tenser 2008). Other Northeastern dialects include Polish Romani of the sub-ethnic group of the *Polska Roma* 'Polish Roms' (Matras 1999), Lithuanian Romani of the *Litovska Roma* 'Lithuanian Roms' (Tenser 2005), and Latvian Romani of the *Lotfitka Roma* 'Latvian Roms' (Mānušs et al. 1997), which is also spoken in Estonia.

Northeastern Romani is a fairly homogeneous group with a shared layer of German and Polish influence. Typical features include the decomposition of aspirated consonants into clusters with /x/ (e.g. /čh > čx/), the shift of /a/ and /e/ to /i ~ y/ (e.g. genitive -*kir*- < *-*ker*-, *syr* 'how' < *sar, comparative -*edyr* < *-*eder*), idiosyncratic forms such as *pšal* or *špal* 'brother' (< *phral) and *gaba*- or *baga*- 'to sing' (< *giljab-), the innovative negative pronouns *n'ičhi* or *n'iso* 'nothing', the 3PL personal pronoun *jone* 'they', the 1PL future marker -*asam*, generalization of the negator *na* at the expense of the prohibitive *ma, and the take-over of the 2PL perfective by the 3PL -*e*.

Northwestern Romani

Northwestern Romani encompasses the Romani dialects of western and northern parts of Europe. It consists of four discrete subgroups: Sinti-Manuš Romani, British Romani, Scandinavian Romani, and Finnish Romani.

Sinti-Manuš arose in German-speaking areas and is nowadays mostly spoken by Romani populations who call themselves *Sinti*, etc., in Germany (e.g. Sowa 1902; Finck 1903; Holzinger 1993), Italy (Soravia 1977; Franzese 1985), and France (Formoso and Calvet 1987), and by those who refer to themselves as *Manuš* in France (Valet 1991). Smaller Sinti communities also live elsewhere in western, central, and eastern Europe (e.g. Mészáros 1980 for Hungary). British Romani was spoken in parts of Britain until the second half of the nineteenth century and is documented in two forms: Welsh Romani (Sampson 1926) and English Romani (Smart and Crofton 1875); see also Matras (2010). Scandinavian Romani is likewise extinct and can only be uncovered from Para-Romani varieties documented in Denmark (Miskow and Brøndal 1923), Sweden (Carling et al. 2014), and Norway (Wiedner 2017). Finnish Romani is spoken as a non-native language by the Finnish *Kaale*, many of whom also live in

Sweden (e.g. Bourgeois 1901; Thesleff 1901; Valtonen 1972; Granqvist 2007, 2011, 2017).

Typical of Northwestern Romani is the deaspiration of /čh/, widespread aphaeresis of /a/ (e.g. *sva* 'teardrop' < *asva, *v-* 'to come' < **av-*), palatalization and affrication in *dži, dzi, zi* (< *ogi) and the word's semantic extension ('heart' < 'soul'), the contraction in the indefinite *kek* 'any, none' (< *kaj-jekh), inherited transitive markers *-ar-* (*-er-*) and *-av-* (*-ev-*) used for adaptation of some loan verbs, and the loss of synthetic middle marking. The Northwestern dialects also have numerous lexical traits in common, including productive onomasiological genitives (e.g. *grajengro* 'horse dealer') as well as a layer of (West) Slavic and German loanwords. Moreover, the Northwestern dialects are characterized by numerous retentions that are rarely attested in other Romani dialects, examples being the indefinites *či(či)* 'anything, nothing', *čimoni* 'something', and *komoni* 'somebody'. Other features, such as the debuccalization of /s/ in Sinti and Finnish Romani, are restricted to different subgroups within Northwestern Romani (cf. Boretzky and Igla 2004, pp. 277–289; Igla 2005; Matras 2010, pp. 60–88).

Iberian Romani

Iberian Romani is a group of extinct Romani dialects that used to be spoken in the Iberian Peninsula before their transformation into Para-Romani varieties. The process of their disappearance probably started as early as around 1600 (cf. Bakker 2005) and lasted until the nineteenth century. The longest surviving Iberian Romani dialect seems to have been spoken in Catalonia and is sporadically documented in sources from the nineteenth century that were analysed by Ackerley (1914–1915). Otherwise, Iberian Romani can only be reconstructed from Para-Romani varieties based on Spanish, Catalan, Basque, and (Brazilian) Portuguese (cf. Krinková 2015).

Iberian Romani underwent sound changes that had been triggered by contact with languages of the Iberian peninsula, such as the loss of distinctive aspiration, a tendency to palatalization of alveolars before /i/, and a peculiar development of sibilants (e.g. /š > x/, except for the Brazilian dialect). Iberian Romani also had a special possessive verb that had developed from Proto-Romani **ther-* 'to hold' and copular forms based on *sin-*. Slavic loanwords in Iberian Romani are indicative of contact with (West) Slavic languages that must have occurred by the fifteenth century at the latest. See Krinková (2015) for more details.

13.4 Diachronic Interpretation of Variation

13.4.1 Modelling Divergence and Convergence

Two models of linguistic divergence have been employed to account for the patterns of cross-dialect variation in Romani, a genealogical one and a diffusion one:

The proponents of the genealogical (or 'genetic' or dialect branching) model (esp. Boretzky 1998; Boretzky and Igla 2004; Boretzky 2007), which is basically an application of the cladistic or tree model of language divergence (*Stammbaumtheorie*), argue that most, if not all, of the present-day dialect groups of Romani are subgroups in a genealogical sense or dialect *branches* (this term will be used if the genealogical nature of a dialect group is to be implicated). In other words, they argue that all varieties of a dialect branch have developed through divergence from a reconstructable proto-dialect, which was spoken in a *Urheimat* (e.g. southern Poland for the proto-dialect of the Northeastern branch, cf. Boretzky 2007, p. 321), and that linguistic variants spread primarily through speaker migrations. Boretzky's view of Romani dialect history is perhaps best summarized in a graphical schema, which shows six separate migration routes of Romani speakers out of Asia Minor or extreme southeast Europe, corresponding to six out of the seven present-day dialect branches (Boretzky and Igla 2004, p. 367). (The only dialect branch that is not assumed to have resulted from a separate migration of Romani speakers into Europe is the South Central group, for which see below.) The proponents of the genealogical model suggest that the split of Proto-Romani into dialect branches was an early, pre-European, development (e.g. Boretzky 1995, pp. 73–75; Boretzky and Igla 2004, p. 292), possibly even a result of separate migration waves of Romani speakers from India (e.g. Boretzky 2007, pp. 318–319). The latter hypothesis, however, is hardly compatible with the presence of a layer of shared grammatical as well as lexical Grecisms in all dialect groups, which indicates that Romani was still relatively homogeneous during its contact with Byzantine Greek (cf. Matras 2002, pp. 19, 21–23).

The proponents of the (geographical) diffusion model (esp. Matras 2002, pp. 214–218; 2005; Matras 2010, pp. 40–56), which is basically an application of the wave model of language divergence (*Wellentheorie*), argue that the present-day patterns of Romani cross-dialect variation result, to a considerable extent, from a relatively late, Early Modern (esp. sixteenth to seventeenth century) period, geographical diffusion within Europe of linguistic innovations from several focal areas, i.e. centres of diffusion. Matras (2005, pp. 11–13) suggests that diffusion from several major focal areas, viz. one in or around Germany, one in the Balkans, and a lesser one in Transylvania and Wallachia, has affected large geographical areas ('diffusion spaces'), which are separated by transitional zones: the so-called Great Divide between the German and Balkan focal areas and the so-called Southeastern Divide around the Transylvanian–Wallachian focal area. Matras (2010, pp. 49–55) further elaborates on these suggestions, adducing additional observations on focal and relic zones. Importantly, the diffusion model entails that the boundaries between the present-day dialects have mostly emerged due to differentiation in situ. In this approach, the dialect groups are viewed as, in effect, clusters of varieties that show a high degree of synchronic linguistic similarity and their taxonomy as representing a 'reference grid' of convenience (e.g. Matras 2005) and an 'economical inventory of reference terms' (Matras 2010, p. 55). The diffusion model is compatible with the view (e.g. François 2014, p. 170) that dialect groups defined by participation in the diffusion of linguistic innovations need not be discrete and may intersect.

To be sure, there are studies that make use of a combination of genealogical and diffusion-based hypotheses (e.g. Heuvel and Urech 2014) and even the proponents of the two competing models acknowledge that both speaker migration and geographical diffusion of linguistic innovations are required to account for Romani cross-dialect variation in its complexity. On the one hand, Matras (e.g. 2002, p. 215; 2005, pp. 7–8, 19; 2010, pp. 47–48; 2013, p. 240) is well aware of the role of speaker migration for the present-day distribution of linguistic variants. On the other hand, Boretzky and Igla (2004, p. 301; also Boretzky 2007, p. 318) admit that there are instances of diffusion in Romani diachrony, including some over large geographical spaces. Also, while the theoretical status of the so-called dialect conglomerations, a term Boretzky and Igla (2004) use with reference to their Northern and South Balkan I groups (see Sect. 13.3.2) and describe as referring to dialect 'arrangements' (*Gefüge*) looser than the regular dialect groups or *families* (p. 17), is unclear, it seems that the term reflects a lesser confidence in, or even agnosticism with regard to, the genealogical nature of such a dialect group. Thus, the difference between the two models is one of contrasting emphasis on the general role of different divergence mechanisms in Romani diachrony and one of diachronic interpretation of concrete instances of cross-dialect variation and dialect groupings.

An example of the latter is the view of the origin of the South Central group of Romani, which shares numerous features with both the geographically distant Arli (South Balkan) dialects to the south and the adjacent

North Central dialects to the north. The diffusion-based approach allows that the isogloss cluster between the two Central groups developed in situ, i.e. through gradual accumulation of linguistic innovations at a presumed social and/or cultural boundary. Specifically, Matras (2002, p. 223) suggests that the South Central features shared with the dialects south of it may be an outcome of geographical diffusion, presumably from the south. Boretzky, in contrast, argues that the South Central group developed due to an out-migration of some speakers of South Balkan Romani from the western Balkans to Hungary and their subsequent contact with speakers of the North Central group (e.g. Boretzky 1999a; Boretzky and Igla 2004, p. 304; Boretzky 2007, pp. 322, 328). Elšík (2003, pp. 56–57, 59; also 2006b) supports the migration view, noting, however, the development of transitional varieties between the two Central groups through, presumably recent, short-distance diffusion and thus linguistic convergence due to dissolution of cultural boundaries. Matras (2010, p. 49) admits that speaker migration might have been involved, suggesting that there might have been a displacement of Romani speakers from present-day Croatia northwards.

In addition to linguistic divergence, the opposite process of linguistic convergence is also relevant in Romani dialectology. First, geographical diffusion of linguistic innovations, as a rule, results in the convergence of those varieties that share the innovations (as well as in the divergence of those varieties that become differentiated by the innovation) (François 2014, p. 169). Second, whenever migration brings speakers of divergent dialects into a single area, there is a potential for the establishment of linguistic interaction between individual speakers or speaker communities of distinct sub-ethnic backgrounds, which may result in bidialectism and inter-dialect borrowing (e.g. Boretzky 1995; Elšík 2003; Friedman 2017a) or even dialect levelling or koineization (cf. Matras 1994; Friedman 2017a, p. 33). Leggio and Matras (2017) describe a variety in an advanced stage of koineization, with a relatively stabilized combination of features of divergent origin, suggesting that dialect levelling represents a theoretical alternative to both the genealogical and the diffusion models of Romani cross-dialect variation.

13.4.2 More on the Genealogical Model

The presumed genealogical nature of most, if not all, of the Romani dialect groups in the genealogical model requires, first of all, that they are established on the basis of innovations vis-à-vis Proto-Romani, since retentions are *not* indicative of a genealogical subgrouping (e.g. Campbell 1998,

p. 197). For example, the presence of the lexeme *kaliko* 'tomorrow, yesterday' in the so-called Northern dialects and, at the same time, in no other Romani varieties (Bakker 1999, p. 189) does not represent any evidence for a genealogical nature of this dialect group, since the lexeme, given its Indo-Aryan origin (cf. CDIAL 3014), must be a retention from Proto-Romani. Nor can dialect branches be established on the basis of (phenomenologically) identical innovations that are historically independent (e.g. Campbell 1998, p. 197). For example, the spirantization of the affricate /dž/ [dʒ] into palato-alveolar /ž/ [ʒ] in Lovari and southern Vendic, as in *džuv > žuv* 'louse', does not imply that these two dialects have anything in common diachronically, since the innovation can easily be shown to have occurred independently, i.e. in different places and at different times. The structural evidence for the independent occurrence is that, unlike in Lovari, the spirantization only affected initial and intervocalic instances of the affricate in Vendic (Bodnárová 2015, p. 64); and, unlike in Vendic, it must have proceeded via an alveolo-palatal /ź/ [z] in Lovari (cf. Boretzky 2003, p. 19; Boretzky and Igla 2004, p. 48).

Even if identical innovations in a group of varieties *are* historically connected, they are not necessarily indicative of a genealogical nature of the group, since they may have spread by geographical diffusion across the varieties. For example, the fact that all South Central varieties have simplified the Proto-Romani cluster /nṛ/ in *manṛo* 'bread' to /r/ does not necessarily mean that one should reconstruct a Proto-South-Central form *maro*. Since a simple rhotic has developed here in all Romani varieties spoken traditionally—i.e. excluding relatively recent, Vlax-speaking, immigrants—in a large continuous area stretching from northwestern Europe to the western Balkans, it is very likely that the innovation has diffused geographically (Matras 2002, p. 226; 2005, p. 13), affecting all the South Central varieties on the way (see, however, Boretzky and Igla 2004, p. 47 for an opponent view).

Thus, the only valid evidence for a genealogical nature of a dialect group are innovations that can be shown to be shared within the group due to inheritance from the branch's proto-dialect, i.e. to have developed when the proto-dialect was still spoken by a relatively homogeneous speech community. In practice, this amounts to showing that a shared innovation is unlikely to have spread to and/or within the group through geographical diffusion. The ideal candidates are those innovations that are not only general (or can be shown to have been general in the past) within the dialect group but also exclusive to it, or at least absent from those dialect groups that were geographically adjacent at the time of the innovation. An example of such an innovation is the palatalization of the initial /t/ of Proto-Romani *tiro 'your SG', which is reflected in all Vlax varieties and, at the same time, in no other Romani varieties, and which thus allows the reconstruction of the Proto-Vlax form *t'iro (Elšík 2000, p. 80).

Despite the methodological importance of inherited shared innovations, proponents of the genealogical model (e.g. Bakker 1999; Boretzky 1999a, b, 2003; Boretzky and Igla 2004) often characterize the presumed branches by lists of synchronic internal similarities and external differences, without the due focus on, or even irrespective of, the diachronic status of these linguistic features (cf. Matras 2002, p. 215; 2005, pp. 8–9; Elšík 2006a). Sometimes, moreover, the diachronic evaluation of a linguistic development appears to be incorrect. Boretzky (2007, p. 326), for example, assumes that the loss of the noun *lurdo* 'soldier' in the South Central branch as well as in his South Balkan I branch represents a shared innovation, while it is in fact clear that innovations here are the different lexical replacements of *lurdo* (if indeed this was the Proto-Romani word for 'soldier'), through lexical borrowing or semantic change (e.g. 'soldier' < *'mounted, risen'), which are distinct between the two branches and even within them (cf. Arli *askeri*, Vendic South Central *ninco*, non-Vendic South Central *lukesto*).

Matras (2005, p. 9) is, in addition, also critical of what he calls the 'classificatory inconsistency' of the genealogical model, where the different dialect branches are *not* defined by an identical set of linguistic features, with those that are taken to be relevant for one group being sometimes irrelevant for another group. However, the genealogical model must draw on whatever structural evidence there is for a potential genealogical relationship, irrespective of the wider cross-dialect relevance of the linguistic structure in question. For example, the South Central group (cf. Elšík et al. 1999, p. 346; Elšík et al., in preparation) and the Arli dialect (cf. Boretzky 1996a, p. 15) share an irregular formation of the sociative case form of the person interrogative, viz. *kas-aha* and *kas-aja* (< *kas-aha*) 'with whom', respectively, which must have developed through a non-trivial morphological analogy (cf. Proto-Romani *kas-sa*). While the formation of the sociative of the person interrogative has no dialectological relevance elsewhere in Romani, the fact that the above idiosyncratic innovation is shared by the two groups and is, moreover, exclusive to them is a highly relevant piece of evidence for a potentially genealogical nature of the South Central–Arli connection (which, interestingly, is not mentioned in Boretzky 1999a, 2007; Boretzky and Igla 2004; Boretzky et al. 2008, pp. 60–65). Cross-dialect consistency of diagnostic features may only be achieved in synchronic models of dialect classification.

Given the central role of the notion of proto-dialects in the genealogical model, one may regret that so little reconstruction of actual proto-dialect forms has been attempted (cf. Matras 2005, p. 7). In other words, the genealogical nature of the internally coherent Romani dialect groups appears to be, to a significant extent, taken for granted (cf. Matras 2005, pp. 8–9), rather than firmly established, by the proponents of the genealogical model. There are, of course, interpretative consequences to employing the presumed dialect branches as an analytic point of departure. For example, whoever believes that the variant -em- of the 1SG perfective suffix is a Proto-Vlax innovation vis-à-vis Proto-Romani *-jom- (e.g. Boretzky 1995, p. 74; Boretzky and Igla 2004, p. 156), is bound to invoke inter-dialect interference to explain the presence of the 'non-Vlax' variant -om- in a dialect that they consider to have developed from Proto-Vlax. Thus, Boretzky (1995, p. 88) suggests that -om- in Bukovina Vlax is a borrowing from the non-Vlax Romani dialects of Ukraine, while Boretzky and Igla (2004, p. 156) consider -om- in this and a few other Vlax varieties to have been borrowed from North Central Romani. (The alternative, non-genealogical, view would be that the innovation *-jom- > -em- spread by geographical diffusion that pre-dated the various out-migrations of Vlax Roms from Romania, without affecting some dialects commonly considered to be Vlax. The present-day distribution of the change in the Romani dialects of Romania [cf. Matras 2013, pp. 214–215; Heuvel and Urech 2014, pp. 60–61] appears to support its diffusion origin.)

Moreover, inter-dialect interference may also be invoked with regard to *entire* varieties and dialect groups (e.g. Boretzky and Igla 2004, p. 300), including those that are geographically and structurally transitional between two or several 'well-behaved' groups and thus do not fit well with a genealogical classification into branches. For example, Ukrainian Romani (see Sect. 13.3.3) is considered by Boretzky and Igla (2004, pp. 237–238) to be originally a dialect of Northeastern (specifically Russian Romani) origin, which acquired a massive Vlax admixture after its speakers migrated to the south. While inter-dialect interference certainly does occur in some Romani speech communities (e.g. Vekerdi 1971; Boretzky 1995; Elšík 2003; Heuvel and Urech 2014, p. 48; Friedman 2017a), there is always a risk that the assumption of dialect mixing in an a priori genealogical model might be just an all-mighty conceptual trick, whereby varieties that do not possess the whole set of 'defining' features of a presumed dialect branch are considered to be mixed by default (Elšík 2006a, p. 98).

It needs to be emphasized that access to geographically detailed linguistic data may be crucial for the genealogical modelling of Romani cross-dialect variation. Innovations that can be shown not to have occurred in *all* varieties of a presumed dialect branch are non-indicative of the genealogical nature of the branch, as they must have spread by geographical diffusion (or else developed in a genealogical sub-branch of the relevant branch). Boretzky (2007, p. 327), for example, observes that *all* North Central dialects[2] have undergone a consonant metathesis in the Proto-Romani root *asv-* 'teardrop', although there are further sound changes in some varieties (cf. *avs-* and also *aps-*, *japs-*, *haps-*, and more). Given that, in addition, the metathesis does not occur in any of the neighbouring dialect groups, i.e. it is exclusive to the North Central group, one might be tempted to reconstruct a metathesized Proto-North-Central form *avs-*. However, additional dialect data (Elšík et al., in preparation) show that various non-metathesized forms (e.g. *asv-*, *asm-*, *asl-*, *jasv-*, *jašv-*) occur not only in some of the so-called Transitional North Central varieties, which often show diffusion from the adjacent South Central varieties (cf. Elšík et al. 1999; Elšík 2003, 2006b) and which thus may be argued to possess the non-metathesized forms secondarily, but also in the varieties on the southeastern periphery of the North Central area, where the lack of metathesis most likely represents a retention from Proto-Romani. In other words, while metathesis is almost general within North Central, geographically detailed data indicate that it must have spread through geographical diffusion.

13.4.3 More on the Diffusion Model

The distinction between retentions and innovations is as important for the diffusion model as it is for the genealogical one, as only the latter may diffuse. In his diffusion-based outline of Romani dialectology, Matras (2005) focuses on the role of those innovations that 'spread through large geographical spaces' (p. 9), presumably because they are likely to reflect the *earliest* divergent developments within Romani. The differing dialectological importance of different innovations in this approach derives from the patterns of their geographical distribution rather than from their structural linguistic character. The entire dialectological landscape of Romani is geographically dissected by means of a score of 'major isoglosses', which correspond to a set of diagnostic linguistic features that are relevant across all the dialects (Matras 2005, p. 7). Retentions of Proto-Romani features may be restricted to geographical peripheries of the Romani-speaking area (e.g. Matras 2010, p. 53). The fact that there are numerous wide-ranging innovations whose geographic distribution is best explained through diffusion

416 V. Elšík and M. Beníšek

does not, of course, entail that diffusion can account for all geographical patterns of cross-dialect variation within Romani. In other words, concrete diffusion-based hypotheses must always be confronted with competing, migration-based, hypotheses.

For geographical diffusion of linguistic innovations to have occurred, there must have been regular linguistic interaction between the relevant speech communities, which, at least until recent advances in technology, necessitated geographical proximity, and/or regular patterns of social contact. Some criticism of concrete diffusion-based claims targets this prerequisite. For example, Boretzky (2007, p. 332) argues that Matras' (2002, p. 223) suggestion that the linguistic features shared by Arli and the South Central dialects may have spread by diffusion from the south (see Sect. 13.4.1) is untenable since it would have had to proceed through areas 'void of Roma', as there is no evidence, according to Boretzky, of Roms in and around Bosnia, before the immigration of the Vlax Roms. However, in Bosnia, Podrinje, and Sandžak, there is sufficient evidence of a pre-Vlax population of long-settled Roms, sometimes called *Bijeli Cigani* 'White Gypsies' or even *Bijeli Arlije* 'White Arli', who have by now assimilated linguistically, culturally, and even ethnically to the local Slavic population (e.g. Đorđević 1903, pp. 6–7; Uhlik 1956, pp. 194–195; Sikimić 2018, pp. 103–104). Thus, the diffusion of linguistic innovations towards the north could have been mediated by this Romani population, i.e. before their loss of Romani (in an unknown period but certainly by the beginning of the twentieth century).

Distinct innovations diffusing from a single focal area may have different geographical distribution (Matras 2005, p. 10; 2010, p. 55), and indeed, this is what is expected in a diffusion model (e.g. Heuvel and Urech 2014, p. 51). Therefore, while it is hardly possible to motivate the precise spatial location of individual isoglosses ('why a given innovation stopped at the place it stopped' in Boretzky's words, 2007, p. 321), the diffusion model should strive to provide an extralinguistic motivation for thick and geographically concentrated bundles of isoglosses, many of which coincide with the boundaries between the consensus dialect groups. The lack of extralinguistic correlates for a deep dialectal boundary may be, in principle, taken as an argument for a migration-induced, and so genealogical, origin of that boundary (cf. Boretzky 2007, p. 319; Heuvel and Urech 2014, pp. 51–52).

For example, given that there is a thick and relatively concentrated bundle of isoglosses between the North Central and the South Central dialects that runs for over 400 kilometres across southwestern and south central Slovakia (e.g. Lípa 1965; Boretzky 1999a; Elšík et al. 1999; in preparation.) and, at the same time, no physical, geographical or administrative boundary, either present or past, corresponding to this bundle (Elšík 2006b), the following question must not remain unanswered, should a diffusion-based explanation be upheld: What kind of social or cultural boundary existed between the Romani speakers on either side of the bundle to allow such a deep in situ differentiation? Matras (2005, pp. 20–21) suggests that the Great Divide (see Sect. 13.4.1), which, he claims, 'separates the Northern from the Southern Central varieties', may have developed due to interrupted contact between Romani populations on either side of the divide in connection with the rivalry between the Habsburg and the Ottoman empires during the Early Modern period (cf. also Matras 2013, p. 206). Nevertheless, unlike the linguistic boundary between the North Central and the South Central groups, the Great Divide is *not* a concentrated isogloss bundle (*contra* Leggio and Matras 2017, p. 177) but a large transitional zone between two distant focal areas (Matras 2005, p. 11). Moreover, only three out of the eight isoglosses that are used to define the Great Divide (cf. Matras 2005, pp. 11–13) are at the same time relevant for the North–South Central boundary (viz. the southern apocope of final /n/ in *-ipen* and *-iben*, the northern prothesis of /j/ in the nominative third person pronouns, and the northern non-indicative copula root *av-*). (Matras [2010, p. 49] concedes that migration might have been responsible for the clear division between the two Central groups.)

The general condition for the development of overlapping diffusion spaces, which are often coextensive with the consensus dialect groups, is formulated as 'group-internal coherence', over a prolonged period of time, of speaker populations in the period following settlement (Matras 2005, pp. 18, 21), which reflects the development of regional group identities (cf. Matras 2010, p. 41). Matras (1999, 2005, p. 18) observes that the greater coherence of Romani populations in the regions more remote from the Balkan source of Romani migrations and demic diffusion derives from the lesser density and the greater isolation of these populations.

We have suggested (Sect. 13.2.2) that co-territorial dialects of distinct sub-ethnic groups of Roms may require distinct layers of geographical representation, in which case isoglosses need to be indexed to distinct dialect groups. *Inter alia*, this reflects the fact that geographical diffusion of structural innovations may (but need not) be selective with regard to the sub-ethnic affiliation of the speakers. For example, the diphthongization of long close-mid vowels, e.g. *dejl* (< *dēl*) 'God' and *louve* (< *lōve*) 'money', in the Lovari-type Vlax dialects of Austrian Burgenland (Cech and Heinschink 1998, p. 4) and western and central Slovakia (e.g. Wagner 2012, pp. 13, 24) but not of eastern Slovakia and most parts of Hungary is an innovation that, in all likelihood, spread by geographical diffusion between Vlax Romani communities, without, however, affecting the Central Romani dialects of the relevant area, which retain long monophthongs (Elšík et al., in preparation). In his pilot analysis of the patterns of cross-dialect variation in Romani of Romania, Matras (2013, p. 234) also concludes that 'group affiliation plays a role in the diffusion of linguistic structures', with groups affiliation being defined as 'a network of contacts among dispersed communities who share certain interests through common occupation patterns, values, customs, inter-marriage and so on'. The diachronic interpretation of cross-dialect patterns in Matras (2013) thus combines the spatial aspect of diffusion within several geographic zones with the social aspect of diffusion within several sub-ethnic networks of speakers.

13.5 Conclusions and Prospects

Though all Romani dialects share a structural core, the degree of cross-dialect variation within Romani is remarkable and often entails a lack of inherent inter-dialect intelligibility. Romani exhibits intricate patterns of cross-dialect variation, especially due to a complex interplay between geographical and migration-induced (sub-ethnic) dimensions of linguistic variation. Romani dialects have been classified especially from a diachronic perspective, i.e. with a focus on the origin and development of the synchronic patterns of cross-dialect variation, and there is an emerging consensus on a concrete taxonomy of Romani dialect groups. The synchronic patterns of cross-dialect variation have received competing diachronic interpretations. While the genealogical model ascribes great importance to long-distance migrations of speakers and assumes a genealogical nature of dialect groups, the diffusion model identifies social and geographical diffusion of linguistic innovations as the major source of cross-dialect variation, viewing dialect groups as clusters of synchronically similar varieties that have developed in situ. A combination of diffusion-based and genealogical hypotheses is required to account for the patterns of Romani cross-dialect variation in its complexity, as is due attention to convergence processes such as inter-dialect borrowing and dialect levelling.

Romani dialectology is a vibrant field of inquiry, both in terms of theoretical and methodological discussions and in terms of its empirical basis. Given that geographically detailed linguistic data may be crucial for diachronic modelling, the continuing documentation and description of undocumented and undescribed Romani varieties are, of course, the basic desideratum for Romani dialectology. Nevertheless, the discipline also urgently needs to widen its horizons: structural linguistic variation due to social factors is in need of basic research; perceptual dialectology is all but non-existent; there are no empirical studies of dialect intelligibility; and the various dialectometric methods are yet to be applied to Romani data.

Notes

1. A mention should also be made about the 'Romani Morphosyntax Database' (RMS), an online database based at the University of Manchester. It serves as a source of data for many otherwise undescribed Romani dialects that have been documented through fieldwork documentation with the help of a reverse translation elicitation questionnaire. Cf. https://romani.humanities. manchester.ac.uk/rms/ (accessed on 11 December 2018).
2. By mistake, Boretzky (2007, p. 327) switches the South Central and the North Central groups in his discussion of this example.

References

Ackerley, Frederick G. 1914–1915. The Romani speech of Catalonia. *Journal of the Gypsy Lore Society*, n.s., 8: 99–140.

Ackerley, Frederick G. 1941. Bosnian Romani: Prolegomena. *Journal of the Gypsy Lore Society*, 3rd ser., 20: 84–99.

Adamou, Evangelia. 2010. Bilingual speech and language ecology in Greek Thrace: Romani and Pomak in contact with Turkish. *Language in Society* 39: 147–171.

Adamou, Evangelia, and Amalia Arvaniti. 2014. Greek Thrace Xoraxane Romani. *Journal of the International Phonetic Association* 44 (2): 223–231.

Angăčev, Ilija. 2008. *Kratka morfologija na ciganskija dialekt na Ljaskovec*. Veliko Tărnovo: Faber.

Ascoli, G.J. 1865. *Zigeunerisches*. Halle: Heynemann.

Baghbidi, Hassan Rezai. 2003. The Zargari language: An endangered European language in Iran. *Romani Studies*, 5th ser., 13 (2): 123–148.

Bakker, Peter. 1999. The Northern branch of Romani: Mixed and non-mixed varieties. In *Die Sprache der Roma: Perspektiven der Romani-Forschung in Österreich im interdisziplinären und internationalen Kontext*, ed. Dieter W. Halwachs and Florian Menz, 172–209. Drava: Klagenfurt.

Bakker, Peter. 2005. Notes on the genesis of Caló and other Iberian Para-Romani varieties. In *Romani in contact: The history, structure and sociology of a language*, ed. Yaron Matras 1995, 125–150. Amsterdam: John Benjamins.

Bakker, Peter, and Yaron Matras. 1997. Introduction. In *The typology and dialectology of Romani*, ed. Yaron Matras, Peter Bakker, and Hristo Kyuchukov, vii–xxx. Amsterdam: John Benjamins.

Baranja, Samanta. 2013. *Amari čhib. Naš jezik. Slovnica prekmurske romščine*. Ljubljana: Pedagoški inštitut.

Barannikov, Aleksej P. 1934. *The Ukrainian and South Russian Gypsy dialects*. Leningrad: Academy of Sciences of the USSR.

Beníšek, Michael. 2017. Eastern Uzh varieties of North Central Romani. PhD thesis. Prague: Charles University.

Bodnárová, Zuzana. 2009. *Gramatický náčrt romského dialektu maďarské obce Versend. Diplomová práce*. Praha: Univerzita Karlova.

Bodnárová, Zuzana. 2015. Vend Romani: A grammatical description and sociolinguistic situation of the so-called Vend dialects of Romani. PhD thesis. Prague: Charles University.

Boretzky, Norbert. 1986. Zur Sprache der Gurbet von Priština (Jugoslawien). *Giessener Hefte fur Tsiganologie* 3 (1–4): 195–216.

Boretzky, Norbert. 1993. *Bugurdži. Deskriptiver und historischer Abriß eines Romani Dialekts*. Wiesbaden: Harrassowitz.

Boretzky, Norbert. 1994. *Romani: Grammatik des Kalderaš-Dialekts mit Texten und Glossar*. Wiesbaden: Harrassowitz.

Boretzky, Norbert. 1995. Interdialectal interference in Romani. In *Romani in contact: The history, structure and sociology of a language*, ed. Yaron Matras, 69–94. Amsterdam: John Benjamins.

Boretzky, Norbert. 1996a. Arli: Materialen zu einem sudbalkanischen Romani-Dialekt. *Grazer Linguistische Studien* 46: 1–30.

Boretzky, Norbert. 1996b. The 'new infinitive' in Romani. *Journal of the Gypsy Lore Society*, 5th ser., 6 (1): 1–51.

Boretzky, Norbert. 1998. Areal and insular dialects and the case of Romani. *Grazer linguistische Studien* 50: 1–27.

Boretzky, Norbert. 1999a. Die Gliederung der Zentralen Dialekte und die Beziehungen zwischen Südlichen Zentralen Dialekten (Romungro) und Südbalkanischen RomaniDialekten. In *Die Sprache der Roma: Perspektiven der Romani-Forschung in Österreich im interdisziplinären und internationalen Kontext*, ed. Dieter W. Halwachs and Florian Menz, 210–276. Drava: Klagenfurt.

Boretzky, Norbert. 1999b. *Die Verwandtschaftsbeziehungen zwischen den Südbalkanischen Romani-Dialekten. Mit einem Kartenanhang*. Frankfurt-am-Main: Peter Lang.

Boretzky, Norbert. 2000. South Balkan II as a Romani dialect branch: Bugurdži, Drindari, and Kalajdži. *Romani Studies*, 5th ser., 10 (2): 105–183.

Boretzky, Norbert. 2003. *Die Vlach-Dialekte des Romani. Strukturen – Sprachgeschichte – Verwandtschaftsverhältnisse – Dialektkarten*. Wiesbaden: Harrassowitz.

Boretzky, Norbert. 2007. The differentiation of the Romani dialects. *Sprachtypologie und Universalienfoschung* 60 (4): 314–336.

13 Romani Dialectology 421

Boretzky, Norbert. 2012. *Studien zum Wortschatz des Romani*. Veliko Tarnovo: Faber.

Boretzky, Norbert, and Birgit Igla. 2004. *Kommentierter Dialektatlas des Romani. Teil 1: Vergleich der Dialekte. Teil 2: Dialektkarten mit einer CD Rom*. Wiesbaden: Harrassowitz.

Boretzky, Norbert, and Petra Cech. 2016. *Der Romani-Dialekt von Prilep-Makedonien*. Graz: Karl-Franzens-Universität Graz.

Boretzky, Norbert, Petra Cech, and Birgit Igla. 2008. *Die Südbalkanischen Dialekte (SB1) und ihre innere Gliederung. Analyse und Karten*. Graz: Institut für Sprachwissenschaft.

Bourgeois, Henri. 1901. Esquisse d'une grammaire du romani finlandais. *Atti de la Reale Academia delle Szienze di Torino* 46: 541–554.

Calvet, Georges. 1982. *Lexique tsigane. Dialecte des Erlides de Sofia*. Paris: Publications Orientalistes de France.

Campbell, Lyle. 1998. *Historical linguistics: An introduction*. Edinburgh: Edinburgh University Press.

Carling, Gerd, Lenny Lindell, and Gilbert Ambrazaitis. 2014. *Scandoromani: Remnants of a mixed language*. Leiden: Brill.

CDIAL = Turner, Ralph Lilley. 1962–1966. *A comparative dictionary of Indo-Aryan languages*. London: Oxford University Press.

Cech, Petra. 2006. *Dolenjska Romani: The dialect of the Dolenjski Roma in Novo Mesto and Bela Krajina, Slovenia*. München: Lincom.

Cech, Petra, and Mozes F. Heinschink. 1996. *Sepečides-Romani*. München: Lincom.

Cech, Petra, and Mozes F. Heinschink. 1998. *Basisgrammatik. Arbeitsbericht 1 des Projekts 'Kodifizierung der Romanes-Variante der Österreichischen Lovara'*. Vienna: Romano Centro.

Cech, Petra, and Mozes F. Heinschink. 1999. *Sepečides-Romani. Grammatik, Texte und Glossar eines türkischen Dialekts*. Wiesbaden: Harrassowitz.

Cech, Petra, and Mozes F. Heinschink. 2001. A dialect with seven names. *Romani Studies*, 5th ser., 11 (2): 137–184.

Cech, Petra, and Mozes F. Heinschink. 2002. Vokabular der Dolenjski Roma aus Novo Mesto und Bela Krajina, Slowenien. *Grazer Linguistische Studien* 58: 1–42.

Čerenkov, Lev N. 2008. Cyganskaja dialektologija v Ukraine. Istorija i sovremennoe sostojanie. Naukovi zapysky. *Zbirnyk prac' molodych věnych ta aspirantiv* 15: 489–503.

Cherenkov, Lev N. 2005. The Plaščuny and their dialect—Preliminary notes. In *General and applied Romani Linguistics: Proceedings from the 6th International Conference on Romani Linguistics*, ed. Barbara Schrammel, Dieter W. Halwachs, and Gerd Ambrosch, 43–47. München: Lincom.

Cortiade, Marcel. 1991. Romani versus Para-Romani. In *The margin of Romani: Gypsy languages in contact*, ed. Peter Bakker and Marcel Cortiade, 1–15. Amsterdam: Instituut voor Algemene Taalwetenschap.

Courthiade, Marcel. 1998. The dialect structure of the Romani language. *Interface* 31: 9–14.

Djonedi, Fereydun. 1996. Romano-glossar. Gesammelt von Schir-Ali Tehranizade. *Grazer Linguistische Studien* 46: 31–59.

Đorđević [Gjorgjević], Tihomir R. 1903. *Die Zigeuner in Serbien. Ethnologische Forschungen I*. Budapest: Thalia.

Elšík, Viktor. 2000. Dialect variation in Romani personal pronouns. In *Grammatical relations in Romani: The noun phrase*, ed. Elšík Viktor and Yaron Matras, 65–94. John Benjamins: Amsterdam.

Elšík, Viktor. 2003. Interdialect contact of Czech (and Slovak) Romani varieties. *International Journal of the Sociology of Language* 162: 41–62.

Elšík, Viktor. 2006a. Review of [Boretzky and Igla 2004]. *Romani Studies*, 5th ser., 16 (1): 95–100.

Elšík, Viktor. 2006b. Romani dialectology of a microregion: The "transitional" North–South Central Romani dialects of Gemer, Slovakia. Paper presented at the 7th International Conference on Romani Linguistics, Prague, 14–16 September.

Elšík, Viktor. 2008. Review of [Angäčev 2008]. *Romani Studies*, 5th ser., 18 (2): 212–216.

Elšík, Viktor. 2009. Loanwords in Selice Romani: An Indo-Aryan language of Slovakia. In *Loanwords in the world's languages: A comparative handbook*, ed. Martin Haspelmath and Uri Tadmor, 260–303. Berlin: Mouton de Gruyter.

Elšík, Viktor, and Yaron Matras. 2006. *Markedness and language change: The Romani sample*. Berlin and New York: Mouton De Gruyter.

Elšík, Viktor, Milena Hübschmannová, and Hana Šebková. 1999. The Southern Central (ahi-imperfect) Romani dialects of Slovakia and Northern Hungary. In *Die Sprache der Roma: Perspektiven der Romani-Forschung in Österreich im interdisziplinären und internationalen Kontext*, ed. Dieter W. Halwachs and Florian Menz, 277–390. Drava: Klagenfurt.

Elšík, Viktor, Michael Beníšek, and Zuzana Bodnárová. In preparation. The linguistic atlas of Central Romani. Manuscript. Prague: Charles University.

Finck, Franz N. 1903. *Lehrbuch des Dialekts der Deutchen Zigeuner*. Marburg: N. G. Elwert.

Formoso, Bernard, and Georges Calvet. 1987. *Lexique Tsigane: dialecte sinto piémontais*. Paris: Publications Orientalists de France.

François, Alexandre. 2014. Trees, waves and linkages: Models of language diversification. In *The Routledge handbook of historical linguistic*, ed. Claire Bowern and Bethwyn Evans, 161–189. London and New York: Routledge.

Franzese, Sergio. 1985. *Il dialetto dei Sinti Piemontesi: note grammaticali e glossario*. Torino: Centro Studi Zingari.

Franzese, Sergio. 1986. *Il dialetto dei Rom Xoraxané. Note grammaticali. Glossario*. Turin: Centro Studi Zingari.

Friedman, Victor A. 2013. Compartmentalized grammar: The variable (non)-integration of Turkish verbal conjugation in Romani dialects. *Romani Studies*, 5th ser., 23 (1): 107–120.

Friedman, Victor A. 2017a. Seven varieties of Arli: Skopje as a center of convergence and divergence of Romani dialects. *Romani Studies*, 5th ser., 27 (1): 29–45.

Friedman, Victor A. 2017b. The Arli of Skopje: A perceptual dialectological approach. In *Das amen godi pala Lev N. Čerenkov: Romani historija, čhib taj kultura* (Grazer Romani Publikationen, 5), ed. Kiril Kozhanov, Mikhail Oslon, and Dieter W. Halwachs, 210–220. Graz: Universität Graz.

Gilliat-Smith, Bernard J. 1913–1914. The dialect of the Drindaris. *Journal of the Gypsy Lore Society*, n.s., 7: 260–298.

Gilliat-Smith, Bernard J. 1915–1916. A report on the Gypsy tribes of North East Bulgaria. *Journal of the Gypsy Lore Society*, n.s., 9 (1): 1–55, 9 (2): 65–109.

Gjerdman, Olof, and Erik Ljungberg. 1963. *The language of the Swedish coppersmith Gipsy Johan Dimitri Taikon: Grammar, texts, vocabulary and English word-index*. Uppsala: Lundequistska Bokhandeln; Copenhagen: Ejnar Munksgaard.

Granqvist, Kimmo. 2007. *Suomen romanin äänne- ja muotorakenne*. Helsinki: Suomen Itämainen Seura ja Kotimaisten kielten tutkimuskeskus.

Granqvist, Kimmo. 2011. *Lyhyt Suomen romanikielen kielioppi*. Helsinki: Kotimaisten kielten tutkimuskeskus.

Granqvist, Kimmo. 2017. Finnish Romani and its dialectology. In *Das amen godi pala Lev N. Čerenkov: Romani historija, čhib taj kultura* (Grazer Romani Publikationen, 5), ed. Kiril Kozhanov, Mikhail Oslon, and Dieter W. Halwachs, 221–237. Graz: Universität Graz.

Grant, Anthony P. 1995. Plagiarism and lexical orphans in the European Romani lexicon. In *Romani in contact: The history, structure and sociology of a language*, ed. Yaron Matras, 53–68. Amsterdam: John Benjamins.

Halwachs, Dieter. 2002. *Burgenland-Romani*. München: Lincom.

Hancock, Ian. 1988. The development of Romani linguistics. In *Languages and cultures. Studies in honor of Edgar C. Polomé*, ed. Mohammad Ali Jazayery and Werner Winter, 183–223. Berlin: Mouton de Gruyter.

Hancock, Ian. 1995. *A handbook of Vlax Romani*. Columbus: Slavica.

Heuvel, Wilco van den, and Evelyne Urech. 2014. Romani dialect variation in Transylvania: Migration and diffusion. *Romani Studies*, 5th ser., 24 (1): 43–70.

Holzinger, Daniel. 1993. *Das Romanes: Grammatik und Diskursanalyse der Sprache der Sinte*. Innsbruck: Institut für Sprachwissenschaft der Universität Innsbruck.

Hübschmannová, Milena, Hana Šebková, and Anna Žigová. 1991. *Romsko-český a česko-romský kapesní slovník*. Praha: Státní pedagogické nakladatelství.

Hutterer, Claus Jürgen (Miklós), and György Mészáros. 1967. *A Lovari Cigány Dialektus Leíró Nyelvtana. Hangtan, Szóképzés, Alaktan, Szótar*. Budapest: Kiadja A Magyar Nyelvtudományi Társág.

Igla, Birgit. 1996. *Das Romani von Ajia Varvara. Deskriptive und historisch-vergleichende Darstellung eines Zigeunerdialekts*. Wiesbaden: Harrassowitz.

Igla, Birgit. 1997. The Romani dialect of the Rhodopes. In *The typology and dialectology of Romani*, ed. Yaron Matras, Peter Bakker, and Hristo Kyuchukov, 147–158. Amsterdam: John Benjamins.

Igla, Birgit. 2005. Sinti-Manuš: Aspects of classification. In *General and Applied Romani linguistics: Proceedings from the 6th International Conference on Romani Linguistics*, ed. Barbara Schrammel, Dieter W. Halwachs, and Gerd Ambrosch, 23–42. München: Lincom.

Kaufman, Terrence. 1979. Review of Weer Rajendra Rishi, multilingual Romani dictionary. *International Journal of the Sociology of Language* 19: 131–144.

Kenrick, Donald S. 1967. The Romani dialect of a musician from Razgrad. *Balkansko Ezikozanie* 11–12: 71–78.

Kenrick, Donald S. 1969. Morphology and lexicon of the Romani dialect of Kotel (Bulgaria). PhD thesis. London: University of London.

Kochanowski, Vania de Gila. 1963. *Gypsy studies*. New Delhi: International Academy of Indian Culture.

Kopernicki, Izydor. 1930. *Textes tsiganes. Contes et poésies avec traduction française* (= Prace Komisji orjentalistycznej, 7). Kraków: Polska Akademja Umiejętności.

Krinková, Zuzana. 2015. *From Iberian Romani to Iberian Para-Romani varieties*. Prague: Charles University.

Leggio, Daniele V. 2011. The dialect of the Mitrovica Roma. *Romani Studies*, 5th ser., 21 (1): 57–114.

Leggio, Daniele V., and Yaron Matras. 2017. Variation and dialect levelling in the Romani dialect of Țăndărei. *Romani Studies*, 5th ser., 27 (2): 173–209.

Lípa, Jiří. 1963. *Příručka cikánštiny*. Praha: Státní pedagogické nakladatelství.

Lípa, Jiří. 1965. *Cikánština v jazykovém prostředí slovenském a českém: k otázkám starých a novějších složek v její gramatice a lexiku*. Praha: Nakladatelství Československé akademie věd.

Lípa, Jiří. 1968. O nevěrohodnosti ciganologa H. v. Wlislockého. *Slovo a slovesnost* 29 (4): 407–411.

Lípa, Jiří. 1979. Cases of coexistence of two varieties of Romani in the same territory in Slovakia. *International Journal of the Sociology of Language* 19: 51–57.

Mann, S. E. 1933. Albanian Romani. *Journal of the Gypsy Lore Society*, 3rd ser., 12: 1–14, 147–152.

Mann, S. E. 1935. South Albanian Romani. *Journal of the Gypsy Lore Society*, 3rd ser., 14: 174–184.

Mānušs, Leksa, Jānis Neilands, and Kārlis Rudevičs. 1997. *Čigānu-latviešu-anglu etimoloģiskā vārdnīca un latviešu-čigānu vārdnīca*. Rīga: Zvaigzne ABC.

Marushiakova, Elena, and Vesselin Popov. 2004. Segmentation vs. consolidation: The example of four Gypsy groups in CIS. *Romani Studies*, 5th ser., 14 (2): 145–191.

Matras, Yaron. 1994. *Untersuchungen zu Grammatik und Diskurs des Romanes. Dialekt der Kelderaša/Lovara*. Wiesbaden: Harrassowitz.

Matras, Yaron. 1999. The speech of the Polska Roma: Some highlighted features and their implications for Romani dialectology. *Journal of the Gypsy Lore Society*, 5th ser., 9 (1): 1–28.

Matras, Yaron. 2002. *Romani: A linguistic introduction*. Cambridge: Cambridge University Press.

Matras, Yaron. 2004. Romacilikanes: The Romani dialect of Parakalamos. *Romani Studies*, 5th ser., 14 (2): 59–109.

Matras, Yaron. 2005. The classification of Romani dialects: A geographic-historical perspective. In *General and applied Romani linguistics: Proceedings from the 6th International Conference on Romani Linguistics*, ed. Barbara Schrammel, Dieter W. Halwachs, and Gerd Ambrosch, 7–22. Lincom: Munich.

Matras, Yaron. 2010. *Romani in Britain: The afterlife of a language*. Edinburgh: Edinburgh University Press.

Matras, Yaron. 2013. Mapping the Romani dialects of Romania. *Romani Studies*, 5th ser., 23 (2): 199–243.

Mészáros, György. 1976. The Cerhāri Gipsy dialect. *Acta Orientalia Academiae Scientiarum Hungaricae* 30 (3): 351–367.

Mészáros, György. 1980. *A magyarországi szinto cigányok: történetük és nyelvük*. Budapest: Kiadja a Magyar nyelvtudományi társaság.

Miklosich, Franz. 1873. *Über die Mundarten und die Wanderungen der Zigeuner Europas III*. Wien: Karl Gerold's Sohn.

Minkov, Michael. 1997. A concise grammar of West Bulgarian Romani. *Journal of the Gypsy Lore Society*, 5th ser., 7: 55–95.

Miskow, Johan, and Viggo Brøndal. 1923. Sigøjnersprog i Danmark. *Danske studier* 1923: 97–145.

Oslon, Mixail V. 2018. *Jazyk kotljarov-moldovaja. Grammatika kelderarskoho dialekta cyganskogo jazyka v russkojazyčnom okruženii*. Moskva: Jazyki slavjanskoj kul'tury.

Paspati, Alexandre. 1870. *Études sur les Tchinghianés ou Bohémiens de l'Empire Ottoman*. Constantinople: Imprimérie Antoine Koroméla.

Pobożniak, Tadeusz. 1964. *Grammar of the Lovari dialect*. Crakow: Państwowe wydawnictwo naukowe.

Puchmayer, Anton J. 1821. *Románi Čib, das ist: Grammatik und Wörterbuch der Zigeuner Sprache, nebst einigen Fabeln in derselben. Dazu als Anhang die Hantýrka oder die Čechische Diebessprache*. Prag: Fürst-erzbischöflichen Buchdruckerey.

Rozwadowski, Jan. 1936. *Wörterbuch des Zigeunerdialekts von Zakopane. Słownik cyganow z Zakopanego*. Krakow: Polska Akademja Umiejęności.

Sabaini, Astrid, Mozes F. Heinschink, and Dieter W. Halwachs. 2015. *Kalderaš Romani*. München: Lincom.

Sampson, John. 1926. *The Dialect of the Gypsies of Wales. Being the older form of British Romani preserved in the speech of the clan of Abram Wood*. Oxford: Oxford University Press.

Sarău, Gheorghe. 1998. *Dicţionar Rrom (Spoitoresc)—Român*. Bucureşti: Editura Kriterion.

Schulman, Veronica Olga. 2010. A grammatical description of the Sofades Romani variety. PhD thesis. Manchester: University of Manchester.

Sechidou, Irene. 2011. *Balkan Romani: The dialect of Ajios Athanasios/Greece*. München: Lincom.

Sergievskij, M. V., and A. P. Barannikov. 1938. *Cygansko-russkij slovar'. Okolo 10000 slov s priloženiem grammatiky cyganskogo jazyka*. Moskva: Gosudarstvennoe izdatel'stvo inostrannyx i nacional'nyx slovarej.

Sikimić, Biljana. 2018. Kovači u Sandžaku. In *Romi Srbije u XXI veku*, ed. Tibor Varadi, 101–117. Beograd: Srpska akademija nauka i umetnosti.

Smart, Bath C., and Henry Thomas Crofton. 1875. *The Dialect of the English Gypsies*. London: Asher & Co.

Soravia, Giulio. 1977. *Dialetti degli Zingari Italiani* (= Profilo dei dialetti italiani, 22). Pisa: Centro di studio per la dialettologia italiana & Pacini.

Soravia, Giulio. 1983. Note grammaticale del dialetto dei Rom Xoraxani. *Lacio Drom* 19 (2): 31–34.

Soravia, Giulio, and Camillo Fochi. 1995. *Vocabolario sinottico delle lingue zingare parlate in Italia*. Roma: Centro Studi Zingari; Bologna: Istituto di Glottologia.

Sowa, Rudolf von. 1887. *Die Mundart der slovakischen Zigeuner*. Göttingen: Vandenhoeck und Ruprecht's Verlag.

Sowa, Rudolf von. 1902. *Wörterbuch des Dialekts der deutschen Zigeuner*. Leipzig: Deutsche morgenlandkudliche Gesselschaft.

Tcherenkov, Lev N. 1999. Eine kurzgefasste Grammatik des Russischen Kalderaš-Dialekts des Romani. *Grazer Linguistische Studien* 51: 131–166.

Tenser, Anton. 2005. *Lithuanian Romani*. München: Lincom.

Tenser, Anton. 2008. Northeastern group of Romani dialects. PhD thesis. Manchester: University of Manchester.

Tenser, Anton. 2012. A report on Romani dialects in Ukraine: Reconciling linguistic and ethnographic data. *Romani Studies*, 5th ser., 22 (1): 35–47.

Thesleff, Arthur. 1901. *Wörterbuch des Dialekts der finnländischen Zigeuner*. Helsingfors: Finnische Litteratur-Gesellschaft.

Toropov, Vadim G. 2009. *Crimean Roma: Language and folklore*. Ivanovo: Unona.

Uhlik, Rade. 1956. Iz ciganske onomastike. Imena plemena i narječja. Glasnik Zemaljskog muzeja u Sarajevu. *Istoria i etnografija* 11: 193–209.

Uhlik. Rade. 1973. Govori jugoslovenskih Cigana u okviru balkanskog jezičkog saveza. *Godišnjak X, Centar za Balkonološka ispitivanja* 8: 53–108.

Urech, Evelyne, and Wilco van den Heuvel. 2011. A sociolinguistic perspective on Roma group names in Transylvania. *Romani Studies*, 5th ser., 21 (2): 145–160.

Valet, Joseph. 1991. Grammar of Manush as it is spoken in the Auvergne. In *In the margin of Romani: Gypsy languages in contact*, ed. Peter Bakker and Marcel Cortiade, 106–131. Amsterdam: Instituut voor Algemene Taalwetenschap.

Valtonen, Pertti. 1972. *Suomen mustalaiskielen etymologinen sanakirja*. Helsinki: Suomalaisen Kirjallisuuden Seura.

Vekerdi, József. 1971. The Gurvari Gipsy dialect in Hungary. *Acta Orientalia Academiae Scientiarum Hungaricae* 24 (3): 381–389.

Vekerdi, József. 1984. The Vend Gypsy dialect in Hungary. *Acta Linguistica Hungarica* 34 (1–2): 65–86.

Vekerdi, József. 2006. An 18th-century Transylvanian Gypsy vocabulary. *Acta Orientalia Academiae Scientiarum Hungaricae* 59 (3): 347–360.

Vencel', Tatjana V., and Lev N. Čerenkov. 1976. Dialekty cyganskogo jazyka. *Jazyki Azii i Afriki I*, 283–332. Moskva: Nauka.

Wagner, Peter. 2012. A grammar of North West Lovari Romani. PhD thesis. Prague: Charles University.

Wentzel, Tatjana W. 1988. *Die Zigeunersprache. Nordrussischer Dialekt*. Leipzig: Verlag Enzyklopädie.

Wiedner, Jakob. 2017. Norwegian Romani: A linguistic view on a minority language in the north of Europe. PhD thesis. Oslo: University of Oslo.

Windfuhr, Gernot L. 1970. European Gypsies in Iran: A first report. *Anthropological Linguistics* 12: 271–292.

Wlislocki, Heinrich von. 1884. *Die Sprache der transsilvanischen Zigeuner*. Leipzig: Wilhelm Friedrich.

14

Language Policy and Planning in Romani

Dieter W. Halwachs

14.1 Introduction

Language policy and planning (LPP) refers to the development of programs and strategies designed to create an official language, i.e. the statutory language of the government and administration of a sovereign state that is implemented by law via the educational system. Research has been traditionally linked to the activities of state agencies in regulating the status of officially recognised language varieties (Kaplan and Baldauf 1997) and to resulting sociolinguistic processes and their consequences for the linguistic behaviour of communities and individuals (Spolsky 2003). Postcolonial research criticises the role of the state agency in identity building (Anderson 1983) and consequently also in language planning (Wright 2004). More recently, research on LPP has gone beyond state-sponsored activities to local and regional levels and included the role of single actors in shaping policy at local institutions (Liddicoat and Baldauf 2008; Davies and Ziegler 2015) in a 'post-nationalist' era (Heller 2011). These developments and approaches also shape research on Romani LLP that always has to consider the complicated sociolinguistic situation of the speakers of this language.

D. W. Halwachs (✉)
Plurilingualism Research Unit, University of Graz, Graz, Austria
e-mail: dieter.halwachs@uni-graz.at

© The Author(s) 2020
Y. Matras and A. Tenser (eds.), *The Palgrave Handbook of Romani Language and Linguistics*, https://doi.org/10.1007/978-3-030-28105-2_14

14.2 The Sociolinguistic Situation of Romani

Up to now, Romani mainly functions in informal domains, whereas the dominant majority languages prevail in written formal use. Its sociolinguistic status reflects the social situation of its speakers: politically, economically as well as culturally marginalised, ethnically stigmatised, discriminated and persecuted to the point of genocide, Roms often could make their living only in small and separated groups at the fringes of society, a situation which explains both their geographical and sociocultural heterogeneity. Romani functions almost exclusively as an intra-group variety in the social microcosm of private and everyday life. Its use in the social macrocosm of everyday life is limited to inter-group contacts. Communication in formal domains is dominated by the respective majority language which also dominates the social macrocosm.

In many cases, majority languages are also used together with Romani as an intimate variety in the social microcosm. The linguistic repertoire of Romani speakers always shows a functional distribution between dominant majority languages and Romani.[1]

Whereas majority languages cover the public domains of language use, Romani varieties are limited to informal domains. Thus, at least the adult members of Romani speech communities are always multilingual with majority languages often dominating not only in formal but also in informal domains of language use. Consequently, Romani has to be characterised as a functionally restricted, dominated language.[2]

Its limited functionality does not make Romani an endangered language. If the complementary functional distribution between the linguistic varieties remains stable in the repertoire, Romani is passed on as an intimate variety. However, functional stability and language transmission require sociocultural continuity. In homogeneous speech communities with largely endogamous, multi-generation households, internal social cohesion and solidarity between extended families, Romani, like any other ethnic language, commonly prevails in the social microcosm. Thus, children are socialised with the in-group variety and in addition they acquire fluency in the dominant language when growing up, as they start interacting with community outsiders. Among the Roms, homogeneity primarily results from exclusion on the grounds of stigmatisation and discrimination. These often trigger self-isolation that, again, intensifies separation. Thus, social differentiation is a crucial factor in language maintenance. Emancipatory efforts may trigger social changes that evolve into economic and political participation. The price for socio-economic integration is sociocultural assimilation that affects group

14 Language Policy and Planning in Romani 431

cohesion and, consequently, language use as well as language transmission. This process is similar to dialect loss among local speech communities of majority languages. The breaking-up of homogeneous rural communities caused by social changes leads, among other things, to the dominance of regional and supra-regional varieties and often causes the abandonment of local dialects. Thus, social mobility results in functional language change. As a rule, integrative measures among Romani speech communities increase the dominance of the respective majority language and reduce both the functionality and vitality of Romani. The maintenance of Romani as a primary factor of ethnic identity is determined by functionality and by such emotive parameters as language attitude and consciousness among individual speakers or speech communities. However, as long as Romani functions as an intra-group variety and is used for the socialisation of Romani children that guarantees its use in domains of everyday life, it remains a vital language.

Based on 'intergenerational language transmission', the 'UNESCO Atlas of the World's Languages in Danger' categorises Romani as 'definitely endangered' because 'children no longer learn the language as mother tongue in the home'.[3] This assessment applies to some speech communities, but there are many others with a different 'degree of endangerment'. Dependent on the specific situation, Romani varieties conform to all five degrees of the UNESCO Atlas: Welsh Romani as described by Sampson (1926) is most probably 'extinct'; Sepečides Romani of Izmir (Cech and Heinschink 1999) where 'the youngest speakers are grandparents, and older [who] speak the language partially and infrequently' is 'critically endangered'; Burgenland Romani (Halwachs 2013) which 'is only spoken by grandparents and older generations; while the parent generation may understand it, [but does] not speak it to children or among themselves' is 'severely endangered'; many other varieties are 'definitely endangered' as 'children no longer learn the language as mother tongue in the home' and some even only 'vulnerable' because 'most children speak the language, but it may be restricted to certain domains (e.g. home)' as it is the case with many Vlax and Balkan Romani communities with sociocultural continuity. To label Romani as definitely endangered seems to be an assessment based on incomplete information.

The same characterisation, incomplete information, holds for the description given in the Ethnologue:[4] 'Romany [rom], a 'macrolanguage of Romania' subsumes eight individual languages: 'Balkan Romani [rmn] (Serbia), Baltic Romani [rml] (Poland), Carpathian Romani [rmc] (Slovakia), Kalo Finnish Romani [rmf] (Finland), Sinte Romani [rmo] (Germany), Vlax Romani [rmy], Welsh Romani [rmw] (United Kingdom)' and 'Tavringer Romani [rmu]' which is defined as a 'mixed language' of Sweden. As the ISO 639-3 letter codes—[rom], etc.—are used in electronic language coding, these labels, although erroneous, cannot be neglected.[5] Five of these 'languages' are treated equally on the 'Expanded Graded Intergenerational Disruption Scale' (EGIDS).[6] They are classified as 'developing' which corresponds to grade 5 and defines these 'Romani languages' as 'in vigorous use, with literature in a standardised form being used by some though this is not yet widespread or sustainable'. 'Vlax Romani' is seen as 'threatened' which complies with grade 6b defined as 'used for face-to-face communication within all generations, but […] losing users'. 'Welsh and Tavringer Romani' are on the edge of extinction (grade 10 'extinct'). They are classified as 'dormant' (grade 9) and defined as languages that 'serve as a reminder of heritage identity for an ethnic community, but no one has more than symbolic proficiency'. Irrespective of the classification of Romani as a macro-language with eight languages, the status information regarding their vitality is not only incomplete but also incorrect. Finnish Romani may be in a similar situation as some Carpathian (=Central) varieties; however, both differ significantly from many Balkan varieties, which show vitality similar to a lot of Vlach varieties.

As Romani is a heterogeneous cluster of varieties with a multiplicity of speech communities and a high diversity of particular sociolinguistic situations, reliable evidence on development and vitality is only possible to collect for individual varieties. Only a basic definition allows an assessment of Romani in general, i.e. a language is vital, if a community uses it as the primary means of communication in private and everyday life. As this description matches the sociolinguistic situation of a good number of Romani communities, Romani remains—as already stated above—a vital language. For LPP purposes, such general descriptions are of minor importance. However, as both Ethnologue and the UNESCO Atlas are respected and often consulted resources, their insufficient and inaccurate information might have a negative impact on decisions in Romani LPP.

14.3 Romani LPP

Until the second half of the twentieth century, LPP was closely linked to the ideology of the ethnic nation-state. Strategies and activities were focused on the standardisation or modernisation of a language, how to lend it official status and the implementation of policy measures (Table 14.1). The latter aimed at linguistic homogeneity and the shift of speakers of other languages to the national standard language. In the aftermath of the political and humanitarian disasters during the first half of the twentieth century, de-colonialisation and democratisation resulted in the development of the concept of the ethnic nation-state into that of the civic nation-state. Whereas the citizens of an ethnic nation-state are idealised as members of a homogeneous state-nation, the definition of citizenship in a civic nation-state is not inevitably ethnicity based. While one ethnic group dominates in many civic nation-states, the possibility for the integration of members of other groups as citizens on an equal basis is legally guaranteed. Thus, ethno-cultural diversity becomes, at least in principle, part of national self-perception. In this context, even marginalised people like the Roms are recognised as ethnic groups and given the possibility for linguistic emancipation, i.e. the use of their ethnic language in formal public domains like education and the media. Thus, in the second half of the twentieth century, Romani, together with various other minority languages, became part of LPP efforts. However, as Roms never ruled over territory or exerted political power over speakers of other linguistic varieties, which is the primary condition for the development of an administrative acrolect, Romani has not developed a standard variety following the patterns of traditional LPP. Strategies and problems of language planning 'beyond the state' including the situation of Romani were first dealt with in Matras and Reershemius (1991). The first notable effort to codify Romani, however, happened in the context of the general language policy of the early Soviet Union.

14.3.1 Early Codifications

Early Soviet ethnopolitics guaranteed each people the right to use their language in a defined geographic area, i.e. an autonomous republic (SSR), region (Oblast) or district (Okrug). This policy aimed at the development of various languages to be used for alphabetisation and education as well as in professional life and public communication with the final goal of ideological mobilisation. Although the Roms did not succeed in being allocated their territory, they participated in this process. A group of Romani activists lobbied for the recognition and inclusion of Romani culture (see O'Keefe 2013) and started, among other things, text production in Romani, including one of the first literary works by a Rom, Alexander Germano's *Ruvoro* 'wolf cub' (see Zahova, this volume). The story appeared in the first issue of the *Romani Zoria* 'Romani dawn' magazine in the autumn of 1926 in Moscow. The 1927 Decree on Creating a Gypsy Alphabet by following

434   D. W. Halwachs

Table 14.1 Language policy and planning goals (Hornberger 2006)

Types	Extra-linguistic aims		Linguistic aims
	STATUS PLANNING about uses of language	ACQUISITION PLANNING about users of language	CORPUS PLANNING about language
POLICY PLANNING APPROACH on form	• Officialisation • Nationalisation • Standardisation • Proscription	SELECTION —————→ language's formal role in society • Group • Education/School • Literary • Religious • Mass media • Work	CODIFICATION language's forms • Graphisation • Documentation • Standardisation of corpus • Standardisation of auxiliary code
CULTIVATION PLANNING APPROACH on function	• Revival • Maintenance • Spread • Interlingual communication: international, intranational	IMPLEMENTATION ◀——— language's functional role in society • Reacquisition • Maintenance • Shift • Foreign language/second language/literacy	ELABORATION language's functions • Modernisation (new functions): lexical, stylistic • Renovation (new forms, old functions) • Purification • Reform • Stylistic simplification • Terminology unification

the Russian model has to be seen as the starting point of the codification of North Russian Romani.[7] During the following years, several hundred Romani texts were published, many of them translations: ideological pamphlets, novels and poetry, education materials and also language textbooks, which were prepared for the teaching of Romani children and for promoting Romani literacy in adults. Neither the level of dissemination of written Romani nor the impact of education and teaching in and of Romani can be evaluated and might not have reached beyond an extended group of activists and their families. In 1937, this policy was replaced by Russification, or rather assimilation, which put an end to the ethnoliberal phase of the early Soviet Union.

'The Soviet practice set the model for what was to become the common pattern of country-based literacy in Romani' (Matras, forthcoming).[8] Around the Prague Spring of 1968, a group of Romani writers in cooperation with academics started a codification process mainly for literary production. They created a writing system based on Czech and Slovak for East Slovak Romani, a variety widely used in the territories of former Czechoslovakia (see Hübschmannová and Neustupný 1996). In the countries of former Yugoslavia, Romani also became part of cultural productions starting from the 1960s. Aleksandar Petrović's film 'I Even Met Happy Gypsies' (srb. *Skupljači perja* 'The Feather Gatherers', 1967) was one of the first mainstream productions to use Romani together with a majority language.[9] Serbo-Croatian Latin orthography was introduced as the model for written Romani; sibilants were marked by carons {č,š,ž}, palatalisation by {đ}, etc. In line with the federal structure of the Yugoslavian state—republics and autonomous regions, nowadays most of them independent states—early literary activities followed a decentralised pattern: Macedonian activists suggested a two-variety approach with Arlije and Džambazi/Gurbet as the two sources (Kepeski and Jusuf 1980). Kosovo mainly used Arlije, however, not only in literary production but also for the first weekly Romani TV production which was aired in February 1986 in Priština (Friedman 2014, p. 6). In Vojvodina, the local Sremski Gurbet variety has been codified for literary productions and education in both Latin and Cyrillic writing (cf. Dimić 1989). In Serbia, today's Central Serbia, the Belgrade Gurbet educational and political elite used their variety for literary production and the first radio broadcast in Romani in 1980 (Friedman 2014, p. 5). In contrast to Romani writing modelled on the writing of the co-territorial majority language, Hungarian writers have used Lovara Romani with English-based digraphs {ch, sh, zh} rather than the Hungarian equivalents {cs, s, zs} from the 1980s onwards. Other initiatives for Romani literacy worth mentioning are the Finnish-based 1970s graphisation of Kaalo, the Romani variety of the first immigrants to Finland, the Kaale, and text production following academic transliteration conventions by Swedish Kalderaš in the late 1980s. All these graphisation initiatives and literary productions have provided the basis for further Romani LLP activities.

14.3.2 Self-Organisation and Linguistic Emancipation

Self-organisation among the Roms gained momentum during the second half of the twentieth century and continues to this day. Activists not only stress the reality of a common history of all Romani groups but also claim a shared cultural identity that strongly focuses on language. The more Romani is seen as an identity factor, the stronger the perception that language loss equates to future identity loss. Furthermore, the reduced functionality of Romani is regarded as a shortcoming when compared to dominant majority languages. Consequently, the development of a written standard becomes part of the political agenda on both international and national levels of self-organisation. Such top-down strategies not only aim at functional expansion into formal domains but—probably even more importantly—the emancipation of Romani as a symbol of the equality of its speakers with the dominant majority. In contrast, bottom-up initiatives primarily stress

436   D. W. Halwachs

language maintenance, which is mostly understood as the use of the Romani variety of a particular group of speakers in all domains of everyday life. Status enhancement and functional expansion are secondary goals. However, as the use of Romani in school and the media is considered essential for language maintenance, the development of both function and status is on the agenda of grass-roots initiatives as well. The underlying common goal of all LLP activities is 'a normative orthography, grammar, and dictionary for the guidance of writers and speakers in a non-homogeneous speech community' (Haugen 1959, p. 8).

14.3.3 Romani LLP at an International Level

Discussions for the creation of an international Romani standard and especially its orthography emerged in the 1970s (see Ljungberg and Scherp 1979), mainly in the context of the International Romani Union (IRU). At the Fourth World Romani Congress in Poland in 1990, a group of only around 30 delegates decided on a 'standard' orthography (IRU 1991). In line with the ethnic nation-state ideology, IRU accepted a Declaration of Nation that claims a non-territorial nation status for the Romani population of Europe at the Fifth World Romani Congress in 2000. Consequently, the Romani standard of 1990 has to be seen—at least for IRU activists—as the official national language of the non-territorial Romani nation.[10]

As orthography is always central to Romani LPP, the writing system of the IRU standard is especially controversial. It was created by Marcel Courthiade and was first presented at a conference in Sarajevo in 1986 (Courthiade 1989). Among other peculiarities as, for instance, the caron with vowels labelled *ćiriklo* 'bird' for marking palatalisation {ǎ,ě,ǐ,ǒ,ǔ}, this alphabet introduces meta-graphemes {θ,ç,ʒ,q} which stand for two or more sounds to cover dialectal variation. For instance, the Greek letter {θ} denotes both dental stops, /t/ and /d/, for consistency of the locative and ablative case endings: *kheres-te/-tar* : *kheres-θe/-θar* 'in/from a house' and *kheren-de/-dar* : *kheren-θe/-θar* 'in/from houses' (cf. Courthiade 1992). Besides graphisation, language planning focuses on status. The main functional goal is the use of Romani in international communication. Consequently, corpus planning concentrates on modernisation. Some neologisms of this standard which are in line with language-internal creativity are widely known today, for instance, the calque *maśkarthemutno* 'international' (< *maśkar* 'between' + *them* 'land, country') which is used alongside the loan *internacionalno*. However, some far-fetched creations like *xurdelin* 'playground, kindergarten' (<*xurdo* 'small/baby') are usually only listed in the standard-specific dictionary (Courthiade 2009, p. 174).[11] This orthography together with most of the lexical innovations was almost exclusively used in IRU declarations and publications of the early 1990s—written, edited or supported by activists who were lobbying for this standard. However, its primary function was not communicative but remained highly symbolic. Matras (1999, p. 496) defined this 'mobilising-rallying' function as 'the shaping of a text in such a way that would demonstrate ideological commitment and political allegiance and identification' with the political strategies and goals propagated by the IRU, its members and supporters. From the late 1990s onwards, the use of this standard more and more has been confined to teaching materials produced by the Romanian Ministry of Education (see below) and publications with the involvement of its leading proponent (e.g. Rézmŭves et al. 2003).

14.3.4 Romani LLP at the Regional Level

Due to the heterogeneity of Romani within the boundaries of some individual states, LLP at the regional level is a complex task that follows various strategies and patterns (cf. Matras 2005a). In countries with a numerically and/or politically strong Romani speech community, the Romani variety of that community is often the one that is codified and (almost) exclusively used in public.

Belgrade-based speakers of Central Serbian Gurbet Romani lead the political movement in the Republic of Serbia for decades. Consequently, this variety has been declared as standard (Đurić 2012) and prevails in formal public domains, first of all in the media but also in education. However, with the growing participation of other, also numerically significant speech communities in the process of emancipation, this dominance is being challenged. Not only Arlije speakers, who numerically increased dramatically through migration from Kosovo, but also speakers of Sremski Gurbet, who politically dominate in the Autonomous Region of Vojvodina, criticise the supremacy of Central Serbian Gurbet, which they perceive as an imposed 'Gurbetisation'. The current Serbian situation has been shaped by the early literary use of Romani in former Yugoslavia outlined above.

The same holds for the situation in Slovakia where the overwhelming majority of Roms uses East Slovak Romani. As speakers of this variety dominate the public discourse, it has been declared as the local Romani standard, using the literary codification of the late 1960s in then Czechoslovakia

438   D. W. Halwachs

as a basis. Consequently, speakers of Vlax and Southern Central varieties, numerically insignificant and marginalised in the political movement, are effectively excluded from linguistic emancipation in Slovakia. A similar case is observed in Hungary, where the early literary Romani codification of the primarily Budapest-based Lovara elite serves as a standard in education and the media. Although most other Hungarian Romani groups are linguistically now assimilated, the remaining speakers of South Central Hungarian Romani are excluded, not only from Romani education but also from media. Thus, possible revitalisation efforts for their variety are limited to the local level, without any institutional support.[12]

Whereas LLP activities and strategies in Serbia, Slovakia and Hungary have been initiated by either an educated and political influential Romani elite and/or the representatives of a numerically dominant group, public Romani use in Romania has been initiated and is led by the state, more precisely by the Ministry of Education (Sarău 1994). The Romani standard used is, more or less, based on the variety of the Romanian Kalderaš, a politically but not numerically dominant group in the country. Orthography follows the international Romani alphabet proposed by the IRU's Warsaw resolution (see above). Various borrowing strategies are applied for lexical modernisation: e.g. *primarĭa* < Romanian *primăria* 'town hall', *print-isarel* < English 'to print', *lekh-ipe* < Hindi *lekh* 'writing, orthography' (Sarău 1992). Considering the heterogeneity of Romani in Romania and the fact that several Romani communities have undergone language shift, the decision for a national standard is understandable, especially in cases of children who learn Romani as a second or rather foreign language. Its obligatory use, however, causes problems for some pupils with Romani as their first language, because they are potentially confronted with a variety that is quite different from their mother tongue. Furthermore, text production outside the educational context and its actors does not follow the standard orthography and the modernised lexicon, but rather relies on group-specific varieties with international academic and/ or Romanian writing conventions (e.g. Cioabă 1994).

The development of a Romani standard in Macedonia follows a majority approach that may be described as a harmonisation process involving several varieties (Friedman 1995, 1999, 2005). Except for the town of Tetovo, where Bugurdži/Kovači hold the majority, speakers of Arlije varieties dominate in all other cities and larger Romani settlements of the country. Consequently, their linguistic varieties serve as the basis of the standardisation process which has produced a generalised Arlije Romani with 'certain grammatical, phonological, and especially lexical additions (and modifications) from all the Romani dialects of the Republic of Macedonia such as

14 Language Policy and Planning in Romani   439

Džambazi, Bugurdži, Gurbet, and others' (Friedman 1995, p. 181). This approach is in line with an ongoing 'natural' process, namely the use of Romani in the municipality of Šuto Orizari, a district of Skopje almost entirely inhabited by Roms of different dialectal backgrounds with speakers of Arlije varieties in the vast majority; other parts of Macedonia inhabited by Roma show a similar intra-ethnic composition. The proposed standard variety more or less parallels the ongoing koineisation of the various Romani dialects on the basis of Arlije varieties in these settlements in everyday communication. Pedagogical materials as well as original and translated poetry and prose for both adults and children have been published in this regional standard. It is used in journals, radio broadcasts, TV programmes and other public domains, such as politics but also in health care and social work. Compared to the limited functionality of the educational standard imposed in Romania and the predominant symbolic functions of the artificial standard propagated by the IRU's Warsaw Declaration, the Macedonian Romani standard also has communicative functions in public life. These result primarily from its connection with the linguistic reality of its target group. The standardisation process is paralleled by the communicative practice of the vast majority of Romani speakers in everyday life. If various numerically small groups of Romani speakers act independently in their political activities for emancipation, LPP activities aiming to create a single standard variety stand little chance of success. For example, Sweden's Romani population is composed of at least five different groups: Resande 'travellers' came to Scandinavia in the early sixteenth century. They perceive their 'Romani'—often labelled Scandoromani, which linguistically is a Swedish ethnolect with Romani elements—as a tabooed in-group marker, which has to be kept secret from the majority population. Shortly after, Kaale reached Finland, some of whom nowadays live in Sweden. Many of their community elders have the same language attitude as the Resande. At the end of the nineteenth century, Kalderaš arrived via Russia. From the 1960s, Roms from Eastern and Southeastern Europe migrated to Sweden. Due to their active participation in the emancipation process, Lovara mainly from Slovakia and Arlije from the Balkans, many from Kosovo, are publicly most visible among the later migrants. Thus, Swedish Romani includes Scandoromani, spoken by the Resande, the Finnish-characterised Kaalo, South Balkan Arlije Romani, which is influenced by Turkish and South-Slavic languages. as well as the Northern Vlax varieties of the Kalderaš and Lovara.[13] With virtually no possibility for the acceptance of a common standard, Språkrådet, the advisory body for the languages and language policy in Sweden, opted for a plurality approach, i.e. the codification and public use of all varieties, at the

D. W. Halwachs

discretion of the speakers. On its website, all five varieties are listed together with the 'Swedish Romani Alphabet' used for all these varieties.[14] The council oversees, among other things, the production of dictionaries; however, these ca. 30.000 Swedish lexemes have been translated and published so far only for Arlije (Lexin 2007). Furthermore, the Swedish National Agency for Education (Skolverket) offers teaching materials for Kaalo, Arlije and Kalderaš Romani.[15] Together with Lovara Romani, the latter two are also the ones used most frequently in journals and regular broadcasts of Sveriges Radio.

Like many other Western European countries with Romani migrants, Austria shows a heterogeneity similar to that of Sweden. However, it combines the plurality strategy with the dominance approach. Although the so-called allochthonous varieties of both migrant workers of the 1960s and 1970s and recent migrants—Arlije, East Slovak, Kalderaš and others—are codified and used in publications and education, Burgenland Romani, endonymically Roman, is the dominant variety in Austria. It is a Southern Central variety, which is almost exclusively spoken in Austria's easternmost federal state, Burgenland. As Sinti treat language as a tabooed in-group marker that has to be kept secret from non-group members and Lovara as a relic from times of true Romanšago 'Romaniness', Burgenland Romani is the only autochthonous variety with a presence in public discourse and the media. Thus, it is legally protected and enjoys the highest status in politics and administration.

14.3.5 Romani LPP at the Local Level

Whereas the dominance approach often follows the top-down strategy of imposing a standard, Romani LPP in line with the plurality approach almost as a rule results from grass-roots initiatives at the local level.

A rather prominent example of a local bottom-up approach is the codification of the above-mentioned Burgenland Romani. Triggered by fears of identity loss in the context of self-organisation for emancipation, the Burgenland Roms' initiative primarily seeks language maintenance. Because of sociopolitical changes—the Roms were recognised as a national minority of Austria in 1993—the codification process has been supported by the authorities and focused primarily on the integration of the language into the educational system. Orthography and lexical modernisation are based on German as the dominant language. Writing conventions are presented in a primer, which is the first book in Burgenland Romani. It introduces, among others, the German multigraphs {sch,tsch,dsch} instead of {š/ž,č,dž} commonly used in Romani writing. Aspiration is marked in line with the international convention as {ph,th,kh}. Text production started with the transcription of oral literature and translations of canonical texts, first of all, prayers. Teaching materials and text collections, which rely on a glossary and a basic grammar, concluded the codification process.

Within one decade, from the 1990s to the early 2000s, the status of Burgenland Romani has changed from an almost unknown strictly oral in-group variety disowned by its speakers to the group's primary identity marker and the most known variety of an officially recognised Austrian minority language.[16] It is now used in printed and electronic media, on the Internet, at public events, but not in administration, legal contexts or on topographical signs. Speakers do not demand the use of Romani in these domains. Administration and the judiciary are generally associated with German as the dominant language, whereas topographical usage is rejected because of fears that such a demand could provoke adverse reactions from the majority population.

Similar single-dialect LLP initiatives have been carried out in various regions of Europe, relating to Kaalo in Finland, Prekmurje Romani in Slovenia, the local Arlije-like variety of Prizren in Kosovo and others.

14.3.6 Romani LPP Between Ambition and Reality

Aims and objectives pursued in Romani LPP often differ significantly from the results achieved, particularly in cases of top-down measures initiated by activists of national and international umbrella organisations in cooperation with supranational organisations and national or regional institutions.[17]

The policy pursued in status planning regarding language use at the international, national and regional levels aims at the standardisation, in the case of the IRU strategy even for the nationalisation of Romani. Acquisition planning targets all formal domains for potential language users. Consequently, corpus planning aims at codification—graphisation and standardisation of a corpus—as well as the functional elaboration of Romani, i.e. lexical modernisation as a prerequisite of regular public usage. The primary functional goal of most codification initiatives is literacy or rather the development of a literate style for language use in national and international communication. However, outcomes differ significantly. If at all, the status of Romani only changes to officialisation as a national minority language, with standardisation, let alone nationalisation as unattainable desiderata. However, even a little improvement in status may contribute to language maintenance. Although it is marginally used in public domains,

Romani's formal role in society remains more or less limited to in-group communication. Whereas the corpus planning goals of graphisation and to some extent of lexical modernisation are achieved in some cases, corpus standardisation usually stops at a basic level of documentation of the variety in question. Although acquisition planning aims for the implementation of a literary style among speakers, efforts contribute, if at all, to language maintenance and, in a few exceptional cases, also to the reacquisition of Romani. The functional status of Romani as a possible means of communication in formal domains at national and international levels between Romani speakers also remains limited to in-group exchange among Romani activists.

Contrary to top-down approaches where ambition and reality of Romani LPP differ considerably, local bottom-up initiatives more often achieve what their proponents aim for. Status planning usually concentrates on officialisation and standardisation for language maintenance and acquisition through education, whereas prospective use of Romani in the media, first of all, targets the particular speech community. Corpus planning aims at graphisation, documentation, in rare cases also standardisation and modernisation to assist language maintenance and to provide a basis for possible revitalisation initiatives. As Roms have never been in a position to set up the relevant institutions to implement a linguistic standard by law, status and corpus planning measures targeting standardisation will fail in most of the cases. All the other aims and objectives of local grass-roots initiatives—officialisation, graphisation, documentation and modernisation to support language maintenance—are realistic goals if the variety in question is used in everyday life at the local level. However, goals are, almost as a rule, only met if the relevant state authorities are supportive of the use of Romani in the media and, even more importantly, in education which is virtually always in the focus of Romani LPP.

14.4 Romani in Education

In contrast to the role of national languages in educational systems, the functionality of a minority language is by no means to be taken for granted in this domain. The difference between the sociopolitical status of a dominant majority language and that of Romani sometimes obstructs and even prevents its use in education. The associated discrepancy between homogeneous written national standards and heterogeneous spoken community languages further contributes to this situation. Although often triggered by concerns about language loss and embedded into cultural activities, Romani language teaching is always part of the political agenda in the struggle for equal opportunities and equal rights. The driving forces behind the various

14 Language Policy and Planning in Romani 443

education initiatives are in most cases also involved in codification and standardisation activities that range from local (bottom-up) grass-roots to national (top-down) initiatives (see also Halwachs 2012).

An example of a relatively successful grass-roots initiative for the teaching of Romani is the case of Burgenland Romani. An investigation by the Austrian presidency about the fate of concentration camp survivors triggered, among other things, the founding of the first Austrian Romani NGO in the south of Burgenland, in Oberwart/Felsőőr/Borta/Erba, in the late 1980s.[18] Young Roms initiated this first step towards self-organisation for emancipation with the help of dedicated social workers, artists and intellectuals from the region. Soon, aside from social and political issues, activities focused on culture, and the continuous decline in the use of Burgenland Romani was, for the first time, perceived as a loss and, consequently, has been interpreted as a symptom of the ongoing cultural assimilation. To counteract language loss and impending assimilation, an initiative to codify and subsequently teach Burgenland Romani was initiated in the early 1990s. After the first printed outputs (grammar, primer, textbook), extra-curricular lessons for Romani pupils started in the framework of the NGO's activities.

Soon, with changes in the sociopolitical situation, the Roms were recognised as a national minority in December 1993. In the following year, the school administration of the federal state of Burgenland extended the law on minority language education to Romani. In February 1995, after four Roms were killed by a pipe bomb placed in front of their settlement in Oberwart by a politically motivated perpetrator, the situation of the Burgenland Roms was brought to the attention of the general public. This incident (among others) made promoting the teaching of Romani in schools politically attractive and resulted in a range of formal measures taken by the authorities for Burgenland Romani. However, most of the initiatives to implement Romani into education remained declarative. While the responsible authorities at the federal level (the department for minority promotion at the Federal Chancellery and departments of the Ministry of Education) contributed financially, it was the collaborative work of NGOs with an academic project that ultimately yielded the prerequisites for Romani teaching, supplying teaching materials, syllabus and teacher training for Romani speakers.

As a result of this collaboration, the teaching of Romani started in autumn 1997 in the form of out of school lessons at the NGO level with Romani children who were looked after in the context of a learning aid programme. It took two more years until all legal problems were solved and Romani lessons finally started at Oberwart primary school. However, these two-hour weekly lessons were elective. Parents were asked to enrol their children who then stayed for the after-school hours for these regular classes. In the following years, this model was only expanded to the lower secondary schools in Oberwart and the primary school in the neighbouring village of Unterwart/Alsóőr/Dolnja Borta/Telutni Erba. Further expansion at primary and lower secondary level was hampered, mainly owing to a scarcity of resources, small class sizes, a lack of initiative and interest on the part of both Roms and authorities. At upper secondary and tertiary levels, so far only lessons at the multilingual grammar school in Oberwart and some irregular courses at university level have been offered.

In contrast to the elective subjects at the primary and lower secondary level, these courses primarily target non-Roms. Although all prerequisites for its use at all levels of education are present, Burgenland Romani teaching at school declined during the 2000s because of the dramatical decline in numbers of pupils. Currently, it is not used in formal education at all. Most probably, the variety with the lowest number of speakers in Austria, in all locations, it fails to meet the threshold of five children whose parents opt for Romani teaching, even if schools work together. However, since this language planning approach—although publicly financed and carried out by an academic institution—was initiated and born by a grass-roots codification initiative, this decline in formal teaching has been compensated by extra-curricular activities that bring together families and their neighbours. Including language-competent elders, committed stakeholders use Romani as a living language and thereby pass it on to weaker speakers as well as children and adults without any language competence. It remains open to what extent such informal teaching activities counteract language loss. The most important effect is their contribution to a positive Romani image, especially among children and teenagers. Ethno-cultural awareness and pride raise self-consciousness and self-esteem, thus supporting the emancipation and social integration of young Roms.

The example of Burgenland Romani suggests that bottom-up initiatives which succeed in the implementation of Romani in education depend on productive collaboration between NGOs and authorities with a positive attitude towards ethnolinguistic diversity. Compromises and joint efforts on both sides can offer the possibility for Romani to be considered part of the education system. However, being part of the system does not automatically mean that Romani is integrated into the regular curriculum. On the contrary, and not only in the Burgenland case, it is taught, almost as a rule, as part of extra-curricular activities and often only in the framework of lessons on Romani history and culture. Romani as a language of instruction is even less common than Romani as a subject; it is not used at all as a language of schooling. If a teacher is competent in Romani—which is quite exceptional—the language might be used with children from a migratory background whose mother tongue is Romani and who have minimal competence in the majority language. In such cases—e.g. the involvement of Romani assistants in Viennese schools and educational advisers of Romani background in Hamburg—Romani functions as an auxiliary language to acquire the majority language which is a precondition for educational participation.

A case of Romani teaching triggered by a national (top-down) initiative is the approach that is used in Romania. In 1990, the country's Ministry of Education and Research initiated Romani teaching at three secondary schools.[19] In the beginning, teaching was scheduled for three hours per week; it was then extended to four hours at the request of pupils and parents. Parallel to this initiative, measures were taken to attract Romani students to become primary school teachers. Furthermore, the University of Bucharest introduced a practical course on Romani history, culture and language. It later led to the foundation of a university department of Romani language and literature. Subsequently, in cooperation with NGOs involved in education, the authorities started to employ (unqualified) ethnic Romani teachers (BA graduates with a Romani background). Over the following twenty years, Romanian authorities in cooperation with NGOs and Romani communities have developed a sustainable framework for Romani teaching at various levels of education with all the necessary prerequisites: a legal framework with a school inspectorate, a national syllabus, as well as teacher training and teaching materials. Nowadays, Romani parents can choose between education for their children in Romanian or Hungarian, depending on the local tradition and the individual Romani family. Moreover, parents may request lessons on Romani language, literature, history and traditions for three or four hours a week for their children. The number of students, classes and participating schools are impressive and have no parallels anywhere else in the world. Romani teaching not only draws on employed staff but also on volunteers; however, their number by no means covers the actual needs. A potential shortcoming of this centralist approach is the Romani variety used for teaching. Romania opted for a top-down solution to Romani teaching, decided to use a standard and chose the one proposed by the Romani Union in 1990. As outlined above, this standard uses a unique alphabet with unique letters and diacritics as well as neologisms with formation principles that are marginal in Romani or have not been present or used at all before (see above). Opting for an international standard seems reasonable given that different Romani varieties are spoken in Romania and that, with several Romani communities having undergone language loss, many children learn Romani as a second language. This standard's compulsory use, however, causes problems for competent Romani speakers. Many perceive it as alien compared to their mother tongue. Moreover, its use in Romani classes is often criticised by local activists and teachers, mainly because neither pupils nor their language-competent parents can identify with the taught variety. They find this standard too different from the local varieties and even, to some extent, incomprehensible. Also, since it is almost exclusively used in the classroom and has practically no functions either in everyday life or in formal public contexts, it is often regarded as being of no use for the pupils' future lives.

The dominance approach in Romani LLP, the decision to use a standard variety or the one with the highest number of speakers, can also be found in other countries: in Slovakia and the Czech Republic, with predominantly speakers of East Slovak Romani; in Kosovo and Macedonia with speakers of mainly Arlije varieties and others.

Local grass-roots initiatives, such as the one in Burgenland, more often occur in countries with some numerically small indigenous speech communities that have been present on the particular state's territory for centuries like the Roms of Burgenland that together with Sinti and Lovara have the status of an indigenous population group. The situation in neighbouring Slovenia with Prekmurje, Dolejnski and Krajina Sinti Romani is quite similar. However, in both countries, Austria and Slovenia, Sinti do not participate in linguistic emancipation process, as they do not want their language to be present in public; this kind of attitude is common among Sinti communities throughout Europe. Although the Finnish Kaale share to some extent the language attitude of the Sinti, teaching among this group developed from a group-internal initiative promoting language and identity maintenance to a public effort with strong top-down support. As Kaale are the only indigenous group of Finland with only minimal numbers of recent migrants from other groups of Romani speakers, the Finnish approach resembles the regional single-variety strategy of Romania and the other countries mentioned in this context. Furthermore, to use only one codified variety in Romani teaching is in line with the prerequisites of any education system that is tailored for the teaching of standardised languages, the national language as well as foreign national languages.

A pluralistic and integrative approach for mother tongue and minority language teaching is alien to any national education system that aims primarily to achieve linguistic unification through the implementation of a standard that is, in most cases, legally specified. To impart, preserve and strengthen ethnic or local group-specific identity through language teaching is, as a rule, far beyond the core areas of responsibility of formal education.

Only in countries with a civic nation-state ideology and an awareness of ethnolinguistic plurality, minority language teaching can be perceived as a definite asset for social cohesion. Sweden has at least partially followed this approach; the authorities provide teaching and information materials for several groups of Romani speakers. The Council of Europe's Curriculum Framework for Romani of the (CFR) is based on a similar pluralistic approach.[20] It provides a basis for developing syllabuses and curriculum guidelines, textbooks and other learning materials in Romani. Furthermore, the CFR aims to strengthen the use of Romani as the mother tongue in education. Its publication was followed by an implementation project that produced teaching materials in various Romani varieties and teacher training modules that used strategies developed by the Council.[21] Promoted by the European Centre for Modern Languages—a division or rather partial agreement of the Council—during the current post-project phase, these materials are used as suggestions and recommendations to implement Romani teaching at the national level. This supranational initiative for Romani teaching has to be seen in the context of the Council of Europe's general measures to support the Romani movement.[22]

14.5 Romani Protection at the European Level

Due to a phase of quite liberal attitudes towards plurality and the rights of minorities in European politics during the 1990s, the recognition of the Romani movement at the supranational European level coincided with the development of instruments for minority protection like the European Charter for Regional or Minority Languages (ECRML). The Charter was adopted as the world's only supranational convention for language protection in 1992 by the Committee of Ministers of the Council of Europe and entered into force in 1998. The Charter defines regional or minority languages as different from the varieties of the official language(s) of a state and as traditionally used by nationals of that state. It explicitly excludes the languages of migrants even if they have the citizenship of their country of residence (Council of Europe 1992). This basic blueprint for the definition of a European minority language is fully applicable to Romani. Against the background of the criteria mentioned, Romani has to be described as different from all official languages of Europe used all over Europe since the Middle Ages by nationals of all nowadays states of Europe. Consequently, Romani should be protected as a minority language by the ECRML in all ratifying countries. However, not all of these countries so far have recognised Romani and some, despite officially recognising it, opted for the minimum protection as a non-territorial language.[23]

Signed by 33 countries by the end of 2017, the ECRML has been ratified so far by 25 countries of which only 16 have recognised Romani as a traditionally used minority language on their territory: Austria, Bosnia and Herzegovina, the Czech Republic, Finland, Germany, Hungary, Montenegro, the Netherlands, Norway, Poland, Romania, Serbia, Slovakia, Slovenia, Sweden and Ukraine. Reservations that affect the protection of Romani range from the somewhat anxious emphasis on the obvious, that only the Romani language of the speakers traditionally residing in the country is protected, to the exclusion of non-territorial languages from the ratification and the simple assertion that Roms have no traditional presence in a country. Austria ratified the ECRML 'with regard to Romany in the Land Burgenland'[24] and only protects the numerically smallest group of Romani speakers on a fraction of its territory. Croatia avoided the recognition of Romani as an official minority language by excluding non-territorial languages explicitly from its ratification instrument.[25] Denmark responded to the request of the Committee of Ministers to 'clarify the issue of the traditional presence of the Romani language' saying that there is 'a lack of historical presence of Roma in Denmark' and that 'only temporary habitations can be evidenced in the historical records'. Furthermore, ongoing migration is often used against the autochthonous status of groups of Romani speakers, sometimes even the whole Romani population in a country. To disprove these incorrect evaluations and to demonstrate that Romani is spoken traditionally in a specific European region sometimes prove almost impossible. Because of social exclusion, Roms have been prevented from owning land and property and, thus, often cannot legally prove their traditional presence. Reservations to grant Romani the official status always have to be seen against the background of the low sociopolitical status of the Roms in general. They are people without an effective lobby. This also explains the reduced level of protection under the Charter, which above all becomes evident in the ratification instruments of the 16 countries. Only in six countries and in the German Federal State of Hesse, Romani enjoys special protection under the Charter, whereas in all other countries and federal states of Germany it is only generally protected under Part II of the ECRML. Part II applies to each language traditionally spoken on the territory of a state that has ratified the Charter regardless of whether the state explicitly lists the particular language or not. It comprises the basic principles that are vital for the preservation of a regional or minority language (RML) that demand resolute action to promote RMLs and encourage their use in public and private life. The ratifying state also has to make provisions for teaching to both speakers and non-speakers and for research at universities or equivalent institutions. Additionally, ratification includes the obligation to promote mutual understanding between all the country's linguistic groups and to take measures for relevant transnational exchanges between speakers of the same language. Furthermore, the state has to take measures for the prohibition of all forms of unjustified distinction, exclusion, restriction or preference relating to the use of an RML and intended to discourage/endanger its maintenance/development (Council of Europe 1992, Article 7).

The evaluation reports of the ECRML so far considered only three out of the ten obligations listed for Romani as fulfilled. The maintenance or development of links between groups using RMLs has been fulfilled by ten, the promotion of study and research at tertiary level by twelve and the promotion of mutual understanding between linguistic groups by eleven out of the sixteen countries that have recognised Romani as RML on their territory. The other commitments are, if at all, only partly fulfilled which leaves the vast majority of legal obligations towards Romani under the Charter as not adequately implemented and, consequently, unfulfilled.[26]

Only six countries have guaranteed special protection for Romani under Part III of the Charter: Bosnia and Herzegovina, Hungary, Montenegro, Poland, Serbia, Slovakia and the German Federal State of Hesse. For valid ratification under Part III, the ratifying state has to select 35 out of 68 undertakings in seven fields: education, judiciary, administration and public services, media, cultural activities and facilities, economic and social life, trans-frontier exchanges. The obligations chosen by the individual states indicate a low level of commitment which is warranted by rather vague formulations in the text of the Charter, such as to apply measures to those who so request/wish in a number considered sufficient' or 'to allow, to encourage, to favour' measures for the protection of Romani. However, the fulfilment rate is even lower than in the case of the general protection under Part II. There are two main reasons for these shortcomings: ratifications neglect the sociolinguistic situation of Romani and/or choose an equality approach for all traditional minority languages spoken on their territories. Montenegro chose the same protective measures for Albanian and Romani; Poland applies identical undertakings for Armenian, Belorussian, Czech, German, Hebrew, Karaim, Kashub, Lemko, Lithuanian, Romani, Russian, Slovak, Tatar, Ukrainian and Yiddish; Bosnia and Herzegovina even apply a slightly higher protection to Romani than to its other 14 RMLs, among them state languages of the region like Albanian, Macedonian and Romanian.

The significant difference in status between languages with a kin state and stateless languages is not taken into consideration at all. Ratification instruments assigning functions in the domains of administration and public services, the judiciary and economy to a dominated minority language without any literary tradition are short-sighted. Even if the necessary LPP measures are initiated in parallel, which happens in exceptional cases and event then to an insufficient extent, problems remain. Besides the fact that Romani lacks the necessary terminology—if present, it would be borrowed from dominant national or international languages—speakers are accustomed to using the particular majority language in these domains. Non-fulfilment of undertakings in these fields should be obvious to all reasonable pre-ratification considerations. In the case of the ratification in Hesse, the authorities even disregarded the language attitude of the Sinti and committed themselves to the public presence of their language which the Sinti themselves perceive as a tabooed in-group marker. However, such over-ambitious ratifications neglecting the reality of language users are not exclusively limited to Romani but are almost a general pattern in ratification instruments of the ECRML.

The Charter protects Romani at the legal level, improves its status and visibility and thus contributes indirectly to the emancipation of its speakers. However, sustainable impact on its use in formal domains of administration, education, the judiciary and the media remains marginal. The underlying problem is the fact that ratifications are above all politically motivated and never really tackle the linguistic needs of the Roms by taking the sociolinguistic situation of Romani varieties and their speech communities into account. This shortcoming challenges both state parties in the fulfilment of their obligations and the Committee of Experts of the ECRML in its evaluation reports and commentaries. Despite such problems, which hamper the implementation of the ECRML, it is—as already mentioned above—the only legally binding instrument for the protection of Romani as a European minority language and has contributed to its recognition at national levels as well as in supranational European contexts.

14.6 Summary and Conclusions

Depending on the character of the relevant driving forces in Romani LPP, which range from local bottom-up to regional and global top-down initiatives, either individual dialects are codified and functionally expanded, or a standard is created. In the vast majority of cases, dialects, sometimes also dialect clusters, are merely fixed in writing and only lexically elaborated.

14 Language Policy and Planning in Romani   451

Artificial standards are modelled on characteristic features of Romani or on those of dominant languages, and sometimes, they are even mixed with particular innovations. As a rule, expanded dialects and created standards, as well as their in-between variants, are tailored to the requirements of spoken and written use in formal public domains. Despite initiatives for the creation of a general Romani standard, the overall trend has gone towards finding local and regional solutions with only some degree of unification in writing and vocabulary by using existing materials of similar Romani varieties across group boundaries and national borders. This situation reflects the heterogeneity and non-territorial character of the language as well as the geographical dispersion and the minimal political influence of its speakers. Thus, language planning efforts and their respective outcomes reflect the outlined sociolinguistic situation of Romani and have to be described as de-central and pluralistic (Matras 2002, p. 257). However, each single LPP initiative is often guided by only one or a few persons, who dominate the codification process. Most of these individuals involved in Romani LLP are also political activists. They use their version of Romani in meetings from local to international level and distribute and promote their literary variety on these occasions and beyond. In this way, they become part of an ongoing harmonisation process which is giving rise to an international Romani variety based to some extent on internationally disseminated Vlax varieties. Especially Kalderaš, but also speakers of other Vlax varieties such as Gurbet and Lovara, dominate international Romani politics together with speakers of Balkan dialects, above all, dialects of Arlije. Although these varieties serve as a basis, the variety used in international communication among activists remains, primarily, a product of polycentric language planning based on linguistic pluralism. Matras (2005a, p. 38) lists three principles of linguistic pluralism for written Romani, which can be employed for both the spoken and written use of Romani in formal domains: In regional pluralism, different forms of literary Romani are used in different regions without making transnational communication impossible. In contextual pluralism, individual users of Romani are able and willing to choose between different forms of literate Romani in different contexts. In functional pluralism, the efficiency of communication is the only criterion for the choice of linguistic variants, whether phonological forms, morphemes, lexemes and their spelling, or syntactic structures and pragmatic patterns. The latter, functional pluralism, is the main driving force behind the ongoing koineisation of an international Romani variety which is based on the multitude of LPP initiatives for linguistic emancipation.

The common practical objective of these LLP initiatives is the use of Romani in education and the media. Whereas use in the media is, above

D. W. Halwachs

all, geared towards raising the prestige of the language through public visibility, Romani teaching additionally seeks to achieve language maintenance. As numerically small speech communities are especially prone to language shift and to becoming monolingual in the dominant language, local grassroots organisations are trying to preserve Romani for in-group communication through teaching initiatives. However, formal language training can never entirely compensate for informal language use and language transmission through socialisation. Although sometimes part of the political agenda, language use in administration and the judiciary is never at the forefront of emancipatory efforts. Speakers are accustomed to dominant languages being used in these domains, which, compared to education and the media, might also be seen as less prestigious. As is the case with many minority language communities, their repertoires show a reciprocal functional distribution between minority and majority language(s). Whereas the minority language functions, quite frequently together with the respective majority language in private and everyday life, the formal public domain is almost exclusively dominated by the latter. Compared to the dominant languages that have developed both spoken and written literate styles, stateless minority languages often remain stylistically limited to patterns of oral language use with communicative functions mainly in informal domains and almost solely symbolic functions in formal domains of language use. If this general situation of stateless languages is not taken into consideration, ambition and reality in Romani LPP will always differ significantly, and protective measures will remain purely nominal. It is not the obligation of a state to save minority language communities from language shift. However, on the background of Human Rights, a state must provide the necessary framework that enables citizens to decide about their language use freely. Provided this condition is met, and the sociolinguistic situation of the respective language is taken into consideration, sustainable results for both language maintenance and its functional expansions will be possible. As these preconditions do not exist at all for Romani LPP, the gap between ambition and reality persists, and the expansion of Romani into formal public domains will remain mainly symbolic.

Notes

1. A language is considered dominant if it prevails in public domains of language use in a state. A language is dominated if its speakers mainly use another language in (formal) public domains.
2. To consider a language that does not function in all domains of usage as threatened or even defective generalises the sociolinguistic situation of

dominant languages and neglects the communicative reality of many marginalised speech communities.

3. See http://www.unesco.org/languages-atlas/en/atlasmap.html. Accessed 21 April 2018.

4. See https://www.ethnologue.com. Accessed 21 April 2018.

5. As the ISO 639-3 letter codes—[rom], etc.—are used in electronic language coding, these labels, although erroneous, cannot be neglected.

6. See https://www.ethnologue.com/about/language-status. Accessed 21 April 2018. EGIDS is an expanded and modified version of Fishman's Graded Intergenerational Disruption Scale (GIDS, see Fishman 1991, pp. 87–111).

7. For a grammar of North Russian Romani, see Ventzel (1964). Rusakov (2013) describes its expansion into "Soviet Standard Romani".

8. Matras (forthcoming) addresses the same topic under the title "The Standardization of a Stateless Language". Other papers that served as reference and source are Halwachs (2003, 2011, 2017).

9. The Romani national anthem *Gelem, Gelem*—originally composed and written by Žarko Jovanović in 1949—became popular through this film.

10. LLP terminology—corpus planning, graphisation, officialisation, status planning, and others—used in the further description follows the definitions summarised by Hornberger (2006). Table 14.1 includes all these terms.

11. In contrast to this artificial unification approach, ROMLEX, the most extensive lexical resource of Romani, contains data that are representative of the variation in the Romani lexicon and offer, among other things, almost complete coverage of the basic lexicon of Romani. ROMLEX currently covers 27 Romani varieties with 17 translation languages; see http://romani.uni-graz.at/romlex. Accessed 27 April 2018.

12. It has to be noted that Hungary distinguishes two languages of the Roma Nationality: Romani, more precisely the Lovara Romani standard, and Beás, which is an old diaspora variety of Romanian spoken by Roms who have undergone language shift, most probably even before they left the Romanian language area.

13. For variety classification, see Matras (2005b, 2002, pp. 214–237).

14. See http://www.sprakochfolkminnen.se/sprak/minoritetssprak/romska.html. Accessed 3 May 2018.

15. See https://www.skolverket.se/om-skolverket/andra-sprak/nationella-minoritetssprak. Accessed 3 May 2018.

16. For more detailed information, see Halwachs (2013).

17. For an overview of the LPP processes and terminology used in the following, see Table 14.1.

18. Although the region is quadrilingual, only the German and Hungarian toponyms—Oberwart and Felsőőr—are officially in use. However, the Burgenland Croatian and Romani ones—Borta and Erba—are known and used by the particular speech communities.

19. The following description is based on http://gheorghesarau.wordpress. com/2009/10. Accessed 16 May 2018.
20. The CFR (Council of Europe 2008) is based on the Common European Framework of Reference for Languages (CEFR) which "provides a common basis for the elaboration of language syllabuses, curriculum guidelines, examinations, textbooks, etc. across Europe. It describes in a comprehensive way what language learners have to learn to do in order to use a language for communication and what knowledge and skills they have to develop so as to be able to act effectively. The description also covers the cultural context in which language is set. The Framework also defines levels of proficiency which allow learners' progress to be measured at each stage of learning and on a life-long basis" (Council of Europe 2001: 1).
21. The project Quality Education for Romani in Europe (QualiRom) was implemented by a consortium of university institutions in cooperation with educational institutions and Romani NGOs in Austria, Czech Republic, Finland, Serbia and Slovakia. See http://qualirom.uni-graz.at. Accessed 16 May 2018.
22. See also Matras (2013, 2015) for a critical and elaborated discussion of how the framework emerged.
23. Territoriality as a criterion for the definition of minority languages is highly questionable. Languages, above all, are linked to speech communities that consist of mobile individuals. This shortcoming is rooted in the nineteenth century, when minorities were perceived as rural, conservative, immobile relics of another (archaic) culture with another language. This anachronism is, nevertheless, still common sense in European minority (language) politics.
24. Citations in the context of the discussion of the ECRML from evaluation and state reports, from the text of the Charter and ratification instruments of the ratifying countries, are taken from https://www.coe.int/en/web/european-charter-regional-or-minority-languages. Accessed 16 May 2018.
25. Croatian authorities do not neglect Romani in general. There is support for Romani-speaking communities, in both education and the media. However, Romani is excluded from the protection under the Charter.
26. For a detailed account of Romani under the Charter, see Halwachs et al. (2015, pp. 37–59).

References

Anderson, Benedict. 1983. *Imagined communities: Reflections on the origin and spread of nationalism*. London: Verso.

Cech, Petra, and Mozes F. Heinschink. 1999. *Sepečides-Romani*. Wiesbaden: Harrassowitz.

14 Language Policy and Planning in Romani

Cioabă, Luminiţa. 1994. *O angluno la phuveako*. Sibiu: Editura Neo Drom.

Council of Europe. 1992. *The European Charter for Regional or Minority Languages (ECRML)*. https://www.coe.int/en/web/conventions/full-list/-/conventions/rms/0900001680695175. Accessed 10 February 2019.

Council of Europe. 2001. *The Common European Framework of Reference for Languages (CEFR)*. https://rm.coe.int/1680459f97. Accessed 10 February 2019.

Council of Europe. 2008. *A Curriculum Framework for Romani (CFR)*. https://rm.coe.int/a-curriculum-framework-for-romani-developed-in-co-operation-with-the-e/16805a2ab9. Accessed 10 February 2019.

Courthiade, Marcel. 1989. O kodifikaciji i normalizaciji romskog zajedničkog jezika. In *I Romani Čhib thaj kultura*, ed. Sait Balić et.al., 205–221. Sarajevo: Institut za Proučavanje Nacionalnih Odnosa.

Courthiade, Marcel. 1992. Research and action group on Romani linguistics. *Interface* 8: 4–11.

Courthiade, Marcel. 2009. *Morri Angluni Rromane Ćhibăqi Evroputni Lavustik*. Budapest: Romano Kher.

Davies, Winifred V., and Evelyne Ziegler (eds.). 2015. *Language planning and microlinguistics: From policy to interaction and vice versa*. Basingstoke: Palgrave.

Dimić, Trifun / Димић, Трифун. 1989. *Ramosarimaski thaj drabarimaski kultura / Рамосаримаски тхај двабаримаски култура*. Novi Sad.

Đurić, Rajko. 2012. *Standardizacija romskog jezika*. Sarajevo: Udruženje Kali Sara Romski Informativni Centar.

Fishman, Joshua A. 1991. *Reversing language shift*. Clevedon: Multilingual Matters.

Friedman, Eben. 2014. *Roma in the Yugoslav successor states*. Flensburg: ECMI.

Friedman, Victor A. 1995. Romani standardization and status in the Republic of Macedonia. In *Romani in contact: The history, structure, and sociology of a language*, ed. Yaron Matras, 203–217. Benjamins: Amsterdam and Philadelphia.

Friedman, Victor A. 1999. The Romani language in the Republic of Macedonia: Status, usage, and sociolinguistic perspectives. *Acta Linguistica Hungarica* 46 (3/4): 317–339.

Friedman, Victor A. 2005. The Romani language in Macedonia in the third millennium: Progress and problems. In *General and applied Romani linguistics*, ed. Barbara Schrammel, Dieter W. Halwachs, and Gerd Ambrosch, 163–173. Proceedings from the 6th International Conference on Romani Linguistics. Munich: Lincom.

Halwachs, Dieter W. 2003. The changing status of Romani in Europe. In *Minority languages in Europe: Frameworks, status, prospects*, ed. Gabrielle Hogan-Brun and Stephan Wolff, 192–207. Houndmills: Palgrave.

Halwachs, Dieter W. 2011. Language planning and media: The case of Romani. *Current Issues in Language Planning* 12 (3): 381–401.

Halwachs, Dieter W. 2012. Romani teaching: Some general considerations based on model cases. *European Yearbook of Minority Issues* 9 (1): 249–269.

456   D. W. Halwachs

Halwachs, Dieter W. 2013. *The Burgenland Romani experience*. Manchester: RomIdent. http://romani.humanities.manchester.ac.uk/virtuallibrary/librarydb/web/files/pdfs/372/Paper14.pdf. Accessed 16 May 2018.

Halwachs, Dieter W. 2017. Languages, plurality, and minorities in Europe. In *Minority languages in education and language learning: Challenges and new perspectives*, ed. Jelena Filipović and Julijana Vučo, 19–42. Belgrade: Beograd University.

Halwachs, Dieter W., Simone W. Klinge, and Barbara Schrammel-Leber. 2015. *Romani, education, segregation and the European Charter for Regional or Minority Languages*. Graz: GLM.

Haugen, Einar. 1959. Planning for a standard language in modern Norway. *Anthropological Linguistics* 1 (3): 8–21.

Heller, Monica. 2011. *Paths to post-nationalism: A critical ethnography of language and identity*. Oxford: Oxford University Press.

Hornberger, Nancy. 2006. Frameworks and models in language policy and planning. In *Language policy: Theory and practice*, ed. Thomas Ricento, 24–41. London: Blackwell.

Hübschmannová, Milena, and Jiří V. Neustupný. 1996. The Slovak and Czech dialect of Romani and its standardisation. *International Journal of the Sociology of Language* 119: 109–123.

IRU. 1991. I Alfabèta e Standardone Rromane Ćhibaqiri. *Informaciaqo Lil E Rromane Uniaqoro* 1 (2): 7–8.

Kaplan, Robert B., and Richard B. Baldauf. 1997. *Language planning from practice to theory*. Clevedon: Multilingual Matters.

Kepeski, Krume, and Šaip Jusuf. 1980. *Romani grammatika*. Skopje: Naša Kniga.

Lexin. 2007. *Svensk-Romskt/Arli Lexikon – Švedikano-Romano/Arlikano Leksikoni*. Institut för Språk och Folkminnen, Språkrådet.

Liddicoat, Anthony J., and Richard B. Baldauf. 2008. Language planning in local contexts: Agents, contexts and interactions. In *Language planning in local contexts*, ed. Anthony J. Liddicoat and Richard B. Baldauf, 3–17. Clevedon: Multilingual Matters.

Ljungberg, Erik, and Lambert Scherp. 1979. *Contribution á la discusion sur l´orthographe de la langue Tsigane*. Stockholm: Garnisonstryckeriet.

Matras, Yaron. 1999. Writing Romani: The pragmatics of codification in a stateless language. *Applied Linguistics* 20 (4): 481–502.

Matras, Yaron. 2002. *Romani: A linguistic introduction*. Cambridge: Cambridge University Press.

Matras, Yaron. 2005a. The future of Romani: Toward a policy of linguistic pluralism. *Roma Rights* 1 (2005): 31–44.

Matras, Yaron. 2005b. The classification of Romani dialects: A geographical-historical perspective. In *General and applied Romani linguistics*, Barbara Schrammel, Dieter W. Halwachs, and Gerd Ambrosch, 7–26. Proceedings from the 6th International Conference on Romani Linguistics. Munich: Lincom.

14 Language Policy and Planning in Romani

Matras, Yaron. 2013. Scholarship and the politics of Romani identity: Strategic and conceptual issues. *European Yearbook of Minority* 10 (2011): 209–245.

Matras, Yaron. 2015. Transnational policy and 'authenticity' discourses on Romani language and identity. *Language in Society* 44: 295–316.

Matras, Yaron. Forthcoming. The standardization of a stateless language. In *The Cambridge handbook of language standardization*, ed. Wendy Ayres-Bennett and John Bellamy. Cambridge: Cambridge University Press.

Matras, Yaron, and Gertrud Reershemius. 1991. Standardization beyond the state: The case of Yiddish, Kurdish and Romani. In *Standardization of national languages*, ed. Ulrich von Gleich and Ekkehard Wolf, 103–123. Hamburg: UNESCO.

O'Keefe, Brigid. 2013. *New Soviet Gypsies*. Toronto: University of Toronto Press.

Rézműves, Melinda, Courthiade Marcel, and Hajnalka Klein. 2003. *Rromane lila – Romani letters – Cigány levelek. József főherceg cigány nyelvű levelezése a XIX. századból*. Budapest: Romano Kher.

Rusakov, Alexander Y. 2013. The Soviet standard Romani language of 1920s–1930s: Linguistic characteristics in a socio-cultural context. *Acta Linguistica Petropolitana. Vol. IX Part* 3: 315–330.

Sampson, John. 1926. *The dialect of the Gypsies of Wales*. Oxford: Clarendon.

Sarău, Gheorghe. 1992. *Mic dicționar Rom-Român*. București: Kriterion.

Sarău, Gheorghe. 1994. *Limba Romani: Manual pentru Clasele de Învățători Romi ale Școlilor Normale*. București: Editura Didactică și Pedagogică.

Spolsky, Bernard. 2003. *Language policy*. Cambridge: Cambridge University Press.

Ventcel, Tatjana V. 1964. *Cyganskij jazyk (severnorusskij dialekt)*. Moskva: Nauka.

Wright, Susan. 2004. *Language policy and language planning: From nationalism to globalization*. Houndmills: Palgrave.

15

Romani Bible Translation and the Use of Romani in Religious Contexts

Wilco van den Heuvel

In this chapter, I discuss the practice of translation into Romani—past and present—of religious texts, especially (parts of) the Bible. Translations always reflect the context in which translating takes place. My discussion is to be understood in relation to religious and linguistic dimensions of these translation practices and the challenges associated with them.

I begin with a brief overview of Romani translation history from the first part of the nineteenth century to the 1990s (Sect. 15.1). Section 15.2 describes how the rapid growth of Neo-Protestant churches, especially since the early 1990s, led to an expansion of the use of Romani in religious domains. However, the extent to which Romani is used is dependent on local social environments, which are highly diverse, ranging from Romani being used in every religious domain to Romani not being used at all. Against this background, Sect. 15.3 presents a brief overview of Bible translation activities since the 1990s. Sections 15.4 and 15.5 describe some of the main challenges in Romani Bible translation and provide illustrations from existing projects and translations of how these challenges are being handled or might be handled. The chapter closes with an assessment of almost 180 years of Romani Bible translation and makes some tentative suggestions as to what we might expect for the future of this dynamic movement.

W. van den Heuvel (✉)
VU University, Amsterdam, The Netherlands

© The Author(s) 2020
Y. Matras and A. Tenser (eds.), *The Palgrave Handbook of Romani Language and Linguistics*, https://doi.org/10.1007/978-3-030-28105-2_15

459

15.1 Religious Texts from 1800 to the 1990s

Apart from a number of wordlists and grammatical descriptions, there are very few written sources in Romani from before the nineteenth century (Bakker 2011, pp. 193–194).[1] The first Romani translations are probably those of the Lord's Prayer into different forms of Romani (Adelung 1806). Soon after, in 1837, we see the first publication of an entire Bible book into a form of Para-Romani. Since then, translators into different varieties of Romani have produced dozens of translations of Bible portions and related biblical materials and, from 1984 onwards, over a dozen translations of the New Testament and even the whole Bible. It is outside the scope of this chapter to provide a complete overview of all that has been published.[2] This section presents a selection of the publications that appeared between 1837 and the 1990s, dividing them into three periods. The first two, discussed in Sects. 15.1.1 and 15.1.2, are characterised by the prominent role of the British and Foreign Bible Society (BFBS) as commissioner, publisher and distributor of the translation.

15.1.1 George Borrow's 1837 Translation into Caló and Other Nineteenth-Century Translations

The 1837[3] translation of the Gospel of Luke by George Borrow into Caló, revised in 1872, is described on the website bible.com—where many publications can be accessed online—as 'the first book ever published in any Romani language'.[4] While it is probably true that this is the first Bible translation intended for any group of Roma, Caló is better identified as a Para-Romani variety, that is a language variety that has preserved a substantial part of the Romani lexicon, but uses the grammatical system of neighbouring languages (Bakker 1995; 1998, pp. 71 and 80; see also Bakker, this volume).

Borrow had been influenced by the Evangelical revival in England in the early nineteenth century (Cressy 2016). As an agent of the BFBS, he started translating the Bible into Caló in the Spanish town of Badajoz, close to the Portuguese border (Canton 1904, p. 240). He allegedly finished his translation with the help of illiterate Gypsies by reading the Spanish aloud to them (Ridler 1981, pp. 330–331). Whether this translation reflects the language as it was actually spoken at the time, however, is questionable (Bakker 1998, p. 84).

Borrow's Caló Bible is one of the many translation initiatives of the first half of the nineteenth century, which saw a surge of new Bible Societies, BFBS being one of the first and certainly the biggest. By 1834, the BFBS,

15 Romani Bible Translation and the Use of Romani ... 461

founded in 1804, had printed over 8 million volumes in 157 languages. This reflected their policy 'to encourage the wider circulation of the Holy Scriptures' (Browne 1859, p. 10).

The Caló translation was revised in 1872. In addition, in the second half of the nineteenth century a translation of the book of Solomon was published, translated into a form of Sinti as spoken in northern Italy. The book, *I Ghiléngheri Ghília Salomunéskero*, was translated by James Pincherle and published in Trieste in 1875. It is probably the earliest example of an Old Testament Bible book translated into Romani.[5] A final example of a nineteenth-century translation is a collection of parts of the Gospels translated into a Sinti dialect of Germany. Although the translation was completed in Friedrichslora in 1836, it was not published until 1911. It appeared, edited by Finck, under the title *Paramisa—amare raieskr Jezus Christi Duk te meripen*, with Theodor Urban Publishers in Striegau (Matras 1999b, pp. 482–483). It should be noted that this is one of the few publications (possibly the only one) from this period where BFBS was not involved as a publisher.

15.1.2 The Early Twentieth Century

BFBS published a second translation of the Gospel of Luke in 1912. The translator was Bernard Gilliat-Smith, well known for his classification of Romani dialects into Vlax and non-Vlax (Matras 2002, p. 219; 2005b, p. 9). While working as Vice-Consul in Varna, Bulgaria, Gilliat-Smith had spent time with Bulgarian Roma and translated the Gospel of Luke into what he called the Erli dialect of Balkan Romani, as spoken by Muslims.[6]

Over twenty years later, in 1936, Gilliat-Smith also played a role in the publication of the translation of the Gospel of Luke into the Gurbeti Erli dialect as spoken in Bosnia. At Gilliat-Smith's endorsement, who at the time worked as British consul in Leningrad, BFBS decided to publish a manuscript that had been translated by the Serbian linguist Rade Uhlik.[7]

While the Caló and Erli translations were initiated and at least partly translated by non-Roma, in the 1930s a number of projects were undertaken in which Roma played a greater role. One of these is the translation of the Gospel of John into a Baltic Romani variety in 1933. The translator, Janis Lejmanis, was a Latvian Rom and a member of the Orthodox Church. His translation was checked both by an educated Rom from Latvia and by the Scottish scholar Sir Donald MacAlister (1854–1934).[8] Also noteworthy are the translations by the Bulgarian Rom A. Atanasakiev of the Gospels of

Matthew (1932) and John (1937) (Slavkova 2007a, p. 220). A final example is the translation of the Gospel of John into Lovari by Jaija Sattler in 1930. Sattler was born in 1902 into a Romani Lovari horse-trading family in Saxony (Miskow 1931). Although he had received no linguistic training, an article in *The Journal of the Gypsy Lore Society* in 1931 praised his translation as 'a competent piece of work upon which both the translator (…) and the publishers are to be congratulated' (Ackerley 1931, p. 93). Sattler worked as a Bible Society bookseller and sold his own translation, travelling through Germany and Central and Eastern Europe, visiting various Kalderash and Lovari settlements.[9]

15.1.3 1970–1990s: The First Complete New Testaments and More Bible Portions

The 1930s and the Second World War were a turbulent period. Sattler was only one of many Roma who were persecuted and murdered. No Bible translations were made until the early 1970s when Bible portions into Romani with commissioners other than BFBS began to emerge. In Finland, Kristillisen Kirjallisuuden published the Gospel of Mark in 1970, translated by the linguist Pertti Valtonen at a time when the Romani language was becoming a topic of growing interest both for academics and for language activists. One year later, the Finnish Bible Society published the Gospel of John in Finnish Romani (Granqvist 2010, p. 252).

Some ten years later, in 1984, International Gypsy Publications Inc (Seattle, USA) published the first entire Romani New Testament.[10] Following some earlier translations of individual Bible books,[11] this New Testament was the first major Bible translation into Kalderash (also known as Kelderash). This variety of Vlax is understood widely in Europe and the Americas as a result of extensive migration (Matras 2014, pp. 38 and 170). The initiator of this translation, Ruth Modrow, was an American missionary, at one time working with SIL. She 'lived with [the Roma] in different countries on different continents'.[12] The translation was made with the help of Tosha, Stevo and Loulou Demeter.[13]

Matéo Maximoff's translation in 1995 was the second complete Kalderash Romani New Testament and was published by the United Bible Societies (UBS). UBS was founded in 1946 to support the work of national Bible Societies, taking on the role played earlier by the BFBS.[14] The introduction to the New Testament refers to Modrow's translation as an earlier work in Kalderash, written in an 'easy American Romani language'.

15 Romani Bible Translation and the Use of Romani ... 463

From this introduction, one may conclude that UBS saw Maximoff's translation as an improvement on Modrow's work though the latter was taken into account.[15] Maximoff also finished the Old Testament, but it has never been published.[16]

The Kalderash New Testament was a major work by Maximoff in his mother tongue. Earlier he had published Bible portions and had written many books in French. Maximoff was a famous Romani writer, who had taught himself to read and write. He wrote the great majority of his works in French (Zahova 2014, p. 45), in a period in which, in the words of Milena Hübschmannová, 'the publication of Romani books was unimaginable'.[17] That Maximoff decided to translate the Bible into his mother tongue is surely connected to his conversion to Christianity in 1961 and his work as an Evangelical pastor after that. Maximoff's conversion, in turn, fits into the rapid growth of the Romani Pentecostal movement in France, which I will discuss below.

Since the 1990s, there was a rapid growth in the number of translation activities and publications. This was due in large part to the opening up of Eastern Europe after the fall of communism and the subsequent spread of Neo-Protestant Christianity among Roma, especially in many of the countries of Eastern Europe. In 1990, several years before Maximoff published his translation in France, the Serbian Evangelical movement *Dobra Vest* published the first New Testament in Gurbet (mentioned in Friedman 2001b, p. 4). Bulgarian Adventists in turn published a New Testament in Erli in 1995 (Slavkova 2007a, p. 215; 2007b, pp. 201–205). This takes us to the mid-1990s and later. Below, I examine the wider religious context within which these new translation activities were taking place.

15.2 Romani in Religious Contexts

An exhaustive discussion of past religions would be beyond the scope of this chapter. However, the Romani language reflects the influence of religion in earlier historical times. Almost all varieties have words that reflect the period of the Christian Byzantine Empire (eleventh to fourteenth century), partly building on earlier, non-Christian terminology. It was probably during this period that, for example, *bolel* (< Old Indo-Aryan [OIA] *buḍyati 'dive, immerse') came to be used for the Christian concept of baptising, *trušul* (< OIA *triśūla 'trident') for 'cross', *rašaj* (< OIA *r̥ṣi 'priest') for a Christian priest and that the Iranian loanwords *khangeri* and *bezex* came to be used for 'church' and 'sin' (cf. Sabaini and Schrammel-Leber 2011, pp. 54–55).[18] Other religious concepts, e.g. *svato* 'holy' (< Slavic), reflect more recent influences and are often derived from the language of wider communication with which the Roma were in contact. All this religious terminology, built up in the past, is part of the lexicon that can be used by translators. We will meet some of these terms again in the section describing translation challenges below.

Before we turn to the influence of the Romani Pentecostal movement, it is important to note that the general tendency of Roma in historical perspective has been to adhere to the most influential and powerful religions of the region in which they live (Matras 2014, p. 95). Thus, Roma have generally been Roman Catholic in Spain, Lutheran in Germany, Orthodox in Romania and Muslim in certain parts of the Southern Balkan. From this perspective, the growing influence of the Pentecostal movement is a remarkable phenomenon.

The Romani Pentecostal movement is often said to have its origin in the 1950s in France, with the work of Clément le Cossec. Beginning with a small group of converts in the early 1950s (Matéo Maximoff being one of them), the number of baptised Roma had grown to over 30,000 by the end of the 1970s. While the first conversions were among the Manush, from the 1960s onwards Kalderash Roma also converted to Pentecostal Christianity (Slavkova 2007a, p. 214; Ries 2007, p. 26). More and more Roma turned to Neo-Protestant forms of Christianity, which went hand in hand with a steady growth of Neo-Protestant congregations, many of which consisted largely or exclusively of Roma church members. The growth intensified after the fall of communist regimes in Eastern Europe and has received attention from sociologists, anthropologists, theologians and ethnologists (e.g. Slavkova [2007a, pp. 214 and 239], Atanasov [2010], and Thurfjell and Marsh [2014]).

The growth of Neo-Protestantism has led to a surge of religious songs, Bible portions, leaflets, videos and the like and has opened a new domain of religious Romani in both written and spoken forms. At the same time, the production of Romani literature has been booming outside of the religious domain as well (Zahova 2014, pp. 6 and 54; present volume). Although new domains have been created, the actual use of Romani is highly dependent on the local situation and may vary considerably. The following paragraphs describe the use of Romani in several geographical regions: Transylvania; a village in Southern Romania; Bulgaria; Eastern Slovakia; and Latin America.

15.2.1 Use of Romani: A Comparison of Several Settings

Transylvania has strong historical ties to the Habsburg Empire and Hungary. It has been part of Romania since 1918. Congregations to which Roma adhere are sometimes ethnically diverse and there are also several dozen Neo-Protestant congregations made up almost exclusively of Roma.[19] In most of these congregations, Romanian or Hungarian is used for Bible reading, preaching and prayers. In some congregations, church members may pray in Romani during the 'open prayer time' when each member of the congregation is free to say their own prayer. Singing is generally in Romani as well as in Romanian or Hungarian. In a survey conducted by SIL between 2007 and 2009 (van den Heuvel and Urech 2011, 2014), one of the main reasons given for not using Romani was the presence of people who do not know Romani, Roma as well as non-Roma. It is worth noting that more than half of all Romanian Roma do not speak Romani (Fleck and Rughiniş 2008, p. 52).[20] While the use of Romani in church is limited, its use increases in less formal activities like Bible studies in smaller groups. Certain Adventist churches, all ethnically mixed, have a special activity in their services in which people form small groups to study passages of the Bible and they discuss it in their own language.[21]

The situation in Sadova, Southern Romania, is similar to that of Transylvania, in that there is little use of Romani in church services. The village has four Neo-Protestant congregations, Baptist, Adventist and Pentecostal, all attended exclusively by Roma, and a second Pentecostal church attended by both Roma and non-Roma. The first-mentioned Pentecostal congregation generally uses Romani for preaching, praying and announcements, while singing and Scripture reading are mostly done in Romanian. In the Baptist church, on the other hand, reading, preaching and most of the praying are generally done in Romanian, while only some announcements are occasionally made in Romani. This has been common practice at least for the last decade, though it may change when newly translated materials are integrated into the services.

A different picture emerges with the situation in Bulgaria as described by Slavkova (2007a). She argues that the possibility of reading the Bible in Romani is one of the reasons Roma are attracted to the rapidly growing Neo-Protestant movement. Slavkova's findings are based on open interviews and group conversations and on her own participation in religious services (Slavkova, p.c.; see also Slavkova 2012 on her methodology).

For Slovakia, 1989 marked the beginning of a 'religious revolution', which led, among others, to the establishment of a number of Pentecostal congregations, most of them in the east of the country (Podolinská 2014, pp. 89–90). My information on Romani religious language use in Slovakia is limited to data about a number of these churches in Eastern Slovakia, provided by Lisa van Vuuren (p.c.). Before the introduction of the New Testament in Eastern Slovak Romani, Roma used to pray and sing in Romani, then read the Bible in Slovak—as they still do for Old Testament readings—and then preach in Romani. Since the appearance of the Slovak Romani New Testament in 2014, they now also read the Bible in Romani in some churches. The Slovak Bible Society, in cooperation with The Word for the World, is in the process of publishing a bilingual Slovak–Romani New Testament (Lisa van Vuuren, p.c.).

For Latin America, reliable numbers on Romani adherents to Neo-Protestant churches are lacking, but it is clear that since the 1980s, the Romani Pentecostal movement has been growing (Ries 2007, p. 29; Bernal 2014, p. 217). Data on the use of Romani in Latin America, however, are scarce. Bernal's overview shows that there is a network of Roma Neo-Protestant churches all over Latin America, within which there is frequent interaction as well as regular contact being maintained with Neo-Protestant Roma congregations in Europe. '[These] contacts fortify the use of the Romani language by bringing about the creation of some kind of standard for it' (Bernal 2014, p. 221). Carrizo-Reimann (2011, p. 172) also mentions Romani language standardisation, which cannot, however, be seen as independent evidence since he bases his statement on interviews with Bernal. Carrizo-Reimann describes the practice in the Iglesia Evangelica Misionera Biblica in Buenos Aires. When singing, the young men, who are in charge of the music, usually combine Latin American rhythms with Romani lyrics. Romani is also used in discussions between the pastor and certain 'important men from the community' following the pastor's reading of the Scripture, which is done in Spanish (Carrizo-Reizmann 2011, p. 170). It is possible that several Latin American Romani churches also have their Bible reading in Romani. Although the details of the reception of the New Testament are not known, I do know that the Chilean Bible Society, Brazilian Bible Society and UBS had sufficient reason to continue to translate the rest of the Bible and are about to release the Old Testament (Neil Rees and Francesco Viguera, p.c.).

As for Europe, here too there are cases of 'fortification of the language' or language revitalisation through relations among churches. In Britain and Norway, for example, the arrival of Pentecostal immigrants from Central and

Eastern Europe has contributed to a revival of Romani language and culture. The immigrants were warmly welcomed by their 'brothers and sisters' who were encouraged to learn Romani and to engage with documentary material on Romani history (Matras 2014, pp. 98–99). Some of the immigrants in Britain have been motivated to learn Romani in order to evangelise in Central or Eastern Europe (Matras 2010, pp. 157–165) and BFBS has received several requests for a new Romani Bible Translation (Neil Rees, p.c.). This has been happening in a context where Romani had gradually been replaced by Anglo-Romani (Matras 2010).

15.2.2 Some Tendencies in the Use of Romani in Religious Contexts

Even though the use of Romani may vary in different social and geographical settings, some general tendencies can be identified. First, the number of Roma who use Romani in religious contexts has been continually increasing since the 1950s.

Second, it is clear that Romani is more likely to be used orally than in written form. It is very unusual for a congregation to read from a Romani translation and use a language of wider communication in other religious domains. In other words, among the different uses of religious Romani, reading is the least frequent.

Third, through the increase in the use of social media and the new long-range migration of Roma from Eastern to Western Europe, religious practices in Romani are being shared trans-locally. It is not hard to find videos of church services, Romani religious songs, baptisms, etc., and some of these have been shared extensively. Trans-local sharing of Romani religious language is more than a marginal phenomenon, see, e.g., the data and analysis by Leggio and Matras, who note that religious (largely Pentecostal) videos constitute one of the three main categories of YouTube videos posted on the Internet (Leggio and Matras 2013, p. 8).

Fourth, music is an important marker of identity, unifying both Roma who use and those who do not use Romani in other domains. Both the style of music and the language used are significant. That the language may be an independent marker of identity is seen in the case of the Transylvanian Gabor, who have translated classic hymns into Romani and produced audio CDs with Gabor choirs singing these hymns in the same musical style in which they are usually sung in Hungarian. Sometimes the style of music rather than the language serves as a marker of identity. One might argue that

468 W. van den Heuvel

this is the case, for example, for Lautari converts who sing *muzică lăutărească* in church and use the Romanian language (see Beissinger 2017, pp. 8–9, and the references to YouTube recordings there).

Finally, even though Romani is more likely to be used orally than in texts, there has been an increase in the production of Romani religious literature, both translations of (parts of) the Bible and other Christian literature. I discuss this in more detail in later sections.

15.3 Bible Translation Since 1990

From the mid-1990s, new Romani Bible translation activities were initiated in a variety of countries, from Russia in the very east to Chile in the very west (Marushiakova and Popov 2014; Bernal 2014). While this proliferation is surely related to the rapid growth of the Romani Neo-Protestant movement, it is significant that at the same time the number of non-religious publications has also been increasing rapidly (Zahova 2014, p. 59; this volume). Tables 15.1 and 15.2 give an overview of NTs and entire Bibles that have been published since the publication of the first Romani New Testament in 1984.

Tables 15.1 and 15.2 show only some of the Romani publications that have appeared. In addition to the NTs listed, dozens of translated Bible portions were produced in many Romani varieties.

Table 15.1 Overview of Romani New Testaments published since 1984

Year	Variety	Orthography	Translator(s)	Commissioner
1984	Kalderash	Roman	Ruth Modrow, with helpers	Seattle: International Gypsy Publications Inc.
1990	Gurbet	Roman	Trifun Dimić	Novi Sad: Dobra Vest
1995	Kalderash	Roman	Matéo Maximoff	Société biblique française/UBS
1995	Sofia Romanes[a]	Cyrillic	Suljo Metkov	Bulgarian Adventist Publishing House
2001/2002	Baltic	Cyrillic	Valdemar Kalinin	GBV/UBS/CBF
2003	Lovari	Roman	Vesho-Farkas Zoltán	Szent Jeroros Katolikus Bilbiatársulat
2007	Chilean Vlax	Roman	Juan and Jorge Nicolich, Carlos Hérnandez	Chilean Bible Society
2010	Sinti	Roman	Armin and Ursula. Peter with Sinti assistants (initiator Railo Weiss)	Romanes-Arbeit-Marburg e.V. and Bible League International
2014	Eastern Slovak	Roman	Marek Olah	The Word for the Word Slowakia
2015	Southern Vlax	Cyrillic	Unknown	MREE

[a]This term is used as self-reference by its speakers (Keith Holmes, p.c.)

15 Romani Bible Translation and the Use of Romani ...

Table 15.2 Overview of entire Bibles in Romani

Year	Variety	Orthography	Translator(s)	Commissioner
2014	Kalderash	Roman	Matéo Maximoff	Not published
t.a.	Baltic[a]	Cyrillic	Valdemar Kalinin	Unknown
	Chilean Romani	Roman	Juan and Jorge Nicolich, Carlos Hérnandez	Chilean Bible Society

[a]*Source* https://midibible.org/en/publishing/europe/romani-baltic/, accessed 31 October 2017

15.4 Intermezzo: The Limited Use of Romani Bible Translations

Notwithstanding the existence of many Romani Bible translations, there is little evidence that these translations are used to any great extent.[22] For those involved in Romani Bible translation, this surely is an issue that asks for an explanation: Why is it that so few Romani translations are used? One may want to ask, for example, whether Romani is for all Romani-speaking Roma the language in which they would like to read the Bible. Another question is whether translations have been produced with the intention to be used extensively. Some Romani linguistic publications suggest that the function of (certain) Romani Bible translations is mainly 'emblematic': to show that Romani is a real language, worthy of having its own translated Bible (Matras 1999a, p. 105). While this may be the case for some translations, one should not make uncritical generalisations from those cases. Any careful analysis of the function of translations should, in my view, distinguish between the intended function of a translation and its acquired function. An interesting question, then, would be whether the emblematic function is an intended function or, an acquired function, or both.

The limited use of Bible translations might also be partially explained by the way in which stakeholders have dealt with the many challenges faced in Romani translation. These challenges form the topic of the following section.

15.5 Challenges in Romani Bible Translation

In this section, I describe challenges that every Romani translation project encounters. I do this not in order to propose solutions to these challenges, but to offer some analytical tools that might help to address them. My aim in this section is twofold: first, I offer some insights into the complexity of

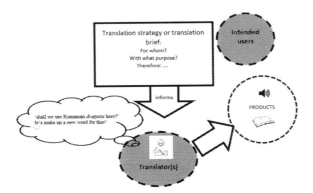

Fig. 15.1 The core of a translation process

translation processes, and second, I describe different ways in which stakeholders have dealt with or might deal with these challenges.

Figure 15.1 illustrates a possible translation process. The translator makes decisions, such as whether or not to use a loanword, or a neologism. In this process of translation and decision-making, the translator is guided by a translation strategy or translation brief, which may be more or less explicit. She or he proceeds with a more or less well-defined group of intended users in mind.

Translator(s) and intended users are the key stakeholders in the process; the process cannot take place without them. Excluding automated translation, translation is done for people by people. In most translation processes, there are, however, more stakeholders involved, like Bible Societies, churches and missionary organisations. To illustrate the complexity of translation, we can consider the roles involved, distributed in several ways among the stakeholders. It might be that the same role is filled by different stakeholders or that the same stakeholder plays more than one role. Figure 15.2 provides an example of a translation process and of a possible division of roles among stakeholders. It shows a church that initiates the process and a Bible Society as the commissioner, that is the party that (formally) asks the translator to produce a particular text for a particular purpose and intended users (Nord 1997, p. 20). The formulation of the translation brief is the result of negotiations between the Bible Society, a missionary organisation, the church and representatives of the intended users. Both the Bible Society and the missionary organisation share expertise with the translator(s), e.g. in the form of linguistic and exegetical training or translation training or in the form of consultant help. In this case, the Bible Society is responsible for the

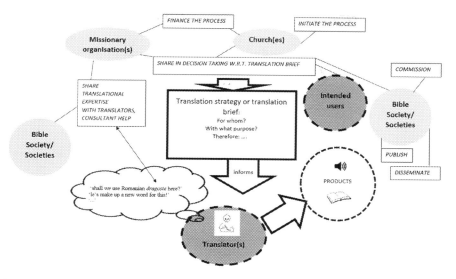

Fig. 15.2 Example of a translation process

publishing and the dissemination of the translation. In many projects, the interplay of the several stakeholders constitutes a major challenge.

15.5.1 For Whom and for What Purpose?

There are language communities in the world whose social and linguistic makeup is much less complex than that of 'the Roma' worldwide. The typical marginalised 'people groups' to which mission organisations have directed their translation efforts in many parts of the world have had more clearly defined sets of intended users, much smaller populations and more easily defined purposes and methods for a Bible translation project. The question of stakeholders, too, has been much less complex.

Roma, in contrast, are a vast and complex group. There are millions of Roma, living in various parts of the world, speaking different varieties of Romani or not using Romani at all, fluent in languages of wider communication, adherents of different religions and church denominations, with no central political or religious authority uniting the group as a whole. Whether or not translating into Romani is seen as a challenge will depend on who you ask. It seems not to have been a problem for those translators who have translated the Bible into their own language variety and were not too concerned about who exactly would be using the translation.[23] On the other hand, for missionary organisations that see it as their goal that all Roma should have access to the Bible in Romani, the situation presents a major challenge.

The questions 'for whom' and 'for what purpose' are fundamental for all the translation issues discussed below. They affect decisions whether or not to use loanwords (see Sect. 15.5.2), which texts to translate (see Sect. 15.5.3), how to deal with religious terminology (see Sect. 15.5.4) or what orthography to use (see Sect. 15.5.5).

15.5.2 Languages of Wider Communication and the Use of Loanwords

Virtually all Roma are bilingual and incorporate lexical items and grammatical forms of the language of wider communication into their daily speech. In many Romani translations, therefore, translators have decided to use such loans. Although Romani has established loans, many are shared only by a few varieties. As a result, a translation intended for Roma with Romanian as their language of wider communication may not be acceptable for speakers of a nearby variety who speak Bulgarian as their language of wider communication, even though their varieties may be highly similar when it comes to the Romani core and shared loans.

The acceptability of a variety other than one's own is based on more than intelligibility; language also has a symbolic or emblematic function, serving as an expression of one's identity (see, e.g., Friedman 2017 for the emblematic function of dialectal differences). Not only loans from a language of wider communication, but also Romani grammatical forms and lexical items from a variety other than one's own may be considered unacceptable, not so much because they are unintelligible, but rather because they are considered as not fitting local Romani identity: 'that is not how we speak *here*' or even 'that is how *they* speak, not how *we* speak'.

15.5.3 Source Text

In most Romani translation projects, existing Bible translations in languages of wider communication play a significant role; in some, existing translations into Romani are equally relevant. This section describes the motivations for using those translations and the associated challenges.

Considering the role of existing translations into languages of wider communication, it should be noted that the terminology and exegetical decisions (decisions with regard to the meaning and explanation of the Greek or Hebrew source text) used in these translations are often part of an established tradition. Therefore, if a translation is to be used in existing Christian communities, translators must decide whether to follow this terminology and explanation or not.

Second, the use of traditional translations may facilitate the translation process. They may be a welcome source of support, especially for translators who lack the expertise to directly access the source texts in the original languages. Moreover, if translators have not been trained in English, they cannot access the exegetical and translation handbooks that are commonly used and therefore remain dependent on sources provided by other project members, like translation instructions, exegetical suggestions or even proposed formulations. In such situations, the use of authorised translations may help translators to be less dependent on the input from other project members.

Coming to existing translations into Romani, translations into one variety may be used as a resource for translation into another variety. Significant differences between varieties may impede automated transposition, but nonetheless, an existing text can fruitfully be used as a guide. The translation into Transylvanian Romani briefly discussed in Sect. 15.5.5 below is a good example; it relies on an existing translation into Oltenian Romani. Although the translation into Transylvanian Romani did require some rethinking, many translation choices did not need to be reconsidered, which accelerated the translation process. Because of the differences in word order between the two varieties, however, automatic word for word translation was impossible.

Finally, one of the challenges with regard to source texts follows from the fact that different church traditions may hold different opinions as to what is the original or authoritative text; church denominations may have appropriated a traditional translation as their own authoritative one. This will often lead to discussions among the translation project members as to which 'original' should be followed. That this may lead to different results is illustrated by the fact that two parallel trial translations were published by the Romanian Bible Society in 1996. The translation of Matthew into Ursari Romani was largely based on the Gala Galaction, an authoritative translation in the Romanian Orthodox Church, while the translation of Mark into Kalderash was largely based on the translation by Dumitru Cornilescu which is authoritative in Romanian Neo-Protestant circles.[24]

15.5.4 Translation Strategy and Biblical Terminology

The target language in a project may lack a lexical equivalent for a lexeme in the source language (Greek, Hebrew). If this is so, then the

474   W. van den Heuvel

following options, among others, are open to the translator (cf. Sabaini and Schrammel-Leber 2011, p. 52 for option 1–3):

(1) to use a loanword from the language of wider communication;
(2) to expand the meaning of an existing Romani word;
(3) to create a new Romani word, on the basis of the existing Romani lexicon;
(4) to use a descriptive phrase describing the concept.

Sabaini and Schrammel-Leber show how different Romani varieties and translations render the terms 'baptise', 'holy' and 'bless'. From the examples they give, option 1, the use of loanwords, is most common, while option 2 is also attested. As an example of the latter, they mention *bolel*, a Romani word originally meaning 'dive' or 'immerse', which came to be used to render the concept of 'baptise', probably already before the sixteenth century (Sabaini and Schrammel-Leber 2011, p. 55). As an example of option 3, they mention Sofia Erli *khangirljalo* 'baptised', derived from *khangeri* 'church', and Macedonian Arli *trušurisarel* 'baptise'.

Table 15.3 shows how six different translations have taken one of these options to translate the terms 'baptise' (Greek: *baptizo*) and 'Holy Spirit (Greek *to pneuma to hagion*) in Luke 3:22.

GS, VK, L and M all use a form of *bolel* for 'baptise' and a combination of Slavic-derived *sfjáti* or *svento*, etc., with *duxo* (Romanian *duh* or Slavic *duhu*) for 'Spirit', the loans being examples of option 1. S, on the other hand, does not use *bolel*, as the word has been lost (Ursula Peter, p.c.), but also avoids the use of German-derived *tawfǝvel*. Instead, it takes option 4 and renders it as the descriptive phrase *thowel an o pani* 'wash in the water'. For 'Holy Spirit', Sinti renders *Debleskro Duxo* 'Spirit of God'. This again reflects the absence of a Slavic-derived *svento*, etc., and the avoidance of a German-derived term. The avoidance of German loans was a policy of the project, motivated by Sinti's reluctance to use them (Ursula Peter, p.c.).

Table 15.3 Translations of 'baptise' and 'holy spirit' in six publications

Author; variety; year	Baptise	Holy spirit
Borrow, George (GB); Caló; 1836	*muchobelado*	*el Peniche*
Gilliat-Smith, Bernard (GS); Erli; 1912	*boljárdas*	*sfjáti Duxós*
Valdemar Kalinin (VK); Baltic; 2002	*boldepe*	*Svento Duxo*
Zoltán, Vesho-Farkas; Lovari (L); 2003	*boladepe*	*Sunti Duho*
Maximoff Kalderash (M)	*boldo*	*Svinto Duxo*
Sinti (S)	*thowas an o pani*	*Debleskro Ducho*

Option 1, finally, might also be reflected in the Caló translation of this verse, but this is far from clear.[25]

15.5.5 Orthography

Despite several attempts to introduce an international Romani orthography, the bulk of Romani publications use orthographies that are not meant to serve as an international standard (Matras 2005a, p. 8). Orthographies tend to be a mixture of international writing conventions (see below) and features of the orthographies of regional languages of wider communication. In designing an orthography, then, it is not only the particular, local Romani phonology that needs to be taken into account, but also who are the intended readers and which language of wider communication they use.

Romani varieties may differ phonologically in the number of phonemes that are distinguished and in the allophonic variation manifested by these phonemes (see Baló, this volume). Some significant phonemic variations are the presence vs. absence of a phonemic difference between plain /r/ and continuations of historical /ř/ (as uvulars, or uvalar trills), between aspirated and non-aspirated stops and between palatalised (or jotated) and non-palatalised variants of the alveolars /d/, /t/, /n/ or /l/, or even the velars /k/, /g/ and the trill /r/ (Baló, this volume; Friedman 2001a).

As soon as it has been decided which phonemes should be distinguished, the next step is to establish which signs should be used to represent these phonemes. While it is rather common to base orthographies at least partly on the orthography used for the regional language of wider communication,[26] in the Romani context the matter is complicated by several attempts that have been made to create an international, standardised, orthography (see Halwachs, this volume).

If the language of wider communication is written in non-Roman script, translators sometimes decide to use a non-Roman script for Romani. This was done in the 2002 and 2014 New Testament and Old Testament translations by Valdemar Kalinin who used the Cyrillic script for his translation into 'Baltic Romani', to be used in Belarus and surrounding regions.

There is a tendency for translators to use Cyrillic characters when the language of wider communication is written in Cyrillic, but this practice is not always followed. Gilliat-Smith, working with Bulgarian Roma, wrote his 1912 translation of John in Roman script, using Czech-style diacritics. In present-day Bulgaria, we find several competing orthographies, one of them based on Cyrillic and others using other orthographic conventions (Friedman 1997, p. 185). In addition to (modified) Roman and Cyrillic orthographies, Romani has also been written in Arabic and even in Devanagari (Bakker and Kyuchukov 2000, pp. 110–112; Leggio, this volume), but there is no evidence of the use of these orthographies for Bibles or Bible-related publications.

I now turn to orthographies that use the Roman script. Consider example 1, which presents a number of verses from trial publications of Genesis 12, 15 and 22 into two forms of Romani, published as part of a translation project with major input from SIL. The lines in bold italics show a translation intended to be used in parts of Southern Romania and the lines in plain italics show a translation intended for use in parts of Transylvania. Both of these orthographies, when tested, were acceptable to the intended users and preferred above the official Romani promoted by the Romanian Ministry of Education (see Halwachs, this volume).

(1)

Hai	***gea***	***ando***		***them***		***kai***	***si***	***te***	***sikavav***	***les***	***tuke.***
the	*dzsá*	*ká*	*kodo*	*them*	*szávo*				*szikávoho*	*lész*	*tuké.*
and	go	to	that	land	which	that	FUT	FUT	I show	it	to you

'And go to the land that I will show you (Gen 12:1)'

Dikh	***man***	***ni***	***dean***	***man***			***ceave .)***	***Hai***	***o***	***robo (...)***
„Dikh		*ná*	*dinyán*	*mán*	*ciné*		*csáve.*	*the*	*moro*	*manus*
look	to.me	not	you.gave	me	small		children	and	my	man

'Look, you haven't given me children, and the slave / the man (...)(Gen 15:2)'

Na	*kadava*	*si*	*te*	*lel*	*kire*	*bukea,*	*hai*	*kodova*	*kai*	*înklela*	*anda*	*tute,*
not	this.one	FUT	FUT	receives	your	things,	and/ but	that.one	that	will.come.out	from	you,

hai	*kodova*	*lela*	*kire*	*bukea.*	*(...)*
and/but	that.one	will.receive	your	things.	

'Not this one will receive your things, but the one that will come out of you, he will receive your things (...) (Gen 15:5)'

Dikh	*o*	*ceri*	*hai*	*ghin*	*e*	*steale*	*te*	*daştisa*	*te*	*ghines*	*len?*
see	the	sky	and	count	the	stars	if	you. could	COMP	count	them

'Look at the sky and count the stars, if you can count them. (15:6)'

O	***Del***	***kerdea***	***man***	***te***	***asau,***	***orkon***	***aşunela***	***si***	***te***	***asan***	***manţa***
the	God	made	me	to	laugh	whoever	will.hear	FUT	FUT	laugh	with.me

'God made me to laugh, whoever will hear will laugh with me. (21:6)'

15 Romani Bible Translation and the Use of Romani ...   477

These few verses are sufficient to illustrate that the orthography for the Southern Romania variety is largely based on Romanian. The postalveolars ʃ and ʒ are spelled {ş} (*daştisa*) and {j} (*ujo* 'clean', not in this passage), respectively, while the (post)alveolar affricates /dʒ/, /tʃ/ and /ts/ are represented as {ge/gi} (*gea*), {ce/ci} (*ceave, atunci*) and {ţ} (*manţa*),[27] respectively. The voiced velar stop /g/ is written as {gh} before the front vowels /e/ and /i/, and as {g} elsewhere. The phoneme /j/ is rendered as {i} or {e}, and the centralised vowels /ɨ/ and /ə/ are represented as {î} and {ă}, respectively.

The Transylvanian orthography, on the other hand, heavily depends on Hungarian orthography, one of the languages of wider communication in that area. The main differences between this orthography and other Romani orthographies are the following: the rendering of the vowel /a/ as {á} (*mán*), the distinction between the vowels /e/ and /ɛ/, rendered as {é} and {e}, respectively (cf. *csavé* 'children' in Gen. 15: and *the* 'and'), and the orthographical representation of the sybillants plus affricates as {sz} for /s/, {cs} for /tʃ/ and {csh}, as in *szikávoho, csáve* and *dzsá*, respectively.

As far as international conventions are concerned, Matras (2005a, p. 10) discerns two main tendencies. One is 'to use the diacritics {č, š, ž} along with other conventions, such as values of {x, j, ph, th, kh}'. The other is to avoid diacritics by using the combinations {ch, sh, zh} instead. The following passage (Luke 3:21–22), from published translations, shows the difference between the two approaches.

Example 2 has been taken from the Lovari Bible translation of 2003, which is a Hungarian-Romani bilingual intended for use in Hungary. Example 3 is a verse from Maximoff's 1995 translation into Kalderash.

(2)

haj	*kado*	*glaso*	*ashundyilas*	*anda*	*cheri:*	*Tu*	*san*	*muro*	*kamado*	*shavo,*
and	this	voice	was.heard	from	sky	you	are	my	beloved	son

ande	*tute*	*pherdyol*	*muri*	*voja.*
in	you	is.fulfilled	my	joy

(3)

ai,	*žikin*	*vo*	*řudil,*	*o*	*čerik*	*puterdilo,*	*(...)*
and	when	he	prays	DEF	sky	opened	

Ai	*jekh*	*hango*	*ašundilo*	*anda*	*o*	*čerik:*
and	ART	voice	was.heard	from	DEF	sky

Tu	san	muřo	Šiav	kai	si	mange	drago;
you	are	my	Son	that	is	to.me	beloved

ande	tute	me	thodem	sa	miři	dragostia.
in	you	I	put	all	my	love

'And when he prayed, the sky opened (...), and this voice / a voice was heard from the sky: you are my beloved son, in you all my joy has been fulfilled / in you I put all my love'.

Neither the Lovari nor the Kalderash translation follow the conventions of the alphabet of their readers' language of wider communication, in contrast to the trial translations discussed above. The Lovari translation avoids all 'Hungarianisms' and all diacritics, and it follows the international convention of using {ch, sh, zh} (in *cheri* 'sky', *shavo* 'son' and *uzharel* 'he cleans' respectively (the latter not in the passage cited here). Again, unlike the Transylvanian translation, it follows international conventions in the representation of the vowels, avoiding the use of {é} and {á}, even in the few loanwords from Hungarian, e.g. *predikalisarel*, from Hungarian *prédikál* (Luke 8:1).

Maximoff's translation, on the other hand, uses diacritics to represent the sibilants and affricates {č, š(i), ž} (in *čerik* 'sky', *Šiav* 'son' and *žikin* 'when') as well as for {ř}, representing the present-day continuation of Early Romani /ř/ (Matras 2002, p. 50). The use of diacritics matches international conventions, such as the use of {x} (in *Duxo* 'spirit')[28] and the use of {j} for /j/.

15.5.6 Which Medium and in Which Format?

In a context where many intended users of a translation are illiterate[29] and not familiar with the practice of reading, it is not surprising that translations are often enriched with helps for readers or published in other media than the traditional print form. Where people are familiar with a translation in the language of wider communication, a bilingual might be expected to have the translation in the language of wider communication on one side of the page and a Romani translation on the other side, as in the Lovari translation of 2003, or in several of the prepublications into Oltenian Romani. Project members may decide to produce Bible portions accompanied by images, questions about the text or footnotes. These choices all depend on the experience and knowledge of the intended users and the purpose of the translation.

Already since the late 1970s, the Romani Neo-Protestant movement has made use of audiovisual material with religious content and religious music (Matras 2010, p. 159). In line with this, and more recently, written translations have often been accompanied by audio versions, appearing on CDs or on the Internet. The former was done, for example, in the Sinti translation project, and examples of the latter can be found in publications of short stories in several Romani varieties. Digital versions of written texts can be found on the website bible.com/versions and recently through the UBS Romani app.[30] Audio versions of several Romani Bible translations can be found on the website of 'Faith comes by hearing' or at www.bible.is, and several examples of video recordings can be found on YouTube.[31] Another example of video material is the Jesus DVD in Romani, which contains synchronised versions of the Jesus film in five different varieties of Romani, and contains the text of Luke, usually heavily leaning on existing Romani translations.[32]

Finally, it should be noted that alongside the Bible or portions of the Bible a variety of other Romani religious publications have been created, like children's Bibles, study booklets, leaflets, songbooks and other religious books (see, e.g., Slavkova 2007a, pp. 220–221).

15.6 Inventories, Dissemination and Local Appropriation

Romani Bible translation has been taking place in a variety of Roma communities and a considerable volume and variety of material has been published. In recent years, various inventories have been made of what has been produced and of projects that are currently in operation. Examples of such inventories can be found in Bakker and Kyuchukov (2003), Kalinin (2014) and in an electronic database set up by SIL Eurasia.

In recent decades, Christian mission organisations have aspired to work with communities in ways that foster local partners' full engagement alongside the mission agency in naming stakeholders, setting goals and planning projects. Whether such aspirations actually become practice will vary from agency to agency and from community to community. Such an approach could entail significant local involvement in Bible translation by Roma church leaders and ordinary church members.[33] Given the complexity of the Romani religious landscape and the absence of central authorities as described above, such an approach could lead to a further localisation of translation projects, with products made for specific local purposes. This would effectively constitute a continuation of the trend set in Romani Bible translation historically. At the same time, given the ease with which materials are shared via the Internet by members of transnational communities and

480 W. van den Heuvel

given the increasing availability of inventories of translations, use of religious Romani will only increase and diversify. As I have already described, Romani songs, videos and Bible booklets have found their way into the network of Roma churches and have been adapted to serve local functions. In the same way, new publications (print and non-print) are likely to keep on getting adapted locally to serve ever-changing needs.

15.7 Summary

In this chapter, I have described the history of Romani Bible translation and have shown the significance of the growth of the Neo-Protestant movement among Roma since the 1950s. Throughout I have paid special attention to the socio-religious and socio-linguistic dimensions of Bible translation.

Romani Bible translation, of course, has a much longer history than the seven decades that I have discussed in more detail. For more than a century before that, beginning in 1837, BFBS was commissioning and publishing Romani translations. Then, from the 1970s there was a rapid growth of Bible translation activities closely linked to Neo-Protestantism. UBS, national Bible Societies and missionary organisations took on major roles in this period.

In this chapter, I have also provided a framework within which the complexities of Romani Bible translation can be analysed. Essential in this framework is the axiom that most translation decisions can eventually be traced back to the question for whom and for what purpose. It is this point that explains why translation in a Romani setting has been so challenging. Given the immense diversity of Roma in terms of their languages of wider communication, their religious backgrounds and their use of Romani, and further, given the lack of a central Roma authority, the decisions for whom and for what purpose require painstaking negotiation between various stakeholders. These negotiations have a diversity of outcomes and have, through history, led to dozens of different translations published in a variety of forms and media.

Acknowledgements I want to thank the following people for sharing from experience(s) with me or for reading earlier versions of this chapter: Keith and Mary Holmes, Netherlands, CBF. Lourens de Vries, UBS/VU University Amsterdam; Barbara Schrammel, Austria, University of Graz; Sofiya Zahova, Reykjavik, Vigdís Finnbogadóttir Institute; Magdalena Slavkova, Bulgaria, Bulgarian Academy of Sciences; Neil Rees, UK, BFBS; Lisa van Vuuren, Slowakia, The Word for the World; Ursula Peter, Germany, Romanes-Arbeit-Marburg e.V; Jelle Huisman, Croatia, Roma Bible Union; Todd Price, Hungary, Pioneers; Lesley Fast,

Netherlands, SIL; Marlute van Dam, Romania, SIL; Zoltán Barabás, Romania, SIL; and David and Sari Gardner, Romania, SIL.

Notes

1. While Bakker (2011) argues for a prayer from 1622 to be written in Romani, Adiego (2016) convincingly shows that it must be a forgery.
2. The most elaborate overviews to date are found in Bakker and Kyuchukov (2003), in which the authors have indicated which of the publications are of a religious nature, and in Kalinin (2014). See also Sect. 15.6.
3. The overleaf of the translation states in Caló that the book was completed in 'the winter of the year of the Lord 1836' (Ridler 1981, p. 329), which explains why Slavkova (2007a, p. 213) mentions 1836 as the publication date. However, the year 1837 appears on the title page as the publication date, although the gospel was in fact not ready until early 1838 (Ridler 1981, p. 330).
4. https://www.bible.com/ur/versions, accessed 22 November 2018.
5. https://www.bible.com/ur/versions, accessed 6 December 2018.
6. https://www.bible.com/ur/versions, accessed 22 November 2018.
7. https://www.bible.com/ur/versions, accessed 22 November 2018.
8. https://www.bible.com/ur/versions, accessed 22 November 2018.
9. https://www.bible.com/ur/versions, accessed 22 November 2018.
10. Although this is the first entire New Testament ever published, Derek Tipler of the UK had finished a New Testament manuscript which was almost ready to be published in 1982 (possibly by Living Bible International) when he suddenly died. He was not a Rom, but had become part of the community of Roma and travelled with them in Europe (Neil Rees, p.c.).
11. For example, a translation of Mark by Derek Tipler published in 1977, or Maximoff's translation of Ruth published in 1983.
12. Letter by Ruth Modrow to SIL, dd. 23 January 2007.
13. The text is available online at http://jesusfellowship.uk/bible/Romani+NT, accessed 22 November 2018.
14. http://www.mundus.ac.uk/cats/38/292.htm, accessed 22 November 2017.
15. Ande 1984 sa e Nevi Vasta sas ramone ande jekh **kovli** shib romani amerikaki. Aver parti nai lasiarde sas ramone ka o Living Bibles International, kai dine le dragosa ka kado kai ramol akana kathe, o Mateo Maximoff (5). Le United Bible Societies kamen te sa naisin ai prinziaren e butji kai kudala kerde angal.
16. The book of Ruth and the book of Psalms, however, were published in 1979 and 2004, the latter in combination with the New Testament. A copy of the Old Testament as translated by Maximoff can be found in the archives of BFBS in Cambridge (Neil Rees, p.c.).

17. http://rombase.uni-graz.at/cgi-bin/art.cgi?src=data/pers/maximoff.en.xml, accessed 22 November 2018.
18. While the examples were taken from Sabaini and Schrammel-Leber (2011), I used Turner's dictionary as a source for the reconstructed forms. See http://dsal.uchicago.edu/dictionaries/soas/; this comparative dictionary of Indo-Aryan languages from 1962 to 1966, by Sir Ralph Lilley Turner, was accessed 22 November 2018.
19. Precise data, however, are lacking. In a document probably written in 2002, most likely not published, Rusu and Tarnovschi mention a total of at least 33 congregations. Comparison of the census data from 2002 to 2011 reveals that the number and percentage of self-declared Roma belonging to Neo-Protestant denominations (Pentecostal, Adventist and Baptist) have risen dramatically, from 8% (43,820 Neo-Protestants out of 535,140 self-declared Roma) in 2002 to 14% (86,870 Neo-Protestants out of 621,573 self-declared Roma in 2011). Not all of these, however, attend ethnically segregated churches.
20. Cf. the national census in Romania of 2011, in which only 40% (245,677 out of 621,573) of all self-declared Roma declared to have Romani as their mother tongue.
21. According to Marlute van Dam (p.c.), who used to attend Adventist congregations during the period when she lived in Targu Mures (2015–2017), this is common practice in at least one congregation in Targu Mures, while it also used to be common practice in the period in which I did my fieldwork there (2007–2009). It is also attested in Craciunesti, close to Targu Mures (Fabian Jakobs, p.c.; Sari Gardner, p.c.), but it is unclear to what extent this practice is representative of Adventist congregations at other places.
22. The only research on Romani Bible use that I know of is the survey by SIL in Romania, 2007–2009, in which the author was one of the surveyors. There we found very few examples of Romani Bible translations actually being read. Examples of Romani Bible reading, however, are reported for Slovakia.
23. There are probably quite a few translators who initiated a project on their own, translating into the variety of their own community, e.g. the translation into Lovari by Sattler (1931). I also know of a more recent case of an individual in Transylvania who had translated the entire New Testament on his own and wanted it to be published without any checking by others.
24. See the descriptions of 'evanghelia pala o MarCo 1996' and 'evanghelia pala o Matei 1996' on bible.com/versions, accessed 22 November 2018.
25. In *muchobelado*, the suffix *-ado* probably reflects the Spanish gerund suffix *-ando*, which leaves us with a stem *muchobel*, the origin of which is not clear. Just as unclear are the origins of *Peniche* for 'Spirit' or *el* for 'holy'.
26. See Malone (2004, p. 38) for a discussion of factors to be taken into account when creating an orthography with and for speakers of a minority language.

27. It might be argued that *ţ* in *manţa* represents phonemic /s/, realised as ts due to its phonological environment following /n/, but the following *ţ* further down in the leaflet is clearly phonemic: *beş ăk ţîra, hai gîndisao* 'sit down for a moment, and think'.
28. Whereas the Lovari translation has *duho* here, it uses {x} at other places, e.g. in Mark 1:6 *xalas* 'he went'.
29. See, e.g., Baucal (2006, pp. 207–208), who writes that, according to a national assessment study in Serbia, around 50% of Roma students in the sample do not develop basic language literacy. For the situation in Romania, see Fleck and Cosima, who say that from a sample of over 1000 respondents from all over Romania, 22% of all household members aged 14 or over appeared to be illiterate (2008, pp. 16 and 167).
30. https://apps.apple.com/us/app/romani-bibles/id1469625145?ls=1. https://play.google.com/store/apps/details?id=bible.global.romani. It also has an accompanying webpage https://romani.global.bible. This includes many Romani translations from UBS and BFBS archives, starting with Calo in 1837.
31. https://www.youtube.com/watch?v=O0yGq5BYtxM, accessed 22 November 2018, had 66 views, while https://www.youtube.com/watch?v=zQtdaSk-kuE, another video from the same series, accessed 22 November 2017, had 1586 views.
32. A search on 'Jesus Film Romani' on YouTube (22 November 2018) gives several recordings of the entire film, e.g. a Hungarian-Slovak version with over 2000 views, a Balkan Romani version with 12K views, a Western Kalderash version with 37K views and a version dubbed in Polish Roma, with almost 200K views.
33. SIL Eurasia, for example, has of late made such an approach more explicit in their internal and external communication (Lesley Fast, p.c.).

References

Ackerley, Frederick G. 1931. O Woyako-Hiro katar o Jesuskasko Christuskasko banasgimmo ä Johannestor. *Journal of the Gypsy Lore Society*, 3rd ser., 10 (2): 92–102.

Adelung, Johann Christoph. 1806. *Mithridates, oder allgemeine Sprachenkunde*, vol. 1. Berlin: Vossische Buchhandlung.

Adiego, Ignasi-Xavier. 2016. Romani or pseudo-Romani? On the Lord's prayer in 'Nubian' by Jean-Baptiste Gramaye (1622). *Romani Studies*, 5th ser., 26 (2): 175–186.

Atanasov, Miroslav A. 2010. *Gypsy Pentecostals: The growth of the Pentecostal movement among the Roma in Bulgaria and its revitalization of their communities.* Lexington, KY: Emeth Press.

W. van den Heuvel

Bakker, Peter. 1995. Genesis of Caló. In *Romani in contact: The history, structure and sociology of a language*, ed. Yaron Matras, 1–21. Amsterdam: John Benjamins.

Bakker, Peter. 1998. Para-Romani versus secret languages: Differences in origin, structure and use. In *The Romani element in non-standard speech*, ed. Yaron Matras, 69–96. Wiesbaden: Harrassowitz Verlag.

Bakker, Peter. 2011. A new old text in Romani: Lord's Prayer, 1622. *International Journal of Romani Language and Culture* I (2): 193–212.

Bakker, Peter, and Hristo Kyuchukov, eds. 2000. *What is the Romani language?* Hatfield: University of Hertfordshire Press.

Bakker, Peter, and Hristo Kyuchukov. 2003. *Publications in Romani, useful for Romani language education*. Preliminary and experimental edition.

Baucal, Aleksandar. 2006. Development of mathematical and language literacy among Roma students. *Psihologija* 39 (2): 207–227.

Beissinger, Margaret. 2017. Balkan Romani musicians and the Evangelical Church: Occupation, faith, and identity. Presentation at the Gypsy Lore Society at Nicosa, Cyprus, August–September.

Bernal, Jorge M. Fernandez. 2014. Romani communities and churches in South America. In *Romani Pentecostalism: Gypsies and charismatic Christianity*, ed. David Thurfjell and Adrian Marsh, 217–230. Frankfurt: Peter Lang.

Browne, George. 1859. *The history of the British and Foreign Bible Society, from its institution in 1804, to the close of its jubilee in 1854*, vol. I. London: Bagster and Sons.

Canton, William. 1904. *History of the British & Foreign Bible Society*, vol. II. London: John Murray.

Carrizo-Reimann, Agustina. 2011. The forgotten children of Abraham: Iglesia Evangelica Misionera Biblica Roma of Buenos Aires. *Romani Studies*, 5th ser., 21 (2): 161–177.

Cressy, David. 2016. Evangelical ethnographers and the English Gypsies from the 1790s to the 1830s. *Romani Studies*, 5th ser., 26 (1): 63–77.

Fleck, Gábor, and Cosima Rughiniş (eds.). 2008. *Come closer: Inclusion and exclusion of Roma in present-day Romanian Society*. Bucharest: Human Dynamics.

Friedman, Victor. 1997. Linguistic form and content in the Romani-language press of the Republic of Macedonia. In *The typology and dialectology of Romani*, ed. Yaron Matras, Peter Bakker, and Hristo Kyuchukov, 181–196. Amsterdam: Benjamins.

Friedman, Victor. 2001a. Romani multilingualism in its Balkan context. *Sprachtypologie und Universalienforschung* 54: 146–159.

Friedman, Victor. 2001b. The Romani indefinite article in its historical and areal context. In *Was ich noch sagen wollte. A multilingual festschrift for Norbert Boretzky on the occasion of his 65th birthday*, ed. Birgit Igla and Thomas Stolz, 287–301. Berlin: Akademie Verlag.

Friedman, Victor. 2017. Seven varieties of Arli: Skopje as a center of convergence and divergence of Romani dialects. *Romani Studies*, 5th ser., 27 (1): 29–46.

Granqvist, Kimmo. 2010. Two hundred years of Finnish Romani linguistics. *Studia Orientalia* 108: 245–264.

Kalinin, Valdemar. 2014. Romanés (Romani) Bible translation and some remarks on translating biblical texts. In *Romani Pentecostalism: Gypsies and charismatic Christianity*, ed. David Thurfjell and Adrian Marsh, 241–246. Frankfurt: Peter Lang.

Leggio, Daniele Viktor, and Yaron Matras. 2013. Social networks as centres of language codification: Romani on YouTube. RomIdent Working Papers 32. http://romani.humanities.manchester.ac.uk/virtuallibrary.

Malone, Susane. 2004. *Manual for developing literacy and adult education programmes in minority language communities*. Bangkok: UNESCO.

Marushiakova, Elena, and Veselin Popov. 2014. The Gypsy revival movement: "New churches" in the territories of the former Soviet Union. In *Romani Pentecostalism: Gypsies and charismatic Christianity*, ed. David Thurfjell and Adrian Marsh, 41–53. Frankfurt: Peter Lang.

Matras, Yaron. 1999a. Sprachplanung und Spracheinstellung im Romanes. In *Die Sprache der Roma. Perspektiven der Romani-Forschung im interdisziplinären und internationalen Kontext*, ed. Dieter W. Halwachs and Florian Menz. Klagenfurt / Celovec: Drava.

Matras, Yaron. 1999b. Writing Romani: The pragmatics of codification in a stateless language. *Applied Linguistics* 20 (4): 481–502.

Matras, Yaron. 2002. *Romani: A linguistic introduction*. Cambridge: Cambridge University Press.

Matras, Yaron. 2005a. The status of Romani in Europe. Report submitted to the Council of Europe's Language Policy Division, October. https://romani.humanities.manchester.ac.uk/downloads/1/statusofromani.pdf.

Matras, Yaron. 2005b. The classification of Romani dialects: A geographical-historical perspective. In *General and applied Romani linguistics*, ed. Dieter Halwachs, Barbara Schrammel, and Gerd Ambrosch, 7–26. Munich: Lincom Europa.

Matras, Yaron. 2010. *Romani in Britain: The afterlife of a language*. Edinburgh: Edinburgh University Press.

Matras, Yaron. 2014. *I met lucky people: The story of the Romani Gypsies*. London: Penguin Books.

Miskow, Johan. 1931. Jaija Sattler and the gypsies of Berlin. *Journal of the Gypsy Lore Society*, 3rd ser., 10 (2): 86–91.

Nord, Christiane. 1997. *Translating as a purposeful activity: Functionalist approaches explained*. Manchester: St Jerome Publishing.

Podolinská, Tatiana. 2014. Questioning the theory of deprivation: Pentecostal Roma in Slovakia. In *Romani Pentecostalism: Gypsies and charismatic Christianity*, ed. David Thurfjell and Adrian Marsh, 89–107. Frankfurt: Peter Lang.

Ridler, Ann. 1981. Sidelights on George Borrow's Gypsy Luke. *Bible Translator* 32 (3): 329–337.

Ries, Johannes. 2007. *Welten Wanderer: über die kulturelle Souveränität siebenbürgischer Zigeuner und den Einfluss des Pfingstchristentums*. Würzburg: Ergon.

Sabaini, Astrid, and Barbara Schrammel-Leber. 2011. Die Bedeutung religiöser Texte für die funktionale Expansion des Romani. *Sociolinguistica* 25: 51–65.

Slavkova, Magdalena. 2007a. Evangelical gypsies in Bulgaria: Way of life and performance of identity. *Romani Studies*, 5th ser., 17 (2): 205–246.

Slavkova, Magdalena. 2007b. *Evangelical gypsies in Bulgaria*. Sofia: Paradigma [in Bulgarian].

Slavkova, Magdalena. 2012. Doing ethnographic fieldwork among Gypsies in home country and abroad. In *Промене идентитета, културе и језика Рома у условима планске социјално-економске интеграције* (The change of Roma identity, culture and language conditioned by planned socio-economic integration), ed. Т. Варади and Г. Башић, 223–239. Beograd: САНУ.

Thurfjell, David, and Adrian Marsh (eds.). 2014. *Romani Pentecostalism: Gypsies and charismatic Christianity*. Frankfurt: Peter Lang.

Turner, Ralph. 1962–1966. *A comparative dictionary of the Indo-Aryan languages*. London: Oxford University Press.

van den Heuvel, Wilco, and Evelyne Urech. 2011. A sociolinguistic perspective on Roma group names in Transylvania. *Romani Studies*, 5th ser., 21 (2): 145–160.

van den Heuvel, Wilco, and Evelyne Urech. 2014. Romani dialect variation in Transylvania. *Romani Studies*, 5th ser., 24 (1): 43–70.

Zahova, Sofiya. 2014. *History of Romani literature, with multimedia on kids' publications*. Sofia: Paradigma.

Part V

Language Use

16

Romani in Child-Directed Speech

Pavel Kubaník

The chapter covers several issues connected with acquisition of languages in (Para-)Romani-speaking communities (see also Bakker, this volume). The introduction discusses the scarcity of sources covering these topics in Romani linguistics. In the second section on acquisition of Romani, the focus is more on competence of children acquiring the language, while the other parts concentrate more on input of Romani and language socialization. Within the context of communities where Romani is used as a main language of socialization both structural and discursive phenomena of CDS are described. In contexts where other languages are used in communication with children more substantively than Romani, the focus is mainly on function and cultural context of Romani-derived insertions in CDS.

16.1 Introduction

This chapter deals with the topic of using Romani within child-directed speech (CDS), i.e. in specific context of interactions with addressees with low but rapidly growing knowledge of language and norms of its use. It will cover studies done in contexts of speech communities which use Romani as

---

P. Kubaník (✉)
Romani Studies Seminar, Charles University, Prague, Czech Republic
e-mail: pavel.kubanik@ff.cuni.cz

© The Author(s) 2020
Y. Matras and A. Tenser (eds.), *The Palgrave Handbook of Romani Language and Linguistics*, https://doi.org/10.1007/978-3-030-28105-2_16

a main language of socialization as well as in communities which use mainly other languages in CDS, but still use some Romani-derived features in this context.

The number of studies written on these topics is very small. Studies of language acquisition and language socialization in different minority or non-Western societies started to be published only in the 1970s and 1980s, respectively (Slobin 1985, pp. 4–5; Schieffelin and Ochs 1986), and so far the topic has attracted just a couple of linguists interested in Romani (see below). Although Matras (2002, p. 240) mentions 'growing interest in the study of discourse styles in Romani', fifteen years after this note there is still a lack of studies on using Romani in general, including CDS. Moreover, different aspects of Romani childhood still remain neglected topics in many other parts of Romani studies (although some anthropological monographs contain some comments on childhood and socialization, see, e.g., Engebrigsten 2007). The only exception could be the area of education of Romani children—paradoxically we have more studies on secondary socialization of Romani children in schools than on their primary socialization in families and this paradox also has its linguistic counterpart. Although the Bibliography of modern Romani linguistics lists 51 sources which somehow apply to child language (Bakker and Matras 2003, p. 340), most of these studies are more interested in the knowledge of particular national languages among Romani children. We can therefore infer that in the case of children with Romani as L1, their second language competence is studied without thorough academic knowledge of L1 acquisition, socialization and development in Romani speech communities.

Although Romani in CDS seems to be a topic on the fringe of academic interest, different facets of this phenomenon can be seen as very substantial. Studying acquisition of Romani can help with more proper diagnosis of cognitive problems of children for whom Romani is the mother tongue. In general, studying minor phenomena in language use can also help to reveal some features that are pertinent to more general linguistic enquiry. Attention to language use in child-focused interactions can also be a helpful means for studying primary socialization both in communities that use Romani as a main language of socialization and in communities that are shifting away from using Romani in everyday interaction.

This chapter, aside from focusing on the few published studies and conference papers, also presents short comments on the topic scattered in sources which are not primarily focused on Romani within CDS and sometimes uses yet unpublished data from my own research.

16.2 Acquisition of Romani

As of yet, there is no comprehensive study of the process of Romani language acquisition or language development of children who live in families and speech communities where Romani is used as the main language of socialization. There are only several articles that focus on certain phenomena of the language acquisition process.

In recent years, Hristo Kyuchukov and his various collaborators used a specially developed test to measure some features of competence of Romani children in Romani (Kyuchukov 2014; Kyuchukov and de Villiers 2014; Kyuchukov et al. 2016, 2017). The Romani language assessment test (ROMLAT) focuses on the ability of children to understand and use wh-questions (e.g. to be able to correctly understand a sentence containing more than one wh-word), wh-complements, passive constructions as well as morphological markers for gender, number, tense and aspect. The latter items were tested through the Wug Test (Berko 1958), i.e. by using nonsense words to test how children are able to apply grammatical rules to them. In several experiments, this battery of tests was used to assess the competence of over 150 Romani children (3–6 years old) from different European countries who spoke Romani as their dominant language and learned the official language of their countries while attending kindergartens (Kyuchukov et al. 2017).

The main conclusion of the tests is, not surprisingly, that the older the children are, the better their result in all of the characteristics measured, i.e. their competence in Romani increases with age. The results achieved in testing groups of children with Romani as L1 are, according to the authors, similar to the results obtained when testing groups of speakers of other languages.

The increase in Romani competence with age was revealed by the same author via other testing methods as well—consulting standard vocabulary lists with the children's parents, linking nouns and verbs with pictures (Kyuchukov 2014; see also Kolmanová 2007 for the same method used with Romani children from Slovakia) and testing comprehension and production of verb tenses both in Romani and in L2 of Romani children from Bulgaria and Slovakia (Kyuchukov 2015).

These findings more or less explicitly target the assumption that Romani children are cognitively underdeveloped when they start their school attendance—an assumption that often appears in public discourse; for example, in Slovakia some teachers of Romani children claim in the media that the children are unable to communicate either in Slovak or in Romani, despite the fact that the teachers themselves are not competent in Romani (see Polgáriová and Liptáková 2012; Kačová 2017, p. 6). Kyuchukov argues that if the cognitive development of Romani-speaking children is assessed, it should be done using their L1 in testing methods (Kyuchukov et al. 2017).

There is no reason to assume that Romani children should be an exception from the rule that children are able to acquire the basics of language(s) in early childhood. It is also obvious that the study of acquisition of Romani can be developed to serve other purposes than to counter stereotypically tinted arguments on Romani-speaking children in education. However, if we stay in the educational sphere, as Kyuchukov does, expanding research on the acquisition of Romani could be helpful in diagnosing real language or cognitive problems that children with Romani as their L1 might be facing.

Moreover, the bilingualism of children who live in families where Romani is used should be more thoroughly considered in those studies that primarily focus on competence in the language of school instruction. These studies sometimes fail to mention whether the Romani children in the sample are bilingual or not (Dolean et al. 2016), or to consider their level of competence in Romani (Mesárošová and Orosová 1995).

This ignorance of the actual (in)competence of Romani children in Romani can also lead to the assumption that the problems of Romani pupils with the language of instruction are caused mainly by the fact that the language of instruction is an L2 for these children, and therefore, it risks missing other real factors responsible for such problems. In Hungary, for example, a large part of Romani school-aged children are native speakers of Hungarian. According to Réger (1999b), the absence of literacy events (i.e. different occasions when a child works with texts) during the language socialization of these children can play a rather significant role in their language problems in school which their teachers have to deal with.

16.3 Child-Directed Speech in Romani

The term CDS will refer in this chapter to the sum of utterances that are addressed to a child. As such, the term differs from child speech (i.e. utterances made by children themselves). Sometimes CDS also stands for a specific speech register (called baby-talk, motherese, etc.); here, baby-talk will be seen as a specific phenomenon which could be part of the term within the broader definition of CDS. Baby-talk exists in the majority of the world's languages (Ferguson 2004 sees it as a possible linguistic universal) and has been described for some Romani varieties (see below).

In the discussion of CDS in Romani, Sect. 16.3 will cover studies implemented in the context of speech communities that use Romani as the main language of socialization. Here, attention will focus both on the structural characteristics of baby-talk in Romani (Sect. 16.3.1) and on the cultural context of CDS within child socialization (Sect. 16.3.2). Section 16.4 will focus on studies based on research in communities that use mainly other languages in CDS, but still use some Romani-derived features in this context.

16.3.1 Simplified Register

The most characteristic feature of CDS across different speech communities is the set of simplifications at different levels of linguistic structure. Although there are speech communities that do not use simplified register in CDS because of various cultural ideologies, or use CDS features in a limited way (Ochs and Schieffelin 1984), it can be assumed from several documented cases that speakers of Romani are not such an exception (Andrš 2010; Kubaník 2012b; Réger and Berko Gleason 1991). Throughout this section, I will use the term 'unmarked Romani' as a term of contrast to the simplified register ('marked' variety).

In a comprehensive structural and discourse-based description of baby-talk in a Northern Central Romani variety from Eastern Slovakia (Kubaník 2012b), I found many features common to other baby-talk registers as described by Ferguson (1964, 2004). On the level of prosody, the speakers used exaggerated contours (e.g. when caretakers call on children) and played with the rhythm of the language (e.g. segmentation of utterances into rhythmically spoken syllables). On a phonological level, typical phonological shifts were observed, for example the change /r>l/ and a reduction of consonant clusters (*pindroro>pintolo* 'little leg'). Another phonological feature is a common CVCV structure in specific words (see Table 16.1: A1–4, D5–8 and others). A distinctive morphological feature of baby-talk is the reduplication of syllables and the reduction of some morphemes both of which involved specific lexicon (*nono < rukono* 'dog'; see also Table 16.1: A1–2, B8–11, C8–9, D5–8 and others). In Romani baby-talk, like in other instances of such a register, specific lexicon can be categorized into several domains related to the child's world, childcare and socialization (bodily functions, kinship terms, etc.). To illustrate this, Table 16.1 presents baby-talk words from two Northern Central and two Northern Vlax varieties of Romani recorded by different researchers in four neighbouring European countries.

Table 16.1 Baby-talk lexicon in four varieties of Romani

		English	A Northern Central Romani, Eastern Slovakia (Kubaník 2012b)	B Northern Central Romani, Western Ukraine (Beníšek, person.com)	C Northern Vlax Romani (Kelderaš) Romania, Banat (Andrš 2010)	D Northern Vlax Romani (Lovari), Hungary (Réger, Berko Gleason 1991)
Kinship	1	mother	*mama* (daj)	*mama* (mama, daj)	–	–
	2	father	*dada* (dad)	*apos* (apos, dad)	–	–
	3	child	*popa* (čhavoro)	(voc.) *ľaľu, bapko (for both boys and girls), puťku (only for boy)* (čhavóro)	–	–
Body and bodily functions	4	food/eat	*(kerel) pap(k)a* (xal)	*(kerel) papa/hamham* (xal)	*(kerel) papa*	–
	5	meat	–		–	*cici*
	6	water	–		–	*tutu*
	7	drink	*bumbu* (pijel)		–	–
	8	sleep	*(kerel) džidži/ džidža/ džudžu* (sovel)	*(kerel) čuču* (sovel)	*kerel haynani /lala/ nana/nani*	*kerel lulu*
	9	urinate	*(kerel) piš* (muterel)	*(kerel) pipi, piš* (muterel)	*kerel pipi*	–
	10	defecate	*(kerel) e-e / keke* (xinel)	*(kerel) aa, kaka* (xinel)	–	–
	11	hurt	*buba* (dukhal)	*bibi, bubu* (dukhal)	–	–
	12	breast	*titi/titka* (čuči)	*cici (also for bottle and pacifier)* (čuvči)	*cici*	
Qualities	13	nice	<u>*tete/čeče*</u> (šukar)	*čeča, čečáno* (šukár)	–	–
	14	dirty	*fuj, e-e* (džungalo)	*kakáno* (džungálo)	–	–
	15	hot	*kiš* (kerado)	*žiži* (kerado)	–	–

(continued)

Table 16.1 (continued)

	English	A Northern Central Romani, Eastern Slovakia (Kubaník 2012b)	B Northern Central Romani, Western Ukraine (Beníšek, person.com)	C Northern Vlax Romani (Kelderaš) Romania, Banat (Andrš 2010)	D Northern Vlax Romani (Lovari), Hungary (Réger, Berko Gleason 1991)
Activities	16 kiss	*(kerel/del/čumidel) bol božťk* (čumidel)	*(kerel / del) bo, boču, ćjom(k)a* (čumidel)	*(del) pupa, midel*	—
	17 stand	*Toju* (imp.) (terdžuvl; imp.)			
	18 clap	*kerel ťapki/ťapkuški*	*bumbum, tapitapi, tapitapiručki* (kľapkinel)	—	—
	19 go out	*džal pa* (džal avri)	*džal tata/táta* (džal avri)	—	—
	20 bite	*kerel kiš kerel kusaj* (danderel)	*(kerel) kis* (danderel)	—	—
	21 beat	*kerel bi* (marel)	*(kerel) bax, bi, pif, puf; čapinel* (marel)	—	*pok-pok kerel*
Animals, things, creature	22 cat	*miňu(š)* (mačka)			
	23 dog	*nono / havo* (rukono)	*havhav, konóro* (rukono, rukonóro)	—	—
	24 sweets	*Čuču* (gul'ipen, bonboni)	*koko, oo* (gul'ipen)	*bobo*	—
	25 toy	*tete/čeče* (hračka)			—
	26 spook	*Bobo* (mulo)	*Hu, vova, babajka* (mulo)	*babao*	—

Table 16.1 shows baby-talk variants which differ substantially from their equivalents in unmarked speech (see words in parenthesis in columns for the two Northern Central varieties). Some of the words listed in Table 16.1 can be used in different grammatical functions; for example, *buba* (Table 16.1: A11) can be used as a noun in *dikhes buba?* 'do you see the wound' or as a verb in *so buba (tut)* 'what hurts (you)'. In the table, we can find frequent examples of collocative expressions formed with basic verbs like *kerel* 'to do' or *del* 'give' (see, e.g., rows 16, 18, 20 and 21 in Table 16.1). Correspondence in form and meaning across the four varieties of Romani can be found only in a few examples (rows 4 and 9 in Table 16.1). This is probably caused by areal diffusion of baby-talk words across different languages (Ferguson 1964, p. 111) from which they were borrowed into Romani; that is, Latin baby-talk *pappa* 'food' (Ferguson 1964, p. 104) was borrowed into Romanian, Slovak or Hungarian and from these languages into particular varieties of Romani. Homonyms are more common, i.e. correspondence only in form, but not in meaning, which is the result of the same phonological and morphological rules of baby-talk registers across languages.

The variety described in my article (Kubaník 2012b) borrows much of its lexical items from Slovak (see underlined words in the fourth column in Table 16.1); however, morphological rules that are commonly applied to items borrowed into Romani are not always involved in this process. Some expressions are only 'copied' from Slovak without any morphological marking (*havo* < Slovak *havo* 'dog'). In other cases, Romani uses items from Slovak in a way that is not common either in Slovak or in unmarked (i.e. not simplified) Romani. For example, Romani baby-talk uses (*kerel*) *bo* 'kiss' < Slovak *bozk* 'kiss', which is a form that is not used in common Slovak or its baby-talk in any dialect (Ondráčková 2008). Unmarked Romani uses the unborrowed (inherited) *čumidel* (verb) or *čumidipen* (noun) '(to) kiss'. Only in CDS, which is open to language play, can the Slovak diminutive morpheme -*k*- be incorporated into Romani baby-talk words: *džidži* / *dži-č-k-a* 'sleep'; *titi* / *tit-k-a* 'breast'. Some collocative expressions of Romani CDS are formed with imperative forms of Slovak verbs: Romani *ker* 'do.IMP' + Slovak *kusaj* 'bite.IMP' or *bij* 'beat.IMP' > *ker kusaj* 'bite.IMP', *ker bi* 'beat.IMP'.

Analogous specific handling of contact language items was noticed in the case of the CDS simplified register of Vlax speakers in Hungary: some phonological changes, which appear in Romani-internal CDS items, were extended to borrowings from Hungarian and even to code-switched Hungarian items, although those changes are not used by native speakers of Hungarian; for example, *öcsönöm* 'thank you' is a form used only in Romani baby-talk, and it is never used in Hungarian, although it is derived from Hungarian *köszönöm* (Réger and Berko Gleason 1991, p. 604).

In the use of a simplified register in the variety I described (Kubaník 2012b), I did not notice any gender division—either among adult men and women, or among children aged four and above, who were using the register actively. The same was observed among Vlax Roma in Hungary (Réger and Berko Gleason 1991, p. 604), while Kyuchukov (2014, p. 212) noticed that fathers more often than mothers use the unmarked variety of Romani instead of the simplified CDS and argued that fathers can therefore function as a 'bridge' towards more complex language forms.

The features of Romani baby-talk that were mentioned above are not limited to this particular speech register. Agha (2004, p. 37) argues that despite the fact that specific registers involve a specific repertoire of forms, boundaries of registers do not depend on these sets of forms, but on the 'social-semiotic processes' (i.e. how speakers link particular forms to stereotypical identities or practices). Forms that are characteristic of the practice of talking to children can therefore be used in different situational contexts. Because of existing stereotypical links, the forms can change the meaning of an utterance based on the context (see also Ferguson 1964, p. 111). In the speech community where I did my research, people with intellectual disability were sometimes addressed in speech using features common in baby-talk. Equally, when the speaker wanted to express their dominance over an older child, he/she could use features of the simplified register that would be otherwise inappropriate (Kubaník 2012b, p. 77). In the first case, the 'baby-talk forms' were used to index the addressee's lower cognitive development and in the second one the forms indexed social hierarchy—both features are present in the conceptualization of 'small children' in the locality of the research.

In other situations, forms which in a particular context seem to be part of the stereotype of talking to children do not index this context, or they do so in a limited way. For example, diminutive forms, which are typical of Romani and other baby-talk registers, are commonly used out of the context of CDS in Northern Central Romani in Eastern Slovakia (which to some extent differs from the situation of unmarked Czech). The case can be illustrated by the use of typical phraseological expressions with the verbs *xal* 'to eat' or *čarel* 'to lick' (e.g. *xav tro jiloro* 'I eat your little heart'). While these idiomatic forms are most commonly used in the context of CDS as an expression of an emotional bond with the child, they can also be used in other situations to express emotionality, for example in requests. Kubaník (2012b, p. 77) mentioned this type of idiomatic expression in prayers (compare with Gilliat-Smith 1915–1916, p. 8).

It should be mentioned that such expressions are quoted in texts about speakers of different dialect groups of Romani—Vlax dialect speakers from Hungary (Réger and Berko Gleason 1991) and Romanian Banat (Andrš

P. Kubaník

2010, p. 52), speakers of Northern Central dialects of Eastern Slovakia (Kubaník 2012b), Sinti dialect speakers in Italy (Tauber 2004) and sedentary Muslim Roma in north-east Bulgaria (Gilliat-Smith 1915–1916). This type of phraseological expression therefore seems to be an archaism, which may have been used by speakers of Early Romani before they spread from the Balkans to other European regions, and major dialect groups evolved. CDS as one of the main domains of its use, and a quite conservative (Ferguson 1964, p. 104) and intimate one, could be one of the reasons for preservation of this language strategy.

16.3.2 Language Socialization

Language socialization is a theoretical framework which views socialization and language acquisition as mutually interconnected phenomena. It focuses on how languages are used during socialization and how the children are socialized to use languages (Ochs and Schieffelin 1984; Duranti et al. 2011). The use of Romani in CDS will be approached in this section as part of a broader cultural context of the speech communities in question.

Norms of parenting reflect and help to sustain the moral standards of a community (LeVine and New 2008, p. 3). Although in each generation some innovations can be accepted, the time of early childhood and cultural models of interaction with small children seem to be a rather conservative area, and probably all the more so within societies in which extended families (parents, grandparents, aunts, cousins) are the main locus of (language) socialization.

Linguists and anthropologists who have mentioned Romani childhood in their texts highlight the participation of children in almost all activities of their community (e.g. Engebrigsten 2007, pp. 53–56; Tauber 2004, pp. 8–11). In the communities studied, children grow up exposed to a rich variety of input sources and regularly interact with people of different age, sex and status (Réger and Berko Gleason 1991, p. 604).

Inspired by De León (2011), I noticed that Romani children in the village of Eastern Slovakia where I was doing my research are most often positioned in open niches, that is, not limited to exclusive face-to-face interactions with their caretakers, before they start to walk safely. These positions enable them to observe their surroundings and, thus, to get used to a multiparty participation framework, from a very early age (Kubaník 2012a, b).

One of the common tasks of older children in different Romani communities is to take care of younger children (e.g. Engebrigsten 2007, pp. 53–56;

16 Romani in Child-Directed Speech   499

Kubaník 2012b). Therefore, children of different ages can interact within child groups, which is relevant for language socialization. In these settings, children can develop their competence in different registers of both Romani and the language of (future) school instruction, for example through collective role-play (see, examples, in Réger 1979, p. 62; Tauber 2004, pp. 8–11; Kubaník 2015).

One of the speech genres involved in language socialization of Romani children is teasing (Réger 1999a; Kubaník 2014; notes and examples also in Tauber 2004, pp. 10–11; Kyuchukov 2016; Kyuchukov 2014, p. 214). Teasing holds a prominent position within studies of language socialization in general (Eisenberg 1986; Miller 1986; Schieffelin 1986; Moore 2011), and studies in Romani linguistics are inspired by this tradition. Teasing can be defined as a set of conversational sequences in which the first sequence can challenge or frighten the child, but the child should recognize through reading contextualization cues (Gumperz 1982, pp. 130–153) in the evolving interaction that the initial 'intention' was not meant seriously.

Réger (1999a), working with just a fragment of her rich data corpus on interaction with children, used the analysis of just two recordings to show how small children are actively involved in the teasing of their younger siblings. These findings support the observation of high frequency of this genre with CDS. Sequences used to tease children progressively become routines and as such can serve as milestones for more developed forms of teasing with a more active participation of the children themselves (Réger 1999a, p. 302). During my own research, I observed the same process: routines used to tease preverbal children became part of playful quarrels in which, in particular, little girls were involved and instructed by their caretakers.

In Example 1, Džiba (age 1 year; 8 months) is prompted by her mother Barka to resist playful provocations by her older cousin Veronka (age 2;4).

Example 1 (Kubaník 2017, p. 33)

1		((Veronka runs around Džiba))
2	Džiba=>Veronka: -kereš.	// -you doing.
3	Veronka=>Džiba ((points at Džiba)): So kereš.	// What are you doing.
4	Dži=>Ve: Kere.	// Home.
5	Barka=>Dži: Phen Džibo - dža khere.	// Džiba, say—go home.
6	Dži: Kaja.	// This (naughty) one.
7	Ve: Dža khere dža khere dža khere.	// Go home go home go home.
8		(Ve runs at Dži and runs away)
9	Barka: Dikh koja, dikh, imar lake doavľa.	// Look, that one, she's going crazy now.
10	Dži=>Ve: Khere. Khere.	// Home. Home.

500   P. Kubaník

In this example, two little cousins inspire each other which utterance from the established set of teasing phrases (e.g. *so* /*keres*/, /*dža*/ *khere* or *kaja*) to use (see the turn taking in lines 2–4). Although Džiba's mother prompts her daughter to use a certain provocative phrase (line 5), Džiba chooses another one (line 6), which is, however, also adequate to use in the situational context. In the context that is already understandable to Džiba, she is competent enough to choose from a set of phrases that are connected with such a situation. Both cousins are competent in this type of situation, which at least partly suggests the frequency of similar situations in their socialization. The example also shows that children themselves are actors (not only objects) of socialization when reacting to each other's utterance.

It is also interesting that some frequent expressions occurring in teasing routines use grammatical features which are only slowly evolving at that particular age (1;8). *Kaja* 'this one' marks gender (f.), number (sg.) and source of knowledge about referent (-*a*- stem indicates that the referent is part of the extra-linguistic speech situation; see Matras 2002, p. 103). In similar contexts with other participants, Džiba correctly uses this type of utterance in masculine (*kada*) or plural (*kale*). This is not to say that Džiba has already fully acquired the marking of gender and number, but in some routine instances she is already able to apply it.

Adults use these demonstratives as a form of directive, i.e. speech acts with a function to appeal to the addressee (Searle 1976), quite frequently (see line 9). Although it is used to reprimand someone specific, there is nothing in the morphology of the demonstrative that points to a concrete person or misconduct directly (as opposed to the use of imperative or 2SG). Taken literally it only calls attention to a person and his/her behaviour, and the participants have to guess from the context who or what was wrong. To sum up, the example shows that participation in cultural routines such as teasing facilitates not only the acquisition of some grammatical features (Ochs and Schieffelin 1995) but also the acquisition of cultural preferences in regard to the way that certain speech acts (e.g. disagreement) should be expressed.

Andrš (2010, p. 56) notices that in the community of Roms in Banat, children are prompted to behave impudently towards their adult relatives (the same behaviour is portrayed in Stewart 2005, pp. 57–58). This discursive strategy is also present in Romani communities in which Roms shift away from using Romani in CDS and intentionally use other languages when talking with children. In situations when playful impudency towards adults is prompted from children, elements of Romani can be used more frequently despite the general attitude disfavouring the use of Romani (Kubaník 2016).

According to Réger (1999a), teasing interactions influence socialization of gender roles, and variability of interaction (switching of topics, roles of speakers or relationships between speaker and addressee) influences the development of communicative competence. Réger takes teasing as an important manipulative means used by adult Roms both in intra-ethnic communication within a basically egalitarian Romani community and in interactions with more powerful non-Roms. In my article (Kubaník 2014, p. 102), I note that in the Romani community of Eastern Slovakia, the ability to rhetorically 'put down' the partner in communication by manipulating the intention of his or her previous statement is appreciated. Teasing in CDS helps to nurture an ability to read the intention of the speaker (to be attentive to contextualization cues that can modify what is conveyed verbally), as well as to teach the techniques of manipulating the intention of the speaker to achieve different goals.

The fact that two-year-old children are prompted to tease others and instructed on how to react to teasing by others can also be interpreted as a mark of importance of this genre in the socialization of Romani children. The act of prompting itself often marks what is important for caretakers to adopt (Moore 2011, p. 213).

During teasing, certain cultural values of the community can be challenged (e.g. respect towards elders with corresponding norms of language etiquette; Kubaník 2014, p. 114; Andrš 2010, p. 56). Children are encouraged to overstep these rules, but if they adhere to the particular prompts, their behaviour can be corrected in the subsequent conversational turn. In this way, teasing can bring about situations that are convenient for learning culturally adequate norms of conduct.

Réger and Berko Gleason (1991) make a connection between CDS and the oral culture of the community with its frequent dialogical features such as testing questions used in storytelling. Children become familiar with these features within both CDS and adult performance of oral culture and are able to perform some elaborated genres of oral culture already at the age of ten–twelve.

In connection with the above, it should be mentioned that language socialization is not limited to children (and CDS), because a person learns throughout his/her life how to communicate with different communities and participate in different practices in which he/she would like to be involved. Hajská (2012; also Hajská and Poduška 2006) observed a process of language socialization of adult women from the Rumungro group (Northern Central dialect) into the community of their husbands, speakers of Northern Vlax varieties from a nearby village. Rumungro wives were

502   P. Kubaník

gradually better able to perform Vlax identity including grammatical and communicative competence in a Vlax variety of Romani. As they became older, they performed their new identity automatically and acted as strict supervisors of the next generation of Rumungro wives in the community.

16.4 CDS in Romani

The European Commission estimates that there are between ten and twelve million Roms living in Europe.[1] According to Matras (2002, p. 238), the most conservative estimate of the number of speakers of Romani worldwide is 3.5 million. Thus, there are many Romani communities where Romani is not spoken. Even in such communities and families some Romani or Romani-derived features can still be in use, and these will be discussed in this section. While in Sect. 16.4.1 the focus will be on families where Romani is still used but its use is intentionally restricted within CDS, Sect. 16.4.2 will focus on the acquisition of Para-Romani, i.e. varieties of the majority languages with a more or less stable admixture of Romani-derived lexicon (see Bakker, this volume).

16.4.1 Romani CDS in Communities that Are Shifting Away from Romani

The current situation of Romani among Central Romani speakers in the Czech Republic is perhaps the best described case of an ongoing language shift in communities of former Romani bilinguals, although the same shift is happening in other countries as well (see, e.g., Halwachs 2005 for Austria; Zahova 2013 for Montenegro).

In the Czech Republic (CR), the majority of the Romani population consists of families that migrated (and to a certain extent still migrate) to Czech towns and cities mainly from rural isolated settlements in Slovakia. More frequent contact with non-Roms together with an attempt to achieve a better life for their children leads these families to the decision to use Czech in CDS instead of Romani. The immediate hope is to facilitate children's school enrolment and success (Hübschmannová 1979), for which competence in Czech at a native level is necessary. According to recent research (Kubaník et al. 2010, 2013), just one-third of Romani children in CR have no problems speaking Romani, another third understands

16 Romani in Child-Directed Speech 503

Romani to some extent (but can speak only with difficulties) and the final third understands only several basic words and phrases. Research also revealed that competence in Romani increases with children's age (Kubaník et al. 2013, p. 70).

In my research (Kubaník 2016), I observed more closely the situation in one Romani family of recent migrants from a rural Slovak Romani settlement, who currently live in Prague. In this family, Romani, although not used in CDS, was still the major language of interaction among adults. The use of Romani particularly in CDS was seen by this family as a marker of backwardness, particularly in respect of Roms from Slovak rural settlements. In this family, children did not speak Romani, and active competence in Romani was not expected from the children (on the contrary, it sometimes served as a secret language of the parents). Due to this practice, children were to some extent excluded from some parts of family life, e.g. from some discussions by adults, which is not the rule in other Romani communities (see above).

Despite that attitude, some Romani items were still present in CDS even in this family. Romani was used by adults in CDS particularly in teasing, shaming, commanding or threatening the children, i.e. in situations where the speaker demonstrates his/her power over the addressee (self-assertive talk in terms of Garrett 2005).

In the following example, Jana, who intentionally used only Czech with her children (Vašek 6, Táda 4, Lenka 3, Tomáš 2), tries to comfort them, while they are each occupied by another activity. Czech utterances are directly translated into English, and Romani utterances are in original *in italics* and translated *in italics* after // double slash. Underlined utterances are pronounced with noticeably higher emotional emphasis (louder, in higher tone) then the rest.

Example 2 (Kubaník 2016, p. 244)

1 Vašek=>author: There's something spilled on the floor.
2 Jana=>Vašek: (Yeah) I'll wipe it,
    let it be.
3 ((Ja wants to wipe the place close to where Va stands))
4 Ja=>Va: *Dža Vašek*.   //   *Go Vašek.*
5 ((Lenka sponges down the table, water is dripping on the place which Ja just wiped up))
6 Ja=>Le: *Lenko ma ker kade pre phuv, ta s'oda s- s'oda tu kada keres?*
                          //   *Lenka don't make a mess on the floor,*
                          oh what is this - what are you doing?

7	Le=>Ja: I'll wipe it up. And it won't be wet.
8	((Táda is barking for fun))
9	Ja=>Ta: Táda, more quietly.
10	((Le probably tears the sponge))
11	Ja=>Le: *Tu rozčhines Leno? Tu rozčhines?* Are you stupid?
	// *You tear it, Lena? You tear it?*
12	((Ja goes to a computer, the children try to switch it on))
13	Ja=>Ta: But that won't go that way, Táda. You see? Wait ()
14	((To runs in, climbs on a box near the computer table, wants to touch the keyboard))
15	Ja=>To: *De. Imar avľal?* Just try to push and I'll hit you.
	// *Stop. You're here already?*

In this short example, Jana addresses in turns all of her children; in communication with Lenka, Vašek and Tomáš, she uses both Romani (lines 4, 6, 11, 12) and Czech (lines 2, 11, 12). Romani is used at moments when the mother commands the children or bans something in the form of both imperatives (lines 4, 6, 15) and rhetorical questions (which serve as threats; lines 6, 11, 15). This function is marked not only by code-switching but also by the higher tone and volume of these utterances.

In this function, Romani is often used in terminal statements after which no reaction is expected. Using Romani does not stimulate any further conversational exchange in Romani; however, Romani utterances are (or should be) understood (at least from the context) by the children. In the family, the use of Romani in CDS more usually signalled negative affect than positive and this functional anchoring and social hierarchy in the family restricted, to certain extent, the use of Romani by the children. In the same function, the children could use what they knew from Romani only when speaking to their peers or younger children (which they sometimes did).

Even in a situation when the caretakers and the others around the child take up the practice of not using Romani in CDS, Romani items can still interfere with the language of children indirectly. Bořkovcová (2006) analysed the structure and use of the so-called Romani ethnolect of Czech, i.e. a variety of Czech with strong interferences from Romani (and Slovak which was the contact language of the oldest generation of ethnolect speakers in Bořkovcová's study). Romani-derived items include not only direct lexical insertions and switches (see above), but also grammatical and semantical calques, omission of reflexive pronouns and use of plain instrumental where prepositional case is obligatory (or vice versa), etc. In Example 3, some of these interferences are marked in bold.

16 Romani in Child-Directed Speech

Example 3 (Bořkovcová 2006, p. 127)

I já se bojim, ale třeba jsou určitý **mrtvoly**, *nebo lidi, který vidim a vůbec* **na mě strach nedávaj**. *Třeba jak tady hodně říkaj, že dyž de mrtvola, že* **máš proklínat**, *prostě nadávat a* **vyhánět**. /.../ **Zdálo se mi s tátou** *a von říkal: „Já vim, Cigáni to dělaj. Voni jim nadávaj,* **voni jim proklínaj**...'

I'm afraid too, but maybe there are some **corpses**, or people which I can see and they **don't drop any fear on me**. For example as they say frequently here, that if the **corpse** goes, you should **spell, scold** and **drive out**. /.../ **I dreamed with father** and he told: „I know, Gypsies do that. They are scolding them, they **curse to them**…"

The above excerpt from a speech in the Romani ethnolect of Czech includes numerous interferences from Romani: the Czech term *mrtvola* 'corpse' as used here does not refer to a dead body, the only possible meaning in Czech, but to a ghost (*mulo*—in Romani 'dead body, ghost'); the Romani-contaminated idiomatic expressions *dávat strach* lit. 'to drop a fear' (=strike fear) and *zdát se s někým* lit. 'to dream with someone' (=to have a dream about someone) are loaned translations from Romani (*mukel dar*, *džal mange suno /dadeha/*) for idioms that are constructed differently in Czech; the verbs *proklínat* 'curse' or *vyhánět* 'drive out' are used without an object in the Romani ethnolect but are transitive in Czech.

The above-cited narrative was recorded from a woman respondent from Prague whose parents did not speak Romani (their L1) with her, but instead used the Romani ethnolect of Czech in CDS. Romani was not used in her family even in later years, but she managed to acquire some competence in Romani from other members of the Romani community in her neighbourhood, which was typical for her generation on the whole (Bořkovcová 2006, p. 29).

Bořkovcová (2006, p. 57) mentions that some ethnolectal items that can convey emotional weight, e.g. intonation, are more frequently used within CDS. She also observed that for the oldest generation (born in the 1930s) of people who migrated to the Czech territories in the 1950s, the ethnolect was the only variety of Czech they were able to use, while among the youngest generation of respondents in her study (born in the 1980s) speakers are able to switch between the ethnolectal and a common variety of Czech (Bořkovcová 2006, p. 110; see also Kubaník 2016, pp. 242–243).

It can be assumed that due to their emotional weight, Romani items could be used in CDS frequently even when Romani is not used as a regular means of communication in Romani families.

16.4.2 CDS with Romani in Para-Romani Speech Communities

While in Sect. 16.3, which concentrated on the use of Romani in interactions with children in Romani-speaking communities, the major focus was put on structural and discursive features of CDS as a particular register of Romani, the remarks about the functional use of the Romani ethnolect of Czech in Sect. 16.4.1 shifted the topic to how a particular register and its functions are acquired. This final content section continues in this direction, concentrating on the acquisition of Para-Romani varieties and their (possible) use in CDS.

From a structural point of view, Para-Romani varieties can be characterized as a lexical layer of Romani embedded into the discourse of another language (Matras 2002, p. 243). In this respect, it differs from the above-mentioned ethnolect (at least for now) which is still in contact with inflected Romani (speakers can be bilingual in Romani and the ethnolect) and Romani interferences in the ethnolect are not only lexical, but also phonological, syntactic, etc.

As a lexical layer of another language, Para-Romani can be seen as a register of the other language. This was already mentioned by Kenrick (1979, pp. 111, 115) for Anglo-Romani. Agha (2004) defines language registers as sets of language items, which are stereotypically linked by speakers to a particular social practice or identity. In a quite similar way, Matras (2010) points to the potential of Romani-derived lexical items embedded in English discourse to index a common set of beliefs and cultural concepts. In his view, Anglo-Romani works as a discursive device that can influence the interpretation of the whole utterance by the addressees.

Comments on the use and acquisition of the Para-Romani varieties can be found in only a few texts. Gamella et al. (2015) in their study pay attention to current competence in Caló among different generations of Spanish Gitanos, Kenrick (1979) gives a short outline of Anglo-Romani and its use, and Matras (2010) in his monograph reconsiders the same Para-Romani variety from the perspective of its function.

Gamella et al. (2015) and Kenrick (1979) both agree that Para-Romani is not learned in childhood. The two works agree that the most substantial domain of Para-Romani use is community gatherings related to traditional professions or (in the past decades) evangelical congregations. This domain of use can postpone the acquisition of Para-Romani varieties to the phase of more active participation in such activities. According to Kenrick (1979, pp. 118–119), a six-year-old child from an Anglo-Romani speech community understands about ten expressions derived from Romani. Kenrick argues that such a small vocabulary set can be explained by concerns of the caretakers about possible disclosure of the secret code. Other reasons according to the author include the fact that children are not allowed to speak in the presence of adults and finally that children do not need to know Anglo-Romani because they are not part of the most substantial domain of its use that lies outside the family circle.

Nevertheless Kenrick considers the use of Para-Romani to be a strong marker of ethnic identity and therefore explains its acquisition in adolescence as a kind of rite of passage (Kenrick 1979, pp. 118–119) after which the different ethnic identity can be performed more adequately than in the previous period.

Some of Kenrick's observations would imply that Para-Romani is acquired in adolescence and excluded from CDS. However, both recent texts on Para-Romani in Spain and Britain feature examples of the use of Para-Romani in which speakers seem to link Para-Romani items with childhood and CDS.

Example 4 (Gamella et al. 2015, p. 69)

La *chuquela* es cunado le dicen a los niños chicos son muy malos: ¡Que *chuquelo sinela*!

The *chuquela* is when they say to little children that they are behaving badly. You are very bad!

Example 5 (Matras 2010, pp. 138–139)

Ol the obben coz when the raklis jels I'm gonna mor yas

„Eat the food coz when the girls go I'm gonna kill you"

The examples above do not show records of first-hand interaction, but speakers' reflections on some types of possible use of Anglo-Romani (Example 5) or Caló (Example 4). While in the Caló example children are mentioned as model addressees for this kind of utterance, in the Anglo-Romani example my interpretation is more speculative—it only shows a clear difference in the status of speaker and the addressee which could be traced to caretaker-child interaction. Para-Romani items are used in both examples as directives, which should move the addressee to act in another way—e.g. by shaming (Example 4) or threatening (Example 5). The use of such specific linguistic items for this function can be caused by the specific emotional weight of these items. Simultaneously, it can also be hypothesized that using Romani-derived items can function as a discursive device which should signal that the whole utterance should be interpreted in the specific context of cultural beliefs and values of a particular group (Matras 2010, pp. 132–133).

To add another insight into my speculation about the use of Para-Romani in CDS, Gamella et al. (2015, p. 81) also mapped the speakers' knowledge of different Caló items. The authors show that particular semantic fields (kinship, body parts, transgression and authority) are more widely known than others (animals, instruments, professions). The more familiar domains can be linked to CDS (see semantic fields in Table 16.1). Some of the well-known words (e.g. for genitals or excrements) can even be seen as being more common in CDS than in other situations. For example, Gay Y Blasco (1999, p. 71) observed that the terms for genitals are not taboo terms among Gypsies in Madrid when interacting with children. Quite to the contrary, referring to children's genitals or even touching, grabbing or kissing these parts of their bodies is a common feature of displaying affection towards children. It can be speculated that Romani-derived terms might be used in these cultural-specific affective displays, although Gay Y Blasco quotes only Spanish terms when describing these situations.

Matras gives one exceptional example of using Para-Romani item in child speech, i.e. an utterance by a child itself.

Example 6 (Matras 2010, p. 136)

> A four-year-old girl draws the attention of her aunt, who is sitting among a group of adults in the trailer, after she had taken, silently and at first unnoticed, a piece of bread from a dinner tray that was being prepared for guests. Her aunt asks her, in a very friendly and not at all accusing tone, where she got the bread from. The girl smiles and says somewhat shyly: 'I *chored* it' ('I stole it').

Example 6 is a rare instance of capturing natural interaction when Para-Romani is used by a four-year-old girl. As Matras notes (2010, p. 136), the verb *chore* 'to steal' is not an instance of using Para-Romani in cryptical function here because the people around the girl can understand it. According to Matras, it is used to evoke the adequate emotional key between the speaker and her addressee.

In this sense, the example touches on the core of language socialization— what is socialized in this interaction is not vocabulary and grammar (it is probable that the girl knows the English term 'steal'), but how particular language items can index culture-specific meanings.

My hypothesis is that despite the fact that Para-Romani is, according to the researchers, acquired mainly during adolescence in these communities, Para-Romani items can also be routinely used in CDS (see also Bakker 1998, pp. 87–88 for some casual examples from nineteenth-century sources on Anglo-Romani). The semantic fields of individual words, the function of Para-Romani items as a link between speech forms and specific cultural concepts and the conservative nature of the domain of language socialization of little children can support this hypothesis. However, as mentioned above, there are only a few studies of how Para-Romani is used and until now none of the existing studies paid attention to CDS.

16.5 Conclusion

This chapter focused on Romani from the point of view of its use in CDS and gathered existing information about the acquisition of Romani. Features of CDS were observed both in communities in which Romani serves as a main language of socialization and in communities which use only some Romani-derived items in this context. In the final part, this information was used to hypothesize about the possible use of Para-Romani varieties in CDS.

Studying Romani in CDS means to a certain extent observing the language from the periphery of its use. On the other hand, the topic can be seen as very substantial as well. CDS is a domain in which Romani, and communicative competence in the language, is (or is not) passed on to the next generation. Acquisition of Romani as the L1 of children is also a very significant topic for the educational sphere and for the diagnosis of language and cognitive problems of children with Romani as L1. The purpose of this chapter was to gather partial knowledge about Romani language acquisition, CDS and language socialization, but it is clear that all these important and interesting topics still await thorough research. Romani speech communities across the world are variable in many ways, which could be a great challenge for comparative research of these topics.

Focusing on using Romani in different contexts or focusing on different registers of Romani can also help to see Romani speech communities as internally structured. A closer look at using Romani in CDS shows that Romani, as any other language, is varied not only in geographical or historical terms, but also in terms of different identities and social practices which can be indexed by using specific linguistic items in a particular context. In this way, focusing on culturally adequate language use can reveal new insights into studies of various social and cultural phenomena.

Acknowledgement The work was supported by the European Regional Development Fund-Project "Creativity and Adaptability as Conditions of the Success of Europe in an Interrelated World" (No. CZ.02.1.01/0.0/0.0/16_019/0000734).

Note

1. http://ec.europa.eu/justice/discrimination/roma/index_en.htm.

References

Agha, Asif. 2004. Registers of language. In *Companion to linguistic anthropology*, ed. Alessandro Duranti, 23–45. Oxford: Blackwell.

Andrš, Zbyněk. 2010. Některé aspekty kultury banátských Rromů prizmatem rumunské kalderašské rromštiny [Some aspects of culture of Roms from Banat from a point of view of Romanian Kalderaš Romani]. PhD thesis, Univerzita Karlova v Praze, Filozofická fakulta, Ústav etnologie, Praha.

Bakker, Peter. 1998. Para-Romani languages versus secret languages: Differences in origin, structure, and use. In *The Romani element in non-standard speech*, ed. Yaron Matras, 69–96. Wiesbaden: Harrassowitz.

Bakker, Peter, and Yaron Matras (eds.). 2003. *Bibliography of modern Romani linguistics: Including a guide to Romani linguistics*. Amsterdam, Philadelphia: John Benjamins.

Berko, Jean. 1958. The child's learning of English morphology. *Word* 14 (2–3): 150–177.

Bořkovcová, Máša. 2006. *Romský etnolekt češtiny. Případová studie* [Romani ethnolect of Czech. A case study]. Praha: Signeta.

De León, Lourdes. 2011. Language socialization and multiparty participation frameworks. In *The handbook of language socialization*, ed. Alessandro Duranti, Elinor Ochs, and Bambi B. Schieffelin, 81–111. Oxford: Wiley-Blackwell.

Dolean, Dacian, Ioanna Tincas, and Crina I. Damsa. 2016. Enhancing the pre-literacy skills of Roma children: The role of socio-economic status and Classroom interventions in the development of phonemic awareness. *The New Educational Review* 45 (3): 39–51.

Duranti, Allesandro, Elinor Ochs, and Bambi B. Schieffelin (eds.). 2011. *The handbook of language socialization*. Oxford: Wiley-Blackwell.

Eisenberg, Ann R. 1986. Teasing: Verbal play in two Mexicano homes. In *Language socialization across cultures*, ed. Bambi B. Schieffelin and Elinor Ochs, 182–198. Cambridge: Cambridge University Press.

Engebrigsten, Ada I. 2007. *Exploring gypsiness: Power, exchange and interdependence in a Transylvanian village*. New York: Berghahn Books.

16 Romani in Child-Directed Speech 511

Ferguson, Charles A. 1964. Baby talk in six languages. *American Anthropologist* 66: 103–114.

Ferguson, Charles A. 2004 (1978). Talking to children: A search for universals. In *First language acquisition: The essential readings*, ed. Barbara C. Lust and Claire Foley. Oxford: Wiley-Blackwell.

Gamella, Juan F., Cayetano Fernández, and Ignasi-Xavier Adiego. 2015. The long agony of Hispanoromani. The remains of Caló in the speech of Spanish Gitanos. *Romani Studies* 25 (1): 53–93.

Garrett, Paul B. 2005. What a language is good for: Language socialization, language shift, and the persistence of code-specific genres in St. Lucia. *Language in Society* 34: 327–361.

Gay Y Blasco, Paloma. 1999. *Gypsies in Madrid: Sex, gender and the performance of identity*. Oxford and New York: Berg.

Gilliat-Smith, Bernard (Petulengro). 1915–1916. Report on the Gypsy tribes of North-East Bulgaria. *Journal of the Gypsy-Lore Society* 9 (1): 1–112.

Gumperz, John J. 1982. *Discourse strategies*. Cambridge: Cambridge University Press.

Hajská, Markéta. 2012. „Ame sam Vlašika, haj vorbinas vlašika!" (My jsme Olaši a mluvíme olašsky!). Nástin jazykové situace olašských Romů z východního Slovenska v etnicky smíšené komunitě ["We are Vlax Roms and therefore we speak Vlax Romani!" Outline of language situation of Vlax Roms from Eastern Slovakia]. *Romano džaniben* 19 (2): 35–53.

Hajská, Markéta, and Ondřej Poduška. 2006. Interdialectal code switching and the maintenance of social prestige. 7th International Conference on Romani Linguistics, Prague, 14–16 September. Abstract available at http://ulug.ff.cuni.cz/7icrl/ses1.php#HajskaPoduska. Accessed 12 December 2017.

Halwachs, Dieter W. 2005. Roma and Romani in Austria. *Romani Studies* 15 (2): 145–173.

Hübschmannová, Milena. 1979. Bilingualism among the Slovak Roms. *International Journal of the Sociology of Language* 19: 33–49.

Kačová, Veronika. 2017. Jedným z najväčších snov každého človeka je pocit ľudskej dôstojnosti [One of the biggest dreams of everyone is the feeling of human dignity. An interview with the teacher of Romani children Alexander Jakubčo]. *Romano hangos* 12 (1): 6–7.

Kenrick, Donald. 1979. Romani English. *International Journal of the Sociology of Language* 19: 111–120.

Kolmanová, Martina. 2007. Výzkum jazykových dovedností dětí v romském a slovenském jazyce [Research of linguistic competence of children in Romani and Slovak]. *Romano džaniben, jevend* 14 (2): 28–45.

Kyuchukov, Hristo. 2014. Acquisition of Romani in a bilingual context. *Psychology of Language and Communication* 18 (3): 212–225.

Kyuchukov, Hristo. 2015. Why Roma children form Slovakia do not know Slovak tenses? In *Človek a jeho jazyk. 3. Inšpirácie profesora Jána Horeckého* [Man and his language. 3 Inspirations of Professor Ján Horecký], ed. Mária Šimkova, 407–411. Bratislava: SAV.

Kyuchukov, Hristo. 2016. Adult-child communication in Roma families. *Problemi na ustnata komunikaciya* 10 (1): 303–311.

Kyuchukov, Hristo, and Jill de Villeirs. 2014. Roma children knowledge on Romani. *Journal of Psycholinguistics* 19 (1): 58–65.

Kyuchukov, Hristo, Milan Samko, Dagmar Kopcanova, and Peter Igov. 2016. The knowledge of Romani and school readiness of Roma children. *East European Journal of Psycholinguistics* 3 (2): 50–62.

Kyuchukov, Hristo, Jill de Villiers, and Andrea Takahesu Tabori. 2017. Why Roma children needs assessment in Romani. *Psychology of Language and Communication* 21 (1): 215–243.

Kubaník, Pavel. 2012a. Language use in a Romani community in Eastern Slovakia, with special attention to language socialization and child directed speech. 10th International Conference on Romani Linguistics, Barcelona, 5–7 September.

Kubaník, Pavel. 2012b. Dětský registr romštiny [Romani baby-talk]. *Romano džaniben* 19 (1): 61–80.

Kubaník, Pavel. 2014. Škádlení dětí v romské osadě [Teasing of children in Romani settlement]. In *Registre jazyka a jazykovedy (II). Na počesť Daniely Slančovej*, ed. Jana Kesselová, Mária Imrichová, and Martin Ološtiak, 110–115. Prešov: Filozofická fakulta Prešovskej univerzity v Prešove. Available at http://www.pulib.sk/web/kniznica/elpub/dokument/Kesselova4/subor/Kubanik.pdf.

Kubaník, Pavel. 2015. Hra na knížky. Poznámky k akvizici slovenštiny v Gavu [Playing the books. Notes on acquisition of Slovak in Gav]. In *Čierno-biele svety. Rómovia v majoritnej spoločnosti na Slovensku*, ed. Tatiana Podolinská and Tomáš Hrustič, 374–397. Bratislava: Ústav etnológie SAV, VEDA.

Kubaník, Pavel. 2016. Using Romani in language socialization in a Czech Rom family. In *Roma: Past, present, future*, ed. Hristo Kyuchukov, Elena Marushiakova, and Vesselin Popov, 238–249. Munich: Lincom.

Kubaník, Pavel. 2017. "Nebijte se, hádejte se." Socializace asertivity v Gavu ["Don't beat each other, just have a quarrel." Socialization of assertivity in Gav]. *Romano džaniben* 24 (2): 21–44.

Kubaník, Pavel, Jan Červenka, and Helena Sadílková. 2010. Romština v ČR – uchování jazyka a jazyková směna [Romani in CR—Language maintenance and shift]. *Romano džaniben* 16 (2): 11–40.

Kubaník, Pavel, Helena Sadílková, and Jan Červenka. 2013. The competence in and the intergenerational transmission of Romani in the Czech Republic. In *Romani V. Papers from the annual meeting of the Gypsy Lore Society, Graz 2011*, ed. Barbara Schrammel-Leber and Barbara Tiefenbacher, 61–80. Grazer Romani Publikationen 2. Graz: Grazer Linguistische Monographien.

LeVine, Robert, and Rebecca S. New (eds.). 2008. *Anthropology and child development: A cross-cultural reader*. Oxford: Blackwell.

16 Romani in Child-Directed Speech 513

Matras, Yaron. 2002. *Romani: A linguistic introduction*. Cambridge: Cambridge University Press.

Matras, Yaron. 2010. *Romani in Britain: The afterlife of a language*. Edinburgh: Edinburgh University Press.

Mesárošová, Margita, and Jeanette Orosová. 1995. Rozvijanie rečových spôsobilostí rómskych detí v slovenskom jazyku v nultych ročníkoch zâkladnej školy [Developing speech abilities in Slovak in preschool Romany children]. *Psychológia a patopsychológia dieťaťa* 30 (4): 352–365.

Miller, Peggy. 1986. Teasing as language socialization and verbal play in a white working class community. In *Language socialization across cultures*, ed. Bambi B. Schieffelin and Elinor Ochs, 199–212. Cambridge: Cambridge University Press.

Moore, Leslie C. 2011. Language socialization and repetition. In *The handbook of language socialization*, ed. Allesandro Duranti, Elinor Ochs and Bambi B. Schieffelin, 209–226. Oxford: Wiley-Blackwell.

Ochs, Elinor, and Bambi B. Schieffelin. 1984. Language acquisition and socialization: Three developmental stories and their implications. In *Culture theory: Essays on mind, self, and emotion*, ed. Richard A. Shweder and Robert A. LeVine, 276–322. New York: Cambridge University Press.

Ochs, Elinor, and Bambi B. Schieffelin. 1995. The impact of language socialization on grammatical development. In *The handbook of child language*, ed. Paul Fletcher and Brian MacWhinney, 73–94. Oxford and Cambridge: Blackwell.

Ondráčková, Zuzana. 2008. Detské slová v slovenčine a ich charakteristika [Child words in Slovak and their characteristics]. In *Štúdie o detskej reči*, ed. Daniela Slančová, 251–305. Prešov: Filozofická fakulta Prešovskej univerzity.

Polgáriová, Erika, and Eleonóra Liptáková. 2012. Otvorený list učiteliek z východného Slovenska [Open letter from teachers from Eastern Slovakia]. Published 12 June 2012. Available at http://janmacek.blog.sme.sk/c/301577/Otvoreny-list-uciteliek-z-vychodneho-Slovenska.html#ixzz1zWjGqCWY. Accessed 11 November 2018.

Réger, Zita. 1979. Bilingual Gypsy children in Hungary: Explorations in "natural" second-language acquisition at an early age. *International Journal of the Sociology of Language* 19 (5): 59–82.

Réger, Zita. 1999a. Teasing in the linguistic socialization of Gypsy children in Hungary. *Acta Linguistica Hungarica* 46 (3–4): 289–316.

Réger, Zita. 1999b. Gypsy children's language problems, their chances to manage school. In *The Roma education resource book: Educational issues, methods and practice, language and culture*, ed. Csaba Fényes, Christina McDonald, and Anita Mészáros, 169–173. Budapest: Open Society Institute—Institute for Educational Policy.

Réger, Zita, and Jean Berko Gleason. 1991. Romāni child-directed speech and children's language among Gypsies in Hungary. *Language in Society* 20 (4): 601–617.

Searle, J.R. 1976. A classification of illocutionary acts. *Language in Society* 5: 1–23.

Schieffelin, Bambi B. 1986. Teasing and shaming in Kaluli children's interaction. In *Language socialization across cultures*, ed. Bambi B. Schieffelin and Elinor Ochs, 165–181. Cambridge: Cambridge University Press.

Schieffelin, Bambi B., and Elinor Ochs (eds.). 1986. *Language socialization across cultures*. Cambridge: Cambridge University Press.

Slobin, Dan Isaac (ed.). 1985. *The crosslinguistic study of language acquisition. Volume 1: The data*. Hillsdale and London: Lawrence Erlbaum Associates.

Stewart, Michael. 2005. *Čas Cikánů* [Time of the gypsies]. Brno and Olomouc: Barrister a Principal, Univerzita Palackého v Olomouci.

Tauber, Elizabeth. 2004. Sinti Estraixaria children at school, or how to preserve 'the Sinti way of thinking'. *Romani Studies* 14 (1): 1–23.

Zahova, Sofiya. 2013. Gypsies/Roma in Montenegro: Group identity and the role of language. In *Romani V. Papers from the Annual meeting af the Gypsy lore society, Graz 2011*, ed. Barbara Schrammel-Leber and Barbara Tiefenbacher, 81–96. Graz: Grazer Romani Publikationen.

17

Romani on the Internet

Daniele Viktor Leggio

17.1 Introduction

The Internet has opened up a new domain of language use in which features of oral communication are expressed in writing and in which new, medium-specific features emerged (Herring 2002; Crystal 2006). Originally designed to only support English, the Internet soon catered to other standardised languages. Meanwhile, users speaking non-standardised languages are taking advantage of the flexibility and openness of the new technology, leading to the emergence of forms of spontaneous, unguided literacy (Danet and Herring 2007). In multilingual virtual spaces, language choice has also become a key element in the presentation and performance of users' identities (Lee 2016). Romani speakers are among those that contributed to the proliferation of languages on the Internet and to the emergence of new forms of literacy.

The appearance of Romani content on the Internet is part of a wider process of domain expansion, which started in the late 1960s and then facilitated by the democratisation of Eastern European countries since the 1990s (cf. Hübschmannová 1995; Matras 2005; Friedman 2005). More recently, the RomIdent project (2010–2013) examined how this process is contributing to the development of a modernised Romani identity.[1] The project highlighted the role of Romani rights activists and NGOs in the proliferation of

---

D. V. Leggio (✉)
University of Manchester, Manchester, UK
e-mail: daniele.leggio@manchester.ac.uk

© The Author(s) 2020
Y. Matras and A. Tenser (eds.), *The Palgrave Handbook of Romani Language and Linguistics*, https://doi.org/10.1007/978-3-030-28105-2_17

written forms of Romani. On their websites, these actors use Romani and its Indian origins to portray the Roma as a unified ethnic minority, rather than a problematic social group, in order to gain support for their demands for political recognition and protection from racism (Hughes 2013, p. 2; Matras 2015, p. 299). The project also highlighted how the usage of written Romani is not necessarily embedded into attempts to influence public debates about the Roma. Rather, on interactive platforms such as chat rooms and forums, Roma individuals use written Romani to replicate the conviviality of face-to-face encounters (Leggio 2015, p. 110). Despite these differences in the uses and discursive representation of Romani, the project has shown how the development of the language does not conform to traditional models of expansions into new domains. Romani expansion has been described as a polycentric process, in which approaches range from spontaneous, idiosyncratic contributions by individual speakers to structured efforts, such as corpus-based codification of single dialects or attempts at creating regional, national or international standardised Romani varieties (Halwachs 2011, p. 397). This, however, does not prevent speakers from claiming personal, individual ownership of written Romani. Rather, the flexible and pluralistic attitudes of Romani speakers towards spoken language use result in an acceptance of structural and orthographic variation (Matras 2015, p. 312).

Acceptance of structural and orthographic variation has been described as a practice within forms of *vernacular literacy*, that is forms of reading and writing that do not conform to the norms dictated by institutions such as education, law and religion (Iorio 2016, p. 167). The RomIdent project, however, did not address the question whether the textual products of the polycentric and pluralistic process of Romani expansion can be consistently described as examples of vernacular literacy, in other words, whether they show some adherence to practices that are similar to the institutional literacy norms of the other languages spoken by the Roma.

In the following article, I will draw on data from the RomIdent project to explore to what extent Romani texts on the Internet do or do not conform to institutional literacy practices. The RomIdent data were collected over a three-year period (2010–2013) mostly from Web 1.0 platforms, that is static web pages and interactive spaces, allowing for both asynchronous (newsletters, forums) and synchronous (chat rooms) one-to-many communication. Private channels allowing for one-to-one communication, whether synchronous or asynchronous, were not investigated. At the time of data collection, the presence of Romani content on social media networks, or Web 2.0 platforms where static content and interactive facilities coexist, was limited to Wikipedia and YouTube. However, later publications describing

Romani content on Facebook will be also considered. The RomIdent research team, of which I was part, paired the collection of texts with ethnographic observations in all the interactive spaces studied. Following a brief review of the literature on the multilingual Internet and the early stages of domain expansion of Romani, I describe Romani usage on the different Internet platforms, paying particular attention to how users vary in their adherence to institutional literacy practices. At the same time, the identities represented or performed by Romani users in different virtual spaces will be also discussed. What emerges is a picture of a lively Romani Internet scene, roughly divided between activist spaces and community spaces. In the activist spaces, we can observe closer adherence to institutional literacy practices, in large part due to the need to engage with non-Romani audiences around sensitive topics such as discrimination and political representation. In community spaces, by contrast, where the audience is comprised exclusively of fellow Roma engaging in private conversations, vernacular literacy practices dominate. The domain expansion of Romani thus offers an example of how, in the absence of a centralised authority, the blurring of institutional and vernacular literacy practices can support the usage of minority languages outside their traditional domains.

17.2 The Internet as a New Language Domain

The introduction of the World Wide Web in 1990 made a number of computer-mediated communication (CMC) platforms accessible to a wide audience. Whether used for asynchronous (i.e. emails, mailing lists, bulletin boards) or synchronous (i.e. chat rooms, instant messaging) communication, Internet technologies opened up a new domain of language use.

Since the Internet's origin was in the United States, the initial focus of research was on the use of English and the way in which Internet communication, although largely textual, shows features traditionally conceived as characteristic of oral registers. This register, described as 'Netspeak' (Crystal 2006), is characterised by creativity and playfulness. It involves the expressive use of capitalisation (to convey shouting), of emoticons (to convey the writer's mood), of written-out sounds ('hahaha' for laughter), of acronyms ('lol' for 'laughing out loud'), unconventional spellings ('u' for 'you') and modified spelling to represent dialectal pronunciation (Sebba 1998, 2003). It responds to constraints imposed by some technologies on the number of transmissible characters and also allows for speed typing and compensates for the lack of typical face-to-face extra-linguistic cues.

17.2.1 The Multilingual Internet

The attention to English CMC reflected its dominance during the early years of the Internet (Lee 2016). Early studies on the use of other languages on the Internet showed that English was adopted as the Internet *lingua franca* by speakers of other languages (cf. the contributions to Wright 2004a). These studies also highlighted the increasing presence of prestigious, standardised languages and difficulties in the use of smaller, non-standardised ones. This led Wright to conclude that the Internet was not 'providing a space for diversity in language practice' (2004b, p. 12) and to suggest that standardisation would be needed for smaller languages to be effectively used across the platforms provided by the Internet.

However, further research, while confirming the role of English as *lingua franca*, has shown that multilingual Internet users showed the same creativity and playfulness characteristic of English 'Netspeak', in overcoming the orthographical constraints imposed by the Internet on their languages (Danet and Herring 2007; Lee 2016). In the case of languages such as Cantonese (Lee 2007), Arabic (Palfreyman and Al Khalil 2007) and Greek (Themistocleous 2010; Tseliga 2007), users employ innovative and non-conventional spellings alongside established transliteration norms. Furthermore, Tseliga (2007, p. 135) notes how users strongly oppose the standardisation of these novel codes and rather show a high degree of tolerance towards variability and appreciation for lack of strict norms. Similar attitudes towards standardisation have also been observed among speakers of highly stigmatised and non-standardised languages such as Jamaican Creole, Nigerian Pidgin (Deuber and Hinrichs 2007) and Mauritian Creole (Rajah-Carrim 2009). As a result, shared writing norms are spontaneously emerging on the Internet, often leading to spellings that increasingly differ from those proposed by language planning experts (Deuber and Hinrichs 2007, p. 23).

Multilingual Internet users also frequently switch between English and their own languages. Some scholars have claimed that English, as the *lingua franca* of the Internet, marks values like assimilation and rootlessness, while in turn switching into other languages indexes indigenous culture and thus authenticity (Paolillo 1996, 2001; Georgakopoulou 1997, 2004; Sperlich 2005). Androutsopoulos (2006, 2007) further notes that, on commercial websites catering to a multi-ethnic audience based in Germany, users favour German but switch into their home languages and into 'appropriate social styles of English from the global flow of media discourse' (Androutsopoulos 2006, p. 541) which help to align them to various subcultures (i.e. music fans, Turkish-Germans). Each language and style come to index multiple cultural affiliations and are used as icons of individual identities, including but not limited to ethnicity.

With the introduction of social media networks in the mid-2000s, the opportunities for users to employ innovative spellings, code-switching and mixing for self-positioning and identity performance have drastically increased (Lee 2016). However, when communication through these channels is private and interlocutors known, the strategical deployment of linguistic resources allows users to index different facets of their individual identities, i.e. serious, professional vs. private, playful (Lee 2014). When communication is public, users have been observed to take into consideration the extent to which they want to forefront their global or local identities. Often, the co-deployment of English and other languages results in the presentation of 'glocal' identities which embrace elements of global culture while retaining a sense of local identity (Lee and Barton 2011).

These characteristics of the multilingual Internet have led Iorio (2016) to argue that multilingual online practices, being largely based on written communication, are forms of vernacular literacy. Voluntary and self-generated, they stand in stark contrast to the institutional literacy supported by language authorities. However, 'the rise of digital networking technologies and the new opportunities that they provide' (Iorio 2016, p. 168) is increasingly blurring the distinction between institutional and vernacular literacy. The fact that, contrary to earlier conclusions (Wright 2004b, see above), literacy in non-standardised and even endangered languages is successfully promoted through the Internet (Sperlich 2005; Deuber and Hinrichs 2007; Rajah-Carrim 2009) is a clear indication of such blurring.

17.3 Romani Literacy from Printed to Digital Media

The development and spread of Romani literacy offer an unparalleled opportunity to observe the progressive blurring of institutional and vernacular literacy practices. With the exception of the Soviet propaganda and educational material published in the USSR in the 1930s (Matras 1999) and the collection of poems by Polish Romni Papusza in 1956 (see Zahova, this volume), it was only towards the end of the 1960s that Roma started to write their language. This development was facilitated, in the West, by the emerging awareness of minority rights (Ruiz Vieytez 2001) and, in socialist countries, by the relative tolerance afforded by the Prague Spring.

Romani intellectuals on both sides of the Iron Curtain mobilised along eth-no-nationalistic lines and started to campaign for the recognition of Romani rights (Matras 2015).

Since the fall of the Berlin Wall, various NGOs that included the pro-motion of Romani among their objectives also started to produce texts in Romani (Hübschmannová and Neustupný 1996; Matras 1999, 2004) while a number of European countries launched national programmes for the promotion of Romani (cf. Friedman 1995, 1996, 1997; Granqvist 2006; Halwachs 2012 and this volume). Friedman (2005) and Halwachs (2011) note that Romani expansion followed a polycentric model, in which texts adhered to institutionalised language planning programmes but remained limited in their reach to single states or regions.

Literacy in Romani, however, remained limited to activists and intel-lectuals and texts such as news periodicals, translations of world literature, literacy primers, collections of Romani fairy tales and of original poetry con-tinued to symbolically support the struggle for sociocultural equality and sociopolitical integration (Matras 2015). Yet the need to coordinate efforts among different NGOs led their members, whose command of English was relatively poor, to use Romani in correspondence among themselves. As a result, the written language also started to acquire communicative functions (Matras and Reershemius 1991; Matras 1999).

These communicative functions and the variation in grammatical and orthographic norms are a clear instance of vernacular literacy practices. Matras has characterised this hybrid form of domain expansion as 'linguis-tic pluralism', an approach removed from the control of power centres and characterised by a tolerant stance towards language variation in phonological shape, lexicon and spelling (Matras 2004, p. 13).

The blurring between institutional and vernacular literacy had thus already started before any Romani content was available on the Internet. Romani started to appear on the Internet as the Next Page Foundation (NPF), an offshoot of the Open Society Institute, between 2001 and 2010 financially supported Roma NGOs in creating websites and mailing lists in Romani.[2] From that moment onwards, the domain expansion of Romani has almost exclusively occurred through virtual media.

17.3.1 Activist Newsletters

E-mailing to and between NGO representatives was already an established means of communication (Matras 2004) by the time the late Valery Novoselsky, with financial support from the Next Page Foundation and

Original text	Translation
JANES ROMANES ! - MISHTO AVELAN !	KNOW ROMANI ! WELCOME !
Mashkar le gadjende leski shib si le Romeski zor!	Among the non-Roma their language is the Roma's strength
This announcement group is aimed to provide Romani (Gypsy) organizations and individuals with the international news on Romani language (Romanes). Moderator of this group is the member of the International Romani Union.	
This listserv is supported by a grant from The Open Society Foundations (OSF).	

Fig. 17.1 Group description of Romane Nevipena

later other initiatives by the Open Society Institute, founded the Roma Virtual Network (RVN) in July 1999. Run single-handedly by Novoselsky, RVN 'aimed to provide the international Roma community and friendly non-Roma organizations and individuals with useful information on Roma issues in variety of languages [sic.]' (RVN[3]). RVN coordinated a consistent number of Yahoo and Google newsletters. The most active among them, and typical of the uses of newsletters made by Roma and pro-Roma activists, was Romane Nevipena[4] '*Romani news*' (Leggio 2011a). Figure 17.1 shows its welcome message.

The opening of the message, written in a Vlax-like variety and using English spelling conventions, clearly displays the symbolic and rallying functions that written Romani serves among activists (Matras 2015).

The newsletters coordinated by RVN were used to circulate announcements about funding opportunities (in English or another European language) or about the activities of NGOs and cultural institutions. The latter kinds of announcements were also circulated through other channels to reach non-Romani audiences. They were thus always composed in English or in a European language and then translated into Romani. These translations tended to show Vlax-like features and their spelling was either English or academic based, following a trend observed among activists to converge on shared norms (Hancock 1993; Halwachs 2011; Matras 2015).

Other common bilingual messages were seasonal holiday greetings, regularly enriched by static and, later, animated images. In these messages, Romani was not always a literary translation and dialectal and orthographical preferences showed more variation than the announcements. Romani was favoured in new users' introductions, eulogies for charismatic figures of the Romani movement, discussions about the planning of activities and debates about the outcomes of such activities. A frequent topic of discussion was the standardisation of Romani. Various models were discussed at length; however, none was ever embraced. Rather, each contributor was generally consistent in their contributions in using both their spoken variety and a spelling based on the official language of their country, although showing some degree of mutual accommodation. Members of the International Romani Union were also active on RVN, but they never joined the debates on standardisation, nor made use of the standard proposed by Courthiade and embraced in the 1970s by their organisation (cf. Matras 2005, 2015). However, an Indian contributor employed it consistently and frequently expressed the idea that a standardised language would be crucial in strengthening the connection between the Roma and their Indian homeland.

In the newsletters coordinated by RVN, we can see a continuation of the blurring between institutional and vernacular literacy that had characterised the early domain expansion of Romani. Emails circulated both within and outside RVN showed a stricter adherence to institutional forms of literacy, with a fairly consistent Romani used in translations with clear symbolical functions. The emails sent exclusively to a Romani audience served primarily communicative functions and also strengthened the internal group solidarity. In them, Romani was favoured, multi-modality was often common and variation in spelling and choice of variety was the norm among contributors.

RVN had remained a popular channel of communication for Roma activists even as more and more NGOs and individuals started to use Facebook. However, following the premature death of Novoselsky in August 2016,[5] all the groups he was coordinating have become inactive.

17.3.2 Web 1.0: Websites, Forums and Chat rooms

The Romani websites created with the financial support by the Next Page Foundation were used to promote the activities of NGOs. Developed first in the national language of the country in which they were based, they regularly featured English and Romani versions, although the latter two were often not updated regularly. In some cases, NGOs that had published periodicals during the 1990s also moved their publications from print to online format (Leggio 2011a).

A typical example of this is the news portal Romea.cz,[6] operated by the Czech Romani NGO registered under the same name. The site is devoted to the promotion of stories of successful integration of Roma from various countries and denounces cases of discrimination against both Roma and non-Roma. In its editorials and comments, it calls for national and international institutions to act against such cases and also contributes to the commemoration of Roma persecution during World War II. The default language of the website is Czech, but an English version is also available. Czech news deemed relevant for an international audience is translated into English and vice versa. The content of the two versions is thus slightly different, although maintaining a uniform tone. Until 2008, a Romani version was also available and contained both translations from the other two and original contributions that were translated into Czech and English. Romea.cz stopped producing content in Romani as the Next Page Foundation support expired. At least until 2011, articles in Romani were archived on the page dedicated to *Romano Vod'i* 'Romani Soul', the monthly magazine published by the same NGO predominantly in Czech with occasional contributions in Romani. All materials in Romani were written following the model used by the Svaz Cikánù-Romù (Union of Roma, cf. Hübschmannová 1995; Hübschmannová and Neustupný 1996), although spelling varied between contributions and, occasionally, even within the same contribution.

The choice of news and the content of editorials on Romea.cz call attention to the ongoing discrimination faced by Roma and the need to keep the memory of persecution. At the same time, the presentation of Roma as successful, active individuals challenges narratives of victimisation. The intended audience for this content is clearly a non-Romani one, as further confirmed by the preference for the national language and English. Similar discursive and language choice patterns have also been identified by Szczepanik (2015) on websites run by Polish Roma NGOs primarily targeting national audiences.

Some Romani intellectuals also used websites to promote their work, as in the case of Jusuf Suleiman, a translator and writer from Macedonia (Leggio 2011a). The default language of his site, at the time of writing no longer accessible, was in English, but versions in Macedonian and Romani were also available. The site listed the author's works, provided excerpts from them and a facility to order hard copies. As Suleiman's early works, the website was initially written in Macedonian and then translated into Romani, employing the official Romani spelling used in Macedonia (cf. Friedman 2005), and English.

524   D. V. Leggio

Original text
"... I come from people who is in constant cosmic exile and I pretend to be a sovereign citizen from the Earth. I have the word as the only weapon against isolation, and the written thought is a proof of my civilisational being... "

Fig. 17.2 Jusuf Suleiman's personal website

In his self-presentation (Fig. 17.2), Suleiman hinted at his Romani origins, by referring to the Roma diasporic condition and his personal feelings to be 'a sovereign citizen from the Earth'. He also stated that 'the written thought is a proof of my civilizational being [sic.]' hinting at the symbolic usage of written Romani. Symbolic functions of Romani were also visible in some of the guestbook messages in Romani (Fig. 17.3) expressing solidarity and appreciation for the effort to affirm Romani culture on the world stage.

In both messages, the Vlax-like variety common among activists (see above) is used and spelling is based on the Macedonian standard. However, it shows instances of simplification typical of CMC in Slavic languages (/s/ for /š/, /z/ for /ž/, /c/ for /č/ and /ć/ cf. Hentschel 1998), together with English-like solutions (/sh/ for /š/) in one of them.

A similar Vlax-like variety can also be found in the translations of official documents dealing with Roma and human rights (i.e. the UN Universal

Original text	Translation
Jusufe, phrala	Jusuf, brother
But, but sukar so iklilo tiro suzo lil	it is very, very good that your nice site has been launched
Grattan	Grattan
#4 - Grattan Puxon - 12/10/2010 - 06:50	
ekziekutivo direktori	executive director
But,But shukar web rig so kamel te kerel afirmacia i Rromani kultyura thai chib.Pacav, so, akava si kotor barvalipe savo si dzivdo 1990.bers ani Europa .	Really,Really good website that wants to promote the Romani culture and language. I believe, that, this is an example of richness that is lively since the year 1990 in Europe
Phralikane O Ismet Jasarevic Centro askala afirmacia thai integracia o rromani khetanipen	With brotherly love Ismet Jasarevic Askali center for affirmation and integration romani togetherness
#3 - Ismet - 10/16/2009 - 10:28	

Fig. 17.3 Messages in Romani, guestbook on Jusuf Suleiman's site

Declaration of Human Rights[7]) and on institutional pages dedicated to initiatives to support Roma inclusion, such as the Decade of Roma Inclusion (cf. Brüggemann and Friedman 2017) whose website is no longer available. In these texts, most of them translated by the Austrian activist Mozes Heinschink, the spelling is consistent within each text and it is either using English-like solutions or the academic orthography.

As in the case of RVN, on sites like the ones above, the blend of institutional (i.e. translations, news) and vernacular (i.e. variation in orthographic and grammatical norms) literacy practices continues to serve primarily symbolic functions as part of the ongoing struggle for Roma recognition. A common feature of this kind of website is also the propagation of narratives about 'the true Roma' aimed at debunking views of the 'gypsies' as a problematic social group (cf. Hughes 2013). Activist websites thus constitute a perfect example of the use of the Internet to challenge stereotyping discourses about minorities (cf. Mitra 2001).

Many of these websites disappeared as financial or institutional support was discontinued in 2011. In some cases, such as the domains used by the Czech NGO Dženo Organizacija[8] or by the Decade of Roma Inclusion,[9] their domains have been taken over and are often used for scam advertising. Their proliferation throughout the 2000s, however, contributed to popularising the idea that Romani could be written and successfully used on the Internet even among Roma not involved in activism. For example, Roma musicians performing mostly for their own communities created websites to promote themselves. Very often these websites also hosted forums and live chat rooms based on standard technical templates. Until the rise in popularity of Facebook, these platforms attracted large audiences of mostly young Roma, including members of Roma groups that have often refused to engage with state or EU-supported efforts aimed at writing Romani, like the Sinti (Matras 2004).[10]

In Leggio (2015), I have shown how, in line with the practices of other ethnic communities, these non-activist Roma sites are run for and by peers to recreate the conviviality and solidarity of face-to-face interactions. I observed how on Radio Romani Mahala (RRM),[11] an online radio and chat room created by Kosovo Roma residing in France, the playful use of all the community languages, of 'Netspeak' conventions (see Fig. 17.4) and the music broadcasted by the site owners contributed to recreate the atmosphere of community celebrations.

Both the site creators and the chat room users used the various elements in their linguistic repertoires to perform various aspects of their individual and group identities. Romani indexes the ethnic ties shared by users, while

D. V. Leggio

Original text	Translation
Sadi Styler: {oooo} (gott diesen senger hat hals schmerzen)	{oooo} (god this singer has a sore throat)
U1: /Bajramo-vs-Mirsadi-2009 by grupa gio boys/	/Bajramo-vs-Mirsadi-2009 by grupa gio boys/ [request for a song]
Sadi Styler: {hahaha}	{hahaha}
MiiLKa_qoKoLLaDa*: (ABER DER ANDRE VOLL DIE STIMME)]	(but the other [has] a powerful voice)
MiiLKa_qoKoLLaDa*: (MAN)	(the man)
10 messages cut	
ROMANI MAHALA: ASUN CERKUSI SAR CILABOL O ADMIR {HAHAHA}	you bitter people listen at how Mirsad sings {hahaha}
MiiLKa_qoKoLLaDa*: JASHA{AAA}	jasha{aaa} [exclamation used by singers to encourage dancing]
16 messages cut	
MiiLKa_qoKoLLaDa*: JOJ MANCEN TE ASUNEN MO /EX/ SAR GILABOL	hey do you want to listen how my /ex/ sings
Sadi Styler: {oooo} (gotttt)	{oooo} /god/
17 messages cut	
MiiLKa_qoKoLLaDa*: PISIN PO YOUTUBE [ex-boyfriend's name] (18:38:43)	write [ex-boyfriend's name] on youtube
12 messages cut	
ROMANI MAHALA: MILKA ASUN SO CEROL KATE O DEMAJLI <ALLAHILE>	milka listen to what demajli does here <oh my god>
3 messages cut	
MiiLKa_qoKoLLaDa*: SI 2 JEK LOLI MAICA JEK KALI MAICA MUNRO /EX/ SI KOJA (MIT) KAI MAICA	there are 2 one red shirt one black shirt my /ex/ is the one /with/ the black shirt

Fig. 17.4 Exchanges on RRM

Serbo/Croatian, Albanian, Turkish, French, German and Italian index both their condition as a diaspora and personal rootedness in different countries. Global identities are also flagged through the use of Qur'an Arabic, English and features of Netspeak (Leggio 2015, p. 110).

Furthermore, I have linked the cosmopolitan openness displayed in these performances of 'glocal' identities to the lack, among RRM users, of any prescriptive attitude (Leggio 2013). Non-standard forms of established languages, showing features of 'Netspeak' or imperfect acquisition, went absolutely unchallenged. Similarly, both Romani dialects spoken by the Mitrovica Roma, a Gurbet and an Arli variety, were employed. Mirroring the prevalence of Gurbet speakers in the Mitrovica Roma community at large (cf. Leggio 2011b), users employing only Gurbet forms were the largest group, followed by those only employing Arli features and, finally, users showing mixed repertoires. Similarly, users' spellings drew from the orthographies of the various major languages in their repertoires, although a consensus pattern, influenced by the avoidance of accented characters used only in certain orthographies, emerged through repeated action.

Websites, forums and chat rooms like RRM, unlike the activist websites, appear as spaces where users can 'be Roma with other Roma' rather than engaging in the presentation of 'the true Roma' to non-Roma. Not having to engage with external audiences, as in the case of emails for RVN members only, users and producers of non-activist websites fully depart from institutional literacy practices. Linguistic pluralism does not simply allow them to expand Romani into new domains, but it also shapes their use of languages other than Romani: all languages in the users' repertoires are employed simultaneously. This mirrors spoken code-switching rather than conforming to the institutional norm of parallel translations found on activist websites. Similarly, the standard norms of those other languages are creatively manipulated and adapted to the constraint imposed by the Internet, without constituting a barrier for mutual understanding.

What is common across all kinds of Romani websites is that, since the early 2010s they have seen a decrease in usage: forums and chat rooms are barely active and websites are updated irregularly as both producers of content and users have shifted to Web 2.0 platforms.

17.3.3 Web 2.0: Wikipedia, YouTube and Facebook

One of the first Web 2.0 platforms to see users contributing content in Romani was Wikipedia. Following the launch of a subdomain for the creation of a Wikipedia in Romani[12] in March 2006, a single contributor, Desiphral, started to upload content and within two months renamed the page Vikipidiya.[13] All of his contributions focused on Romani history and language, emphasising the importance of the Indian origin of the Roma. He consistently employed both the Devanagari and Latin (using English-like solutions rather than academic conventions) alphabets and resorted to Hindi to introduce neologisms and to replace loanwords from European languages.

As more people started to contribute, the number of articles written only in the Latin alphabet rapidly increased. These articles, often translations of other Wikipedia entries not dealing with Romani topics, employed different orthographic conventions and retained borrowings from European languages and resorted to English for neologisms. Desiphral, as the subdomain administrator, repeatedly removed or edited many of them to conform with his English-based and Devanagari orthographies and Hindi-based lexicon. These actions led to a vivid discussion between contributors in 2007 and 2008.[14] Other contributors, most of them stating their credentials as activists, argued that, although the Indian origin of the Roma was an important element to emphasise, Wikipedia should be used to make a wider range of information accessible to Roma users. To achieve this, they repeatedly stated, the existing practices of Romani speakers, even if not conforming to institutional literacy practices, had to be followed when producing content for Wikipedia. They saw Desiphral as pursuing a personal language planning project that was making Romani impossible to read, not just for non-Roma but for Roma as well. In his defence, Desiphral stated that the choices of Devanagari and Hindi roots were justified as they linked Romani to its Indic origins. Furthermore, he offered the example of Serbo-Croatian as a language that used a parallel writing system. The entire discussion was carried out in English, but for a single contribution in Romani accompanied by English translation, consisting of a violent attack on Desiphral (Fig. 17.5).

As the dispute escalated, Wikipedia moderators intervened[15] and ruled that Desiphral should not use Devanagari or Hindi roots without the pre-emptive consensus of other contributors, nor should he arbitrarily remove or edit content (Leggio 2011a).

However, Desiphral persisted in his actions, leading in 2012 to his ban from Wikipedia and the decision to remove all the Romani content using the Devanagari script.[16] Since that moment, a message on the revised homepage[17] invites speakers of Romani to contribute to the revival of the project, although at present it seems that not much content has been added over the last few years.

Original text

Ashun DILEA, kon chi zhanel Romanes san tu, ke thos divaya ke konik anda e Rom mothol. Tu san ferdi yekh chorho gazho indiano dilo ke kamel le Romen te aven dile sar tut. Kon chi del atveto san tu, ke nashti phenes savo dialekto lian sar "chiri" Romani shib. Intaine del varekon duma tusa. Zhanes mishto ke nai chi yekh Rom ke ramol kodo alfabeto dilo ke tu kames (thai shoxa si te avel chi yekh). -- Listen, you idiot, who does not speak Romani is you, as you write improperly. You are only a poor fool, you are not Rom but an Indian gadjo that wants Roma to become as you like. Who does not give answers is you, that have not specified which dialect is that you take for "your" Romani language. It's idle to speak with you. You know perfectly that there is not a single Rom using the stupid alphabet that you want to impose (and never will be any). [Time stamp and user-name not shown]

Fig. 17.5 Romani message, with English translation, from Vikipidiya discussion page

As a crowd-sourced encyclopaedia, Wikipedia strictly adheres to institutional literacy practices on its front pages. Desiphral's attempt to implement a parallel Latin/Devanagari writing system was an example of a relatively formal literacy practice and as such conformed to institutional conventions. However, its rejection by the other contributors and their requests to accept existing practices show how the blurring of institutional and vernacular literacy practices has become a widely accepted reality for Romani speakers using the language on the Internet. Furthermore, the discussion on the Vikipidiya back pages highlights how the other contributors, while still recognising and accepting a link between Romani and a common Indian identity, were not willing to compromise ease of access for the wider Roma population by implementing a complex writing system.

While Wikipedia mostly attracted Roma activists, a Web 2.0 platform that has been also used by lay Roma is YouTube. Leggio and Matras (2017) have shown how Romani speakers not involved in activism tend to create networks within YouTube that replicate communities that share a tradition of face-to-face oral communication. They also note how the majority of such communities are now dispersed across the globe following successive waves of migration. Like in the case of RRM (see above), within each network the immediate spoken variety of the users is employed alongside all the other languages experienced by the users. The orthographies employed also show the tendency observed on RRM to draw from the norms of national languages and to avoid characters that are not shared among such languages. On YouTube, however, users interact in various networks. Each network, Leggio and Matras argue, acts as a centre for innovations in the selection of Romani varieties and orthographies. However, the participation of individuals in multiple networks, and the common constraints on the availability of characters under which they operate, results in a rather homogeneous, although still varying, orthography. Despite dialectal and spelling differences, communication across different networks is not hindered. This, they suggest, is allowing individuals to establish connections across previously distinct, and often geographically distant, Romani groups. This happens when users share other interests, such as certain music genres, and practices, such as belonging to the Pentecostal church. However, the authors argue that, as observed in the case of non-activist websites, YouTube networks are spaces in which a common Romani identity is performed by and for peers, rather than for outsiders. As evidence of this, Leggio and Matras take the avoidance, on the part the users of the YouTube networks, of the solutions used in activist orthographies to represent Romani specific sound. The representation of aspirated stops and of the traces of retroflex articulations has always been considered of extreme importance by activists as a way to represent the Roma as a unified nation, since it allowed to emphasise the distinctiveness of Romani and the Indic origin of its speakers (cf. Matras 2015).

A similar use of social networks for the re-establishment of communities dispersed by migration has been observed by Beluschi-Fabeni et al. (2017) among the Korturare of Romania. Videos of the complex funeral rites of this community are shared on YouTube, allowing distant relatives and friends to express their condolences in the comments section. The introduction of live videos and video conversations on Facebook has furthermore allowed members of the community that are unable to physically attend a funeral to be present and interact with those gathered around the mourned. Unfortunately, the authors do not comment on the languages used and how they are written in the comments.

I have only conducted some casual observations of the Facebook profiles of Romani speakers I met on RRM. My impression is that they continue to engage in exactly the same practices I have described above. The tone of posts and conversations is still predominantly jocular and convivial. Code-switching between Romani and other languages they know is common, and all languages are represented using unconventional orthographies.

Similarly, the use of Romani on YouTube channels or Facebook pages and groups explicitly linked to NGOs and activism has not been systematically explored; thus, it is not possible to say for certain if it reflects the practices observed on their websites. However, a quick look at some publicly accessible pages, such as that of Romea.cz on Facebook[18] or the YouTube channel of Mundi Romani,[19] an Open Society-funded series of Romani documentaries, suggests that this might be the case. On both social networks, fixed expressions in Romani are used for symbolic purposes within texts in English or one of the major European languages, both in the posts of page owners and in the comments.

17.4 Romani Literacy Practices Between Activist and Non-activist Virtual Spaces

It seems clear that, on both Web 1.0 and Web 2.0 platforms, there is a clear distinction between activist and non-activist spaces. In the former, content producers, whether owners of the space or simple users, engage non-Roma audiences to present, debate and ultimately reframe 'Romani identity'. The identity narratives produced within such spaces regularly converge in representing the whole Roma population as a single diaspora of Indian origin, often putting aside distinctions based on religious affiliation, country of origin and residence, class and so on (cf. Hughes 2013). The use of virtual spaces to publicly negotiate and re-negotiate the identity of an imagined whole group is common to many diasporas (Mitra 2001), particularly among individuals in positions of material or cultural privilege within the group (Gajjala 2002). The Romani case, in addition, allows to observe how this kind of use and the background of individuals involved have an effect on their adherence to institutional literacy practices. The need to engage non-Roma requires individuals to use either English, as the Internet *lingua franca*, or the national language of the country in which the activism takes place. Furthermore, the very nature of a struggle for human and cultural rights requires individuals to interact appropriately in institutional domains, limiting the use of vernacular practices. At the same time, Romani becomes a symbol of commonality and a rallying point in the struggle against discrimination and marginalisation. Its use, however, has to conform, as much as possible for a non-standardised language, to the institutional literacy practices characteristic of public debates. The publication of parallel translations, the use of Romani for site and page names, the insertion of slogans and solidarity formulae in Romani within messages in other languages allow precisely for that. At the same time, strict adherence to a standardised version of Romani, while advocated by some individuals, is not considered crucial. Institutional and vernacular literacy practices are thus blurred, although the institutional ones remain the main means of interaction between Romani activists and their intended audiences.

Non-activist virtual spaces, rather than serve as platforms for the public presentation of Roma identity, are used to create or maintain a sense of unity and shared belonging among a specific group of peers, generally known to each other through face-to-face interactions. When peers are not previously known, they are self-identified on the basis of shared participation in particular cultural practices or of common origin, although these are always rooted in specific times and places, rather than in the mythical Indian 'homeland' of the activists. Non-activist virtual spaces thus appear as community spaces in which people meet to jointly replicate offline practices, whether ludic or ritual. In doing so, they tap into their whole linguistic repertoires in order to indexically perform their individual identities, including but not limited to ethnicity. These community spaces are removed from any centre of power and their users do not seek to involve outsiders in them. The need to abide by institutional requirements concerning the use of written language, seen in activist spaces, is therefore absent in community spaces.

This results in a lack of effort and interest to adhere to institutional literary practices and in the overlap of vernacular practices ranging from flexibility in orthographic representation, through coexistence of different varieties of Romani and use of 'Netspeak' features, to continuous switching and mixing between Romani and other languages.

As exemplified by the discussions on the back pages of Vikipidiya, individuals involved in the activist scene are not only aware, but even accepting of such vernacular literacy practices. This suggests that even they, when engaging other Roma, might dispense with a more formalised use of written Romani. The coexistence and acceptance by language users of such a plurality of literacy practices is a confirmation of how linguistic pluralism can positively support previously spoken-only languages in new domains.

17.5 Future Directions

As mentioned above, Romani use on Facebook and YouTube has been barely explored. Even less is known about Romani on other Web 2.0 platforms such as Twitter, Flickr, Instagram or blogging sites. Furthermore, even the studies conducted so far have focused only on the uses of Web 2.0 platforms and on the spelling of Romani: the different repertoires at the users' disposal and how they are mobilised within each platform have not been discussed in any detail.

At the same time, the study of CMC has now moved from a focus on technologies and virtual spaces to a focus on individual users (cf. Androutsopoulos 2015; Lee 2014). Ethnographic investigations on how, on a personal basis, Roma engage with different users and on different platforms, on how individuals use their linguistic repertoires in each situation, on when and how they dispense with institutional literacy practices and, finally, on each user's awareness of their own behaviours and attitudes will be a welcomed addition to the growing literature on multilingualism and new technologies.

Notes

1. https://romani.humanities.manchester.ac.uk/virtuallibrary/about.html, accessed 13 June 2019.
2. http://npage.org/rubrique57.html, accessed 8 January 2019.

3. https://www.linkedin.com/pulse/20141002161533-65600778-introduction-of-roma-virtual-network-rvn, accessed 16 December 2017.
4. https://groups.yahoo.com/neo/groups/Romane_Nevipena/info, accessed 13 June 2019.
5. http://www.errc.org/blog/in-memory-of-valery-novoselsky-1970-2016/124, accessed 13 June 2019.
6. http://www.romea.cz/, accessed 13 June 2019.
7. http://www.ohchr.org/EN/UDHR/Pages/Language.aspx?LangID=rmn1, accessed 13 June 2019.
8. http://www.dzeno.cz, accessed 13 June 2019.
9. http://www.romadecade.org, accessed 13 June 2019.
10. http://www.zigeuner.de/, accessed 13 June 2019.
11. http://romani-mahala.beepworld.de/, accessed 13 June 2019.
12. https://rmy.wikipedia.org/w/index.php?title=Sherutni_patrin&oldid=1, accessed 13 June 2019.
13. https://rmy.wikipedia.org/w/index.php?title=Sherutni_patrin&oldid=2947, accessed 13 June 2019.
14. http://rmy.wikipedia.org/wiki/Vakyarimata:Sherutni_patrin, accessed 13 June 2019.
15. https://en.wikipedia.org/wiki/Wikipedia:Requests_for_comment/Desiphral, accessed 13 June 2019.
16. http://meta.wikimedia.org/wiki/Proposals_for_closing_projects/Closure_of_Romany_wikipedia, accessed 13 June 2019.
17. https://rmy.wikipedia.org/wiki/Sherutni_patrin, accessed 13 June 2019.
18. https://www.facebook.com/pg/sdruzeniromea/posts/?ref=page_internal, accessed 13 June 2019.
19. https://m.youtube.com/channel/UC9iP8WfhIm5FXPPsSkoI1eg, accessed 13 June 2019.

References

Androutsopoulos, Jannis. 2006. Multilingualism, diaspora, and the Internet: Codes and identities on German-based diaspora websites. *Journal of Sociolinguistics* 10 (4): 520–547.

Androutsopoulos, Jannis. 2007. Language choice and code switching in German-based diasporic web forums. In *The multilingual Internet*, ed. Brenda Danet and Susan Herring, 340–361. Oxford: Oxford University Press.

Androutsopoulos, Jannis. 2015. Networked multilingualism: Some language practices on Facebook and their implications. *International Journal of Bilingualism* 19 (2): 185–205.

Beluschi-Fabeni, Giuseppe, Elisabeth Gómez-Oehler, and Vasile Muntean. 2017. Funerale 2.0. Riti digitali ed emigrazione dei Rom Korturare. *Zapruder* 42 (1): 98–105.

Brüggemann, Christian, and Eben Friedman. 2017. The decade of Roma inclusion: Origins, actors, and legacies. *European Education* 49 (1): 1–9.

Crystal, David. 2006. *Language and the Internet.* Cambridge: Cambridge University Press.

Danet, Brenda, and Susan Herring (eds.). 2007. *The multilingual Internet.* Oxford: Oxford University Press.

Deuber, Dagmar, and Lars Hinrichs. 2007. Dynamics of orthographic standardization in Jamaican Creole and Nigerian Pidgin. *World Englishes* 26 (1): 22–47.

Friedman, Victor A. 1995. Romani standardization and status in the Republic of Macedonia. In *Romani in contact: The history, structure and sociology of a language*, ed, Yaron Matras, 203–217. Amsterdam: Benjamins.

Friedman, Victor A. 1996. Romani and the census in the Republic of Macedonia. *Journal of the Gyspy Lore Society*, 5th ser., 6 (2): 89–101.

Friedman, Victor A. 1997. Linguistic form and content in the Romani-language press in the Republic of Macedonia. In *The typology and dialectology of Romani*, ed. Yaron Matras, Peter Bakker, and Hristo Kyuchukov, 183–198. Amsterdam: Benjamins.

Friedman, Victor A. 2005. The Romani language in Macedonia in the third millennium: Progress and problems. In *General and applied Romani linguistics*, ed. Barbara Schrammel, Dieter W. Halwachs, and Gerd Ambrosch, 163–173. Munich: Lincom Europa.

Gajjala, Radhika. 2002. An interrupted postcolonial/feminist cyber ethnography: Complicity and resistance in the "cyberfield". *Feminist Media Studies* 2 (2): 177–193.

Georgakopoulou, Alexandra. 1997. Self-presentation and interactional alliances in e-mail discourse: The style- and code-switches of Greek messages. *International Journal of Applied Linguistics* 7 (2): 141–164.

Georgakopoulou, Alexandra. 2004. To tell or not to tell? Email stories between on- and off-line interactions. *Language@Internet* 1: 1–38.

Granqvist, Kimmo. 2006. (Un)wanted institutionalization: The case of Finnish Romani. *Romani Studies* 16: 43–62.

Halwachs, Dieter. 2011. Language planning and media: The case of Romani. *Current Issues in Language Planning* 12 (3): 381–401.

Halwachs, Dieter. 2012. Functional expansion and language change: The case of Burgenland Romani. *Romani Studies* 22: 49–66.

Hancock, Ian. 1993. The emergence of a union dialect of North America Vlax Romani and its implications for an international standard. *International Journal of the Sociology of Languages* 99: 91–104.

Hentschel, Elke. 1998. Communication on IRC. *Linguistik Online* 1 (1). Retrieved on 3 September 2019 from https://bop.unibe.ch/linguistik-online/article/view/1084/1773.

Herring, Susan. 2002. Computer-mediated communication on the Internet. *Annual Review of Information Science and Technology* 36: 109–168.

Hübschmannová, Milena. 1995. Trial and error in written Romani in the pages of Romani periodicals. In *Romani in contact: The history, structure and sociology of a language*, ed. Yaron Matras, 189–205. Amsterdam: Benjámins.

Hübschmannová, Milena, and Jirí V. Neustupný. 1996. The Slovak-and-Czech dialect of Romani and its standardization. *International Journal of the Sociology of Languages* 120: 85–109.

Hughes, Philippa. 2013. Language and the representation of Romani identity on websites. RomIdent Working Papers 23, University of Manchester, Manchester. Retrieved on 9 March 2019 from https://romani.humanities.manchester.ac.uk/virtuallibrary/librarydb//web/files/pdfs/378/Paper23.pdf.

Iorio, Josh. 2016. Vernacular literacy: Orthography and literary practices. In *The Routledge handbook of language and digital communication*, ed. Alexandra Georgakopoulou and Tereza Spilioti, 166–179. London: Routledge.

Lee, Carmen. 2007. Linguistic features of email and ICQ instant messaging in Hong Kong. In *The multilingual Internet*, ed. Brenda Danet and Susan Herring, 184–208. Oxford: Oxford University Press.

Lee, Carmen. 2014. Language choice and self-presentation in social media: The case of university students in Hong Kong. In *Language and digital media*, ed. Philip Seargeant and Caroline Tagg, 91–111. London: Palgrave Macmillan.

Lee, Carmen. 2016. Multilingual resources and practices in digital communication. In *The Routledge handbook of language and digital communication*, ed. Alexandra Georgakopoulou and Tereza Spilioti, 118–132. London: Routledge.

Lee, Carmen, and David Barton. 2011. Constructing glocal identities through multilingual writing practices on Flickr.com. *International Multilingual Research Journal* 5 (1): 39–59.

Leggio, Daniele Viktor. 2011a. The Romani Internet: Language codification and identity formation. Annual Meeting of the Gypsy Lore Society, Graz, Austria. Available at http://romani.humanities.manchester.ac.uk/virtuallibrary/publications.html.

Leggio, Daniele Viktor. 2011b. The dialect of the Mitrovica Roma. *Romani Studies* 21 (1): 57–113.

Leggio, Daniele Viktor. 2013. Lace avilen ko radio: *Romani language and identity on the Internet*. School of Arts, Languages and Cultures, University of Manchester, Manchester. Retrieved on 9 March 2019 from https://www.academia.edu/8766428/Lace_avilan_ko_radio._Romani_language_and_identity_on_the_Internet_Full_thesis_.

Leggio, Daniele Viktor. 2015. Radio Romani Mahala: Romani identities and languages in a virtual space. In *Virtual citizenship? Roma communities, inclusion policies, participation and ICT tools*, ed. Alfredo Alietti, Martin Olivera, and Veronica Riniolo, 95–114. Milan: McGraw-Hill Education.

Leggio, Daniele Viktor, and Yaron Matras. 2017. Orthography development on the Internet: Romani on YouTube. In *Creating orthography for endangered languages*, ed. Mari C. Jones and Damien Mooney, 119–140. Cambridge: Cambridge University Press.

Matras, Yaron. 1999. Writing Romani: The pragmatics of codification in a stateless language. *Applied Linguistics* 20 (4): 481–502.

Matras, Yaron. 2004. The future of Romani: Toward a policy of linguistic pluralism. *Roma Rights Quarterly* 1: 31–44. http://romani.humanities.manchester.ac.uk/downloads/2/Matras_Pluralism.pdf.

Matras, Y. 2005. *The Status of Romani in Europe*. Report submitted to the council of Europe's language and policy division, October 2005. Retrieved on 11 September 2019 from http://romani.humanities.manchester.ac.uk/downloads/1/statusofromani.pdf.

Matras, Yaron. 2015. Language and the rise of a transnational Romani identity. *Language in Society* 44 (3): 295–316.

Matras, Yaron, and Gertrud Reershemius. 1991. Standardization beyond the state: The cases of Yiddish, Kurdish and Romani. In *Standardization of national languages: Symposium on language standardization*, ed. Utta von Gleich and Ekkehard Wolff, 103–123. Hamburg: UNESCO Institute for Education.

Mitra, Ananda. 2001. Marginal voices in cyberspace. *New Media & Society* 3 (1): 29–48.

Palfreyman, David, and Muhamed Al Khalil. 2007. "A funky language for teenzz to use": Representing Gulf Arabic in instant messaging. In *The multilingual Internet*, ed. Brenda Danet and Susan Herring, 43–63. Oxford: Oxford University Press.

Paolillo, John C. 1996. Language choice on soc.culture.punjab. *Electronic Journal of Communication* 6 (3).

Paolillo, John C. 2001. Language variation on Internet Relay Chat: A social network approach. *Journal of Sociolinguistics* 5 (2): 180–213.

Rajah-Carrim, Aaliya. 2009. Use and standardisation of Mauritian Creole in electronically mediated communication. *Journal of Computer Mediated Communication* 14: 484–508.

Ruiz Vieytez, Eduardo Javier. 2001. The protection of linguistic minorities: A historical approach. *International Journal on Multicultural Societies* 3 (1): 44–54. UNESCO. www.unesco.org/shs/ijms/vol3/issue1/art1.

Sebba, Mark. 1998. Phonology meets ideology: The meaning of orthographic practices in British Creole. *Language Problems and Language Planning* 22 (1): 19–47.

Sebba, Mark. 2003. Spelling rebellion. In *Discourse constructions of youth identities*, ed. Jannis Androutsopoulos and Alexandra Georgakopoulou, 151–172. Amsterdam: John Benjamins.

Sperlich, Wolfgang B. 2005. Will cyberforums save endangered languages? A Niuean case study. *International Journal of the Sociology of Languages* 172: 51–77.

Szczepanik, Marta. 2015. Cultural uniqueness, memory of the traumatic past and struggle for equal opportunities in the present: A study of self-representations of the Polish Roma on the Internet. In *Virtual citizenship? Roma communities, inclusion policies, participation and ICT tools*, ed. Alfredo Alietti, Martin Olivera, and Veronica Riniolo, 135–145. Milan: McGraw-Hill Education.

Themistocleous, Christiana. 2010. Writing in a non-standard Greek variety: Romanized Cypriot Greek in online chat. *Writing Systems Research* 2 (2): 155–168.

Tseliga, Theodora. 2007. "It's all Greeklish to me!": Linguistic and sociocultural perspectives on Roman-alphabeted Greek in asynchronous computer-mediated communication. In *The multilingual Internet*, ed. Brenda Danet and Susan Herring, 116–141. Oxford: Oxford University Press.

Wright, Sue (ed.). 2004a. Multilingualism on the Internet. *International Journal on Multicultural Societies* 6: 1: UNESCO Social and Human Sciences. Retrieved on 3 December 2017 from www.unesco.org/shs/ijms/vol6/issue1.

Wright, Sue. 2004b. Introduction. *International Journal on Multicultural Societies* 6 (1): 5–13.

18

Romani Language Literature

Sofiya Zahova

18.1 Introduction

Romani language literature experienced several remarkable developments during the twentieth and twenty-first centuries. Original literature works written in Romani were first published during the interwar period (1918–1939), and today Romani language literature has emerged in new digital forms. In almost all countries where Roma live, books and other publications in various Romani dialects have been produced. There has been a significant increase in the usage of Romani in books, translations and periodical publications written and produced by and for Roma in the decades after 1989. A correspondence between the Romani political movement and Romani literature production is also observable, both nationally and internationally. Romani literature pieces share features that go beyond the borders of a country or a region. These circumstances allow us to speak of Romani language literature as a heterogeneous and multifaceted yet still collective phenomenon.

The term 'Romani language literature' refers to written works that target Romani reading audiences. These can be either monolingual (Romani) or bilingual/multilingual publications in which Romani is one of the languages of publication. I suggest a wide and inclusive definition of literature that

---

S. Zahova (✉)
University of Iceland, Reykjavík, Iceland
e-mail: zahova@hi.is

© The Author(s) 2020
Y. Matras and A. Tenser (eds.), *The Palgrave Handbook of Romani Language and Linguistics*, https://doi.org/10.1007/978-3-030-28105-2_18

goes beyond traditional classifications and consider materials in various genres and categories published in Romani, including folklore, periodicals, oral histories, testimonies, essays, Internet publications, etc. This broad definition would also include Romani language translations of religious texts and educational materials, but these will not be the focus of this chapter as they are discussed by van den Heuvel in this volume.

It is important to note that Romani language literature does not fully overlap with Romani literature. The former includes publications in Romani language, including Romani language translations of literature written by non-Roma, while the latter refers to literary works written by Roma in various languages, including Romani. Many Romani authors write and publish in a majority language of the state in which they live. Literary works published by Roma authors in languages other than Romani, indeed, outnumber those written in Romani. While the focus here is placed on Romani language literature, the historical tendencies discussed offer a general interpretational method applicable to Romani literature as a whole.

Romani language literary texts, like most literary artefacts, were neither created nor do they exist autonomously. Thus, it is preferable to assess tendencies, bearing in mind the context surrounding Romani language literary production and the key factors which impact it, instead of trying to comprehensively review or provide an account of all works and authors, which is impossible in any case. The historical approach is appropriate and effective since the various developments of Romani language literature are inseparable from the respective historical periods during which they took place (both nationally and internationally) along with their political contexts.

18.2 Historical Overview: From National to Transnational Developments

Although Romani language literature is a rather recent phenomenon, its development is neither unique nor without parallels among minority-language literatures. While written records of the Romani language were created in earlier centuries, the first literary pieces demonstrating a transformation from oral to written and subsequently printed texts took place only during the nineteenth and the early part of the twentieth centuries. This transformation repeats a pattern through which other European vernacular languages also developed printing traditions in the process of nation building in the eighteenth and nineteenth centuries (Anderson 2006, pp. 70–71). The first Romani language printed texts featured folklore materials collected and published by folklorists and Bible translations into Romani dialects. Often the persons collecting folklore materials and studying the Romani communities were also responsible for publishing Bible translations in collaboration with native speakers. Publications by Bernard Gilliat-Smith (1911, 1912), who researched Bulgarian Roma, and by Rade Uhlik (1937; Bible. Luke 1938) in Yugoslavia are examples of such tendency.

Romani language literature might be considered belated or underdeveloped only if compared with the written traditions of other communities and languages that are strongly associated with their own nation state. However, if compared with the literary traditions of other state-less ethnic and linguistic communities in Europe (e.g. the Saami in Northern Europe or the Aromanians in the Balkans), Romani language literature publications appear quite timely and 'normal'—such groups, like the Roma, had their folklore recorded in the nineteenth and twentieth centuries, while the production of literary fiction started only after World War II (Gaski 1998, pp. 10–12; Kahl 2002, pp. 147–151).

The development of Romani language literature can be separated into four distinct periods (Zahova 2016, pp. 82–83). The first period began with the emergence of written texts in Romani in the late nineteenth and early twentieth centuries and continued during the period in which the Soviet state established an initiative for publications in Romani. The second period corresponds to the second half of the twentieth century when works by Romani authors were published in many European countries, although publishing in Romani was still sporadic and dependent on national policies towards the Roma. The third period began during the 1980s, following rising concerns of governments and intergovernmental institutions, such as the Council of Europe, about the education of Romani/Gypsy children. This period was characterized by a significant increase in Romani language literary production for the purposes of education. The fourth period—starting at the end of the 1990s—saw the internationalization of the Romani language literature scene, which reached beyond national or regional borders. All four periods are characterized by Romani language literature's fundamental intertwining with the respective policies of the state, region, or historical period.

18.2.1 The Emergence of Romani Literature

While there were some sporadic efforts prior to the 1920s, the birth of Romani language literature is commonly connected to the period

1925–1938, when a large-scale state-supported initiative for book publishing in Romani was established in the Soviet Union. This initiative was part of a greater political platform of the Soviet regime targeted at smaller ethnic communities (*narodnosti*) whose political and social integration would be achieved through the development of their language and culture. The Soviet policies of the time offered opportunities for the 'advancement' of communities and the development of nationality consciousness in unison with the new Soviet regime (O'Keeffe 2013, pp. 33–35). As a result, languages—Romani among them—with no prior publications became literary through formulating systems of spelling, publishing original and translated books, and producing of textbooks. Between 1931 and 1938, nearly 300 titles were published in Romani, and around 20% of them were original works (poetry and short stories) by Romani authors. The Cyrillic script and the North Russian dialect were the base for the standard language applied in these publications. The activists Aleksandr Germano, Nikolaj Pankov, Nina Dudarova, Olga Pankova. Mihailo Bezljudsko, Rom Lebedev, and Evdokia Orlova produced both original texts and translations during this time (Cherenkov 1975; Rusakov and Kalinin 2006), including educational materials, political propaganda, and classical literary works. Even the original works by Romani authors were dominated by the glorification of the new regime and the 'new era' in the life of Gypsies and all the people in the state, exemplified by such titles as *About the Soviet power* (Dudarova 1929), *New life* (Bezljudsko 1932), and *New Roma are coming* (German 1933).

Despite the fact that these publications were produced over a period of 13 years, and their distribution and impact were limited to a rather small circle of educated Roma in the bigger cities, the Soviet Union state initiative for Romani publications from the 1920s to 1930s remains unmatched in the history of Romani publishing in terms of the number of titles, print run, and variety of genres produced (Rusakov and Kalinin 2006). This period ended with a sharp turn in Soviet policies on the status of minority cultures, including Romani. Government policy towards Gypsies changed radically in 1938 when decisions related to ethnic communities, including the Roma, were left to the authorities of their place of residence (Marushiakova and Popov 2017, p. 52).

During the same period, elsewhere in Europe, Romani language publications continued to appear as folklore materials, for example in periodicals such as the *Journal of the Gypsy Lore Society*. Romani civil organizations that appeared in the interwar period in some European countries used Romani language only in the titles of their periodicals to flag Romani identity. For example, *Romano lil* (Romani Newspaper) appearing in the

18 Romani Language Literature

Kingdom of Yugoslavia or *O Rom* (The Roma) in the Kingdom of Romania (Achim 2004, p. 157; Acković 2014, pp. 69–73) each published a few issues in the early 1930s. Still, the language of publication of these periodicals was not Romani.

18.2.2 Developments in Eastern Europe after World War II

During the post-war period, original works by Romani authors appeared in many European countries. While Romani culture was reflected in these works, few were written in the Romani language. The developments in this, the second period of Romani language literature, remained within the borders of the individual nation states and Romani language publishing depended on the various national policies towards the Roma. The developments in Western and Eastern (communist) Europe will be treated separately since the Eastern European Roma formed a considerably higher percentage of the population of the states they lived in and, generally, had a higher level of social integration in various social fields such as education and labour, compared to Western European Roma. According to a classification proposed by Elena Marushiakova and Vesselin Popov (2008), in the socialist states in the second half of the twentieth century Roma-related policies can be separated into two types depending on the general nation-building strategies. The first consists of ethno-national policies that aimed to create a single (ethno)nation, which included measures specifically targeted at minority groups, including Roma (such policies were characteristic for Bulgaria, Romania, Hungary, Poland, Albania), who were expected to merge into the ethno-nation. The second type were post-imperial policies that aimed not at the creation of a single ethno-nation but at a hierarchical structure of ethnic/national communities, usually in a federative state structured on the territories of former empires. Examples of such policies in which Romani literature production appeared as result of federative nationalities policies are the Soviet Union and the Yugoslav federation. In fact, the Romani language publishing initiative of the Soviet Union, discussed above, is an example of a post-imperial policy towards ethnic/national groups, since Roma were not targeted specifically but as one of the Soviet ethnic communities without a literary tradition. The ethno-national paradigm, which generally aims to create a national identity formed around the principle one people–one language–one territory, has been characteristic of most of the countries in Eastern Europe during the post-war period. In these countries, public demonstrations of Romani identity and usage of Romani language were not allowed. Thus, in countries like Hungary, Bulgaria, and Romania, Romani authors published as part of the national literature canon in the languages of the state and their Romani background was not officially mentioned, although it was often well-known unofficially. Romani authors, however, had chosen topics related to the Romani culture and way of life and published Romani language words or phrases in the narratives or in the direct speech of their characters (see, e.g., *The colour of smoke* by Menyhért Lakatos 2015). In addition, some folklore materials in Romani were published in Hungary, for instance (Berki and Görög-Karady 1985).

While a considerable number of Romani language titles were produced in the Soviet Union, these publications were distributed within the borders of the union and their effect was limited in time. The most famous Romani poet of the twentieth century is the Polish Romni Bronisława Wajs—better known by her Romani name Papusza (Doll). Papusza wrote in the Romani language, and her poetry collection *Songs of Papusza* was published in 1956 in a bilingual (Romani/Polish) edition. It was edited and annotated by Jerzy Ficowski, a long-term researcher of the Polish Gypsies and government advisor on Gypsy issues, who also published the most extensive study on Gypsies in the Polish territories.

Like the Soviet state during the 1920s–1930s, the Socialist Federative Republic of Yugoslavia in the 1960s saw the creation of conditions in which Romani literature and culture production was stimulated. Yugoslav ethnic policies were designed around a hierarchical structure where the different communities in the federation were classified into three main groups— nations, nationalities, and ethnic groups (Bertsch 1977, p. 92). Roma were considered an ethnic group and, as such, had certain rights related to Romani cultural production. The involvement of the Yugoslav Roma activists within the international Romani movement (Marushiakova and Popov 2005) and the federation's support for the development of Romani identity politics led to Romani language literature production, primarily in the form of bilingual poetry books by Romani authors in all Yugoslavian republics and provinces, including works by Rajko Djurić (Serbia), Jovan Nikolić (Serbia), Mehmed Saćip (Kosovo), Iljaz Šaban (Macedonia), and Ruždija-Ruso Sejdović (Montenegro). Only the work of Alija Krasnići went beyond the poetry genre to include short stories, tales, and dramas in Romani. Other Yugoslav-born Roma, including Semso Advić and Rasim Sejdić, who started their literary activities in the Yugoslav federation in the 1970s, published Romani language works in bilingual editions in Italy where they lived as immigrants during the 1980s (Zahova 2014, pp. 29–30).

Translations into Romani included works by Roma authors who originally wrote in another language. Jovan Nikolić, for instance, wrote poetry in Serbian, but his works were usually published in bilingual editions with Romani translation (Nikolić 1982). Two Romani translations of mainstream propaganda books about the Yugoslav leader Josip Broz Tito were also published: *Amen sam e Titoske o Tito si amaro* (We are Tito's, Tito is ours) as translated by Šaip Jusuf, a Romani activist and linguist from Macedonia (Zdunić et al. 1978), and *Po Tito* (About Tito) published after the Yugoslav leader's death in 1980 and translated by a team of activists led by Sait Balić (Balić et al. 1980).

In another federation, Czechoslovakia in the late 1960s, as a result of the Prague Spring and the general course for political liberalization and the creation of 'socialism with a human face', the conditions for Romani literary production also emerged (Hübschmannová 1991). The Slovak Roma founded the Union of Gypsy-Roma in Brno in 1969 and soon established the union's journal *Romano lil* (Romani Newspaper, 1970–1973), which became a place for publishing Romani language literature—mainly poetry and short stories—by writers such as Tera Fabiánová, Andrej Pešta, Andrej Giňa, František Demeter, and Jaroslav Fabián. The first bilingual collection of Romani poetry *Romské písně/Romane Gil'a* (Romani poems) was published in 1979. Other publications in both Romani and the Czech language consisted of folklore materials edited and commented by Milena Hübschmannová, who also cooperated with Romani authors, stimulating them to write and publish in Romani (Šebková 2003).

In Hungary in the 1980s, during the so-called Kadar era, two Romani newspapers that provided space for works by Hungarian Gypsies were published, *Rom som* (I'm Rom) and *Romano nevipe* (Romani news). Although the general assimilationist policy did not tolerate attempts to develop an ethnic or nationalist Roma identity, in the 1980s Kadar's Hungarian regime did permit cultural expression, and Roma were allowed to perform their songs and dances. In fact, several associations were set up by the state to finance and control Roma activities (Crowe 1991).

18.2.3 Developments in Western Europe after World War II

Romani language literature in Western Europe was quite rare until the 1980s. Roma in Western European states were publishing in the respective majority languages and wrote primarily novels and memoir literature.

The reason for the absence of Romani language literature in the area was not a lack of knowledge of Romani language as all Western Europe Romani authors were fluent Romani speakers (and Matéo Maximoff for example published folklore materials and religious translations in his own dialect, Kalderash Romani). The first reason was that these authors wished to counteract non-Roma majority narratives with Romani-created ones (Toninato 2014, pp. 74–76). Additionally, until the 1970s, Romani language publishing was unpopular among publishers who were aiming at producing works that had a clearly targeted audience. Both of these factors affect the production of Romani language literature in Western Europe to this day.

While in earlier periods recorded Romani folklore was published primarily by non-Roma, after World War II folklore and oral history narrations in Romani were published also by writers or researchers of Romani background. Apart from the *Journal of the Gypsy Lore Society*, two other periodicals, *Etudes Tsiganes* (published since 1955 in France) and *Lacio Drom* (published from 1965–1999 in Italy), became a space for publishing folklore material and oral history narratives by Roma from both Western and Eastern Europe (e.g. Vanya de Gila Kochanowski, Leksa Manush, and Matéo Maximoff all published oral stories in *Etudes Tsiganes*).

Romani novelists of the 1950s–1970s included Matéo Maximoff in France, José Heredia Maya in Spain, Veijo Baltzar in Finland, and Ronald Lee in Canada. Writing and publishing in the respective majority languages, these authors, however, mentioned Romani words related to customs and beliefs in the works. For example, in Maximoff's works, we find terms such as *o bang* (the Devil), *o mulo* (the dead), and *pativ* (honour, respect). Family relation terms were also often kept in Romani and accompanied by explanatory footnotes, like *kako* (uncle, an elderly male), *teta* (aunt, an elderly woman), *dej* (mother), *sastro* (father-in-law), *xenamika* (in-laws), *bori* (bride, daughter-in-law), *rom* (man, husband), and *zamutro* (son-in-law). Greetings and curses were also frequently presented in Romani.

The genre of memoirs or autobiographical narratives was most common among Roma and Sinti in Germany, Austria, and Italy. Memoir literature in the German-speaking countries often dealt with the topic of the Romani Holocaust, which should be viewed in the context of the political, scientific, and public discourse on the topic after the 1970s, including its importance in the international Romani movement (Kapralski 1997). In the 1980s, Philomena Franz (1985), a German Sintiza, and Ceija Stojka (1988), an Austrian Lovara Romni, independently of each other, each published an account of their lives before, during, and after the concentration camps. As pioneering examples of Sinti and Roma women writing from the perspective of Holocaust survivors, the two authors are often compared to each other (Blandfort 2013, pp. 108–109). One major difference in their narrations is that Franz wrote in German and did not provide words or phrases in the Sinti dialect, while Stojka included many Romani language phrases in her text (published without editing, accompanied by German translations), particularly when recalling her mother speaking.[1]

In the 1970s, the Swedish government started implementing measures for educating Romani children and adults. In the course of this strategy, publications by Romani authors gained state support. While the most prominent among them, Katarina Taikon, published in Swedish, some Romani language works also appeared. Among them were the twelve-poem epic *O Tari thaj e Zèrfi* (Tari and Zerfi) by the Lovara Rom Władysław Jankowicz-Mikloš (1983) and a collection of Kalderash folklore in Romani and Swedish by Monica Caldaras and Dragan Caldaras (1983). Earlier Kalderash folklore materials were also published by Swedish researchers collaborating with Johan Dimitri Taikon (Gjerdman and Ljungberg 1963).

Romani language brochures intended as learning materials for children were also produced in some Western European countries, including for example *Mo Romano lil* (My Romani book, 1971) in the UK, *Amari šib* (Our language, Scherp 1979) in Sweden, and *Amarí čhib, amaro barvalipé* (Our language, our treasure, 1980) in Italy.

18.2.4 Romani Language Literature on the Rise

In the third stage, since the 1970s the Council of Europe has had active involvement in issues affecting Roma, Gypsies, and Travellers especially regarding access to education. Various debates have taken place and recommendations for Romani language, culture, and education of Gypsy children in Europe have been issued (Liégeois 1987, 1994). In the early 1990s, two conventions—the European Charter for Regional or Minority Languages and the Framework Convention for the Protection of National Minorities—demonstrated the Council of Europe's commitment to the protection of national minorities (see Halwachs, this volume). In the 1990s, Romani activism was on the rise along with expanding discourse on Romani issues from other European institutions and international organizations (Kapralski 1997, pp. 276–277; Acton 2006, pp. 29–30). Roma rights were an important topic in the course of the democratization of Eastern European countries. Following ratification of the above-mentioned conventions, some Western countries (for instance, Sweden, Finland, and Austria) started adopting regulations regarding both the status of Roma as a minority group and Romani language education.

Both the International Romani Union (IRU) and international donors and programmes, as well as national governments, identified the Romani language as an important resource for Romani identity that had to be preserved and developed. In the course of this strategy, activities for publishing in Romani and books by Roma were subsidized by foundations, international organizations, local and national government, and non-governmental organizations (Matras 2005). Since the 1990s, there has been a significant expansion of Romani language literature, with considerable production in Eastern Europe and an increasing number of publications in Western Europe as well (Bakker and Daval-Markussen 2013, p. 4).

In this period, the main players in publishing Romani literature in Eastern Europe became the non-governmental Romani or pro-Romani organizations, which were supported by international donors, often with Open Society funding, to develop activities in support of Romani culture. In all Eastern European countries, Romani language books consisting of folklore, poetry, and short stories appeared. In many places, for the first time, Romani language children books, both original texts and translations, were also published. Authors who had earlier published in another language, for example the famous Slovak Romani poet Dezider Banga (2012), translated their own verses and published them in Romani. Hungarian and world Romani poetry written before 1989 was also collected, translated, and published in Romani during this time (Rom Som 1995). Books of short stories and collections of Romani authors' works were also published in Romani in Slovakia and Czech Republic (Hübschmannová 1990; Sadílková 2009). In Romania, where no Romani author was known during the communist period, poetry by Luminiţa Cioabă (1994) appeared, published by her own non-governmental organization, Neo Drom.

While the majority of Romani language literature titles appearing in Eastern Europe were published by non-governmental cultural/educational/human rights organizations or the authors themselves, with the help of grants from donors supporting the development of Romani culture and literature, Romani language literature in Western Europe was commonly published by professional publishing houses specializing in minority literatures and non-commercial publishing. Countries that extended minority status to Roma and ratified the Council of Europe Charter also supported the production of Romani language materials. Publishers with a significant record of

Romani literature publishing include Drava (Austria), the *Interface* collection developed in cooperation between the University of Hertfordshire Press (UK) and *Centre de Recherches Tsiganes* of the University of René Descartes in Paris, Podium (Sweden), and Wallâda (France).

Authors with Yugoslav background who migrated to Western Europe as part of the labour or Yugoslav war migrations, published their works in their new countries of residence, Romani being one of the languages of publication (e.g. Ferida Jašarević in Sweden, Ilija Jovanović in Austria, Jovan Nikolić in Germany, and Semso Advić in Italy and later in Sweden). Italy, for the first time, saw publications of original poetry written by Italian-born Romani authors (Spinelli 1988, p. 19). Romani language started to be used more often in works by Romani authors, who have been publishing in other languages, to manifest Romani identity (Lee 2009; Baltzar 2000; Caldaras 2015).

Sweden is one of the countries where after 2000, when the Roma were recognized as a minority group, impressive number of Romani language books have been published (Rodell Olgaç 2013, pp. 199–200). This was possible due to the state-supported publishing of Romani language works targeted to Romani children (as both curricular and extracurricular materials, including picture books), which were released in all Romani dialects spoken in the country.

18.2.5 Going International, Going Digital

Prior to the 1990s, Roma authors were mainly published and known within the borders of the state they lived in. In stage four, since the end of the 1990s common features of internationalization have emerged, including globalized and Internet technologies that make communication across borders easier; many international events providing opportunities for contacts between authors; translation and distribution of publications across borders, particularly within the area of a common geographical, cultural, or linguistics space (such as the territories of former Yugoslav, Soviet federations, or Czechoslovakia); donors and programmes for Romani language literature production; and curricular or extracurricular programmes for education of Romani children developed at European level. This period is also marked by a strong influence of Romani political activism on Romani literature production (Zahova 2014, pp. 65–96). In fact, the figure of the Romani author and that of the Romani activist often overlap, as Roma involved in national or international political activism use writing as one of the means to communicate their ideas in public.

Writing, translation, and distribution of Romani language publications take place not only nationally, but across borders at international events, for example. Romani writers have also undertaken activities to network and present Romani literature as a common phenomenon at cultural and political forums (e.g. poetry readings were made at IRU assemblies). Organizations that unite Romani authors and promote Romani literature were also established. The Roma PEN Centre, a member of the world writers' organization PEN, was established in Berlin in 1996, with Rajko Djurić serving as its president. The centre was active for about a decade, published several newsletter issues, and held an international competition for literary works on the Holocaust (in 2003). In 2002, in Helsinki, the Roma novelist Veijo Baltzar initiated the establishment of the International Romani Writers Association that existed for a few years (until 2008) and gathered Romani authors from both Eastern and Western Europe. The International *Amico Rom* competition for literature has also taken place since 1994 in the framework of a culture festival of the same name, managed by Santino Spinelli and open to Romani and non-Romani authors. Another annual *International festival of Romani poetry* was launched in 2016 by the Romani poetess Luminiţa Cioabă in Sibiu, Romania.

The internationalization and globalization of the Romani movement have not only influenced the development of Romani literature. There is, in fact, a very direct personal link as the figure of the Romani author and Romani activist commonly overlaps. Romani writers are, with rare exceptions, members of the Roma *intelligentsia*—people who are at the same time activists (in the field of human rights, education, culture, etc.), collectors of folklore, educators, linguists, scholars, or artists in the general sense. Thus, in their literary or any other kind of work engaged with Romani issues, they promote ideas relating to the Romani movement, or their own ideas, about the Roma. Their writings are often charged with political statements and generalizations, and the individual narration is usually closely related to collective destiny (involving common expressions such as 'We the Roma', 'us the Roma', 'all the Roma', etc.). Among those who are acclaimed as both activists and writers (internationally or nationally) are Šaip Jusuf, Matéo Maximoff, Katarina Taikon, Ceija Stojka, Rajko Djurić, Ian Hancock, Hristo Kyuchukov, Lilyana Kovatcheva, Ljatif Demir, Santino Spinelli, Jorge Bernal-Lolo, and others.

Since the year 2000, Romani literature has gone digital. This process has taken different forms and a short typology of such forms in which Romani language literature is published on the Internet or released in other digital formats is presented here. The first type are digitized old (printed) books and materials. The largest such corpus so far is a collection including most of the Soviet books from the 1920s to 1930s digitized by the National Libraries of Finland and Russia and available online.[2] The second type of digital material consists of e-books in PDF format, aimed to ensure a wide distribution of works that are the outcome of non-commercial projects.[3] Kindle editions of Romani language literature have not appeared yet, although some books in English written by authors of Romani background are offered as Kindle editions (Marafioti 2012; DiRicchardi-Reichard 2013; Lakatos 2015). The third type of such material is that published on websites and platforms devoted to Romani culture/literature where usually Romani and non-Romani texts are presented by authors from the same geographic, historical, and linguistic space, such as former Yugoslavia, Soviet Union, or Czechoslovakia.[4] The fourth type, completely recent form, consists of social media platforms on which authors post short literary texts in Romani, where such a post generates emoticons and comments, also in Romani, by other writers or lay Roma from around the world. Finally, there are audio recordings of Romani literature—audio books on CD as a single edition (e.g. Hans Caldaras reading Katarina Taikon's book series *Katizi* in Romani) or accompanying print editions, for example *Marie Claude—Jekh řomani šej* (Maria Claude—a Romani girl) by Ramona Taikon-Melker and Amanda Eriksson (2010). The Swedish National Radio programme *Radio Romano* has also produced audio versions of literary pieces in Romani.

18.3 Theorizing Romani Literature

Looking at the growing scholarship on Romani literature, two distinct approaches to the subject can be distinguished. On the one hand, there are those that adopt a historical approach and are based on providing accounts of the Romani literature production and authors' life paths, along with outlines of socio-political factors. On the other hand, there are studies that adopt the methods of the field of literary theory and comparative literature and focus on case studies of authors and theoretical interpretations of literary works. In these latter studies, however, Romani language literature was not often considered separately from Romani literature written in other languages. Romani language literature production was specifically reviewed in studies focusing on Romani language usage, including its use in publications

(Matras 1999, 2002, 2005) and in Romani children's eduction (Bakker and Kyuchukov 2003; Bakker and Daval-Markussen 2013).

The first comprehensive international study on this topic was *The Literature of Roma and Sinti* by Rajko Djurić (2002), which provided accounts of national developments up until the 1990s. The emergence of publications in Romani and by Roma authors was also discussed in studies about Roma history in various countries (Marushiakova and Popov 1997, pp. 121–123; Achim 2004; Acković 2014, pp. 251–332) or in general (Crowe 1995; Kenrick 1998). Several studies focused on reviewing literature by Romani authors in a national or regional context(s), e.g. Soviet Union literature (Cherenkov 1975; Rusakov and Kalinin 2006), Kosovo poets (Courthiade 1985), Hungary (Crowe 1991), Czechoslovakia (Hübschmannová 1991; Šebková 2003; Sadílková 2009), and Macedonia (Friedman 1999; Kurth 2008). Italian Sinti book publishing activities and narratives were interpreted by Paola Trevisan (2008). Considerable research on famous Roma authors was also produced by the University of Graz within its Rombase project (romani.uni-graz.at/rombase/) and in the Roma history and culture factsheets project co-funded by the Council of Europe (Romani Project Graz/Michael Wogg). A general historical overview of European Romani literature was conducted by Paola Toninato (2014) and myself (Zahova 2014). Both studies aimed to interpret Romani literary development while also considering their entanglement with the identity politics of the time.

Several issues of *Etudes Tsiganes* (number 9, 1997; number 36, 2008; number 37, 2009) were devoted to Romani literature as a phenomenon that demands a comparative investigation and theoretical interpretation. The issues' editor Cécile Kovacshazy discussed critical literature and arts theories that contribute to the interpretations of Romani literature and also reflected on an earlier discussion (Eder-Jordan 1993) to consider whether, given the diversity of languages and authors' backgrounds, one should speak about Romani literature or Romani literatures (Kovacshazy 2009, pp. 4–5).

Recently, Romani authors' works published in German and French were analysed by literary scholars (Blandfort 2015; French 2015), and Romani literature has also been interpreted within the frameworks of Holocaust (Blandfort 2013) and Diaspora studies (Toninato 2014), as well as in the context of post-colonial theory (Kovacshazy 2009, 2011). Scholars have also analysed certain Romani literary works in relation to the socio-political situation and orality of Romani culture (Eder-Jordan 1993; Kurth 2008). The interrelation between orality and writing is an important factor and has been discussed in earlier publications as well (Courthiade 1985; Karpati 1989).

Critical gender theory has also been employed in interpreting the works of certain Romani women writers (Scheinostová 2010; French 2015; Tahirović-Sijerčić 2016).

A prevailing discourse in Romani literary scholarship supposes that, regardless of their national context, which should not be underestimated, Romani literary works share similarities related to the Romani background of the authors and the authors' ambitions to represent or to build a collective memory. The relevance of the *minor literature* concept, as framed by Gilles Deleuze and Félix Guattari (Deleuze and Guattari 1986), has often been stressed upon in this context as Romani literature has always been highly politically charged, self-representative, and used to express generalizing collective value(s).

18.4 Genre Diversity and Genre Merging: Prevailing and Missing Genres

As mentioned above, the classification of genres typically employed in literary studies is not productively applicable to Romani language literature, as traditional genres are often blurred. For example, folklore story and authors' narrative are entangled, and one book can function as memoir, testimony, and folklore. A picture book/short story/graphic novel can be a memoir and/or an educational material, and a picture book may, at the same time, be suitable for both children and adults.

A stricter distinction can be made regarding the genres in which Romani language literature is often published and those in which it does not typically appear. Folklore materials, poetry, and short stories are published in Romani or in bilingual/multilingual editions. Memoir literature, including testimonies and oral history, is only sometimes published in Romani (along with parallel translations). However, at the time of writing, there are no Romani language novelettes or novels. Children literature (original and in translation), on the other hand, is published primarily in Romani, often with parallel texts in other languages.

Folklore materials like (fairy-)tales, legends, and other forms of narratives recorded among Romani communities are the most common outlet of Romani language literature. They are either published by researchers, with annotations, comments, and information about the narrator, or published by Romani authors who may also re-interpret them. The model of folklore material production repeats a well-known pattern developed in the nineteenth and early twentieth centuries, which follows the Herderian model for national emancipation through the collection and publishing of folklore materials, dictionaries, narratives about customs, and traditional songs representing 'the national spirit'. Such materials are newly published or reprinted (as for example Barbu Constantinescu's Romani folklore from Romania). Collections of Romani tales were also published by Romani education and language activists, including, for example, Gheorghe Sarău and Petre Copoiu in Romania (Copoiu 1996), Ljatif Demir in Macedonia (Demir 1996), Mikael Demetri and Angelina Dimiter-Taikon (2002) in Sweden, and Jossif Nunev (2003) in Bulgaria.

Established researchers of Romani culture, who have also been collectors of folklore, have edited volumes of Romani folklore. Elena Marushiakova and Vesselin Popov have published five volumes of the *Studii Romani* series with materials presenting the folklore, culture, and language of the Roma communities in Eastern Europe (Marushiakova and Popov 1994–1997). The Romani Project research group at the University of Graz has published a series of Romani folklore collected by Mozes Heinschink, classified mainly by Romani variety, e.g. collections of Lovara tales, of Gurbet tales, Arli folklore materials, Kalderash tales and narratives, etc. (Cech et al. 2001; Heinschink et al. 2006).

Folklore has also influenced publications in other genres. Romani language short stories (by Andrej Gina or Georgij Tsvetkov, for example) are often based on modifying or rewriting narratives and beliefs common among the author's community. Often, a community narrative is taken and adapted by an author, who exercises their own creative licence, thus producing a new story. Romani language short stories are published in almost all countries where Roma live. In countries like Norway and Argentina, where Romani language books were once very rare, the first Romani language tales and stories collections by Roma have recently appeared (Gjerde 1994; Bernal 2005; Lakatosova et al. 2016). There are also contemporary authors' stories that are not based on folklore, such as many of those written by the Czechoslovak Roma (Kramářová and Sadílková 2007) or those by Alija Krasnići (2005) in Serbia.

Poetry continues to be a genre favoured by Roma writers, and many activists have published poetry books, apparently proving musician, lecturer, and poet Santino Spinelli's suggestion that 'every Roma is a poet' (Spinelli 1997, p. 9). In Bulgaria, for a period of 15 years after 1990, around ten Romani language poetry books were published along with a trilingual (Romani, Bulgarian, English) collection of Bulgarian Roma poetry (Parushev 2002). Apart from the increasing number of original Romani language poetry, there are also Romani translations of verses previously published in another language. During the 1990s, in many countries for the first time, Romani children's poetry books began to appear, including, for example, *Mirikle* (Beads) by Sejdo Jašarov (1996) in Macedonia and *Da bâdem umnichki / Te ovas gozaver* (Let's be clever) by Ata Becheva (2004) in Bulgaria.

The considerable quantity of poetry produced during this time led to the publication of Romani language poetry anthologies, usually in several languages (typically Romani, the language of the country of publication, and/or English). These anthologies present and organize Romani poets and their works within the borders of nation states—such were published in Hungary (Rostas-Farkas 1993), Italy (Spinelli 1993), and Bulgaria (Parushev 2002)—or former federations, as for example Yugoslavia (Šainović and Balić 2001; Krasnići 2016). Romani language anthologies of world Romani poetry were, for instance, published in Hungary (Rom Som 1995), Sweden (Lundgren 2002), and Italy (Spinelli 1995–1997).

While Romani language phrases and words often appear in published memoirs or biographies, such works are usually written and published in a majority language. The few examples of Romani language literature in this genre include Lilyana Kovacheva's books about Romani activism and political personalities (Kovatcheva 2001, 2008), a picture book about the life of Nadja Taikon (Mannerfelt and Eriksson 2003), and Fred Taikon's memoir, which was published as a children book (Taikon 2017). Alyosha Taykon's *From coppersmith to nurse: Alyosha the son of a Gypsy chief* was also published in Kalderash Romani, which was a translation of the original Swedish-language edition (Taykon and Lundgren 2003).

To date, although there are Roma novelists (such as Matéo Maximoff in France, Veijo Baltzar in Finland, Ľudovít Didi in Slovakia, Zlatomir Jovanović in Serbia, and Georgi Parushev in Bulgaria), no Romani language novel has appeared in print and only one unpublished manuscript is known to me, written by Alija Krasnići in Gurbet Romani. The lack of Romani language works in these genres is a combination of the writers' wish to reach wider audiences and the publishers' market-logic that favours higher-return investments and the ability to target potential readers. This lack is, however, not at all a reflection on the authors' inability to write in Romani.

The corpus of Romani language literature includes various translations. Among them are children's classics, such as *Snow White and the Seven Dwarfs, Emil and the Bad Tooth, Pippi Longstocking*, the children's picture books series about Spot the Dog by Eric Hill, and even a translation of the Disney production *Shrek*, published in the Drandari dialect in the Bulgarian periodical *Andral*. Romani translations of adult literature comprise translations of world classics (Federico García Lorca), of the works of national poets (e.g. a collection of poems by the Bulgarian national hero and revolutionary poet Hristo Botev was translated into Drandari Romani dialect), and the works of Romani authors originally written in other languages (e.g. *Kosovo mon amour*, a drama text by Jovan Nikolić and Ruždija Russo Sejdović, originally written in Serbian, was translated into Romani for a theatre production and book publication), as well as popular scientific books, such as *Berša bibahtale* (Unhappy years) by Grattan Puxon and Donald Kenrick (1988), *Tikni historija e Romengiri* (Short history of the Roma) by Rajko Djurić and Ljatif Demir (2005), and *I Romani kultura* (The Romani culture) by Elena Marushiakova and Vesselin Popov (2012).

Although periodicals produced by Roma organizations are usually published in a majority language, many are issued as bilingual editions and reserve some pages for presenting Romani language literature. Some such bilingual periodicals with international distribution and a rather long record of publishing include *Romano lil* (Romani magazine) and *Čhavrikano lil* (Children's magazine) in Serbia, *Romano hangos* (Romani voice) in the Czech Republic, *Romano centro* in Austria, and *Romani glinda* (Romani mirror) in Sweden.

Children's literature is published primarily in Romani or in bilingual editions. Some works in the genres of poetry, memoir, or short stories can also be classified as children's literature for extracurricular reading. In textbooks and anthologies produced for the education of Romani children, Romani authors' works are presented in Romani. In countries where Romani is taught in schools, there is also state support for children's books. Sweden can be considered the country with the highest quality of Romani children's literature. Skolverket, an agency within the Swedish Ministry of Education responsible for minority children's education, supports Romani language children's books in which each title normally appears in the main Romani dialects spoken in the country (Kalderash, Arli, Kale, Lovara). An overlap between the comics/graphic novel genre and educational materials (Glaeser et al. 1998) or books (Lundgren and Taikon 2005) is also noticeable.

18.5 Common Themes and Narratives

The internationalization of Romani literature and its interrelation with the Romani movement, as well as the increasing production of Romani language titles, allow for the interpretation of certain similarities and commonalities, without underestimating national contexts. A typology of commonly met

18 Romani Language Literature

motifs, narratives, and topics across Romani language literature can thus be suggested. In folklore publications, there are often common motifs, such as the so-called Roma-creation myth, the lost Romani kingdom, the curse placed upon Romani people, the wise and poor Rom, legends related to the origin of a custom or a celebration as well as descriptions of rituals, and stories about ghosts and dead people (*mulo* and *čohano*), etc.

One of the common motifs appearing in poetry concerns Romani identity vis-a-vis 'the other'—many Roma poets have, for example, a poem called *I am Rom* or discuss what it is like to be *kalo* (black) in a world of *parne* (white people). The theme of Rom-Gadje relations and the injustices and prejudices that Roma face because of their ethnic background is also customary. Another commonly encountered topic relates to the idea of a lack of a sense of belonging as stated in the poem *Without a home, without a grave* by Rajko Djurić. The poem provided titles for several Romani poetry international collections and—according to the author—is a favourite piece of the Romani-speaking audience:

> Without a house or a grave
> 0-0-0
> goes my endless lament
> 0-0-0
> to my father-o
> my graveless father
> my homeless people
> toys of the wind
> dregs of the world
> Where then
> Where then from here?
> 0-0-0
> to my mother-o
> gentle mother
> where is there a stone
> on which to raise me up
>
> that I might call your name?
> The sky is our cover
> and wherever I fly
> the ground is barren
> without a heart.
> Where then

> Where then from here?
> … a life of wandering
> forwards, backwards
> along the roads
> that time forgot. (Hancock et al. 1998, pp. 143–145)

Interestingly, many Romani language poems explore the 'special' Romani perception of and connection to the natural and supernatural. While some reiterate the romanticizing discourse on the free-spirited Gypsies, often encountered in artistic pieces created by non-Roma, others—for example, the poems of Papusza and Luminiţa Cioabă—reveal complex sensitivity towards metaphorical images and archetypes (Earth, Forest, Wind, Sky) without falling into the trap of clichés that exoticize Roma. Some poetry narrations describe and reflect upon important customs—the poem *I bori našli* (The bride ran away) by Mihail Georgiev (2009, p. 10), for example, narrates the wedding day of a girl married by her parents to a man she has not chosen herself, while Luminiţa Cioabă describes fortune-telling rituals in her poem *Drabarimos* (Cioabă 2016, pp. 26–27).

A recurrent narrative intertwined with the idea of a common trans(national) Romani identity, which has been on the rise since the 1990s, concerns the Roma as victims of World War II. This narrative is frequently reflected even in the poetry of authors whose families were not concentration camp captives or Holocaust victims, but who express solidarity with those who suffered there. Alija Krasnići, for example, edited a bilingual *Anthology of poetry about Jasenovac* (Krasnići 2000), while Santino Spinelli is the author of a short poetry text engraved at the entrance of the memorial site to the Sinti and Roma victims of National Socialism in Berlin.

In Romani language memoirs, the customary first-person-singular narrative voice (about the individual and his/her family) often shifts to a first-person-plural voice in order to make generalizing claims on behalf of all Roma ('We the Roma', 'us the Roma', 'all the Roma'). Memoir literature often discusses topics of importance for the Romani national movement, such as the idea of the Roma as a 'trans-border national minority' (Marushiakova and Popov 2005), of Romani origins from India, and the Roma as victims of World War II. In a recently published picture book from Sweden, the transformation of the first-person narrative occurs when a nine-year-old Romani girl first learns about the suffering experienced by Romani children during World War II. The sorrowful history of the Roma (*nekežime historia*) is related to her by her aunt Ramona while visiting a museum exhibition:

My aunt Ramona told me that we the Roma have a sorrowful history. She wanted to show me more about this, so she took me with her in a museum to see photos about the Roma and photos about the Second World War. We dressed in our most beautiful clothes when we went there.

There were photos of kids at my age. They were caught captives in the camps and *[they]* did not give them to eat. And because of this with the time many were dying. I was full of sorrow when I was thinking about them. I couldn't understand why they did that to the Roma. We are not bad people.[5] (Taikon-Melker and Eriksson 2010, pp. 32–33)

Memoirs also describe the Romani way of life in a manner that challenges stereotypical images and common misconceptions about the Roma, such as the observed hygienic habits in some Roma groups versus the image of the 'dirty Gypsy', the strict rules for behaviour within Romani families and communities versus the image of the 'careless' and 'free Gypsy', or the wealthy family life versus the image of the 'poor Gypsy'.

18.6 The Value of Romani Literature

While it is encouraging that Romani language literature has seen significant growth in the decades after the 1990s, there are still many challenges regarding the production, distribution, reception, and access to this literature.

One problem faced by the authors of Romani language books and their publishers is the low market value of their works. Mainstream publishers attempting to target readers are often not interested in Romani language texts, or even in bilingual editions, because of the assumed low interest among readers and the poor sales figures expected. Thus, Romani language literary production is typically funded not directly by publishers but by grants from various donors. During the transition process in Eastern Europe, these foundations and programmes, mainly from the Open Society network, offered grants to Roma and pro-Roma organizations, while in Western Europe and in some Eastern European countries (such as Romania) funds often came from national institutions (educational and school agencies) to support minority-language books as a part of a larger strategy for educating Romani children. Romani language literature is, thus, dependent on local and political circumstances and is commonly published by non-governmental organizations, non-commercial publishers, or educational institutions. According to some US-based Roma activists and experts, the lack of such donors and programmes in the USA is the reason for the absence of books in Romani language in the country and for the small number of titles published by Roma authors there.

Dependency on external funding has made Romani language publishing—which already has a short history—quite unsustainable. In many of the Eastern European countries in which, during the 1990s, a Romani language literature boom was observed, after entering the EU, international funding for Roma-related activities decreased, Romani non-governmental organizations ceased to exist, and some Roma authors and activists even relocated to Western European countries as labour migrants. For example, in Bulgaria in the decade after the 2007 EU entry, only a couple of Romani language titles were published.

Another issue, originating in the fact that Romani publishers are primarily non-governmental organizations or other entities with no experience in publishing (even individual authors who self-publish their own books), concerns the way this literature is created, marketed, and distributed. Often the sole aim is to produce a book published in Romani, and there are no efforts directed towards addressing certain age groups, producing an attractive text and cover, editorial work on the content, or other similar concerns. A major issue for many Romani language literary titles is the lack of any distribution. The dissemination of the works is usually undertaken by the authors, or organizations that publish the titles, at national or international events or during meetings with other activists or experts (Matras 1999, p. 498). Some efforts for book promotions have been made but reading events designed to attract audiences have not been sufficient.

Both Romani language literary publishers and booksellers have been criticized for not placing Romani language editions in bookshops. In fact, the lack of such editions in bookshops is not only the result of the devaluation of Romani literary production by the booksellers. Many donors supporting such editions set conditions so that the subsidized books must be given for free but not sold. This further prevents titles in Romani from appearing in the bookshops in those cases when the booksellers would otherwise be interested in selling Romani language books.

Ironically, although a strategic goal behind supporting Romani language literature has been to preserve Romani language literary works, the preservation of the Romani literature itself often poses a problem. Today it might be quite challenging to find a copy of a Romani language book published, for instance, in Eastern Europe a decade ago. The lack of professional publishing experience among those who first produced the books meant that many Romani language titles have not been deposited in public or national libraries and were not assigned ISBN. Furthermore, there are even some authors and translators who themselves do not have copies of the Romani language titles they have written or translated only a few years earlier.

Other issues related to the perceived value of Romani language literature include the lack of reading habits among Roma, insufficient Romani language literacy, the diverse content of the publications with which only a particular group can identify, among others. These issues are relevant when discussing how many Roma, apart from Romani activists and Romani culture researchers, actually read Romani language books. However, the question of whether Roma identify with Romani literature, whether it makes them proud, and whether they find it valuable yields a rather positive answer. Yaron Matras suggests a typology of the Romani codification functions, according to which 'emblematic' texts are those which are intended to elicit emotional identification on the part of the addressee (Matras 1999, pp. 495–496). This emblematic function is particularly relevant when we speak about Romani literature and embedding of the Romani language in it. When we examine countries with a longer record of Romani language publishing (such as the countries of former Yugoslavia and Sweden), we see that many Roma in these countries are aware of Romani language literature, know the names of Romani authors, and are quite proud of the fact that this literature exists. This tendency is very clear when Romani language publishing goes hand in hand with Romani language production in other spheres of culture and in media. Furthermore, on the Internet, Roma search for and disseminate information about Romani language literature from around the world among both Roma and non-Roma. For example, several posts in the closed Facebook group *Our Romani culture*, administrated by Bulgarian Roma, have been devoted to famous Romani authors such as Papusza. Despite the many challenges in producing, distributing, and accessing Romani literature, its symbolic value concerning Romani identity and self-esteem is indisputable.

18.7 Conclusion

Romani language literary production experienced several remarkable developments during the past century. Throughout its existence, it has always been dependent on the policies towards the Roma or minority groups as a whole instigated by the respective countries. By the 1980s, developments on a national scale began to take place within the individual countries. In Eastern European countries, as previously in the Soviet Union during the interwar period and in Yugoslavia and Czechoslovakia after the 1970s,

Romani language literature was increasingly produced and circulated. In Western Europe, however, with few exceptions, there were no Romani language books, although folklore materials in Romani were published in periodicals devoted to studies of the Roma/Gypsies. Despite the rise of the Romani international movement during the 1970s, there were few signs of cross-border literary activities.

Since the end of the 1980s, a significant growth of Romani language literary production can be observed in almost all genres, as well as in other publications (media, educational materials, etc.), with considerable production coming out of Eastern Europe and the emergence of Romani language titles in Western Europe. The profound influence of the Romani movement and ideas about the history and symbols of 'the Romani nation', as formulated by activists of the Romani movement at national and international levels, is noticeable across all genres of Romani literature. Despite the general growth of Romani literary production and its international dissemination, national policies are still a key factor. Countries where Roma are recognized as a minority group can typically claim a sizeable measure of Romani language literary production (Sweden, for instance), while others (like Greece), despite being home to a considerable Romani-speaking population, have no Romani language literature due to the lack of policies stimulating such production in the country.

Romani literary writers often feature among those Romani activists fulfilling leadership roles within Romani political movements, both nationally and internationally. Networking among these activists-writers through trans-border activities in Europe or in other common geographical and cultural spaces (in federations such as Yugoslavia, Soviet Union, or Czechoslovakia) led to the internationalization of the Romani literary scene. This process has been facilitated by the increased usage of Internet technologies and various forms of mobility. Romani literature is now accessible in digital formats as well as traditional print forms.

The digital era may offer new possibilities to solve some familiar challenges faced by Romani publishers and writers. It may allow both publishers and writers to reach wider audiences through digital platforms and also to better preserve the Roma literary heritage, since, as mentioned above, titles by Roma authors have often not been properly distributed and deposited in libraries, making it difficult to read and access these works. 'Going digital' may represent and stimulate the interest in the Romani language and its literature among younger generations who, having mastered the Romani language orally, now have better opportunities to read, write, and post in Romani on the Internet in forums or on social media, and to communicate with their relatives and communities on a global scale.

Notes

1. One possible interpretation of this difference arises from the fact that there was an official position of the Head of the Central Council of German Sinti and Roma, Romani Rose, and during these years, it was thought that the Sinti language should be kept within the community and no publications or phrases using it should be published. This was not the case with Romani, especially in Austria, where the processes for recognition of the language and cultural rights of the Roma within the country began during the 1980s.
2. https://fennougrica.kansalliskirjasto.fi/handle/10024/86980.
3. http://npage.org/rubrique31.html.
4. http://gypsy-life.net/literatura.htm#15, kher.cz, http://sveske.ba/en/content/antologija-romske-poezije.
5. Muři bibi e Ramona phendás mange ke áme le řom si amén jekh nekežimé história. Voj kamélas te sičuváv maj but pa godó, thaj voj las man pésa kaj jekh muzéo te dikhás pe patréci pa le řom thaj patréci pa o dújto lumiáko marimós. Amé lam pe aménde amaré maj šukár gadá kána gelám koté.

   Koté sas patréci pe gláti kaj sas sa gadjá terné sar mánde. Von areslé phandadé ánde le kámpuri thaj či dine len te xan. Thaj gadjá pe vurmería merénas but. Me nakežísájlem kána dávas man gíndo pe lénde. Me či ačarávas sóstar von kerdé godjá le řoménsa. Amé či sam nasúl manúš.

References

Achim, Viorel. 2004. *The Roma in Romanian history*. Budapest: Central European University Press.

Acković, Dragoljub. 2014. *Pisani svetovni i duhovni tekstovi na Romskom i o Romima*. Beograd: Rrominterpress.

Acton, Thomas. 2006. Romani politics, scholarship, and the discourse of nation-building. In *Gypsies and the problem of identities: Contextual, constructed and contested*, ed. Adrian Marsh and Elin Strand, 27–37. Istanbul: Swedish Research Institute in Istanbul.

Anderson, Benedict. 2006. *Imagined communities: Reflections on the origin and spread of nationalism*. London/New York: Verso.

Bakker, Peter, and Aymeric Daval-Markussen. 2013. Romani identity in Romani language teaching materials: Visual and linguistic aspects. RomIdent Working Papers. Working paper No. 21. http://romani.humanities.manchester.ac.uk/virtuallibrary. Date Accessed 21 October 2017.

Bakker, Peter, and Hristo Kyuchukov. 2003. Publications in Romani, useful for Romani language education. Preliminary and Experimental Edition. October.

Balić, Sait, Jovan Kesar, and Rajko Đurić.1980. *Po Tito šelbrešutnipe pindžardol*. Niš: O kidipe amalipengo Rom SR Srbijako.

Baltzar, Veijo. 2000. *Phuro*. Helsinki: Tammi.

Banga, Dezider. 2012. *Le Khamoreskere čhavora / Slniečkove deti*. Bratislava: Luludʻi.

Becheva, Ata. 2004. *Da bâdem umnichki / Te ovas gozaver*. Sofia: Iktus.

Berki, János, and Veronika Görög-Karady. 1985. *Berki János mesél cigány és magyar nyelven / Tales of János Berki Told in Gypsy and Hungarian*. Budapest: MTA Néprajzi kutató csoport.

Bernal, Jorge (O Lolya Le Yonosko). 2005. *Le Paramícha le Trayóske (Los cuentos de la vida)*. Buenos Aires: Gobierno de la Ciudad de Buenos Aires.

Bertsch, Gary K. 1977. Ethnicity and politics in socialist Yugoslavia. *Annals of the American Academy of Political and Social Science* 433: 88–99.

Bezljudsko, Mihailo. 1932. *Njevo dzhiibjen*. Gilja, Moskva: Terny gvardija.

Bible. Luke. 1938. *O Devlikano Ramope e Sumnale Lukahtar, nakhadino pe Ŕromani čhib kater Rade Uhlik, sikamno*. Parnoforo: Englezongo thaj Aver Themengo Biblijako Amalipe.

Blandfort, Julia. 2013. Remnants of Auschwitz—Romani narratives and the aesthetics of Holocaust. *The Holocaust in History and Memory* 6: 107–116.

Blandfort, Julia. 2015. *Die Literatur der Roma Frankreichs*. Mimesis: Romanische Literaturen der Welt. Berlin: Walter de Gruyter.

Caldaras, Hans. 2015. *I betraktarens ögon*. Stockholm: Bladh by Bladh.

Caldaras, Monica, and Dragan Caldaras. 1983. *Zigenarmor berättar: traditionella zigenska sagor återberättade på svenska och romani*. Stockholm: Fabel.

Cech, Petra, Christiane Fennesz-Juhasz, Dieter W. Halwachs, and Mozes F. Heinschink. 2001. *Fern von uns im Traum … – Te na dikhas sunende … Märchen, Erzählungen und Lieder der Lovara – Lovarenge paramiči, tertenetura taj gjila*. Klagenfurt: Drava Verlag.

Cherenkov, Lev. N. 1975. *Cyganskaja literatura. V: Literaturnaja enciklopedija*, tom 8, 408–410. Moskva: Sovetskaja enciklopedija.

Cioabă, Luminiţa Mihai. 1994. *O angluno la phuveako*. Sibiu: Editura Neo Drom.

Cioabă, Luminiţa Mihai. 2016. *O dii la phuweako / Sufletul pămăntului / The soul of the Earth*. Bucharest: Editura centrului naţional de cultură a Romilor.

Copoiu, Petre. 1996. *Povesti tiganesti / Romane paramica*. Bucharest: Kriterion.

Courthiade, Marcel. 1985. Between oral and written textuality: The lila of the young romani poets in Kosovia. *Lacio Drom* 6: 2–20.

Crowe, David. 1991. The Roma (Gypsies) in Hungary through the Kadar Era. *Nationalities Papers* 19: 297–311.

Crowe, David. 1995. *A history of the gypsies of Eastern Europe and Russia*. Palgrave Macmillan.

Deleuze, Gilles, and Félix Guattari. 1986. *Kafka: Toward a minor literature*. Minneapolis and London: University of Minnesota Press.

Demetri, Mikael, and Angelina Dimiter-Taikon. 2002. *Pay zuvindo. Romane sityarimata haj divano – Romska ordspråk och talesätt*. Stockholm: Skolverket.

18 Romani Language Literature

Demir, Ljatif. 1996. *Chavengere paramisjora*. Skopje: NIP Studentski zbor.

DiRicchardi-Reichard, Rinadlo. 2013. Born as Sinto Gypsy, must I now become a Romani? Kindle Edition.

Djurić, Rajko. 2002. *Die Literatur der Roma und Sinti*. Berlin: Edition Parabolis.

Djurić, Rajko, and Latif Mefaileskoro Demir. 2005. *Tikni historija e Romengiri / Kratka istorija na Romite*. Skopje: Rkec Darhia.

Dudarova, Nina. A. 1929. *Palo vlast' sovetjen. E biblioteka vash nabut sykljakirde manushenge*. Moskva: Centrizdat.

Eder-Jordan, Beate. 1993. *Geboren bin ich vor Jahrtausenden… Bilderwelten in der Literatur der Roma und Sinti*. Klagenfurt: Drava.

Franz, Philomena. 1985. *Zwischen Liebe und Haß*. Herder: Freiburg im Breisgau.

French, Lorely. 2015. *Roma Voices in the German-Speaking World*. London: Bloomsbury.

Friedman, Victor A. 1999. The Romani language in the Republic of Macedonia: status, usage, and sociolinguistic perspectives. *Acta Linguistica Hungarica* 46: 317–339.

Gaski, Harald. 1998. *Skriftbilder: samisk litteraturhistorie*. Kárášjohka/Karasjok: Davvi girji.

Georgiev, Mihail. 2009. Mo vogi / Dushata mi. Sofia.

German, Aleksandr V. 1933. *Dzhjana njevje roma*. Moskva: Profizdat.

Gilliat-Smith, Bernard. 1911. Jek biav. *Journal of the Gypsy Lore Society*, 2nd ser., 5: 75.

Gilliat-Smith, Bernard. 1912. *E Devleskoro sfiato lil. E Isus-Xristoskoro džiipe thai meribe e sfjatone Lukestar*. London: British and Foreign Bible Society.

Gjerde, Lars. 1994. *The orange of love and other stories: The Rom-Gypsy language in Norway*. Oslo: Scandinavian University Press.

Gjerdman, Olof, and Erik Ljungberg. 1963. *The language of the Swedish coppersmith gipsy Johan Dimitri Taikon: Grammar, texts, vocabulary and English word-index*. Uppsala: A.-B. Lundequistska Bokhandeln.

Glaeser, Ursula, et al. 1998. *Amen Roman Siklojas*. Oberwart: Verein Roma.

Hancock, Ian, Siobhan Dowd, and Rajko Djurić, eds. 1998. *The roads of the Roma: A PEN anthology of Gypsy writers* (Pen American Center's Threatened Literature Series). Hatfield: University of Hertfordshire Press.

Heinschink, Mozes F., Milena Hübschmannová, Astrid Rader, and Dieter W. Halwachs. 2006. *Von den Hexen – E Čoxanend'i. Märchen der Gurbet-Roma – Gurbetond'e paramiča*. Klagenfurt: Drava Verlag.

Hübschmannová, Milena. 1990. *Kale ruži (česko-romská sbírka prózy a poezie romských autorů)*. Hradec Králové: KKS.

Hübschmannová, Milena. 1991. Birth of Romany literature in Czechoslovakia. *Cahiers de litterature orale* 30: 91–97.

Jankowicz-Mikloš, Władysław. 1983. *O Tari thaj e Zerfi*. Stockholm: Skolöverstyrelsen.

Jašarov, Sejdo. 1996. *Mirikle*. Skopje: Shkupi.

Kahl, Thede. 2002. The ethnicity of Aromanians after 1990: The identity of a minority that behaves like a majority. *Ethnologica Balkanica* 6: 145–169.

566   S. Zahova

Kapralski, Slawomir. 1997. Identity building and the Holocaust: Roma political nationalism. *Nationalities Papers* 25 (2): 269–283.

Karpati, Mirella. 1989. La tradizione romani fra oralità e scrittura. *Lacio Drom* 1: 30–34.

Kenrick, Donald. 1998. *Historical dictionary of the Gypsies*. London: The Scarecrow Press.

Kovacshazy, Cécile. 2009. Pour une définition des littératures tsiganes / romani. *Etudes tsiganes* 37 (1): 4–7.

Kovacshazy, Cécile. 2011. Une ou des littératures romani/tsiganes? Littératures d'Europe centrale et orientale? *Etudes tsiganes* 43: 5–9.

Kovatcheva, Lilyana. 2001. *O Rom dzhanel o drom*. New Delhi: [s.n.].

Kovatcheva, Lili. 2008. Shakir Pashov. *O apostolo e romengoro 1898–1981/ Shakip Pashov. Apostolât na romite v Bâlgarija 1898–1981*. Sofia: Kham.

Kramářová, Jana, and Helena Sadílková, eds. 2007. *Čalo voďi – antologie prozaických textů romských spisovatelů z ČR*. Brno: Brno: Muzeum romské kultury.

Krasnići, Alija (ed.). 2000. *Jasenovac: antologija pesama o Jasenovcu / Jasenovac: antologija e diljendi katar o Jasenovac*. Kragujevac and Gnjilane: Memorijalni centar Roma za holokaust studije.

Krasnići, Alija. 2005. *E bahh paćardi ćorrimasa*. Kragujevac: Maškaripe e rromane kulturako / Centar za kulturu Roma.

Krasnići, Alija (ed.). 2016. *Antologija e rromane poezijaći ane varekanutni Jugoslavija / Antologija romske poezije u nekadašnoj Jugoslaviji*. Subotica: Rromane pustika - Romske knjige.

Kurth, Gérald. 2008. *Identitäten zwischen Ethnos und Kosmos: Studien zur Literatur der Roma in Makedonien* (Forschungen zu Südosteuropa. Sprache - Kultur - Literatur). Weisbaden: Otto Harrassowitz Verlag.

Lakatos, Menyhért. 2015. *The color of smoke. An epic novel of the Roma*. Williamstown, MA: New Europe Books.

Lakatosova, Maria Barinka, Robert Lorentsen, and Balder Carstens Hasvoll. 2016. *Romske eventyr og historier / Paramiči taj čače historiji*. Oslo: Solum.

Lee, Ronald. 2009. *E Zhivindi Yag / The living fire*. Toronto: Magoria Books.

Liégeois, Jean-Pierre. 1987. *Gypsies and travellers: Dossier for the intercultural training of teachers*. Strasbourg: Council of Europe.

Liégeois, Jean-Pierre. 1994. *Roma, Gypsies, Travellers*. Strasbourg: Council of Europe.

Lundgren, Gunilla. 2002. Bi kheresko bi limoresko. Utan hus utan grav. Romska Sånger och dikter. Stockholm: Wahlstrom & Widstrand.

Lundgren, Gunilla, and Sofia Taikon. 2005. *Sofia Z-4515*. Stockholm: Tranan/ Podium.

Mannerfelt, Karine, and Ann Eriksson. 2003. *Nadja Taikon. Tjejen från Tanto. É šei anda Tanto*. Stockholm: LL-förlaget.

Marafioti, Oksana. 2012. *American Gypsy: A Memoir*. Farrar, Straus and Giroux: Kindle Edition.

18 Romani Language Literature

Marushiakova, Elena, and Vesselin Popov. 1994–1997. *Studii Romani*, Vol. I–IV. Sofia: Druzhestvo za izsledvane na malcinstvata "Studii Romani".

Marushiakova, Elena, and Vesselin Popov. 1997. *The gypsies (Roma) in Bulgaria*. Frankfurt am Main: Peter Lang.

Marushiakova, Elena, and Vesselin Popov. 2005. The Roma—A nation without a state? Historical background and contemporary tendencies. In *Nationalismus across the globe: An overview of the nationalism of state-endowed and stateless nations*, ed. Wojciech Burszta, Tomasz Kamusella, and Sebastian Wojciechowski, 433–455. School of Humanities and Journalism: Poznan.

Marushiakova, Elena, and Vesselin Popov. 2008. *State policies under Communism. Factsheets on Roma history*. Strasburg: Council of Europe. http://romafacts.uni-graz.at/index.php/history/prolonged-discrimination-struggle-for-human-rights/state-policies-under-communism. Date Accessed 19 October 2017.

Marushiakova, Elena, and Vesselin Popov. 2012. *I Romani etnokultura: Palunipe thaj akana. Katalogo*. Sofia: Paradigma.

Marushiakova, Elena, and Vesselin Popov. 2017. Politics of multilingualism in roma education in early soviet union and its current projections. *Social Inclusion* 5 (4): 48–59.

Matras, Yaron. 1999. Writing Romani: The pragmatics of codification in a stateless language. *Applied Linguistics* 20 (4): 481–502.

Matras, Yaron. 2002. *Romani: A linguistic introduction*. Cambridge: Cambridge University Press.

Matras, Yaron. 2005. The status of Romani in Europe. Report submitted to the Council of Europe's Languages policy division, October 2005. http://romani. humanities.manchester.ac.uk/downloads/1/statusofromani.pdf. Date Accessed 19 October 2017.

Nikolić, Jovan. 1982. *Dosti khatinendar / Gost Niotkuda. Pesme*. Vršac/Vîrset: Bibloteka Kov.

Nunev, Jossif. 2003. *Romski prikazki / Romane Paramisya*. Sofia: Stigmati.

O'Keeffe, Brigid. 2013. *New Soviet Gypsies: Nationality, performance, and selfhood in the early Soviet Union*. Toronto: University of Toronto Press.

Papusza. 1956. *Piesni Papuszy*. Wroclaw: Ossolinski.

Parushev, Georgi, ed. 2002. *Antologija na romskata poezija / Antologija e romane poezijake / Anthology of Roma poetry*. Sofia: Biblioteka Zhitan.

Puxon, Grattan, and Donald Kenrick. 1988. *Berša bibahtale*. London: Romanestan Publications.

Rodell Olgaç, Christina. 2013. Education of Roma in Sweden—An interplay between policy and practice. In *Die Bildungssituation von Roma in Europa. Studien zur International und Interkulturell Vergleichenden Erziehungswissenschaft 16*, ed. Sabine Hornberg and Christian Brüggemann, 197–213. Münster: Waxmann.

Romani-Project Graz/Michael Wogg. Roma literature. Roma culture factsheets. Council of Europe. http://romafacts.uni-graz.at/index.php/literature/roma-literature/roma-literature. Date Accessed 19 October 2017.

568   S. Zahova

Romské písně: Sborník romské poezie / Romane giľa: Genďi ramaňa poeziatar. 1979. Praha: Obvodní kulturní dům v Praze 8.

Rom Som. 1995. *Romane Poetongi Antologia / Anthology of Gypsy poets / Ciganyok Költök Versei*. Budapest: HTSART Kiadó.

Rostas-Farkas, Gyorgy (ed.). 1993. *Maladyipe / Találkozás*. Budapest: Muforditasok.

Rusakov, Aleksandr, and Valdemar Kalinin. 2006. Literatura na ciganskom jazike v SSSR: 1920–30-e gody. In *Issledovaniya po severnorusskomy dialektu ciganskogo jazyka*, Ol'ga Abramenko, 266–287. Saint Petersburg: Anima.

Sadílková, Helena. 2009. La littérature romani en République Tchèque: sources et état actuel. *Etudes tsiganes* 36: 182–203.

Šainović, Kardija, and Osman Balić. 2001. *Jabuka u srcu / Phabaj ano ilo / Apple in the heart*. Niš: Smotra kulturnih dostignuća Roma Srbije.

Scheinostová, Alena. 2010. Ženská romská próza jako zápas o sebevyjádření. In *Česká literatura v perspektivách genderu*, ed. Jan Matonoha. Praha: Academia – Nakladatelství Akropolis.

Scherp, Lambert. 1979. *Amari šib*. Stockholm: Skolöverstyrelsen.

Šebková, Hana. 2003. Počátky romské literatury v České a Slovenské republice. http://www.iliteratura.cz/Clanek/10183/sebkova-hana-pocatky-romske-literatury-v-ceske-a-slovenske-republice, Date Accessed 21 October 2017.

Spinelli, Santino. 1988. *Gilì Romanì. Canto Zingaro*. Roma: Lacio Drom.

Spinelli, Santino. 1993. *Romanipè / Ziganità, Raccolta di Poesia Zingara*. Chieti: Zolfanelli/ Marino Solfanelli Editore.

Spinelli, Santino, ed. 1995–1997. *Baxtalo drom / Felice cammino*, 3 vols. Lanciano: Edizioni Tracce.

Spinelli, Santino. 1997. Introduction. In *Baxtaló drom / Felice cammino. Vol. 3: Antologia delle migliori opere del 4° Concorso Artistico Internazionale "Amico Rom"*, 9–12. Lanciano: Thèm Romanó.

Stojka, Ceija. 1988. *Wir leben im Verborgenen. Erinnerungen einer Rom-Zigeunerin*. Wien: Picus.

Tahirović-Sijerčić, Hedina. 2016. *Rodni identiteti u književnosti romskih autorica na prostorima bivše Jugoslavije*. Sarajevo: Federalno ministarstva obrazovanja i nauke.

Taikon-Melker, Ramona, and Ann Eriksson. 2010. *Marie Claude – Jekh řomani šej / Marie Claude – en romsk tjej*. Huddinge: ERG förlag.

Taikon, Fred. 2017. *Barnen på Tanto. Tantoindianerna / Le gláti po Tanto. Le tantoindiánura*. Stockholm: ERG förlag.

Taykon, Alyosha, and Gunilla Lundgren. 2003. *From Coppersmith to Nurse: Alyosha the son of a Gypsy chief*. Trans. Donald Kenrick. Centre de Recherches Tsiganes / University of Hertfordshire Press.

Toninato, Paola. 2014. *Romani writing: literacy, literature and identity politics*. New York: Routledge.

18 Romani Language Literature

Trevisan, Paola. 2008. *Etnografia di un libro. Scritture, politiche e parentela in una comunita di sinti.* Roma: CISU Edizioni.

Uhlik, Rade. 1937. *Romane gjilja / Ciganske pesme.* Prijedor: Vučen Štrbac.

Zahova, Sofiya. 2014. *History of Romani literature with multimedia on Romani kids´ publications.* Sofia: Paradigma.

Zahova, Sofiya. 2016. Romani literature: Historical developments and challenges of internationalization. In *Roma culture: Myths and realities,* ed. Elena Marushiakova and Vesselin Popov, 81–126. Munich: Lincom Academic Publisher.

Zdunić, Drago, Niro Vavpotić, and Tone Pavcek. 1978. *Amen sam e Titoske, O Tito si amaro.* Ljubljana: Univerzum.

Author Index

Abercrombie, Amelia 3, 332
ab Hortis, Samuel Augustin 71–73
Abramenko, Olga 156, 200, 266, 271, 276
Achim, Viorel 543, 552
Ackerley, Frederick G. 17, 232, 281, 293, 375, 405, 408, 462
Acković, Dragoljub 543, 552
Acton, Thomas 362, 367, 547
Adamou, Evangelia 3, 4, 97, 119, 124, 139, 188, 190, 198, 200, 234–236, 240, 319, 332, 336, 338, 339, 343–345, 348, 370, 405
Adelung, Friedrich von 74
Adelung, Johann Ch 87, 460
Adiego, Ignasi-Xavier 4, 6, 50, 55, 59, 69, 86, 357–359, 366, 373–376, 378, 380, 481
Agha, Asif 497, 506
Aichele, Walther 28
Alexopoulou, Theodora 204
Anderson, Benedict 429
Andersson, Pierre 374, 379
Andrews, Avery D. 204
Androutsopoulos, Jannis 518, 532

Andrš, Zbyněk 493, 494, 497, 500, 501
Angǎčev, Ilija 391
Antonovska, Svetlana 234
Archaimbault, Sylvie 74
Ariste, Paul 119, 156
Arvaniti, Amalia 119, 124, 139, 188, 198, 338, 339, 405
Ascoli, Graziadio 59, 401
Atanasov, Miroslav A. 252, 464
Auer, Peter 333

Bacmeister, Hartwig 74, 75
Baghbidi, Hassan Rezai 400
Bakker, Peter 2–4, 17, 61, 62, 109, 156, 219, 331, 333, 334, 354–359, 362–364, 367, 369, 371–374, 376, 379, 395, 396, 398, 399, 401, 408, 412, 413, 460, 476, 479, 481, 489, 490, 502, 509, 548, 552
Balić, Sait 545, 555
Baltzar, Veijo 546, 550, 555
Banga, Dezider 548
Baranja, Samanta 403

© The Editor(s) (if applicable) and The Author(s) 2020
Y. Matras and A. Tenser (eds.), *The Palgrave Handbook of Romani Language and Linguistics*, https://doi.org/10.1007/978-3-030-28105-2

572 Author Index

Barannikov, Aleksei Petrovič 2, 88, 272, 273, 282, 286, 405–407
Barthélémy, André 55, 57
Bashir, Elena 14, 40
Baucal, Aleksandar 483
Becheva, Ata 555
Beissinger, Margaret 468
Beluschi-Fabeni, Giuseppe 530
Benišek, Michael 188, 215
Berger, Hermann 25
Berki, János 544
Berko, Jean 491
Berlin, Brent 110
Bernal, Jorge M. 466, 468, 554
Bertsch, Gary K. 544
Bezljudsko, Mihailo 542
Bhatia, Rishi Gopal 232
Bickel, Balthasar 223
Björckman, Samuel P. 67
Blandfort, Julia 547, 552
Bloch, Jules 2, 21, 32, 35, 36, 156
Bodnárová, Zuzana 121, 122, 127, 129, 134, 136, 138, 145, 170, 188, 306–308, 310–313, 315–323, 325, 340, 391, 403, 412
Borde, Andrew 50, 52, 53, 57–59, 75, 86, 88
Boretzky, Norbert 2, 14, 20, 25, 27, 28, 32, 35, 36, 38, 52, 58, 88, 93, 94, 98, 100, 101, 110–113, 120, 121, 125, 130, 132, 133, 138, 142, 149, 151, 156, 157, 159, 167, 198–200, 202, 203, 208, 213, 231, 244, 249, 255, 263–265, 267, 268, 270, 271, 273–280, 283–294, 306, 309, 312, 315, 316, 322, 331–334, 336, 346, 353, 357, 365, 366, 369, 391, 393–395, 397, 399–406, 408–416, 419
Bořkovcová, Máša 504, 505
Borrow, George 460
Bosworth, Clifford Edmund 373

Bourgeois, Henri 408
Brenzinger, Mathias 369
Briggs, George Weston 15
Browne, George 461
Bryant, Jacob 75, 377
Brøndal, Viggo 358, 407
Bubeník, Vít 19, 26, 31, 32, 34, 35, 37, 172, 199, 222, 287, 306, 317
Bunis, David M. 238
Burridge, Kate 334
Büttner, Christian Wilhelm 71, 73, 74

Č

Caferoğlu, Ahmet 358, 359
Caldaras, Hans 549, 551
Caldaras, Monica 547
Calvet, Georges 89, 104, 400, 407
Campanile, Enrico 108
Campbell, Lyle 411, 412
Canton, William 460
Canut, Cécile 1
Čarankoŭ, Lev N. See Cherenkov, Lev N.
Cardona, George 14
Carling, Gerd 67, 371, 374, 378, 379, 407
Carrizo-Reimann, Agustina 466
Cazes, Hélène 76
Cech, Petra 89, 156, 199, 203, 238, 240, 254, 278, 280–282, 285, 287, 289, 292, 293, 308, 310, 311, 315–318, 391, 400, 402, 405, 417, 431, 554
Čerenkov, Lev N. See Cherenkov, Lev N.
Červenka, Jan 274
Charnon-Deutsch, Lou 359
Chatterji, Suniti Kumar 31
Cherenkov, Lev N. 262, 266, 272, 274, 282, 362, 397, 404–406, 542, 552
Cioabă, Luminiţa Mihai 438, 548, 550, 558
Coelho, F. 367
Comrie, Bernard 157, 195, 204, 217

Author Index

Conde, José Antonio 361
Copoiu, Petre 554
Corbett, Greville G. 194
Cortiade, Marcel 71, 73, 77, 355, 357, 398, 436, 437, 522, 552
Courthiade, Marcel. *See* Cortiade, Marcel
Cressy, David 460
Crevels, Mily 219
Cristofaro, Sonia 206
Crofton, Henry 50, 51, 53, 59, 76, 366, 371, 373, 407
Crowe, David 545, 552
Crystal, David 515, 517

Dallı, Hüseyin 239
Danet, Brenda 515, 518
Dankoff, R. 62, 63, 248
Daval-Markussen, Aymeric 368, 548, 552
Davies, Winifred 429
De León, Lourdes 498
Deleuze, Gilles 553
Demeter, Nadezhda G. 261, 266, 274, 282
Demetri, Mikael 554
Demir, Ljatif 550, 554, 556
Deshpande, Madhav 28
Deuber, Dagma 518, 519
Dimić, Trifun 435, 468
Dimmendaal, Gerrit J. 355
DiRicchardi-Reichard, Rinadlo 551
Dixon, Robert M. 205
Djonedi, Fereydun 400
Djurić, Rajko 437, 544, 550, 552, 556, 557
Dolean, Dacian 492
Đorđević, Tihomir R. 416
Douglas, John 75
Dowsett, Charles 100
Draganova, Desislava 240, 243, 245

Dryer, Matthew S. 223
Dudarova, Nina 542
Duranti, Allesandro 498
Đurić, Rajko. *See* Djurić, Rajko

Eder-Jordan, Beate 552
Ehrenborg, H. 67
Eisenberg, Ann R. 499
Ellis, Burcu Akan 235
Eloeva, Fatima A. 157, 267, 272, 278, 283, 289
Elšík, Viktor 3–5, 17, 18, 20, 25, 27–30, 32, 36, 38, 50, 91, 93, 97, 101, 106, 121, 122, 128, 141, 150, 155, 156, 159, 160, 163–170, 172, 178, 181, 182, 188, 189, 194, 214, 216, 223, 231, 233, 234, 237–239, 262, 266, 268, 272, 273, 279, 281, 288, 291, 292, 306–325, 330, 332, 340, 346, 347, 354, 391–394, 396, 401, 403, 411, 413–418
Emeneau, Murray Barnson 16, 17
Engebrigsten, Ada I. 490, 498
Etzler, Allan 67

Ferguson, Charles A. 493, 496–498
Finck, Franz N. 14, 17, 67, 407, 461
Fishman, Joshua A. 453
Fleck, Gábor 465
Formoso, Bernard 89, 104, 407
François, Alexandre 410, 411
Franz, Philomena 546
Franzese, Sergio 405, 407
Fraser, Angus 18
French, Lorely 552, 553
Friedman, Eben 525

574 Author Index

Friedman, Victor A. 2, 4, 25, 31, 62, 63, 134, 137, 149, 156, 157, 164, 190, 199, 206, 208, 231–238, 240, 241, 244, 247, 248, 250–252, 267, 277, 281, 283, 284, 289, 292, 332, 335, 336, 338, 370, 392, 395, 405, 411, 414, 435, 438, 439, 463, 472, 475, 515, 520, 523

G

Gabarri, Israel 373, 379
Gajjala, Radhika 531
Gamella, Juan F. 356, 360, 366, 378, 379, 506–508
Ganander, Christfrid 70
Gardner, David J. 119, 121, 122, 125, 311
Garrett, Paul B. 503
Gaski, Harald 541
Gay Y Blasco, Paloma 508
Georgakopoulou, Alexandra 518
Georgiev, Mihail 558
German, Aleksandr V. 542
Gilliat-Smith, Bernard J. 28, 233, 241, 264, 270, 276, 282, 397, 398, 401, 461, 475, 497, 498, 541
Gjerde, Lars 554
Gjerdman, Olof 2, 373, 374, 405, 547
Glaeser, Ursula 556
Göksel, Aslı 240, 241
Graffunder, Alfred 17
Grannes, Alf 233
Granqvist, Kimmo 17, 119, 138, 139, 163, 332, 336, 370, 393, 408, 462, 520
Grant, Anthony P. 25, 404
Greenberg, Joseph H. 355
Grienig, Gregor 261
Grierson, George Abraham 2, 16, 20, 21, 40
Grigorova, Evelina 119, 339

Gumperz, John 499
Gvozdanović, Jadranka 281

H

Haig, Geoffrey 198
Hajská, Markéta 501
Halwachs, Dieter W. 1, 2, 4, 89, 202, 203, 306, 307, 316, 323, 332, 403, 431, 443, 453, 454, 475, 476, 516, 520, 521, 547
Hamp, Eric P. 40
Hancock, Ian F. 2, 14, 20, 25, 26, 40, 98, 100, 107, 108, 262, 264, 331, 333, 334, 354, 367–369, 396, 398, 405, 521, 550, 558
Harris, Alice C. 128
Haspelmath, Martin 91, 97, 195, 233, 336, 347
Haugen, Einar 331, 436
Heine, Bernd 336
Heinschink, Mozes F. 89, 199, 203, 238, 263, 268, 278, 280–282, 285, 287, 289, 292, 293, 308, 310, 311, 315–318, 391, 400, 402, 405, 417, 431, 525, 554
Heller, Monica 429
Hentschel, Elke 524
Herin, Bruno 14
Herring, Susan 515, 518
Hervás y Panduro, Lorenzo 86
Heuvel, Wilco van den 4, 395, 404, 405, 410, 414, 416, 465, 540
Hill, John M. 69
Hill, Nathan W. 255
Hock, Hans Henrich 14
Holzinger, Daniel 2, 147, 156, 202, 333, 407
Hornberger, Nancy 453
Hualde, José Ignacio 136
Hübschmann, Heinrich 98
Hübschmannová, Milena 37, 156, 172, 268, 272, 273, 279, 287, 306,

317, 403, 434, 463, 502, 515, 520, 523, 545, 548, 552
Hughes, Philippa 516, 525, 531
Hutterer, Miklós 306–310, 312, 313, 322, 323, 405

Iggesen, Oliver A. 194
Igla, Birgit 2, 14, 20, 27, 28, 32, 36, 38, 88, 94, 98, 101, 110–113, 120, 124, 132, 145, 149, 156, 157, 190, 192, 197, 198, 231, 235, 240, 251, 264, 266, 271, 273, 275, 277–281, 284, 286–288, 292, 309, 312, 313, 315, 316, 332, 334–336, 353, 357, 358, 369, 393, 399–402, 404, 405, 408–414
Iorio, Josh 516, 519
Irvine, Francis 377
Ivanov, Ivan 240

Jašarov, Sejdo 555
Ješina, Josef 274, 278, 279
Jordan, Charles Etienne 67, 68
Jusuf, Šaip 235, 435, 545, 550

Kačová, Veronika 492
Kahl, Thede 541
Kahraman, S. 62
Kalina, Antoine 272, 273, 278, 279
Kalinin, Valdemar 468, 469, 474, 475, 479, 542, 552
Kaplan, Robert B. 429
Kappler, Matthias 248
Kapralski, Slawomir 546, 547
Karpati, Mirella 552

Kaufman, Terrence 331, 333, 344, 367, 373, 398
Kazazis, Kostas 234
Keenan, Edward 204
Kenrick, Donald S. 2, 362, 364, 367, 369, 371, 373, 401, 506, 507, 552, 556
Kepeski, Krume 235, 435
Kiefer, Ferenc 318
Kluge, Friedrich 373
Kluyver, A. 50, 54, 55
Knauer, Georg Nicolaus 50–52, 58
Kochanowski, Vania de Gila 2, 26, 397, 546
Kolliakou, Dimitra 192
Kolmanová, Martina 491
König, Werner 104
Kopernicki, Isidore 273
Koptjevskaja-Tamm, Maria 31, 106, 157, 163, 192, 193
Kostov, Kiril 2, 250, 264, 266, 274, 277, 279, 280, 288, 289, 293
Kovacshazy, Cécile 552
Kovatcheva, Lilyana 550
Kralčák, Ľubomír 265
Kramářová, Jana 554
Krasnići, Alija 544, 554, 555, 558
Krinková, Zuzana 373, 379, 408
Kubaník, Pavel 4, 493, 494, 496–503, 505
Kuiper, Franciscus Bernardus Jacobus 15
Kurth, Gérald 552
Kuteva, Tania 336
Kyuchukov, Hristo 4, 248, 476, 479, 491, 492, 497, 499, 550, 552

Labov, William 240
Laederich, Stéphane 362
Lakatos, Menyhért 544, 551

Author Index

Lakatosova, Maria Barinka 554
Lazzeroni, Romano 108
Leblon, Bernard 59
Lee, Carmen 515, 518, 519, 532
Lee, Ronald 546, 549
Leggio, Daniele Viktor 3, 4, 188, 270, 273, 279, 288, 292, 332, 392, 405, 411, 417, 467, 476, 515, 516, 521–523, 525, 526, 528, 529
Leland, Charles Godfrey 39
Lemon, Alaina 4
Leschber, Corinna 332
Lesný, Vincent 14
LeVine, Robert 498
Lewis, G. 240
Lewis, Martin 3
Liddicoat, Anthony J. 429
Liégeois, Jean-Pierre 547
Lípa, Jiří 164, 279, 281, 391, 393, 403, 404, 416
Ljungberg, Erik 2, 405, 436, 547
Lorimer, David Lockhart Robertson 14
Ludolfus, Iob 65, 86
Lundgren, Gunilla 555, 556

M

Macalister, Robert Alexander Stewart 14
MacRitchie, David 50, 51
Malchukov, Andrej 195
Malone, Susane 482
Mann, S. 405
Mannerfelt, Karine 555
Mānušs, Leksa 17, 27, 407
Marafioti, Oksana 551
Marsden, William 75
Marushiakova, Elena 4, 17, 393, 468, 542–544, 552, 554, 556, 558
Masica, Colin P. 14, 20, 23, 26, 27, 29–32, 37

Matras, Yaron 1–6, 14, 16–20, 23, 25, 26, 28, 30–32, 34–36, 38, 39, 52, 53, 61, 66, 73–75, 87, 90, 93, 95, 97–99, 102, 103, 105, 107–110, 112, 120, 122, 124, 126, 128, 131, 133–135, 137–139, 141–143, 145–151, 156, 159–161, 163–165, 167, 168, 170–173, 178, 182, 187–191, 196, 197, 202–204, 206, 207, 216–218, 221–223, 231, 233, 234, 237–240, 249, 252, 254, 262, 264, 266, 267, 271–275, 277, 278, 280, 283–285, 287–289, 292, 293, 306, 310, 312–314, 316, 319, 321, 322, 324, 330–339, 341–348, 354–357, 360, 362, 364–373, 376, 378–380, 391–394, 396, 398–401, 404, 405, 407–418, 433, 434, 437, 451, 453, 454, 461, 462, 464, 467, 469, 475, 477, 478, 490, 500, 502, 506–508, 515, 516, 519–522, 525, 529, 530, 548, 552, 560, 561
Mayrhofer, Manfred 15
McDaniel, Dana 3
McGowan, Alan 60, 61, 363
McLane, Merrill F. 356, 366
Meakins, Felicity 355
Megiser, Hyeronimus 64
Meli, Giulia 106
Mesárošová, Margita 492
Messing, Gordon M. 233, 235, 251
Mészáros, György 306–310, 312, 313, 318, 321–324, 404, 405, 407
Meyer, Anna-Maria 4, 262, 264, 265, 268, 271, 273, 282, 291, 338, 340
Michel, Francisque 374
Miklosich, Franz 20, 21, 25, 27, 28, 38, 50, 52, 53, 56, 59, 76, 88, 126, 263, 397

Author Index 577

Miller, Peggy 263, 499
Miltner, Vladimír 156, 271
Minkov, Michael 267, 271, 280, 284, 400
Miskow, Johan 358, 407, 462
Mišeska-Tomić, Olga 275
Mitra, Ananda 525, 531
Montoya, Juan Ramón 373, 379
Moore, Leslie C. 499, 501
Münster, Sebastian 86
Muysken, Pieter 378
Myers-Scotton, Carol 356, 367, 370

N

Nichols, Johanna 223
Nikolić, Jovan 544, 545, 549, 556
Nord, Christiane 470
Nunev, Jossif 554

O

Ochs, Elinor 490, 493, 498, 500
Okely, Judith 1
Ondráčková, Zuzana 496
Orengo, Alessandro 94, 100, 101
Oslon, Mixail V. 19, 26, 30, 405
O'Keeffe, Brigid 4

P

Padure, Cristian 344
Pallas, Peter Simon 74, 75, 87
Pančenko, Januš Aleksandrovič 279
Paolillo, John C. 518
Parushev, Georgi 554, 555
Paspati, Alexandre G. 63, 64, 112, 236, 396–398, 400
Paul, Hermann 368
Payne, John 193
Payne, Mark 4
Pereltsvaig, Asya 3

Petulengro. *See* Gilliat-Smith, Bernard J.
Piasere, Leonardo 60
Pirttisaari, Helena 156
Pischel, Richard 21, 30
Plank, Frans 157, 193
Pobożniak, Tadeusz 2, 405
Podolinská, Tatiana 466
Polgáriová, Erika 492
Poplack, Shana 263
Popov, Veselin 4, 17, 393, 468, 542–544, 552, 554, 556, 558
Pott, August Friedrich 1, 25, 27, 38, 50, 55, 57, 76, 87–89, 109, 331
Przyluski, Jean 15
Puchmayer, Anton J. 284, 403
Puscher, Wilfried 271
Puxon, Grattan 556

R

Rácová, Anna 264, 265, 267–272, 278, 279, 282, 286, 288, 291–293
Rajah-Carrim, Aaliya 518, 519
Ranking, D. 60
Réger, Zita 332, 359, 492–494, 496–499, 501
Reinecke, John E. 368
Rézműves, Melinda 437
Ridler, Ann 460
Ries, Johannes 464, 466
Rijkhoff, Jan 334
Rishi, Weer Rajendra 26
Rodell Olgaç, Christina 549
Rostas-Farkas, Gyorgy 555
Rozwadowski, Jan 403
Ruch, Martin 73
Rüdiger, Johann Christian Christoph 38, 49, 73–75, 87
Ruiz Vieytez, Eduardo Javier 519
Rusakov, Aleksandr Yur'evič 157, 267, 272, 278, 282–284, 286, 289

Author Index

S

Sabaini, Astrid 405, 474
Sadílková, Helena 548, 552, 554
Šainović, Kardija 555
Samer, Helmut 261
Sampson, John 2, 14, 21, 27, 32, 35, 38, 51, 53, 57, 61, 75, 88, 89, 106, 113, 199, 232, 353, 354, 407, 431
Sarău, Gheorghe 401, 438, 554
Sasse, Hans-Jürgen 196, 369
Scala, Andrea 4, 14, 25, 27, 98, 100, 101, 103, 105, 109, 136, 147, 337, 346, 365
Scheinostová, Alena 553
Scherp, Lambert 436, 547
Schieffelin, Bambi B. 493, 498, 499
Schmid, Wolfgang P. 37, 156
Schrammel, Barbara 156, 318, 464, 474, 482
Schrammel-Leber, Barbara. *See* Schrammel, Barbara
Schuchardt, Hugo 368
Schulman, Veronica 400
Schultze, Benjamin 74
Schulzius, Benjaminus. *See* Schultze, Benjamin
Searle, J. 500
Sebba, Mark 517
Šebková, Hana 268, 272, 273, 279, 286, 552
Sechidou, Irene 238, 286, 357, 400
Semiletko, V'jačeslav 266, 272, 274
Sergievskij, Maksim Vladimirovič 88, 276, 286, 292, 407
Sharma, Ram Sharan 15
Sikimić, Biljana 416
Silverman, Carol 4
Šiškov, Stoju N. 233
Škaljić, Abdulah 233
Skendi, Stavro 253
Skok, Petar 253
Slavkova, Magdalena 462–465, 479

Slobin, Dan Isaac 490
Smart, Bath C. 366, 371, 373, 407
Soravia, Giulio 27, 39, 88, 94, 113, 401, 402, 405, 407
Southworth, Franklin 20
Sowa, Rudolf von 285, 403, 407
Sperlich, Wolfgang B. 518, 519
Spinelli, Santino 549, 550, 554, 555, 558
Spolsky, Bernard 429
Stewart, Michael 3, 6, 500
Stojka, Ceija 546, 547, 550
Stolz, Thomas 218
Stump, Gregory 157
Suleiman, Jusuf 523, 524
Sutherland, Anne 3
Swadesh, Morris 93
Szczepanik, Marta 523

T

Tadmor, Uri 91, 93, 233, 336, 347, 355
Tagare, Ganesh Vasudev 26
Tahirović-Sijerčić, Hedina 553
Taikon, Fred 555
Taikon-Melker, Ramona 551, 559
Tálos, Endre 19, 27, 28
Tauber, Elizabeth 3, 498, 499
Taykon, Alyosha 555
Tcherenkov, Lev Nikolaevič. *See* Cherenkov, Lev N.
Tekin, Talat 248
Tenser, Anton 147, 188, 206, 207, 218, 263, 269, 276, 284, 293, 336, 343, 406, 407
Themistocleous, Christiana 518
Theokharidēs, Petros D. 233
Thesleff, Arthur 17, 408
Thomason, Sarah Grey 331, 344, 356, 367, 373
Thurfjell, David 464
Toninato, Paola 546, 552

Author Index 579

Toropov, Vadim Germanovič 25, 265, 266, 272, 273, 400
Trevisan, Paola 552
Triandaphyllidis, Manolis A. 358
Tseliga, Theodora 518
Turner, Ralph Lilley 2, 14, 17, 21–24, 27, 28, 32, 33, 38, 40, 482
Tzitzilis, Christos 25

Uhlik, Rade 277, 402, 416, 461, 541
Urech, Evelyne 395, 404, 405, 410, 414, 416, 465

Valet, Joseph 407
Vallmitjana, Juli 375
Valtonen, Pertti 27, 70, 89, 112, 408, 462
van der Voort, Hein 2, 357
Vekerdi, József 15, 65, 88, 122, 312, 323–325, 402, 404, 414
Vencel', Tatjana V. *See* Ventcel, Tatjana V.
Ventcel, Tatjana V. 2, 264, 270, 274, 276, 293, 397, 407
Verhoeven, Elisabeth 220
Versteegh, Kees 355, 365
Vulcanius, B. 50, 58, 76, 86–88

Wagner, Max L. 57
Wagner, Peter 405, 417
Wallaszky, Paullus 72
Weinreich, Matthias 14
Wentzel, Tatjana W. *See* Ventcel, Tatjana V.
Wiedner, Jakob 4, 312, 317–319, 323, 338, 340, 407
Willems, Wim 1, 72, 73
Windfuhr, Gernot L. 400
Windstedt, E. 68
Wogg, Michael 202, 203, 306, 307, 323, 552
Wohlgemuth, Jan 157
Wolf, Siegmund A. 27, 88, 106
Woolner, Alfred C. 2, 15, 21, 22, 31, 32, 156
Wlislocki, Heinrich von 404
Wright, Susan 429

Zahova, Sofiya 4, 433, 463, 464, 468, 480, 502, 519, 541, 544, 549, 552
Zdunić, Drago 545
Zoller, Claus Peter 23, 24, 40

Dialect Index

A

Abruzzian 96, 102, 103, 136, 147, 159, 183. *See also* Southern Italian
Agia Varvara 145, 172, 173, 176, 177, 182, 192, 216, 235, 237, 239–241, 251, 335, 336, 405
Ajia Varvara. *See* Agia Varvara
Ajios Athanasios 160, 161, 169, 238, 400
Angloromani 3, 54, 61, 75, 264, 331, 356, 362, 364, 366–369, 371, 372, 376, 378, 379
Anglo-Romani. *See* Angloromani
Apennine. *See* Southern Italian
Arli
    Florina Arli 241, 246
    Karditsa Arli 237
    Kosovan Arli 138, 146, 278
    Kriva Palanka Arli 249–251
    Macedonian Arli 137, 146, 198, 235, 273, 289, 343, 474
    Montenegrin Arli 272
    Prilep Arli 273
    Skopje Arli 160, 161, 238, 248
Arlije. *See* Arli

B

Bačkačjke 279
Balkan group 393
    North Balkan 410
    South Balkan 402, 410
Basque 17, 55, 71, 338, 356–358, 362–364, 373, 374, 408
Bergitka 140, 262, 264, 265, 277, 291, 343
Bohemian 57, 58, 180, 183, 273, 274, 283–285, 403
British 54, 61, 62, 75, 234, 339, 340, 367, 368, 399, 407, 460, 461. *See also* Angloromani; English Romani; Welsh
Bugurdži 138, 140, 199, 236, 266, 268, 273, 283, 366, 401, 438, 439
    Kosovan Bugurdži 265, 267, 275
    Serbian Bugurdži 267
Burgenland. *See* Roman

C

Calabrian 96, 102. *See also* Southern Italian

Dialect Index

Caló 56, 232, 356, 359, 360, 362, 365, 366, 368, 369, 371, 373, 374, 376, 378, 379, 460, 461, 474, 475, 481, 506–508
Catalonian 57, 232, 377. *See also* Iberian
Central group 20–24, 393
   Northern/North Central 111, 399, 404, 411, 415, 417, 419
   Southern/South Central 111, 399, 409–411, 413, 419
Cerhari 321
Crimean 55, 57, 89, 94, 140, 170, 193, 201, 239, 241, 273, 398, 400
Čurari 130, 138
Čurarja Arlije 287
Čuxny. *See* Lotfitka
Czech 403. *See also* Bohemian

D

Dolenjska. *See* Hravati
Dortika 357, 358
Drindari 270, 398
Džambazi 435, 439

E

Eastern Slovak. *See* East Slovak
East Slovak 54, 136, 139, 141, 169, 206–216, 219, 220, 222, 232, 264, 265, 267–270, 273, 274, 277, 279, 282, 285, 286, 288, 291, 293, 394, 403, 417, 434, 437, 440, 446, 464, 466, 468, 493–495, 497, 498, 501
English Romani 331, 341, 344, 347, 367, 368, 407. *See also* Angloromani; British
Epiros 159, 169, 183
Erli 89, 107, 110, 275, 279, 400, 461, 463, 474
   Rhodope Erli 281
   Sofia Erli 192, 199, 221, 222, 236, 275, 474

F

Finikas 357
Finnish 54, 56, 70, 112, 127, 132, 135–141, 145, 148, 160, 163, 169, 195, 213, 222, 309, 365, 370, 398, 407, 431, 446, 462. *See also* Kaalo

G

Gabor 121, 125, 137, 147, 198, 201, 467
Geygel Yürük 359
Gurbet
   Belgrade Gurbet 435
   Bosnian Gurbet 277
   Croatian Gurbet 273
   Kosovan Gurbet 273, 279, 288
   Sremski Gurbet 435, 437
Gurvari 127, 130, 136, 139, 147, 313, 316, 325

H

Hravati 280

I

Iberian 57, 58, 64, 69, 71, 379, 398, 399, 408. *See also* Caló; Catalonian
Istrian. *See* Hravati

K

Kaalo 439–441. *See also* Finnish
Kalajdži 132, 137, 193, 222, 233, 241, 278, 401
Kaldarash. *See* Kalderaš
Kalderaš
   Romanian Kalderaš 438
   Russian Kalderaš 175, 176, 282
   Serbian Kalderaš 176, 177, 264, 267, 275, 276
   Swedish Kalderaš 435

Dialect Index   **583**

Kale 103, 435, 556. *See also* Kaalo; Welsh
Kangljari 138, 142, 144, 151, 188, 189, 405
Kaspichan 160, 183, 391
Kelderaš. *See* Kalderaš
Kišinevcy 145
Korturare. *See* Kurturare
Kumanovo 128, 140, 280
Kurturare 189, 196, 530
Kərəmidarea 145, 147

L

Laeši 201
Laješa. *See* Laeši
Latvian. *See* Lotfitka
Lingurari 132, 137, 138
Lithuanian 54, 107, 121, 125, 127, 131, 133, 134, 139, 143, 148, 170, 188, 200, 217, 218, 268, 270, 276, 340, 397, 407, 449
Lotfitka 131, 135, 140, 145, 147, 263
Lovara. *See* Lovari
Lovari
   Austrian Lovari 158, 173, 174
   Russian Lovari 140
   Slovak Lovari 159, 163, 173, 174
Lovari Čokeši. *See* Lovari, Russian Lovari

M

Manuš 108, 125, 128, 134, 162, 205, 216, 265, 362, 407
Manuša Čurjarja 273, 287
Mečkari 122, 137, 140, 191
Mexican 344
Mexican Vlax. *See* Mexican
Molisean 199, 201, 341, 401. *See also* Southern Italian
Molise. *See* Molisean

N

Northeastern group 148
North Russian 54, 125, 134, 262, 263, 265–267, 270–272, 274, 276, 278, 279, 283–287, 289, 293, 370, 434, 453, 542
Northwestern group 146

P

Plaščuno 404
Polish. *See* Polska Roma
Polish Xaladytka 127, 279
Polska Roma 121, 129, 133, 134, 136, 138, 144, 145, 147, 189, 203, 207–212, 214–216, 218–220, 268, 270, 277–279, 283, 407
Prekmurje 303, 305, 403, 441, 446
Prilep 112, 169, 173, 175, 176, 276, 279, 280, 400

R

Roman 440, 468, 469, 475, 476
Romis. *See* Dortika
Romungro
   Central Romungro 142
   Hungarian Romungro 122, 124, 127, 141–144, 148
   Romanian Romungro 124, 127, 143, 144
Rumelian 63, 237, 238, 247
Rumungro. *See* Romungro
Ruska Roma. *See* North Russian
Russian. *See* North Russian

S

Šanxajcy 137
Scandoromani 3, 374, 378, 439
Selice 97, 157, 158, 167–183, 311, 312, 316, 317, 320, 322, 332, 347, 355, 391, 396

584 **Dialect Index**

Sepeči 94, 156, 157, 166, 170, 171,
173, 174, 176, 177, 183, 199,
203, 236, 238, 240, 241, 245,
246, 283
Sepečides. *See* Sepeči
Serres. *See* Ajios Athanasios
Servi. *See* Servy
Servy 125, 128, 134, 139, 140, 145,
213, 274, 276, 278, 279, 406
Sinti
Austrian Sinti 201
German Sinti 107, 156, 160, 162,
174, 180, 202, 216, 322
Hungarian Sinti 305, 316–318, 321,
322, 326
Lombard Sinti 96, 106, 108, 109,
191, 201
Piedmontese Sinti 89, 96, 104–106,
285
Romanian Sinti 146
Venetian Sinti 96
Skopje Barutči 249–251, 255
Slovene. *See* Hravati
Sofia Erli. *See* Erli, Sofia Erli
Southern Italian 102, 107, 136
South Italian. *See* Southern Italian
Spanish. *See* Caló
Spoitori 189, 199, 241
Šušuwaje 198, 201

T

Texan 262, 264

U

Ukrainian 132, 140, 142, 160, 191,
213, 215, 270, 272–274, 280,
284, 286, 293, 340, 344, 399,
403, 404, 406, 414, 494, 495
Ursari 131, 132, 145, 189, 398, 473
Uzh 179
Eastern Uzh 166, 392
Uzhhorod. *See* Uzh

V

Velingrad Yerli 277, 278
Vend 122, 127, 129, 131, 138, 145,
169, 175–178, 183, 188, 306,
307, 311–313, 315–322, 391,
402
Versend 168, 175–177, 232, 308, 316,
403
Vlax group 64, 144
Northern Vlax 127, 133, 214, 406,
439, 493, 494, 501
Southern Vlax 129, 133, 214, 246,
293, 406, 468
Vlaxurja 128, 140, 201, 276, 405, 406

W

Welsh 53, 61, 66, 88, 106, 109, 157,
163, 172–177, 180, 199, 206,
216, 264, 285, 354, 360, 377,
398, 407, 431
West Slovak 124, 128, 272, 273, 283,
285

X

Xaladytka. *See* North Russian
Xandžari 140, 276
Xoraxane 122, 134, 137, 139, 142,
145, 151, 190, 198, 200, 203,
233, 241
Xoraxani. *See* Xoraxane

Y

Yerli 400
Velingrad. *See* Velingrad Yerli

Z

Zargari 159, 163, 167, 174, 177, 398

Subject Index

ablative 30, 31, 146, 148, 163, 194, 218, 221, 222, 238, 251, 276, 316, 436
  replacement of 238
  used on interrogatives 211
accusative 31, 127, 163–165, 195, 200, 217, 221, 292, 320. *See also* oblique, independent
acquisition 111, 217, 332, 441, 442, 489–492, 498, 500, 502, 506, 509, 526. *See also* socialization, language
active participle 37, 161
activism 6, 525, 529–531, 547, 549, 550, 555. *See also* political movement
adjectival participle. *See* active participle
adjectives
  borrowing of 95, 325
  derivation of 17, 87, 149, 158, 171, 175, 176, 179, 180, 183, 315
  inflection of 35, 36, 159, 161, 163, 165–167, 180, 181, 183, 267, 340, 354

  position of 128, 180
adpositions 31, 195, 221, 222, 323, 324, 345, 346. *See also* prepositions
adverbial clauses 209. *See also* conditional
  anteriority 209
  posteriority 209
  simultaneity 177, 209, 346
adverbs
  de-adjectival 167, 170, 171
  de-nominal 156, 171, 175, 177
  derivation of 17, 171, 176, 177, 268, 316
  extensions 176, 177
  of manner 176, 177, 316
  of place/location 93
  phasal 267, 268, 294, 345
  temporal 175, 177, 203, 209, 267, 268, 294, 324
affricates 120, 123, 124, 126, 133–135, 140, 236, 272, 306, 395, 406, 412, 477, 478
agentive 31, 34, 174, 236, 315, 339
  borrowed suffixes 173

© The Editor(s) (if applicable) and The Author(s) 2020
Y. Matras and A. Tenser (eds.), *The Palgrave Handbook of Romani Language and Linguistics*, https://doi.org/10.1007/978-3-030-28105-2

586 Subject Index

agglutinative 31, 236, 243, 314, 340, 341, 358, 362
agreement, of adjectives 164–166, 181, 194, 402
aktionsart 156, 158, 172, 281, 283, 314, 318, 319, 336, 340, 343
Albanian 107, 110, 122, 231, 233–238, 248, 252, 253, 273, 279, 286, 339, 340, 345, 449, 526
animacy 163, 204, 221
animals, terms for 347
anticausatives 171
Apabhraṃśa 14, 30, 32
apocope 19, 29, 34, 406, 417
Arabic 59, 90, 91, 364, 373, 476, 518, 526
archaism 52, 64, 148, 498
areal development 2, 272, 392–394, 496. *See also* linguistic area
argot. *See* secret language; slang
Arli 254
    Kosovan Arli 273
Armenian 14, 28, 90, 94, 100, 101, 103, 111, 449
    Iranian influences on 25, 85, 90, 98, 100, 101, 337, 365
Aromanian 233, 234, 248, 541. *See also* Balkan Romance
Aśokan inscriptions 14, 22, 26
aspect 4, 19, 58, 85, 120, 149, 155–159, 161, 162, 168, 181, 183, 206, 234, 236, 281, 283, 284, 332, 337, 418, 490, 491, 525
aspiration 120, 134, 307, 354, 441, 479
    loss of 134, 408
    transfer of 19, 28
athematic morphology 168, 333, 338. *See also* xenoclitic
Atlas of Central Romani 3
auxiliaries 37, 255, 283–285, 292, 322, 344, 445

B

baby-talk 492, 493, 496, 497
Balkanisms 2, 231, 277
Balkan Romance 103, 231, 232, 237, 252
benefactive 31, 217, 221, 275
Bengali 15, 75
bilingualism 85, 89–91, 102, 103, 105, 247, 329, 330, 363, 395, 492
    bilingual publications 539, 545
body parts, terms for 347
broadcasting, in Romani 435, 439, 440, 525
Bulgarian 206, 232, 233, 240, 244, 250, 262, 264, 266, 267, 271, 273–275, 277, 279–281, 284, 286–289, 293, 294, 339, 340, 346, 391, 397, 401, 461, 463, 468, 472, 541, 554–556, 561
Burushaski 25
Byzantine Greek 25, 168, 222, 223, 231, 333, 337, 409

C

calques 107, 113, 178, 235, 244, 250, 251, 270, 343, 436, 504
cant 58
case layers 30, 31, 314
    Layer I 125, 133, 164, 166
    Layer II 30, 135, 164
causal clauses 209, 324
causative 37, 157, 171, 172, 287, 317, 340
Central Indo-Aryan 21–23, 337
Central NIA 33
Ceylon 72, 73
child language 490
clitic 35, 199, 240, 241, 246, 336, 344, 361, 377
code mixing. *See* language mixing
codeswitch. *See* code switching

code switching 504, 519, 527, 530
coins, terms for 364
colour, terms for 110, 267
comitative. *See* instrumental
Common Romani 52, 90, 391, 529. *See also* Early Romani; Proto-Romani
comparative (degree) 321
   borrowing of 167, 237
compartmentalisation, morphological 181
competence, in Romani 444, 445, 489–492, 499, 502, 503, 505, 509
complementation 37, 188, 208
complementiser
   borrowing of 322, 346
   factual 292, 338
   non-factual 206, 285, 338
compounding 155, 170
   of nouns 179
   of verbs 38, 178
computer-mediated communication (CMC) 517, 518, 524, 532
conditional
   borrowing of particles 209, 210, 346
   clause 201, 202, 206, 208
   particle 288, 293, 295
   use of tense 281
conjunctions 2, 201, 211, 212, 288, 290–292, 295, 337, 360, 361
   borrowing of 291, 344, 346
consonant cluster
   assimilation of 308
   assimilation of OIA 27
   reduction of 120, 128, 130, 149, 493
   retention of OIA 22
   simplification of 146
converb 19, 37, 159, 177, 178, 213, 285
convergence 5, 63, 165, 202, 232, 237, 252, 335, 336, 338, 339, 342, 347, 369, 409, 411, 418
conversion (word-formation) 155, 179
   word-class 180

copula
   borrowing of 156
   negative 159, 216
   perfective origin of 36, 142, 159, 162, 401
   subjunctive forms of 159, 160, 162
copular auxiliary. *See* copula, subjunctive forms of
Council of Europe 447, 449, 541, 547, 548, 552
counterfactual 157, 162, 163
creole 331, 368, 369, 378
Croatian 254, 263, 264, 271, 272, 279, 285, 287, 288, 292, 294, 303, 402, 453, 454, 526
Croatian Gurbet 132
Cyrillic 435, 468, 469, 475, 476, 542
Czech 266, 271–273, 279, 284, 294, 475, 497, 502–506, 523, 545
Czechoslovakia 304, 434, 437, 545, 549, 551, 561, 562

Dardic 20, 21, 23, 24, 29, 337
dative
   borrowing of 295
   reflexive 275, 286, 294
   replacement of 238
   used on interrogatives 211
declarative 160, 206, 343, 443
declension 87, 181, 199, 247, 375
definite article 32, 129, 156, 166, 167, 188, 190, 191, 193, 194, 222, 266, 274, 277, 291, 294, 308, 338, 361, 375, 390, 402
   doubling of 192
   loss of 189, 223, 277, 342
definiteness 167, 204, 221
demonstrative 19, 32, 40, 91, 93, 130, 132, 138, 156, 166, 167, 188–190, 193, 194, 277, 280, 322, 338, 343, 359, 362, 500

588   Subject Index

Desiphral 527–529
Devanagari 476, 527–529
devoicing 19, 27, 136, 140, 271, 294
dialectal variation 5, 18, 19, 35, 168, 436
diffusion 5, 390, 396, 409, 496
  of borrowed morphology 339
  of innovations 392, 393, 410, 411, 415, 416, 418
digital (publications) 2, 539
diminutive 29, 106, 134, 170, 174, 176, 182, 253, 270, 274, 339, 390, 497
diphthongs 104, 131, 132, 138, 148, 150, 339
direct object 31, 159, 163, 195, 199, 205, 323
discourse markers 345
ditransitive 195, 199
Dōm 14, 15
Domari 14, 15, 17, 35, 95, 240
Dravidian 15–17, 73
Ḍumāki 14

Early Proto-Romani 14, 18, 19, 22, 24, 25, 34, 36, 37, 39
Early Romani 5, 13, 18, 20, 38, 52, 102, 103, 105, 110, 120, 204, 222, 237–239, 247, 266, 274, 285, 306, 307, 309, 310, 313, 314, 336, 337, 342, 365, 366, 478, 498. *See also* Common Romani; Proto-Romani
education 2–4, 265, 429, 433–435, 437–440, 442–447, 449–452, 454, 490, 492, 509, 516, 519, 540–543, 547–550, 553, 554, 556, 559, 562
Egyptians 53, 57, 58, 61, 63, 64, 86, 252, 255

elision 120, 126–128, 144–147, 164
emblematic 469
  use of language 371, 472, 561
  use of texts 561
enclitic 23, 34, 159, 164, 165, 280
English 3, 53, 61, 95, 234, 252, 331, 339, 341, 354, 357, 359, 362, 364, 367–373, 376–378, 390, 397, 435, 438, 473, 494, 503, 506, 508, 515, 517–528, 530, 531, 551, 554, 555
ergativity 19, 31, 34, 222
ethnolect 391, 439, 504–506
ethnonyms 14, 17, 106, 107, 391, 395, 401
euphemism 334
evidentiality 159, 161, 244, 248, 281, 289
experiencer 220, 221
external possession 188, 219

Facebook, use of Romani on 522, 532
factitive 171, 172
fairy tales 520
feminine marker 274, 339
Finnish 136, 140, 309, 339, 343, 435
focus particles 214, 268, 269, 323, 345
folklore 540–542, 544–548, 550, 553, 554, 557, 562
French 55–57, 67, 74, 77, 105, 106, 124, 223, 338, 357, 362, 364, 463, 526, 552
frequentative 157, 172, 176, 317. *See also* iterative
fricatives 27, 28, 120, 122–124, 135, 137–140, 144, 148, 306, 309, 395
future tense 36
  analytic 314, 322, 401

Subject Index   **589**

geminates 27, 28, 124, 141, 142, 308, 309
gender (grammatical) 19, 159, 266, 314, 321
 loss of distinction of 165, 320, 343
genealogical model (of dialectal variation) 390, 396, 411, 413, 414, 418
genetic 3, 5, 65, 73, 223, 398, 409. *See also* genealogical model (of dialectal variation)
 relationship between languages 73–75, 87
genitive adnominal 192, 194. *See also* possessor
genitive
 borrowing of 157, 341
 derivations 157, 179, 183
 nominalizations of 180, 183
 phonological distinction in 163
 suffix, harmony of 18, 31, 133, 134, 164, 180
geographical diffusion model (of dialectal variation) 3, 392, 409–412, 414–418
Georgian 25, 100
German 17, 52, 55, 57, 58, 62, 64, 65, 69, 71, 74, 85, 86, 104, 106, 107, 111, 113, 124, 183, 202, 214, 216, 264, 303, 304, 306, 309, 311, 313, 318, 321, 322, 335, 336, 339, 343, 345, 363, 397, 407, 408, 410, 440, 441, 448, 449, 453, 474, 518, 526, 546, 547, 552, 563
 borrowings from 66, 178, 319, 333, 346
 secret languages 372, 373
gerund 213, 482
Gospels 460–462, 481. *See also* New Testament
gradual grammatical borrowing 367

grammaticalisation 216, 319, 336, 338
Great Divide, the 112, 410, 417. *See also* geographical diffusion model(of dialectal variation)
Greek
 adaptation markers 149, 150, 168, 169, 316
 adjectival derivational suffixes 337
 definite article 190, 192, 194, 223, 338, 343
 function words 112, 345
 lexicon 101, 102, 107, 112, 124, 315, 333, 337, 357, 365
 nominal morphology 102
 numerals 101, 109, 177
 phonemes 339
 syntactic typology 18, 338
 verb inflection 342

hiatus 120, 129, 130, 145
Hindi 15, 17, 20–23, 29, 35, 39, 438, 527, 528
Holocaust 546, 547, 550, 552, 558
Hungarian 4, 66, 72, 73, 97, 121, 122, 134, 142, 149–151, 166, 168–173, 176–178, 206, 264, 266, 287, 303–326, 335, 338–341, 343, 345, 346, 357, 359, 362, 390, 391, 397, 403–405, 438, 445, 453, 465, 467, 477, 478, 483, 492, 496, 545, 548
 writing system 315, 435

idiomatic expressions 497, 505
imperative 34, 61, 159, 161, 162, 182, 281, 496, 500, 504
 borrowing of 289
 negator 38, 214, 215, 293

Subject Index

imperfective 241, 242, 281, 282. *See also* aspect
inchoatives 171
indefinite article 188, 190, 191, 194, 361, 374
  loss of 342
indefinites
  borrowing of 216, 278, 337, 403
  impersonal 342
  markers 177, 214, 216, 316, 337, 340, 345, 374, 403, 408
indirect object 195, 199, 220, 358
infinitive 37, 70, 159, 213, 240, 241, 247, 281, 306, 314, 319, 322, 402, 404, 406
  borrowing of 295, 322, 337, 395, 403
  new infinitive 213, 223, 244, 284, 285, 294, 344, 395
instrumental 31, 32, 35, 74, 146, 163, 194, 218, 221, 276, 313, 324, 504
inter-dialectal (contact) 111, 326
International Romani Union (IRU) 436–439, 441, 522, 548, 550
internet 4, 441, 467, 479, 515–520, 525, 527, 529, 531, 540, 549, 551, 561, 562
interrogatives 32, 33, 112, 130, 138, 151, 165, 166, 223, 248–251, 268, 279, 280, 320, 324, 337, 413
  borrowing of 346
intonation 119, 313, 339, 505
intransitive 35, 121, 142, 145, 161, 169, 171, 172, 182, 195, 217, 249, 283, 285, 286
inversion 336, 343
Iranian 13, 25, 28, 37, 85, 90, 91, 98–102, 112, 182, 213, 284, 337, 365, 463
irrealis 36, 158, 208, 209, 312

isoglosses 104, 111, 112, 285, 393, 394, 411, 415–417
Italian 56, 59, 60, 86, 102, 105, 135, 136, 138, 141, 338, 339, 341, 346, 364, 401, 402, 526, 549, 552
iterative 172, 283, 317, 318. *See also* frequentative

J

jotation 52, 142, 143, 272, 307
  morphological 120

K

Kashmiri 23
kinship, terms for 93, 94, 96, 113, 493
  and EGO 95, 97
  borrowing of 233, 347
Konkani 29
Kurdish 25, 99

L

Lahnda 23, 29
language maintenance 332, 430, 436, 440–442, 452
language mixing 336, 354, 370. *See also* mixed languages
language play 496
Late Proto-Romani 13, 15, 17–20, 28, 30, 32, 35, 36, 38, 39
Latin 51, 56, 64, 66–68, 70–74, 435, 466, 496, 527, 529
Latin America 464, 466
Latvian 54, 110, 127, 133–135, 141, 147, 156, 168, 172, 175, 179, 182, 183, 219, 220, 336, 407, 461
linguistic area 326, 401
linguistic pluralism 451, 520, 527, 532

Subject Index

literacy 2, 3, 253, 262, 434, 435, 441, 483, 492, 515–517, 519, 520, 522, 525, 527–529, 531, 532, 561

loan verbs, adaptation of 266, 408

locative 30, 31, 135, 163, 194, 217, 219, 221, 222, 241, 249, 436
  borrowing of 238
  replacement of 218, 238

Lom 15

Lomavren 14, 15, 17, 357, 369

Low German 357, 358, 390, 391

M

Macedonian 137, 149, 232–235, 237, 238, 248–251, 253, 255, 271, 272, 275–277, 280, 283, 284, 286, 288, 289, 292–294, 344, 435, 439, 449, 523, 524

Malabar 72, 73

Marathi 29, 35, 75

masculine, endings for 106, 265–267

matrimonial use of ethnonym 16

mediopassives 35, 142, 145, 149, 272. *See also* middle verbs

memoirs 545, 546, 553, 555, 556, 558, 559

metathesis 99, 120, 147, 415

Middle Indo-Aryan (MIA) 13, 14, 17–19, 21–23, 25–37, 219, 332, 337

middle verbs 35, 161, 178, 182. *See also* mediopassives

migrant dialects 335, 402, 405

minority language 378, 433, 441–443, 446–450, 452, 454, 482, 517

mixed languages 2, 3, 14, 70, 331, 333, 334, 336, 348, 355, 356, 362, 363, 365–367, 369, 370, 375, 378, 379, 432. *See also* language mixing

modals 160, 201, 203, 206, 254, 284, 285, 404
  borrowing of 288, 295, 337, 342, 346
  impersonal 205, 206, 286, 342

musicians 15, 400, 525, 554

N

nasals 19, 21, 23, 24, 27, 28, 31, 36, 122, 123, 144, 146, 307

nature, terms for 347

negation
  negative indefinites 214, 216
  negators 38, 214, 216, 293

negotiating identity 531

neologisms 234, 235, 436, 445, 470, 527

Neo-Protestant 459, 463–466, 468, 473, 478, 480. *See also* Pentecostal

Nepali 15, 20, 21, 24, 29

neuter gender 26
  loss of OIA 30

New Indo-Aryan (NIA) 14, 23, 25–32, 34, 35, 37, 38, 40, 223, 270, 336

New Testament 460, 462, 463, 466, 468, 475. *See also* Gospels

Next Page Foundation (NPF) 520, 522, 523

nominalization 183
  abstract 156, 173
  onomasiological 180, 183

nominative, markers for 29–31, 149, 163, 164, 168, 181, 338, 340

non-perfective 33, 34, 158–161, 169, 177, 182, 254, 404. *See also* present, tense

non-territorial 5, 436, 448, 451

noun derivation 173, 174

noun inflection. *See* case layers

Subject Index

novels 434, 545, 553
numbers, of speakers 355
numerals
    borrowing of 109
    compound forms of 179
    ordinal 166, 337

object doubling 199, 290, 292
oblique, independent 31, 194, 217,
    219, 221. *See also* case layers,
    Layer I
oikoclitic 29, 168, 169, 173–175, 181,
    247, 254, 333. *See also* thematic
    morphology
Old Indo-Aryan (OIA) 13, 17–19,
    21–25, 27–37, 108, 109, 122,
    136, 206, 310, 463
Old Testament 461, 463, 466, 475,
    481
Open Society Institute 520, 521
orthography. *See* writing system
Ossetian 25, 99, 147

Pahari 20, 21, 23
palatalization 52, 63, 64, 339, 401,
    406, 408, 413
palatals 126, 272, 307, 339
Panjabi 16, 20, 23, 29
Papusza 519, 544, 558, 561
paragoge 120, 147, 402
Para-Romani (PR)
    Angloromani 61, 62, 331, 353, 354,
      356, 366–369, 373, 374, 376
    Basque 363, 373, 374, 408
    Catalan 357, 358, 373, 374, 376,
      408
    functions of 354, 356, 371,
      506–509
    genesis of 363, 367, 369, 372

    Spanish 357, 359, 373, 374, 506,
      508
    Swedish 357, 366, 373, 374
Pashto 98, 99
passive 33, 34, 37, 340, 360, 491
    analytic 37, 286
    auxiliary 37, 283, 285
past participle 36, 283, 285
Pentecostal 463–467, 482, 529. *See also*
    Neo-Protestant
perfect, tense 244, 246, 283, 314
perfective
    aspect 158, 159, 161, 162, 169, 284
    classes of verbs 182
    stem 33, 34, 52, 138, 142, 144,
      146, 161, 162, 169, 281, 282,
      401
    suffixes 34, 35, 161–163, 169, 182,
      414
periphery, geographical 415
Persian 25, 99, 100, 124, 235, 373,
    390
personal pronouns 32, 127, 131, 132,
    147, 165, 280, 361, 362, 375,
    407
    borrowing of 340, 376
    in Para-Romani 359, 376
person concord 127, 131–133, 139,
    145, 146, 148, 341, 377
    borrowing of 149
phonetics 15, 99, 100, 104, 107, 120,
    271, 272, 274, 294, 311, 321,
    339
    borrowing of 263, 272
phonology 4, 20, 27, 70, 91, 119, 232,
    236, 271, 274, 294, 306, 326,
    338, 354, 367, 369, 376, 475
    borrowing of 263
pidgins 368, 369, 378
place names 106, 107, 364, 365
pluperfect, tense 36, 159–161, 163
pluralistic (approach to language diver-
    sity) 447

Subject Index   593

poetry 434, 439, 520, 542, 544, 545, 548–550, 553–558
polar questions 339
Polish 66, 137, 138, 150, 163, 191, 214, 215, 219, 263–265, 268, 271, 273, 276, 279, 280, 284, 288, 291, 294, 295, 335, 336, 339, 340, 343, 397, 403, 407, 519, 523, 544
political movement 437, 438, 539, 562. *See also* activism
possessive pronouns 280, 312, 360, 361
possessor 31, 192, 193, 219, 221. *See also* genitive adnominal
post-alveolar
    affricates 27, 39, 123, 124, 135, 138, 140, 144, 307
    graphemic representation of 307
    sibilants 22, 124, 139, 141
postpositions 31, 164, 166, 192, 223, 249, 251, 314, 323, 343, 390
    borrowing of 238, 251
Prākrits 14, 15, 19, 22, 24, 30
prefixation 170, 274, 281, 282, 321
prepositions 129, 165, 167, 188, 192, 217, 223, 251, 276, 277, 324, 359, 361, 375, 504
    borrowing of 251, 275, 290, 291, 295, 337, 346, 347, 376
    replacement of case marking by 238
present, tense 36, 37, 127, 131, 133, 139, 146, 148, 161, 162, 213, 240, 243, 246, 249, 337, 338, 374. *See also* non-perfective
present/future 36, 159, 160, 242, 244, 314
privative 158, 174, 176, 179
progressive 159, 240–242, 499, 519. *See also* imperfective
pro-nouns 163, 165, 166, 173, 181
prosody 338, 493
prosthesis 27, 99, 120, 147, 417

Proto-Romani 5. *See also* Common Romani; Early Romani
    ethnonyms 14, 15, 391
    language contact 14
    nominal morphosyntax 29
    phonology 14, 19, 25, 26, 32, 39, 158, 182
    pronominal forms 31
    reconstruction of 14, 18, 19, 38, 156, 413, 414
    verbal morphosyntax 33
Proto-Vlax 413, 414
public, use of Romani 430, 433, 437–439, 441, 446, 451, 543
publications, in Romani 3, 50, 76, 262, 437, 440, 447, 460, 461, 463, 468, 469, 475, 476, 479, 480, 516, 531, 539–545, 547, 549–552, 554–557, 561–563
purpose clauses 201, 208, 212

Q

quantifiers 155, 188, 191, 270, 324, 325, 345
    borrowing of 294, 347

R

Radio Romani Mahala (RRM) 525–527, 529, 530
Rajasthani 20, 21, 29
Rājpūts 26. *See also* warriors
realis 208, 209
recognition, official, of Romani 55, 433, 447, 448, 450, 516, 520, 525
reduplication 170, 270
    of root 157
    of syllables 493
reflexive 275. *See also* dative, reflexive
    borrowing of 295, 320, 341
    constructions 285, 286, 402

594   Subject Index

personal forms of 286
register 357, 492, 493, 496, 497, 499, 506, 509, 517, 523
relative clause 204–206, 223, 337, 338
relativiser 33, 324, 337
relexification 369, 376, 378
remoteness marker 243, 403
resumptive pronoun 199, 205, 337. *See also* object doubling
retroflex 19, 22, 28, 39, 120, 136, 307, 529
rhotic 15, 21, 28, 412
Romance 103, 105, 106, 147, 357, 368, 373. *See also* Balkan Romance
Romane Nevipena 521
Romanian 131, 132, 135, 138, 146, 174, 177, 206, 214, 264, 271, 278, 286, 313, 321, 326, 338, 343, 345, 404, 405, 445, 449, 465, 468, 472–474, 497
    borrowing from 125, 206, 335, 340, 345, 346, 406, 438, 496
    orthography 438, 476, 477
Romano Lil 542, 545, 556
Roma Virtual Network (RVN) 521, 522, 525, 527
Rotwelsch 58, 66, 69, 87, 372, 373
Russian
    borrowing from 170, 263–266, 268, 272, 273, 278, 283, 287–289, 336, 340, 346
    calquing from 270, 271, 292
    orthography. *See* Cyrillic

S

salience, of lexicon 93
    cognitive 91, 93
    cultural 91, 93
Sanskrit 13, 15, 16, 33, 70
school 132, 169, 203, 262, 265, 436, 443–445, 490–492, 499, 502, 556, 559

secret language 334, 364, 371–373, 503. *See also* slang
semi-vowels 120, 137, 138, 145, 273
Serbian 262, 271–274, 277, 279, 287, 294, 303, 342, 437, 461, 463, 545, 556
    borrowing from 234, 264, 279, 288, 289
Shina 29, 30
Sindhi 23, 29
Sinhalese 73
slang 59, 86, 87, 331. *See also* secret language
Slavic
    borrowing from 208, 211, 236, 262–265, 267–270, 281–283, 287, 288, 290–292, 294, 295, 340, 346, 395
    Slavic aspect 281–283, 294
    writing system 315, 475. *See also* Cyrillic
Slovak 71, 150, 156, 171, 175, 180, 218, 219, 264, 265, 268–272, 274, 279, 282, 284, 286, 287, 304, 306, 307, 311–313, 317, 318, 321, 434, 449, 466, 468, 492, 503, 504, 545, 548
    borrowing from 209, 266, 279, 288, 291, 295, 335, 340, 347, 354, 496
Slovene 167, 176, 206, 272, 278, 280, 284, 285, 295, 303, 305, 341, 391, 399, 402, 403
    borrowing from 263, 287
Slovenian. *See* Slovene
socialization, language 489–493, 498, 499, 501, 508, 509
Soviet Union 106, 433, 434, 542–544, 551, 552, 561, 562
Sprachbund. *See* linguistic area
stops (consonants) 22, 28, 120, 122–124, 136, 147, 149, 307
stress 71, 90, 120, 125, 127, 128, 132, 134, 136, 149–151, 192, 272,

Subject Index

273, 294, 312, 313, 326, 339, 354, 402–404, 435, 553
subjunctive 36, 159–162, 213–215, 241–244, 247, 285, 342
subordination 201, 247
subordinators 208, 209, 211, 323, 324, 326, 346. *See also* conjunctions
superlative (degree) 321
  analytic 167
  borrowing of 158, 167
suppletion 165
  of affixes 158, 181
  of copula 159
Swedish 67, 357, 362, 366, 373, 374, 379, 439, 440, 547, 555
syllable structure 28, 120, 148
syncretism 157, 160, 164, 284

T

teasing (speech genre) 499
tense-aspect-mood (TAM) 156, 159, 160, 162, 236, 240–242, 322
thematic morphology 168. *See also* oikoclitic
topicality 196, 197, 199
transitive 35, 159, 169, 171, 172, 182, 220, 266, 285, 286, 317, 369, 408, 505
transitivising. *See* valency alteration
translation, into Romani 60, 459, 472, 473, 541, 545
transliteration 39, 435, 518
transnational 3, 449, 479
Transylvania 303, 395, 404, 410, 464, 465, 476, 482
truncation 120
Turkish 4, 62, 107, 122, 172, 174, 231–255, 273, 335, 336, 338, 340, 341, 345, 346, 357–359, 362, 370, 391, 400, 405, 439, 526
  borrowings from 156, 157, 233, 251
  verb inflection 342

U

Ukrainian 262, 272–274, 284, 294, 340, 406, 449
unevenly mixed languages 370
U-turn hypothesis 369

V

valency alteration 314
vernacular literacy 516, 517, 519, 520, 522, 529, 531, 532
Vikipidiya 527–529, 532
vocative 16, 53, 56, 57, 68, 158, 163, 164, 181, 194, 233
  borrowing of 238, 274
voicing 23, 24, 136
vowels
  central 121, 122, 339
  lengthening of 126
  reduction of 120, 402

W

warriors 26, 107, 108. *See also* Rājpūts
Western Pahari 23, 29, 30
wh-questions 201
Wikipedia in Romani 527. *See also* Vikipidiya
word order
  borrowing of 326
  interrogative clauses 201, 202
  main clauses 196
  subordinate clauses 201
World War II (WWII) 235, 402, 403, 523, 541, 546, 558
writing system 19, 71, 72, 434–436, 438, 440, 468, 469, 472, 475–478, 482, 525, 527–530

X

xenoclitic 168, 169, 173–177, 181, 183, 247, 254, 333, 338, 406. *See also* athematic morphology

596 Subject Index

Y

yes-no questions. *See* polar questions
Yugoslavia 88, 101, 107, 398, 405,
434, 437, 541, 543, 544, 551,
555, 561, 562

Z

zero (marking) 30

Printed in the United States
by Baker & Taylor Publisher Services